The publisher gratefully acknowledges the generous support
of the Ahmanson Foundation Humanities Endowment Fund
of the University of California Press Foundation.

BERENIKE AND THE ANCIENT MARITIME SPICE ROUTE

THE CALIFORNIA WORLD HISTORY LIBRARY

Edited by Edmund Burke III, Kenneth Pomeranz, and Patricia Seed

*For Marijke,
with best wishes,
Steve*

BERENIKE AND THE ANCIENT MARITIME SPICE ROUTE

Steven E. Sidebotham

UNIVERSITY OF CALIFORNIA PRESS
Berkeley   Los Angeles   London

University of California Press, one of the most distinguished university presses in the United States, enriches lives around the world by advancing scholarship in the humanities, social sciences, and natural sciences. Its activities are supported by the UC Press Foundation and by philanthropic contributions from individuals and institutions. For more information, visit www.ucpress.edu.

University of California Press
Berkeley and Los Angeles, California

University of California Press, Ltd.
London, England

Library of Congress Cataloging-in-Publication Data

Sidebotham, Steven E.
    Berenike and the ancient maritime spice route / Steven E. Sidebotham.
        p.   cm.   (The California world history library ; 18)
    Includes bibliographical references and index.
    ISBN 978-0-520-24430-6 (cloth : alk. paper)
        1. Baranis (Egypt)—Antiquities.   2. Baranis (Egypt)—Antiquities, Roman.   3. Excavations (Archaeology)—Egypt—Baranis.   4. Spice trade—Egypt—Baranis—History.—To 1500.   5. Trade routes—Egypt—Baranis—History.—To 1500.   6. Baranis (Egypt)—Commerce—History.   7. Port cities—Egypt—History—To 1500.   8. Eastern Desert (Egypt)—Commerce—History.   9. International trade—History.—To 1500.   10. Baranis (Egypt)—Social life and customs.   I. Title.
    DT73.B375S4   2011
    932—dc22   2010038906

Manufactured in the United States of America

19 18 17 16 15 14 13 12 11
10 9 8 7 6 5 4 3 2 1

The paper used in this publication meets the minimum requirements of ANSI/NISO Z39.48-1992 (R 1997) (Permanence of Paper).

CONTENTS

FIGURES

PREFACE AND ACKNOWLEDGMENTS

A book of this type demands a wide-ranging knowledge of numerous disciplines and aspects of antiquity over an extended period of time and broad geographical area. I do not possess such a breadth or depth of knowledge. Therefore, friends and colleagues have read and commented on some of these chapters at various stages of their writing, making numerous suggestions for improvement. Others have provided important bibliography, which I would otherwise have missed. Those who should be acknowledged include, in alphabetical order: S. A. Abraham, C. E. P. Adams, A. Avanzini, H. Barnard, M. Bishop, L. Blue, S. M. Burstein, L. Casson, P. J. Cherian, J. P. Cooper, M. H. Crawford, H. Cuvigny, F. De Romanis, R. Fattovich, D. F. Graf, S. Gupta, J. A. Harrell, A. M. Hense, R. A. Lobban, M. M. Mango, A. Manzo, V. A. Maxfield, S. C. H. Munro-Hay, L. Okamura, G. Parker, D. P. S. Peacock, J. S. Phillips, D. T. Potts, I. Roll, H. Schenk, A. Sedov, V. Selvakumar, P. Shajan, P. Sheehan, F. Stone, R. J. A. Talbert, P. Tallet, R. I. Thomas, R. S. Tomber, S. L. Tuck, G. Tully, C. Ward, W. Z. Wendrich, E. Wheeler, F. C. Wild, J.-P. Wild, H. T. Wright, and C. Zazzaro. Michael Peppard shared his manuscript on a papyrus dealing with Berenike in the Yale University collection. Carey Fleiner provided invaluable assistance by formatting portions of the bibliography from rather cryptic notes. Martin Hense prepared the maps and drawings. I took all the photos.

I especially want to thank the cheerful and efficient staff of the interlibrary-loan section of Morris Library of the University of Delaware who, over the years, obtained hundreds of articles and books for this research.

My wife, Mary Sidebotham, endured my preoccupation and, eventually, obsession with completion of this project. Her patience and help with numerous computer problems associated with writing this book saved me many hours of frustration.

There is always the vexed question of ancient and modern site names and place-names and the transliteration of their current nomenclature from Arabic or Greek into English. Often the names as they appear in Arabic on maps are not the same as spoken in the region, or are pronounced very differently, by the indigenous Ma'aza, 'Ababda, and Bisharii Bedouin. The most commonly used Bedouin names/pronunciations are used here. With regard to the *el-/al-* prefix in Arabic place-names, I have opted for *al-*. If an author has spelled his name with *el-*, then that spelling has been retained. If transliterated from the Greek, *k* rather than *c* has been used.

J. M. Kistler, *War Elephants* (Westport, CT, and London); A. Bülow-Jacobsen, *Mons Claudianus: Ostraca graeca et latina*, vol. 4, *The Quarry-Texts. O. Claud. 632–896 (DFIFAO 47)*, (Cairo: 2009); J. E. Hill, *Through the Jade Gate to Rome: A Study of the Silk Routes during the Later Han Dynasty 1st to 2nd Centuries c.e.* (Seattle: 2009); and R. McLaughlin, *Rome and the Distant East: Trade Routes to the Ancient Lands of Arabia, India and China* (London and New York: 2010) came to my attention too late for use in this book.

Finally, I dedicate this book to all participants in the Berenike project, both foreign staff and our beloved 'Ababda Bedouin workmen.

July 2010
Newark, Delaware

ABBREVIATIONS

AAE	*Arabian Archaeology and Epigraphy*
AASOR	*Annual of the American Schools of Oriental Research*
ADAJ	*Annual of the Department of Antiquities of Jordan*
AÉ	*L'Année épigraphique,* Paris, 1888–.
AESC	*Annales; économies, sociétés, civilisations*
AHSS	*Annales Histoire, Sciences Sociales*
AJ	Josephus, *Jewish Antiquities*
AJA	*The American Journal of Archaeology*
AJP	*The American Journal of Philology*
ANRW	*Aufstieg und Niedergang der römischen Welt*
AntW	*Antike Welt*
ARCE	The American Research Center in Egypt
ASAE	*Annales du Service des Antiquités de l'Égypte/Annales du Service des antiquités égyptiennes*
ASP	*American Studies in Papyrology*
ATN	*Archaeological Textiles Newsletter*
AUC	American University in Cairo
AW	*The Ancient World*

BAR	*British Archaeological Reports*
BASOR	*Bulletin of the American Schools of Oriental Research*
BASP	*Bulletin of the American Society of Papyrologists*
BFAFU	*Bulletin of the Faculty of Arts Fouad I University*
BIFAN	*Bulletin de l'Institut français d'Afrique Noire*
BIFAO	*Bulletin de l'Institut français d'Archéologie Orientale*
BJ	Josephus, *Jewish War*
BJRL	*Bulletin of the John Rylands Library*
BSAA	*Bulletin de la Société Archéologique d'Alexandrie*
BSFE	*Bulletin de la Société française d'Égyptologie*
BSFFA	*Bulletin de la Société française des fouilles archéologiques*
BSG	*Bulletin de la Société de Géographie*
BSkGÉ	*Bulletin de la Société khédiviale de Géographie d'Égypte*
BSOAS	*Bulletin of the School of Oriental and African Studies*
BSRAA	*Bulletin de la Société royale d'archéologie d'Alexandrie*
BSRGÉ	*Bulletin de la Société royale de Géographie d'Égypte*
CA	*Current Anthropology*
CB	*The Classical Bulletin*
Cd'É	*Chronique d'Égypte*
CIL	*Corpus Inscriptionum Latinarum*
CNRS	Centre national de la Recherche scientifique
CNWS	Centre for Non-Western Studies, Leiden University
Cod. Theo.	*Codex Theodosianus*
CP	*Classical Philology*
CQ	*Classical Quarterly*
CRAI	*Comptes-rendus des Séances de l'Académie des Inscriptions et Belles-Lettres*
CY	*Chroniques yéménites*
DFIFAO	*Documents de Fouilles de l'Institut français d'Archéologie Orientale*
DOP	*Dumbarton Oaks Papers*
EA	*Egyptian Archaeology*
EES	Egypt Exploration Society
ÉFEO	École française d'Extrême Orient
EW	*East and West*
FIFAO	*Fouilles de l'Institut français d'Archéologie Orientale*

GJ	*The Geographical Journal*
GM	*Göttinger Miszellen*
GR	*Greece and Rome*
IESHR	*Indian Economic Social History Review*
IFAO	Institut français d'Archéologie Orientale
IGRR	*Inscriptiones Graecae ad res Romanas pertinentes*, ed. R. Cagnat, Paris, 1911–.
IJNA	*The International Journal of Nautical Archaeology*
JA	*Journal Asiatique*
JAES	*Journal of African Earth Sciences*
JAOS	*Journal of the American Oriental Society*
JARCE	*Journal of the American Research Center in Egypt*
JAS	*Journal of Archaeological Science*
JCHS	*Journal of the Centre for Heritage Studies*
JEA	*Journal of Egyptian Archaeology*
JEBH	*Journal of Economic and Business History*
JESHO	*Journal of Economic and Social History of the Orient*
JFA	*Journal of Field Archaeology*
JHS	*Journal of Hellenic Studies*
JIOA	*Journal of Indian Ocean Archaeology*
JJP	*Journal of Juristic Papyrology*
JMMM	*Journal of Minerals, Metals, and Materials*
JNES	*Journal of Near Eastern Studies*
JÖB	*Jahrbuch der österreichischen Byzantinistik*
JRA	*Journal of Roman Archaeology*
JRAS	*Journal of the Royal Asiatic Society of Great Britain and Ireland*
JRGS	*Journal of the Royal Geographical Society*
JRS	*Journal of Roman Studies*
JSAS	*Journal of South Asian Studies*
JWH	*Journal of World History*
MAAR	*Memoirs of the American Academy in Rome*
MBAH	*Münstersche Beiträge zur antiken Handelsgeschichte*
MDAIK	*Mitteilungen des deutschen Archäologischen Instituts Abteilung Kairo*
MÉFRA	*Mélanges de l'École française de Rome Antiquité*
MIFAO	*Mémoires de l'Institut français d'Archéologie Orientale*

NARCE	Newsletter of the American Research Center in Egypt
NC	The Numismatic Chronicle
NH	Pliny the Elder, Natural History
O. Bodl.	Greek Ostraca in the Bodleian Library at Oxford and Various Other Collections, ed. J. G. Tait. Vol. 1. London, 1930.
O. Brüss.	Ostraka aus Brüssel und Berlin. Ed. Paul Viereck. Berlin, 1922
O. Did.	Didymoi: Une garnison romaine dans le désert Oriental d'Égypte, ed. H. Cuvigny. Vol. 2, Les Textes. Cairo, forthcoming.
O. Did. Inv.	= O. Did.
OGIS	Orientis Graeci Inscriptiones Selectae, ed. W. Dittenberger, Leipzig, 1903–1905.
O. Krok.	Ostraca de Krokodilô: La correspondance militaire et sa circulation (O. Krok. 1-151), by H. Cuvigny. Cario, 2005.
O. Petrie	Greek Ostraca in the Bodleian Library at Oxford and Various Other Collections, ed. J. G. Tait. Volume 1. London, 1930.
PBSR	Papers of the British School at Rome
P. Cairo Zen.	C. C. Edgar, Zenon Papyri, 4 vols. (Catal. Gén. des Antiq. égypt. du Musée du Caire 79), 1925–1931.
P. Eleph.	Elephantine Payri. ed. O. Rubensohn. Ägyptische Urkunden aus den Kgl. Museen zu Berlin: Griechische Urkunden. Sonderheft. Berlin, 1907.
P. Giess.	Griechische Papyri im Museum des Oberhessischen Geschichtsvereins zu Giessen. Bd. I, Hefte 1–3. ed. O. Eger, E. Kornemann, and P. M. Meyer. Leipzig, 1910–1912.
P. Lond.	Greek Papyri in the British Museum. Vols. 1 and 2 ed. F. G. Kenyon, vol. 3 ed. F. G. Kenyon and H. I. Bell, vols. 4 and 5 ed. H. I. Bell. London, 1893–.
P. Mich.	University of Michigan Papyri. Published in TAPA 53 (1922):134.
P. Oxy.	Oxyrhynchus Papyri, ed. B. P. Grenfell and A. S. Hunt. London, 1898–.
PRGS	Proceedings of the Royal Geographical Society
PSAS	Proceedings of the Seminar for Arabian Studies
PSI	Papyri greci e latini, Publicazioni della Societá italiana per le ricerca dei Papyri greci e latini in Egitto, Florence, 1912–.
RA	Revue Archéologique
RAA	Revue des Arts Asiatiques
RAAO	Revue d'assyriologie et d'archéologie orientale
RAO	Recueil d'archéologie orientale

RAR	*Rock Art Research*
RB	*Revue Biblique*
RÉ	*Revue d'Égyptologie*
RÉA	*Revue des Études anciennes*
RHR	*Revue de l'Histoire des Religions*
RN	*Revue numismatique*
SB	*Sammelbuch griechischen Urkunden aus Ägypten*, ed. F. Preisigke and F. Bilabel, Strassburg-Berlin-Leipzig-Heidelberg, 1913–1934.
SHAJ	*Studies in the History and Archaeology of Jordan*
SRAA	*Silk Road Art and Archaeology*
SRGÉ	Société royale de Géographie d'Égypte
TAPA	*Transactions of the American Philological Association*
TIMM	*Transactions of the Institution of Mining and Metallurgy*
WA	*World Archaeology*
WO	*Das Welt des Orients*
ZAE	*Zeitschrift für Allgemeine Erdkunde*
ZÄS	*Zeitschrift für ägyptische Sprache und Altertumskunde*
ZDMG	*Zeitschrift der deutschen Morgenländischen Gesellschaft*
ZDPV	*Zeitschrift des deutschen Palästina-Vereins*
ZPE	*Zeitschrift für Papyrologie und Epigraphik*

1

INTRODUCTION

There was a "global economy" thousands of years before the term became fashionable in the late twentieth century.[1] Yet, it is difficult to know where to begin to study this phenomenon or how it functioned and affected people's lives in the centuries straddling the turn of the Common Era. The extant, best-known written sources for the last few centuries B.C.E. and early centuries C.E. are predominately from the "western/Roman" perspective and picture the Mediterranean basin as the center of the trade. This network and the Romanocentric view of it are, however, much more complicated. The images and ideas that peoples had of themselves and of distant trading partners are complex and not easily understood, and changed over time. It would be best to start with the investigation of a single city, one that owed its existence to the economic boom of its age. Berenike, a port on Egypt's Red Sea coast (figure 1-1), is the ideal microcosm to study in order to come to grips with ancient "Old World" commerce and its impact on those who participated in it.

Berenike was one of many hubs in the extensive Old World economic network of the first millennium B.C.E. and first millennium C.E. that concatenated east and west. This intricate, far-flung web reached from at least Xian in China westward and overland along the numerous caravan routes, known collectively as the Silk Road, through Central Asia, South Asia, and the Near East, eventually ending at its westernmost termini on the eastern coasts of the Black Sea and the Mediterranean.[2] Another link, the Trans-Arabian Incense Route, connected southern Arabia with ports on the southeastern Mediterranean seaboard and on the Persian Gulf.[3] The Maritime Spice Route was the southern land-cum-maritime counterpart of the central Asian Silk Road. It supplemented and complemented

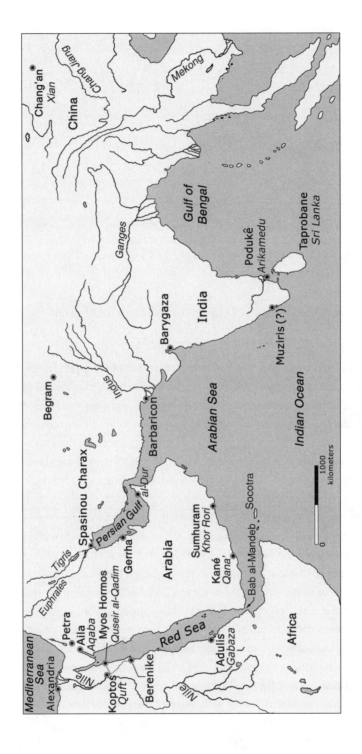

FIGURE 1-1

Map of the southeastern Mediterranean Sea, the Red Sea, the Persian Gulf, the Indian Ocean, and surrounding land masses. Drawing by M. Hense.

but was never a major competitor of the more northerly and more famous terrestrial route. The Maritime Spice Route connected China, Korea, and Southeast Asia to the Persian Gulf, Arabia, and Africa by sea via South Asia and to the Mediterranean via the Red Sea and Egypt.[4] It also complemented and to some extent competed with the Trans-Arabian Incense Route. Another route joined sub-Saharan regions to the Mediterranean littoral of North Africa.[5] The Amber Route, the only ancient long-distance trade network solely within Europe, linked the Mediterranean—primarily through the northern Adriatic port of Aquileia—with the amber-producing areas of the Baltic Sea.[6]

Berenike itself was an important conduit in the southern Maritime Spice Route, which served long-distance commerce ranging from the Mediterranean basin, Egypt, and the Red Sea on the one hand to the Indian Ocean, including the African coast, the Indian subcontinent, Sri Lanka, and to a lesser extent the Persian Gulf and perhaps beyond on the other. Varieties of merchandise, both prosaic trade goods and more exotic items, passed through Berenike; peoples from many parts of the ancient world, both inside and beyond the boundaries of the Greco-Roman Mediterranean, passed through the city or made it their home.[7]

The commodities, material possessions, records, and structures that people left behind are concrete testimony to this trade. Merchants, travelers, and mariners also conveyed knowledge and ideas—which, however, have left few if any physical traces—and medical, philosophical, astrological-astronomical, and religious concepts whose practices have left some material remains. These ideas and concepts influenced what people believed and how and what they thought far more and longer than any altars or temples they may have left behind. These abstract "commodities" also passed both ways along the Berenike conduit linking east with west, and south (sub-Saharan Africa) with north (Mediterranean).

Several emporia on the Nile served Berenike (figure 1-2). Archaeological surveys have yet to identify an ancient track leading to Syene (modern Aswan), about 260 km to the west, though circumstantial evidence suggests that at least one such route existed in antiquity. Our archaeological projects at Berenike and throughout the Eastern Desert of Egypt have surveyed the major ancient routes leading to Apollonopolis Magna (modern Edfu), 340 km toward the west-northwest; and to Koptos (modern Quft), about 65 km farther north from Edfu on the Nile. According to Pliny the Elder (*NH* 6.26.102–104), Koptos was a twelve-day overland journey from Berenike. Reaching Berenike from anywhere on the Nile necessitated crossing expanses of rugged, mountainous deserts. The traveler hoping to journey between the Nile and Berenike had to deal with an unforgiving hyperarid environment, which was often the haunt of bandits seeking refuge from authorities on the Nile, of tax evaders and other malcontents, and of local "nomads" who, when possible, robbed wayfarers or extorted protection money from them.[8] Most of those traveling between Berenike and the Nile did so in caravans of donkeys and camels supplied with guides, occasionally military escorts, and adequate food and water supplies—much of the food and water obtained en route. The Koptos Tariff, an inscription dated May 90 C.E.,

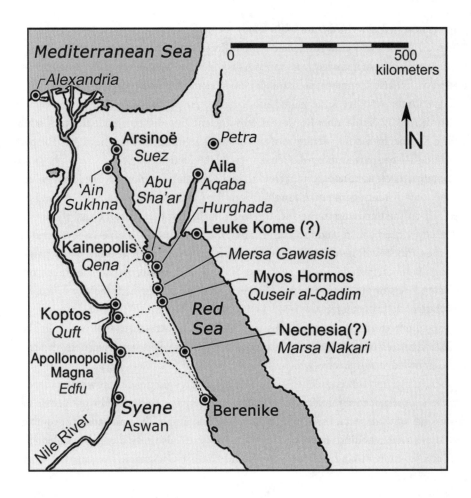

FIGURE 1-2

Map of the Nile valley and the Red Sea coast. Drawing by M. Hense.

records tolls to be paid to make the desert crossing;[9] there were also undoubtedly "unofficial" arrangements available that allowed wayfarers to obtain food and water for themselves and their baggage animals, and occasionally shelter at fortified caravansaries (*praesidia*) along the routes. Most likely, due to costs or lack of personal contacts, the average traveler probably could not take advantage of these amenities on a regular basis (see chapters 7 and 8).

Today's entrepreneurs travel to their destinations in hours, or a day or two at most, in relative comfort and security. Their ancient counterparts did not. By sailing or trekking overland long distances for weeks, months, or even years per single round-trip journey, ancient voyagers and merchants were also making other important contributions: the discovery and documentation of distant lands and peoples. In this sense these earlier mariners and businessmen were amateur geographers, ethnographers, and anthropologists.[10]

They charted and described unknown or little-understood peoples and places. Some of their reports were very fanciful and amateurish; others were keenly astute and surprisingly accurate. These included "geographies" and *periploi*—handbooks compiled of sailing conditions, ports, wind patterns, reef and island locations, and peoples and products of distant lands.

Drawing upon earlier sources, Herodotus wrote accounts about India and the "east" in the fifth century B.C.E.[11] Alexander the Great's campaigns of the 330s and 320s B.C.E. in "eastern" lands sparked interest in these regions in subsequent centuries among many dwelling in the Mediterranean. Historians recounted various aspects of Alexander's adventures,[12] and although some of these accounts survive in whole or in part, others are lost, their authors known to us by name only, or were paraphrased by later writers.[13]

Although Ptolemaic monarchs sought mainly gold from the Eastern Desert of Egypt, their major activity in more southerly regions of the African Red Sea coast was the acquisition and transportation of ivory, and of war elephants with which to counter their Seleucid adversaries in the Near East. These pachyderms, captured in areas of what are today Sudan and Eritrea, were taken to elephant-hunting stations along the Red Sea coast.[14] The animals were then loaded onto specially designed ships called *elephantegoi* and dispatched to more northerly ports in Egyptian territory, Berenike being the favored landfall. Thence they were marched overland to one of the Nile emporia, where, after training, they were incorporated into the military as the ancient equivalent of tanks. (Acquisition and transportation of elephants is discussed at length in chapter 4.) Although the Ptolemaic rulers were also interested in and had some diplomatic and commercial contacts with South Arabia and India, we have no evidence that this contact was maintained on an extensive scale or on a regular basis.

After the annexation of Egypt as a Roman province in 30 B.C.E. there was increased interest in the *Erythra Thalassa*— viz. the Indian Ocean—and, to a lesser extent, the Persian Gulf as well as the Red Sea.[15] Roman commerce, however, was different from that of the Ptolemies; Roman mercantile activity was greater in scope and more civilian and commercial in nature. The Roman Empire was many times the size of the Ptolemaic both in geographical extent and in population. Therefore, it stands to reason that the quantities and varieties of items exchanged via the Red Sea emporia after the Roman annexation of Egypt were substantially greater than in the Ptolemaic period. Given the disinclination of ancient writers and the dearth of detailed commercial documents from this Roman-era trade, one cannot determine precisely the volumes or costs; both were quite substantial.

Clearly, Berenike played an important role in the vibrant Old World global economy that bound west with east and south with north, both by sea and by land. For that reason, to study this city allows a better understanding of some portion of this vast, ancient commercial network. From a still far from complete understanding of this microcosm of international trade, one can explore Berenike's role in the larger economic picture of the ancient world approximately two millennia ago in the Maritime Spice Route and the overland Silk Route and Trans-Arabian Incense Route. What Berenike reveals is a microcosm of the larger economic picture of the ancient world two millennia ago.

There were a number of ports on the Mediterranean and the Red Sea that bore the sobriquet Berenike. The one examined here was named after the queen of Ptolemy I Soter, who established the Ptolemaic dynasty, and the mother of Ptolemy II Philadelphus, founder of this important Red Sea emporium.

2

GEOGRAPHY, CLIMATE, ANCIENT
AUTHORS, AND MODERN VISITORS

The remains of Berenike Trogodytika[1] lie approximately 825 km south-southeast of Suez and about 260 km east of Aswan (figure 1-2). In the third century B.C.E. Ptolemaic authorities founded a settlement here, at the interface of the Eastern Desert and the Red Sea. Initially in the Ptolemaic era military and diplomatic, and later economic and government administrative, interests were the main impetus to founding and maintaining the community. Eventually Berenike evolved into a bustling metropolis and grew to enormous importance in the first century C.E. and later, when it became an integral part of the ancient global economic network.

The Red Sea is, in geological terms, a long, narrow, and recent marine feature created about 25–30 million years ago when the African and Eurasian landmasses pulled apart. The Red Sea is almost completely enclosed except at its southern end, where a 26–29 km–wide strait, the Bab al-Mandeb (Gate of Tears),[2] connects it to the Indian Ocean. Surface currents, which peak in the winter, flow northward from the Indian Ocean into the Red Sea with a speed up to half a knot, reaching as far north as Myos Hormos (Quseir al-Qadim).[3] In the north, the Suez Canal is a recent artifact linking the Red Sea to the Mediterranean. Measuring about 2,250–2,350 km long north–south, including its extensions into the Gulfs of Suez and Aqaba,[4] by about 350 km east–west at its widest,[5] the Red Sea is a geographical extension of the Indian Ocean, but because of minimal water circulation between the two bodies, the Red Sea is warmer and the evaporation rate higher, and it is, therefore, saltier than the Indian Ocean.[6] Tides in the Red Sea vary from over 2 m near Suez to imperceptible in other locations.[7] Jagged coral reefs fringe much of the coastline, beyond which the sea drops off precipitously to depths reaching 2,300 m or more.[8]

Although the Indian Ocean and the Red Sea have some flora and fauna in common, the Red Sea has developed some unique species of fish as a result of its almost complete isolation.[9] After the Suez Canal opened in 1869, some Red Sea fish used it to migrate to the Mediterranean; the reverse also occurred, though not to the same extent.[10]

Its topography suggests that commerce and communication within the Red Sea naturally tended to be along the lines of the shortest sailing distances—that is, west–east between Africa and the Arabian Peninsula. Although there is some evidence of this, the predominant directions of sailing and, hence, of communications and commerce were mainly along its northwest–southeast axis. This is due in part to the desert environment along the eastern (Arabian) coast of the Red Sea and to the fact that most merchandise sought by Egypt was either from the African side or from the extreme southern end of the Arabian coast. Contact with these regions, therefore, necessitated generally north–south sailing patterns.

In the Red Sea north of 18°/20° north latitude, prevailing winds are usually northwesterly and at times can be quite strong. A newly deciphered papyrus likely from the Arsinoite Nome (Fayum), purchased by Yale University and dated June 5, 97 C.E., confirms the problems ships had when approaching Berenike against these strong contrary winds.[11] In the southern third of the Red Sea, wind patterns and strengths are more variable and can, generally, be stronger than in the north.[12]

Berenike's location at the boundary of the Red Sea and the Eastern Desert provided avenues of trade, communication, and conveyance of basic resources to and from the port, but also posed barriers to reaching it. The Eastern Desert south of the Nile Delta and north of the Sudanese border covers approximately 206,000 km². Plains of varying widths slope down from the Red Sea mountain watershed toward the Nile and the Red Sea. These mountains comprise igneous and metamorphic basement rocks, formed about 550–900 million years ago, with some sedimentary deposits, which run parallel to the Nile and the Red Sea.[13] The highest peak is Gebel Shayib al-Banat at 2,184 m.[14] Generally east–west-running wadis (valleys or seasonal watercourses) carry rainfall toward the Nile and the Red Sea and dictate locations of water supplies, especially wells and springs. These wadi systems also determine directions of most human and animal movement through the region.[15]

Annual precipitation is minimal in the northern Red Sea, varying from about 5 mm at Quseir to approximately 27–28 mm at Eilat; farther south at Suakin and Massawa this increases to 44 mm per annum.[16] In Egypt's Eastern Desert most rain falls in rare, heavy downpours every few years in mountainous areas west of the Red Sea coast. Depending upon the side of the watershed on which the rain falls, the resulting precipitation eventually flows either west toward the Nile or east in the direction of the Red Sea. This rainfall leads to occasional devastating flash floods (*seyal/suyul* in Arabic). The destruction wrought by these *suyul* and their incredible power are graphically visible in wadis throughout the Eastern Desert and along the Red Sea coast. Uprooted trees, toppled houses, washed-away vehicles, undercut or heavily eroded roads and railway beds, reports of many drowned humans and animals, and dense clumps of vegetation washed 2 m and higher against low-lying acacia trees or clinging to craggy wadi walls are omnipresent reminders of these deluges.[17] Available evidence indicates that rainfall levels were similar during the period when Berenike operated.[18] Examination of ancient authors, including Aelius Aristeides (*Egyptian Discourse* 36.32 and 36.67), indicates how desiccated the region was in Roman times.

One can appreciate the enormous efforts and matériel expended to establish a community at Berenike and maintain its infrastructure to enable people to live and work in such a hostile environment. Berenike was founded in the first half of the third century B.C.E. and lay abandoned before about 550 C.E. Subsequently, until modern times, few people seemed to know its whereabouts, though transients occasionally camped there for brief periods.[19]

Berenike's location south of Ras (Cape) Benas (see figure 5-6) was carefully considered. Whereas the cape did not protect the port from powerful northerly winds, it did block the strong, southerly alongshore current that partially caused the harbor at Berenike to silt up (from sediment moving along the shore) and boats anchored offshore to drift. Ras Benas was also an excellent landmark for those sailing along the coast.

The ruins of Berenike cover an area of about 300–350 m north–south by approximately 670 m east–west (figure 2-1).[20] The remains lie mainly atop an extinct coral reef,[21] which rises about 2 m above sea level, with the overlying ruins reaching just over 7 m above sea level in the center of the site. Visible at ground level today are fragments of walls made of chunks of coral the size of baseballs or even basketballs, which form outlines of buildings of the latest period of the city and of the streets and alleys that separated them. Thousands of small artifacts, mainly potsherds, litter the surface.

Berenike was situated between two wadis, which during the occasional heavy rains, mainly between October and December,[22] convey large volumes of water and sediments from sandy, gravelly plains and mainly metamorphic mountains that rise about 15–20 km west of the site. The seaward terminus of Wadi Mandit formed the northern harbor of Berenike, and the eastern end of Wadi Umm Salim al-Mandit created its southern harbor. The latter seems to have been the more important.

The sandy wadi outflow was a mixed blessing. On the one hand, sediments carried by occasional heavy rains through the wadis that emptied into the harbors generated turbid water that prevented the growth of coral reefs offshore, and the erosive currents created accessible natural embayments or *mersas*.[23] The heavy flow of freshwater into these natural harbors also killed or stunted the growth of otherwise blocking reefs.[24] This lack of reefs facilitated the development of natural harbors somewhat protected from strong winds and currents, with accesses unimpeded by the dangers that coral reefs would otherwise have posed to maritime traffic. This phenomenon was not unique to Berenike, but is common along both the Arabian and African coasts of the Red Sea[25] and is one that the ancients soon noticed and learned to exploit when choosing a site for a harbor or roadstead.

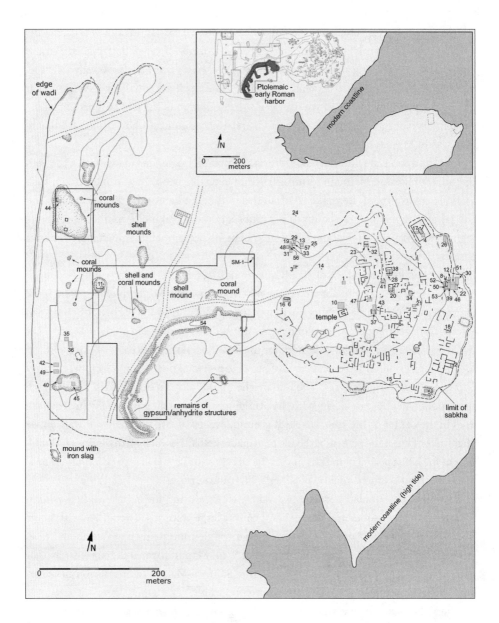

FIGURE 2-1
Berenike, plan of the site. Drawing by M. Hense.

Yet, the same conditions that created these optimal situations for port location also caused problems throughout Berenike's history and, eventually, were probably partially responsible for its ultimate demise. Over the centuries large volumes of sediments washed from the wadis into the harbor basins and eventually silted them up, rendering them unusable except for the shallowest-draught vessels. Long before the early nineteenth century the northern harbor at Berenike had completely disappeared under waterborne sediments and windblown sand; by the mid 1990s the southern harbor was so shallow that numerous sandbars were visible, and at low tide one could easily wade across it.

In addition, the sea level has also changed since antiquity. Some geologists agree that the level of the Red Sea has risen 1–2 m during the last two millennia or so, whereas others see minimal changes.[26] This ongoing phenomenon would have created problems and challenges for Berenike with regard to harbor location and maintenance, and to the placement of buildings in the city at different periods in history. Assuming that there has been a 1–2 m change in sea level, ancient Berenikeans would have had to deal with two diametrically opposed natural phenomena: on the one hand, a rising sea level, which threatened to flood lower areas of the city closest to the sea; on the other, local silting of the harbors, which counteracted and more than offset rising sea levels. This latter tendency—which would have been the Berenikeans' major concern and one that they could, to some extent, have dealt with—required either dredging or the physical displacement of the city eastward toward the receding, seaward-moving coastline. For reasons not yet understood, the responsible powers seem to have opted for movement of the city closer to the sea rather than dredging the harbors, which they were fully capable of doing, in both the Ptolemaic and Roman periods. This eastward migration of the settlement points to a rapid (in geological terms) sanding up of the coastal area, protected from the currents to some extent by Ras Benas throughout the Ptolemaic and Roman periods.

Floodwater and sediment runoff created problems in the harbors themselves. Yet, unlike other ancient desert peoples of Libya and the Near East—especially the Nabataeans, who developed ingenious technologies for efficiently acquiring, managing, storing, and distributing rainwater and groundwater for drinking, cooking, washing, industry, and irrigation[27]—there is no evidence yet of how the residents of ancient Berenike attempted to manage water resources. Our fieldwork at Berenike is bound to discover their efforts eventually; it is inconceivable that they would not have undertaken them, since water acquisition, storage, conservation, and distribution methods were well known and essential to those manning the *praesidia* lining the transdesert routes linking Berenike and the Nile (see chapters 7 and 8). The irregularity of the precipitation and the unpredictability and destructive nature of the floods may have made such endeavors extremely difficult nearer the Red Sea coast at ports like Berenike.

The nearest sources of substantial amounts of potable water for humans residing at Berenike were the large wells *(hydreumata)* sunk at intervals, 7–8.5 km west-northwest and southwest of the city. Deemed so important, the *hydreumata* were fortified inside *praesidia* and were supplied with protective military garrisons (see chapters 7 and 8).

LACK OF PROVISIONS: FOOD, WATER, WOOD

There were three basic resources critical to the city's residents: food and water for inhabitants and livestock, and for provisioning the ships; and timber/wood for limited construction and ship repair. Wood, and animal dung, would also have been used as fuel for fires, both industrial and domestic.

Limited documentation from excavations of the Ptolemaic (third to second century B.C.E.) industrial area of Berenike indicates that much of the city's protein food derived from the Nile valley, and to a lesser extent the Red Sea.[28] Wild game played little part in the diet of residents at any time in Berenike's history.[29] There must have been, as in Roman times (late first century B.C.E. to mid-sixth century C.E.), some local cultivation of grains, fruits, vegetables, and legumes, but there is little direct evidence of this.[30]

The more permanent, long-term needs of the Ptolemies and Romans to sustain large numbers of people and animals in desert regions for more extended periods than their Pharaonic predecessors led them to build upon that earlier knowledge. This necessitated sophisticated strategies for the storage, distribution, and use of water. These efforts grew extensively after the arrival of the Romans and their expanded interest and presence in the Eastern Desert, especially in early and late Roman times—the eras of greatest population density, at any time in the region's history (see chapters 7 and 8).

A human living in or traveling through the Eastern Desert requires a minimum of about four to six liters of water a day for drinking in the summer, less in the cooler months, when engaged in moderate levels of exertion. Increased levels of physical activity require consumption of proportionally more water. Our surveys and excavations over the years have noted that additional use for bathing, cooking, and so on raises that total to about fifteen to twenty liters per person per day in the summer and less in the winter.[31] Donkeys and camels, the primary pack animals used in the region, require varying amounts of water depending on a host of factors (discussed in chapter 7). Numerous dated ancient graffiti found along the Eastern Desert roads and at sites along them indicate that travel and residence in the region were perennial,[32] though perhaps somewhat greater during the cooler months. Wind patterns in the Red Sea and directions of the monsoon winds in the Indian Ocean dictated sailing schedules between the Red Sea ports and those in the Indian Ocean, whether toward India or toward the African coast; these winds also influenced the times of year during which people traveled through the Eastern Desert.

The effort that went into maintaining Berenike is impressive considering the difficulties of providing for its population and provisioning ships that embarked on lengthy voyages from the port or that required extensive repair after landing there. Berenike would not seem to be an ideal location for an important emporium. In addition to adverse weather, with almost constantly blowing winds carrying stinging and blinding sand, swarms of biting and annoying insects—both terrestrial and airborne—scorpions, termites, snakes, large spiders, mice, and rats, there was the constant issue of acquiring adequate supplies of food and water. Furthermore, travel to and from Berenike presented numerous challenges. Access would have been difficult both by sea and by land. The strong prevailing northerly winds of the region[33] required highly skilled seamanship in heavy oceangoing vessels. Coral reefs fringing the coast, with resulting shallow waters, were, and are still, extremely hazardous and caused numerous shipwrecks.[34] Piracy was, at times, also a serious problem in the Red Sea—so much so that some departing merchant ships hired archers to be placed on board for protection.[35] A dearth of maps—together with the poor quality of those that may have been available, due to the inability of cartographers to measure longitude accurately[36]—plus a lack of reliable methods for measuring time at sea prior to the eighteenth century compounded the hazards of maritime travel.[37]

AUTHORS IN THE PTOLEMAIC AND ROMAN PERIODS ON BERENIKE AND THE EAST

Numerous ancient authors reported on Berenike and the city's contacts with other areas of the ancient world. These reports range in date from the second century B.C.E. into the sixth century C.E.[38]

Agatharchides of Knidos wrote *On the Erythraean Sea* in the second century B.C.E., but using sources from the preceding century.[39] Little or nothing of his original work survives, though Diodorus Siculus in the first century B.C.E., Strabo at the turn of the Christian era, and Photius in the ninth century paraphrase him.[40] Agatharchides provides important information on the Red Sea and some of its prominent emporia.

Strabo, writing his *Geography* in the last decades of the first century B.C.E. and the early decades of the first century C.E.,[41] had read Agatharchides as well as the geographers Eratosthenes of Cyrene and Artemidorus of Ephesus, and used of some of their information.[42] Strabo, however, provided additional data, some of it firsthand and very practical, for travelers in the Eastern Desert and the Red Sea. Strabo's was a period of intense Roman interest in the area. In his day Berenike, and a more northerly Egyptian Red Sea port at Myos Hormos, were the premier emporia of the region.[43]

Roman emperors sent out several expeditions in these years to learn more about the east and sub-Saharan Africa, for reasons both political—the Parthians were Rome's main adversaries in the Middle East and the eastern Mediterranean region—and economic: an attempt to circumvent the Parthians as middlemen in the lucrative trade between the east and the Mediterranean world, or at least to dilute their influences on and profits derived from this commerce. The Romans, however, were not averse to launching military expeditions to further their commercial and diplomatic objectives; Augustus learned of the wealth of southern Arabia, one source of much frankincense and, indirectly, of myrrh, and dispatched an unsuccessful military expedition, whose commander, Aelius Gallus, was a good friend of Strabo's, to gain control of it in 26/25 B.C.E. (see chapter 9).[44] It is probably no coincidence that embassies between eastern peoples (primarily various Arab and Indian states) and Rome began in earnest soon thereafter.[45] Although a military failure, the expedition brought diplomatic and, it appears, economic benefits to Rome in its wake.

Another traveler, also Augustan in date, was Isidore or Dionysus from Charax, near Basra, at the head of the Persian Gulf. He surveyed the caravan routes down the Euphrates into Parthian territory and into Central Asia and, according to Pliny the Elder (*NH* 6.31.141), wrote a report called *Parthian Stations,* a portion of which survives.[46] This impetus seems to have been preliminary due to Augustus sending his grandsons Gaius and Lucius on geographical expeditions to the east at the turn of the Christian era.[47] In their writings, contemporary Roman literati and poets reflected the Romans' fascination with things "eastern"—mainly Arabian, Indian, and Chinese—and hinted that Rome should control these remote lands as part of her *"imperium sine fine."*[48] Also at about this time, Juba of Mauretania wrote a book on the Erythraean Sea, which Pliny later cited throughout his own *Natural History.*[49] It seems that during the age of Augustus there was much interest, either state sponsored or independently inspired, in the exploration of the "east," likely for commercial purposes.

A few decades after Strabo, Cornelius Celsus wrote an encyclopedia, including a section entitled *De Medicina*—the only part of the book that survives. In it he routinely lists ingredients of prescriptions for various ailments, ingredients that include pepper, frankincense, and myrrh among others.[50] The regularity with which he notes these items—imported from India, South Arabia, and the Horn of Africa, respectively—indicates their relative abundance and overall affordability. Celsus's account demonstrates that commerce between these regions and the Roman world via the Red Sea ports, especially Berenike and Myos Hormos, was substantial at this time. Dioscorides, who wrote *Materia Medica* just after the middle of the first century C.E., cites an abundance of botanical data used in pharmacology. Comparing his information with that of half a century earlier indicates much greater knowledge of those species useful in the medical profession and, ergo, an increase in their importation to the Mediterranean world.[51]

Sometime between approximately 40 and 70 C.E. a nameless author, probably a sea captain or experienced navigator, wrote in Koine Greek the *Periplus Maris Erythraei*. It is a practical handbook that notes the winds, port locations, political situations, peoples, and products available and desired at harbors on the Red Sea and on the Arabian, African, and Indian coasts of the Indian Ocean, as well as some on the Persian Gulf; it survives only in a tenth-century copy.[52] The author of the *Periplus* noted what other first-century C.E. authors and the archaeological record at Berenike and elsewhere show: this was a peak period of contact between eastern lands and the Mediterranean basin, and Berenike was an important player in these economic and cultural exchanges.

Seneca (*Natural Questions* 6.8.3–5) and Pliny (*NH* 6.35.181 and 12.8.19) report an expedition that apparently reached into areas of the Sudd, a marshy region of southern Sudan.[53] Seneca's sources were two Roman centurions who accompanied the exploratory effort. The purpose of this reconnaissance remains unknown, but economic motives may have been considered.

About the time that Seneca recorded this African adventure, Pliny the Elder, writing in his encyclopedic *Natural History* sometime between about 50 and 77 C.E., documented the Romans' increased knowledge of and interest in "eastern" lands.[54] He provides a long account of merchandise that Romans acquired from India, Arabia, and elsewhere, and notes what those peoples wanted in return from the Mediterranean world. He also records a detailed price list for these commodities, presumably for sale in the city of Rome. Pliny clearly had more information available to him than did Strabo several decades earlier. Berenike figured as an important Red Sea trade port in Pliny's writings, as it had in Strabo's.

Though imprecise, Pliny's writings indicated (*NH* 6.26.100–101 and 104) that, sometime before his day, westerners had learned about the monsoons in the Indian Ocean, the exploitation of which made voyages from the mouth of the Red Sea to India and coastal sub-Saharan Africa and back much faster and, therefore, more cost-effective in commercial terms.[55] They called these monsoons "Hippalus" winds, after the ship's helmsman of Eudoxus of Cyzicus, who sailed likely sometime late in the second century B.C.E.[56] The "discovery" of the monsoons by westerners probably occurred in the later second century B.C.E., though peoples of the Mediterranean did not exploit them extensively until the first century C.E.[57] By using the monsoons, westerners could sail across open water in the Indian Ocean and avoid the time-consuming coast-hugging navigation that they had used previously to reach South Asia; such bold undertakings, however, were substantially more dangerous. These Hippalus winds also facilitated voyages down Africa's Indian Ocean coast.

This fascination with things "eastern" and "exotic" continued.[58] In the middle of the second century C.E. Claudius Ptolemy published his *Geography*, which provided thousands of locations for ports, inland cities, and other points of geographical interest and importance in the known world. In Ptolemy's case, this extended from beyond Britain in the northwest to Southeast Asia (the Golden Chersonese).[59] He was, of course, most accurate in the Mediterranean basin.[60] His was a remarkable accomplishment based upon travelers' reports and on his predecessor Marinus of Tyre, whom Ptolemy cites but who is otherwise unknown.[61] Although Ptolemy incorrectly estimated distances between toponyms, he was the first scholar whose work survives to use concepts of longitude and latitude and degrees and seconds, and these have come to be essential for all modern maps. Ptolemy's major errors were an underestimation of the size of the world by about 25 percent and his assumption that Africa and eastern lands met in the distant south, forming an enclosed lake: the Indian Ocean. By extension, his former errors led to distortions of east–west distances and incorrect locations for many of his place-names.[62] Nevertheless, his influence extended into the sixteenth century, and he was the acme of ancient "western" geographical knowledge.[63] It can be no coincidence that Ptolemy's *Geography* appeared during or shortly after the period of the maximum extent in size and prosperity of the Roman Empire and at the height of its commercial contacts with distant lands. Ptolemy's detailed list of Red Sea ports includes Berenike, as well as one mentioned in no other surviving ancient source: Leukos Limen. The location of Leukos Limen has never been accurately determined. (More will be said about this in chapter 9.) All later extant ancient geographical writings pale in comparison with the breadth of Ptolemy's knowledge. Thereafter, ancient "classical" authors merely paraphrased and, in some cases, misunderstood and distorted the geographical and ethnological knowledge known to their predecessors.

There were also maps and itineraries produced in Roman times, including the *Antonine Itinerary*, the *Peutinger Table*, and the much later *Ravenna Cosmography*. (More will be said about these as well as other ancient geographical sources in chapter 8.)

One of the latest pre-Islamic authors dealing with the topic was Cosmas Indicopleustes, an Egyptian monk who, in the mid sixth century C.E., wrote *Christian Topography*. Books 2 and 11 of this opus provide insights into travel on the Red Sea and Indian Ocean.[64] Much of what Cosmas recorded was fanciful, though his description of an eastern ocean bordering China was quite accurate (*Christian Topography* 11.16).[65]

DARING EARLY MODERN VISITORS

Basic problems that plagued the ancients traveling to and from Berenike and surviving there for extended periods also troubled modern visitors.[66] The earliest modern traveler to record his experiences was the Portuguese Dom Joam de Castro. In 1541 de Castro was navigating in the Red Sea with an armada to protect Portuguese interests in the region and in India from the intrigues of the Egyptian Pasha Soliman; much of his mission entailed raiding and destroying Egyptian coastal towns. De Castro's surviving account indicates that he was aware of Berenike. Yet, although he sailed close to the ancient remains on April 10, 1541, he failed to find them.[67]

In the eighteenth century the French traveler J. B. B. d'Anville recorded both the observations of de Castro and those of ancient authors who wrote about Berenike, but he, too, was unable to locate the ruins.[68] Finally, Giovanni Belzoni "discovered" the remains of Berenike in 1818. In 1820 he published his preliminary remarks about the site and a drawing he made of temple ruins in the middle of the ancient city.[69]

Throughout the remainder of the nineteenth century, western travelers journeyed to Berenike. These included J. G. Wilkinson, who in 1826 drew the first plan of the site. He paced it out, not using any more precise measurements; nevertheless, his map is remarkably accurate and was the only one available until the Berenike Project began to draw a measured plan of the site in 1994.[70]

Nineteenth-century visitors, following Belzoni's and Wilkinson's accounts, were attracted to the highest point of the city, the location of the most famous building in Berenike: a temple dedicated to Serapis and several other Egyptian gods. This is the edifice that Belzoni sketched in 1818. The Greek-born, Cairo-raised Giovanni d'Athanasi, an Arabic and Turkish interpreter for the British consulate and an employee of the Egyptophile Henry Salt, also passed by the site and partially cleared the Serapis temple, probably as part of Belzoni's original team.[71] Other travelers, in addition to Belzoni, d'Athanasi, and Wilkinson, also attempted to clear the temple, thereby revealing hieroglyphic inscriptions on the interior walls and recovering statue fragments, offering tables, and other texts inscribed in Greek. This led J. R. Wellsted, who visited Berenike in the first half of the century, to comment upon the extremely fragile state of the reliefs inside the Serapis temple, which had been exposed, no doubt, partially by winds and certainly by the labors of previous visitors.[72] Later in the century the German explorer H. Barth also paid a visit.[73] The German botanist G. Schweinfurth[74] also traveled by Berenike, as did the Russian W. Golénischeff;[75] the American Colonel Purdy, working for the Egyptian government;[76] and R. E. Colston,[77] as well as the Frenchmen E. A. Floyer,[78] G. Daressy, and others.[79] Several of these visitors also cleared the Serapis temple, though none indicates how much work he actually undertook in this endeavor.

Logistical constraints greatly limited what these travelers could accomplish in their short visits, which was to clear the most conspicuous building on the site: the temple dedicated to Serapis and other Egyptian gods. Limited to nonexistent water supplies in Berenike's environs severely curtailed the amount of time they could spend at the ruins. They had to either trek back to acquire potable water from a source often at a great distance from Berenike or have camel trains sent to procure adequate amounts of water and food. These nineteenth-century adventurers must have marveled at the ability of the ancients to live and work in such a hostile environment for centuries when they could last so little time there themselves.

Yet, despite these drawbacks even in modern times, both Egyptians and foreigners recognized that Berenike's general location was a good one from a commercial point of view. In 1897 the Egyptian government commissioned J. Raimondi to conduct a survey and feasibility study for constructing a railroad between the eastern end of Ras Benas and Kom Ombo on the Nile.[80] A trunk line was to run from near Berenike, join the Ras Benas–Kom Ombo line, and proceed northwest to the Nile. This Red Sea–Nile railway was planned to hook up with the Luxor–Aswan railroad, which had been opened earlier that same year. A major issue for Raimondi's survey was the availability of potable water for the projected railroad. Although fieldwork demonstrated the value of a modern Red Sea port in the region of Berenike, nothing ever came of Raimondi's plan, due, in part, to the logistical problems that the construction of such a railroad would have encountered.

Theodore Bent and his wife visited the site at the end of the nineteenth century as part of a larger trip throughout the Red Sea area and conducted "sundry excavations" at Berenike, but they did not tarry long.[81]

Travelers in the twentieth century were no less enthusiastic when visiting Berenike than their nineteenth-century predecessors had been. The geologist J. Ball wrote about Berenike.[82] As part of his duties for the Survey of Egypt—a department of the Egyptian government—between the World Wars, G. W. Murray visited Berenike in the 1920s and provided a description of the site. He also investigated and wrote about other ancient remains in the vicinity of Berenike, and about the artifacts he collected.[83]

There have been modern geological field studies conducted throughout the Eastern Desert and in the vicinity of Berenike, especially in the earlier part of the twentieth century, to determine the types of minerals present and the feasibility of extracting and shipping them economically.[84] Though some of these reports led to the opening, or reopening, of mines and quarries, none of these are in close proximity to Berenike, no doubt due to the logistical difficulties their working would have entailed.

None of these nineteenth- and early-twentieth-century visitors, however, undertook systematic, long-term, scientific surveys or excavations at Berenike or in its environs. This was due to the same physical limitations that the ancients had to overcome. It was one thing to spend a few days or even a week or perhaps longer at the ruins with a small team, often with extensive camel trains or a ship offshore loaded with supplies; it was quite another to mount a full-scale expedition with a large staff to study the site in detail over an extended period of time. The reluctance of earlier visitors was not due to lack of interest; numerous practical and financial problems prevented meaningful investigations.

THE LOGISTICS OF EXCAVATING AT BERENIKE

When the University of Delaware–Leiden University/UCLA consortium first began drawing a map of the visible remains at Berenike and started excavations in 1994, we had a relatively small expedition, but the practical problems to be surmounted to remain in the field were considerable. Our team came to have empathy with earlier travelers and an immense respect for the ancients who had made Berenike their home. Berenike itself now lies about 8 km east of the main paved north–south Red Sea coastal highway linking Shalateen to Marsa Alam, Quseir, Safaga, Hurghada, and points north. After 1996 this road was repaved and well maintained. Originally Berenike was difficult for us to locate, but eventually the daily influx of 'Ababda Bedouin pickup trucks carrying excavation workers created well-used abraded dirt tracks between the paved highway and the ancient site. Thus, our supply and communication problems were far less burdensome than they had been for earlier visitors. Nevertheless, they were still daunting. In the first few seasons of fieldwork all nonpotable water (used for bathing, laundry, cleaning pottery and other artifacts, and cooking) came by truck from Bir Jahaliya, about 113 km to the south; and drinking water and food came from Quseir, about 300 km to the north. Rationing of precious water resources was paramount. Several years later the project procured nonpotable water from a desalinization plant at Hammata, a small village about 40 km to the north. Although this alleviated the water situation somewhat, we still depended upon the water truck arriving several times a week from Hammata for resupply. Lack of telephones afforded little option when the truck did not arrive except to drive to Hammata and request that water be sent as soon as possible.

Our camp at Berenike is not on an electrical grid. Although probably more expensive than a traditional gasoline- or diesel-powered electrical generator, solar panels were our choice during the 1994–2001 seasons due to environmental concerns and the need for a low-maintenance source of power. Placed upon the roof of our storage magazine and connected to twelve-volt truck batteries on the courtyard floor below, the panels functioned reasonably well except on cloudy days. They usually generated sufficient electrical supplies to operate computers for the registry and for writing reports and to allow minimal lighting in the magazine itself for evening work. During the brief 2009–2010 excavation seasons we used a gasoline-powered generator a few hours each day. All other illumination throughout camp was by candle, kerosene lantern, or flashlight. All meals, cooking, bathing, toilet use, and sleeping took place in tents pitched adjacent to the storage magazine during the 1994–2001 seasons. During the 2009 season we cooked and ate in the magazine.

In addition to all these "inconveniences," during our 1994–2001 excavations medical facilities were nonexistent, and telephonic or other communications with the outside world were sporadic. There was no cell-phone communication in this part of Egypt at that time, nor was there fax or e-mail access. Only in a dire emergency did officers at the nearby Egyptian military base allow us to use their phones.

Despite logistical problems, chronic financial shortages, the intemperate climate, and poor living conditions, conducting research at Berenike offers a wealth of information to those willing to excavate, study, and live there. Problems that kept earlier visitors from working for extended periods at Berenike also protected the site from later redevelopment, with the exception of some minor and superficial damage done by bulldozers or front-end loaders to parts of the mound in the early 1970s.

Another potential danger is the construction of tourist resorts in the region north of Ras Benas and the concomitant increase in visitors to the site. Since we were forced to halt excavation by the Egyptian military after our 2001 season and could no longer afford to pay guards after 2005, there was no way to protect the site from the ravages that uncontrolled tourism wrought. Needless to say, lack of protection also left the site open to plunder by antiquities hunters and vandals. More recently, there has been some robbing of sections of the site by unknown persons.

Such a situation is extremely unfortunate, since the hyperarid climate allows an amazing degree of preservation, especially of organic remains, that cannot be found in other areas of the ancient Mediterranean world. In fact, the extensive array of finds recovered from the excavations affords an amazingly detailed glimpse of the day-to-day activities of Berenike's ancient residents, and of the long-distance trade that was their bread and butter.

In ten seasons of fieldwork at Berenike between 1994 and 2001 and briefly in 2009–2010 we excavated only about 2 percent of the surface of the site and much less than that of its depth. In one trench alone, investigated between 1996 and 2000, we excavated down over 4 m and still did not reach the bottom, but only to the level of the late first century B.C.E.; there is probably still about 250 years' worth of site history to uncover in this trench alone.

Despite our digging so little of the site, our painstaking methods of excavation, recording, and detailed study have paid huge dividends. Vast quantities of both organic and inorganic artifacts and ecofacts (finds of natural substances such as botanical remains, bones, and seashells, as opposed to man-made objects) ranging from large buildings to seeds and the exoskeletons of insects that died in trash dumped nearly two thousand years ago have, when analyzed, revealed many aspects of daily life at Berenike and of the long-distance trade that was the main raison d'être of the city. We have recovered tantalizing clues identifying ethnic and socioeconomic groups residing at Berenike in different periods and have revealed what their daily lives were like—including what they manufactured in the town, the items traded, their diets, the pets they owned, the types of clothing and jew-elry they wore, the languages they spoke, the gods they worshipped, the places they lived and worked and how these were furnished and decorated, and the way at least some of them were buried. The relationships that different ethnic groups had with one another, and both de facto and de jure with the government and its various representatives, and methods the government and private entrepreneurs used to monitor, protect, promote, and profit from the lucrative commerce have also been documented, though they remain only partly understood. Something is known about the nearby desert settlements and the distant lands both within the Mediterranean basin and well beyond it to the east that were in contact with Berenike. Despite all this, we have only scratched the surface. We have raised as many questions as have been answered.

The following chapters will examine many facets of Berenike and the relationships the port had with the immediate hinterland, with more distant communities in the East-ern Desert, with emporia along the Nile, and with trading partners many hundreds or thousands of kilometers away in the Mediterranean, the Red Sea, and the Indian Ocean.

3

PRE-ROMAN INFRASTRUCTURE
IN THE EASTERN DESERT

PRE-PTOLEMAIC ERA

To communicate with the Red Sea ports in Egypt including Berenike, it was necessary to build roads linking the Nile to emporia on the coast and to provide those routes with water and protection to accommodate merchants, other civilian and military-government travelers, and their pack and draft animals.

Numerous graffiti, which from the Archaic/Early Dynastic period (Dynasties 1–3; 2920–2575 B.C.E.) on included hieroglyphic and pictorial scribblings, are found adjacent to pre-Dynastic and prehistoric rock art.[1] Routes throughout Egypt, including the deserts, had existed since prehistoric times—millennia prior to the unification of Egypt in about 3000 B.C.E. This is evident from numerous petroglyphs, and from finds of early stone tools, graves, and human settlements—some of the latter found in caves (like Sodmein, about 35 km west northwest of Quseir)[2] or on high ground—preserved throughout the desert.[3] Visitors from the Nile valley and denizens of the region traveled between the Nile and the Red Sea in search of game and plant foods, and to exploit its mineral resources, especially chert, but also other soft and especially hard stones as well as metals.[4] Tools and weapons found throughout the region are also depicted in rock art: hunters armed with spears or bows and arrows chasing their prey.[5] By engaging in these "artistic" practices, people followed a universal human urge to leave graffiti attesting their presence or passing—a characteristic that long predates the invention of writing. The oldest graphic activity thus far recorded in the Nile valley dates to the period of Neolithicization, not during the great Holocene wet phase (12,000–8000 before present, B.P.), but to the mid-

Holocene arid phase (8000–7000 or 7500–6500 B.P.).[6] Throughout the Neolithic (fifth millennium B.C.E.) and the Predynastic periods (about 4000–3000 B.C.E.), mankind continued to leave his mark by carving on boulders and rock faces and, to a lesser extent, by painting in hues of red and ochre with mineral or plant-based pigments.[7]

Locations for these etchings were at naturally shaded rest stops along well-trodden routes or near water sources where humans and the prey they sought tended to gather and linger. The oldest dated petroglyphs in Egypt depict bovines and, possibly, fish traps.[8] Other favorite graphic subjects of these prehistoric desert wanderers were animals they hunted or hoped to hunt or capture. Popular illustrations included gazelles, ibexlike quadrupeds, and ostriches, but also long-horned cattle and, occasionally, giraffes and, perhaps, elephants; even leopard hunting seems to be shown.[9] The early inhabitants also left carvings representing "sickle-shaped" or square boats and ships.[10] We do not know if these depict vessels on the Nile or the Red Sea. Nor are we certain of the purpose of these drawings. There may have been magical, ritualistic, or religious motivations; in some cases they may have been simple doodlings having no particular significance to the artist who made them.[11]

These early travelers and residents in the Eastern Desert discovered the most convenient routes that passed by or led to the purest and most dependable water sources, optimal hunting grounds, most desirable places to live, and best sources of usable stone—all of which later generations continued to exploit. As the region became drier following the end of the Holocene wet phases, about seven thousand years ago, eventually evolving into a hyperarid climate, people continued to live in and travel to or through the Eastern Desert. Naturally, they tended to use traditional well-known routes and to tap whatever perennial water sources had been noted and used by previous generations for millennia.

The knowledge gained by nomads residing in the Eastern Desert—the location of mineral resources, shelters, plants, hunting grounds, and water sources—was passed on through oral tradition, but for the inexperienced inhabitants of the Nile valley, the deserts represented hazardous environments. Narmer's name appears on rock surfaces in the Eastern Desert.[12] The earliest surviving evidence of Pharaonic-era construction activity in the Eastern Desert, however, is the unfinished Old Kingdom (2649–2152 B.C.E.)[13] dam, possibly constructed by Cheops (reigned 2551–2528 B.C.E.) during the Fourth Dynasty, in Wadi Gerady, about 30 km east of Cairo.[14] Its purpose remains enigmatic; perhaps it provided mud, which facilitated the movement of wooden sleds hauling blocks from a nearby alabaster quarry to the Nile.[15] Old Kingdom and earlier dynastic sherds have been documented from Gebel Zeit adjacent to the Red Sea, about 50 km south of the modern town of Ras Gharib.[16]

Middle Kingdom (2040–1640 B.C.E.) inscriptions refer to events along Wadi Hammamat. Texts record two expeditions—one sent by Mentuhotep III (reigned 1957–1945 B.C.E.) and comprising three thousand men,[17] and another sent by Mentuhotep IV (reigned 1945–1938 B.C.E.) and made up of ten thousand men[18]—engaged in quarrying and well-digging. There was also activity in Wadi Hammamat during the New Kingdom (1550–

1070 B.C.E.).[19] In addition, from the Middle and New Kingdom periods comes archaeological evidence for the exploitation of galena at Gebel Zeit.[20]

About 16 km southeast of the galena mines are petroleum seeps that provided bitumen used in mummification. Studies of pottery found near the seeps indicate their exploitation from the first through sixth centuries C.E. Chemical trace analysis of bitumen from one mummy, however, documents that it was used at least as early as the ninth century B.C.E.[21] It would be surprising if, given their proximity to the Middle and New Kingdom galena mines, the petroleum seeps had not been known and exploited in those periods as well.

Given the treacherous reputation of Egypt's deserts for the average Nile dweller, it is likely that that maps were produced to assist travel to and work in the region. One of the earliest maps found in Egypt may depict Wadi Hammamat. The map, drawn in color on a papyrus now in the Egyptian Museum in Turin, Italy, and dated to the reign of Ramses IV (1163–1156 B.C.E.),[22] depicts gold mines and quarries likely in Wadi Hammamat. The gold mines, a well, a cistern, an earlier stele of Seti I (reigned 1306–1290 B.C.E.), plus thoroughfares radiating from the wadi are depicted. Several roads lead to the sea, while others snake deeper into the desert or lead to the Nile valley. But there is also evidence that in earlier times, travelers to the Eastern Desert may have used maps. Archaeological survey work has, in addition to recording rock art depicting animals, hunters, and boats, found rather abstract representations. Although earlier surveyors were aware of some of these marks,[23] their significance has only recently become clear, when compared to certain wadi systems on modern maps. One of the abstract signs bears a striking resemblance to a modern map of Wadi al-Atwani, Wadi Atshan, and Wadi Hammamat. Another appears to depict the main wadi system connecting Wadi Barramiya north to near the Laqeita well west of Wadi Hammamat, while a third also appears to be a depiction of a map of the region between Wadi Hammamat and Wadi Barramiya.[24] We cannot be certain of the dates of these abstract representations: perhaps they are prehistoric; maybe they are more recent. Rock art is notoriously difficult to date, although recently the use of accelerator mass spectrometry (AMS) carbon 14 dating of organic matter enclosed in rock varnish may enable the determination of an age range for rock drawings.[25]

In the Pharaonic period hieroglyphic inscriptions, often with the name and regnal year of the king, were added to the palimpsest.[26] Thus, we know more of the fate of the men sent out by Pharaoh Ramses IV on several desert quarrying expeditions, since they may have used the Turin map. One expedition comprised 8,368 men—a clear indication of the importance and scale of these endeavors.[27] That 900 perished graphically illustrates the harsh realities of travel and work in this hostile, hyperarid region.[28] Overcoming the dangers and difficulties of the Eastern Desert was prestigious.[29] Pharaohs sent quarrying expeditions from the Old Kingdom on,[30] and although the leaders of these projects proudly bear witness to them in autobiographies inscribed on their tomb walls, we have, in many cases, neither literary nor archaeological evidence of the sizes or appearances of these expeditions. The routes they took can be partially reconstructed from the location and identification of quarries and mines they exploited and from inscriptions and graffiti left along the way.

Wadi Hammamat was famous throughout the Pharaonic period both for its gold and for its *bekhen* stone—a smooth, grayish green chlorite siltstone used to make vessels and sculpture, and found nowhere else in Egypt.[31] Its east–west orientation also made this wadi an excellent thoroughfare between the Nile at Koptos and the Red Sea near modern Quseir. For several kilometers flanking either side of the modern paved road about midway between the Nile and the Red Sea, which in the narrow traverse of the Wadi Hammamat itself follows the course of the ancient route, are hundreds if not thousands of inscriptions and petroglyphs depicting animals and hunters. The inscriptions and graffiti document everything from accounts of alternately proud and bored leaders of Pharaonic-period quarrying expeditions to recent "Mohammed was here" commemorations. These appear in hieroglyphs, Greek, Demotic, Latin, Coptic, Arabic, and other languages. Many are dated, and some recount in detail exactly what the dedicant was doing in this remote spot.[32]

The Wadi Hammamat inscriptions also bear witness to pre-Ptolemaic maritime expeditions.[33] We glean most information on the famous expedition sent by Hatshepsut (reigned 1473–1458 B.C.E.) to Punt from reliefs and inscriptions on her funerary temple at Deir al-Bahri. The location of Punt, somewhere in the Horn of Africa or southern Arabia, is still debated. It could be a geographical designation that shifted or expanded throughout history as the Egyptians explored farther southward.[34] Wherever Punt was, it is clear that Hatshepsut's expedition sought exotic commodities, especially myrrh and frankincense.[35] Hatshepsut's expedition passed across the Eastern Desert along one of the established routes, but which one remains a mystery. Her men probably set out from Wadi Gawasis (figures 1-2 and 8-1), about 23 km south of Safaga, the only location on the Red Sea coast of Egypt that has unequivocal evidence of shipping to and from Punt dating to the Pharaonic period; the remains there are from the Old Kingdom, possibly the First Intermediate period, primarily the Middle Kingdom and early New Kingdom eras.[36] Excavations inside several rock-cut galleries at Wadi Gawasis recovered sixty to eighty coils of rope; cedar timbers that are the remains of planks and decking, with mortise-and-tenon fastenings; and wooden boxes labeled with the names of pharaohs and "PUNT."[37] Another predominantly Middle Kingdom–era site with rock-cut galleries for boats and copper-smelting facilities has recently been identified near 'Ain Sukhna south of Suez (figure 1-2).[38] In addition to its copper-smelting activities, the site lay at the end of a route from Memphis to the Red Sea coast with links to copper-mining operations in Sinai at Serabit al-Khadim.

In more northerly reaches of the Eastern Desert, in Wadi Umm Balad, and in Sinai, copper mining took place. Sinai was also the source for turquoise and malachite, mined as early as the Predynastic period and throughout the Old and Middle Kingdoms.[39] Other important regions were Wadi Allaqi, extending initially in a southeasterly direction from Aswan, for its gold in the Middle and New Kingdoms;[40] Wadi al-Hudi, especially in the Middle Kingdom for its amethysts;[41] and the region between Marsa Alam and Edfu, where comparatively large deposits of cassiterite (tin dioxide, SnO_2, which is about 85 percent tin) have been located, which were probably exploited beginning in the Old Kingdom.[42] Tin was a critical component mixed with copper to manufacture bronze, the most widely made and used metal in this period.

The frequency and size of these quarrying and mining expeditions would argue for a regular road system during the Pharaonic period. However, although routes to and from the Nile and these desert locations are, in general, known due to the presence of graffiti, pictographs, and wells, there is no evidence that any of these were paved or guarded except when these expeditions were sent out at irregular intervals. Paved roads were not unknown to the ancient Egyptians, the oldest and most famous being the Old Kingdom road leading from basalt quarries at Gebel Qatrani (Widan al-Faras) in the Western Desert north of Fayum Oasis to Lake Moeris (modern Lake Qarun), from where the large basalt slabs were transferred from sledge to ship.[43] The road is relatively straight and can be followed over its full length of 11.5 km. Where best preserved it is 2.1 m wide and built of local limestone and basalt cobbles.

Another road, about 15 km long, joins a travertine quarry at Hatnub in the Eastern Desert to Tell al-Amarna on the Nile, the location of Akhenaton's capital during the Eighteenth Dynasty. It is not paved, but it has a built-up roadbed with stone embankments in some places. Exploitation of the quarry took place in the Old, Middle, and New Kingdom eras. Thus, the road must have been built and maintained sometime within this broad time frame as well, though no more specific dating is possible.[44]

Final examples of possible pre-Ptolemaic desert roads—though they, too, could be partly Roman in date—appear near the Gebel Gulab quartzite or siliceous sandstone quarry on the west bank of the Nile opposite Aswan. The routes are likely associated with that quarry, which was active during the New Kingdom and in Roman times, though the roads themselves—2.8–3.5 m wide—are likely New Kingdom.[45] Some segments preserve built-up roadbeds similar to those appearing at the Hatnub quarry, while other lengths have stone embankments or flagstone paving—the latter similar to that joining the Old Kingdom basalt quarry in Gebel Qatrani to Lake Moeris, noted earlier in this chapter. Some cleared sections of the Gebel Qatrani roads[46] closely resemble those of Roman date that can be seen all over the Eastern Desert (see chapter 8).

To understand better the courage and logistics it took either to cross the desert to reach the harbors on the Red Sea shore, or to provide for a large party working the quarries and mines, it should be noted that the primary pack animals used before the Ptolemaic period were donkeys. Donkeys have an incredible resilience but must drink at regular intervals. Camels, which can go without water for extended periods and for which there is both faunal and archaeological evidence in Pharaonic times, were probably not introduced into Egypt and used on a regular basis until the later Persian or early Ptolemaic period and do not appear to have been in widespread use until Ptolemaic times.[47] In hot weather a pack donkey must drink about ten liters of water per day (see chapter 7).[48] Ancient Egyptians used donkeys to travel deep into the most arid regions of Egypt, including the Western

Desert, by establishing routes with base camps around clusters of water jars. These were presumably filled by donkey trains to replenish the water supply so that an expedition on the return journey would find water waiting in a prearranged place.[49] Pre-Ptolemaic expeditions into the Eastern Desert may have used a similar system of prepositioned water supplies along some of the longer and more difficult routes. There is evidence for this practice in the Eastern Desert along at least the Abu Sha'ar–Nile road in Roman times.[50]

As they undoubtedly did for road building, quarrying, and mining activities in the Eastern Desert, the Ptolemies and Romans most likely took Pharaonic practices as their model for water-resource acquisition and management as well. Unfortunately, we know little of how Pharaonic authorities dealt with this issue. Earlier we mentioned that the Turin papyrus map showed a well and a cistern. Also depicted is a wall, undoubtedly made of local stone, that surrounds the well, probably to protect it from infilling by sediments washed through the area during the infrequent heavy rains.[51] Possibly, too, this protective wall kept animals from approaching too close and from falling in and thereby polluting the well. Wells dug today throughout the region by Bedouin rarely use such protective walls. The cistern, located near the well and the gold mines on the map, may have been associated with gold-crushing and gold-washing operations. There is no indication on the Turin map of the sizes of the well or the cistern, and no constant scale seems to have been employed;[52] perhaps these depictions were merely map symbols indicating the general presence in this area of a number of wells and cisterns. Unless some or all of the water needed by thousands of laborers was painstakingly brought from the Nile, about 84 km to the west, it more realistically would have been supplied locally. A single well would not suffice, and many must have been sunk in different areas up and down the wadi, their contents deposited in cisterns scattered about the working and residential areas of the laborers; these have long since disappeared, washed away or filled in by water and windborne sand.

Two New Kingdom inscriptions, dating from Seti I (1306–1290 B.C.E.) and located on a rock face near his temple at al-Kanaïs (figure 3-1) about 46 or 47 km east of the Nile, describe the excavation of wells.[53] Here later in Ptolemaic and Roman times was an important *praesidium* with wells *(hydreumata)* and cisterns *(lakkoi)*[54] that serviced traffic on the roads between Apollonopolis Magna and Berenike as well as between Apollonopolis Magna and Marsa Nakari on the Red Sea. Dedicated along with the rock-cut temple here and in conjunction with the foundation of a settlement, Seti's inscriptions indicate the excavation of wells to service travelers journeying between the desert gold mines and the Nile. The dearth of water had led to languishing mining operations, which the wells were designed to rectify.[55]

Seti I's son and successor, Ramses II (ruled 1290–1224 B.C.E.), was one of many pharaohs who dispatched expeditions to the gold-mining region in Wadi Allaqi, southeast of Aswan. An inscription, found on a stele at the village of Kubban, discusses digging a well in the Eastern Desert to support gold-mining operations there. Seti I had earlier attempted, unsuccessfully, to excavate a well along this same road; representatives of Ramses II were ultimately able to achieve this feat, finding water at a depth of about 6 m.[56]

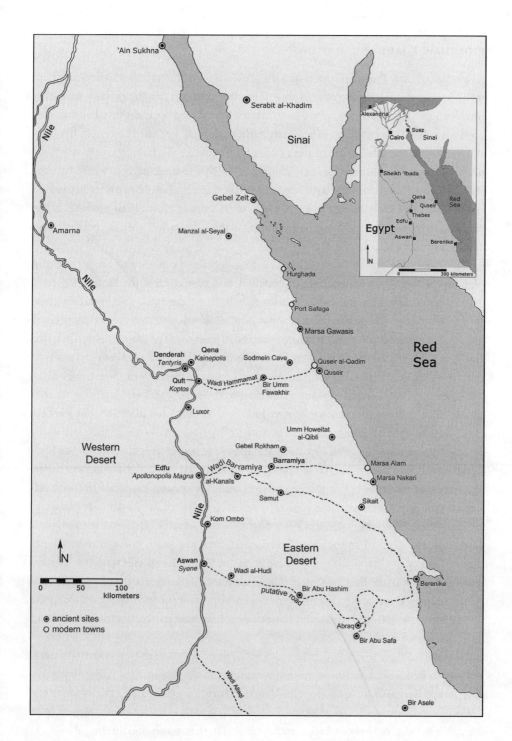

FIGURE 3-1

Map of the Eastern Desert of Egypt and adjacent Red Sea coast. Drawing by M. Hense.

PTOLEMAIC ROADS AND STATIONS

As a result of early Ptolemaic interest in the acquisition of elephants and ivory (see chapter 4), and increased mining of gold and other mineral resources, theirs was a more regularized approach to and systemization of Eastern Desert road networks than had occurred previously. With the creation of Ptolemaic harbors along Egypt's Red Sea coast, the Eastern Desert was included in the country rather than considered a foreign area to which expeditions were sent. Roads were extended from the Nile to these harbors with a regularity of purpose not previously seen or needed. Most of these Nile–Red Sea routes also passed near mining or quarrying settlements, which used them to export their products to the Nile and to import necessities—food, clothing, wine—from the Nile and, perhaps, also from ports on the coast.

The Ptolemaic period preserves the earliest definitive evidence of an overarching plan for the long-term penetration, exploitation, and protection of the Eastern Desert.[57] The Ptolemaic government and its proxies refurbished older roads and built new ones; they fortified road stations and watering points. Cairns—deliberately created mounds of stones—or squared towerlike structures marked at least some of the routes and assisted travelers on their journeys. Though there is no evidence that the Ptolemies used any type of milestones or distance-marking devices along roads in the Eastern Desert, such signposts seem to have been used along roads close to the Nile. The hieroglyphs carved into stones close to those Nile roads may have indicated distance and direction, but whether these were of Ptolemaic or earlier date is unclear.[58]

It is uncertain whether Ptolemaic desert routes were paved. Irregular, destructive flash floods in wadis of the Eastern Desert probably washed away most of the evidence. Nevertheless, it seems unlikely that too much effort would have been expended in constructing a thoroughfare that was used mostly by relatively lightweight human pedestrian and animal—especially donkey and, to a lesser extent, camel[59]—traffic. There has been long and heated debate about when the camel was domesticated and when it was introduced into Egypt,[60] but by the Ptolemaic period there is no doubt that the species was an important beast of burden in the Eastern Desert. Although wheeled transport existed from the New Kingdom period onward,[61] wagons were not an important mode of transport along the Ptolemaic Eastern Desert roads, and most evidence for their use comes from the Roman era (see chapter 8).[62]

We know of three major Ptolemaic roads in the Eastern Desert, as well as shorter routes, leading to Red Sea ports and to mining operations in the region. One major thoroughfare linked Berenike to Apollonopolis Magna.[63] Fortified stations and cairns identified and marked the route. It was along this highway that most elephants transshipped from Berenike to the Nile likely walked (see chapter 4). There was a second thoroughfare, linking Marsa Nakari (perhaps ancient Nechesia) on the Red Sea to Apollonopolis Magna.[64] Numerous gold-mining operations also used this route, which was furnished with unwalled stops possessing wells and fortified Ptolemaic strong points. There appears to have been a third road, though the evidence is not extensive, between Koptos and Myos Hormos (about 6–8 km north of modern Quseir) on the coast. Along this route some Ptolemaic graffiti in Demotic and an inscription in hieroglyphs have been found.[65] One station at Bir Sayyala was called Simiou, a place-name that was perhaps derived from the moniker of one of Ptolemy II's officers, a man named Simmias,[66] put in command of an elephant-hunting expedition, who may have passed here en route to or from his assignment. Recent finds of Ptolemaic pottery and coins at Myos Hormos,[67] as well as Ptolemaic (or possibly early Roman) temple blocks in the Ottoman/French fort and some of the houses at Quseir,[68] may point to a Ptolemaic-era port in this same region.

The Ptolemaic road station's most ubiquitous manifestation was a fortification with one or two round or oval-shaped cisterns built of stone and lined with waterproof lime mortar. The cisterns were the focal points and dominated the small interior spaces of these installations. In the Ptolemaic period cisterns were filled with water from a well, sometimes inside, but mostly nearby and outside the walls. Some early Roman fortified water stations preserve evidence of a channeled water runoff from nearby mountains, but we have no indication at this point that the Ptolemies used this method. Unfortified road stations also had one or more cisterns. One of these stations, at Bir 'Iayyan on the Marsa Nakari–Apollonopolis Magna route, preserves several inscriptions, one of which recorded precisely who built it (Ptolemy II Philadelphus), when it was built (257 B.C.E.), and its distance from the Nile (461 stades or 97.7 km).[69] This suggests a high degree of control by the Ptolemaic government, keen to advertise its authority to desert travelers even at the smallest stations.

Ptolemaic road stations were, generally, smaller than their Roman counterparts. It is doubtful that the personnel of these forts and smaller, unfortified road stops allowed visitors and their animals regular and uncontrolled access to water reservoirs. The danger of pollution or uncontrolled consumption would have been too great. Given the small internal areas of many Ptolemaic-period walled installations, there must have been mechanisms for removing the water and conveying it outside, where it was consumed. There is evidence of this practice in the Roman period (see chapter 7), but none that we have seen from Ptolemaic times.

In the Ptolemaic period, as in the Roman (see chapter 8), there were undoubtedly also military, paramilitary, or police patrols sent out from emporia on the Nile, from the Red Sea ports, and from desert garrisons that conveyed messages between stations and monitored the movements of travelers through and activities of indigenous peoples in the region. These would have been mounted patrols, probably using camels or horses or both, as circumstances dictated. Unfortunately, we know little about them. A graffito left by troops at al-Kanaïs dated May 22, 254 B.C.E., during the reign of Ptolemy II, indicates the presence of a garrison there. This mid-third-century B.C.E. account names each of only fifteen men.[70] If this represents the entire strength of the unit, then it was indeed small and cannot have been expected to send out anything except modest-sized patrols for limited periods, ranging not far from the fort. In times of real trouble these men must have

FIGURE 3-2
Fort at al-Kanaïs. Photo by S. E.Sidebotham.

relied on support from the Nile valley about 46 or 47 km away. This station at al-Kanaïs (figure 3-2) accommodated traffic on the heavily used Ptolemaic road between Berenike and Apollonopolis Magna as well as that between Marsa Nakari and Apollonopolis Magna, and gold mines scattered along or near that highway.[71] Numerous graffiti found at al-Kanaïs, including the one that depicts an elephant and that dates perhaps to between 270 and 264 B.C.E.,[72] provide some indication of how busy this route was during Ptolemy II's reign.

Another inscription, purportedly from Koptos, dates from October 2, 130 B.C.E., during the reign of Ptolemy VIII (Euergetes II) and his queen and wife, Cleopatra III. It was dedicated by Soterichos son of Ikadion from Gortyne on Crete, who was *strategos* of the Thebaid. The text describes security provided to mining operations in the desert and to those conveying products, including incense, imported via the Red Sea ports from southern Arabia. This implies that there were Ptolemaic troops stationed along one of the desert routes, but we do not know which road, that coming from Berenike or Myos Hormos; nor are we informed of the number of soldiers involved.[73] Based upon paltry evidence, we might argue that Ptolemaic desert garrisons and patrols were probably smaller than their Roman successors, but we are not certain whether they were organized along lines similar to those of the Romans, for whom we have more information.

The Ptolemaic approach to dealing with roads, forts, and patrols may have differed from the Roman military's handling of affairs, certainly in the size and scope of their desert operations. Later Ptolemaic organization depended more on private enterprise, which followed stricter control under the first two Ptolemies.[74] The lessening of central power during the later Ptolemaic period enabled an increase in private enterprise, such as tax farming, protection, and trade. One might surmise that this development would be reflected in the physical remains of the Ptolemaic way stations, which do not follow a strict design but are adapted to the landscape. A striking example is the Roman modification program to the Ptolemaic way station at Vetus Hydreuma: from an organically shaped rounded fortification to a straight-angled Roman *praesidium*. Subsequent chapters will examine how the Romans exploited and protected this region.

4

PTOLEMAIC DIPLOMATIC-
MILITARY-COMMERCIAL ACTIVITIES

Ptolemaic strata excavated at Berenike produced archaeological evidence that corroborates and adds to information preserved in ancient literary sources. The segment of an elephant tooth, mentioned later in this chapter, is evidence for live pachyderms in the city, as may be a V-shaped ditch, possibly the remains of an elephant retaining pen (see chapter 7). Pottery from Phoenicia and Rhodes signals possible imports of wine and oil from those regions. We cannot determine whether these were consumed at Berenike, used as trade goods, or destined as provisions for the ships' crews or for outposts farther south along the Red Sea coast. It does indicate, however, that the Ptolemaic trade network covered important regions of the eastern Mediterranean, the East African coast, and South Arabia.

In addition to elephants, ivory, and the mining of amethysts, iron, gold, and some other minerals,[1] the Ptolemies had other interests in the Eastern Desert, the Red Sea, and beyond, though initially these were secondary to elephant and ivory acquisition and gold mining. Goods from South Arabia, a hub for trade with Mesopotamia, India, and the East African coast, traditionally followed the desert route north through the Arabian Peninsula and from there across to Mediterranean ports such as Gaza (figure 4-1). After Alexander the Great, much of this northern area fell to the Seleucids. From the Ptolemaic perspective, trade had to be rerouted to avoid or minimize Seleucid control; direct contact with the source was far preferable to commerce controlled by middlemen. Finds from excavations conducted throughout Ptolemaic Egypt and in parts of the eastern Mediterranean in Hellenistic contexts have unearthed products from and inscriptions left by peoples from

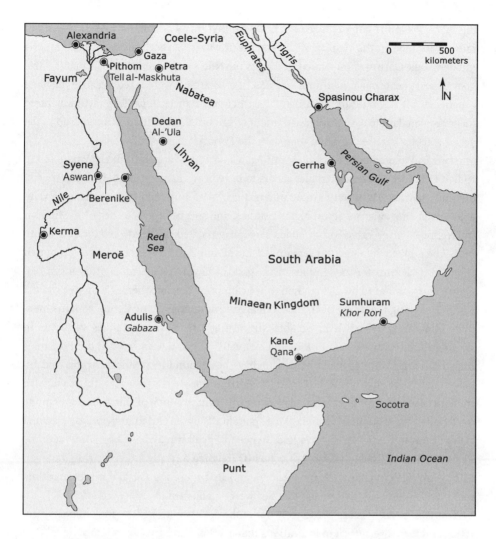

FIGURE 4-1

Map of Egypt, the Near East, and Arabia in Ptolemaic and early Roman times. Drawing by M. Hense.

southern Arabia and India; these, together with descriptions of ancient authors and records on papyri and ostraka, have given us clues as to what these peoples were like.[2] Much transactional information appears in the archive of Zenon, manager of Apollonius, who was both businessman and *dioiketes,* "treasurer general," of Ptolemy II.[3] Zenon and Apollonius corresponded mostly about legal issues and newly developed land in the Fayum, but this exchange also mentions regions of southern Arabia as sources of incense.[4] Zenon mainly traveled between Philadelphia, a newly founded agricultural village in the Fayum, and Memphis and Alexandria; his only trip abroad took him to Palestine. The Zenon papyri occasionally mention the "harbor Berenike" and transactions with Trogodytes residing there. From the context it seems, however, that this was not the Red Sea port, but rather a location in the vicinity of the Fayum. It was a "harbor" either on Lake Moeris (modern Lake Qarun) or on a canal leading to the Nile. One scholar suggests that the Trogodytes were seasonal agricultural workers.[5] Perhaps they were hired because they had experience with agriculture in difficult desert circumstances. One Trogodyte was hired for seventeen days to assist with a shipment of imported garlic used as a test crop in the desert soil of a land-reclamation project in the Fayum.[6]

Trade in Ptolemaic times from South Arabia, or transshipped from elsewhere in the Indian Ocean via southern Arabia, seems to have been mainly in frankincense, myrrh, calamus, saffron, cassia, cinnamon, and textiles.[7] Also imported from India were valuable woods, precious and semiprecious stones, and special breeds of dogs.[8] A Minaean inscription survives, carved on a wooden sarcophagus dated 264 B.C.E. and found at Memphis. The casket contained the remains of Zaydil bin Zayd, a merchant who "imported myrrh and calamus for the temples of the gods of Egypt." A second-century B.C.E. Minaean altar was found on Delos, though we cannot be certain whether it arrived via the Red Sea or along the terrestrial trans-Arabian caravan routes.[9] One Zenon papyrus mentions Minaean and Gerrhaean weights, suggesting that the incense trade was active in the mid third century B.C.E. in Ptolemaic Egypt.[10] We do not know what the Ptolemies traded in return, though Ptolemaic coins have been found in southern Arabia and India.[11] There were attempts by Ptolemaic authorities, apparently unsuccessful, to cultivate frankincense and myrrh within their territory.[12] Perhaps much of this commerce in the third century with southern Arabia came sporadically by sea and more regularly overland via the caravan routes up to Gaza and thence to Egypt; it may have been only with the Ptolemaic loss of Coele-Syria to Antiochus III (reigned 223–187 B.C.E.) during the reign of Ptolemy V Epiphanes (210/204–180 B.C.E.) that more regular and direct maritime routes with southerly areas of the Red Sea were established.[13]

This commerce was not completely under the direct control of the Ptolemaic government, and there are sufficient indications that private merchants were also active.[14] One example is an interest-free loan made by Arkhippos in about 150 B.C.E. to five merchants sailing to Punt.[15] No one is certain of Punt's location. It was either in southwestern Arabia (modern Yemen) or in the Horn of Africa (Somalia), likely the latter, and may have been a term whose geographical parameters changed over history.[16] That the loan was interest free strongly suggests that Arkhippos himself had direct involvement in the voyage, undoubtedly to secure aromatics.

The Ptolemaic government heavily taxed imports, from 25 percent up to 50 percent of their value in some cases.[17] Apparently, to avoid the onerous burdens entailed in collecting the duties itself, the government often auctioned to tax farmers the right to collect them.[18] This guaranteed the government revenue without its having to undertake all the effort, time, and money that would have been necessary to expend in collecting these taxes itself. The Romans used a similar tax-farming technique, though not universally, across their empire.

Conversely, there is in those "eastern" lands evidence of limited Ptolemaic commercial and diplomatic exchanges. Ptolemaic contacts with some Arab groups, especially the Nabataeans (see chapter 11) and Lihyanites (in northwestern Saudi Arabia), related to caravan trade coming from southern Arabia.[19] Although we can detect Ptolemaic artistic and linguistic influences among the Lihyanites, the Ptolemies seem to have viewed the Nabataeans as competitors in the lucrative transit trade arriving at the Mediterranean from the incense-bearing lands in southern Arabia and points beyond. Ancient sources refer to the Ptolemies periodically battling Nabataean "pirates" in the Red Sea who preyed on their shipping.[20] It is not clear whether these Nabataeans acted as privateers, were under official royal Nabataean orders, or were freebooters.[21] The Nabataeans may also have occasionally raided the Egyptian Red Sea coast.[22] In response to these and other threats, by 130 B.C.E. if not earlier, an inscription relates that the Ptolemies placed archers aboard some of their vessels as protection;[23] Pliny the Elder writes that this security measure continued into Roman times.[24] It is clear, however, that expanding Ptolemaic commercial interest in the Red Sea can be detected not only in their defensive efforts against and punitive responses to these Nabataean attacks, but also by the appearance in the third century B.C.E. of a Ptolemaic official styled *ho epi tes libanotiches* ("overseer of the incense traders")[25] and stationed at Gaza. The creation of this office suggests that the importation of aromatics from southern Arabia into Egypt was substantial enough, and probably sufficiently lucrative, to require official Ptolemaic protection and regulation.[26]

Strabo (*Geography* 2.3.4–5) writes that toward the end of the second century B.C.E. Eudoxus of Cyzicus, a ship captain employed by the Ptolemies, seems to have "discovered" the existence of monsoon winds in the Indian Ocean, something long known to those who dwelt along its littoral.[27] Alternatively, the *Periplus* (57) attributes western discovery of the monsoons to a skipper named Hippalos, after whom the winds were named. The *Periplus* does not mention when this event took place.[28] Pliny the Elder (*NH* 6.26.101 and 104) is also vague, saying only that the Hippalos winds provided the most advantageous way of sailing to India.

The "discovery" of the monsoons and their exploitation by "western" sailors drastically reduced travel times and, therefore, costs between Red Sea ports in Egypt and the Indian subcontinent for Ptolemaic and later Roman ships when they were in the Indian Ocean. The powerful Indian Ocean monsoon winds blow from the southwest between June and September or October, the time of sailing to the west coast of India, and between May/June and September, the seasons of sailing to southern India from Egypt. Returning from India to the mouth of the Red Sea required departure from ports there sometime between November and March/April (figure 4-2). If sailing from the Red Sea to East Africa, one left between November and April and returned between May and September. The round-trip voyage to India from the Red Sea was rough and very dangerous, and though the actual sailing time might have been only two to three months or so one way, the entire journey took about a year because of the need to wait for the shift in the monsoons. A round-trip voyage between the Red Sea and Indian Ocean ports on the African coast also entailed

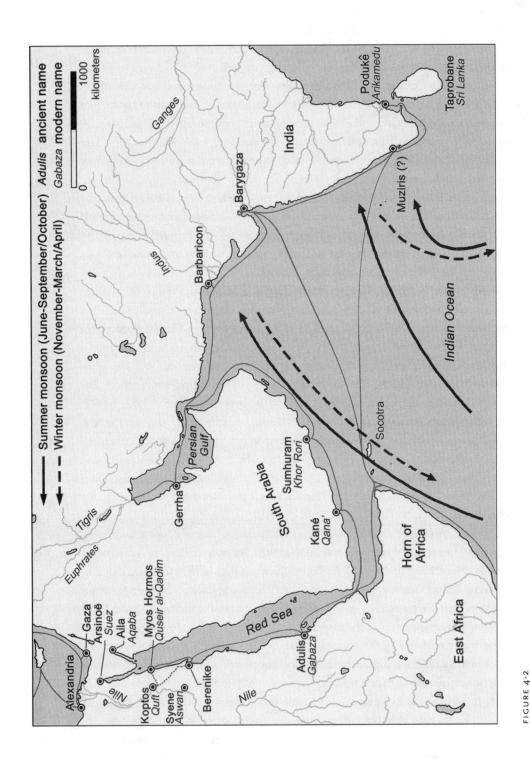

FIGURE 4-2

Map of monsoon patterns in the northwestern Indian Ocean. Drawing by M. Hense.

relatively short sailing times, was quite easy, but took about two years, due to the wait for a shift in the monsoon winds.[29] The appearance of the office of "Strategos and Epistrategos of the Red Sea and Indian Ocean" suggests that these regions were of sufficient enough interest—undoubtedly commercial, but also diplomatic—to the Ptolemaic government that an official dealing with them was required. We are uncertain when this office was established and whether its functions were administrative, military, or economic; perhaps it encompassed all three. Dates for its creation ranging from soon after Eudoxus's voyage—that is, about 116/110/109 B.C.E.—on have been proposed.[30]

Ptolemaic contacts with India were more sporadic and deemed less vital than those with southern Arabia or other areas of the African coast of the Red Sea. Inscriptions found in India indicate that the Mauryan king Aśoka (reigned ca. 265–228 B.C.E.), grandson of Candragupta, first king of that state,[31] maintained diplomatic relations with at least five contemporary Hellenistic monarchs, and references to these individuals help date the Indian inscriptions in which they appear.[32] In his Thirteenth Rock Edict, Aśoka lists these "western" rulers: Antiochus II (reigned 261–246 B.C.E.), Ptolemy II Philadelphus, Antigonus Gonatas of Macedonia (ruled 276–239 B.C.E.), Magas of Cyrene (reigned ca. 258–250 B.C.E.), and an Alexander. The latter could have been either Alexander of Corinth (reigned 252–244 B.C.E.) or Alexander of Epirus (reigned 272–255 B.C.E.). Pliny the Elder (*NH* 6.21.58) mentions that a man named Dionysus was Ptolemy II's ambassador to the Mauryan court, and we later discuss the Seleucid ambassador Megasthenes' description of elephant gathering in India in his day. Unfortunately, we cannot gauge the nature and frequency of these exchanges or who initiated them.[33] Later, in the 130s B.C.E., there were also Ptolemy VIII's embassies to incense-bearing lands.[34]

In addition to diplomatic exchanges, there appears to have been limited commercial interaction between the eastern Mediterranean and areas of India in Hellenistic times and between Ptolemaic Egypt and India; a few "Classical Greek," Ptolemaic, Seleucid, and other coins of western "Hellenistic" date have been found in India, but numismatic evidence suggests that whatever commerce took place between the two areas was neither extensive nor intensive.[35] Ptolemaic–"Indian" contacts may have been more diplomatic than commercial in nature, involving gift exchanges between rulers and a rather low level of truly commercial interaction using barter.[36] It would be interesting to know more about the types and quantities of products the Indians and the Ptolemies and other "westerners" exchanged or traded with one another in this period. In the fourth century B.C.E. Theophrastus says little specific about western importation of Indian plants or plant products, which suggests that the market for these was not great at that time. It is not clear what the Mediterranean and Near East had to offer the Indians; perhaps the South Asians desired some of the same items in Hellenistic times that they imported in the early Roman period. These are described in the *Periplus* and by Pliny, and included wines, textiles and fancy Mediterranean red coral, bullion, and a variety of human cargoes, among other items.

If they ever entertained the idea, the Ptolemies were never able to dominate trade between southern Arabia, the Horn of Africa, or beyond on the one hand, and the Mediterranean basin on the other. Some scholars attribute this to Arab and other middlemen obfuscating the provenances of these commercial products. It was in their interest to keep Egyptian and other "western" trading partners in the dark about the sources of precious goods. If Ptolemaic merchants were to cut out the middlemen and start direct trade relations with the producers, or local Indian merchants, South Arabian harbors stood to lose much of their trade.[37] Thus, the sources of incense, cinnamon, and other resins and spices were not disclosed, and the discovery of the trade routes in the late Ptolemaic period is a story involving a successful degree of economic disinformation by middlemen.

Arabia matched on land the long tradition of Egyptian interest in and exploitation of the Red Sea. Parallel to the Red Sea coast, the western regions of the Arabian Peninsula had long-established overland caravan routes.[38] Using these tracks, donkeys and, after their domestication somewhere in Arabia probably in the second millennium B.C.E., one-humped camels,[39] traveling in caravans, conveyed the wealth of southern Arabia and the Horn of Africa to the eastern Mediterranean. This was primarily frankincense and myrrh—gum resins bled from the trunks of trees cultivated in those regions—plus any cargoes transshipped to southern Arabia from other points in the Indian Ocean. We do not know the sizes of these caravans.[40] Smaller ones traveled faster, but might have been more vulnerable to bandits, than the slower-moving but better-protected larger ones. Whatever the caravans' sizes, those braving these antique trade routes had to overcome adverse weather including sandstorms, intense heat and dearth of food and water, robbers, nomadic raids, and the inevitable payment of protection money to allow unmolested passage.[41] These caravan routes continued long after the advent of Islam in the seventh century C.E.[42]

Pliny the Elder (*NH* 12.32.64–65) describes a trip of sixty-five stages (likely measured in days) for a caravan to reach Gaza on the Mediterranean coast from southern Arabia, a distance of 1,487.5 Roman miles (2,198.5 km) or an average speed of just under 23 Roman miles (about 34.2 km) per day. This relatively modest pace suggests that this may have been the typical speed of a larger caravan rather than a faster-moving smaller one. By the time a caravan reached Mediterranean ports, Pliny writes (*NH* 12.32.65), one camel load cost an incredible 688 denarii. A denarius was about one and a half day's pay for a Roman legionary at that time.[43] Pliny does not mention what the original price of this camel load was prior to the start of the journey, nor does he indicate the size of the caravan. The travel time he records may be an average depending upon the number of transport animals and travelers and the kinds of problems encountered by any given caravan. There is little reason to doubt, however, that it was a journey of similar length prior to Pliny's day. The high costs, great dangers, and long duration of such trips did not dissuade merchants and transporters, suggesting that enormous profits were at hand that, they believed, more than compensated for the risks taken. Nor did the relatively cheaper costs of maritime transport versus overland conveyance induce large numbers to abandon the age-old overland Arabian caravan routes. The sea-lanes had their own liabilities: storms, pirates, dangerous reefs and shoals, and the ever-present perils of shipwreck resulting in death for crews and passengers, and the total loss of huge and expensive cargoes.

THE PTOLEMIES AND AFRICA: IVORY AND ELEPHANTS

India and southern Arabia were not as important to the Ptolemies as was the Red Sea coast of eastern Africa, where ivory and war elephants were the main items sought. Elephants appear in rock art in the Eastern Desert from an unknown, but likely early, date;[44] these depictions suggest that these animals were indigenous at that time. Use of ivory, both elephant and hippopotamus, for decorative purposes was an Egyptian practice dating to Pharaonic times.[45] Thus, the Ptolemies continued a long tradition. It was only natural, in conjunction with the capture of elephants used in warfare, that the Ptolemies also sought ivory. This trade in ivory, in addition to increased exploitation of gold sources and, to a lesser extent perhaps, amethyst mines of the Eastern Desert, helped to defray expenses entailed in elephant acquisition, transportation, and training.[46] Inscriptions from Delos dating to the reign of Ptolemy II record a dramatic drop in the price of ivory reaching markets in the Mediterranean, which suggests that substantial quantities were available at that time.[47] Acquisition of ivory on a massive scale and its sale on the open market may have been part of a Ptolemaic policy to help defray the costs of their massive Mediterranean fleet and their elephant "trade" and training program. It reflects relatively intensive Ptolemaic activities in northeastern Africa and suggests that elephant and ivory acquisition was well organized on a large scale by the reign of Philadelphus.

THE PTOLEMIES AND ELEPHANTS

One weapon all Greek and Macedonian commanders came to know in their wars with the Persians and "Indians" during Alexander's eastern campaigns was the elephant. Although they had been seen previously,[48] Plutarch records (*Life of Alexander* 60.10) that the Macedonian king feared elephants. Horses of the Macedonian cavalry balked at approaching the pachyderms, put off especially by the smell, but also by the appearance of large numbers of elephants arrayed against them.[49] Elephants were present at the Battle at Gaugamela in 331 B.C.E., though we are uncertain whether Darius III actually deployed them.[50] By 326 B.C.E. Alexander himself had accumulated about 126 elephants, though he seems never to have used them in battle.[51] There is no evidence that he deployed them when fighting Porus at the Battle of the Hydaspes River (Jhelum, a branch of the Indus, in Pakistan) in 326 B.C.E., though Porus did.[52]

As a result of their experiences, Alexander's successors soon began incorporating these animals in calculations of their own battlefield tactics.[53] Elaborate training procedures for the beasts and the eventual placement of custom-made and custom-fitted crenellated battlements, created of materials that remain unknown to us (probably lightweight yet strong), for troops placed atop the backs of the pachyderms provided soldiers with great moving platforms from which they rained missiles down on their opponents.[54] We are not certain when "western" armies first fitted portable castles atop elephants—probably sometime in the 270s B.C.E. during Pyrrhus of Epirus's war against Roman forces in Italy.[55]

This idea of placing towers or turrets atop the elephants seems to have been a Hellenistic Greek invention rather than an Indian one.[56] Plutarch (*Life of Pyrrhus* 15) says that Pyrrhus's pachyderm contingent numbered twenty, of which only two made it to shore after a storm had ravaged his invasion fleet.[57] It was the first time the Romans laid eyes on the beasts—which, Pliny tells us (*NH* 8.6.16), they termed "Lucanian oxen," since they first saw them in that region of Italy. Pliny has left a fairly lengthy description of elephants in his day (*NH* 8.1.1–8.13.35).

These elephant-mounted walls plus the intimidating size and power of the beasts promised great tactical advantages to those who possessed and used them effectively against enemy infantry and cavalry or even against other elephants. Controlling the animals in battle proved extremely difficult, however, and Arrian (*Anabasis* 5.17.5) reports that at the Battle of the Hydaspes River, elephants inflicted as many casualties on "friendly" forces as on Alexander's when they turned and fled from the mêlée back through Indian ranks.[58] Although we possess no detailed accounts of later battles of the Ptolemies and Seleucids, it is likely that friendly forces suffered as much from their own elephants as had the Indians from theirs at the Hydaspes. Such seems to have happened, for example, to the Ptolemaic left flank against the Seleucids at the Battle of Raphia in 217 B.C.E.[59] It occurred later to the Romans as well; Appian (*Wars in Spain* 46) provides a description of the problems of stampeding elephants used by the Romans in battle at Numantia in Spain in the mid second century B.C.E.

Nevertheless, despite the great costs entailed in their capture, training, maintenance, and deployment, and the practical problems of using them in battle, no self-respecting third- or second-century B.C.E. army in the Near East, Asia Minor, Egypt, parts of Greece, Italy, or North Africa was deemed complete without elephants;[60] they were the ancient equivalent of armored units. Not all ancient authorities, however, agreed on the utility of elephants in battle. Asclepiodotus, a lesser-known military historian writing in the first century B.C.E., indicates (*Tactics* 1.3) that elephants were not by nature well adapted for warfare. Since he wrote from a theoretical point of view and had little if any practical battlefield experience, we are not sure how much weight to give to his observations. On the contrary, Julius Africanus (*Kestoi* 1.18), in the early third century C.E.,[61] notes the great shock value of elephants in battle and describes tactics one should use to counter them.[62]

Representations of both Indian and African elephants alone or outfitted in military garb or in martial settings adorned items including contemporary coinage,[63] silver plates, wall paintings, and tomb decorations, and their images also appeared as large sculptures and small statuettes found in many parts of the Mediterranean world, the Near East, and deep into modern Sudan.[64] Column capitals sculpted in the form of Asian elephant heads decorated the Great Temple at Petra.[65] The phases of construction and use of this structure are not yet securely understood, but current opinion is that the edifice was initially erected in the first century B.C.E., subsequently altered and enlarged perhaps into the second century C.E., and used until abandoned sometime in the third or fourth century C.E.[66]

Clearly, elephantomania had seized much of the ancient Mediterranean world and Near East during the course of the third century B.C.E. and later.

According to Diodorus Siculus (18.33.1–18.36.5), Perdiccas, one of Alexander's former lieutenants, invaded Egypt in 321 B.C.E. with a force that included elephants. He was defeated by Ptolemy I Soter and ultimately killed by his own troops.[67] Ptolemy probably captured some elephants from his deceased opponent. Then, at the Battle of Gaza in 312 B.C.E., Ptolemy I, joined by Seleucus I, who had been forced to flee his realm, captured forty-three Indian elephants from Demetrius Poliorketes, son of Antigonus Monopthalmos,[68] thereby augmenting his elephant units. These Indian elephants would have eventually passed away, as did whatever goodwill that had once existed between the Ptolemies and the Seleucids. With the end of somewhat civil relations between the two states sometime early in the third century B.C.E., Ptolemaic access to Indian elephants became a thing of the past.[69] Naturally, the Seleucids, who controlled overland access to India, tried to prevent their Ptolemaic adversaries from acquiring the Indian species, and the Ptolemies were, thereby, forced to locate alternate sources. Although they denied their Egyptian adversaries access to Indian pachyderms, that species appears on coins minted by Tarentum in celebration of its alliance with Pyrrhus of Epirus against the Romans.[70] Though Pyrrhus was a protégé of the Ptolemy I and perhaps of Philadelphus,[71] the depiction of the pachyderms on the Tarentine coins is Indian, perhaps deriving via Egypt if not directly from the Seleucids. Certainly when Pyrrhus launched his war in 280 B.C.E. against the Romans in support of Tarentum, Ptolemaic penetration into those regions of Africa that later produced elephants for their military was either in its infancy or had yet to take place at all. Thus, it may be that those Indian beasts in Pyrrhus's possession came to him from the Ptolemies but had been initially captured from Demetrius at the Battle of Gaza described earlier.

For the Ptolemies, finding a comparable species with the size, power, and intelligence of an elephant was not an option; they demanded elephants. Strategically outflanking the Seleucids to bring Indian elephants from the subcontinent by sea rather than overland to Egypt, however, was clearly not feasible, or if possible it would have been extremely hazardous, would have resulted in an unacceptably high attrition rate of elephants, ships, and crews, and would certainly have been prohibitively expensive.[72] An alternate source had to be found closer to home. Beginning with Ptolemy II Philadelphus or perhaps even as early as the latter part of Ptolemy I Soter's reign (323–282 B.C.E.), the Ptolemies turned to Africa to obtain elephants.[73] The African species captured by the Ptolemies was transported by sea to Egypt, usually to Berenike, and thence marched to the Nile.

Graffiti and pictographs in the Eastern Desert allude to the transdesert conveyance of elephants that landed at Berenike. Depictions of at least two elephants—one painted in red with a human rider, probably a mahout, and the other a graffito of an elephant alone—appear on rock outcrops in a wadi near the Ptolemaic-Roman hilltop fort of Abraq, southwest of Berenike.[74] Abraq seems to have straddled at least one road linking Berenike to

FIGURE 4-3

Rock outcrop at al-Kanaïs with a Ptolemaic-era petroglyph of an elephant. Photo by S. E. Sidebotham.

Syene (Aswan),[75] and the appearance of elephant pictographs here suggests that this was one route along which the pachyderms might have been led to the Nile.

An inscription, together with a graffito of an elephant, left by Dorion at al-Kanaïs during the reign of Philadelphus, probably in the period 270–264 B.C.E., attests the transport of the beasts from Berenike to Apollonopolis Magna along that desert thoroughfare (figure 4-3).[76] Interestingly, however, the pachyderm depicted here is Indian, not African, suggesting that the artist knew that elephants passed by al-Kanaïs but had not actually seen the African variety.[77] A Hungarian expedition identified two other elephant graffiti in the vicinity of Bir Menih,[78] a site near the Berenike–Koptos road.[79] Koptos replaced Apollonopolis Magna as Berenike's main Nile entrepôt sometime in the early Roman period.[80] It is, therefore, odd to find elephant graffiti along this Roman-period route, since the large-scale importation of elephants from Africa via the Red Sea seems to have ended during the late third or second century B.C.E. Perhaps these latter drawings represent prehistoric rather than Ptolemaic elephants,[81] since the Ptolemaic and later Roman routes partly followed well-established and long-used desert tracks.

Another inscription, dated 260/259 B.C.E., on a stele erected in conjunction with the opening of a canal linking the Red Sea and the Nile and found in the northeastern Nile Delta at Pithom (Tell al-Maskhuta), near the Greek settlement of Heroonpolis, reports on

Philadelphus's elephant-gathering efforts in Africa.[82] The elephants displayed in Ptolemy II's grand procession in Alexandria held at some unknown date, but likely early in his reign,[83] may have been a mix of Indian ones, obtained years earlier from the Seleucids, and some of the more recently captured African species.[84]

An inscription of about 246 B.C.E., at the beginning of the reign of Ptolemy III Euergetes I (246–221 B.C.E.), and originally set up at Adulis on the Red Sea coast but surviving only in a sixth-century copy by Cosmas Indicopleustes (*Christian Topography* 2.58),[85] states that both "Troglodytic" and "Ethiopian" elephants were used in a war in Asia Minor. The text also claims that these animals were first obtained by Euergetes and his father, Ptolemy II; there is no mention of Ptolemy I.[86] We do not know whether the designations "Troglodytic" and "Ethiopian" refer only to the geographic locations from which the pachyderms were obtained or whether they indicate different types of elephants that were available.

There was likely a connection between the Ptolemaic search for sources of ivory, of iron for armaments, and of gold from the desert on the one hand and the need to pay to fortify the military with pachyderms on the other. The timing of these events cannot be accidental. While the Ptolemies were moving into regions of the Eastern Desert, they were also busy, from the reign of Ptolemy II on, if not earlier, extending roads into the area, building ports on the Red Sea coast, and also digging a canal joining the Nile to the Red Sea. All of these activities must have been complementary to one another and cannot be viewed in isolation (see chapter 9).

In order to control gold-mining areas, the Ptolemies launched an attack overland via the Nile into Nubia in about 275 B.C.E., which may have led to their domination of important auriferous assets in the Wadis Allaqi and Gabgaba and adjacent regions east and southeast of Syene (Aswan).[87] Areas of the Eastern Desert north of Berenike and west of Hurghada preserve numerous remains of Ptolemaic gold-mining operations.[88] These were major sources of revenues for the Ptolemaic state and military. This aggressive policy of controlling important areas of Egypt's Eastern Desert and perhaps northern Sudan may have been one facet of an overall strategy. We have no contemporary or later documents that suggest this strategy, but it would have been a sensible one, since the Ptolemies required gold in order to subsidize the great expenses entailed in acquiring elephants. Ivory, either a by-product of elephant hunts gone badly, or deliberately harvested in tandem with the capture of live beasts, would also have defrayed expenses entailed in the capture, shipment, training, and maintenance of elephants. Some indigenous peoples—specifically, the Asachae and Trogodytes known as *elephantomachoi*—hunted elephants for food, and ivory gathering was a by-product of these activities.[89] Undoubtedly, some of the ivory that made its way into Ptolemaic hands came from these peoples. It was logical for the Ptolemies to piggyback efforts to import live elephants with the procurement of gold, ivory, precious stones, and iron from the same general region.

Projection of power in the arena that the Ptolemies considered most important—that is, the Aegean and eastern Mediterranean—required a substantial military presence. The

Ptolemies could not hope to field native troops in numbers comparable to those of the Seleucids due to great differences in the sizes of their respective populations, except, perhaps, by employing mercenaries.[90] Thus, they sought to even the playing field if not tip the military balance of power in their favor through naval superiority if not supremacy. Since their Mediterranean and Aegean interests lay in the islands and coastal areas of mainland Asia Minor and the Levant, their emphasis on naval power is understandable. Athenaeus (*Deipnosophistai* 5.203d), in the late second or early third century C.E., records that Ptolemy II possessed the largest navy in the eastern Mediterranean and Aegean, totaling some four thousand vessels, a number of which were huge warships. Although this figure is probably greatly exaggerated, to construct, man, and maintain a naval force even one-quarter of this size must have been an expensive undertaking, one whose cost gold from the Eastern Desert and ivory from farther south would have helped to defray.

The Ptolemies also founded elephant-hunting stations—literary sources suggest over a dozen—the bulk of which lay along the African coast of the Red Sea down to the Bab al-Mandeb (see chapter 2).[91] A few of these stations may have lain beyond the Red Sea in the Horn of Africa.[92] Evidence suggests that when sources of elephants nearer to Egypt had been depleted, the Ptolemies were forced to go farther afield. If so, it seems that those more southerly stations functioned later in time.

One hypothesis holds that large savanna elephants may have been brought to Egypt occasionally from Kenya and Tanzania.[93] These must have been rare and exceptional imports indeed, given their huge sizes and the great distances over which they had to be transported—perhaps sought more for the ivory of their larger tusks than for the animals themselves.

High-ranking officials commanded these elephant-gathering expeditions, which must have been elaborately organized, given the complicated logistics involved and the great importance the Ptolemaic government placed upon the success of these endeavors. Eventually men with the rank of *strategos* were put in charge,[94] which underlines both the importance and military character of these activities. One such *strategos*, Lichas, son of Pyrrhos from Acarnania in Greece, left a dedication honoring Ptolemy IV Philopator (221–205 B.C.E.), his queen and sister Arsinoë III, and Serapis and Isis. This inscription was found at Apollonopolis Magna, an appropriate location given that this was the Nile terminus for those conveying pachyderms from Berenike after their traumatic voyage from more southerly points on the Red Sea coast.[95] One scholar suggests that Ptolemaic elephant hunts in Africa were haphazard under the earlier Ptolemies and were not systematized until the reign of Philopator.[96] Yet, this does not appear to have been the case.

Locations of a few of these coastal stations may have been identified in modern times, but certainly none has been excavated. Correcting this oversight would provide important information on the organization of the elephant hunts, something missing in the extant ancient written accounts. Some of these larger Red Sea stations along the coasts of Sudan and Eritrea would also have been havens for ships engaged in other ventures in the Red Sea and Indian Ocean, especially trafficking in precious woods and aromatics.

Many coastal foundations dealing with Ptolemaic elephant gathering bear Ptolemaic royal family names or those of high officials involved in organizing and conducting the expeditions. The names of these stations included the Harbors of Antiphilos, the Isle of Straton, the Altars of Konon, the Lookout Post of Demetrios, the Grove and Harbor of Eumenes, the Island of Philip, the Hunting Ground of Pythangelos, the Lookout Post of Leon, and a number of Berenikes as well as others.[97] Their precise locations are uncertain, though a large one named Ptolemais (Epi)Theron (Ptolemais of the Hunt)[98] probably lies south of modern Port Sudan (see chapter 9). We do not know how many other elephant-hunting stations founded by the Ptolemies still operated in Roman times. During the stations' zenith in the third and perhaps early second centuries B.C.E., hunting parties sent into the hinterland from these enclaves captured the elephants, but probably not without great danger and loss to both themselves and their quarry.

We are not completely certain how Ptolemaic elephant-hunting parties operated, but Megasthenes—an older contemporary of Alexander the Great who served as a governor in the empire and later (between about 302 and 291 B.C.E.) as ambassador from the Seleucids to Candragupta, the first king of the Mauryan state in India[99]—left descriptions of India that may provide some clues.[100] Megasthenes' accounts in his *Indika,* now lost, survive in writings of later savants, including Diodorus Siculus, Strabo, Pliny the Elder, and Arrian. According to Strabo (*Geography* 15.2.9 cf. 16.2.10), Candragupta traded five hundred Indian elephants—undoubtedly an exaggeration[101]—for territory from his western neighbor Seleucus I.[102] Strabo's account (*Geography* 15.1.42–43) and Arrian's (*Indika* 13.1 to 14.9) preserve descriptions of how Indian elephants were captured and domesticated in Megasthenes' day. Strabo's and Arrian's descriptions of the Indian techniques may have been similar to methods used by the Ptolemies in Africa, but we cannot be certain, because only the briefest fragments survive detailing African methods of elephant capture. Unplaced fragments of ancient texts, possibly from Agatharchides, preserved later most likely in Pliny (*NH* 8.1.1–8.13.25), suggest that in Africa (presumably North Africa) elephants wandered into pits and were extracted from these.[103] Elephants were available at that time from the Atlas Mountains in modern Morocco.[104] Ptolemaic elephant-gathering expeditions in East Africa seem to have used an enclosure method similar to that of the Indians, described later in this chapter, but those elephants caught or lured into these traps by Ptolemaic hunters may have been starved until they submitted and could be tamed;[105] this was one technique used in India, as we shall see shortly.

The Indian system, recorded by Strabo and Arrian (copying or paraphrasing Megasthenes), involved entrapment of wild male elephants by luring them into a large enclosed area where domesticated female elephants were located. This occurred at night. Or, a mahout riding a tame elephant beat a wild elephant, which was alone or separated from its herd, with an iron whip, thereby forcing it into an enclosure. We should probably view this last account with skepticism, since it is highly unlikely that a feral elephant would allow a human riding a tame beast to approach near enough or remain sufficiently close to allow it to be goaded into an enclosure unless a number of mahouts commanding domesticated elephants encircled the target elephant, thereby forcing it into the retaining area. Strabo and Arrian (Megasthenes) continue: Once the feral elephants were inside this large "corral," the bridge joining it to the outside was removed or blocked and the quarry cornered. Tame elephants then battled the newly corralled feral males, and these were also worn down through food deprivation. A man then dismounted and bound the feet of the object elephants, which were then beaten by the tame ones. Once these fell, men fastened the necks of the wild elephants to those of the tame ones and also inserted thongs into their necks so that through pain and starvation they finally submitted. Strabo is quite clear that the Indians did not want elephants that were too old or too young, but only those mature and large enough, and presumably sufficiently healthy, to be trained for immediate use. Since elephants have life spans similar to those of humans and some-times longer, the age of captured elephants would have been of some concern. We as-sume that the Indians captured not only males but also females, as indicated by the fact that females were used as lures for wild males.

Meroitic peoples, in whose territory much Ptolemaic elephant gathering took place, may have employed a similar system, or there may have been several techniques. Ptole-maic officials and hunters sent to acquire the beasts would have consulted, been trained by, or hired indigenous experts, or carefully observed and imitated local acquisition meth-ods. Perhaps in some instances elephants already trained by Meroitic handlers were traded to the Ptolemies[106] early on for their immediate deployment, thereby allowing time to train newly captured ones. There is archaeological evidence that Meroitic peoples may have used elephants in battle and that this was known to the Ptolemaic elephant gather-ers, who would have sought their advice and assistance.[107] In any case, hunters then con-veyed recently captured feral elephants to the coast, where they probably underwent some pacification and detraumatizing prior to placement on board specially designed ships called *elephantegoi*[108] (which we discuss later) for the treacherous journey north. Nor can we be certain, in the African scenario, whether mainly male or female elephants were gathered, and whether only adult or also juvenile and infant elephants were collected. If the Ptolemies wanted to establish their own breeding program in Egypt, both male and female elephants would have been captured, perhaps juveniles and infants as well on occasion. If they knew anything about the social relationships elephants have with one another, the Ptolemies would have seen the wisdom of having elephants of both genders and various ages grouped together. This may have made the training process easier.

We can only estimate the numbers of elephants captured during these hunting oper-ations. No figures survive from the few papyri dealing with this issue, but we may glean some idea from accounts of ancient historians who describe battles in which numbers of elephants are listed. For example, Polybius recounts the Battle of Raphia in 217 B.C.E. between the Ptolemaic and Seleucid forces. He says (*Histories* 5.79.2 and 13) that Ptole-maic forces fielded 73 African elephants against the Seleucids' 102 larger Indian ones on that occasion.[109] In no surviving records are the numbers of elephants recorded in bat-tles excessive—usually in the tens or dozens, exceptionally in the 70s to low 100s. We can estimate that at its zenith the Seleucid elephant corps totaled perhaps 150 beasts.[110] We assume that the figures cited by the ancient authors reflect only elephants that could be put into the field or were deployed in battle and that they do not include others that, for various reasons, were not used. The elephants the Ptolemies and their opponents actually possessed would have been greater than the number they put into the field on any single occasion. These "unseen" elephants would have included infants in captivity; their lactating mothers; any injured, juvenile, sick, or elderly animals; and others still in training. We cannot know what percentage of the total captive herd (both those in the field and those held back from combat) these animals would have represented, but if they were even as much as half, this would still put total Ptolemaic numbers of elephants at about 150, certainly less than 200.[111] These figures, in turn, would have been less than the number of elephants originally obtained, as a result of attrition during their capture, transport, and training. There is no evidence that any ancient "western" armies regularly using elephants could, under any circumstances, field an elephant corps of hundreds of beasts at a time.[112] Ancient "western" sources, though they disagree on numbers, indicate that even Porus, when confronting Alexander at the Battle of the Hydaspes, fielded no more than 200 or so elephants,[113] and he was from a region where elephants were easily acquired. Appian (*Punic Wars* 14.95) reports that the Carthaginians had stables that could accommodate up to 300 elephants and places for their fodder; many of these pachyderms were likely obtained from nearby regions of the Atlas Mountains and the Fezzan in modern Libya.[114]

In connection with discussion of the numbers of elephants the Ptolemies may have possessed, we have some information about the size of one of the elephant-hunting parties, its pay, and the duration of its activities. A papyrus dating from 223 B.C.E., toward the end of the reign of Ptolemy III (246–221 B.C.E.), records that 231 men received a combined salary of 2 talents and 1,860 drachmas for three months' work. That averages about 20 drachmas or 4 silver obols per person per day, very good pay for the time.[115] Who were these people? Was local talent employed rather than conveying at some cost in time and money individuals from Egypt itself to undertake this highly specialized and dangerous work? Whoever they were, they obtained an advance on this amount for the three-month operation, with the balance paid upon completion of the assignment.[116] We cannot be certain why the contract was limited to three months or at what time of year the men undertook their assignment. This may have had to do with the length of time the men needed to finish one job, or it may have coincided with the time of year that the elephants were most easily captured (mating or birthing season?), or perhaps it coincided with some annual elephant migration closer to the coast, or it may have been undertaken during cooler weather or been based on calculating wind patterns and, thus, sailing conditions, in the Red Sea, or a host of these or related factors. The account in this papyrus answers some questions about hunting activities, but it raises several others. Was this the normal or average size of such expeditions, and were the salaries paid and time on the job also typical? How successful were these hunts—viz., on average, how many elephants might they expect to capture in one expedition? Alternatively, how many perished? How were the hunting teams organized? Were the men who captured the elephants responsible for harvesting ivory as well? Were the hunting teams also assigned to care for the animals once they had been conveyed to the Red Sea coastal depots, or was this responsibility delegated to others?

Graffiti scratched on statues of Ramses II (reigned 1279–1213 B.C.E.) at his Abu Simbel temple record the names and hometowns of some Ptolemaic-era elephant hunters. These men were not from Egypt or anywhere in Africa, but from Cyprus and, apparently, Asia Minor. Two of them, Ariston and Boutrys, were from Kourion, whereas a third, Krateros son of Leukaros, was likely from Ionia. The men did not date their graffiti, but they likely carved them sometime in the third century B.C.E. during the zenith of Ptolemaic elephant hunting; perhaps the scribblings were left in connection with Ptolemy II's "Ethiopian" expedition, which passed this way sometime between 280 and 272 B.C.E.[117] It is noteworthy that these elephant hunters' names should appear here when most of the elephant traffic seems to have been via the Red Sea; this indicates that some of the hunters reached areas of elephant habitation overland via the Nile. It also suggests, given their origins, either that little training or talent was needed to hunt the elephants—and we do not know whether these individuals were involved in capturing the beasts or slaying them for their ivory—or that these men had received the training necessary to carry out their tasks; perhaps this was not their first expedition.

In any case, there is no evidence that live elephants were conveyed overland to Egypt; they came via the Red Sea on specially designed ships called *elephantegoi*. Ships built for conveying certain types of animals were not unusual in the ancient world. *Hippagogoi*, horse-carrying transport ships, represent one category, and they are mentioned by writers between the fifth century B.C.E. and the second century C.E. and in a fourth-century B.C.E. inscription found at Piraeus.[118] Though several ancient accounts report transporting elephants by sea, including the Pithom stele noted earlier[119] and Diodorus Siculus (3.40.4), only two surviving ancient written sources mention *elephantegoi* by name. These rare references to the *elephantegos* occur solely in the early to middle Ptolemaic period. One is a third-century B.C.E. papyrus, discussed later, and the other is in Agatharchides (5.85).[120] It has been calculated that voyages in the *elephantegoi* lasted at least a week and more often several weeks to a month depending upon factors including location of the hunting stations, their final ports of call in Egypt, sailing conditions, the sizes and experience of the crews, and the sizes and conditions of the ships.[121] Ports, stations, and other safe landfalls along the African Red Sea littoral were critical to the administrative tasks and logistical support associated with the elephant hunts. It was undoubtedly at these principal ports that practical basic training and initial maintenance and recuperation of the pachyderms took place after their capture and prior to their shipment north by sea. Red Sea stations situated between ports of embarkation and Egypt likely also supported the transport ships that plodded north with their troublesome cargoes. *Elephantegoi* likely could not carry sufficient food and water for crews and their charges to make a nonstop journey; ships traveling some distance probably landed periodically for resupply and rest, and ports sprinkled along the coast would have performed this critical logistical task. Alternatively, but less likely, large transport ships loaded with stores of food and water may have occasionally accompanied the *elephantegoi,* provisioning them as needed, thereby obviating the need to land frequently. Such transfer, at sea, from one ship to another, of heavy containers of fresh water and food, if it took place at all, would have required great skill and must have been a rare occurrence. One papyrus mentions a large grain ship headed south from Arsinoë/Cleopatris/Clysma;[122] perhaps one of its functions was to accompany and supply one or more *elephantegoi* sailing back north.

We have no surviving ancient descriptions of the size or appearance of an *elephantegos.* Yet, we must assume that each vessel was specially designed and built for the purpose at hand, was quite large, and was probably especially wide, to provide added stability in consideration of the size and shifting heavy weight of the cargo; the vessel was undoubtedly fairly awkward in appearance. There may have been several different classes of *elephantegoi* depending upon the number of elephants destined for transport and the travel time and distance of each journey. Perhaps the sizes of these ships increased over time as their ports of departure lay farther south and the journey north to ports in Egypt became longer. To make such long voyages more cost-effective, ever-larger vessels may have been built to carry more elephants and/or more supplies to minimize the number of intermediate revictualing stops that would be required. Each *elephantegos* would probably have conveyed at least several pachyderms if not more to make such journeys worth the cost and effort. One highly speculative modern account holds that such ships carried ten elephants and enough food and water to remain at sea for ten days without putting into port.[123] It would also be important to learn where the Ptolemies obtained their knowledge for the design of these vessels and the methods and materials used in their construction. Ptolemaic shipwrights understood how to design and build massive warships for use in the Mediterranean,[124] and they may have used these large battleships as models for constructing *elephantegoi.* Alternatively, they may have built modified *hippagagoi* to meet the special needs for conveying elephants.[125] Was the design one their own marine architects evolved after much trial and error or modification of ship designs known to them, or did the Ptolemies borrow the design from other peoples and modify it for their own requirements? If the Ptolemies' *elephantegoi* were copied from foreign prototypes, or perhaps initially built by natives living along the coasts associated with the elephants' capture and shipment, the question arises of why indigenous peoples such as the Meroitic would have needed vessels like these in the first place. The location, identification, and excavation of an *elephantegos* would likely answer some of these questions.

For an added degree of safety, *elephantegoi* may have occasionally traveled in groups, though this is uncertain; nor can we estimate how large such convoys might have been. We can imagine the scene when these ships arrived at Berenike with their terrified and seasick charges and exhausted crews. How and where in the port were they unloaded, and where in the city were the elephants kept until healthy enough to begin their journey across the desert to the Nile? We can only speculate—as we do later on in this chapter—though we hope that future excavations might answer these questions with more precision. The discovery of an elephant tooth in Berenike's Ptolemaic "industrial" area and finds of ivory from parts of the Roman-era city indicate that live beasts and their tusks traveled through the port, undoubtedly brought by ship from the more southerly reaches of the Red Sea.[126]

A mosaic pavement in the early fourth century c.e. villa at Piazza Armerina[127] preserves depictions of an elephant and a bull being coaxed onto a ship for transport, presumably from Alexandria, most likely to Ostia.[128] There are images of other animals being loaded onto another vessel, perhaps at Carthage, and also destined for Ostia.[129] Other scenes show the disembarkation of animals including a tiger and an ostrich at a port, presumably Ostia.[130] These creatures were destined for spectacles or destruction in combats between animals of different species or between animals and men *(bestiarii)* held in amphitheaters throughout the empire. The appearance of at least one other animal species being boarded on the same ship as the elephant does not indicate a vessel design specifically for elephants, nor are any *elephantegoi* known from ancient writers to have plied the Mediterranean in the Roman era, but this may be the closest surviving depiction we have, in lieu of an excavated specimen, of what an *elephantegos* in the Red Sea might have looked like.

There is another possible depiction of an *elephantegos* carved as a graffito on a block recycled into the Islamic Bab al-Futuh (Gate of Conquest) in Cairo. It is impossible to date this graffito or determine the provenance of the block on which it is inscribed. It may show an *elephantegos* on the Red Sea. Alternatively, it might represent a Nile ship transporting an elephant or a ship leaving Alexandria with an elephant.[131]

A third possible representation appears on a mosaic in a late first-century c.e. Roman villa at Veii. The mosaic depicts an elephant on a gangplank, with men on board the ship and on the dock pulling at ropes attached to the beast in an attempt to get him on board the vessel.[132] In the case of the Roman mosaics from Piazza Armerina and Veii, the ships onto which the elephants are being loaded may be only large transports, for there is no record of an *elephantegos* from the Roman era. We have no way to establish a Ptolemaic date for the Cairo graffito. So, again, we cannot be certain that the ship depicted was an *elephantegos*. Nevertheless, these visual survivals suggest the possible appearance of an *elephantegos*.

Most ancient written evidence indicates that elephants were offloaded at Berenike, and there is papyrological evidence that *elephantegoi* were outfitted at Heroonpolis in 224 b.c.e.—and likely at Berenike as well—about the time when archaeological evidence indicates that the Ptolemaic industrial area at Berenike was active.[133] Thus, measurements of harbor facilities at Berenike (see chapter 10) may provide some idea of the dimensions of many ships that berthed here.

The size, awkward dimensions, and deep draft of *elephantegoi*, as well as their direction of voyage against strong prevailing north winds in the Red Sea, meant that rowing one of these vessels was out of the question. Diodorus Siculus (3.40.4–8) reports on the ships, noting that they were powered by sails. We might speculate, though we have no evidence, that *elephantegoi* had multiple rudders due to their large dimensions and as insurance in case one broke—supplemented, perhaps on occasion, with oars that could be used in emergencies to keep the ships away from reefs. Because they likely had drafts greater than those of typical merchant or cargo ships or of any galley, they would probably have traveled some distance offshore to avoid shallow waters with their sandbars and dangerous reefs.[134] Yet, tacking these unwieldy ships against strong prevailing north winds must have been a daunting task. Diodorus Siculus (3.40.4–8) reports that many *elephantegoi* were wrecked. Their skeletal hulks were deliberately left dotting islands and shorelines as cenotaphs for their crews and warnings to others passing nearby of omnipresent dangerous sailing conditions. We do not know what percentage of the ships were sunk, how many crews were lost, or how many animals may have died in transit, but every effort must have been expended to keep the elephants alive and as healthy as possible.

Once the ships' live cargoes landed at Berenike or, perhaps occasionally, at some other, more northerly Egyptian Red Sea port, the elephants were undoubtedly allowed a recovery period prior to being marched overland to Apollonopolis Magna. The Pithom stele reports that on at least one occasion during Philadelphus's reign elephants went via the "Eastern Canal" linking the Red Sea to the Nile.[135] This may have been a onetime public-relations stunt. Aside from this passing reference, however, there is no evidence that elephants were transported on a regular basis as far north as Arsinoë/Cleopatris/Clysma for subsequent conveyance by barge along a canal linking that Red Sea port to points along the Nile.[136] The strong prevailing north winds in the Red Sea would have deterred such efforts. Transport ships sailed south from Egypt; one is specifically mentioned carrying grain,[137] and undoubtedly such ships carried other merchandise that was traded or sold to residents of the elephant-hunting stations or peoples living in the hinterlands of those entrepôts. Sailing as far north as Arsinoë/Cleopatris/Clysma with elephants when more southerly ports were available must have been very rare indeed. One station on the Myos Hormos–Koptos road bears the name Simiou, which may derive from Simmias, who Diodorus (3.18.4) mentions was one of the commanders Ptolemy III sent to secure elephants.[138] This suggests that Simmias passed by here, though we cannot be certain of this or of whether, if he did travel this direction, he was en route to his assignment farther south or on the way back with some elephants. In any case, Berenike was clearly the preferred landfall, although on occasion elephants might be disembarked at more northerly ports for a host of practical or other reasons.

We have an account of an *elephantegos* that was shipwrecked—fortunately, as it returned south, and thus had no elephants on board—in 224 B.C.E.; the papyrus recording the event reports that help was on the way as soon as another *elephantegos* could be outfitted at Berenike.[139] Communication between the crew of the wrecked *elephantegos* and officials at some port in Egypt, most likely Berenike, suggests that at least one other ship had accompanied the stricken vessel during its voyage and that the emergency signal to officials in Egypt and their reply to it had been conveyed in this manner. This may suggest, in this instance, that *elephantegoi* traveled in convoy with at least one other ship. In addition to the possibility of these ships sailing north in groups with their charges to ports in Egypt, they were probably guarded, perhaps not on a regular basis but only as needed or deemed necessary, by Ptolemaic naval forces or came in convoy with such vessels as a safety precaution as the opportunity arose. There were a number of Red Sea ports bearing the sobriquet Berenike, so we cannot be certain that our emporium is the one referred to in the letter. That the papyrus in which this mention appears was found in Egypt in the Fayum, however, strongly suggests that our Berenike was indeed the port from which help was to be sent.

Given that the Ptolemaic court had a direct and vested interest in elephant and ivory acquisition and that most of the live animals and their by-products would have reached Egypt by sea, the former aboard *elephantegoi*, we must assume that these transport vessels were part of the logistical side of the Ptolemaic navy in the Red Sea.[140] We have no idea how sizable the Red Sea fleet was, since the bulk of Ptolemaic military effort was concentrated against better-organized and more dangerous foes in the eastern Mediterranean. The Egyptians had a naval presence in the Red Sea since Pharaonic times, and this seems to have grown with the advent of the Ptolemies in proportion to their increased presence and interest in the Eastern Desert and the Red Sea.

An inactive (adult) elephant, such as would have been on board a ship, consumes an average of 45.5 kg of hay, supplemented with vegetables and oats, per day, whereas an active feral African elephant may consume 136.5–227.5 kg of vegetation and spend up to sixteen hours a day obtaining it. An elephant can drink up to two hundred liters of water per day,[141] whereas if it is inactive, and in a relatively cool environment, it would probably drink far less. We must assume that although inactive, the elephants would have been quite stressed while aboard the transport ships, and this would have greatly affected these rates of consumption and the overall state of their health. Thus, providing even the most minimal provisioning for the animals, their caretakers, and ships' crews—plus adding the dangers, stress, and exhaustion of sailing on the Red Sea—probably dictated that an *elephantegos* had to put into shore at least once every few days. An important question then becomes whether the elephants were periodically taken off at these intermediate stops to eat, drink, or otherwise recover somewhat from the voyages before continuing on. Numerous resupply points along the coast would, then, have been necessary. Some of these may have been only temporary stations established during the peak of each elephant-gathering season, which for practical purposes would have been mainly in the cooler winter months, though elephant acquisition at other times of the year might also have taken place depending upon locations of the herds, their breeding cycles, and other considerations. Prevailing wind patterns south of 18°–20° north latitude in the Red Sea blow from the south between October and May,[142] and sailors would have been wise to take advantage of these whenever possible. Perhaps it was at those times that most *elephantegoi* voyaged north to Berenike. The names of these transitory waypoints are lost; others were elephant-marshaling yards or served other trade-related purposes and would have been the larger, more permanent settlements the names of which we noted above. None of these stations, with the possible exception of Ptolemais (Epi)Theron, has been positively identified on the ground, so their sizes and plans, and the degree of effort expended in creating and maintaining them, remain unknown.

African elephants could be trained for military duties, though there seems to be no specification in the ancient sources that the African variety was more difficult to discipline than its Asian counterpart. Of the two major species of elephants in Africa—the larger bush elephant *(Loxodonta africana)* and the smaller forest elephant (*Loxodonta cyclotis*, now extinct in East Africa though present elsewhere on the continent)—it seems that the object of the Ptolemaic hunters was the forest elephant.[143] This species is generally smaller than both the African bush elephant and its Indian cousin, which caused some problems when they met their larger Seleucid counterparts in battle.[144] The forest elephant is, however, easier to train than the bush variety.[145] Whether the "Troglodytic" and "Ethiopian" elephants mentioned earlier in this chapter in the inscription of Ptolemy III/ Cosmas Indicopleustes were both types of forest pachyderms is uncertain. Although their use in battle continued, there is little indication that the Ptolemies imported elephants from the Red Sea region after the reign of Ptolemy IV Philopator (221–205 B.C.E.) or possibly as late as Ptolemy VI Philometor (180–145 B.C.E.).[146] This may have been due either to the presence of adequate numbers imported into Egypt and the establishment of a successful breeding program there and later or, certainly by the late third or second century B.C.E., to the realization that elephants as military tools cost more than whatever real or perceived advantages they might bring to those deploying them. There is also the possibility that the Seleucids may have been cut off from their sources of Indian elephants by the rise of the Parthian state, with its heartland in Iran, at the end of the third century B.C.E. If so, lack of elephants among their rivals due to inaccessibility of traditional Indian sources of supply and failure of any domestic breeding program they may have instituted, and the reduced military threat that the Seleucids then posed, may have convinced the Ptolemies to abandon their own elephant-gathering and -training project.[147] Thus, whatever attempt the Ptolemies made to establish an elephant-breeding program in Egypt was closed down. In any case, we cannot be certain of the success of this endeavor if, indeed, it was ever seriously and consistently implemented.

ROMANS AND ELEPHANTS

Fascination with and curiosity about elephants continued into the Roman period.[148] Though they first saw these animals during the war with Pyrrhus in the early third century B.C.E., the Romans first captured large numbers of the beasts, 140 or 142 according to Pliny (*NH* 8.6.16), from the Carthaginians during the First Punic War in Sicily in 252 B.C.E. The Romans themselves deployed elephants, captured from the Carthaginians during the war with Hannibal in North Africa, in small numbers in the second century B.C.E. in battles against the Macedonian king Philip V at Cynoscephalae in 197 B.C.E. and again against his son and successor, Perseus, at Pydna in 168 B.C.E.[149] They also used them on a limited scale (ten beasts total) in the mid second century B.C.E. in Spain, at the siege of Numantia.[150] Dio Cassius (39.38.2–4) reports the importation of eighteen elephants from Africa to celebrate the inauguration of the Theater of Pompey in 55 B.C.E. Since Ostia at this time probably could not have accommodated any large ship or ships transporting the animals, these likely landed at Puteoli; then they either were loaded onto more numerous and smaller vessels that could land at Ostia or, alternatively, were marched overland from Puteoli to Rome.[151] Julius Caesar's civil-war opponents fielded sixty pachyderms in 46 B.C.E. at the Battle of Thapsus.[152]

Julius Caesar himself or Augustus may have established an elephant-breeding program located somewhere in Italy, probably south of Rome, which persisted at least into the reign of Claudius (41–54 C.E.).[153] At that time, late in the first century B.C.E. and subsequently, successive emperors put elephants on display in various venues as curious beasts of incredible strength and, depending upon their training, great ferocity or docility, as well as of considerable intelligence.[154] Their previous important role in the military had, however, faded to near insignificance, though it had not disappeared completely, by the peak of the Roman Empire in the later first and second centuries C.E.

Ammianus Marcellinus (25.6.1–4) records that Romans faced elephants deployed in battle by their Sassanian adversaries in 363 C.E. It is evident from Ammianus's brief description that the Romans were so unaccustomed to elephants by that time that both their infantry and cavalry were initially thrown into some confusion by their appearance before eventually rallying to win the battle. Several writers in the sixth and seventh centuries C.E., especially Procopius and Theophylactus, report that the Sassanians continued to use elephants in battle, though apparently in small numbers, against their late Roman/ Byzantine opponents.[155] There is little indication of their effectiveness in these engagements. Cosmas Indicopleustes (*Christian Topography* 11.20)[156] relates how the Indian king Gollas took with him to war at least two thousand elephants. Given all we have said above about elephants in battle, this number seems greatly exaggerated.

5

PTOLEMAIC AND EARLY ROMAN
BERENIKE AND ENVIRONS

Excavations at Berenike revealed something about the size, layout, and building methods and materials used to create the port's infrastructure and how these changed over the life of the city. Our project also recovered written documents (in at least twelve different ancient languages, although most texts are in Greek and Latin) and other artifacts and ecofacts that provide insights into those who lived and worked here, the items traded, and other areas of the ancient world with which Berenike was in contact (see chapters 6 and 12). The architecture and materials used to construct Berenike throughout its history must have been partially a reflection of the ethnic building conventions of the city's residents. Yet, these traditions were modified somewhat by the types and quantities of construction materials available both at the emporium itself and in its environs. Very few building materials were imported from the Nile valley; the price would have been prohibitively high.

The early middle Ptolemaic-era industrial area at the western edge of the site has walls comprising limestone chunks and other cobblestones as the primary building materials. Portions of a hydraulic installation indicate extensive knowledge of waterproofing techniques. A V-shaped ditch cut into bedrock also appeared in the Ptolemaic industrial area (see chapter 4). Beneath the early Roman trash dump at the northern edge of the city were Ptolemaic structures made of sand bricks. Other slight evidence of Ptolemaic construction materials appeared in two other trenches. None of the building materials from the Ptolemaic era, however, were used—except limestone, and that quite sparingly—in early or late Roman architecture at Berenike. Nor is there any evidence that inhabitants

FIGURE 5-1
Berenike, late Roman-style building technique using extinct coral heads for walls, which contain numerous niches (Trench BE00/01-41). Scale = 1 m. Photo by S. E.Sidebotham.

of Roman Berenike ever excavated into bedrock. This may suggest that groups living here in Ptolemaic times had access to different materials and had different building traditions than did the city's Roman-era residents.

Ancient literary and archaeological evidence from across the Mediterranean indicates that the early Roman period, until the mid or late second century C.E. at least, was prosperous. Ancient texts, and floral and faunal remains from early Roman Berenike, demonstrate that the port flourished in the first century C.E. as well. Yet, ironically, little architecture dating from either the later Ptolemaic or the early Roman era has been excavated thus far at the site. For the most part, strata containing these structures are quite deep and would be, in some instances, below the late Roman city. Since excavations throughout much of the site have uncovered mainly late Roman structures, and we assume that earlier phases of occupation lie beneath these, only future fieldwork will document more fully late Ptolemaic and early Roman phases of occupation from an architectural perspective. There is an interesting conundrum with any discussion of early Roman Berenike—that period from the Roman annexation of Egypt in 30 B.C.E. until the early second century C.E. There exist an overwhelming preponderance of datable artifacts; hundreds of written documents, predominantly ostraka and papyri (see chapters 6 and 12); small artifacts; and associated floral and faunal remains from this period—mainly though not exclusively from a first-century C.E. trash dump north of the city. The Berenike excavations have also recovered quantitatively more artifacts and other organic remains from early Roman contexts than from any other time in the port's eight-hundred-year existence. Yet, few early Roman buildings have thus far been excavated. This is in stark contrast to the late Roman city, where there is substantial evidence for its physical appearance yet very little in the way of contemporary written documents.

The materials and techniques used to create Berenike changed from the early and middle Ptolemaic period—when evidence from the Ptolemaic industrial area at the western end of the city and from areas beneath the early Roman trash dump indicates that mostly gypsum/anhydrite stone and bricks made of sand were employed—to late Ptolemaic and early Roman times, when what little evidence we have suggests that large limestone boulders and cut stone seem to have been preferred. By late Roman times—from the middle of the fourth century C.E. on, perhaps somewhat earlier—most structures in the city consisted predominantly of fossilized coral heads that were collected and quarried from the surface upon which Berenike was built (figure 5-1).[1] In this later era, door thresholds, quoins of walls, staircases inside edifices, and benches, stairs, and paving stones inside the ecclesiastical structure at the eastern edge of the city were made of gypsum/anhydrite ashlars and other types of cut blocks, many of which had been recycled from earlier Roman edifices in the city (see chapter 13). It seems that throughout the life of the city there were sculptors who used the locally available gypsum/anhydrite for their glyptic artwork. Good examples include a small human head from the Ptolemaic era; a broken statuette of Aphrodite/Venus (figures 5-2a and 5-2b), found in the early Roman trash dump; and a reclining sphinx recycled into the southern wall of the so-called Shrine of the Palmyrenes (figure 5-3) (see chapter 13).

There is little indication of why Berenike's residents switched from using one type of building material to another. The metamorphosis may have had something to do with the change in the ethnic composition of the port's inhabitants, which can be documented from the ceramic, floral, and faunal corpora, but that can provide only a partial explanation. Given the relative dearth of late Ptolemaic and early Roman structures thus far excavated, there is also no reliable information about the most preferred types of building materials in use at the port at that time. Myos Hormos, about 300 km north of Berenike, which flourished from early Roman times, if not earlier, until about the mid third century C.E., was constructed of a hodgepodge of various locally available materials including coral heads, large clamshells, both fired and unfired bricks, cobblestones, and anything else that was readily available.

The late Ptolemaic-era settlement at Berenike (latter half of the second to first centuries B.C.E.) likely differed from that of the early and middle Ptolemaic era in its location and, most probably, in its size. Although it is difficult to determine the physical extent of late Ptolemaic Berenike or the individual sizes and designs of its buildings, the community at that time seems to have abandoned the early and middle Ptolemaic-era industrial zone and moved east, though there is evidence that the harbor south of the indus-

FIGURES 5-2A AND 5-2B

Berenike, front and back of a broken statuette representing Aphrodite/Venus, made of local gypsum/anhydrite, from the first-century c.e. trash dump. Scale = 10 cm. Photos by S. E. Sidebotham.

trial zone may have still been operational in late Ptolemaic and early Roman times. Aside from the harbor, the western limits of the late Ptolemaic settlement seem to have lain somewhere east of the early-middle Ptolemaic industrial zone and west of the area with the Serapis temple. That structure, perhaps built during the reign of Ptolemy VI Philometor or Ptolemy VIII Euergetes II—eras of extensive temple construction elsewhere in Egypt[2]—may have been a focal point of the late Ptolemaic-era city.[3] The Serapis temple was, likely, a legacy of the layout of the late Ptolemaic town and does not appear to have been situated in the center of the early Roman community. Satellite imagery of Berenike and geomagnetic surveying east of the early-middle Ptolemaic-era industrial area in 2008–2009 suggests some degree of orthogonal planning of this part of the city. Since no excavations have been conducted here, it is uncertain whether the subterranean features revealed by satellite and magnetic surveying are Ptolemaic or early Roman or may, in fact, reflect early Roman modifications of a Ptolemaic plan. Ptolemaic settlements were usually orthogonal in plan, following "Hippodamian" tenets,[4] and future excavations in this part of Berenike should clarify this. By the early Roman period, the urban center seems to have shifted east and northeast of the abandoned Ptolemaic industrial zone and toward the ever-receding coastline, with the result that the Serapis temple

FIGURE 5-3
Berenike, stone sphinx made of local gypsum/anhydrite recycled into the late Roman-era southern wall of the Shrine of the Palmyrenes. Scale = 20 cm. Photo by S. E. Sidebotham.

was probably located off-center in the southern or southwestern quadrant of the city by the first century C.E.

Limited evidence suggests that early Roman Berenike's street plan was also orthogonal, but over time, and by the late Roman period, modifications and encroachment of buildings farther into the streets clouded the original layout. The lines of coral that mark the surface of unexcavated portions of the site today, and plans of the town based on these remains, reflect the latest phase of occupation in the fourth, fifth, and into the sixth centuries. The abundance of Roman documents and other items from the early Roman trash dump north of the city suggests that the size of the town increased in comparison with what it had been during the Ptolemaic period. Berenike in the early Roman era seems to have been a lively settlement in spite of its remote location—a twelve-day trip from the Nile at Koptos according to Pliny the Elder (*NH* 6.26.102–103).

Berenike, the southernmost major port in Ptolemaic or Roman Egypt, lay about 150 km south of Marsa Nakari.[5] A coastal survey conducted in 2002 revealed no substantial ancient remains between Berenike and Marsa Nakari, although the Via Nova Hadriana runs parallel to, but some distance inland from, the littoral and connected the two settlements to one another and to Myos Hormos as well as other points north.

The best-known structure at Berenike prior to our excavations was a temple dedicated to Serapis, a Ptolemaic god combining the attributes of Osiris and Apis, and to other deities. This structure was made of locally available white gypsum/anhydrite ashlars attached together using wooden clamps. Located at the highest point on the site, the edifice was cleared by earlier travelers (see chapter 2) several times in the nineteenth and early twentieth centuries. This temple probably dates originally from the second century B.C.E., with active use until at least the 160s C.E. (see chapter 13). We should not be surprised if future excavations in the temple's environs reveal final phases extending into late Roman times.

We undertook limited work in the temple in 2009 only after serious vandalism had occurred during 2007–2008. Our project has, however, excavated an area immediately north and adjacent to the Serapis temple. At the earliest Roman-era levels, excavations revealed indications of a temple courtyard made of beaten earth. Resting on this surface were several deteriorated wooden bowls, items that seem to be present at a number of other cult centers in the city. Also excavated were two large round-bottomed terra-cotta storage jars made in India and buried up to their rims in the courtyard floor. One of these jars preserved the remains of a wooden lid; the other contained 7.55 kg of black peppercorns, clearly an import from southern India (see chapter 12). We must conclude that the presence of the peppercorns in the courtyard indicates that the temple owned them. In other words, not all the items imported from overseas passed through Berenike to onward destinations, at least in early Roman times. Some commodities were consumed by residents of Berenike itself. This (see chapter 12) was true for a number of items imported especially from India into Berenike in all phases of Roman occupation.

As already mentioned, we are not certain precisely when the Serapis temple was initially constructed; nor do we know how long it operated. The temple may have functioned into the fourth or fifth century C.E., since other pagan cult centers were active at that time—suggesting, despite any imperial decrees and the presence at Berenike of a large church in the fifth century C.E., that pagan religious practices continued in the port. Berenike's population was obviously quite eclectic in its religious proclivities.

The only other early Roman structures discovered at Berenike, aside from walls associated with the courtyard of the Serapis temple, and the Ptolemaic and perhaps early Roman harbor works south of the Ptolemaic industrial area, are two seawalls at the eastern edge of the site. Both are approximately contemporary—viz. late first century B.C.E./first century C.E.—and provide a limited and very incomplete glimpse of the configuration of the early Roman port at about the peak of commercial activity.

One seawall appears at the northeastern edge of the city beneath a temple or major public edifice. This structure consisted of coral heads and ashlar blocks, much damaged and partly destroyed. It was 1.30 m wide—quite wide by Berenike standards—and 6.6 m long, but only 0.35 m high.[6] It was oriented northeast–southwest and was a seawall and not a pier that jutted out into the water. We know this because we found evidence of marine activity on the northern side only; here a number of small wooden bollards projected out of the harbor bottom, suggesting that smaller craft tied up alongside the seawall. The southern side seems never to have been exposed to marine activity and appears, instead, to have always been landward facing.[7]

The other seawall, at the eastern edge of the site south of the church, dated from the late first century B.C.E./first century C.E. It comprised large limestone boulders that formed a wall about 1 m wide east–west × 5 m long north–south within the excavated area.[8] Excavations at Berenike thus far have rarely encountered limestone in any form used as a construction material later in Berenike's history. This type of stone seems to have been used mainly, if not exclusively, in Ptolemaic and early Roman times. We do not understand why this was the case.

These remains, combined with the results of a geomagnetic survey undertaken in 1999, indicate that there were at least two bays or inlets, one on the northeast side,[9] where the survey noted absolutely no structures and where excavations documented the seawall— all of which combine to suggest an open area of water. Another, much larger one lay on the southern side of the site with, presumably, a protective seawall running around those portions of the city adjacent to the shore. Geomagnetic surveying detects anomalies in subsurface soil densities. Subsurface walls built of stone will, thus, appear very different from the surrounding sand. This method of detecting subsurface structures is accurate only to depths of about 1 to 1.5 m and is of extremely limited use in a *tel* site with multiple layers of later-over-earlier structures such as we have throughout most of Berenike. Yet, it provides much insight in areas of light and shallow architectural buildup such as in the western, outlying Ptolemaic industrial area, where it helped us situate trenches in 2000–2001. In 2008–2010 we conducted additional magnetic surveying south of the early-middle Ptolemaic-era industrial area, where we believe the Ptolemaic and/or early Roman harbor to have been located. The limited excavations here in 2009–2010 indicate that this was indeed a harbor and that it had been abandoned by the early Roman era. Subsequently, it was converted into industrial trash dumps or light manufacturing areas.

At this point it is uncertain whether there were other inlets. Nor is it clear whether the seemingly small northern inlet accommodated only smaller tender vessels associated with unloading and loading larger ships anchored out in deeper water or more diminutive, coastal-hugging Red Sea tramp steamers. It seems that the more substantial southern harbor served larger merchantmen. Such segregation would have made control for customs procedures much simpler.

Sometime in the Roman period, perhaps early, certainly later, the western portions of the huge harbor works located immediately south/southeast of the early to middle Ptolemaic industrial area had been abandoned and the piers, breakwaters, seawalls, and so on, due to circumstances of harbor silting, were built anew farther east toward the ever-receding coastline. The eastern portions of this large southern harbor may still have operated in Roman times, since basalt ballast from Qana' on the Indian Ocean coast of Yemen[10]—which began to operate only in the first century B.C.E. and whose floruit was the second to fifth centuries C.E.—was identified in this area. Unfortunately, excavations to date have not located identifiable harbor works in any other part of Berenike.

Excavations at Myos Hormos identified a similar silting phenomenon. There the Romans built an ingenious "pier," contemporary with Berenike's seawalls, that comprised large numbers of amphoras imported from the Nile valley, Italy, Rhodes, and the Istrian peninsula.[11] Once emptied of their contents, presumably consumed at Myos Hormos, these jars were recycled for this land-reclamation project.[12] Limited evidence thus far shows that Myos Hormos, perhaps like the early Roman harbor at Berenike, was extremely primitive and jerry-built using whatever materials were readily available. Whatever size and appearance either harbor had was due to the practical issue of moving cargoes through the ports quickly and efficiently; impressing visitors with fancy monuments was not important such as was the case with many of the more prominent harbors in the Mediterranean at this time.[13]

Ostraka from the early Roman trash dump north of the city center may provide insights as to when some of these harbor-construction activities at Berenike took place. Ancient literary sources may also shed some light on this question. Strabo (*Geography* 17.1.45) indicates that Berenike had convenient landing places in his day, thereby suggesting that the emporium was an anchorage or roadstead and not a port with a proper harbor. About six or seven decades later Pliny the Elder (*NH* 6.26.103) seems to indicate that Berenike had a proper harbor. If our interpretation of these admittedly less-than-clear passages is correct, then we might extrapolate that sometime in the first three quarters of the first century C.E. a proper harbor was constructed at Berenike.[14]

The Nikanor Ostraka (see chapters 6 and 9)[15] indicate a spurt of trade activity and quarrying operations in the Eastern Desert during the reign of Tiberius (14–37 C.E.), and it may be that major renovations and enlargements to augment, or replace, the silted-up Ptolemaic facilities began and had progressed sufficiently during his reign and immediately thereafter at Berenike.[16] Most of the identifiable coins (over 41 percent) from excavations at Berenike between 1994 and 2001 and 2009–2010 were minted during the first three-quarters of the first century, contemporary with the early Roman trash deposit.[17] Numerous finds of coins of Tiberius in India and the reintroduction of the tetradrachm in Egypt during his reign all suggest increased mercantile activity at that time,[18] as does the presence of Tiberian-era graffiti carved in Wadi Hammamat along the Myos Hormos–Nile road.[19] Epigraphic evidence suggests that it was also late in the reign of Augustus and early in Tiberius's own tenure that the Roman government solidified its hold over mining and quarrying operations in the Eastern Desert.[20]

Ostraka from the early Roman trash dump, the presence of a hieroglyphic text of Tiberius in the Serapis temple,[21] and inscriptions found at four of the *praesidia* on the road between Berenike and Koptos—at Siket near Berenike, at Khawr al-Jir (probably the ancient Aphrodito), at Khashm al-Menih/Zeydun (ancient Didymoi), and at Laqeita (ancient Phoenicon) (see chapters 7 and 8)—also suggest that the Julio-Claudian and Flavian periods were ones of robust activity at Berenike and along the route joining it to Koptos.[22]

Josephus (*BJ* 2.385) indicates that Egypt was the port for India at that time. His claim is certainly borne out by evidence from excavations at Berenike, at Myos Hormos, in the Roman forts along the Myos Hormos–Nile road, and elsewhere in the region. Thus, although we have yet to uncover many physical remains of early Roman Berenike, a great deal of other evidence, mainly numismatic, ceramic, and epigraphic, seems to point to major construction activity associated with trade in the first century C.E. sometime between the reigns of Tiberius and the Flavians. (We deal extensively with this and other desert installations in the early and late Roman periods in chapter 8.)

Excavations at Berenike have shown that after the early second century C.E. there was a dramatic decrease in the quantity of texts, coins, pottery, and other datable small finds. There is little evidence excavated thus far for activity at Berenike in the later second, the third, or the first half of the fourth century C.E. and nothing that would indicate the physical appearance of ships or harbor facilities or their location at that time. During this period the empire in general, and Egypt in particular, suffered from an economic downturn and political dissonance, which would have hindered, though not brought to a complete halt, trade via Berenike with emporia on the Nile and other points in the Eastern Desert.

Berenike must have suffered a steep decline in activity and a concomitant drop in the size of its population at this time. Political unrest and open rebellion along the Nile,[23] including an attack on the Nile cities of Koptos and Ptolemais by the nomadic Blemmyes;[24] an increase in banditry and Bedouin ("barbarian") activities in the Eastern Desert, which is evident from excavations along the Myos Hormos–Nile road (see chapter 8);[25] and a decline in the international trade passing through Berenike may all have played a role in this decline in the fortunes of the port.

In addition to local, regional, and empire-wide troubles, which would have caused Berenike much economic distress in the later second and third centuries, there were also problems in the Red Sea and Indian Ocean that would have added to the woes of those whose livelihoods were based upon this commerce. There were wars in southern Arabia among the states of Saba', Himyar, and Hadramaut in the second century and the annexation of Qatabanite land by Hadramaut. In the early third century the Kingdom of Himyar was attacked by the Abyssinians, though by 270 C.E. Himyar was victorious, having driven out the Abyssinians and annexing Saba' and Hadramaut (see chapter 13).[26]

Piracy had always been a problem in the Red Sea since Ptolemaic times, as several ancient authors and at least one inscription indicate.[27] There was also uncertainty due to piracy in India in this era; the *Periplus* (53) relates that at certain times piracy in India was more menacing than at others. This would have determined which ports in India were more accessible to merchants and might have influenced which products would be available and their prices.[28]

The appearance in the late second/early third centuries of several inscriptions, however, indicates some activity at Berenike. The aforementioned hieroglyphic text in the Serapis temple commemorating the joint reigns of Marcus Aurelius and his junior partner, Lucius Verus (161–169 C.E.), shows that there were still civic-minded individuals in the

FIGURE 5-4
Berenike, artist's reconstruction of the bronze
statue and the inscription dedicated by Marcus
Aurelius Mokimos (in the Shrine of the
Palmyrenes). Drawing by M. Hense.

city. Several sources indicate that a virulent plague, probably smallpox or measles, struck Egypt and the eastern Roman Empire during the reign of Lucius Verus and lasted several decades.[29] It decimated the population in many places in Egypt and the empire as a whole; this may have caused a dramatic downturn in activity at Berenike as well.

Our excavations documented two other inscriptions from the Shrine of the Palmyrenes, west of the Serapis temple. This cult center was neither as large nor as nicely constructed as the Serapis temple, but made, instead, of walls built of a hodgepodge of extinct coral heads mixed with gypsum/anhydrite blocks recycled from other buildings. One of the coral-head walls preserved a leveling course made of teak timber (see chapters 12 and 13). This small, narrow shrine accommodated a number of religious practices including the Roman imperial cult in the early third century C.E., the Palmyrene deity Yarhibol/ Hierobol, who was one of the important gods in the religious triad of that Syrian Desert caravan city, and possibly Harpocrates (Horus the Child), the son of Isis. In addition, excavations documented over one hundred wooden bowls, similar to those found on the early Roman courtyard floor of the Serapis temple, and a small reclining stone sphinx, noted earlier, reused in a later wall of the building. The wooden bowls probably contained something that comprised "prepackaged" offerings that worshippers could purchase and dedicate. Also unearthed was a small stone altar that preserved burn marks on its top.

FIGURE 5-5
Berenike, bilingual Greek-Palmyrene inscription
dedicating a statue to Yarhibol/Hierobol (from
the Shrine of the Palmyrenes). Scale = 10 cm.
Photo by S. E. Sidebotham.

Associated with this small altar were small, simple pottery bowls. We have not determined
how these bowls were used or how they related to the small altar near which they were
found.[30] Likely they had some ritual function.

One text in the Shrine of the Palmyrenes appears on two squared-off stones that provided part of the base for a bronze statue of an unidentifiable female figure, likely a deity, inside the building. The statue was complete from the knees down, and excavations
recovered numerous fragments that account for about 60 percent of the entire figure,
including an arm holding either a cornucopia or a snake.[31] The inscription beneath the
statue, offered by an auxiliary soldier who was an archer from Palmyra named Marcus
Aurelius Mokimos, indicates that the object of veneration was the Roman imperial cult—
specifically, the Emperor Caracalla and his mother, Julia Domna. The final words of the
dedication provide its precise date: September 8, 215 c.e. (figure 5-4). The imperial cult
was fairly widespread throughout the Roman world and was especially popular in the eastern part of the empire.[32]

The second inscription from this small cult center, which has no date, but whose period of carving we can estimate from the personal names that appear on it, was a bilingual text written in both Palmyrene and Greek in about 180–212 C.E. The Greek text was the longer of the two, with the Palmyrene being rather laconic. It records the dedication of a statue of Yarhibol/Hierobol, made when Aemilius Celer was Roman governor *(Praefectus Montis Bernicidis)* of the region and commander of a military unit called the *Ala Herculiana,* and when Valerius Germanon was *chiliarch* (military tribune/commander of one thousand men) of that unit. The personal name of the artist who "made the [statue of the] greatest god Hierobol" is given: Berichei, who was almost certainly Palmyrene himself (figure 5-5). Portions of a large stone base with sockets for feet and bits of lead used to seal the statue to the base and a life-size bronze hand, which does not appear to belong to the bronze statue of a female noted earlier, may be all that remains of Berichei's masterpiece.

At Koptos, the main Nile terminus for the Berenike road in the Roman period,[33] excavators years ago found inscriptions recording the presence of Palmyrene archers stationed there in the same period as that in which they appear at Berenike—viz. 215/216 C.E.[34] Also at Koptos, a dedicatory inscription to Yarhibol has been documented.[35] These parallel texts from Berenike and Koptos cannot be mere coincidences; they must record individuals of the same unit stationed simultaneously at both cities who patrolled the Koptos–Berenike road.

BERENIKE'S IMMEDIATE HINTERLAND

Within a 40 km radius of Berenike were sites of various dates and functions. Ten *praesidia* ringed Berenike, ranging from 7.2 km to 35 km from the city center. They have been surveyed and a few partially excavated (figure 5-6). All were founded or operated in the early Roman period, no doubt providing an early warning system to the city were it to be threatened by marauders coming from the desert. Given the value of commerce passing through the port in this period, one would expect such protection. We discuss in chapters 7 and 8 three *praesidia* closest to Berenike—two in Wadi Kalalat and one in Siket—that also supplied drinking water to the city and that would, in turn, have relied on Berenike for supplies.

It is not clear why the major unfortified settlements and cemeteries in the environs of Berenike are late Roman in date (discussed in chapter 13) whereas the ten forts/*praesidia* ringing the city from the hilltop fort at Shenshef southwest of the emporium to that in Wadi Lahma/Lahami northwest of the port are overwhelmingly of early Roman foundation. Surface surveys of all of these military installations and partial excavations at some of them indicate that only one or two (in Wadi Abu Greiya/Vetus Hydreuma) appear to have continued to operate in the late Roman era, when Berenike had a renaissance in its economic fortunes. One would expect, then, as in the early Roman period, when Berenike also prospered, that there would have been a need to defend the city and continue to supply it with drinking water. However, this appears not to have been the case, suggesting

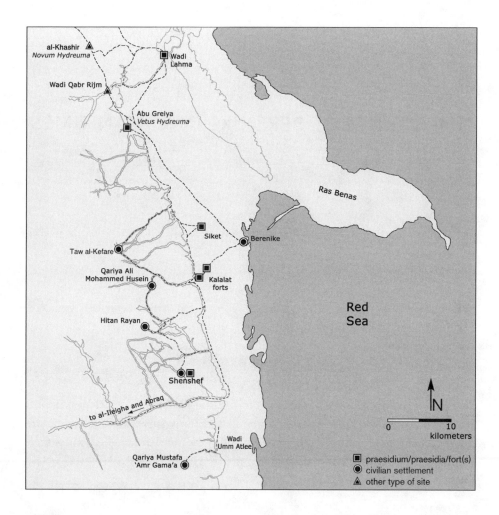

FIGURE 5-6

Map of Berenike and environs. Drawing by M. Hense.

that the garrison defending the port was stationed increasingly in the city itself rather than in outlying installations. Perhaps the presence of rather large, and apparently civilian, late Roman settlements at Shenshef, Hitan Rayan, and Wadi Umm Atlee as well as smaller ones in the environs of Berenike also housed small units of soldiers who left no trace in the archaeological record. If so, this would have obviated, at least in the minds of the authorities, the need for separate military installations at that time. The dearth of evidence about the city's drinking-water sources in the late Roman period remains an important question that future fieldwork hopes to answer.

6

INHABITANTS OF BERENIKE IN ROMAN TIMES

Here we will examine those who lived in Berenike in the Roman period, their professions, religious practices, and the languages they wrote and, likely, spoke. We will also explore how the foods they consumed were, along with other excavated data, indications of their ethnicity and social status.

POPULATION SIZE

Estimating population sizes of ancient settlements, especially larger urban centers, is fraught with pitfalls. At Berenike visible surface remains and excavations reveal predominantly mid- to late fourth- to fifth-century structures. During this late Roman renaissance a population of approximately five hundred to one thousand is likely.[1] In all periods of Berenike's history numbers of residents undoubtedly fluctuated throughout the year, peaking with the arrival and departure of ships; times when the vessels were not in port probably saw some of the city's population drift back to the desert or the Nile valley due to a decline in employment opportunities. No Ptolemaic domestic areas, though some industrial facilities, have been examined. The same is true for the early Roman city, though documents excavated from the early Roman trash dump indicate that the early Roman era was the zenith of the port's prosperity and, therefore, size. This suggests that the city's population was probably greatest at that time. Calculating population numbers for the Ptolemaic and early Roman periods, however, is impossible until excavations document more of these periods of the city's history.

PERSONS, PROFESSIONS, ETHNICITY

People of different regions, ethnic backgrounds, and socioeconomic statuses sought their fortunes in Roman Berenike. They participated in the trade and its infrastructural support. Archaeological finds record their statuses, and graffiti found along the Eastern Desert roads, together with formal inscriptions, ostraka, and papyri found at Berenike itself, provide information on who was involved in the commerce. Some texts record the names of individuals, and from these, scholars can begin to understand who they were and something about their ethnic and social backgrounds. Information on their diet, the textiles, rope, and basketry that they used, and the objects with which they adorned themselves and decorated their houses allows intimate views of their lives. Those who dwelt in Berenike, either briefly or as more or less permanent settlers, came from throughout the ancient world, including Egypt, the Mediterranean, Axum, sub-Saharan Africa, and the kingdoms of southern Arabia, Nabataea, and Palmyra. Indian sailors or merchants, and likely their Sinhalese contemporaries, visited Berenike and either stayed for a few months, arriving in early summer and catching the monsoon back to India in August, or resided there on a more permanent basis.

Texts excavated at Berenike were written on various objects. These texts were primarily on pottery ostraka, with the second most plentiful on papyri; the rest are on stone, plaster amphora stoppers, and so forth. Most ostraka are public documents from the early Roman era and include archives of individuals associated with the Berenike customs house; there is also a corpus, found in 2009 and 2010, that lists members of the Roman military and their involvement in the city's freshwater supply.[2] Most papyri, on the other hand, are private in nature: personal letters, bills of sale, and so on. There are also formal dedications (usually religious) carved on stone made by individuals, and also a smattering of texts written on seashells or stamped on dozens of plaster jar and amphora stoppers used to seal containers of commodities transported to Berenike for consumption there or for onward shipment to other areas of the Red Sea and Indian Ocean.

Collections of texts, some excavated at Berenike and others found in different parts of Egypt, document individuals involved in the trade. The Nikanor Ostraka Archive is that of a family of camel owners from Koptos involved in the transport of goods between the Nile valley and Berenike and Myos Hormos from late first century b.c.e. until the 60s c.e.[3] Ostraka from *praesidia* along the Myos Hormos–Koptos route deal mostly with provisions of the garrisons based there; some refer to trade and transport.[4]

Ostraka from the early Roman trash dump at Berenike consist, in part, of laissez-passer, which indicate that the bearer, or his agent or company, had paid certain taxes at Koptos and that he was allowed to bring a specified amount of goods into the customs area at Berenike.[5] These passes were written in Greek, but from the terminology used it is clear that the organization was Roman. Terms such as *kouintanèsi(o)s* (Latin *quintanensis,* an official who receives the *quintana,* a specific type of tax levy) and *loncheus* (Latin *lancearius,* a lance-bearing soldier) are renderings in Greek of Latin terms. The *quintanensis* was probably a revenue collector, who lived at Berenike, and ostraka provide the names of at least nine persons who held this position.[6] Occurring most frequently is Andouros, a Gallic or Germanic name.[7] Andouros was probably related to the *quintanensis* Pakoibis, an Egyptian name.[8] Egyptian names appearing in the ostraka are mostly theophoric, referring to Egyptian gods venerated in Koptos or Panopolis (modern Akhmim), or their Greek counterparts, such as Min-Pan, Horus-Apollo, Isis-Aphrodite, and Geb-Kronos. Egyptian personal names also reflect veneration of the Egyptian gods Amun, Osiris, Thoth, and Tutu.[9] There are numbers of mixed Egyptian-Greek names, where the grandfather has an Egyptian name, the father a Greek name, and the son either a Greek or an Egyptian name, or vice versa. In the early Roman period this situation probably should not be interpreted as the result of fluctuations in Hellenization or Egyptianization, but rather of a well-established corpus of Greek and Egyptian names that had been used by families for generations.[10]

The Nikanor Archive also provides information on the names of entrepreneurs, trading houses, and personnel who worked for these organizations. The firm of Paminis and his sons, for instance, had agents both at Myos Hormos and at Berenike. Another customer of the Nikanor firm was Marcus Julius Alexander,[11] who was probably the brother of Tiberius Julius Alexander, the prefect of Egypt, and the nephew of the Jewish historian Philo of Alexandria.[12] The Alexanders were members of one of the highest-ranking and richest families in Egypt. They had great interests in the trade, but also exercised important state functions. Marcus's father was probably in charge of the customs of Egypt's eastern frontier. The combination of private and state interests overseen by elite families residing in Egypt was common in both Ptolemaic and early Roman times and further clouds efforts to ascertain the extent of direct official Roman governmental participation in this commerce. The Zenon Archive (see chapter 4) provides a similar picture for the early Ptolemaic period.[13] The opportunities for social mobility for Egyptians or others of non-Greek origin clearly grew in the late Ptolemaic and especially in the Roman period. Apollonius, a high official under Ptolemy II, was Greek, while the family of Philo of Alexandria in the first century C.E. was Jewish. The opportunities for members of (Hellenized) Egyptian families to obtain important administrative posts also increased in the late Ptolemaic and Roman periods, especially when Egyptians later became eligible for Roman citizenship.[14]

Some personal names occurring in the Nikanor Archive also appear in the Berenike ostraka. Berenike ostrakon no. 212 lists transporters of camel loads *(gomoi)*.[15] The leader of the group is Aulos, son of Miresis. The latter is a very uncommon Egyptian name, occurring in the Nikanor Archive in ostraka dated from 41–62 C.E. Miresis and Peteharpochrates were both sons of Nikanor, which would make Aulos, leader of the camel drivers, his grandson.[16] Another name found in the Nikanor Archive and in the Berenike ostraka is Zethos, slave of Tratos, slave of Caesar.[17] Latin names refer mostly to freedmen and slaves of imperial households. Thus, it is apparent that persons stationed at Berenike were members of households of the most influential families of Egypt and of the emperors' retinues.

The Berenike ostraka also preserve Latin names, though sometimes transliterated into

FIGURE 6-1
Berenike, ostraka dealing with the fresh water supply to the city, and a reed pen, from the first-century c.e. trash dump. Scale = 5 cm. Photo by S. E. Sidebotham.

Greek. For example, the Roman centurion Julius Marinus appears on one of these ostraka.[18] Over two hundred ostraka excavated in 2009–2010 reveal activities of the Roman military as it related to the city's freshwater supply (figure 6-1). These documents contain names of Roman soldiers not appearing in the earlier ostraka excavated from Berenike; they are currently being studied.[19] Another ostrakon appears to be a school math exercise.[20]

The Berenike papyri, on the other hand, are primarily private documents. One papyrus contains a land register, though it is not clear where the property is located—near Berenike or in the Nile valley; the latter is more likely.[21] We also have a bill of sale for a white male donkey and its saddle by the owner, Horos, son of Komaros and grandson of Germalos, who seems to have been illiterate. The document is written in a practiced hand, perhaps that of a hired scribe or literate friend, whereas Horos's signature is very clumsy. The price for donkey and saddle is 160 drachmas, and the bill of sale is dated July 26, 60 c.e.[22] This sale, at the height of the sailing season, should not be surprising, since transport would have been in great demand to move freight and people between the Nile valley and Berenike at that time of year. Possibly, the donkey was used for only local and regional transport purposes. This is the only surviving example of a contract for the sale of a donkey from the Eastern Desert in the Roman era.[23]

The names and statuses of some who visited Berenike, although records of their activities do not appear in the city, can be found adjacent to the Berenike–Koptos road. Along this route is a rock shelter frequented by travelers between the stations at Didymoi and Aphrodito who sought protection from the sun. This shelter was first discovered in the late 1930s,[24] and since that time many scholars have studied the site.[25] This portal into Berenike's past contains many graffiti left by travelers, in several languages. Those of most interest are in Latin and Greek. One man, Gaius Numidius Eros, left two inscriptions in Latin; one, dated August 28, 2 B.C.E., notes laconically that he is returning from India.[26]

Another, left by Lysas, freedman of Popilius Annius Plocamus, appears in both Latin and Greek. The Greek text is dated July 2, 6 C.E., while the Latin one was carved on July 5.[27] It is uncertain why the freedman spent three days at this remote location. What makes this text so fascinating is that Pliny records a story (*NH* 6.24.84–85) of a freedman of Annius Plocamus who was a tax farmer. Perhaps acting on behalf of his former owner, this nameless freedman was blown off course, undoubtedly by powerful monsoon winds, to Sri Lanka. Pliny suggests that this occurred during the reign of Claudius (41–54 C.E.), several decades after Lysas inscribed his graffiti. This freedman in Pliny's account learned the local language and so impressed the Sinhalese king with the quality of Roman coins in his possession that the monarch sent an embassy to Rome to learn more about these people. Perhaps the freedman in Pliny's story can be identified with Lysas in the rock shelter. If so, it is difficult to explain the chronological discrepancy between Pliny's story and the inscriptions in the rock shelter. Possibly Pliny heard the story only when he began to compile his *Natural History,* sometime in the reign of Claudius, when, in fact, the event took place decades previously. It is also feasible that the freedman mentioned by Pliny was a different individual from Lysas.[28] The Anni Plocami were prominent in business in Puteoli in the first century.[29] Clearly, their mercantile interests were geographically wide-ranging and long lasting.

There were others. Euphemos, freedman of Lucius Attius Felix, left a dedication to his friend Leonidas, son of Areios, on April 29, 44 C.E., at the rock shelter.[30] Primus Sextus Mevus Celer, a centurion in the twenty-second legion, also rested here.[31] It seems that few high-status Romans crossed the desert to visit or conduct affairs at Berenike in person, so they sent representatives, usually trusted freedmen, to act as their proxies. Others included soldiers who had to follow orders and proceed to Berenike. There are other individuals whose names appear in the rock shelter, also of various statuses or, in some cases, whose statuses cannot be determined.[32] It was clearly a popular unofficial resting place on the Berenike–Koptos road at the height of the port's prosperity in early and late Roman times. Inscriptions also appear along Eastern Desert roads of peoples from the Kingdom of Axum,[33] from South Arabia,[34] and, possibly, from India.[35]

Plaster jar stoppers used to seal the amphoras that conveyed wine, oil, fish sauce, and other products shipped to Berenike and beyond from the Nile valley and elsewhere in the Mediterranean are also informative about individuals involved in this commerce (figures 6-2a and 6-2b). Scores of these ancient bottle caps have been excavated at Berenike, made in all types of materials besides plaster: stone, basketry, mud/clay, wood, cork, potsherds,

Berenike, plaster jar stoppers from the first-century C.E. trash dump. Scale = 10 cm. Photos by
S. E. Sidebotham.

pitch, rope, and grass. The plaster ones are most useful, for they are often stamped or
painted with the names of the owners, perhaps distributors, or persons whose olive presses,
vineyards, and so forth produced the contents. There are scores of these jar stoppers from
Myos Hormos and from the desert quarries at Mons Claudianus and Mons Porphyrites
(see chapter 8).[36]

Most stamped or painted plaster stoppers are early Roman and usually contain personal names and patronymics: Latin, Egyptian, and Greek. The nomenclature on examples from Berenike is male. Latin names include Petronius, Justus, and Julius. Greek and
Egyptian names include Amphiomis, Petarpochrates, and possibly Zenonos.[37] Sometimes
logos accompany the texts. A popular one found at Myos Hormos, at Berenike, and at the
two quarry sites is the *uraeus* cobra. This Egyptian sign appears on stoppers from the first
century B.C.E. into the second century C.E.[38] It may be the symbol of a particular vine-
yard, farm, or estate somewhere in the Nile valley or in the Fayum. Other stoppers have
different designs, including ligatured letters or abbreviations of the names of individuals involved in the trade in commodities contained in the amphoras.[39] Some stoppers from
Myos Hormos mention an *arabarch,* an official with fiscal responsibilities. One is possibly Horus, who may be the *arabarch*'s representative rather than the *arabarch* himself.[40]
Other stoppers from Myos Hormos mention freedmen of Roman emperors.[41]

The process of determining the ethnic background of people in Berenike from writ-

FIGURES 6-3A AND 6-3B.
Berenike, graffiti in a pre-Islamic South Arabian language of the first or second century C.E. Each black and white increment on the scales = 5 cm. Photos by S. E. Sidebotham.

ten and archaeological records is fraught with pitfalls. Ethnicity is not a fixed property, but changes with perceptions people have of themselves or with the identity they want to adopt or project.[42] We suggested earlier that Egyptian and Greek names do not necessarily indicate a level of Hellenization of Egyptian families or Egyptianization of Greek families. The names can be classified as Egyptian, Greek, or Latin, but this does not invariably reveal anything about the ethnic background of those individuals. In the third century C.E., several inscriptions at Berenike list people with Semitic names, such as Berichei—the artist mentioned in the dedicatory inscription to Hierobol. In this case, however, it is not only the name that tells us about Berichei, but explicit references to his Palmyrene origin.[43] The Palmyrene auxiliary archer Marcus Aurelius Mokimos, son of Abdaeus, dedicated a nearly life-size bronze statue of some unidentifiable female accompanied by an inscription in Greek. The text bears a date in the month Thoth of the 24th year of Caracalla, which equates to 8 September 215 C.E. (see chapters 5 and 13).[44]

Different languages found at Berenike in early Roman times are another important clue to the multicultural composition of its demography. Most texts are in Greek, the lingua franca of that time, but formal inscriptions over the gates of some desert *praesidia* and a letter on an ostrakon from one of the *praesidia* at Vetus Hydreuma are in Latin.[45] Demotic rarely occurs.[46] Excavations in 2009 documented two jar fragments of South Arabian man-

ufacture; both contained graffiti, one of which bore letters of a pre-Islamic South Arabian language, the other seemingly a ligatured monogram (figures 6-3a and 6-3b).[47] Palmyrene,[48] Axumite,[49] and perhaps North Arabian/South Arabian or Ethiopic[50] are attested in later periods. A first-century Tamil-Brahmi graffito appears on a fragment of a Dressel 2–4 amphora, the same type of vessel in which wine was transported in massive quantities through Berenike, especially in the first century C.E.[51] The graffito reads "the Chieftain Korran" (figure 6-4)[52] and is, perhaps, an indication of the destination of this vessel. It is not certain that the person who wrote this was present in Berenike. There are other indications that Indian merchants or their agents visited and lived in Berenike and Myos Hormos.[53] Indian pottery found at Berenike, mostly from contexts dated to the late first century B.C.E./ first century C.E., comprises both fine and coarse wares (see chapter 12).[54] Fine wares were probably imported by Indian residents, as were coarse wares, mostly cooking pots with traces of use. The early Roman trash dump yielded large pieces of coarse reed matting, which have been tentatively sourced to North India.[55]

We have little information about persons performing specific jobs, but there is some evidence from the Berenike ostraka, such as the names of men holding the position of *quintanensis*—Andouros, Pakoibis, Peisipmouis, Germanos, Caecilius and Eponychos (acting as a pair), Albius and Theodorus (acting as a pair), and, likely, Peisitheos—who were stationed at Berenike and were probably part of the military who collected revenues levied on goods traded through the port.[56] Although revenue collecting was sometimes a private enterprise, there are indications that Berenike was organized by the Roman military or had a military contingent stationed among its residents.

When one considers the diet of Berenike's inhabitants, there are clear differences evident in various periods of the city's history. The Ptolemaic era was mainly dependent on ovicaprids (sheep and goats) and Red Sea fish for its protein. In early Roman times the varieties of animal protein changed dramatically. Then, in addition to sheep, goat, and Red Sea fish, the early Roman trash dump yielded considerable evidence for the consumption of beef, chicken, and pork. Meat, especially pork, was a staple of the Roman army.[57] There were even such exotics as Nile fish; at least four species of catfish have been identified at Berenike.[58] Escargots *(Helix pomatia)* were probably imported from France or northern Italy[59]—a treat for the higher-status inhabitants of the city.

If dietary evidence from early Roman Berenike points to a Roman or Romanized population, this alone may or may not indicate that some inhabitants were military personnel and, therefore, male (figure 6-5). The discovery in 2009 and 2010, however, of several hundred ostraka noted earlier confirms a substantial Roman military presence in the city in the early Roman period.

There is enough data from the excavations to draw some conclusions about what kind of society existed in Berenike. There were probably families living in the port. Both the Koptos Tariff and texts found at *praesidia* on the Myos Hormos–Nile road refer to women, including prostitutes, with the Tariff recording fees levied on them.[60] Faunal evidence demonstrates that children and women lived in Berenike. Our excavations recovered remains of a prematurely born infant or fetus,[61] the burial of a two-year-old girl,[62] the remains of a six- to nine-year-old child,[63] and the skeleton of a forty- to fifty-year old woman.[64] Thus, the archaeological record does not corroborate an image of Berenike in the early Roman period as a frontier town—desolate, offering few domestic comforts, and inhabited mostly by men. Many fragments of bangles, a large number of beads, and a gold-and-pearl earring found in the excavations also indicate the presence of women.[65] The interior faces of Berenike's rough coral walls were smoothed over with plaster, and some were decorated with high-quality textiles and carpets,[66] perhaps indicating a feminine touch. In addition, glass finds, the consumption of escargots, fancy beads, engraved intaglios for finger rings, and the gold and pearl earring suggest that at least some of the city's inhabitants had access to extremely high-quality commodities.[67]

There are other indications that Berenike was a town where men brought their families and where women could even reside without the protection of a husband. A woman named Hikane wrote a letter to her son Isidoros, whose function was "harbor man," as indicated on the address side of the papyrus. We do not know where Isidoros was sta-

FIGURE 6-5
Berenike, fragment of
a terra-cotta figurine
representing a Roman
auxiliary soldier, from
the first-century C.E.
trash dump. Scale = 5 cm.
Photo by S. E. Sidebotham.

tioned, but contact with the Egyptian homeland was maintained through ships arriving at Berenike. Hikane could have had a scribe write the epistle for her in any village in the Nile valley, but she informs Isidoros that she writes from Berenike and reproaches her son for not having answered her previous letter. Her lament—"Was it for this that I carried you for ten months and nursed you for three years, so that you would be incapable of remembering me by letter?"[68]—has been echoed through the centuries by other parents to their forgetful offspring and has an ageless quality. Then there was Philotera, whose dedication to Zeus carved on two stones during the reign of Nero[69] attests a relatively independent woman with, apparently, a great deal of discretionary wealth.

Women in Roman Egypt, especially widows, could own property and engage in economic activities.[70] The Nikanor Archive mentions Isidora, a female agent stationed in Myos Hormos.[71] Similarly, although we are lacking particulars, it is likely that women were actively engaged in the trade in and passing through Berenike. Hikane's letter does not mention why she was staying in town. In fact, the letter leaves most information about her unsaid. One might surmise from the text that she had at least two sons and two daughters, but we do not know whether she traveled to Berenike with any of her children. No mention is made of a husband, nor do we know how old she was, although as the mother of several adult children she must have been at least thirty-five or forty.

Families also likely resided at Myos Hormos and other Red Sea communities. There is ample evidence for their presence at some of the larger quarries as well.[72] If tolls paid by or on behalf of prostitutes plying their trade recorded in the Koptos Tariff reflect the expected profit of the economic activity of the entrepreneurs traveling to Berenike, prostitution must have been deemed very profitable.

The demography of Berenike should include estimates of the age of the inhabitants—an issue linked to the question of whether there were children and elderly people in residence. These economically less active groups are usually the least visible in the textual record, though they might appear archaeologically in mortuary contexts. There is scant evidence for toys or games. Several round cut potsherds with two holes drilled through the fabric may have been children's toys, which could be strung, wound up by twirling one side of the string, and pulled to create a buzzing sound.[73] Evidence for elderly people is not readily available. There are two reasons to suppose that although people in the first and second centuries c.e. may have brought their families to Berenike, they did not consider Berenike their home but would probably have retired to their villages in the Nile valley or beyond. The first reason is the specific function of the town, geared completely to long-distance trade, which was probably seasonal or had at least a frantic peak during those months when ships arrived and departed. Every settlement requires a support group of professionals who render services to inhabitants engaged in the main economic activity. This broadens the economic base, but evidence from this period shows a dependence on the Nile valley for resources such as food, wood, mats, textiles, and at least some metal. The second reason is the lack of burials dating to the early Roman period. The cemetery, adjacent to the road entering Berenike from the northwest, has so far documented only late Roman burials (see chapter 13). In the lower strata, which our excavations did not reach, there may be earlier tombs, but the size of the cemetery is not in keeping with the size of the town. It is likely that in early Roman times, bodies of many of the deceased were transported back to the Nile valley. As it does with all the other traffic through the Eastern Desert, the Koptos Tariff mentions a price for this activity.[74]

FOOD AND WATER

Inhabitants of early Roman Berenike had access to a large variety of food, most of which was imported from the Nile valley. Earlier in this chapter we provided a brief account of the different meat sources. The early Roman trash dumps north of the city center yielded evidence about how the animals reached the port. Cattle arrived on the hoof. Bone remains of all parts of the cows were found; the animals were young, and mostly male. The lower legs showed no deformations that are usually indicative of animals used for draft purposes. Thus, bovines appear to have been brought in specifically as a meat source. Pigs, mainly young males, were probably slaughtered in the Nile valley and brought to Berenike salted in jars. Not all skeletal parts were found; one would expect to find all parts if the pigs were actually kept in Berenike. Sheep and goats could survive without a problem in Berenike, and probably chickens were kept there, too. Horse and donkey bones are rare. Some of these pack animals undoubtedly lost their lives in Berenike, but they appear not to have been consumed on a large scale, which is an interesting contrast to practices at Mons Claudianus.[75] Camels were clearly multifunctional. They were the most important caravan pack animals but were also a source of protein, as butcher marks on camel bones indicate. Feral desert game did not provide much of the diet; there were meager remains of wild quail and Dorcas gazelle.[76]

Red Sea fish were potentially an excellent source of protein, yet fish made up only a small part of the diet, and turtle and dugong (a manatee-like mammal) were only rarely consumed. Middens of mollusks indicate that shellfish were eaten, but there certainly was a preference for fancier fare, especially suited to a Roman palate: chicken, salted pork, escargot, and *garum*. Excavations found several potsherds with remains of small fish bones that are indicative of this fermented fish sauce. The *garum* was probably a local product. Faunal analysis indicates that the fish species used to make the sauce—small sardines and herring—were caught in the Red Sea and would have produced as pungent a product as the Mediterranean variety.[77] On the other hand, four different types of catfish were transported from the Nile valley to Berenike, suggesting that the Nile fish probably arrived salted or dried for it to remain edible after a twelve-day transdesert journey.[78]

The staple food in early Roman Berenike was wheat, which is also mentioned as an export in the *Periplus* (24, 28). Wheat is, however, never mentioned in the Berenike customs ostraka, and only a passing reference to "grain" appears in a papyrus written by Aphrodite to her husband, Lucius, who is apparently in Berenike, sometime during the third quarter of the first century C.E.[79] Both bread wheat and emmer wheat are found at Berenike in early Roman contexts, as well as barley and rice. Barley was partly used as fodder, because the cereal has been found in camel dung.[80] How one should interpret the occurrence of rice is less clear. It appears often in the first-century dumps and also in later Roman contexts (see chapter 12), but always in small quantities. It was not a staple, but was consumed quite regularly. Wheat and barley were imported from the Nile valley, but the origin of the rice is less clear (see chapter 12). Rice was grown in the Near East at that time; however, it could also have been imported from India. Black pepper, an import product from Kerala or the Western Ghats of southern India, has been found in almost every trench. The city's trash dumps generate ample black-pepper finds, and specimens are often found charred. The discovery of a storage jar containing 7.55 kg of black peppercorns in the courtyard of the Serapis temple suggests the extent to which Indian imports were available to the Berenikeans (see chapters 5, 12, and 13).[81]

Fruit and nuts were also imported from the Nile valley: almonds, walnuts, hazelnuts, apricots, peaches, Egyptian plums, figs, grapes and pomegranate, watermelons in large quantities, dates, pine nuts, doam nuts, and *nabaq* (the fruit of the *Ziziphus spina-christi*) (see chapter 12). The only "fruits" available in the vicinity of Berenike, however, were colocynth, an extremely bitter medicinal plant, and the sugar date, a name that belies the hard plywoodlike fruit of the *Balanites aegyptiaca*.

Lentils, chickpeas, white lupine, and bitter vetch, together with the fava bean, which today is the mainstay of the Egyptian breakfast, were found at Berenike and were probably also imported from the Nile valley,[82] whereas spices, such as coriander and cumin, may have been grown locally in small plots.[83] Using wastewater, and rain, which on rare occasions fell in the Berenike area, and perhaps runoff from the wadis, the inhabitants could have grown some vegetables and fruit. Archaeological evidence for the use of irrigation to produce crops appears at several locations in the Eastern Desert, and current irrigation practices of the 'Ababda Bedouin may provide some idea of how this process took place in antiquity (see chapter 7).[84]

The major resource required to sustain life in Berenike was water. The town would have needed sufficient amounts for its inhabitants and the ships' crews who landed at the harbor, but also to provision ships with water for their outbound journeys. There is a fair amount of archaeological evidence pertaining to the city's water supply in the early Roman period (see chapter 7), but very little during the era of the port's renaissance from the mid fourth century C.E. on. There is no evidence that any of the *praesidia* at Siket or in Wadi Kalalat near Berenike continued to operate in late Roman times. Thus, it is uncertain where the city obtained its drinking water at that time for either its inhabitants or those setting sail for distant lands.

Clearly, given this water situation, whatever cultivation of crops—fruits, vegetables, and some grains—took place at Berenike or in its environs would have been relatively small-scale and would have provided, at best, only meager supplements to larger quantities of imported food.[85] Ostraka excavated from *praesidia* on the Myos Hormos–Nile road indicate that there were irrigated areas producing cultigens tended by troops stationed at those installations,[86] but the military garrisons of these and other desert outposts undoubtedly consumed most or all products that these plots produced, leaving little, if anything, for constant large-scale export to any of the Red Sea ports.

A question rarely considered, but important when dealing with a port of Berenike's status, is that of health and hygiene. In Berenike, where large numbers of people lived and through which many people passed, communicable diseases must have been a problem. Numerous pack animals congregated regularly in nearby *praesidia* that provided water to the city, and were also present in the cramped urban environment; their resulting waste must have attracted huge numbers of disease-carrying flies and other vermin, and the decomposing waste itself eventually would have percolated into the groundwater, thereby polluting it. Humans would not have drunk the groundwater at Berenike, since it was too saline or brackish, but many of the pack animals might have, and we have no knowledge of what intestinal problems this may have caused them. We have no evidence of a typical Roman-style sewage or water-supply system at Berenike. Nor have excavations documented public latrines, which in Mediterranean contexts were often found adjacent to public baths. We can only assume that toilet facilities for humans were rudimentary.

Consumption of groundwater must have led, minimally, to recurrent stomach ailments, and perhaps longer-term health problems, which may be another reason, aside from its brackishness, that most drinking water probably arrived from *praesidia* located in wadis some distance from the city. Ostraka from the Roman quarry site of Mons Claudianus preserve letters indicating health problems—especially of the eyes (probably from the sun and flies) and gastrointestinal systems (from flies and water)—of the troops stationed there.[87] Residents of the Red Sea ports and other desert settlements undoubtedly experienced similar maladies.

No systematic study of the bones of those buried in antiquity at Berenike or Sikait, another site we have partially excavated in the Eastern Desert, has taken place. Looting of most ancient graves makes such future analysis extremely difficult. Nevertheless, a more detailed examination of the causes and effects of such environmental degradation of the Eastern Desert would be very useful in understanding the health and longevity of individuals and populations resident in the area for extended periods of time.[88]

The Roman preoccupation with bathing, as both a hygienic and a social phenomenon, leads to the expectation that Berenike had a number of baths.[89] The only indication, however, that water, possibly the locally available brackish water and rarely that carried in to the city by pack animal from outlying *praesidia,* was used for bathing was the discovery of several glass unguent bottles associated with bathing, and kiln-fired bricks preserving chucks of mortar, from a clearly hydraulic context.[90] The military character of the first- and second-century C.E. occupation of Berenike, however, can be compared with that of other establishments in the Eastern Desert, where several formal bathing facilities have been identified, all in military contexts (see chapter 7).

RELIGION

An important religious structure in Berenike, probably founded in the late Ptolemaic period, was the Serapis temple, which was also dedicated to several other Egyptian gods.[91] The name of Serapis was inscribed on the base of a bust found by Wilkinson in the 1820s, who also reconstructed the god's name on a stone fragment with two inscriptions from the Roman period.[92] Meredith published a description of the temple, using notes of several nineteenth-century visitors who cleared all or part of it, including Belzoni, Wilkinson, Wellsted, Purdy (published by Daressy), and Golénisheff. Our expedition documented portions of the temple in 2009, which had been vandalized sometime in 2007–2008 (figures 6-6a and 6-6b). We then backfilled exposed parts of this building in order to protect it, but there has been no attempt to re-excavate this structure. It was, after all, the only building in town about which anything was published prior to our expedition, whereas the rest of the town awaited exploration. In addition, however, we were concerned that the intervening centuries had further damaged the walls and reliefs, and that consolidation of the walls would prove an extremely expensive task. Wilkinson's notes indicate that the "soft limestone" was so weathered that the reliefs could be removed "by merely passing the hand over them."[93] The temple was, in fact, built not of limestone but of gypsum/anhydrite blocks, a very soft material easily eroded by the steady battering of the

FIGURES 6-6A AND 6-6B
Berenike, two views of the Serapis temple. Photos by S. E. Sidebotham.

northern winds; it flakes off in layers when exposed to water and temperature extremes—both common phenomena in the region. Meredith published as detailed and informed a description of the temple reliefs as was possible from the sometimes conflicting notes of others. From his overview it is clear that most of the temple decoration is early Roman. Tiberius (14–37 C.E.) appears in hieroglyphs on several walls of the hall (Room 1), and perhaps also on the facade. Cartouches on the facade might be those of Trajan (98–117 C.E.) or Domitian (81–96 C.E.).[94] The name of a second emperor depicted on the temple facade, Aurelius Germanicus, could refer to Marcus Aurelius, Commodus, or Caracalla. Wellsted, however, found an unattached fragment in the temple mentioning Marcus Aurelius and his coregent, Lucius Verus (161–169 C.E.), suggesting that the text inside also belongs to Marcus Aurelius.[95]

The sanctuary of the Serapis temple (Room 2) has a depiction of Isis-Hathor, while a goddess with the sun disk between cow horns, perhaps Isis, appears on the facade, and Isis is depicted in the hall (Room 1) and on the walls of the entrance to the sanctuary. Apart from Isis, the name of Horus, son of Osiris, is visible on the facade. In the hall (Room 1) are several scenes featuring Tiberius presenting offerings to Osiris and Isis, to Horus and Isis, to Neith or Mut, to Amun the Great and Mut, Mistress of Ishru (referring to the Mut precinct in Karnak), to Min of Koptos, and to Isis the Great. In the entrance to Room 2, in addition to Isis, depictions of Aroeris (Horus the Elder) and Harpokrates (Horus the Child) occur. In the sanctuary (Room 2) Isis is depicted together with a god with a child's lock and a four-feathered crown with a solar disk; this latter figure may be Harsamtawi or Hor-Shed. Thus, it seems that the main deity of the Serapis temple in Berenike was either Horus, in several forms, the goddess Isis, or perhaps the triad of Koptos that also protected the desert beryl/emerald-mining settlement at Sikait (Mons Smaragdus): Min/Khem, Isis/Aphrodite/Hathor, and Horus the Child.

Although the name of the goddess on the facade is illegible, and we are doubtful whether Isis or Hathor is depicted, she is specified as "she who is in the middle of the great green." Meredith proposes several explanations for this epithet, first by linking the "great green" with green stones—such as beryls from Mons Smaragdus, or turquoise from Sinai (where the quarries were under the protection of Hathor)—as export products through the harbor of Berenike.[96] His second suggestion, to interpret *wadj wer* as the Red Sea, is much more likely.[97] It seems suitable that the epithet of the main deity of a port catering to hazardous long-distance sea voyages refers to the waters on which one was about to set out, or from which one had safely returned. Hathor was often syncretized with foreign goddesses[98]—specifically, with Near Eastern fertility deities.[99] The association of Hathor with the sea and seafaring does not seem to be particularly strong, although seashells certainly have a religious link to sexuality—an association perhaps through their voluptuous shapes— and, thus, affiliation with the goddess.[100] In the Roman period both Hathor and Isis were syncretized with Aphrodite, and perhaps it is her power that, in the minds of the Romans, kept the sailors safe. Isis's connection with safe sailing along the Nile and the celebration of the *Ploiaphesia,* which opened the sailing season in the Mediterranean, would have been easily transferred to maritime activities in the Red Sea by Egyptians as well as those from the classical Mediterranean world;[101] these associations would have made her a very appealing and relevant deity. For Egyptians the triad of Koptos represented well-established deities that belonged to and had protected the entire region since time immemorial. The occurrence of Aroeris (*Hor her,* Horus the Elder) represents a link to another town in the Nile valley to which Berenike was connected by desert road in the Ptolemaic period: Apollonopolis Magna, named after Apollo, the Hellenistic namesake of Horus of Edfu.[102]

In the first room of the Serapis temple Wilkinson found an "altar of libations." It had the form of a miniature double temple pool, with six staircases, and it is now in the British Museum. This specimen is likely late Roman; chapter 13 examines similar temple-pool-shaped altars in late Roman contexts. Excavations just north of the Serapis temple revealed a courtyard that was probably part of the temple complex in the early Roman period. In this courtyard dark brown soil colorations represented the remains of circular wooden objects that had completely decayed.[103] In several pagan shrines at Berenike we found evidence of the use of wooden bowls in temple services. Since most evidence is from the late Roman period, more will be said in chapter 13.

The Shrine of the Palmyrenes, which is neither as large nor as nicely constructed as the Serapis temple, was built of a hodgepodge of fossilized coral heads mixed with gypsum/anhydrite blocks that appear to have been recycled from other buildings. One of the coral-head walls preserved a leveling course made of teak timber (figure 6-7). This small, narrow shrine accommodated several religious practices including the Roman imperial cult in the early third century C.E., the Palmyrene deity Yarhibol/Hierobol, who was one member of the important religious triad of that Syrian Desert caravan city, and possibly Harpocrates, the son of Isis. In addition, excavations recorded more than one hundred wooden bowls[104] similar to those found on the early Roman courtyard floor of the Serapis temple, and a small stone sphinx reused in a later wall of the building (figure 5-3) (see chapters 5 and 13).[105]

Finds from the later second/early third and later centuries from this small shrine included religious inscriptions and dedications made by military personnel; these are discussed further in chapter 13.

Three additional inscriptions provide information on religious activities in Berenike in the first and second centuries C.E. and about the individuals who donated these texts. The first is a dedication to "Isis, the very great goddess," by an interpreter and secretary [name lost] who was the son Papiris. The inscription mentions the emperor Trajan and M. Rutilius Lupus, prefect of Egypt, and dates from between 113 and 117 C.E.[106] Excavations recovered this text on the courtyard floor of a house built during the renaissance at Berenike in the mid to late fourth/early fifth century C.E.

Two other inscriptions, probably recycled as windowsills in the later building in which they were recovered, were identical texts, with dedications to Zeus by Philotera, daughter of Patentais.[107] One was perhaps a "rough draft" where an extra iota (Philoitera) appears,

FIGURE 6-7

Berenike, teakwood beam recycled into the late Roman-era northern wall of the Shrine of the Palmyrenes. Scale = 1 m. Photo by S. E. Sidebotham.

and the other stone a final copy. It is unclear where this inscription originally was placed and why. There is circumstantial dating evidence for this Zeus veneration; on both inscriptions the name of the emperor has been effaced. The words *"diou Kaisarou Sebastou Germanikou Autokratoros"* remain, but on the final inscription one can still make out the words *"Neronos Klau"* in the neatly erased section. The year then, falls between 54 and 68 C.E., while the precise date is 12 Pachon 27 (May 22). Philotera is a Greek name, and almost exclusively occurs in Hellenic contexts,[108] but in this case her father's name was Egyptian, so the family probably was of Greek extraction. As pointed out earlier, this mixing of Greek and Egyptian names through different generations seems to signal, in this period, that the inhabitants of Egypt were comfortable with both traditions. The same seems to be true for their religion and the veneration of Greek and Egyptian gods. The discovery of three texts dating to the first and second centuries C.E. in a fourth- or fifth-century structure indicates recycling of these earlier stones in a centuries-later context. More interestingly, these stones also suggest the existence of other shrines in early Roman Berenike that we have not yet found.

BERENIKE'S POLITICAL SIGNIFICANCE

Berenike's political importance in early Roman times seems to have been greater than it was in the Ptolemaic era. Early Roman Berenike served, for some undetermined length of time, as an important administrative center for the Prefect of Mount Berenike. Some of those who held this office went on to other government posts elsewhere in the empire. Some of their names are extant: Aemilius Celer, who appears on the late second-/early third-century bilingual Greek-Palmyrene inscription dedicated to Yarhibol/Hierobol. Celer was also commander of a mounted unit stationed in the city, the *Ala Heracliana*.[109] Another prefect was Marcus Trebonius Valens, whose name appears in Latin on the massive triangular block carved in 76/77 c.e. found at Siket, the small water station only 7.2 km west-northwest of Berenike.[110] The names of others are preserved on texts found elsewhere in Egypt,[111] but some remain unknown. The prefect, whose headquarters and permanent residence must have been in the city, was also responsible for overseeing the exploitation of many mineral resources of the Eastern Desert, for pearl fisheries, and for the construction and upkeep of many of the desert roads and stations linking Berenike and sister ports to the Nile. There is more discussion of his duties in chapter 8.

Often decisions of the highest ranks spurred action. The prefect of Egypt, Julius Ursus, may have visited Berenike. The trip would have taken about twelve days, and several nights would have been spent camping out *in monte* (in the desert), because *praesidia* linking Berenike to Koptos were too far apart to enable the traveler to find shelter each night; alternately (see chapter 8), many *praesidia* had not yet been constructed. Julius Ursus or his representative indicated the places where these new stations were to be built.[112] We know, therefore, which of these were the first-generation Roman *praesidia*—sometimes built de novo, sometimes refigured Ptolemaic establishments—and which were of the second generation, founded in Ursus's time.

WATER IN THE DESERT AND THE PORTS

Methods used for water acquisition, storage, protection, and distribution in Ptolemaic and Roman times in the Eastern Desert (figure 7-1) were undoubtedly similar to those employed in the Pharaonic era (see chapter 3). The most noteworthy difference was the scale on which these operations were conducted. Ptolemaic activities would have dwarfed earlier ones, with Roman logistical efforts being the most impressive and sustaining of them all.[1]

PTOLEMAIC-ROMAN WATER RESOURCES AND THEIR MANAGEMENT

The critical importance that water played in Ptolemaic and Roman times deserves special examination in more detail. Given the paltry amount of precipitation (see chapter 2), the primary concern for anybody venturing into and living in the Eastern Desert and in the Red Sea ports was finding, accessing, storing, and distributing sufficient quantities of water for sustained periods. Without water, no human activities were possible for more than a day in this hyperarid environment. During fieldwork we came to appreciate what the ancient peoples working and living here must have endured for extended periods and the constant concern they must have had to insure adequate supplies of water.

The real and symbolic importance of water to those traveling into the Eastern Desert from the Nile cannot be overstated. At least one well with an honorary inscription dedicated to Isis between 110 and 30 B.C.E. provides an additional reminder of dangers faced

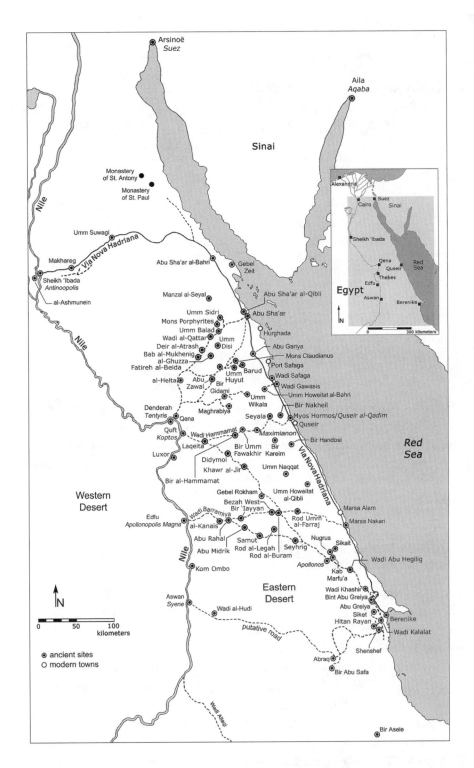

FIGURE 7-1

Map of the more important sites mentioned in this chapter, with place-names.

Drawing by M. Hense.

by the wayfarer leaving Koptos and venturing into the desert.[2] Ancient Egyptians always distinguished between the "Black Land"—that is, the Nile valley and regions irrigated by it—and the "Red Land," the vast and forbidding deserts stretching to the east and west.[3] To leave the former and venture into the latter was a very dangerous proposition.

WATER REQUIREMENTS OF HUMANS AND ANIMALS

A human living in or traveling through the Eastern Desert requires a minimum of about four to six liters of water a day for drinking in the summer, less in cooler months when engaged in moderate levels of exertion. Increased levels of physical activity require consumption of proportionally more water. Our survey and excavation work indicates that additional use for limited bathing, cooking, and so on raises that total to about fifteen to twenty liters per person per day in the summer and less in the winter.[4]

An ostrakon excavated at Mons Claudianus and dating likely to 110 C.E. sometime in the winter provides a detailed account of water distribution to 917 people. Amounts allotted depended upon the type of labor performed and the person's rank. The higher the rank, the greater the water allotment; those expending greater manual labor also received a larger ration.[5] The maximum ration was one *keramion,* about 6.5 liters, while unidentified family members (presumably infants or small children) received about 2.16 liters.[6] Information in this ostrakon accords well with the average water consumption for drinking purposes that we have experienced in the desert during the summer. One must assume that allotments in the ostrakon were for all purposes including drinking, and that amounts were likely greater during the summer.

Although those traveling through and living in the Eastern Desert in Roman times may not have bathed as often as we do on surveys, they used water in ways that our desert surveys do not: for washing clothes, irrigating small gardens, and watering animals. Dated ancient graffiti found along Eastern Desert roads and at sites indicate that travel and residence in the region were perennial,[7] though perhaps greater during cooler months. Wind patterns in the Red Sea and directions of the monsoons in the Indian Ocean dictated sailing schedules between Red Sea and Indian Ocean ports and also influenced the times of year people traveled through the Eastern Desert.

An important issue is water usage among those sailing to and from the Red Sea ports. The *Periplus* (14, 39, 49, 56) notes that those venturing from Egyptian ports to India should leave in July;[8] if they were contemplating travel only to more southerly ports within the Red Sea, departure in September was suggested (*Periplus* 24). Those returning from the Indian Ocean to northern Red Sea ports arrived between November and January.[9] Thus travel between the Nile and the Red Sea ports peaked between mid to late October and mid to late February and again between mid to late June and August/September to take into account these sailing conditions. There would have been, then, only three or four months when traffic between the Nile and the Red Sea ports was reduced: March through May, and part of October; and even at those times inhabitants of these emporia continued to communicate with and require supplies from the Nile valley. These arrived both overland and also by sea from more northerly ports such as Arsinoë/Cleopatris/Clysma and Aila, both of which had easier access to comestibles than did more southerly ports on Egypt's Red Sea coast such as Myos Hormos and Berenike. Perhaps some individuals directly associated with shipping operations, including entrepreneurs and ships' crews, left Berenike and other Red Sea ports at off-peak times of year and returned to the Nile valley, thereby reducing the populations of these emporia, but this is not certain; or if this did take place, it is impossible to gauge how many people were involved. In any case, traffic between the Nile and the Red Sea emporia would have been a year-round affair.

Whenever ships arrived or departed, their crews required water for drinking, cooking, and very limited bathing and laundry, though the latter two activities can occasionally be performed by using saltwater. The amount of water taken aboard varied according to size of the crew, available storage room, and travel time and distance to the next port of call where additional supplies could be obtained. No ship would have loaded all the freshwater required to make a journey between Berenike, Myos Hormos, or some other Egyptian Red Sea port and points farther south on the African Red Sea coast, let alone to more distant destinations in the Indian Ocean. Rates of consumption for the crews would have been similar to those for crossing and working in the desert, which we noted earlier; no ship could carry all the water required for a lengthy voyage.

There is conflicting evidence regarding the timing of mining and quarrying operations in the region, which would have affected water usage. One papyrus seems to suggest that most activity at the mines and quarries occurred during cooler months.[10] Yet, excavations at Mons Claudianus and, to a much lesser extent, Mons Porphyrites produced thousands of ostraka and papyri many of which indicate that operations were conducted perennially.[11] This may also have been the case at other mines and quarries in the Eastern Desert, though there is a lack of specific documentation in these other instances. Water acquisition, storage, protection, and distribution would have been major activities at mines and quarries throughout the year, but especially in the summer.

Excavations at the beryl/emerald-mining settlement at Sikait (ancient Senskis/ Senskete), part of the region known as Mons Smaragdus, focused our attention on water-related issues and made us appreciate the logistical challenges faced by ancient miners.[12] During those excavations our teams were substantially smaller than those that worked these mines in antiquity. Yet, our water-supply problems were ongoing headaches, probably our single most important daily concern. The size of our team in the summer was significantly smaller than in the winter due to the intense heat and the need to consume that much more water per capita than in winter, when we could have a larger group on-site. Admittedly, all our water came from outside, whereas the ancients tapped locally available underground supplies for most or all of their needs. Still, water conservation for the ancient peoples working here, or in any other region of the desert, would have been a constant issue and would have been highly regulated and closely monitored.

ANIMALS

The primary transport and pack animals used in the Eastern Desert in Ptolemaic and Roman times were donkeys and camels.[13] In hot weather a pack donkey must drink about ten liters per day,[14] while a pack camel averages twenty liters per day.[15] On short journeys between the Nile and the Red Sea or between the Nile or the Red Sea and points in the desert, a camel might not consume any water; this was more likely during cooler months, and when carrying a light load.[16] G. W. Murray recorded an extraordinary 128-day period when his camels did not drink during his 1926 visit to Gebel Elba.[17] This was due to cool weather; short, easy daily journeys for the animals; and their consumption of abundant succulent plants.[18] Another advantage of using a camel is its ability to consume water too saline for humans and about five times the salinity tolerated by a donkey.[19] Loss of bodily fluids due to dehydration, relative to surface area, is three times greater in a donkey than in a camel.[20] In fact, a camel can safely lose up to 30 percent of its body weight in fluids, something that no other mammal can sustain.[21] In addition, a heavy-baggage camel can carry a substantial load of 200–325 kg for a normal trip and up to 475 kg for a shorter journey.[22] A. E. P. Weigall, Inspector-General of Antiquities in Egypt from 1905 until 1914, reported that during one trip in the Eastern Desert his riding camels averaged 7.2–8 km per hour and could easily cover about 48–49 km per day; his baggage camels traveled at about 4.8–5 km per hour.[23] Weigall suggested watering camels every second day, but he writes that the animals were still strong after three or four days; he indicates that when pushed, they could travel a week or more "through a land without wells."[24] On the other hand, a donkey can transport only approximately 70–90 kg with a pannier,[25] but a donkey is better able to negotiate stony surfaces than a camel.[26] Thus, time of year, weight of cargo, terrain to be crossed, and availability and degree of salinity of water determined which types of animals were used. Many caravans likely comprised a combination of both camels and donkeys.

The same ostrakon from Mons Claudianus noted earlier also provides information about rations for horses and donkeys, though not for camels. It records that a horse received about twenty-six liters per day and a donkey about half that amount. This ration was for inactive animals during a winter day.[27] These amounts are somewhat more generous than estimates for horses and donkeys working in more recent times.

On short trips, travelers carrying light loads during cooler periods might tote sufficient water from the Nile or the Red Sea coast or one of the desert outposts or settlements to obviate the need for frequent, and perhaps expensive, resupply during their journeys. On longer trips during hotter months, or for long-term residents in the desert or along the Red Sea coast, however, finding, storing, and distributing water was a major concern. From personal experiences on two-week-long surveys involving three or four people, we know that water and gasoline are the two most important items. They take up the most room and weight in the vehicles. Unlike the ancients, who could draw water from *hy-*

dreumata inside or adjacent to *praesidia,* we cannot, and must carry all we require for the duration of the project. Thus, we must ration our supplies very carefully.

Given the minimal precipitation in the Eastern Desert, ranging from 3 to 25 mm per annum today[28]—and it was similar in antiquity, as Aelius Aristeides (*Egyptian Discourse* 36.32 and 36.67) indicates[29]—it was essential that the Ptolemies and Romans had a proactive system for finding, storing, protecting, and distributing water for those residing in and traveling through the desert.

WATER ACQUISITION

Two sources of water in the region in antiquity, as today, were surface-water runoff after rare heavy rains (included here are springs) and subsurface water. Rain is usually very seasonal and unpredictable, peaking in November to early December if there is any at all. Subsurface water is perennial and, therefore, more dependable. There are several sources for acquiring surface-water runoff and subsurface water in the Eastern Desert.

SURFACE WATER

Surface water[30] is easier to obtain than subsurface water, but its quantity, quality, and availability are highly variable; it is an undependable source in the desert. One method of securing surface water is the natural accumulation of rainwater in a *qalt* (plural, *qulut*);[31] another is rainwater runoff from mountains, deliberately channeled by human action into cisterns, water catchments, or smaller, portable containers; and a third is springs.

A *qalt* is a naturally occurring depression in eroded hard stone such as granite and other crystalline rocks. Typically, *qulut* lie along wadi beds or at the bases of seasonal waterfalls. They hold varying quantities of water depending upon the amount of surface runoff that has accumulated in them, their sizes, and their locations in direct sunlight or shade. *Qulut* would not have played a major role as regular and reliable sources of water acquisition for consumption by humans or pack animals, though the Bedouin might have—as they do today—occasionally watered herds of goats, sheep, donkeys, and camels at such places. Most *qulut* are useful only at certain times of year and are often neither easily accessible nor large enough along or near the major ancient roads in the region. Thus, they would not have provided dependable supplies, which greatly limited their usefulness; they were neither major nor regular sources of water in antiquity for travelers or residents in the Eastern Desert.

There is a *qalt* near Umm Disi,[32] west of Hurghada, that was large enough that the author swam in it on August 7, 1997.[33] Accounts of earlier visitors to this remote spot indicate that amounts of water there could vary dramatically from one year to the next—depending, of course, completely upon rainfall. Whereas one visitor saw it bone-dry, another reported that it was brimming with an estimated one hundred thousand liters.[34] The *qalt* at Umm Disi must have been close to its maximum capacity during our August visit. All other *qulut* seen on our surveys were much smaller than that at Umm Disi and would have been dry most of the time except following brief periods of heavy rains. Water in these is often potable initially, but after some time it becomes extremely brackish due to evaporation, or polluted due to animal use.

Other *qulut* noted during our surveys are in a settlement 21.3 km south-southwest of Berenike in Wadi Shenshef. About 1,550 meters down the wadi southeast of the center of this large late Roman settlement were pools with varying amounts of water in them during winter 1996. It is uncertain whether these *qulut* actually provided water to the ancient settlement, though they potentially could have whenever sufficient rain had fallen and accumulated in them.[35]

C. B. Klunzinger, a German physician who lived in Quseir in 1863–1869 and 1872–1875 and was quarantine officer there,[36] discussed water accumulation from waterfalls and rain in *qulut*.[37] A French project reported *qulut* near the ancient beryl/emerald mines at Nugrus and Sikait. One of these, in a small tributary of Wadi Nugrus, was a depression in gneiss that must have contained an impressive amount of water, because the report of the project published in 1900 indicates that the source was sufficient for the entire season for twenty persons.[38] The French noted another *qalt* in a small "affluent" in Wadi Sikait that produced potable water for only a short time.[39] A *qalt* also appears at the base of a dry waterfall at the *praesidium* of Abu Hegilig North on the Berenike–Nile roads;[40] a number of visits by our survey, however, never recorded water in this *qalt*.

Another water source in the Eastern Desert is springs (*'ayn* [pl. *'uyun*] in Arabic). Klunzinger also discussed these briefly.[41] Though these derive from the subsurface, they appear naturally on the surface, so they should be discussed here.[42] Springs usually produce very pure water. Unfortunately, there are few in the Eastern Desert, and they are remote from most areas of substantial ancient habitation or desert roads and supply too little water to be major perennial sources, though they are good supplements, or sources for very limited numbers of people and animals making infrequent visits. F. W. Hume described two of the most noteworthy springs, one in Wadi Qattar and the other in Wadi Dara.[43] One of our surveys visited the spring at Qattar in January 1989 and found it dry. During fieldwork at Sikait in summer 2002 one of our 'Ababda workmen showed us a small spring about 1 km east of the site. He claimed that it produced about ten liters of potable water per day. Hume also noted a spring near Sikait that provided about fifty liters of "excellent water issuing from a rock drop by drop."[44] He did not, however, indicate where in the area he saw this spring, but his description suggests that it was not the same one the workman showed us in 2002.

Farther south is an example, perhaps unique in the Eastern Desert, of an ancient monument built to commemorate a spring conveniently located along an ancient route. In 1832 L. M. A. Linant de Bellefonds visited Bir Abu Safa, about 13 km due south of the Ptolemaic–early Roman fort at Abraq and about 22 km away via an ancient track that passes through Wadis Hodein and Abraq.[45] Originally, Bellefonds was an artist and draftsman making maps and illustrations for European writers and explorers working in Egypt. While

FIGURE 7-2
Bir Abu Safa, facade of
a Ptolemaic-era water
shrine. Photo by
S. E. Sidebotham.

commissioned by Mohammed Ali Pasha to search for sources of gold, Bellefonds discovered the facade of a small temple cut into the face of a large sandstone mountain in Wadi Hodein. He left a brief description and made a drawing of the structure, which has no interior. He believed the facade to be Ptolemaic and cited an inscription preserved above the structure purporting that Ptolemy III Euergetes, who came to the throne in 246 B.C.E., was the builder. Our survey examined the structure and the inscription on the facade, which now preserves only a few Greek letters and the regnal year 19 of a Ptolemaic king we believe to be Ptolemy III (figure 7-2). The source of the spring is rainfall on Gebel Abraq that percolates down to and then flows along the dip slope of a geological syncline. A small trickle of water still pours from beneath the temple facade's western end, flows down a small hill, and pools in front of and beneath the facade. It can be no coincidence that this temple facade and the spring are located in the same place. We do not know how productive this source was in antiquity, but there can be little doubt that this facade was dedicated to water in the middle of the desert.[46] The construction of temples or other monuments associated with water sources in arid regions was fairly common in antiquity, especially in the Hellenistic and Roman periods, and parallels can be found in Tunisia and the Middle East.[47] This structure in Wadi Hodein, however, has no parallel of which we are aware anywhere in Egypt.

There is evidence that several Roman *praesidia* on the Berenike–Nile roads used artificial channels to direct rainwater from nearby mountains to *lakkoi* (cisterns) in adjacent installations below. This can be seen at the early Roman *praesidium* at Abu Hegilig South (figures 7-3a and 7-3b), the early Roman station at Abu Gariya/Umm Ushra, and perhaps at the late fourth-/fifth-century c.e. installation at Abu Hegilig North. There may have been others that have gone unnoticed. Where these water channels are visible, their tops are made of stone, but since none has been excavated, the remainder of the materials used in their construction, whether they had some type of waterproof coating or lining, and their precise appearances and dimensions remain unknown. There is no evidence of wells inside any of these stations with water channels, though they may have tapped wells, now filled in and thus no longer visible, that lay outside their walls. If these stations relied totally on water runoff for their supplies, the runoffs would not have been reliable perennial sources. There probably were long periods when these stations were completely dry and, perhaps, temporarily abandoned or left with only small garrisons that had to fend for themselves or be supplied from another nearby *praesidium* until rain once again fell in the region. It seems more reasonable to conclude that rainwater available at these stations merely supplemented well water.

Aside from natural accumulation in *qulut,* we have evidence of other methods used by peoples residing in the Eastern Desert to capture, channel, and temporarily store the water that raged down wadis during the brief but heavy rains that occasionally fell in the region. At least one Eastern Desert settlement attempted to protect low-lying buildings from floods. There were undoubtedly other communities that did the same. At Shenshef we noted the deliberate placement of stones lining the edges of the lowest embankments on which structures were erected closest to the wadi floor. We are uncertain whether this lining was intended only to retard erosion caused by fast-moving floodwaters, or whether it may also have been part of a mechanism to channel water into some storage facility.[48]

A popular method of capturing surface runoff elsewhere in the ancient Near East, including Libya,[49] Sudan,[50] and Jordan, was the use of *hafayir* (singular *hafir;* literally, "excavation"). These installations take a variety of forms. Some are dams of various sizes built across low ground, sometimes between hills. These may be made of stones or bundles of shrubs placed to catch sediments that then block water. The water may be used for irrigation, or the soil that builds up behind a *hafir* may be the actual field of cultivation. Subsurface dams consisting of trenches filled with fine-grained silts or clays may also have been constructed to facilitate water catchment and use.[51] We have, thus far, documented no use of this type of *hafir* in the Eastern Desert .

FIGURES 7-3A AND 7-3B
Abu Hegilig South,
praesidium with two oval-
shaped cisterns. Photos
by S. E. Sidebotham.

The other type of *hafir* comprises a large circular or oval-shaped structure either cut into or built up (using gravel, rubble, and stone) from the wadi bed to capture surface-water runoff. This form of *hafir* is very inefficient, since the large surface area of the water accumulated in it is subject both to rapid evaporation and to salinization. *Hafayir* were important in water-management plans of the Kushites,[52] and theirs provide the best parallels for the rare examples thus far identified in the Eastern Desert of Egypt. Where datable, they appear to be Ptolemaic or early Roman. Our surveys have identified only a few. There is a large one at Rod Umm al-Farraj[53] and possibly another, the walls south of the *praesidium* at Abu Sha'ar al-Qibli.[54] Alternatively, the walls near Abu Sha'ar al-Qibli may have channeled water for cultivation; Egyptian farmers today use similar methods, as do some of Bedouin in the Eastern Desert.[55] There is possibly another *hafir* near the Ptolemaic–early Roman gold-mining settlement at al-Ghuzza. South of the main settlement is a large triangular-shaped trench open at the western end,[56] which may have captured surface water flowing toward the Red Sea. The feature in Wadi Khashir (ancient Novum Hydreuma)[57] along the Berenike–Nile roads has all the hallmarks of a *hafir* rather than a *praesidium*. Other sites with possible *hafayir* include the forts at Samut, Abu Midrik, and Rod al-Legah on the Berenike–Apollonopolis Magna route, and at Rod al-Buram and Bezah West, both unfortified stations on the Marsa Nakari–Nile road; Rod al-Buram is also on the Berenike–Koptos highway.[58]

SUBSURFACE WATER

Subsurface water[59] was obtained from wells (*bir* [pl. *abyar*] in Arabic). These were excavated either within or immediately outside fortified or unfortified military installations and in or around civilian settlements; water could be drawn directly from them for immediate use, or channeled into adjacent cisterns. Wells have traditionally been major sources of water for those living in and traveling through the region.[60] We have noted a few terra-cotta or stone conduits or pipe systems that carried water from wells to points of storage and distribution for consumption. More will be said about this later in this chapter. Water might also be transported from sources to points of storage and distribution by wagons, pack animals, or human porters—a topic that will also be elaborated on later.

Undoubtedly, the most common and reliable method of water acquisition for the ancients, as for the Bedouin today, was to draw it from wells.[61] These artificially excavated shafts of varying diameters and depths tapped underground aquifers fed by infiltrating rainwater that percolated down and, on the Nile side of the Eastern Desert watershed close to the river, also by groundwater from the Nile.[62] *Hydreumata* and their sanded-up remains survive inside numerous forts in the Eastern Desert from Ptolemaic to late Roman times. Most are generally circular in plan, frequently quite large, and often dominate the center of a fort. One of the most impressive is in a large *praesidium* in Wadi Kalalat, about 8.5 km southwest of Berenike (figures 7-4a and 7-4b). This installation was one source

FIGURES 7-4A AND 7-4B
Wadi Kalalat, large
praesidium interior
with large well *(hy-
dreuma)*. Photos by
S. E. Sidebotham.

of water for Berenike in at least the second century c.e. The wall surrounding the well there is about 32 m in diameter and was approached by a staircase; most of the well and staircase are now buried beneath drifts of windblown sand, precluding any determination of their original depth.[63] We assume that staircases provided access to many *hydreumata* inside *praesidia,* though the only ancient *hydreuma* visible is in an early Roman *praesidium* at al-Zerkah (ancient Maximianon) on the Myos Hormos–Nile road.[64] Most wells, where they are at least partially visible, were lined with cobblestones or fired bricks to minimize internal collapse and maintain some degree of water purity. Wells in *praesidia* on the Myos Hormos–Nile road vary from 3 to 25–30 m deep.[65]

WATER STORAGE, PROTECTION, AND DISTRIBUTION

Water acquisition, storage, protection, and distribution must have been a highly organized, regulated, and monitored activity at large quarry settlements with substantial populations of men, women, and children, such as those at Mons Claudianus and Mons Porphyrites. Mons Claudianus had a bath,[66] as did Mons Porphyrites.[67] In addition, elaborate hydraulic complexes exist in the immediate vicinities of both quarries.[68] In Wadi Ma'amal, where the largest concentration of structures, including temples associated with operations in Mons Porphyrites, are found, there is a large feature called the South Well and related hydraulic channels that lie in the wadi immediately north of the large fort.[69] Graffiti depicting boats or ships carved on pillars surrounding this well may represent the longings of some members of the garrison for the Nile or may indicate contacts with the Red Sea.[70] This well was the major water source for the garrison. The presence of a cistern inside the fort[71] suggests that porters conveyed water from the well up the hill to the fort in leather or terra-cotta containers. There are other hydraulic facilities in the Mons Porphyrites area,[72] one of which included Umm Sidri, the stop heading out of the narrow wadi and ultimately to the road leading to the Nile.[73] There are also hydraulic installations in the Mons Claudianus area,[74] but, like those at Mons Porphyrites, the dimensions of the cisterns and troughs can only be estimated, since they are filled or partially filled with debris obscuring their bottoms and thereby preventing accurate calculations of their capacities. It is impossible to determine individual and collective levels of productivity of the wells supplying these sites, but, given their large sizes and the protection they were afforded, the associated hydraulic channels and cisterns, and the potential numbers of animals and humans they supplied, one must conclude that the amount of water consumed was large and that the supplies were reliable enough to meet constant high demand. The ostrakon from Mons Claudianus discussed earlier lists 917 people requiring water,[75] an impressive number, and when one adds requirements of animals, of farming, and for the repair of tools, the amount of water used each day must have been substantial, and it had to be carefully stored and distributed.

In the early twentieth century the Geological Survey of Egypt reactivated wells associated with some Roman *praesidia*—a process that included re-excavation, relining, and the addition of staircases and concrete basins.[76] Their modern appearances may provide some indication of what their ancient predecessors looked like. Sites where our survey work detected these modern renovations include the Ptolemaic-Roman *praesidium* at al-Kanaïs on the Berenike/Marsa Nakari–Apollonopolis Magna route, where the modern well is probably not at the original location of its ancient counterpart. There are also modern modifications to the station at al-Qattar on the Abu Sha'ar/Mons Porphyrites–Nile road made when, as an "inscription" carved into the wet concrete of one hydraulic tank there indicates, Farouk was emir of Egypt—viz. between 1920 and 1937.[77] Other sites where modern modifications are evident include Abu Greiya on the southern portion of the Mons Claudianus–Nile road just north of the modern asphalt highway about 42 km from Qena,[78] and at the *praesidium* at Abu Zawal (Father/Place of Ghosts), a gold-mining camp, also on the Mons Claudianus–Nile road.[79] The station at Abu Gariya on the Via Nova Hadriana was also remodeled in modern times,[80] as were those at Seyala[81] and Bir al-Hammamat,[82] on the Myos Hormos–Koptos road.

In the mid nineteenth century Richard Lepsius was impressed by the ancient and still-functioning well at Bir al-Hammamat, noting that it was "broad . . . , about 80 feet deep, lined with stones, into which there is a descent by a winding staircase."[83] The Arabs told Lepsius that Christians had built it, and recent archaeological work at nearby gold mines at Bir Umm Fawakhir date that site to the fifth to sixth centuries C.E.[84] Traffic between Bir Umm Fawakhir and the Nile would have used water facilities en route, and the supply at Bir al-Hammamat was a natural stopping point—one those responsible for the miners' welfare would have enhanced to facilitate access to the water. Bir al-Hammamat also supplied Muslim pilgrims performing the hajj, as attested by the remains of a small mosque built into one corner of the *praesidium*.[85] The well itself looks the same today, though clearly the superstructure surrounding it is a more recent addition—of about 1830 or later.[86]

Some *praesidia* probably also obtained supplementary water supplies from extramural wells. The fort at Umm Balad (Domitiane/Kaine Latomia), about 11 km south of Mons Porphyrites, imported water from nearby wells by camel.[87] It is impossible to gauge the number, size, or importance of such potential extramural water sources, since most have long since disappeared, filled in with sand during heavy rains. Geomagnetic surveys of areas where ancient wells might have been situated should locate some of these lost installations, and selective excavation would provide evidence of their sizes, methods of construction, and, if luck is with the excavators, dates of use.

An important reason, but not the only one, for placing unfortified stations and *praesidia* along routes on low ground in the Eastern Desert was to facilitate water acquisition (see chapter 8), storage, and protection, and to regulate and monitor its distribution.[88] This would not have been possible if *praesidia* had been located on high ground. These low-lying forts and stations were not intended to provide security for the entire desert; they had more modest and realistic missions: to protect and provide water, and perhaps on occasion food, animal fodder, and local security, which included guarding routes between stations.[89] They also relayed official and private correspondence among the stations and between terminal points on the Red Sea and the Nile valley (see chapter 8).[90]

Some wells in *praesidia* on the Myos Hormos–Nile road were not always self-sufficient. Some ostraka record private requests of those living in these desert outposts to friends that they should send water; this was done by wagon or pack animal.[91] Ironically, ostraka from some of these same locations indicate that *praesidia* provided water to passing commercial caravans.[92] We are not certain what accounts for this dichotomy in water availability or how often nonmilitary travelers were denied water because little was available. Perhaps a certain quantity was set aside for use solely by the garrison and another amount was designated for consumption by passing civilian caravans. This would have been especially difficult during times of peak summer traffic between the Nile and the Red Sea ports, when departures were most frequent. Possibly passing travelers tapped water only from specific *hydreumata* and *praesidia* where it was most abundant at the time of their passage and as designated by garrisons of those installations—and not necessarily as they needed it. If so, they would have had to plan accordingly. Perhaps one function of signal towers along the route (see chapter 8) was to relay messages regarding the availability of water supplies up and down the length of the road in a bid to assist those stations in need and to warn travelers en route so that they could take extra water with them if necessary.

Placing *praesidia* on low ground was neither unique nor confined to the Eastern Desert but is evident in desert regions of Syria and Jordan.[93] Inscriptions and ostraka indicate that *praesidia* and other watering points along Eastern Desert routes were built, maintained, and garrisoned by the Roman military or its proxies.[94] Many of the fortifications protecting these water sources, and militarization of the Eastern Desert in general, occurred between the Julio-Claudian period and the reign of Hadrian (30 B.C.E.–138 C.E.) as a result of increased problems with *barbaroi* in the region.[95] Perhaps the economic vitality of this period, as reflected in the Red Sea trade and prosperity at the quarries and mines, led to more raids by bandits and others, thereby necessitating construction and refurbishment of many stations.

Elsewhere *hydreumata* provided potable water for nearby ports at Pelusium and Arsinoë/Cleopatris/Clysma.[96] Excavations at Arsinoë documented the problems residents had in procuring potable water from a site close to the sea and noted that much if not all of the port's drinking water came from sources some distance outside the town.[97] Excavations unearthed numerous cisterns, water catchment basins, and channels for acquiring, storing, and distributing water throughout the city.[98] Several *praesidia* located 7.2–8.5 km from Berenike also supplied that city,[99] as described in more detail later in this chapter. Although there is no specific evidence, perhaps Myos Hormos[100] and Marsa Nakari (maybe ancient Nechesia) were provided in a manner similar to that in which Pelusium, Arsinoë/Cleopatris, and Berenike were supplied.

Like modern Bedouin, ancient desert dwellers dug wells in wadi bottoms or wherever the water table was closest to ground surface and where protective walls could be placed around them. Roman garrisons were probably responsible for acquiring water, protecting sources, and maintaining hydraulic installations as well as monitoring water use. They undoubtedly tapped locations where water was purest and most abundant. In doing so, they probably relied on local Bedouin to assist in identifying the best spots. Water from these wells was conveyed as needed into cisterns[101] inside the stations. Where they survive, interior cisterns are made of fieldstones or fired brick coated with thick layers of waterproof lime plaster. The Ptolemaic–early Roman fort in the gold–mining area of Barramiya on the Marsa Nakari–Apollonopolis Magna road is an unusual exception in that the large interior rectangular-shaped cavity was dug into natural bedrock. A cistern and lime-plastered conduits lay inside the southwestern portion of that fort.

A less convenient method entailed hauling water from more remote locations to points where it would be stored, protected, and distributed. Pack animals, wagons, and human porters carrying amphoras, leather bags, or, less likely, wooden barrels[102] could have brought water from more distant points into one or more central water-storage facilities in *praesidia* and at the Red Sea ports. Excavators of Myos Hormos between 1978 and 1982 speculated that this method was used to supply that emporium with potable water from one or more wells at Bir Kareim about 30–35 km southwest of the port.[103] Excavations at Myos Hormos between 1999 and 2003 and surveys in the region noted a track between the port and Bir Nakheil, about 6 km to the west, identified by the presence of numerous rock graffiti and pictographs.[104] A large, and now almost completely destroyed, early Roman *praesidium* at Bir Nakheil[105] may have supplied water to Myos Hormos. This would have been analogous to *praesidia* at Siket and in Wadi Kalalat, which provided potable water to Berenike. The most recent excavators suggested that Bir Nakheil was a source of potable water for Myos Hormos and discounted Bir Kareim because of its distance from the port.[106] However, there were likely at least several sources that the city drew upon, as would have been the case for all the Red Sea ports. Multiple sources in diverse locations insured that there were some reliable, if not always adequate, supplies.

At Berenike we have found no evidence that pipelines or any kind of "aqueduct" supplied the port from *praesidia* in Wadi Kalalat and Siket, though differences in elevation between those sources and the port were such (77.8 meters in the case of Wadi Kalalat) that some type of pipeline or aqueduct carrying water could, in principle, have been used.[107] Water transported to Berenike from these sources, which are within 7.2–8.5 km of the city center, was most likely conveyed using pack animals, wagons, and/or human porters. An ostrakon from Berenike's early Roman trash dump records a letter addressed to Antonius and refers to a water skin sent to him.[108] This suggests that some water may have been transported in this manner to Berenike at least in the early Roman period. Leather water bags *(askoi)* have been found in desert contexts at Mons Claudianus[109] and Mons Porphyrites,[110] and an ostrakon from the *praesidium* at Maximianon on the Myos Hormos–Nile road, dated from the late first/early second century C.E., also refers to an *askos*.[111] Study of leather remains from Berenike should also eventually document their use there. Few sherds have been found on the routes joining *praesidia* in Wadi Kalalat and Siket to

Berenike, suggesting that leather bags may have been the preferred transport container rather than the more fragile and heavier ceramic amphoras or wooden barrels.

Nevertheless, the early fifth-century c.e. writer Palladius (*Historia Lausiaca* 17.11 and 27.1) refers to "Cilician" jars or pots (most likely the Late Roman Amphora I/LRA1) used to carry or store water in more remote desert settlements.[112] Our surveys have recovered large quantities of Cilician- or northern Cypriot–made (LRA1) amphoras from late Roman sites, possibly Christian hermit *(laura)* communities, found throughout the region,[113] and it is likely that ceramic containers, such as reused wine amphoras, were also occasionally employed to haul and store water at Berenike. An ostrakon from Mons Claudianus mentions using an amphora to carry water to the quarries.[114] Egyptians today use large terra-cotta jars called *azyar* (singular *zir*) to store water, which is kept surprisingly cool even in the summer. These are often located along roads to provide travelers with drinking water free of charge. A possibly analogous system—though we do not know details of how supplies were replenished or what, if any, fee was charged—has been documented along one route in the Western Desert from at least the Old Kingdom to Ptolemaic times.[115] Broken amphoras found at route-marking cairns and signal towers along the Abu Sha'ar–Nile road in the Eastern Desert suggest that a similar arrangement was in place there Roman times.[116] We do not know whether the placement of jars and their possible refilling were part of the official, de jure duties of those guarding or using the routes, or if such supply arrangements were more ad hoc or de facto.

Archaeologists have not determined methods used to transport water from *hydreumata* to Pelusium and Arsinoë/Cleopatris. Pack animals transporting ceramic or leather water containers, possibly also wooden barrels, were the most likely means.

WATER STORAGE AND PROTECTION

High evaporation rates and increased salinity of water remaining after evaporation meant that careful storage and protection were critical. Most wells and cisterns probably possessed, and some still preserve, raised perimeter walls made of fieldstones mortared together and plaster coated that minimized debris falling into them and, in the case of extramural wells, prevented waterborne sediments from filling them. Some cisterns preserve evidence of having had protective coverings that minimized the amount of debris falling into them and also lessened evaporation from them. Evaporation would have posed the more serious problem—especially from cisterns, less so from wells, given the relative size of the exposed surface areas that each of these types of hydraulic installations had. Modern average evaporation rate in the Red Sea Governorate of Egypt is 2,500 mm per annum versus an annual precipitation of 3–25 mm.[117] These rates were probably similar during Ptolemaic and Roman times. Water loss at this pace would have quickly depleted supplies, and the water remaining in the exposed cisterns would have become highly saline and nonpotable.

Reliable figures for ancient cistern capacities in the Eastern Desert are difficult to determine due to the cisterns' states of preservation. We do, however, have some idea. At the Ptolemaic site of Abu Midrik on the Berenike–Apollonopolis Magna road, for example, illicit excavations revealed the bottoms of two circular cisterns. One is 4.3 m and the other 4.1 m in diameter at the top; their depths are about 3 m, with slight angles of slope in their centers. Each basin, when full, could hold about forty-four thousand liters, for a total of eighty-eight thousand liters theoretically available from this small to moderate-sized Ptolemaic fort, which has defensive walls with maximum exterior dimensions of about 24 × 26 m. At six liters of water per person per day, this totals about 14,667 days of drinking water for a single human. Consuming fifteen to twenty liters per day for all activities results in 4,400–5,867 person-days of water. One donkey consuming ten liters a day would be supplied for 8,800 days, and a single camel at twenty liters per day would have quantities for 4,400 days. No estimates have been calculated detailing how many humans and animals—including passing elephants in the Ptolemaic period—on average used this station each day and what amounts of water would have been consumed for other activities including cooking, bathing, laundry, and the cultivation of small desert plots. More will be said about desert cultivation later in this chapter. There is no ancient well visible at Abu Midrik, though someone attempted to dig a modern one outside the fort. Whatever the ancient water source for the cisterns at Abu Midrik, there is no way to determine if or when they were always filled to capacity. One would surmise, however, that such large cisterns would not have been built if they had not been occasionally filled.

The early Roman *praesidium* at the quarries in Wadi Umm Wikala (ancient Mons Ophiates) (see chapter 8) preserves a rectangular-shaped cistern with overall internal dimensions of 2.5 × 2.2 × 1.6 m, providing a capacity of 8.8 m³ or eighty-eight hundred liters.[118] Given water requirements noted earlier, when full, this hydraulic feature potentially provided sufficient amounts to accommodate 440–586 people with the minimum daily requirement of water for drinking, washing, and cooking. If these figures for water capacity take into account supplies for draft animals, irrigation of any desert gardens, and repair of tools, the potential number of human consumers would decrease dramatically. Using the figures from our surveys of Wadi Umm Wikala and nearby Wadi Semna, and taking into consideration all factors noted here, we calculated a total Roman-era work force at the quarry of 100–200 people, with probably the lower figure being the more accurate.[119]

Another cistern, now measurable due to recent vandalization, is at Rod Umm al-Farraj, an unfortified Ptolemaic–early Roman station on the Marsa Nakari–Apollonopolis Magna road.[120] The site has several structures plus animal-tethering lines and a rectangular-shaped cistern enclosed by a wall. The small size and low height of the wall suggest that it was intended to prevent animals from approaching the cistern unattended, and perhaps to prevent floods from washing sediments into the basin, but not designed for defense against attack. The cistern's internal dimensions are 2.47 m north–south × 7.18 m east–west × 2.20 m deep. When full, this provided about 39 m³, or approximately thirty-nine thousand liters, of water.

The *praesidium* at al-Muwieh (ancient Krokodilô) on the Myos Hormos–Nile road had cisterns capable of a theoretical maximum capacity of over two hundred thousand liters.[121] It will likely never be known whether and how often this and other reservoirs were filled to capacity, but it is unlikely that they would have been built if they had not at least occasionally been topped off.

The last example is inside the main fort at Mons Claudianus. There, just southeast of the fort entrance, is a two-chambered cistern measuring about 1 m deep; its total capacity was approximately ten thousand liters.[122]

Statistics from five sites of Ptolemaic to early Roman date—Abu Midrik, Wadi Umm Wikala (Mons Ophiates), Rod Umm al-Farraj, al-Muwieh (Krokodilô), and Mons Claudianus—provide some idea of potential capacities. Many Roman-era *praesidia* in the Eastern Desert have external dimensions similar to Krokodilô's or greater than those of the others described earlier, and surface areas of cisterns that are larger, too, though their depths, hence their overall capacities, cannot be estimated. In general, however, these statistics suggest that Roman *praesidia* accommodated larger garrisons and/or larger numbers of transient visitors than did Abu Midrik, Wadi Umm Wikala, Rod Umm al-Farraj, or Mons Claudianus. These figures are, however, far smaller than those gleaned from some Roman water tanks in desert areas of the Hauran in northern Jordan.[123]

Overall, the greater number and size of most Roman-era stations and stops in the Eastern Desert compared to their Ptolemaic predecessors, and the apparent larger size of cisterns contained in most of the Roman stations, suggest that the quantity of travelers and inhabitants was more substantial in the Roman period than it was earlier or later. Cistern sizes at some of the smaller quarries such as those at Umm Balad,[124] Barud (ancient Tiberiane)[125] near Mons Claudianus, Badia',[126] a road station linking Mons Porphyrites to the Nile, and al-Kanaïs[127] are smaller—due, no doubt, to their catering to a very specific clientele. The fort at al-Kanaïs may well have had multiple water tanks, and any estimation of capacities may have to be revised upward if these catchments should ever be discovered and investigated.

The ledges on the peripheries of the cisterns at their tops must have accommodated covers—none of which have been found; probably, we would hypothesize, these were lightweight wooden frames with pieces of cloth, leather, or animal hides sewn together and stretched across them. These would logically have been segmented so that they could be folded back at different points, exposing only some sections of the reservoirs. Such a method would have provided access only to the water needed, without exposing the entire surface area of the cistern to contamination and excessive evaporation. Water tanks in the Ptolemaic, or suspected Ptolemaic, and early Roman stations that may have modified and used earlier Ptolemaic facilities tended to be round or oval in shape, as at Abu Midrik,[128] Abu Hegilig South,[129] Umm Gariya,[130] Seyhrig,[131] Abu Rahal,[132] and Samut (figure 7-5)—all on the Berenike–Apollonopolis Magna/Koptos roads. One cistern at Samut is now covered in sand and no longer visible, but in the 1820s J. G. Wilkinson drew a plan locating it in the western corner of that fort.[133] Where visible, and in the examples that have been examined, Ptolemaic–early Roman cisterns were made of locally available cob-

FIGURE 7-5
Samut, fort on the Berenike–Apollonopolis Magna road. Photo by S. E. Sidebotham.

blestones and small boulders coated with multiple layers of waterproof lime plaster several centimeters thick; they made no use of fired bricks. Plastered basins from which water could be distributed are adjacent to cisterns at Abu Midrik and Abu Rahal. One cistern at Abu Rahal with a basin preserves part of a terra-cotta pipe and what appears to be a decanter or distillation tank, which was probably instrumental in removing heavier silt and other larger debris from the water prior to its dispensation.

Most cisterns in installations that are only Roman in date, with no evidence of earlier Ptolemaic activity, are rectilinear in plan and often comprise basins segmented into two or three compartments. These compartments, where they can be examined, have small channels near their bases that permitted water to flow from one chamber to another, allowing them to fill at fairly even rates; this would also have reduced the likelihood that intense lateral pressure exerted by water filling in one tank would cause that tank to collapse outward into an as yet unfilled adjacent one. A number of cisterns inside Roman *praesidia* are segmented with dividing walls, suggesting that multiple covers were used. The outermost portions of these cisterns comprise fieldstones, with the inner sides closest to the water formed of fired bricks coated with waterproof lime mortar several centimeters thick. There are, of course, exceptions. The rectangular-shaped reservoir at Rod Umm al-Farraj seems to be Ptolemaic to early Roman in date. Ceramic evidence from the

FIGURE 7-6
Siket, triangular-shaped
stone with a Latin inscription, from the gate area.
Photo by S. E. Sidebotham.

two visible rectangular-shaped cisterns at Bezah West, a stop on the Marsa Nakari–Apollonopolis Magna route, is, unfortunately, not datable.[134] The late Classical, Hellenistic,
and possibly early Roman stop at Rod al-Buram[135] on the Marsa Nakari–Apollonopolis
Magna road preserves two rectangular-shaped cisterns; it may also have been a stop on
the Berenike–Koptos route. On the other hand, Bir ʻIayyan, an unwalled early Ptolemaic
water station on the Marsa Nakari–Apollonopolis Magna road, has reservoirs that are both
circular and rectangular in plan, with no surface ceramic evidence whatsoever that the
Romans ever used this stop.[136]

   Excavations at the main gate of the *praesidium* at Siket, 7.2 km west-northwest of
Berenike, produced a triangular-shaped stone 2.46 m long × 1.07 m high × 0.17 m thick,
with a Latin inscription dated 76/77 C.E. The text designates the site as *"hydreuma . . .
praesidium et lacus"* ("well . . . fort and cistern[s]") (figure 7-6).[137] Siket is not on any main
road leading to or from Berenike, though close to the principal one connecting Berenike

to the Nile, and it was very close to Berenike, suggesting that its main function was to supply potable water to the port rather than to travelers en route between Berenike and the Nile.

Neither Pliny nor other itineraries and maps dealing with the Berenike–Nile roads (see chapter 8) mention any site between Vetus Hydreuma and Berenike, even though pottery found at Siket indicates activity there from the first to the third centuries C.E. This also suggests that Siket was not a station used by travelers between Berenike and the Nile. Since wells dug close to Berenike today produce salty or highly brackish water that humans cannot drink—and this was undoubtedly also the case in antiquity[138]— Siket, and two forts in nearby Wadi Kalalat, probably provided much of the drinking water consumed in the city in the early Roman period.[139] Similar Flavian inscriptions appear at other *praesidia* on the Berenike–Koptos road—at Aphrodito,[140] Didymoi,[141] and Phoenicon[142]—suggesting that construction or renovation of stations and water sources along the road was undertaken at that time. It was also in this era that construction of *praesidia* began along the Myos Hormos–Nile road. Recent excavations at the *praesidium* at Umm Balad recovered another inscription recording activity there during the reign of Domitian (81–96 C.E.). Initially the place was called Domitiane. After the emperor's assassination and his *damnatio memoriae*, however, the site was renamed Kaine Latomia (New Quarry).[143]

Excavations at the large *praesidium* in Wadi Kalalat also produced about two dozen fragments of a large Greek inscription from the reign of Trajan (98–117 C.E.) when Servius Sulpicius Similis was governor of Egypt.[144] It remains uncertain whether this text is the original foundation inscription of the fort or, instead, records later repair work. Ceramic evidence from excavations at both the large and small *praesidia* in Wadi Kalalat suggests that the larger one was the earlier of the two.[145] Though the smaller installation, less than a kilometer away, seemingly operated after the larger was abandoned, our excavations recovered no epigraphic evidence indicating its function.[146] Supplying water to Berenike, however, must have been one of its raisons d'être.

Another well appears in an inscription from the reign of Gallienus (259/260–268 C.E.) found on a rock-cut temple dedicated to Serapis, Isis, Apollo, and other deities at the Roman beryl/emerald-mining settlement at Sikait.[147] The well itself does not survive, though the existence in the wadi, near the temple where the inscription appears, of some dilapidated architectural features may indicate some type of monumentalized well.

Palladius's references (*Historia Lausiaca* 17.11 and 27.1) to "Cilician" jars, noted earlier, would apply as much to water storage and protection as to transport. It may have been beyond the abilities of those who dwelt in these modest enigmatic desert communities to build elaborate cisterns, in which case water storage and protection may have been accomplished primarily in ceramic vessels.

It is evident that the excavation of some wells and their protective forts or temples warranted advertisement and commemoration on inscriptions; we must assume, however, that the vast majority of wells sunk in the Eastern Desert received no such accolades.

It is evident from the levels of salinity that humans, donkeys, and camels can tolerate in drinking water, and from the more diverse uses humans make of water than do animals, that any discussion of water distribution must comprise two parts: water for human consumption (drinking, cooking, cleaning, bathing, irrigation, mining/industrial), and drinking water for animals. Our investigations, though not definitive, have noted important differences in the appearances of distribution systems depending on whether water was destined for human or for animal consumption. Unfortunately, less is known about water distribution in the Ptolemaic and Roman periods than about its acquisition, storage, and protection. Many major water-distribution sources from the Ptolemaic and Roman periods derived from inside or near fortified structures, suggesting that the government, primarily through the military, took responsibility for most aspects of water acquisition and, perhaps, assumed sole responsibility for its storage and distribution. By overseeing and administering water supplies, the military also more closely controlled and monitored activities of travelers in the region.

Less certain are rules that governed water use and the permits and fees required by the military that controlled the forts in Wadi Kalalat and Siket in order for Berenike to draw on these freshwater supplies. We do not know whether Berenike had additional sources beyond these, since none of these *praesidia* seems to have continued in use into the late Roman period, when water would have been in great demand at the port—during its renaissance in the mid fourth through fifth centuries C.E. The early Roman ostrakon noted earlier dealing with Antonius and the leather water bag may be a clue that the military required some form of permit to allow people to transport and receive water in Berenike from outlying sources. Excavations in 2009–2010 recovered approximately 240 ostraka written primarily in Greek, some in both Greek and Latin, and at least one only in Latin. They are primarily military and deal with water supply to the city (figure 6-1).[148] It is too early to determine whether the water discussed in these ostraka derived from nearby *praesidia* in Wadi Kalalat or Siket. Evidence suggests, however, that water distribution to the city's residents was, indeed, closely monitored by the Roman military.

Unfortunately, aside from the Mons Claudianus ostrakon listing water rations to 917 persons, nothing is known about the administration of water distribution in the *praesidia* or settlements in the Eastern Desert. There must have been some type of water-rationing system in these locations, though who managed these is not known—probably the military. One must assume that any water provided to ships sailing from Berenike and the other Egyptian Red Sea ports was also carefully monitored, but until more detailed study of the recently discovered Berenike ostraka has been completed, we have no other evidence relating to these activities.

The Koptos Tariff dated May 90 C.E. reflects the sale and use of passes by travelers and their goods crossing the Eastern Desert between the Nile and various Red Sea ports.[149] In addition to being a source of revenue for the government to help defray costs of maintaining the desert garrisons—it also records taxes on prostitutes and dead bodies being carried to the Nile valley for burial[150]—and a means of monitoring travelers in the region, there may have been an additional purpose for such passes. Perhaps the fees recorded in the Koptos Tariff also covered costs of water consumption by travelers in the region. By collecting such fees at central locations on the Nile, possibly also at various Red Sea ports or, less likely, at a few other major desert installations such as the more important quarries and mines, the government guaranteed that it garnered this money. Had travelers paid for water at stops along their itineraries, there was the potential for those residing in the desert garrisons to cheat them and, more important from the "official" point of view, the potential to line the pockets of corrupt soldiers and officials in the *praesidia* along the roads, thereby depriving the government of these revenues. Very few ostraka from *praesidia* on the Myos Hormos–Koptos road, including Maximianon and Krokodilô,[151] and none from Didymoi on the Berenike–Koptos road, deal with water-administration issues, suggesting that a higher authority was responsible for collecting fees for water distribution. Most likely, representatives of the provincial or imperial government exercised authority from key emporia along the Nile or Red Sea coast—possibly, too, on a limited basis from some of the larger imperial quarries and mines. An ostrakon excavated at Didymoi records an official styled *epimeletes hydreumaton* as the one in charge of excavating a well.[152] His duties included estimating the number of men required to dig the well, gathering tools and a forge to make and repair iron tools, and acquiring the oil used in the iron-hardening process.[153] He also appears to have been responsible for the repair of any wells in the Eastern Desert.[154] He was an employee of the Prefect of Mount Berenike.[155]

The Koptos Tariff reflects activities in the late Flavian period and suggests, together with epigraphic evidence from *praesidia* at Didymoi, Aphrodito/Aphrodites, Siket, and Phoenicon, that this was an era of refurbishment, enlargement, and fortification of hydraulic facilities along the Berenike–Koptos road. It was also along the Myos Hormos–Nile road that many installations were built in the period between the Julio-Claudians and the militarization of the region by the early second century C.E.[156] This was a reflection of the growing traffic due to trade passing between the Red Sea ports and emporia on the Nile at that time and to the government's increased interest and concern to protect it; on other roads it would also have signaled expanded operations at quarries and mines. It is unclear, however, what administrative rules might have governed water distribution at Eastern Desert forts with wells and cisterns in the lesser-known Ptolemaic, middle Roman, and late Roman periods.

WATER CONDUITS

Conduits were used for water acquisition and distribution, though the bulk of the evidence, with one possible exception, suggests that most pipelines were for distribution. There must have been numerous examples of piping water from sources to points of storage and distribution in the region in antiquity, but few have been identified or studied; many are no doubt covered by sand or, in some cases, probably no longer survive. We have found short lengths of pipes—or evidence that pipes or conduits once existed— that carried water from *hydreumata* inside *praesidia* to adjacent or nearby cisterns. Examples of sites where pipes or evidence of them have been found include the large fort in Wadi Kalalat near Berenike, at Abu Greiya (ancient Jovis/Dios) on the Berenike–Koptos road, and in the installation in Wadi Safaga on the Via Nova Hadriana.[157] Pipes have also been found at Maximianon on the Myos Hormos road[158] and at Didymoi on the Berenike–Koptos route.[159] There are, however, only two examples of terra-cotta and stone pipes built over distances of several hundred meters or more that have been recognized and studied. One is late Roman, while the other example can be dated no more closely than sometime in the Roman period. Both examples carried water to military installations. One, at the late Roman fort at Abu Sha'ar on the Red Sea coast north of Hurghada, brought water from a well about 1 km southwest of the fort under pressure through a closed system of terra-cotta pipes coated on the outside with plaster. This pipeline entered the fort through the main western gate, but its terminus inside the fort remains uncertain. Excavations in the fort's *principia*, which was converted into a church after the military abandoned the site probably sometime in the late fourth century c.e., recovered terra-cotta water pipes, though not in situ, and this building may have been the terminal of the channel that entered the west gate.[160] There was, undoubtedly, also a branch that bifurcated before reaching the west gate; this latter conduit probably headed north, supplying the extramural bath at Abu Sha'ar with water.[161] There was at least one water-distribution tank made of gypsum ashlars and fired bricks near the well about 1 km southwest of the fort at Abu Sha'ar;[162] it was probably from this reservoir that well water was deposited and then piped to the fort.

The second example, which may be early or late Roman, was a pipeline comprising small cobbles and other stones mortared together, with an internal diameter of 9.5–10.8 cm. It ran east for approximately 477 m from Bir Abu Sha'ar al-Qibli to a small *praesidium*.[163] Excavations recorded part of this site, including two extant oval- to rectangular-shaped water basins outside and abutting the southern exterior wall of the *praesidium*. One was in very ruinous condition, but the second was intact and measured 2.75 m long × 0.70 m wide × 0.50 m deep;[164] it had a capacity of about 960 liters when full. There was a single large open cistern, whose top measured 13.95 m north–south × 13.45 m east–west, of unknown depth inside the *praesidium* in the southeastern corner, made of fieldstones mortared together and coated with waterproof plaster.[165] We cannot be certain of the date of this pipeline linking Bir Abu Sha'ar al-Qibli to the *praesidium*, because this fort was originally on the second-century c.e. Via Nova Hadriana, as indicated by ostraka excavated here.[166] Later it supported operations at the late Roman fort at Abu Sha'ar, which lay about 5.5–6 km to the east. Excavations could not determine whether this smaller installation still functioned and supported the main fort at Abu Sha'ar during the final period of Christian occupation.[167] It likely did, since the Via Nova Hadriana still operated at that point in late antiquity,[168] and the small fort would have continued to serve a convenient and much-needed dual function. Pottery from the small *praesidium* also indicates continued occupation in late Roman times.[169]

Extant remains at some *praesidia* demonstrate that channels made of mortared stone or terra-cotta pipes occasionally conveyed water from wells inside these installations into adjacent cisterns—intended, judging by their sizes. to accommodate smaller to larger numbers of animals—outside the forts. This arrangement is evident at Deir al-Atrash ("Monastery of the Deaf One") on the Abu Sha'ar/Mons Porphyrites–Nile road.[170] It is also visible at Abu Gariya on the Via Nova Hadriana[171] and at Jovis/Dios on the Berenike–Koptos road.[172] There are also extramural water tanks surviving outside the main gate at al-Kanaïs on the Berenike–Apollonopolis Magna and the Marsa Nakari–Apollonopolis Magna roads[173] as well as outside the gate of the lower fort at al-Heita on the Abu Sha'ar/Mons Porphyrites–Nile road.[174] There are sizable but much-damaged remains of hydraulic tanks immediately outside and both east and west of the large *praesidium* in Wadi Kalalat, about 8.5 km southwest of Berenike, though there is no extant evidence indicating how these tanks were filled or by whom they were used.[175] A large unfortified installation in Wadi Abu Shuwehat[176] on the southern route between Mons Claudianus and the Nile emporium at Kainepolis/Maximianopolis (modern Qena) had at least one large well surrounded by a low stone wall, no doubt to keep animals from approaching close to the source. One or more terra-cotta conduits fed water from this well to numerous troughs made of terra-cotta and plaster associated with a series of animal-tethering lines that accommodated traffic hauling stone from Mons Claudianus to the Nile. A small hole part way up and through the eastern perimeter wall at the *praesidium* of Maximianon possibly conveyed water for extramural consumption by animals,[177] or liquefied waste from the fort to the exterior.

Other water conduits or possible conduits survive at Mons Claudianus; another near Vetus Hydreuma, the first major stop on the road from Berenike to the Nile; and a third in Wadi Nakheil near Myos Hormos. Abu Greiya is a popular name for wadis in the Eastern Desert, since it means Father of the Village/Place of a Village. Since there are numerous ruins scattered throughout the region, the epithet, together with its variants—Abu Gariya/Greiya, Umm Gariya/Greiya (Mother of the Village)—is a common one given by the Bedouin to these locations.

There has been debate about the function of the so-called aqueduct leading from the hydraulic complex in Wadi Umm Diqal[178] toward the main settlement at Mons Claudianus. Earlier visitors believed that the long stone walls were the remains of an aqueduct,[179] but recent investigations do not support this identification and suggest, instead, that the walls diverted wadi floods *(seyul/seyal)*; possible parallels have been noted near Bir Nakheil west of Myos Hormos and in Wadi al-Qattar on the Abu Sha'ar/Mons Porphyrites–Nile road, while others can be found in Libya[180] and in the ancient Kingdom of Kush in modern Sudan.[181]

In 1826 J.G. Wilkinson noted a well and a small length of possible aqueduct leading away from it and toward lower ground in Wadi Abu Greiya (ancient Vetus Hydreuma). This well and putative aqueduct lay immediately south and at the base of the mountain atop which perches a facility called "Hilltop Fort Number 5."[182] Recent and repeated survey work has not revealed the conduit or wall that appears on Wilkinson's plan, but comparisons of Wilkinson's numerous other plans and maps of antiquities that he drew in the Eastern Desert with actual remains have proven him to be generally accurate. There is, thus, no reason to doubt his observations on the existence of this wall or conduit, though one might disagree with him about its function. One cannot, of course, determine whether this now-missing feature was a water-diversion wall similar to that at Wadi Umm Diqal or some type of conduit designed to transport water from the well eastward toward two large, low-lying wadi forts about 2 km to the east-southeast. The date of such a feature would likely have been early Roman, since the surface pottery of Hilltop Fort Number 5 was early Roman. If this fort and the well and "conduit" were contemporary, they may have augmented whatever other water supply was available at the main forts in the lower wadi to the east-southeast; it was these latter installations that serviced travelers between Berenike and the Nile. The forts and other structures at Vetus Hydreuma, which were about 25 km north-west of Berenike, comprised the first and largest stop on the road leading from Berenike to the Nile, and it was precisely in the early Roman period that traffic along these routes, resulting from long-distance maritime commerce, would have been at its peak; additional water sources and the need to protect them would have been essential to sustain the increased traffic. Hilltop Fort Number 5 and its putative related well and "aqueduct" may have been part of a wider program of water procurement and management that took place during this trade boom in the Flavian period, as we know from the hundreds of ostraka found in the trash dumps at Berenike and as is clear from first-century C.E. inscriptions found at several sites along this same road, which we discussed earlier.[183]

The nicely constructed double-faced wall comprising mortared cobbles and boulders in Wadi Nakheil has been eroded in several areas by floods. Whether it was intended for flood control or to divert waters for storage and supply remains unknown. The presence of a nearby ancient necropolis might suggest that this barrier was to divert floodwaters away from the cemetery.[184]

OTHER WATER CONVEYANCES

Roman *praesidia* at Deir al-Atrash[185] and possibly the lower fort at al-Heita,[186] both on the Abu Sha'ar/Mons Porphyrites–Nile road; perhaps at Abu Zawal,[187] a gold-mining settlement on the Mons Claudianus–Nile road; maybe at Gerf[188] on the Berenike–Koptos road; and at Abu Sha'ar al-Qibli near the Red Sea coast all have installations that suggest the presence of a water-lifting device. In Egypt this mechanism is called a *shadoof* (*kelon* in Greek and *telo, tolleno,* or *ciconia* in Latin),[189] and it may have been used to convey water from a very shallow well or, in the case of Abu Sha'ar al-Qibli, from a cistern to other tanks or extramural troughs where the water was more easily accessed. There are numerous textual references to their use in Greco-Roman Egypt.[190] A shadoof is a long pole with a bucketlike device at one end and a counterweight at the other, resting on a vertical beam that allows the long pole to dip down into a water source. The counterweight allows the user to lift the water-weighted end up and then pivot the long pole on the vertical upright and pour the water into a nearby location. Shadoofs are useful for raising water from a lower to a higher level in field irrigation. They appear throughout Egypt from Pharaonic times on and are still-visible, though fast-disappearing, features of irrigated areas adjacent to the Nile.[191] They are also in current use in northwestern Romania.[192]

There is evidence that water wheels, *saqqiyas* (*mechane* in Greek), were also used in the Eastern Desert during the Roman period.[193] *Saqqiyas* operated in a rotary fashion using draft animals. The system entails a wheel set above and horizontal to the ground that has cogs meshed to a vertical wheel that drives a third wheel, along the outer diameter of which clay pots are affixed at intervals. An animal walks in a never-ending circle, driving the device, which raises water by using pots attached to the wheel. Excavators at Mons Porphyrites postulated the use of a *saqqiya* at the well below the main fort.[194]

Saqqiya pots, fragments of clay jars resembling them, and ostraka referring to women who operated a water wheel have been found at Mons Claudianus, at Didymoi on the Berenike–Koptos road, and at Maximianon on the Myos Hormos–Koptos road. *Saqqiya* pots and fragments have also been found, especially in late Roman/Byzantine contexts, elsewhere in Egypt.[195] Papyri and other texts record their extensive use throughout Egypt.[196] References to drawers of water, though we cannot be sure if they used animals or a water screw, appear on ostraka excavated from *praesidia* on the Myos Hormos–Nile road.[197]

There is a large station on the Mons Porphyrites/Mons Claudianus/Abu Sha'ar–Nile road that preserves a substantial well hole and elaborate hydraulic facilities and animal-tethering lines to accommodate traffic. This stop now bears the name al-Saqqia, which may suggest the use of such water-lifting devices in Roman times here, too.[198]

WATER FOR IRRIGATION

Archaeological evidence for crop irrigation appears at several locations in the Eastern Desert, and current Bedouin practices may provide some idea of how this process took place in antiquity.[199] Good examples survive at Mons Claudianus,[200] near the small *praesidium* at Abu Sha'ar al-Qibli,[201] at Berenike,[202] and likely also at the gold-mining settlement at Bir Umm Fawakhir.[203] Early Roman ostraka from the village of Persou in Wadi Hammamat on the Myos Hormos–Nile road refer to the cultivation and sale of vegetables, herbs, and poultry to soldiers in nearby *praesidia* at Krokodilô and Maximianon;[204] cultivation of limited quantities of food, especially fruits and vegetables, may have also taken place at other desert locations.[205]

South of the *praesidium* at Abu Sha'ar al-Qibli are low stone walls running generally in an east–west direction.[206] They are not animal-tethering lines and have been interpreted as walls designed to protect crops from strong north winds; though, less likely, these may also have been part of a *hafir*. Water would have been transported, in a manner that remains unclear, from one or more cisterns inside or adjacent to the *praesidium* to the fields, thereby providing a supplemental source of food for those stationed at Abu Sha'ar al-Qibli and, possibly, for the nearby garrison at Abu Sha'ar on the coast.

Recent excavations at Sikait have found evidence that some open courtyards connected to domestic, or likely domestic, structures in areas adjacent to the wadi floor preserve numerous small stone boxes embedded in the ground both singly and in groups.[207] Archaeologically these stone boxes appear in fourth-century c.e. levels and later, and we conclude that they were used to support trellises for growing crops or protecting young plants or tree saplings.[208] Although many of these "trellis" works might have supported plants exposed to direct sunlight, a number were situated close to walls, and whatever greenery they braced would have received only diffuse or indirect sunlight. If our interpretation of these stone boxes as plant-related features is correct, this suggests that Sikait's inhabitants cultivated a variety of plants with different environmental requirements to supplement their otherwise heavy reliance on food imported from the Nile valley and, perhaps, to a lesser extent, from the Red Sea.[209] Future analysis of botanical remains will determine which species were produced on-site.

There are also Christian references to desert cultivation. In the fourth and fifth centuries the *Historia Monachorum in Aegypto* (12.16), together with Athanasius's *Life of St. Antony* (50) and Palladius's *Historia Lausiaca* (7.4), records that many monks and hermits residing in the Eastern Desert had their own gardens, where they cultivated fruits, vegetables, and grain to make bread. Such cultivation and irrigation practices take place today in the Eastern Desert monasteries of St. Antony and St. Paul.[210] Though most of these gardens would have been as close to the settlements as possible, in Judaea some monastery fields were several kilometers distant.[211] Given the large land holdings of some of the monasteries in Egypt, especially from the fifth century on,[212] this may have also been the case, in some instances, in the Eastern Desert.

The practice of desert cultivation was probably more widespread in antiquity in the region than much of the archaeological record suggests. Investigation of pollen appearing in some ancient mud bricks used in structures in the Eastern Desert indicates that their floral residues derived from plants grown in the immediate vicinity.[213] Thus, many mud bricks found at these sites were made on the spot—mixing, deliberately or inadvertently, locally cultivated plant remains. Unfortunately, many sites in the Eastern Desert have not been carefully surveyed for such farming activities, and this kind of evidence would easily be missed during a cursory examination or washed away in the intervening centuries. Yet, Bedouin in the Sinai, and Ma'aze and 'Ababda Bedouin of the Eastern Desert, today all practice desert cultivation, especially of fruits and vegetables and, to a lesser extent, grains.[214] This would have been an important activity at many ancient desert sites as a supplement to foods imported from the Nile valley; few fresh fruits and vegetables especially would have survived the desert trip in edible form. Gardening would also have provided some practical way to pass the time for those stationed or living in the region whose lives were otherwise undoubtedly quite boring much of the time.

Providing water to allow cultivation would probably have been effected, most frequently, by carrying it from a well or cistern to the gardens. One might expect most of desert plots to have been located fairly close to the water used in their irrigation. There is no extant evidence that pipelines, canals, or irrigation ditches were used much, if at all, for this purpose in the Eastern Desert in this period; certainly ditches and canals would leave few traces in the archaeological record. Use of open canals and irrigation ditches would, in any case, have resulted in substantial water loss through infiltration. Increased salinity would, on the other hand, have been minimal in these cases, since water flowing short distances or water poured directly onto the plants would not have been exposed long enough to allow excessive evaporation to take place, which would lead to oversalinization.

INDUSTRY

Industry should be defined in the desert as mainly metalworking and brick manufacture, both of which required water. Chapter 5 briefly discussed such manufacturing and water use in Ptolemaic Berenike. In Roman times at Berenike immediately north of the Serapis temple there is additional evidence of metal and glass working in late Roman times, both of which would have required water.[215]

Christian writers of the fourth and fifth centuries mention some pastimes of desert monks and hermits, including mat, basket, and rope making. The materials used to manufacture these items must have been soaked and softened in water, thereby making them more pliable prior to weaving.[216] This would also have been the case at other times in history. There is evidence of industrial activity, usually metalworking, at sites in the region. During our desert surveys it is not uncommon to find metal, especially iron slag scattered around Ptolemaic forts and Roman *praesidia* and especially at mining and quarrying sites, where metal tools and some weapons must have constantly been made or repaired. Water would have played a critical role in this process.[217] Our surveys found stone molds for making metal items, as well as iron slag, in the Ptolemaic gold-mining center at Abu Gerida and also at the large fort at Samut on the Berenike–Apollonopolis Magna road; at the latter site and in the same location where our survey found the stone mold for toolmaking, we also noted a large hydraulic tank, recently exposed and badly damaged by looters. There is a long open conduit coated with waterproof plaster that runs adjacent to a number of structures at the Ptolemaic–early Roman gold-mining camp at al-Ghuzza, west of Abu Sha'ar, though it is not certain whether this channel carried water for drinking, for irrigation, for metalworking, or for other activities associated with gold-ore processing. Our survey also found a very long, narrow, and nicely constructed hydraulic tank at the Roman gold mines at Bir Semna. A detailed survey and some excavation of the fifth- to sixth-century C.E. gold-mining site at Bir Umm Fawakhir, on the Myos Hormos–Koptos road, revealed a huge community, satellite settlements, industrial areas, roads and paths, and wells and cemeteries.[218]

Diodorus Siculus (3.14.1)[219] records the use of water poured on inclined gold-washing tables in the Eastern Desert in the Ptolemaic period. One would expect that at least the larger mines[220] used this or some similar techniques to wash gold. Although Diodorus does not say so, pouring water on fire-heated rocks in order to crack them more readily to facilitate access to the ore may also have been occasionally practiced. Water was, thus, critical to make or repair tools, for human and animal consumption, and for the cultivation of desert crops to the extent that locally available resources allowed.

Excavations in the Ptolemaic industrial zone at Berenike preserved the remains of a large sloping V-shaped ditch that turned at a right angle. Given the lack of any hydraulic lining and its substantial width, which would have led to greatly increased evaporation, we determined that it likely did not serve a hydraulic function but was, rather, an enclosure for captive elephants awaiting their onward journey to the Nile (see chapters 4 and 5).[221]

Washing metal ores, and their manufacture into finished products, required freshwater. The use of saltwater, obtainable in limitless amounts from the sea at Berenike and the other Red Sea ports, was not an option, because it would have left salt residues in both the ore and finished products, resulting in the production of inferior metal objects. Sudden cooling or quenching using freshwater on copper alloys produced a slightly softer metal.[222] Sudden cooling of iron, by thrusting it into cold water or oil, produced hard, brittle metal.[223] Thus, in all likelihood much if not all metalworking that took place at Berenike and the other Red Sea ports required freshwater that must have been obtained with some effort from wells far enough from the coast to produce both the necessary quantity and quality of water.

Recent excavations at Myos Hormos identified an early Roman metalworking area.[224] Yet the excavators recorded no evidence for water use associated with the workshops uncovered there. Perhaps, in that instance, water was transported and held in movable containers or tanks that have since disappeared.

The Mons Claudianus ostrakon, which records water rationing from the early second century C.E., refers to blacksmiths and bellows men at the quarries and the amounts of water they received.[225] It is not clear whether their allotted quantities included water used in their work as well as for drinking.

BATHING

Few formal bathing facilities have been identified in the Eastern Desert, and all have been found in military contexts.[226] Their presence at some excavated sites suggests that more will probably be identified as archaeological work in the region continues. Archaeologists have found at least seven baths:[227] one associated with the late Roman fort–Christian ecclesiastical complex at Abu Sha'ar,[228] which is discussed later; another at Mons Claudianus;[229] a third at the *praesidium* at Maximianon;[230] and a fourth at the *praesidium* at Didymoi.[231] There was a fifth found adjacent to the main fort at Mons Porphyrites.[232] Others have been identified at Umm Balad (Domitiane/Kaine Latomia)[233] and at Jovis/Dios.[234] It is noteworthy that excavations at Myos Hormos and Berenike, two large civilian settlements, have recovered no remains of baths. There is only circumstantial evidence for a bath at Berenike, either early or late Roman in date, but one would expect that a city of that size would have had such a facility.[235] The find in the center of Berenike of sherds of glass flasks used specifically for bathing, and of kiln-fired bricks preserving chunks of mortar, used in some hydraulic context, points to the possible presence nearby of a bathing facility.[236]

None of the baths noted here was large, but nevertheless, each would have required relatively substantial amounts of freshwater and fuel in order to keep them functioning even on a semiregular basis. We would expect that a bath building at a relatively large urban center like Berenike probably catered to a greater number of patrons than those at the quarry sites and would, consequently, have been bigger than its desert counterparts. Future excavations may document more about this.

HYDRAULIC FACILITIES FOR ANIMALS

Providing adequate water supplies to large numbers of pack and draft animals posed substantial logistical burdens on stations handling traffic between desert quarries and mines and points on the Nile. There is limited evidence that some mine and quarry products were shipped to the Red Sea ports for consumption there or for onward export, but most items would have been sent to the Nile. Routes between the quarries at Mons Claudianus and Mons Porphyrites and the beryl/emerald mines at Sikait all had animal-tethering lines and watering facilities, indicating that the bulk of the traffic was between those centers and the Nile and not to the Red Sea coast. A late-first-century c.e. ostrakon from Didymoi refers to a worker in the emerald mines.[237] This indicates that there was at least some traffic between those mines and the Nile via the road to Koptos in the early Roman period.

In general, animal-tethering lines comprise low walls with extant heights of ca. 0.50–1.0 m. Sometimes the animal lines are directly associated with water troughs; in other instances the water troughs and animal lines lie on different parts of the sites some distance from one another. This spatial separation was probably intended to minimize fouling of the water supply by quickly moving animals away from the troughs once they had consumed their fill and to allow more rapid and efficient circulation of large numbers of animals to and from the water supplies.

TETHERING LINES ON THE ABU SHA'AR/MONS PORPHYRITES–NILE ROAD

The road joining the fort at Abu Sha'ar and the Nile at Kainepolis/Maximianopolis (modern Qena) also accommodated traffic from the quarries at Mons Porphyrites, from smaller ones nearby at Umm Balad and Umm Towat, and perhaps from the gold mines at al-Ghuzza.[238] Toward its western end, from al-Saqqia onward to the Nile, stations on this road also handled some traffic coming from Mons Claudianus, perhaps from the quarries and *praesidium* at Barud (ancient Tiberiane),[239] and from the small quarries at Umm Huyut.[240] Many, but not all, stops and *praesidia* between Mons Porphyrites/Mons Claudianus and

FIGURE 7-7

Abu Greiya on the Mons Claudianus–Nile road, approximately 42 km from the Nile emporium of Kainepolis/Qena. Easternmost fort and extensive animal tethering lines. Photo by S. E. Sidebotham.

the Nile had animal-tethering lines and associated watering facilities.[241] Stations at Umm Sidri,[242] Badia',[243] Qattar,[244] Deir al-Atrash,[245] Bab al-Mukhenig,[246] al-Saqqia,[247] the lower fort at al-Heita,[248] and possibly the fort at al-'Aras had these facilities.[249] Other stops may have originally had them, but no evidence survives; there are no visible animal lines associated with the small fort in Wadi Belih[250] or at the stop at Bir Saleh, which is between the *praesidia* at Deir al-Atrash and at al-Saqqia.[251] Nor are animal-tethering lines visible at the small stop at Atrash Northeast, between Qattar and Deir al-Atrash.[252]

There are indications at Deir al-Atrash, at al-Saqqia, and at the lower fort at al-Heita that the animals were watered in one location and moved to another to rest and eat. This arrangement allowed, as noted earlier, more efficient circulation of large numbers of draft animals and minimized pollution of the water supplies.

TETHERING LINES ON THE MONS CLAUDIANUS–NILE ROADS

Mons Claudianus and satellite quarries at Barud (Tiberiane) and Umm Huyut used two routes to the Nile. For the first 18–20 km after leaving Mons Claudianus and heading toward the southwest there was a single thoroughfare. This passed a small early Roman-era quarry at Fetireh al-Beida, where one branch continued west-northwest to Wadi Qalt al-Naga, and, another 12–15 km past that, a second bifurcated at Abu Zawal, at which point the road proceeded to al-Saqqia, al-Heita, and al-'Aras and then onward to the Nile on the

Abu Sha'ar/Mons Porphyrites–Nile road. A more southerly route from Mons Claudianus via Abu Zawal passed Wadi Abu Shuwehat, with animal–tethering lines and water troughs, and then went on to Abu Greiya, approximately 42 km by modern paved road from Qena. Abu Greiya has two separate forts, part of the westernmost of which is covered by the modern highway, and massive animal-tethering lines (figure 7-7).[253] The ancient route then went to al-'Aras before arriving at Kainepolis/Maximianopolis. The main camp at Mons Claudianus also possesses animal lines for accommodating primarily donkeys and camels.[254]

TETHERING LINES ON THE MARSA NAKARI (NECHESIA?)–NILE ROAD

The Marsa Nakari (Nechesia?)–Nile road linked the small Red Sea port at Marsa Nakari, which may be the ancient Nechesia described by Claudius Ptolemy (*Geography* 4.5.8), with Apollonopolis Magna.[255] At its western end this route coincided with that linking Berenike to Apollonopolis Magna (see chapter 8). This thoroughfare has three stops on it that preserve what appear to be animal-tethering lines. They are, from east to west, Rod Umm al-Farraj, with twelve lines; Rod al-Buram, with approximately twelve lines; and Bezah West with about thirteen lines. In all instances the putative animal-tethering lines are low walls of stones varying in length from 3.1 to 8.2 m and about 0.50 m high, which lay some distance from the water sources. Similar numbers of lines at each site suggest that all three catered to about equal numbers of animals. The appearance of these animal-tethering lines is quite different from that of those on the Abu Sha'ar/Mons Porphyrites–Nile and Mons Claudianus–Nile roads and from that of those recorded farther south on the route joining mining settlements in Wadis Nugrus and Sikait to the Nile, which will be discussed later in this chapter. Those on the more northerly Mons Porphyrites and Mons Claudianus routes, except the one at Wadi Abu Shuwehat, tend to be enclosed by walls,[256] whereas those on the Marsa Nakari–Nile road are simple, open lines roughly in pairs parallel to one another. The walls found at stops on the Marsa Nakari–Nile road generally run east–west, no doubt allowing animals to be tethered to the southern side, affording them and their fodder protection from the generally prevailing northerly winds.

Although there are gold-mining settlements along this main Nile–Red Sea road, or connected to it via trunk routes, it is not clear why there was a need for animal-tethering lines when none appear associated with other gold-mining areas in the Eastern Desert. Perhaps these lines were not intended to serve traffic leading to or from the gold mines at all, but rather facilitated traffic leading to or from a quarry whose existence in the early Roman period has only recently been documented. J. A. Harrell discovered a pegmatitic diorite quarry used in the Predynastic period and exploited, again, in early Roman times at Gebel Umm Naqqat.[257] Our survey discovered and followed the Roman route that headed north from Gebel Umm Naqqat, then west and ultimately south. We had insufficient time to trace the entire course of this road, but its general direction suggests that it likely intersected the Marsa Nakari–Nile road near the sites preserving the animal-tethering lines noted earlier. Perhaps, then, those sites accommodated traffic coming from this distant quarry headed for the Nile along the Marsa Nakari–Apollonopolis Magna road. This remains to be investigated. No stations with animal-tethering lines preserve any indication of defense—something one would think necessary were these stops catering to traffic carrying gold; this may also be evidence that their role was for support of quarry operations at Gebel Umm Naqqat, the stone from which hardly needed guarding. On the other hand, no animal-tethering lines appear farther west along this road, which is strange if the road did, indeed, cater to quarry traffic from Gebel Umm Naqqat. We have, at this point, no explanation for the dearth of animal lines at the more westerly end of the road.

TETHERING LINES ON THE SIKAIT/NUGRUS AND BERENIKE–NILE ROADS

Many scholars have long believed, because of the relative ease with which items like gold ore, beryls/emeralds, amethysts, and other metals and precious and semiprecious stones could be transported, that no elaborate animal-watering or animal-tethering systems, such as those that supported the major quarrying operations en route to the Nile, were required. Our surveys have borne this out except in the case of the beryl/emerald-mining centers in Wadis Sikait and Nugrus, which operated throughout the Roman period, and perhaps earlier, and into the Islamic era and, sporadically, in modern times. Our surveys in that area identified what appear to be animal corrals and watering points at two locations, both near the beryl/emerald mines themselves. One set of five or six huge enclosures, located at the juncture of Wadi Nugrus and the main road to the Nile via Wadi Gemal, lies only 7.9 km from the major mining centers at Sikait and Nugrus.[258] They must have been used to accommodate pack animals bringing supplies and visitors to numerous mines up those wadis and/or carrying emeralds and travelers from them.[259] The other is also close by, at a place our survey discovered and named Wadi Gemal East, no more than a few kilometers farther on the road toward the Nile from the former set of animal lines. A smaller animal-tethering line at Wadi Gemal East may have been equipped with a watering trough. Other animal lines here seem to lack troughs, suggesting—as at Deir al-Atrash and al-Saqqia on the Abu Sha'ar/Mons Porphyrites–Nile road—that at least some animals arriving at Wadi Gemal East were watered and then moved away to rest and eat elsewhere. Neither set was nearly as large or elaborate as those on the routes leading from the Mons Claudianus and Mons Porphyrites quarries. The lines on the Mons Claudianus and Mons Porphyrites–Nile roads, except for Wadi Abu Shuwehat, are rows of low walls enclosed within a surrounding wall. Those on the Marsa Nakari–Nile road comprise short parallel animal lines with no surrounding stone walls. The examples between the emerald mines in Wadis Sikait/Nugrus and the Nile were, on the other hand, generally large, open areas surrounded by walls, without any additional lines inside the enclosed spaces. One possible watering trough at Wadi Gemal East lacks a surrounding wall. We cannot offer any suggestions as to why there should be at least three different design plans for animal-tethering lines in the Eastern Desert, unless their appearance relates, somehow, to the cargoes that were hauled past or the numbers and species of draft animals that used them.

Since it was along the Berenike–Apollonopolis Magna road that the Ptolemies trans-ported many elephants brought by sea to Egypt, one would expect to have evidence of this along that highway. Chapter 4 noted the amounts of food and water that elephants typi-cally consume. Yet, nothing along this route, or any other road examined in the Eastern Desert, specifically points to special accommodations for elephants that can be identified, unless the small station at Abu Midrik, with cisterns capable of holding eighty-eight thou-sand liters, provides some clue. Abu Midrik accommodated traffic between Berenike and Apollonopolis Magna in Ptolemaic times and is the sole station on the road where only Ptolemaic–era pottery has been found. Perhaps the relatively massive cisterns there served, in part, to quench the thirst of pachyderms making their way to the Nile.

Providing adequate water supplies to large numbers of pack and draft animals posed substantial logistical burdens on stations handling traffic between quarries and mines in the desert and terminal points on the Nile. There is limited evidence that some mine and quarry products were shipped to the Red Sea ports for consumption there or onward ex-port, but the vast majority of the items would have been sent to the Nile valley. Routes between Mons Claudianus, Mons Porphyrites, Sikait, and some mines along the Marsa Nakari–Apollonopolis Magna road had animal-tethering lines and animal-watering fa-cilities, indicating that most traffic was between those centers and the Nile and not to the Red Sea coast.

WATER POLLUTION

The use of water associated with mining, quarrying, and industrial activities raises the question of water pollution and what impacts consuming polluted water had on the health of humans and animals residing in the Eastern Desert and along the Red Sea coast.[260] It is not possible to measure precisely either the levels of ancient water pollution or the ad-verse effects such pollution may have had on those who consumed the water, but we have some inkling. Tailings at many gold and beryl mines in the region are extensive, and their residues must have infiltrated into the local groundwater supplies. In stations where large numbers of animals congregated regularly, their droppings must have attracted huge num-bers of disease-carrying flies, and the decomposing waste itself would have eventually penetrated into the groundwater, on which both animals and humans depended.

Consumption of such water must have led, minimally, to recurrent stomach ailments and, perhaps, longer-term health issues. Ostraka from Mons Claudianus preserve letters indicating deaths and health problems, especially of the eyes and gastrointestinal systems of some people living there.[261] One can only imagine how much worse the health situa-tion must have been where water used in the mining and quarrying process percolated into the groundwater, carrying metallic or other pollutants with it.[262] Gold and other mines, especially in places such as Sikait and Nugrus, also had the added effects of workers breathing polluted air in the narrow shafts.[263] In the Sikait-Nugrus area the basement rocks emit low-level radiation.[264] One wonders what negative long-term health effects exposure to this radiation might have caused in those residents.

No systematic study of the bones of those buried in Berenike or Sikait in antiquity has taken place. Most of the graves have been thoroughly robbed, making any such examination extremely difficult and very incomplete. Nevertheless, a more detailed investigation of the causes and effects of environmental degradation of the Eastern Desert would be useful in any study of the health and longevity of populations resident in the area over long periods of time.[265]

CONCLUSION

The methods used for water acquisition, storage, protection, and distribution in Ptolemaic and Roman times in the Eastern Desert were undoubtedly similar to those employed in the Pharaonic period. The most noteworthy differences were the scales on which these operations were conducted. Ptolemaic and especially Roman activities in the region would have dwarfed earlier ones.

It seems the Ptolemaic and Roman governments, mainly through the military, played a major role in managing water resources in the Eastern Desert. Unfortunately, few surviving ancient authors provide insights on how water-management operations were conducted. Thousands of ostraka and papyri provide very little information about this subject, while study of ostraka excavated at Berenike in 2009–2010 that do deal with water supply has only begun. The bulk of what is known, or believed, comes from archaeological, mainly architectural, evidence. Few excavations have been conducted at any of the desert sites, including limited investigations of some *praesidia* on the Myos Hormos road, where ostraka and inscriptions have been found recently. These include stations at Krokodilô, Maximianon, Qasr al-Banat, Bir al-Hammamat, Bir Sayala, and several others, and two on the Berenike–Koptos road: Didymoi and Jovis/Dios. Our limited excavations at *praesidia* in Wadi Kalalat and Siket and in the gate areas of two forts at Vetus Hydreuma have also documented inscriptions and a few ostraka. Only one, from Siket, details the hydraulic function of the site;[266] it provides, however, no insights into methods of water distribution. Most data pertinent to the question of water management in the Eastern Desert in Ptolemaic and Roman times derive from surface surveying; few, aside from the ostrakon found at Didymoi noted earlier and the ostraka excavated at Berenike in 2009–2010,[267] have come from any ancient texts thus far uncovered. Inscriptions and ostraka from some *praesidia* suggest that stations and roads in the Eastern Desert were built, garrisoned, and maintained by the military. Unfortunately, these texts provide no information on how water was acquired, stored, or distributed. Most sites possessed wells or other hydraulic facilities used by garrisons and travelers along the routes. One should conclude from this that most water management at road installations was, therefore, the responsibility of the military in the Ptolemaic and Roman periods. At mines and quarries, the degree of civilian versus military responsibility for water management is not as clear. It would seem that, from the reign of Tiberius on, the imperial government operated most mines and quarries.[268] The military guarded many if not most of these facilities, suggesting that it was also responsible for the management of such a vital resource as water in these locations.

Aside from epigraphic and specific literary evidence that records construction, repair, and refurbishment of hydraulic facilities in the period of Ptolemy II (285/282–246 B.C.E.) and, again, in Flavian times (69–96 C.E.), such activities in the region conducted by other rulers cannot be as securely documented. There must have been additional repair and refurbishment carried out in Ptolemaic times connected with gold mining in the Eastern Desert—and at the Red Sea ports, particularly those associated with the elephant trade. This may be suggested by the appearance in the first century B.C.E. of the special Ptolemaic office of "strategos and epistrategos of the Erythraean and Indian Seas," seemingly related to activities in the region.[269] There was an upsurge in trade, and mining and quarrying, in the Eastern Desert in Augustan and Tiberian times (30 B.C.E.–37 C.E.),[270] with renewed interest, again, in the Flavian era and in the Trajanic and Hadrianic (98–138 C.E.) age;[271] we have evidence from an inscription that the hydreuma in the large praesidium in Wadi Kalalat supplying water to Berenike operated during the reign of Trajan (98–117 C.E.).[272] An inscription from the reign of Trajan has also been recently documented at the praesidium at Jovis/Dios.[273] The construction of many praesidia on the Myos Hormos–Nile road seems to have taken place in the Flavian and Trajanic/Hadrianic periods.[274] The Severan era (193–217 C.E.) also appears to have been one of relatively brisk activity in the region.[275] A renaissance in Red Sea trade, travel, and mining in the Eastern Desert took place in the mid fourth and fifth centuries.[276] It would be reasonable to assume that during these periods additional attention was lavished on road infrastructure and hydraulic facilities so vital to the support of passing traffic. Repairs on an ad hoc basis would, of course, have been carried out as needed. There must have been a large upsurge in water usage also at the mines and quarries in the Eastern Desert, especially in the early Roman period and again in late Roman times.

Though extensive survey work provides a basis for the present discussion, it is not a substitute for careful examination of key sites, whose excavation would pay great dividends on this and other questions relating to life in the region between Ptolemaic and late Roman times.

8

NILE–RED SEA ROADS

An elaborate maritime network concatenated Berenike and other Egyptian Red Sea ports with emporia elsewhere in the Red Sea and Indian Ocean. This maritime web was, however, incomplete without complementary terrestrial transportation points at those ports. Here we will examine these land routes in the Eastern Desert from about 30 B.C.E. until the sixth century C.E. (figure 8-1). The Romans enlarged the earlier infrastructure, especially that of the Ptolemies. Unfortunately, little is known about the Eastern Desert during the transition from Roman to Muslim domination that took place beginning in 641 C.E. This is, in any case, beyond the scope of our present study.

ROMAN ROADS

Between the Roman annexation of Egypt in 30 B.C.E. and the later fifth and sixth centuries C.E. the Eastern Desert and Red Sea coast witnessed the greatest and densest population and most human activity of any period until the second half of the twentieth century. The Romans enhanced the previously existing road networks by refurbishing, enlarging, and extending older Ptolemaic routes and renovating stops and stations along them. In addition, roads, stops, and *praesidia* were constructed and *hydreumata* dug de novo to deal with the increased traffic. The Eastern Desert road system represented only a fraction of the Roman highway network that linked all areas of the empire. This comprised more than 80,000 km of major thoroughfares and approximately 320,000 km of secondary roads.[1] Many of the former were solidly built on deep, well-prepared founda-

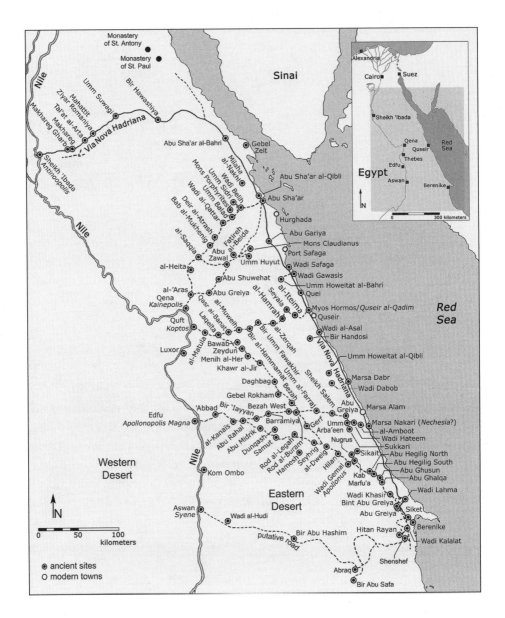

tions topped with huge paving stones.[2] It is impossible to calculate the total length of all other types of roads constructed and used throughout the Roman Empire during its long history.

Roman-era roads and settlements in the Eastern Desert were interconnected and symbiotic and cannot be understood properly apart from each other. We cannot investigate all Roman roads in the region, many thousands of kilometers' worth, nor each of the hundreds of sites; instead, our discussion will examine typical Roman roads and various types of sites, and the relative frequency with which they appear. Thereby one can gauge the overall importance of the kinds of activities they represent. Then one can relate the data to create a picture of interactions and interrelationships that existed among them and Berenike, other Egyptian Red Sea ports, and emporia on the Nile.

The main concern of Augustus—the initial problem he encountered in Lower Nubia—and of later authorities was the maintenance of internal security; there was little fear, except along the Nile valley later on, of invasion from outside Egypt.[3]

Not all Roman roads and sites that once existed in the Eastern Desert have been found and identified; our Ma'aze and 'Ababda guides and informants have provided information on ancient remains and roads that have yet to be visited and that appear on no maps. Therefore, lack of complete data hampers this discussion. Nevertheless, surveys and excavations have identified sufficient numbers and lengths of roads, and sites associated with them, that their overall study, supplemented by ancient written documentation, can provide a general idea of activities in the region in the Roman period.

The length of all Roman-era roads in the Eastern Desert is unknown, nor is it certain that all extant remains were originally constructed at that time; undoubtedly some are Ptolemaic or older, and those now visible are, in some cases, Roman repairs and refurbishments of earlier routes.[4] The number and length of Roman roads seem to have exceeded those of the Ptolemies due to increased levels of activity in the Eastern Desert at that time. Results of our surveys, however, provide a fair idea of the approximate lengths of seven major Ptolemaic and Roman roads in the Eastern Desert: about 2,000–2,200 km. Our surveys have examined all major highways. These "built" or refurbished "Roman" routes often followed Ptolemaic and earlier tracks for at least part of their courses and were mainly products of first- and early second-century c.e. construction efforts, though many, perhaps most, continued in use, and were undoubtedly repaired repeatedly, into late antiquity and beyond. The roads followed major wadi systems that ran generally east–west, avoiding steep gradients wherever possible.[5] Examination of pottery, coins, inscriptions, and building styles of road installations, and references to some road stations on ancient maps and itineraries and in accounts of Roman-era authors, provide clues about Roman road extensions and newly built segments. These major thoroughfares included the following, from north to south:

1. Via Nova Hadriana (Antinoopolis on the Nile–Berenike), approximately 800 km[6]

2. Abu Sha'ar/Mons Porphyrites–Kainepolis/Maximianopolis, approximately 180 km[7]

3. Mons Claudianus–Kainepolis/Maximianopolis (two routes), approximately 120 km/40 km (trunk) total ca. 160 km[8]

4. Myos Hormos–Koptos, approximately 180 km[9]

5. Marsa Nakari (Nechesia?)–Apollonopolis Magna, approximately 240 km[10]

6. Berenike–Koptos, approximately 380 km[11]

7. Berenike–Apollonopolis Magna, approximately 340 km[12]

Table 8–1 lists roads, stops, stations, and wells along their courses and nearby settlements that used them.

There are examples of a Roman proclivity to conjoin desert roads, and some routes were coterminal with others. For example, the last ca. 35 km of the Myos Hormos–Koptos road also served the last 35 km of the Berenike–Koptos road, while the last 75 km or so of the Marsa Nakari (Nechesia?)–Apollonopolis Magna route also served the Berenike–Apollonopolis Magna highway. The first approximately 170 km of the Berenike–Nile roads accommodated the Nile emporia at Apollonopolis Magna and at Koptos. Wherever possible, practicality and frugality led the Romans to tie route systems together, which led to a situation that required fewer forts and garrisons than would have been the case if these roads each had their own courses. This made their construction, repair, and maintenance simpler and cheaper, and it would have been easier to monitor and defend such a network.

These major roads had certain features in common, but they did not necessarily have the same functions or importance. All major roads ultimately linked the Nile to the Red Sea coast, except routes to quarries at Mons Claudianus, Mons Porphyrites, and Mons Ophiates, discussed later in the chapter. All were undoubtedly built by and primarily for the use of the Roman military,[13] and for government business. Most were also important commercial links from Red Sea ports—often via quarries or gold-, beryl/emerald-, and other desert mining centers—to counterparts on the Nile. The Via Nova Hadriana, built in the second century C.E., is an anomaly in this respect. Given its course, which was substantially longer and, therefore, less cost-effective for entrepreneurs to use than the other major, mainly east–west oriented, Nile–Red Sea roads, the Via Nova Hadriana was not a convenient highway for commercial, mining, or quarrying activities. Its major purpose seems to have been administrative; it was the only road that linked all major Egyptian Red Sea ports by land to one another.[14] In this respect the Via Nova Hadriana had a function similar to the Via Nova Traiana in Provincia Arabia.[15]

Evidence from our surveys suggests that there was at least one other major route joining Berenike toward the southwest—via Bir Jahaliya (a well), Abraq (a Ptolemaic–early Roman fort), Bir Abu Hashim (a well and graves), and Wadi al-Hudi (Pharaonic and Roman amethyst quarry and associated forts)—to Syene (modern Aswan);[16] possibly a second bifurcated somewhere near Abraq and headed more southwesterly via a Ptolemaic water temple at Bir Abu Safa, eventually reaching the Nile at or near Syene.[17] Some travelers and our survey, which quizzed local ʿAbabda and Bishareen Bedouin, have concluded that there was probably another track, perhaps multiple routes, linking Berenike to Syene. However, due to the difficulty of obtaining permits from Egyptian authorities, adequate survey work to test this hypothesis has not been undertaken. Limited evidence suggests

TABLE 8-1 Major Ptolemaic-Roman Roads and Stations/Stops in the Eastern Desert

Via Nova Hadriana: Antinoopolis to Berenike

Site Name	Type of Site	Pottery and Other Dates
Antinoopolis (Sheikh 'Ibada)	Nile emporium	Roman-Byzantine
Quarry in Wadi al-'Ibada	Three small limestone quarries	Unknown, likely Roman
Large ramp in Wadi al-'Ibada	Part of road	Unknown, likely Roman
Makhareg Gharb	Unidentified structures	2nd–4th (?) century C.E.
Makhareg	Wells/associated structures	2nd–5th century C.E./lithics (pre-early dynastic)
Tal'at al-Arta	Road station/well	Early Roman–late 4th–5th century C.E.
Large ramp east of Tal'at al Arta	Part of road	Unknown, likely Roman
Mahattit Ziyar Romaniya	Road stop	Late 1st–2nd or early 3rd century C.E.
Umm Suwagi	Cistern/associated structures on road	Early Roman, possibly late Roman
Bir Hawashiya	Well/associated structures on road	Late 1st/2nd to early 3rd (?) century C.E.
Wadi Umm Dhaya	Settlement/quarry (?)	Ptolemaic inscriptions
*Abu Sha'ar al-Bahri	Praesidium/wells on road	Poorly dated early Roman
*Milaha al-Nakhl	Settlement near road	Possibly early Roman/mainly late 4th–5th century C.E.
Abu Sha'ar al-Qibli	Praesidium/wells on road	2nd-5th/6th century C.E.
Abu Sha'ar	Fort near road	4th–late 5th/6th century C.E.
Abu Gariya	Praesidium on road	Late 1st–2nd or early 3rd century C.E.
Wadi Safaga	Praesidium on road	Unknown, probably early Roman
Umm Howeitat/Umm Hayatat	Christian settlement near road	5th century C.E.
*Quei	Praesidium on road	Unknown, likely Roman
Myos Hormos (Quseir al-Qadim)	Red Sea port	Ptolemaic, 1st–3rd century C.E., later Islamic
Wadi al-Asal	De facto road stop/no structures	Ptolemaic
Umm Howeitat al-Qibli	Gold-mining settlement near road	Ptolemaic

Via Nova Hadriana: Antinoopolis to Berenike (continued)

Site Name	Type of Site	Pottery and Other Dates
Wadi Dabob	Gold mine off road	Unknown Ptolemaic/Roman
Marsr Dabr/Marsa Nabiyah	Praesidium on road	Early Roman
Marsa Nakari (Nechesia?)	Red Sea port	Possibly Ptolemaic, 1st–2nd and mid 4th–5th centuries C.E.
Bir Ria'da	Cemetery/well near road	Unknown
Vetus Hydreuma (Wadi Abu Greiya)	Five praesidia on and near road	Ptolemaic, early-late Roman
Berenike	Red Sea port	3rd century B.C.E.–6th century C.E.

Abu Sha'ar-Mons Porphyrites–Kainepolis/Maximianopolis Road

Site Name	Type of Site	Pottery and Other Dates
Abu Sha'ar	Fort/monastery	Early 4th–late 5th/6th century C.E.
Abu Sha'ar al-Qibli	Praesidium/wells on road	2nd–5th/6th century C.E.
Wadi Belih	Praesidium on/near road	1st–2nd century C.E.
Mons Porphyrites/Umm Sidri	Quarry settlement/road station, off road	1st–4th/5th century C.E.
Badia'	Two praesidia/animal tethering lines on road	1st–2nd and 4th–5th centuries C.E.
Umm Balad	Praesidium/quarry	1st–4th century C.E.
Qattar	Praesidium/wells/animal tethering lines on road	1st–4th century C.E.
Wadi Nagat	Monastery/settlement off road	4th century C.E. and perhaps earlier
Atrash Northeast	Road stop	Unknown, likely Roman
Deir al-Atrash	Praesidium/wells/animal tethering lines on road	1st–6th century C.E.
Bab al-Mukhenig	road station/animal tethering lines on road	1st–5th/6th century C.E.
Bir Salah	Stop/well on road	3rd–4th century C.E.
al-Saqqia	Praesidium/wells/animal tethering lines	1st–2nd and 3rd–4th centuries C.E.
al-Heita/Qasr al-Jin	Two praesidia/wells/animal tethering lines	1st–2nd and late 4th–6th/7th (?) centuries C.E.
al-'Aras	Praesidium/well/animal tethering lines	1st–4th century C.E.
Kainepolis/Maximianopolis (Qena)	Nile emporium	Ptolemaic-Roman-(earlier?)-modern

Mons Claudianus-Kainepolis/Maximianopolis Roads

Site Name	Type of Site	Pottery and Other Dates
Mons Claudianus	Quarry settlement	1st–3rd/4th century C.E.
Umm Huyut	Quarry settlement near road	1st–2nd century C.E.
Fatireh al-Beida	Small quarry settlement	Early Roman
Fatireh al-Beida al-Qibli	De facto stop on road	Unknown
Abu Zawal	Gold-mining settlement on/near road	Ptolemaic-Roman
Wadi Abu Shuwehat	Road station/animal tethering lines	Likely 1st–3rd/4th century C.E.
Wadi Abu Greiya	Two *praesidia*/animal tethering lines	Likely 1st–3rd/4th century C.E.
al-ʿAras	*Praesidium*/animal tethering lines	1st–4th century C.E.
Kainepolis/Maximianopolis (Qena)	Nile emporium	Ptolemaic-Roman-(earlier?)-modern
Mons Claudianus (alternate route)	Quarry settlement	1st–3rd/4th century C.E.
Abu Zawal	Gold-mining settlement on/near road	Ptolemaic-Roman
al-Saqqia	*Praesidium*/wells/animal tethering lines	1st–2nd and 3rd–4th centuries C.E.
al-Heita	Two *praesidia*/wells/animal tethering lines	1st–2nd and late 4th–6th/7th (?) centuries C.E.
al-ʿAras	*Praesidium*/well/animal tethering lines	1st–4th century C.E.
Kainepolis/Maximianopolis (Qena)	Nile emporium	Ptolemaic-Roman-(earlier?)-modern

Myos Hormos–Koptos Road

Site Name	Type of Site	Pottery and Other Dates
Myos Hormos (Quseir al-Qadim)	Red Sea port	Ptolemaic, 1st–3rd century C.E. and Islamic
al-Iteima/Duwi/Hammad	*Praesidium*/well	2nd century C.E. at least
Seyala	*Praesidium*/well	2nd century C.E. at least
al-Hamrah	*Praesidium*/well	Early Roman
al-Zerqah (Maximianon)	*Praesidium*/well	1st–2nd century C.E. at least

Myos Hormos–Koptos Road (*continued*)

Site Name	Type of Site	Pottery and Other Dates
Fawakhir (Persou)	*Praesidium*/gold-mining settlement/ quarry settlement	Ptolemaic (inscription)-Late Roman/early Byzantine
al-Hammamat	*Praesidium*/well	At least 2nd century C.E. and Islamic
al-Muweih (Krokodilô)	*Praesidium*/well	Late 1st–2nd century C.E. at least, possibly into 3rd C.E.
Qasr al-Banat	*Praesidium*/well	1st century B.C.E.-early Roman at least
*Laqeita (Phoenicon)	*Praesidium*/wells	(inscriptions of Claudius and Vespasian), at least early Roman
al-Matula	*Praesidium*/well	1st–2nd and 5th centuries C.E. or later
Koptos	Nile emporium	Pharaonic-modern

Marsa Nakari (Nechesia?)–Apollonopolis Road

Site Name	Type of Site	Pottery and Other Dates
Marsa Nakari (Nechesia?)	Red Sea port	Ptolemaic (?), 1st–2nd and 4th–5th centuries C.E.
al-Amboot	Gypsum/anhydrite quarry off road	Early Roman
Wadi al-Amboot	Gold-mining settlement/cemetery	Ptolemaic
Wadi al-'Alam	Cemetery	Late Roman
Double built up road segment	Part of road	Unknown
Wadi Hateem	Settlement	Ptolemaic–early Roman
Umm Arba'een	Several settlements	Late Roman–Islamic
Sukkari	Gold-mining settlement on/near road	Ptolemaic-Roman-Islamic
Umm Mureer	Christian settlement off road	Late Roman
Abu Greiya in Wadi Umm Kharega	Gold-mining settlement on/near road	Ptolemaic
*Sheikh Salem	Road station	Ptolemaic–early Roman
Rod Umm al-Farraj	Road station/animal tethering lines	Ptolemaic–early Roman
Rod al-Buram	Road station/animal tethering lines	Late Classical-Hellenistic-early Roman (?)
Bezah West	Road station/animal tethering lines	Unknown

Site Name	Type of Site	Pottery and Other Dates
Barramiya	Praesidium/gold mines on road	Ptolemaic–early Roman
Bir 'Iayyan	Road station	Ptolemaic
Abu Rahal	Road station	Ptolemaic-early Roman-Islamic
Abu Rahal West	Road station	Ptolemaic-early Roman
al-Kanaïs (Hydreuma to epi tou Paneiou)	Fort/related features	Pharaonic-Ptolemaic-early Roman
'Abbad	Forts	Ptolemaic-early Roman-late Roman
Apollonopolis Magna (Edfu)	Nile emporium	Pharaonic-Ptolemaic-Roman-modern

Berenike–Koptos Road

Site Name	Type of Site	Pottery and Other Dates
Berenike	Red Sea port	3rd century B.C.E.–6th century C.E.
Siket	Praesidium/well off road	1st–3rd century C.E.
Wadi Abu Greiya (Vetus Hydreuma)	Five praesidia	Ptolemaic, early-late Roman
Bint Abu Greiya	Cemetery near road	4th–5th century C.E.
Wadi Lahma	Praesidium off road	Ptolemaic, 1st–2nd and 4th (?) centuries C.E.
Wadi Qabr Rijm/Shea'leq/Mkbea'/Abu Ghurban	Tombs/road stop (?)	Early Roman and 5th century C.E.
Mweillah	Gold-mining settlement off road	Ptolemaic-early Roman (?)
Wadi Khashir (Novum Hydreuma)	Stop on road/hafr	Unknown, probably Roman
Abu Ghalqa	Praesidium	5th–6th century C.E.
Abu Ghusun (Cabalsi)	Praesidium	Late 4th–5th century C.E.
Abu Hegilig South	Praesidium	Early Roman, some late Roman
Abu Hegilig North	Praesidium	Late 4th–5th century C.E.
Wadi Duba'	Beryl/emerald-mining settlement off road	Late 1st century B.C.E.–early 1st century C.E.
Wadi Gemal East	Road station	2nd–4th century C.E.
Wadi Gemal (Apollonos)	Praesidium	1st–6th/7th (?) century C.E.

Berenike–Koptos Road (*continued*)

Site Name	Type of Site	Pottery and Other Dates
Between Wadi Gemal and Gelli	Cemetery	Early and late Roman
Kab Marfu'a/Wadi Gemal North	Beryl/emerald-processing settlement (?)	2nd–5th century C.E.
Kab Marfu'a East	Beryl/emerald processing settlement (?)	2nd–5th century C.E.
Sikait, Middle Sikait, North Sikait, Wadi Umm Harba	Beryl/emerald-processing settlements off road	1st–6th century C.E.—Islamic (perhaps Ptolemaic)
Umm Heiran	Christian settlement off road	Late Roman
Nugrus. Nugrus West, Abu Rushaid (Nugrus North)	Beryl/emerald-mining settlements off road, possible Christian settlement	Early-late Roman
Hilan	Station near road	Early and late Roman
Umm Gariya/Umm Ushra	*Praesidium*	Early Roman
Umm Kebash	Road stop	1st–4th/5th century C.E.
al-Dweig (Falacro ?)	*Praesidium*	Early Roman
Sha'it/Shay'iet	Stop on road	Unknown
Gerf (Aristonis)	*Praesidium*	1st–2nd and 5th–6th/7th (?) centuries C.E.
Rod Legaya	Stop on road	Early Roman (?)
Rod al-Buram	Road station/animal tethering lines	Classical-Hellenistic-early Roman (?)
Bezah	*Praesidium*	1st–2nd and 5th–6th centuries C.E.
Abu Greiya (Jovis/Dios)	*Praesidium*	1st–4th century C.E.
Gebel Rokham/Atafla	Marble quarry	Roman-modern
Daghbag South	*Praesidium*	Early Roman (?)
Daghbag (Compasi?)	*Praesidium*	1st century B.C.E.–early Roman
Khawr al-Jir (Aphrodito)	*Praesidium*	1st–2nd and 5th centuries C.E.
Wadi Menih/Menih al-Heir	Rock shelter with graffiti/petroglyphs	Upper Paleolithic-modern (much Roman)
Menih al-Heir South/Bir Menih	Christian settlement (?)	5th–6th century C.E. settlement (rock drawings = Pharaonic and later)
Bawab	De facto road stop/graffiti	Pharaonic-Roman
Wadi Hima	Stop on road	Uncertain

Site name	Type of Site	Pottery and Other Dates
Khashm al-Menih/Zeydun (Didymoi/Dios)	*Praesidium*	1st–4th and 5th–6th/7th (?) centuries C.E./Mamluk
*Laqeita (Phoenicon)	*Praesidium*/wells	1st century C.E. at least and late Roman
al-Matula	*Praesidium*	1st–2nd and 5th centuries C.E. or later
Koptos (Quft)	Nile emporium	Pharaonic-Roman-modern

Berenike–Apollonopolis Magna Road

Site name	Type of Site	Pottery and Other Dates
al-Dweig (Falacro)**	*Praesidium*	Early Roman
Seyhrig	Fort on road	Ptolemaic–early Roman and Islamic
Hamesh	Gold-mining settlement near road	Early Roman?
Sibrit	Gold-mining settlement	Unknown
Rod al-Legah	Fort on road	Ptolemaic–early Roman
Umm Garahish	Gold mines/road stop	Ptolemaic
Rod al-Gamra	Hard stone quarry	30th Dynasty–Ptolemaic and early Roman
Samut	Fort/settlement on road	Ptolemaic–early Roman
Samut North	Gold-mining settlement	4th–3rd century B.C.E.
Dunqash	Gold-mining settlement	Earlier dynastic and Roman-Byzantine
Elevated road segment	Part of road	Unknown, probably Ptolemaic
Abu Midrik	Fort on road	Ptolemaic
Abu Rahal	Road station	Ptolemaic–early Roman, Islamic
Abu Rahal West	Road station	Ptolemaic, early Roman
al-Kanaïs (Hydreuma to epi tou Paneiou)	Fort/related features	Ptolemaic, early Roman and earlier dynastic
'Abbad	Forts	Ptolemaic, early and late Roman
Edfu (Apollonopolis Magna)	Nile emporium	Pharaonic-modern

* Indicates feature that is no longer extant.

** Stops/sites are the same as the Berenike–Koptos road until ad-Dweig (Falacro) that these roads operated in the Ptolemaic and early Roman periods, though they may have followed earlier courses.

We have also surveyed hundreds of kilometers of other roads in the Eastern Desert that are not included in the tables in this chapter. Some of these are secondary routes leading to small quarries, such as the early Roman one connected to Mons Ophiates in the Wadis Umm Wikala and Semna,[18] discussed later, and trunk routes usually connecting one of the major thoroughfares noted earlier to nearby larger quarries; larger or smaller gold, amethyst, beryl/emerald, or other mines; or water sources. Our surveys have located a road running parallel to the coast south of Berenike; it seems to be an extension of the Via Nova Hadriana, but we have been unable to trace it for more than about 30 km due to lack of proper permits from Egyptian authorities. Where investigated, this route seems to have been in place at least by early Roman times, thereby predating the Via Nova Hadriana itself. From it several secondary routes proceeded westward to mines and other settlements. It may have been an inland branch of this road that eventually led to Abraq and, thence, over to the Nile at or near Syene.

Results of numerous desert surveys indicate that the ancient, especially the Roman, route system in the Eastern Desert was elaborate and sophisticated. It is also evident that additional survey work is necessary to understand better this transportation network. It would be important to know, for example, which and how many of these routes were official—that is, sanctioned and built by the military—and which were "built" by those with nonmilitary, mainly commercial or religious, interests in the region.

PHYSICAL APPEARANCE OF ROADS

Roman roads in the Eastern Desert were, like their predecessors, unpaved. This technique was not unique and was used in the construction of desert roads elsewhere in the Roman period—for example, in Egypt's Western Desert,[19] in Nubia,[20] and in Syria.[21] Roads in North Africa,[22] in Judaea,[23] and in some areas of Arabia[24] were also unpaved— what the Romans would have called *viae terrenae*.[25] There were financial and practical advantages to constructing unpaved roads in desert environments. Costs of building and maintaining such thoroughfares were substantially less than those of paved ones, and would have been largely unnecessary given the relatively firm surface, which was capable of supporting, in most cases, even heavy loads leaving the quarries for the Nile valley. Another consideration is the total unsuitability of paved road surfaces for camels. The slightest amount of sand on paved surfaces creates highly hazardous walking conditions for camels, because the animals' feet easily slip from under them in such circumstances.[26] Rare stretches of surviving pavement seem to have been laid down by modern European (mainly British)-Egyptian mining and quarrying interests in the first half of the twentieth century to facilitate motor transport to and from the areas. Examples of this paving, which comprises smaller stones or cobbles closely set together to provide traction where vehicles might become bogged down in deep sand, were visible at Mons

FIGURE 8-2
Eastern Desert, segment of the Via Nova Hadriana near Antinoopolis. Photo by S. E. Sidebotham.

Porphyrites and also at two places at least along the ancient route between Mons Porphyrites, reopened briefly and sporadically after the Roman occupation, and the Nile at
Kainepolis/Maximianopolis (modern Qena).[27] In the mid 1980s stretches of paving could
still be seen at the base of the ramp in the Lykabettus quarry at Mons Porphyrites; unfortunately, those were destroyed or covered over by flash floods sometime before 1992.[28]
Other paved sections appear in sandy areas in Wadi al-Qattar and between Roman stations at al-Heita and al-'Aras,[29] on the Abu Sha'ar/Mons Porphyrites–Nile road.[30] Remains of a long and well-preserved segment, comprising smaller closely laid stones and
cobbles with curbing, join the Nile at or near Qena and lead to the modern Red Sea port
of Safaga.[31] At first glance this thoroughfare appears ancient, but a closer examination
reveals that it is not; an older Ma'aze guide indicated that the British constructed it sometime just before or during World War II.

  Because Roman highways and lesser tracks in the Eastern Desert were largely if not
totally unpaved and, therefore, would not have been obvious to many travelers using them,
authorities responsible for road construction and maintenance tended, in many instances,
to clear the desired courses of all surface detritus, which was then pushed off to the side,
forming windrows parallel to the route that acted as the road's boundaries. The cleared
surfaces, unhindered by stones and boulders, allowed a faster journey and also readily
identified the roads' courses for travelers. Even today these cleared sections and accompanying windrows are obvious in many places (figure 8-2).[32]

  A very notable feature of many windrows is their relative evenness in size and regularity of appearance for long stretches. This suggests that they were formed not by hand,
or at least not solely by hand, but by some kind of mechanical device. There is no ancient

inscription or other written or archaeological source that discusses how these roads were created. In lieu of this, the following hypothesis may supply the answer. A plausible explanation for the uniformity of size and shape of long segments of windrows is that builders used some kind of road grader. Perhaps this was nothing more than one or more long pieces of relatively heavy timber beams hitched to draft animals and pulled along at an angle that resulted in pushing the light surface debris to the road's edge to form the windrows. In other words, one can envisage something resembling the ancient equivalent of a light bulldozer. We will probably never know whether these hypothetical Roman bulldozers were the sole means used to create the windrows or were supplementary, evening out the more labor-intensive piling of debris by hand.

These major Eastern Desert roads could be relatively modest in width, from just a few meters to an impressive 46.5 m wide. The latter was attained in a stretch of the Via Nova Hadriana north of Wadi Sharm al-Bakary.[33] Our survey found an even more impressive segment on a trunk road leading from Mons Porphyrites past the small fort in Wadi Belih, which then went onward to the Nile; it measures 53 m wide.[34] Traces of windrows are evident for long stretches between Berenike and Vetus Hydreuma, in Wadi Abu Greiya, about 25 km northwest of the port. Despite recent military maneuvers with tracked vehicles in the region of Berenike, there are segments of the telltale Roman windrow road that we have found and studied. These surviving traces, visible through the late 1990s, varied greatly in width, from about 5.1 to 32.3 m, with wider portions nearer Berenike and narrower ones in the vicinity of Vetus Hydreuma.[35] Cairns and graves, either of the road's builders or travelers or both, appear along the margins; some cairns lie well beyond the windrows. The road does not actually go to the lower wadi forts at Vetus Hydreuma (figure 8-3), but passes about 1,250 m northeast of them[36] and continues on past a late Roman cemetery at Bint Abu Greiya.[37] The route then proceeds to the next significant Roman stop on the road at Novum Hydreuma in Wadi Khashir, about 15 km northwest of Vetus Hydreuma. Here no *praesidium* or other buildings survive; instead there is a feature resembling a *hafir* (see chapter 7).

It is not clear why there were substantial variations in widths of the same highway and why greater widths would be necessary, considering that traffic consisted primarily of human pedestrians, and transport and baggage animals. Many route segments in the Eastern Desert were generally wider than their better-known paved counterparts in Roman Italy.[38] There is little evidence for the use of wheeled conveyances in the Eastern Desert; what evidence there is has been found on roads leading primarily from hard-stone quarries, together with traces of the passage of some smaller wagons and chariots along portions of the Myos Hormos–Nile road.[39] One can only speculate on the reasons for constructing such wide road segments. Perhaps work crews living in nearby camps tended to make wider roads to impress superiors, while more modest widths lay some distance from the road crews' camps—and their supervisors' scrutiny—and will have received, therefore, more desultory attention. Perhaps variations in widths indicate that different crews worked simultaneously on constructing the road in several places. Statius (*Silvae*

FIGURE 8-3
Wadi Abu Greiya/Vetus Hydreuma, two forts in the wadi viewed from a third fort on the hill above.
Photo by S. E. Sidebotham.

4.3.49–55) reports that to have been the case in the construction of the Via Domitiana in Italy.[40] Where these telltale windrows survive, not washed away by desert floods or built over by modern asphalt highways or other structures, the courses of the ancient routes are easy to identify.

Not all Roman routes in the Eastern Desert, however, were constructed in this manner; surviving evidence indicates that other methods were used. When windrows are absent, tracing the roads is extremely difficult and can be accomplished only with diligence, using other ancient indicators and having a great deal of luck. Because some Eastern Desert routes crossed mountainous regions, those sections that were not well marked could easily lead unwary or inexperienced travelers astray, with potentially disastrous consequences. Ancient wayfarers may have had local guides; certainly route-marking monuments helped.

Frequently, small cairns built of piles of stones of varying sizes averaging about 0.55–0.70 m × 0.60–0.70 m in diameter, but usually rounded mounds in appearance, peppered the lengths of these routes, especially portions of the Via Nova Hadriana; the cairns were located just inside, atop, or outside windrows.[41] Some sections preserve only cairns and no windrows, in which cases the cairns clearly functioned as route-marking devices for travelers, though their original intent may have been different, as shall be examined later on. Alternatively, there are sections where there are windrows but no cairns.[42] In instances where there are cairns but no windrows or where cairns lie outside the windrows and seem, thereby, to be superfluous if their function was as road markers, there must be other explanations for their placement.

Perhaps the Roman road-building process in the Eastern Desert involved two phases. First, experienced road-building survey teams—elsewhere in the Roman world these were military engineers, and such was likely the case here, too,[43]—were dispatched to determine the general orientation of the proposed route. One might speculate that they marked their courses using cairns of piled stones. Follow-up crews were then free to place the road itself—frequently, but not invariably, the cleared surface with windrows—anywhere within the flanking lines of survey cairns. This might explain why cairns along some road sections lay parallel to, but well outside, the windrows. In instances where lines of cairns survive but there is no trace of windrows, it may be that, for whatever reason, the survey crews' work was never followed up by the actual road builders. Perhaps these instances indicate that the roads were never completely finished. Alternatively, building crews may have determined that portions of a route that the survey teams had staked out with cairns did not require additional attention and thereby saved a great deal of time, effort, and money by subsequently not creating windrows. Our surveys have found evidence of this latter phenomenon during investigations of the Via Nova Hadriana, whose construction began in the second century C.E. Whereas most sections of that road were cleared and preserve windrows, there is a portion between Berenike and Marsa Nakari where cairns survive but there are no windrows. The dearth of windrows may indicate that this stretch was never completed.

It is uncertain which Roman official was responsible for roads in the Eastern Desert. Ultimately it was probably the governor of Egypt, but some other, lower-ranking functionary must have had responsibility for building and maintaining them. Perhaps this was the *Praefectus Montis Berenicidis,* who was also responsible for controlling mines, quarries, and pearl fisheries.[44] It would have been logical for the official overseeing the mineral wealth of the area to have also controlled the roads, whose existence and maintenance would have been so critical to mining and quarrying operations and the movement of military and civilian traffic. This officeholder also appears in ostraka—often orders to the garrisons—excavated from *praesidia* along the Myos Hormos–Koptos road.[45] There has been some debate about where the *Praefectus Montis Berenicidis*—the individual names of at least eighteen of these men are known[46]—might have been posted; Berenike is the most likely location.[47]

SIGNAL-WATCH TOWERS

Some highways, especially in the Roman period, also had signal towers (Greek *skopelos/* plural *skopeloi*).[48] Some bore individual names; one called Isideion/Ision is known, as is

FIGURE 8-4

Myos Hormos–Koptos road, one of the watchtowers *(skopeloi)*. Photo by S. E. Sidebotham.

another, called Ebeion/Ibis, though it is not certain that these were along any of the desert roads; perhaps they lay closer to the Nile.[49] *Skopeloi* are especially evident along the Myos Hormos–Koptos road.[50] Along that route carefully built square-shaped towers—about 3–3.5 m on a side, approximately 2–3 m high, and tapering slightly toward the summit—were made of local fieldstones and were solid, with a slight wall around the top (figure 8-4).[51] Some *skopeloi* examined near Myos Hormos were much smaller—about 1.5 m on a side at the base—whereas others, such as Qasr Hadie, north of Myos Hormos, were much larger.[52] Groups of men sent out in rotation from nearby *praesidia* probably garrisoned the towers, frequently in teams of two or four;[53] where preserved in ancient documents, personal names suggest that these *skopelarioi* (tower guards/lookouts) were often Egyptians.[54] Ostraka from *praesidia* along the Myos Hormos–Nile road, however, indicate that "regulars" served as well.[55] As needed or per some prearranged schedule, at least one of the *skopelarioi* probably climbed a ladder up the tower to send or receive messages. Surveys have identified sixty-five to seventy towers along the Myos Hormos–Nile road; each is intervisible with another or with a *praesidium* immediately to its east or west.[56] Towers appear atop hills and mountains, part way up their sides, or in the bottoms of wadis near where the road passes.

There is evidence that in other parts of the empire, especially in northern Europe, Roman watch and signal towers used flame and smoke, some of the latter of different colors, to send messages.[57] A papyrus from the third century B.C.E. references signal fires, no doubt along the Nile, possibly in watchtowers.[58] Yet, there is no evidence of burning inside *skopeloi* in the Eastern Desert.[59] This suggests that fire and smoke were probably not used for signaling, fuel being scarce in the desert in any case, although a fire pot could have been carried up into the *skopeloi,* which would have left few or no burn marks on the interior faces of surrounding walls.[60] Alternately, torches may have been used, which would have left no burn marks inside the towers; Polybius (*Histories* 10.45.6–47.4) refers to signal torches.[61] Climatic conditions could have affected signaling. Smoke and flames can be obscured or their visibility neutralized by bright sunlight, winds, and windborne sand, all of which are common occurrences in the desert, and are additional arguments against their use in this region.[62] There are ancient literary references to daylight signals using shields moving up and down or possibly other types of reflective surfaces.[63] Given the dearth of evidence indicating the use of smoke or fire, it is more likely that prearranged signals employing brightly colored flags or highly polished metal surfaces, such as mirrors, were employed.[64] A parallel for the use of signal flags comes from the western frontier areas of Han China in periods contemporary with the Roman Empire.[65] Messenger pigeons were likely used as well on occasion.[66]

As shown by the development of an early nineteenth-century British signal-flag system first used by the Royal Navy during the Napoleonic Wars, a surprising variety of messages can be sent over several kilometers, if visibility is good, by using relatively few flags of different colors, shapes, and sizes, arranged in various orders.[67] The Romans may have had a similar, but far simpler, system for using signal flags.[68] Vegetius (*Epitome of Military Science* 3.5) indicates that beams hung on *skopeloi* could be raised and lowered to send prearranged signals.[69] Whatever methods they used, alarms or warnings of trouble could be quickly conveyed or the movement of travelers and their caravans more carefully monitored. We estimate that, by using this system, a simple prearranged signal could be sent between Myos Hormos and Koptos, a distance of about 180 km, probably, under optimal conditions, in just a few hours, certainly in less than a day.[70] It has been estimated that it took a cavalryman about two or three hours to cover the distance between stations on the Myos Hormos–Nile road; riding continuously and changing horses occasionally, a rider could make the trip between Myos Hormos and Koptos in about twenty-four hours.[71] Most signals sent and received were probably local in nature, communicated among several towers and *praesidia,* and were not regularly relayed along the entire length of the road between the Red Sea coast and the Nile. Signals might give an alert of approaching caravans; of dangers, including the appearance of marauders; of the need for help or supplies such as water; and a host of other transmissions. Likely not all messages were "official," and the occasional "unofficial" communication might also have been sent. Ostraka recently excavated at Krokodilô on the Myos Hormos–Nile road indicate that troops used passwords as part of their security precautions.[72]

Little or nothing at the towers themselves allows dating of their construction and use to the Roman period aside from the discovery of a few Roman-era potsherds. Yet, they were clearly interdependent and, in some instances, intervisible with *praesidia* along the route, which are mostly early Roman in date, indicating by association that these signal platforms were also used, if not originally built, at that time. An earlier survey suggested that some towers might have been Ptolemaic constructions, but if so, these were likely remodeled in Roman times.[73] As noted earlier, and as will be discussed later, there is evidence for Ptolemaic use of the road, and there are cairns, less likely towers, of similar design, though of smaller size, on portions of the Berenike–Apollonopolis Magna road that are likely Ptolemaic.[74] Thus, the date of original construction of at least some towers on the Myos Hormos–Nile road may have been Ptolemaic. Excavations indicate that most *praesidia* were built and occupied in the first and second centuries c.e., with one, at Qasr al-Banat, also active in the late second/early third century c.e.[75] The *praesidium* at Krokodilô had at least three occupation phases; in its latest manifestation it probably provided logistical support and communications between the Nile and gold-mining operations conducted at Bir Umm Fawakhir in the fifth and sixth centuries c.e.[76]

There is some indication of Ptolemaic—and perhaps early Roman—activity along or near the Myos Hormos–Nile road that includes graffiti in Wadi Hammamat written in Demotic,[77] a hieroglyphic text inscribed on a pillar from the Min temple in Wadi Umm Fawahkir from the reign of Ptolemy III (246–221 b.c.e.),[78] a surface find of a Ptolemaic bronze coin from the *praesidium* of Maximianon,[79] and some graffiti in Greek from Abu Kuway of the third century b.c.e.[80] The *praesidium* at Bir Sayyala was called Simiou, perhaps derived from Simmias, a general sent by Ptolemy III to hunt elephants and reconnoiter the territory (Diodorus Siculus 3.18.4).[81] This may indicate Ptolemaic activity along the route. Excavations at Myos Hormos recovered Ptolemaic coins and pottery near the harbor,[82] suggesting that the Hellenistic settlement was either inundated by the sea or buried by sediments carried through the wadi. By Roman times Myos Hormos had been moved due to severe silting; an analogous situation occurred at Berenike.

Inscribed and decorated Ptolemaic, or possibly early Roman, temple blocks have been found at modern Quseir.[83] Yet, little of Ptolemaic date has been recorded from the excavations at forts along the road to the Nile. Thus, although it is possible that some watchtowers were originally erected in the Ptolemaic period, in their latest manifestation they seem to be Roman. They may have also been used later, when Myos Hormos revived as a port in the Ayyubid and Mamluk period (late eleventh/early twelfth to fifteenth centuries).[84] Towers along the highway may have continued in use when the newer port at Quseir, 6–8 km south of Myos Hormos, served as an embarkation and disembarkation point for hajjis performing their religious pilgrimage to Mecca, via Jeddah on the Red Sea coast of Saudi Arabia,[85] beginning in the fifteenth or sixteenth century.[86] Pilgrims crossing the desert between Quseir and the Nile valley, and those protecting them, may have used some of these towers. There is evidence that passing Muslim caravans used at least the Roman *praesidium* at Bir al-Hammamat, where remains of a mosque appear in the southeastern corner of the fort.[87] In the post-Roman period there seems to have been no interest in other *praesidia* along the route, since there is no evidence of Islamic occupation at these other installations.

Our surveys noted ancient signal towers on other desert roads—for instance, a few along the Berenike-Nile and the Abu Sha'ar/Mons Porphyrites-Nile routes, and along the Via Nova Hadriana near Myos Hormos—but they are few and far between.[88] Why the Myos Hormos–Nile road had such an extensive signal-tower system, one that survives in a remarkable state of preservation, while other equally important routes in the Roman period did not remains an enigma.

BUILT-UP ROAD SECTIONS AND RAMPS

Other features, though rare, along several of the Eastern Desert routes are built-up road sections and ramps. These also occur on Roman roads in Judaea/Palestine.[89] Well crafted and made of piled-up stones of various sizes and sand, these segments in Egypt's Eastern Desert often bridge narrow wadis; the ramps allow routes more gradual ascents from and descents to areas of vastly different elevations. Such ramped and elevated avenues served a dual purpose: adding another feature to mark the route, and facilitating passage over difficult terrain. Our surveys have found only a few of these on major roads. Two appear along the Via Nova Hadriana. One in the Wadi 'Ibada, not far from Antinoopolis, measures about 85 m long and directs the road around the northern edge of a steep section of the wadi.[90] The other, about 60–70 m long and 4.3–5.1 m wide, lies east of a small road station in Tal'at al-Arta and connects high ground on the east down to a wadi floor in the west.[91] We investigated another elevated road segment along the Berenike–Apollonopolis Magna road between Samut and Abu Midrik. Since both these installations were Ptolemaic, the road segment likely dates from that era as well.[92] Another road segment, possibly unique, is a double built-up one on the Marsa Nakari–Apollonopolis Magna road; this appears between Wadi al-'Alam and Wadi Hateem (figure 8-5).[93] The upper section measures at least 17.1 m long and may have been up to 41.1 m in length, but that is difficult to determine due to soil overburden. The lower section is 42.8 m long. Overall width of the two is 6.5 m. The upper preserves a built-up height of about 0.80 m, while the lower is approximately 1 m high. We do not know why a double construction was required, unless traffic was so substantial that these "causeways" handled human pedestrians and baggage animals going in opposite directions simultaneously. Perhaps they represent a reorientation of the road.

Several massive ramps or slipways survive at Mons Porphyrites. One is approximately 1,700 m long and joins nearby Wadi Ma'amal with the Lykabettus quarries.[94] Other, less impressive ramps lead to the Lepsius quarries[95] and the North-west quarries.[96] Another substantial ramp providing access from the wadi floor to the emerald-mining areas above

FIGURE 8-5

Marsa Nakari (Nechesia?)–Apollonopolis Magna (Edfu) road, double built-up road sections.
Photo by S. E. Sidebotham.

survives in Middle Sikait. Here an approximately 1,600 m–long built-up roadway hugs the sides of the mountains.[97] Another ramp, in Wadi Umm Huweis, about 10 km south of Tiberiane, links the early Roman *praesidium* and quarry at Tiberiane to roads emanating from Mons Claudianus. It measures 54 m long and 2.7 m high.[98] Our surveys have noted, however, that built-up road segments, though more common, are usually much smaller along secondary routes that wind through more mountainous areas, especially in regions where there are mines and quarries. For example, we recently found one perched on a steep side of a mountain path linking the emerald-mining towns of Nugrus and Sikait (figures 8-6a and 8-6b).[99] It was along this same route, and quite close to this latter built-up road section, that we found remains of a bridgelike structure across the midsection of a seasonal waterfall.[100] Along with these built-up road segments, one also occasionally finds that narrow passes through mountainous areas have been artificially widened by hacking or quarrying away stone, or creating steps cut into bedrock—such as we noted, for example, on the route leading to the late Roman settlement at Shenshef 21.3 km south-southwest of Berenike,[101] and joining the beryl/emerald mining center in Wadi Umm Harba to settlements in Wadi Sikait.[102] Sometimes builders supplemented natural terrain with cut-stone blocks as steps, as can be seen opposite Hill Top Fort Number 5 at Wadi Abu Greiya/ancient Vetus Hydreuma, the first major stop on the Berenike–Nile road, about 25 km northwest of Berenike.[103]

FIGURES 8-6A AND 8-6B

So-called Administrative Building at the emerald-mining settlement of Sikait. Photos by S. E. Sidebotham.

Our surveys have also examined several road junctions where at least two highways of different orientations intersect.[104] The Romans referred to a road junction as a *caput viarum*. Our surveys have found junctions along all major roads. Often stops or stations at these junctions are larger and capable of accommodating greater numbers of visitors than other facilities along individual routes. Sometimes, however, the junctions of roads are not marked by any particularly noteworthy stop or station. The Via Nova Hadriana intersects all major highways (except those from Mons Claudianus and Mons Ophiates that head west to the Nile) listed in the table that appears earlier in this chapter. In some cases the crossroad is marked only by a normal-sized stop, such as that at Abu Sha'ar al-Qibli at the intersection with the Abu Sha'ar–Nile road; at other points—for example, close to where it joins the Berenike–Nile road near Vetus Hydreuma—there are five forts. The intersection of the Berenike–Apollonopolis Magna and Marsa Nakari–Apollonopolis Magna roads is near Abu Rahal/Abu Rahal West; neither stop is fortified or substantial, though somewhat farther west on the coterminal route is the *praesidium* at al-Kanaïs. The bifurcation point of the Berenike–Apollonopolis Magna and Berenike–Koptos roads may or may not be at al-Dweig (ancient Falacro?); it is certainly in the vicinity. The *praesidium* at al-Dweig is not that large; one would expect something more substantial at this convergence.

Given the extensive traffic that used Myos Hormos and Berenike in the early Roman period, one would expect the juncture of these two roads leading to Koptos at or near the stop at Laqeita (ancient Phoenicon) to have been sizable. The site today preserves no ancient remains, though there was a *praesidium* here at one time. Travelers visiting Laqeita in the late nineteenth and early twentieth centuries recorded some scant traces and noted two Roman-era inscriptions, one found in a cistern and the second recovered from a well; one dated to the reign of Claudius and the other to a Flavian emperor.[105] Today, in addition to wells, there are some dilapidated structures; the most prominent feature is the tomb of Sheikh Abdullah Sayed Ali. The point of intersection of the Via Nova Hadriana with the Marsa Nakari–Apollonopolis Magna road has never been precisely located; it does not appear to have been at Marsa Nakari, but some 3 or 4 km inland. These examples should indicate that the Romans did not invariably take particular care in marking the junctures of roads, at least in the Eastern Desert.

In one instance, two separate cleared sections of the Via Nova Hadriana climb up the northern side of Wadi Quei and join about 2 km north of the wadi; these may represent separate periods of the road, but this is uncertain.[106] There are also examples along the Via Nova Hadriana where it narrowed, widened, or altered course.[107]

LACK OF MILESTONES

An idiosyncrasy of Eastern Desert roads is the dearth of inscribed milestones. Other Roman provinces preserve milestones in large numbers, which are fairly uniform in appearance. They are usually columnar-shaped markers of stone approximately 2–2.5 m high, sometimes with a squarish base. These signposts were informative, appearing every Roman mile, which is 1,478.5 m (an English mile is 1,609 m).[108] Many were carved with letters highlighted in red paint; some were only painted and others reused. The latter were often recycled and plastered over with new texts painted in red. In numerous instances, especially in the eastern parts of the Roman Empire, milestones appear to be blank. Yet it is likely that these originally bore red paint, or plaster and paint, that have decayed over time.[109] Most that survive are frequently inscribed, often inscribed and painted or only painted, usually in red—with abbreviated texts detailing the reigning emperor and his titles, sometimes the provincial governor, and the distance to and occasionally from the nearest urban areas on the road.[110] They are usually written in Latin, though in the eastern portions of the empire from the mid second century c.e. and especially after Constantine I (reigned 306–337 c.e.), they also appear in Greek.[111] West of Palmyra bilingual Greek-Palmyrene milestones have been found.[112] After their conquest of the Middle East, Muslim Arabs continued to use milestones inscribed in Arabic along the Jaffa–Jerusalem[113] and Damascus–Jerusalem roads.[114] The Roman distance markers occur sometimes in bunches at points where frequent repavings were carried out during the reigns of several emperors and tenures of governors. Where they survive and have not been carried off for reuse in later structures or destroyed, they are important sources of information for dating road construction, use, and repair, and they also indicate which urban areas they linked together.

Thousands of milestones have been found throughout the Roman world. Unfortunately, in the Eastern Desert very few if any inscribed milestones have been identified. One or two possible milestones have turned up in Lower Egypt in and near the Nile Delta, and one or two probable milestones have been found in Nubia.[115] There are also shaped stones that seem to be milestones, probably of Roman date, found in the Western Desert north of Fayum; these may mark a route to Saqqara.[116] Anepigraphic columnar-shaped stones interspersed with occasional squared columns also appear along some roads in Nubia west of the Nile.[117] The reason for the absence of milestones, inscribed or otherwise, in the Eastern Desert is not clear, but this may have been a deliberate policy, which remains unknown to us, rather than an oversight. Whatever the cause, deprived of the important information these monuments provide for reconstructing the history of roads elsewhere in the empire, one can only estimate the ages of the Eastern Desert thoroughfares based upon dating the stations and other mining and quarrying settlements through or near which they passed. The absence of inscriptional milestones along local or regional routes whose courses have been damaged or washed away by infrequent but powerful flash floods over the centuries also deprives scholars of important information about which settlements they linked together and the ancient names of those communities.

Despite the lack of datable Eastern Desert milestones, the relatively pristine condition of many, and the probable survival of at least remnants of most, sites along the roads—sites that have not, in most instances, been altered by later Islamic or modern construction—

allow us to determine fairly confidently when these roads were used, if not precisely when and by whom they were made. In Roman times there was an increase in the number of installations over what had existed previously, and these facilities were generally also larger than their Ptolemaic predecessors. Sometimes the Romans continued to use earlier Ptolemaic-era installations, often enlarging them to accommodate the increased volume of traffic and larger garrisons that used them; for instance, this clearly happened at one of the lower forts at Vetus Hydreuma on the Berenike–Nile road.

On the other hand, there are examples (like Abu Midrik) where the Romans did not continue to use earlier Ptolemaic stations or stops on roads; these seem to have been completely abandoned before Roman times. The reasons for this remain unknown; perhaps local nomadic unrest, political turmoil along the Nile, or lower water tables contributed to abandonment of earlier stations or routes. A good example of this is the Berenike–Apollonopolis Magna road, a trip along which probably took eight or nine days.[118] Although this was the main Berenike–Nile avenue in the Ptolemaic period, our surveys indicate that sometime during the early Roman occupation of Egypt the Apollonopolis Magna branch was abandoned and a longer segment was exploited, extending from Berenike to Koptos, about 65 km farther north on the Nile from Apollonopolis Magna.[119] It was uncharacteristic of the practical Romans to opt for a longer route, especially in the desert, that would have demanded construction of new stations, the addition of new garrisons, and, consequently, greater expenses. The newer and longer route required a twelve-day trip between Koptos and Berenike according to Pliny the Elder (*NH* 6.26.103), and that was probably a fairly quick journey. Other sources, notably an anonymous late Roman/early Byzantine traveler, indicate a trip of thirteen days[120] or more. There must have been some important overriding circumstance that required all this effort. Unfortunately, we do not know what prompted the Roman decision to opt for the route from Berenike to Koptos instead of the shorter, previously used Ptolemaic one from Berenike to Apollonopolis Magna.

ANCIENT GRAVES

Ancient graves and burials of those who died while building, maintaining, or traveling along the roads can be found close to the routes or on hills lining them.[121] These ancient sepulchers supply information on use of the routes. Most graves occur singly or in small groups; occasionally they are found in larger numbers making up discernable cemeteries. Those burials that have been looted often preserve human bones and potsherds scattered close by, likely the broken remnants of grave goods—a practice continued by the indigenous 'Ababda Bedouin today. Rarely, as we found on the Via Nova Hadriana north of Berenike and west of Hammata, an ancient inscribed tombstone provides the name of the deceased—in this case, a Christian named Adidos from Pharan, a city in the Sinai, dating to sometime in the sixth century c.e.[122] Pottery shapes and fabrics allow identification, in many instances, of where the pottery originated. Thus, by examining the broken pots from travelers and from graves near the roads that passed by the stations, we learn, in addition to the dates of activities at the stations, what other areas of the ancient world were in touch directly or indirectly with these remote desert locales.

ROAD-BUILDING COSTS

Scholars have no idea of what it cost to build these desert highways. Much is known about road-building expenses and maintenance in other parts of the Roman Empire. Estimated construction costs reflect outlays for roads paved with large flat paving stones fitted together and laid atop well-prepared and elaborate foundations; they were nothing like the simple cleared desert tracks discussed here. High-quality paved roads cost approximately 500,000 sesterces (125,000 denarii) per Roman mile to build.[123] Evidence from milestones found elsewhere in the empire indicates that these same roads required repair once every twenty to forty years, but such maintenance costs were less, perhaps about 30,000 denarii per mile in Italy in the second century C.E.[124] A denarius was about a day and a half's pay for a Roman legionary throughout much of the first century C.E.[125] Though built by the military, upkeep expenses elsewhere in the empire were the responsibility of local communities through which roads passed.[126] Yet, it is uncertain who was responsible for repair of the Eastern Desert roads. They passed through or near few communities, and those would likely have been unable to provide the resources necessary for road maintenance. The responsibility of maintaining them and the associated *skopeloi* must have fallen on the Egyptian provincial government, which delegated this task to the military. Communities close to the Nile and the Red Sea may have been responsible for upkeep of nearby roads. Whether troops from *praesidia* along these roads occasionally engaged in route maintenance as part of their desert duties or whether civilians from the Nile valley were pressed into corvée service under military supervision remains a mystery, since there are no extant sources that deal with this issue. In any case, road upkeep in much of the Eastern Desert would have been relatively low cost.

DESERT PATROLS IN THE ROMAN PERIOD

Discussion of desert patrols must take into consideration the number and types of troops stationed in and adjacent to the region in the Roman period. Numbers fluctuated, with a peak likely sometime in the first half of the second century C.E., when activity at *praesidia* and quarries seems to have been at or near its zenith.[127] Of the eighty or so forts that have been identified mostly as Ptolemaic and Roman in the region east of the Nile, few have been excavated, and as a result, their more precise periods of use and the sizes of their garrisons can only be estimated. Desert garrisons were a mixture of legionaries sent out in smaller units from parent camps along the Nile[128] and auxiliary troops. This is evident from inscriptions found at Berenike and other settlements, and from quarries and some forts in the region; ostraka from Berenike, from quarries, and from some *praesidia* also refer to legionaries and auxiliary troops. These units have been well studied, and their movements into and out of the region are generally known, though not with precision in every case.[129]

Given our much greater knowledge about Roman than Ptolemaic military activity in the Eastern Desert, there is somewhat more information about Roman than about Ptolemaic military patrols (see chapter 3). Even in this peak time, however, evidence provides little insight into these endeavors. Patrols were likely dispatched from points along the Nile,[130] from Red Sea ports, and from garrisons along the roads. How far afield a patrol normally traveled, its size, mode of transport—horses or camels, most likely—type of armament, and time away from base are unknown or little understood. The contents of Roman-era inscriptions, papyri, and ostraka, together with some Talmudic sources, provide few answers, and most of these come from outside Egypt. Patrols may have been dispatched sporadically and as needed or deemed prudent rather than on a regular basis, especially if the general situation was one of relative tranquillity. These reconnoitering missions gleaned tactical rather than strategic intelligence.

It is doubtful whether these patrols comprised any more than two or three members and certainly not more than a dozen or so, since many of the smaller stations could not have afforded to send large portions of their garrisons away at any one time. Thus, patrols in the Eastern Desert were probably, in general, smaller than those dispatched in other, nondesert areas due to climate, terrain, and dearth of food and water. Additionally, given their scouting nature, large desert patrols would be more easily detected by potential enemies and would be more difficult to supply than smaller ones. It is doubtful that patrols were out for longer than a day or so due to dangers of detection and ambush by bandits or nomads. Decrease in levels of fighting ability due to climate and efforts to erect nighttime defenses would have quickly dulled a patrol's fighting edge.[131]

Nonmilitary travelers such as merchants and camel drivers likely provided the latest information on roads they had recently used. Good intelligence on desert activities would also have been available at markets in Red Sea ports and Nile emporia; the Byzantine manual *Peri Strategikes/De Re Strategica* (42.24–28), written sometime between 565 and 636 by Syrianos Magister,[132] emphasizes the importance of markets as sources of intelligence.[133]

A papyrus dated August 156 c.e. from Contrapollonopolis Magna, on the east bank of the Nile opposite Apollonopolis Magna, records a unit of the *Cohors I Augusta Praetoria Lusitanorum Equitata*. The roster includes 3 decurions, 6 centurions, 145 cavalry, 18 camel riders, and 363 infantry.[134] For practical purposes the infantry were limited to activities near the Nile—as were the cavalry, though to a lesser extent. The presence of 18 camel riders, however, suggests that this Nile garrison dispatched longer-range desert patrols as needed. Their small number, and the likelihood that not all 18 would have been sent on a single mission, suggest that if they were used for desert patrolling purposes, their numerical composition was probably not even a dozen. One assumes that if a patrol needed rapid reinforcement and was not too deep into the desert, the cavalry could be called upon.

Other ostraka indicate the presence of at least one Roman army unit near Thebes.[135] Paleographically these ostraka belong to the second century c.e. It is evident, in this instance, that the Roman military used the local population to conduct desert patrols, per-haps because they had more knowledge of the terrain and the local problems,[136] and had a more vested interest in protecting their own communities; their use also saved money by not employing Roman troops or auxiliaries for this task. Other evidence indicates the use of Egyptians rather than troops from regular military units for various tasks. Part of the wider definition of desert patrols may have included postings to signal towers (skopeloi), especially on the Myos Hormos–Nile road. Ostraka dealing with military gar-risons in the Eastern Desert, including ostraka recently excavated at Krokodilô, suggest that groups of two or four men were sent out to these towers from nearby praesidia.[137] Many of these individuals seem to have been Egyptian. In the Tetrarchic period the Luxor temple complex housed the Legio III Diocletiana,[138] which sent a vexillation of mounted troops (cavalry or dromedary) to garrison the fort at Abu Sha'ar (figure 8-7);[139] troops from this Nile base may also have been sent on rotational duty to other Eastern Desert installations or on patrol duties at that time.

Patrols composed of military personnel are rarely, if ever, mentioned in ancient sources. The twenty-four hundred or so ostraka excavated from praesidia along the Myos Hormos–Koptos road say virtually nothing about patrols. An ostrakon from Krokodilô suggests that a reconnaissance patrol consisted of only two men.[140] A mid-second-century c.e. ostrakon from Mons Claudianus mentions one man sending another man food "with the patrol [caravan or detachment]."[141] He uses the Greek word probole, which might refer to either a formally or informally organized military or nonmilitary group. The term appears in several Mons Claudianus ostraka, all from the second century c.e.[142] Their contexts tell us nothing, unfortunately, about the status or size of these "patrols."

Official mail and orders traveled between stations accompanied by a single mounted escort or courier, presumably with the escort proceeding only as far as the next station, at which point the mail continuing on was carried by another soldier from there in a re-lay fashion until the message reached its destination.[143] Ostraka excavated from praesidia on the Myos Hormos–Nile road indicate that mounted couriers used horses,[144] though ostraka indicate that there were constant problems keeping horses in these desert out-posts.[145] Ostraka alluding to messengers may refer to a military transport service[146] rather than the Roman postal service.[147] How closely modeled the Eastern Desert system was on the "official" Roman one seen elsewhere in the empire is uncertain; it may have imi-tated the Persian or Ptolemaic communication and postal networks.[148]

Ostraka indicate that military escorts of one or two cavalrymen accompanied com-mercial caravans.[149] Providing armed escorts was common practice in other arid domains. For example, in the desert between Palmyra and the Euphrates civic-minded, prominent, and wealthy Palmyrene citizens undertook the obligation at their own expense and were, subsequently, honored with inscriptions and statues along the main colonnaded street of that city; some also promoted Palmyrene financial interests in other ways.[150] There were caravans of different status, of course. One should probably assume that civilian entre-preneurs traveling between the Nile and a Red Sea port paid extra for military security,

Late Roman fort at Abu Sha'ar, overall view of the interior, looking northwest. Photo by S. E.Sidebotham.

as indicated in the ostraka noted earlier. Perhaps some expenses are also represented on the Koptos Tariff.[151] Garrisons along the Myos Hormos–Nile road, and we presume by analogy along other desert highways as well, dispatched patrols and provided security to civilian caravans; there is no indication that desert *praesidia* were customs posts.[152] "Official" caravans—for example, those conveying gold or precious stones from the desert to the Nile or those supplying the *praesidia*—must have also received military escorts, if not regularly, then on an ad hoc basis. It is unlikely that additional private "security" guards" were hired, because Roman officials would have been very reluctant to allow Egyptian civilians, especially from the Nile valley of Upper Egypt, to carry arms.

In view of the dearth of military-related documents dealing with patrols in the proper sense of the term, one wonders whether their frequency was in direct proportion to the perceived threat or to the number of travelers and caravans passing along the roads at any given time, and whether we have simply not excavated any documents dealing with this issue. Or perhaps patrols were sent out on a regular basis regardless of conditions. If military escorts for commercial convoys were dispatched primarily from termini on either the Nile or the Red Sea, it may explain why so few documents dealing with this subject have been found in excavations at desert sites.[153] If this was the case, any record of them would, naturally, be found more frequently either at the Nile or Red Sea emporia.

Possible support for this latter hypothesis comes from the early third century c.e. There are two inscriptions, one from Koptos and the other from Berenike. Both are written in Greek and list auxiliary troops from Palmyra; this suggests that they patrolled between the Nile and the Red Sea coast at least in 215/216 C.E.[154] A third inscription—a bilingual Palmyrene-Greek religious dedication made by troops and also found at Berenike— although undated, appears to have been carved between about 180 and 212 C.E.[155] It would have been sensible for Roman authorities to use troops who had an intimate knowledge of how to live and operate in a desert, and the Palmyrenes, probably archers riding camels, would have been ideal for this purpose.[156] Numerous Palmyrenes lived and worked in Koptos and some at Denderah (ancient Tentyris), as finds of dedicatory inscriptions and tombstones indicate.[157] Palmyrenes had engaged in these activities between their own city and the Euphrates River and points beyond for some time, as we discussed earlier (see also chapter 11).[158] Their city honored them with celebratory inscriptions and statues placed along the colonnaded streets of Palmrya.[159] Grateful merchants at Tentyris made a similar dedication to a Palmyrene named Julius Aurelius, son of Makkaios, for escorting their caravan across the Eastern Desert.[160] Clearly, Palmyrene desert experience was highly valued not only by civilian merchants but also by the Roman military.

The Nabataean Arabs also had desert experience. However, none of the eighty-five or so graffiti written in Nabataean and found in the Eastern Desert, mostly dating between 110 and 266 C.E., indicates that the dedicants were soldiers or had security-related professions; those few designating occupation record a camel driver, a plasterer, a priest, and a patcher of clothes.[161] Nor have inscriptions been found at the Nile or Red Sea emporia stipulating that Nabataeans served in security-related capacities. Nevertheless, both the Palmyrenes and Nabataeans had commercial interests in Egypt, and both are first mentioned in texts there as early as the late first century B.C.E. (see chapter 11).[162]

One early Roman inscription in Latin describes men from a unit stationed in Egypt sometime in the first century C.E. They built and dedicated installations at Apollonos Hydreuma, at Compasi, at Berenike, and at Myos Hormos.[163] Forts are known from desert sites now identified with Apollonos Hydreuma (likely in Wadi Gemal) and Compasi (probably in Wadi Daghbag), but none are evident at the Red Sea cities of Berenike or Myos Hormos themselves unless the inscription refers to forts "near" those emporia by the monikers of the ports themselves. The date for this text has been debated for years, but it is likely from later in the first century,[164] probably reflecting that period between the Flavians and the reigns of Trajan and Hadrian when many *praesidia* along the Berenike– Koptos and Myos Hormos–Koptos roads were built or refurbished. Other Flavian inscriptions in Latin have been found in three *praesidia* near or along the Berenike–Koptos road (at Siket, Aphrodito, and Didymoi) indicating construction or repair of those facilities by the military.[165] Fragments of another Flavian inscription were found at Laqeita (ancient Phoenicon)[166] and, most recently, at the quarry fort at Domitiane/Kaine Latomia near Mons Porphyrites.[167] Fragments of one or more Trajanic inscriptions have been recorded at the large *praesidium* in Wadi Kalalat near Berenike[168] and at Jovis/Dios on the Berenike–Koptos road.[169] Clearly, this was an era of considerable construction and repair of forts and other desert infrastructure. Troops building or repairing facilities in desert regions probably also patrolled at least areas immediately near their construction activities if not farther afield; these would, however, have been secondary missions and normally would not have been deemed worthy of record in any inscriptions.

There are examples of individual soldiers or groups being detached and sent to other garrisons for varying lengths of time both in Egypt and elsewhere, but these instances should be viewed more as examples of what the U.S. military would term TDY (temporary duty) rather than patrols.[170] It is likely, therefore, that the soldiers who recorded their repair and refurbishment of several Eastern Desert *praesidia,* noted previously, in early Roman times were probably on a TDY assignment rather than on patrol.[171]

The few camels noted in ostraka found in excavations along the Myos Hormos–Koptos road seem to have been associated with commercial caravans passing between the Nile and the Red Sea rather than with military activities.[172] This supposition is reinforced by the mid-second–century C.E. "Muziris" papyrus (see chapter 11), which records the transport of almost 7 million drachmas' worth of cargo from Muziris in India to one of Egypt's Red Sea ports and then by camel across to the Nile for transport downriver to Alexandria.[173] Camels also carried urgent messages that had to cross between the Nile and a Red Sea port as quickly as possible.[174] A Trajanic-era ostrakon recently excavated from Domitiane/Kaine Latomia attests a Roman military *dromadarius.*[175] A military camel squadron was stationed at Elephantine (near Aswan) in the mid 290s C.E.[176] Though the date of its introduction to Egypt is debated,[177] the domesticated camel certainly was in common use by Roman times.

Chapter 7 examined the distances and speeds that camels can travel.[178] Nineteenth- and twentieth-century visitors to the Arabian Peninsula recorded their travel times by camel, and it is evident that speeds and distances varied significantly depending upon a multitude of factors. These would include age, type, and health of the camel, the weight of its load and distance covered/length of journey, temperatures, nature of the terrain traversed, amount of rest, food, and water the animal consumed, and so on.[179]

In addition to covering great distances, camels can also carry loads of varying sizes depending upon a number of circumstances. The convex back of the camel allows it to carry heavier loads than a horse can, but it is limited by the weight it can rise with (since it is loaded while resting on the ground). If the load is too heavy a camel cannot rise on its hindquarters. Once its hindquarters are up, however, it will always get up on its front legs.[180] Chapter 7 noted average and exceptional loads borne by dromedaries under various conditions.[181] Military and police regulations for British, French, and Italian forces in northern and eastern Africa in the late nineteenth and early twentieth centuries indicate maximum loads of between 120 and 220 kg per animal;[182] indigenous owners lacking weighing instruments regularly expect a camel to carry in excess of 300 kg for approximately 32–40 km per day for extended periods.[183] Using these statistics, one could realistically project that camels in caravans of the Roman period crossing the Eastern Desert probably worked under similar conditions.

Given these statistics, one would expect that distances between *hydreumata* and *praesidia* along the Eastern Desert roads were about a day's march for a camel. Yet, as the table in this chapter indicates, this was often not the case. Sometimes stations, stops, *praesidia,* and *hydreumata* built and controlled by the military were quite far apart (unless remains of an intermediate station or stop have disappeared totally or have eluded identification); occasionally they were extremely close together. This suggests that their placement took into account more than an average day's march for a laden camel or moderate-sized caravan. Considerations of available and accessible water supplies, optimal placement of fortifications to protect those supplies, and best location with regard to communications—visual/nonverbal as well as written or orally transmitted messages carried by couriers—were paramount in the location of *praesidia* and unfortified stops. Terrain also dictated placement, with closer spacing in more-difficult-to-negotiate mountainous regions and more distant spacing in areas with relatively flat topography. It is evident from the discovery of ad hoc unofficial stops along several roads—the one at Umm Kebash on the Berenike–Nile roads being especially noteworthy—that placement of *praesidia* was not necessarily convenient for all travelers. All that marks Umm Kebash as a regularly used but unofficial stop/campground is the concentration of sherds covering hundreds of meters spanning the first to fourth or fifth century c.e.

ANCIENT MAPS AND GUIDES

All this civilian and military activity suggests a fairly constant flow of traffic along at least the major routes between the Nile and the Red Sea coast and certainly to those mines and quarries, usually larger ones, deemed important or profitable. The latter would certainly have warranted military protection. Aside from use of local guides, who might not have always been willing or available, or marking of routes with windrows or cairns or both, which was not always the case, there were other navigational aides that the tyro desert traveler could use. Voyagers could not rely on milestones, as has already been shown.

There were maps and itineraries listing stops along roads throughout the empire, and these also existed for sections of the Eastern Desert and the Red Sea coast. Yet, one wonders how the traveler could relate his map to distances between stations without the assistance of milestones. It is not clear how accessible these maps and itineraries were to the average traveler, or their cost. Their usefulness was limited, although they would have provided a sense of security to those who were more fearful of the uncertainties facing them. Some maps were very schematic, identifying major topographical and geographical features, but not with precision. Maps more closely resembled sketches indicating general locations of major *praesidia* along the roads.[184] There were no scales of distances, so travelers bereft of any other sources of information, such as milestones, could not determine from the maps themselves the distances and times they had to travel from one point to the next;[185] travel conditions were nowhere listed. Many of these maps may simply be indicators of trade and travel through these regions rather than tools useful to the travelers per se. Sets of earlier Roman maps or lists of stops along major roads, of which only late antique or medieval copies survive, are good illustrations, especially for routes between Berenike and Koptos.[186] The Roman army could also make maps at times, as needed.[187]

Lists of Eastern Desert road stations from the early Roman period, such as those of Strabo (*Geography* 17.1.45) or Pliny the Elder (*NH* 6.26.102–103), would have been of limited use and only for those traveling to Myos Hormos and Berenike, although Pliny's encyclopedia does provide distances between stations on the Berenike–Koptos road in terms of Roman miles: 257. A Roman mile is 1,478.5 m.[188] Thus the distance in Pliny's calculations is about 380 km; it took twelve days to make the trip one way according to Pliny. When one travels along the "road," as we have done many times, there are a number of locations where alternate local routes might be used, thereby changing both distance and travel time; for example, a late Roman/early Byzantine–era graffito found along the road in a small grotto notes that the trip took thirteen days.[189] Thus, any ancient records of distances and times needed to make a journey were only approximations.

Other sources include the *Periplus*,[190] which was useful for maritime travelers and traders but not desert wayfarers. It records distances, local topographical and political conditions, and items traded, but it appears not to have included any maps.[191] Claudius Ptolemy's *Geography* was the most detailed in terms of locating prominent manmade and natural locations. Historians are not certain that Ptolemy made maps himself, but he lists thousands of place-names using latitude and longitude, and indicates various ways maps could be drawn.[192] His work, had it been accompanied by maps, would have been most useful in our part of the world for those traveling in the Red Sea and Indian Ocean areas, since he lists the ports from Arsinoë in the north to well past Berenike Trogodytika in the south as well as some of the more prominent Eastern Desert mountains including Smaragdus (Emerald) and Pentadactylus (Five Fingers) (*Geography* 4.5).[193] He lists ports on the African side of the Red Sea south of Egypt in what he called "Aethiopia"—that is, modern Sudan and Eritrea—and even outside the Red Sea along the Indian Ocean coast of Africa (*Geography* 4.5 and 4.7).[194] He continues on to the southern shores of Arabia, to South Asia, and beyond—to Southeast Asia.[195] Many Roman-era authors refer to the Seres—inhabitants of Sinae and Chryse Chersonesus; these are China and Southeast Asia, respectively.[196] The major problem for anyone consulting Ptolemy was his underestimation of the overall size of the world by approximately 25 percent.[197] Though somewhat useful for those voyaging in the Red Sea , Ptolemy's work was of extremely limited value to anyone crossing the desert between the Nile and the coast.

The *Peutinger Table*, a twelfth- or thirteenth-century copy several times removed from the original Roman map probably of the fourth century C.E., was more useful for those journeying between the Nile and the Red Sea coast.[198] Although some stations listed for the Berenike–Koptos road in the *Peutinger Table* seem to coincide with Pliny's, others do not, and the distances between the stops given in the *Peutinger Table* do not always match those provided by Pliny. It is likely that some stations active in Pliny's day had fallen out of use and been abandoned and, therefore, no longer functioned by the time of the composition of the *Peutinger Table*, and that new stations had been built since Pliny penned his work. Indeed, analysis of surface pottery collected by our surveys at all the stations recorded in Pliny and the *Peutinger Table*, plus sherds from ones neither of them list—probably because they did not yet exist or had ceased to function when Pliny and the *Peutinger Table* were compiled—suggests that not all road stations were used contemporaneously. This is the case with stations lining the Myos Hormos–Koptos road.[199] It is doubtful that Pliny ever visited the region, and one wonders what sources he used to record his information.[200] He must have consulted travelers, official records, or both.

The *Antonine Itinerary*, originally compiled in the late second/early third century C.E., with later ancient additions, seems to have followed, at least in part, the travels of the emperor Caracalla in the early third century.[201] It would have been of limited value to a traveler in the Eastern Desert along the Berenike–Koptos road (*Antonine Itinerary* 172.1–173.4).[202] There is also a late antique/early medieval list called the *Ravenna Cosmography* (2.7),[203] compiled in the early eighth century, probably only a copy of either or both of the two previously mentioned, likely the *Peutinger Table*, although with fewer place-names, and with some place-names that appear on neither. It would have been of limited value to someone crossing the desert; in any case, by the time the *Ravenna Cosmography* was compiled both Berenike and Myos Hormos had ceased to operate.

Table 8–2 compares stops/stations between Koptos and Berenike and their distances from Koptos, as noted by Pliny, the *Antonine Itinerary*, and the *Peutinger Table*.[204]

The maps, itineraries, and lists of road stations, inns, towns, military garrisons, and cities throughout the empire were likely compiled by individuals of varying abilities on official or unofficial missions over long periods of time. Given the huge areas covered, information for some regions may have been quite dated by the time the maps appeared. It would be nice to know the lag time between the actual field observations on which these maps and itineraries were based and their publication. Although the precise dates of compilation of the original versions of these maps are not known, by studying the maps and examining and dating the pottery found during surveys at the stations, historians and archaeologists have some idea of periods when the maps and itineraries might have been used, if not actually compiled—at least for those sections dealing with the Eastern Desert.

If one combines this information obtained from desert surveys with references in Strabo (*Geography* 17.1.45) and Pliny the Elder (*NH* 6.26.102–103), the latter of whom mentions a number of the stations between Berenike and Koptos that were active when he was writing, one can be fairly certain that at least the Eastern Desert portions of these maps were originally compiled sometime in the first century C.E., perhaps updated in the late second to early third. and thereafter copied with little regard to their later relevance or their accuracy. Since Pliny does not mention some stations that appear to have been constructed during his time, he was likely relying on earlier, probably Augustan-Tiberian-era, sources for some of his information. Pliny himself (*NH* 3.2.17) discusses a map of the world set up by Augustus's lieutenant Marcus Agrippa (died 12 B.C.E.) in the Porticus Octaviae in Rome,[205] and he may have used it as an important source of information for his own work. This would explain the total absence of the names of some stations

TABLE 8-2   Stops/Stations and Distances between Koptos and Berenike

Pliny	Roman Miles from Koptos	Antonine Itinerary	Roman Miles from Koptos	Peutinger Table	Roman Miles from Koptos
Coptus	—	Coptos	—	Cenoboscio	
	—		—	Diospoli Q[-?-]tibe	20+
Hydreuma	22	Poeniconon	24	Phenice	12 (32+)
In mountains	—	Dydime	24 (48)	Affrodites	24 (56+)
	—	Afrodito	20 (68)	Dydymos	20 (76+)
Hydreuma	85	Compasi	22 (90)	Compasari	20 (96+)
In mountain	—	Iovis	23 (113)	Dios	22 (118+)
—	—	Aristonis	25 (138)	Xeron	24 (142+)
—	—	Falacro	25 (163)	Philacon	24 (166+)
Apollinis Hydreuma	184	Apollonos	23 (186)	Apollonos	24 (190+)
In mountains	—	Cabalsi	27 (213)	Cabau	27 (217+)
Novum Hydreuma	230		—	—	—
Hydreuma Vetus	237	Cenon Hidreuma	27 (240)	Cenonnydroma	13+ (230+)
Berenice	257	Beronicen	18 (258)	Permicide portum	22 (252+)

NOTE: Figures in parentheses indicate total Roman miles from Koptos. The plus sign (+) in the figures for the *Peutinger Table* indicates that the distance recorded is possibly greater (numbers on the surviving copy of the *Peutinger Table* are not clear enough to be determined with precision).

found during surveys that have produced only late Roman pottery; they were built after Strabo and Pliny wrote, and later sources simply did not know of their existence because, for the most part, they merely copied earlier authors, making no attempt to find out how road conditions had changed in the intervening period.

For example, Strabo (*Geography* 17.1.45) refers briefly to both Apollonopolis Magna and Koptos and their Eastern Desert routes. Yet, he indicates that in his day Koptos was the preferred Nile terminus for roads coming from Berenike and Myos Hormos. He also notes that Myos Hormos was the favored Red Sea port; he does not mention the names of any *praesidia* along the Myos Hormos–Nile route that are prominent features. This suggests, as the archaeological evidence confirms, that those forts had yet to be built at the time he wrote. Peak travel along the Myos Hormos–Koptos road came after Strabo penned his tome. On the other hand, Pliny (*NH* 6.26.102–103) and various maps and itineraries noted earlier in this chapter emphasize the Berenike–Koptos route and record some but not all stations between the two emporia. This is some confirmation of the results of desert surveys, which have demonstrated that the Apollonopolis Magna portion of the Berenike route seems to have fallen out of use in the late Ptolemaic or early Roman period, about the time Strabo was writing, for reasons that are still not understood. The same survey results indicate that as the Apollonopolis Magna route waned, the road leading from Berenike to Koptos came to prominence, especially in the mid to late first century—precisely the period when Pliny was compiling his encyclopedia.[206]

Unfortunately, the results of archaeological fieldwork are often neither straightforward nor easily interpreted. Pottery analysis from desert surveys suggests that some stations on the Berenike–Koptos road were not active at the same time. Ceramic evidence from some *praesidia* indicates use only in the early Roman period and none later, whereas others suggest just the opposite: that they were built and operated only in the late Roman era. Several *praesidia* are so close together, only 8–9 km apart, and the dates of their pottery so very different that we must conclude that one station fell out of use and that, subsequently, one nearby was eventually built to replace it, but the reasons for such moves remain unknown. Good examples of this phenomenon appear at two pairs of stations whose ancient names are unknown or highly questionable at best; both sets appear on the Berenike–Nile roads. One set is at Abu Hegilig North and Abu Hegilig South, separated by only 8 km. Our surveys of Abu Hegilig South produced almost exclusively early Roman pottery, with possible slight evidence of late Roman, whereas at Abu Hegilig North our surveys recovered only late fourth- to fifth-century C.E. pottery, suggesting that the station at Abu Hegilig North replaced that at Abu Hegilig South sometime in late antiquity, apparently centuries after the *praesidium* in Abu Hegilig South had been abandoned. Evidence from Abu Hegilig North suggests that it may not have been completed before it, too, was vacated.

The other pair of *praesidia* occurs at Abu Ghalqa and Abu Ghusun, the latter of which may be the ancient station named Cabalsi in the *Antonine Itinerary* and Cabau by the *Peutinger Table;* Pliny refers to this or some nearby stop as "in mountain," suggesting that no fort existed here at the time of his writing. This pair of forts lay immediately south of the aforementioned Abu Hegilig stations. Our surveys found very little pottery at Abu Ghusun, and what they did find was of the late fourth to fifth century C.E., whereas sherds from Abu Ghalqa, only about 9 km away, were of the fifth to sixth century C.E. When our surveys visited, both these outposts were in poor states of preservation; most of Abu Ghusun had been washed away by desert floods, while Abu Ghalqa, which is only about 500 m south of a modern iron mine, had been reworked by the British in the earlier part of the twentieth century and was also in poor condition. Perhaps Abu Ghalqa replaced Abu Ghusun. Yet, we do not know what caused earlier stations such as Abu Hegilig South and Abu Ghusun to cease operations. Perhaps the wells or water supplies dried up. Both sites in Abu Hegilig seem to have drawn, at least in part, on runoff from adjacent mountains— a very unpredictable method of water acquisition (see chapter 7). It is uncertain why these pairs of stations lay in close proximity or why the earlier ones were abandoned.

In the late third century rebellions at Koptos and throughout the province[207] disrupted trade along the desert roads. The biblical translator and scholar Jerome (*Chronicon* 308F.) notes that Koptos was destroyed in 293 C.E., and temporarily abandoned.[208] This led one modern scholar to posit that a new settlement at Kainepolis/Maximianopolis replaced Koptos as an administrative and commercial center sometime around 294 or 295; the situation at Koptos seems, however, to have returned to normal soon thereafter.[209] There were also upheavals at the southern end of the Red Sea in the third century: a war between Abyssinia and southern Arabia as well wars within southern Arabia.[210] This local, regional, and more remote turmoil certainly had a negative impact on those traveling between Koptos, the Red Sea ports, and other points in the Eastern Desert. Another rebellion in Egypt by the usurper L. Domitius Domitianus just a few years later likely also disrupted commercial activities.[211]

ROMAN SETTLEMENTS IN THE EASTERN DESERT

With the lack of milestones and minimal excavations to obtain information on periods of activity at sites and along roads, optimal dating methods entail the collection and study of potsherds from sites associated with the roads. The provenance of many ceramics can also be determined. This allows one to establish which other locations were in contact with the site where the sherds were found. Occasionally, surveys find few if any datable sherds from some stations, or in rare instances do so only after repeated visits and careful searching for these sometimes elusive ceramic clues. There are pitfalls to using pottery found during surface surveys for dating purposes: the sherds may not represent the entire chronological breadth of activity at a site; there might be gaps in the ceramic corpus. Still, such dating procedures provide important information, which only expensive, time-consuming, and, in many cases, logistically difficult or impossible excavations could improve upon. Occasionally when excavated, some stations reveal datable inscriptions that commemorate their construction or refurbishment; this was the case at *praesidia* near

Berenike[212] and at forts along the Myos Hormos–Nile road,[213] as well as at Didymoi toward the northern end of the Berenike–Koptos road.[214] Another at Jovis/Dios, also on the Berenike–Koptos road, recently yielded a Trajanic text.[215] Study of graffiti carved by residents and passersby and the recovery and analysis of ancient coins occasionally found at the sites also help to date activities. Our surveys have not located or identified all ancient roads and sites originally built or that may still survive in the region.

Roman settlements in the Eastern Desert were connected with the road system and cannot be understood apart from it. We cannot examine each of the hundreds of Roman sites, but rather the types of sites and the relative frequency with which they appear. By doing so we can gauge the overall importance of activities they represent and create a picture of the interactions and interrelationships that existed among them and between them and Berenike, other Egyptian Red Sea ports, and emporia on the Nile.

Roman sites in the Eastern Desert were of two major types. First, there were those with a police-military function, which included water points/wells, *praesidia*, and signal towers. The second major category, primarily civilian sites, included mining and quarrying communities and settlements of unknown function, possibly belonging to Christian hermits. These groups were not mutually exclusive; both depended upon each other and the road system to function.

ROMAN MILITARY SITES

Inscriptions and other documents found along the Nile, at Berenike, at Myos Hormos, and in desert outposts show that the Roman military, including regular troops, auxiliary forces, and police, were responsible for the construction, maintenance, and garrisoning of most if not all of the road-related installations in the Eastern Desert. Those that have been measured and drawn or excavated indicate that, in general, they were larger than their Ptolemaic precursors and had basic features in common, but that some leeway was allowed regarding their sizes, plans, and locations.[216] We do not know how detailed orders were regarding the size, degree of physical uniformity, or locations of these installations. Perhaps, due to the similarity of circumstances where the routes were laid out, the climate, and overall similarity of missions, these forts naturally conformed to a general type seen throughout the empire.[217] Since larger and better-preserved *praesidia* appear to be miniature Roman army camps, it may be that troops building them designed them in a way in which they always built any army camp, and that this accounts for the relative similarity in overall design. Friends and foes alike recognized these as projections of Roman military might into the remotest desert regions and understood the underlying message of the omnipresent nature of Roman power and its enforcement.[218]

Early Roman garrisons stationed along or near the Eastern Desert roads generally built rectilinear-shaped forts of varied sizes made of locally obtainable cobbles and small boulders laid without mortar or with an ephemeral mud binder, much of which has eroded away due to wind and water.[219] Rarely, those *praesidia*, which are more semicircular or oval in plan or had one end so designed, may have originally been Ptolemaic constructions, with subsequent rectilinear-shaped enlargements added in Roman times. Examples of such hybrids include one at Vetus Hydreuma, noted earlier, and another at al-Kanaïs—both on the Berenike–Nile roads. These were more reminiscent of their Ptolemaic predecessors upon which later Roman constructions may well have been erected. Yet, the fort in Wadi Semna—built to support the Mons Ophiates quarries in Wadi Umm Wikala, and constructed and used only in the early Roman period—was also somewhat semicircular in plan.[220]

Our surveys have recorded approximately eighty forts of all periods between the Nile and the Red Sea coast; most of these appear to be Roman, and a few Ptolemaic or Ptolemaic-Roman. At least five more have completely disappeared;[221] there may be others that have been destroyed or have yet to be found. The smallest, a hilltop fort at Vetus Hydreuma on the Berenike–Nile roads, measures only about 21.4 m × 9.85 m (external dimensions), whereas one of the largest—in Wadi Gemal, also on the Berenike–Nile roads—preserves walls that measure approximately 119 m × 78 m. These are not the full lengths, since portions of some of the walls, the entirety of two others, and most of the interior buildings of this fort have been washed away. Its internal area, however, was at least 0.92 hectares, making it one of the largest military facilities in the Eastern Desert.[222] These *praesidia* served various functions, but especially guarding water supplies along roads, circulating messages, monitoring traffic, and assisting passing military and civilian commercial caravans; some *praesidia* guarded mines and quarries or other settlements. They also defended against banditry and nomadic raids, though the ability to distinguish between the two activities is nearly impossible.[223] A Roman novel, probably written in the second century C.E.,[224] uses the Eastern Desert as a setting for banditry, likely an accurate reflection of the general situation at the time.

Many of these military installations had protective patron deities. Excavations at *praesidia* along the Myos Hormos–Nile road demonstrate that Athena was particularly popular, with others like Apollo, the Dioscuri (twins Castor and Pollux), Pan, Serapis, Tyche (Fortuna), and Philotera, the deified sister of Ptolemy II, also represented.[225] Once other stations on the Eastern Desert roads are excavated it will likely be evident that these and other deities acted as those installations' apotropaic guardians as well.[226]

Due to the installations' dilapidated states and the fact that the vast majority have not been excavated, the original heights of defensive enceintes for most forts can only be estimated—perhaps 2–4 m—while those of larger garrisons, like that in Wadi Gemal, were undoubtedly greater. Our excavations estimate that the outer walls of the late Roman fort at Abu Sha'ar were probably about 3.5–4 m high, while the adjacent towers rose to approximately 5.3 m above ground level.[227] Surveys and excavations have shown that fort walls were accessible by staircases or perhaps wooden ladders placed at points around the interior, which allowed egress to catwalks and parapets. There was usually a single large gate, and sometimes also another smaller portal, into a fort; larger forts undoubtedly had more entrances. Two forts in Wadi Kalalat and a small one at Siket near Berenike had multiple entrances, albeit in all three cases the second entrance was small and had been blocked off sometime in antiquity while the forts were still in use.[228] The fort at Abu Sha'ar, whose walls enclose an area measuring about 77.5 m × 64 m, had two main entrances, one on the west and another on the north, and at least one smaller portal at the southwestern corner of the fort associated with a tower, which had been blocked in antiquity.[229]

Defensive towers often appear at the exteriors of the four corners of a fort and flanking a main gate. If the fort was large, defensive towers might also be found along the exterior faces of the walls between the corner towers and flanking other gates as well, such as at Abu Sha'ar,[230] at the large fort in Wadi Kalalat,[231] and at the large *praesidium* of Apollonos in Wadi Gemal.[232] These towers usually appear to be round or oval in plan in the early Roman period, and in late Roman manifestations tend to the square or rectilinear; they might vary substantially in size even in the same installation. The towers are usually close enough together to provide enfilading fire to each other. Some of the towers may have originally been rectilinear in plan but in their tumbled conditions appear to be round or oval. As with the parapets, staircases from inside the fort provided access to towers. When there is no evidence of a staircase, possibly a portable ladder was used.

The center interior of most Roman *praesidia* invariably had a large well *(hydreuma)* sunk into it; the sides of these *hydreumata* were reinforced with stones or kiln-fired bricks to prevent collapse and preserve somewhat the integrity of the water supply. Stone staircases, some spiraling, descended into the *hydreumata*. There were often stone or kiln-fired brick cisterns lined with waterproof lime mortar in which well water could be stored for subsequent use. These cisterns appear inside the defensive walls, often in a corner, for use by the garrison. Many cisterns, troughs, and tanks also exist outside some *praesidia*—for example, the large one in Wadi Kalalat about 8.5 km southwest of Berenike[233]—to accommodate travelers and animals that the garrison wanted to keep outside the installations. Water could be conveyed from interior catchments to exterior ones via channels or carried by humans or pack animals, presumably in leather bags, clay water jars, or, less likely, wooden barrels (see chapter 7).

Abutting the interior walls of a fort and freestanding from the fort walls were accommodations for troops, storage rooms for food and equipment, stables for their mounts, occasionally pigsties (such as at Krokodilô and Didymoi, *praesidia* on the Myos Hormos–Koptos and Berenike–Koptos roads, respectively),[234] and, in several instances at least, a small intramural bath (at the *praesidia* of Maximianon on the Myos Hormos–Koptos road, at Didymoi, at Umm Balad, and at Javis/Dios).[235] In some larger, better-preserved, and more fully excavated *praesidia* are headquarters buildings (at Maximianon and Qasr al-Banat on the Myos Hormos–Nile road),[236] kitchen facilities with areas for grinding grain and perhaps olives, and, at Abu Sha'ar, an extramural bath building.[237]

With few exceptions, facilities that guarded the routes and water supplies along them lay on low ground. Rarely did a fort perch on a hilltop, mountain summit, or other high ground.[238] Common sense and basic tactics would, in normal military circumstances, dictate location of defenses on higher ground. If the mission of these garrisons had been to protect, control, or monitor vast areas of the Eastern Desert, then, prima facie, many should have been situated on elevated terrain that commanded the most extensive views. That so few were thus located suggests that Roman strategy in the Eastern Desert had more limited and achievable goals. It was neither necessary, nor possible or desirable, to control the entire Eastern Desert, but only its key assets. Limited water resources and logistical difficulties of supplying garrisons also dictated that these forts be relatively few in number and, generally, small in size.

The assets the military focused upon included command of the major route systems/communications networks and the water resources along their courses; water was to be found in wells sunk on low ground, not on mountaintops. Another part of the strategy included protection of nodes of mineral wealth deemed important enough to exploit. Though these demands required a fairly elaborate and impressive architectural and human infrastructure, this strategy of limited control relieved a great deal of pressure, saved a great deal of money, and obviated the need to have larger numbers of troops stationed in the region. This is one reason, as ancient writers and documents tell us, that bandits, tax evaders, and other malcontents regularly fled to the desert from the densely populated areas along the Nile:[239] they knew that they were generally beyond the reach of authorities as long as they remained clear of the local points of control and the communication lines that linked them together. This same strategy seems to have been prevalent with the Roman army throughout much of its history in different areas of the empire.[240]

In the Roman period and earlier and among knowledgeable Bedouin today, one could and can find a modicum of water with a fair degree of certainty by digging down a few meters or so in the bottoms of many wadis. Thus, wayfarers singly or in small groups did not have to travel along the main routes. It was, however, the rare voyager who strayed from the trodden path. Indigenous peoples knew where the water was or was not available in any given season or from one year to the next; their existence and that of their herds of sheep, goats, camels, and donkeys depended upon this knowledge. Thus, they could avoid most road stations and their overly inquisitive garrisons, who sought to control their movements. However, the average Nile denizen, Red Sea port resident, or itinerant merchant from father afield, fearful of straying too far off, did travel these roads and was carefully watched and taxed in the process.

Ancient documents provide only scrappy information about the sizes of these desert garrisons. None was huge; perhaps the largest, not attached to a quarry or mine but simply a *praesidium*, lay in Wadi Gemal (ancient Apollonos Hydreuma), accommodating only a few hundred at most. Most forts probably housed only a few dozen or a few score men and their mounts, in some cases less. Based upon a Nikanor ostrakon from the first century C.E.,[241] one scholar estimated the size of the garrison at Apollonos Hydreuma. Predicating calculations upon the amount of grain supplied to that installation, he put the garrison at about 35 men.[242] This sum, based on an ostrakon dated to the reign of Tiberius (14–37 C.E.), must be prior to the construction of the huge *praesidium* whose remains are now visible there, which may be the one referred to in the Latin inscription noted earlier, likely constructed in Flavian times or somewhat later.[243] Otherwise, this estimate would be way off the mark, for this was one of the largest forts in the region, with an approximate area of 0.92 hectares. With extant walls of at least 119 m × 78 m, 35 men could not possibly have controlled so vast a fort. An original figure of about 215 soldiers, which the same scholar estimates as too great for such a small site, is probably, in fact, more accurate.[244] The fort at Abu Sha'ar, based on the number and sizes of the barracks rooms, may have housed about 150–200 men, possibly less.[245] *Praesidia* on the Myos Hormos road perhaps accommodated anywhere from as few as 15 men upward.[246] An ostrakon of 109 C.E. from Krokodilô suggests a garrison of 11–15 men (3–5 cavalry and 8–10 infantry); yet, this seems too small for the size of the *praesidium*.[247] Another scholar estimates that the fort in Wadi Belih (near Mons Porphyrites), which is only about one-sixth the size of Krokodilô, had a garrison of 15–18 cavalry or 28–36 infantry.[248] An ostrakon from Mons Claudianus, written in the winter, probably in 110 C.E., lists water rations for 917 people, 60 of whom were soldiers.[249] Ostraka from forts along the Myos Hormos–Koptos road indicate that those garrisons were a mix of cavalry and infantry,[250] with virtually no mention of camel-borne troops.[251] A recently discovered ostrakon of Trajanic date found at Domitiane/Kaine Latomia does, however, mention a Roman military *dromadarius*,[252] as do documents from Mons Claudianus.[253] On balance,[254] the extant information indicates that many desert *praesidia* were built in the period between the Flavian emperors and the reigns of Trajan and Hadrian—an era when there was an upsurge in "barbarian" activity in the region.[255]

Pliny (*NH* 6.26.103) writes that forts at Vetus Hydreuma on the Berenike–Nile road accommodated up to 2,000 persons! This must be a gross exaggeration, and one scholar interprets this passage, quite oddly, to mean that the *praesidia* at Vetus Hydreuma kept watch over an area of two Roman miles.[256] G. W. Murray estimated that the garrisons of the five *praesidia* at Vetus Hydreuma totaled about 250 men.[257] In lieu of ancient documents, the only method to estimate garrison sizes is to measure the areas of fort interiors and calculate from these. Ostraka indicate that civilians also dwelt in some or all of the *praesidia* on the Myos Hormos–Nile road; there are few if any recognizable extramural civilian settlements associated with these installations, so we can be fairly certain that most nonmilitary personnel, though not necessarily passing travelers, lived inside the forts.[258] These desert garrisons were commanded by auxiliary troops who held a rank no more senior than centurion or decurion and sometimes a *duplicarius* or *sesquiplicarius*. In ostraka the commander of the *praesidium* is usually addressed as *stationarius*.[259]

Ostraka, mainly excavated along the Myos Hormos–Nile road, suggest that the length of service a soldier could expect at one of these forlorn locations was at least three to seven months.[260] A graffito near al-Mweih on the Koptos–Myos Hormos road indicates a five-month stay.[261] One Trajanic-era papyrus describes an eighteen-month posting at Pselkis.[262] In other desert areas, including Nubia, Syria, and Libya, service in remote forts might be eighteen months to three years.[263] It is not certain, however, that such lengthy tours of duty applied to Egypt's Eastern Desert.

Quarries and mines, their related settlements, and late Roman communities of uncertain function, but possibly used by Christian recluses, form the second major category of habitation in the Eastern Desert. No matter how close to the Red Sea, all quarries, except the most local and clearly exploited for use in the immediate vicinity, sent their products primarily to the Nile valley and derived from the Nile valley most of their supplies and manpower requirements. There were also contacts with the Red Sea coast, but on a modest scale. The recovery of Red Sea fish remains and shells at many desert sites indicates limited commercial contacts, probably at the personal level, between those living at the quarries and the Red Sea ports.[264] Some products from the mines and quarries have been recovered at the Red Sea ports—for example, beryls/emeralds from mines in the Sikait-Nugrus region found at Berenike and Marsa Nakari[265]—indicating two-way, albeit apparently limited, contact between coast and hinterland. Settlements close to some of the Red Sea ports were, however, heavily dependent upon coastal emporia for many imported goods.

Quarries Mineral exploitation of the Eastern Desert was at its zenith during the early Roman period, with the extraction and export of hard stones from at least thirteen quarries,[266] especially in the first three or four centuries C.E. and, in the case of Mons Porphyrites, possibly into the fifth century. This process began late in the reign of Augustus and early in that of Tiberius, when three inscriptions indicate that the central government brought the mines and quarries under its supervision. Suetonius (Tiberius 49.2) and Pliny the Elder (NH 36.11.55) also note Augustan and Tiberian interest in minerals in general and the mines and quarries of the Eastern Desert in particular.[267]

Places like Mons Porphyrites,[268] Mons Claudianus/Klaudianon (figure 8-8),[269] Mons Ophiates,[270] Domitiane/Kaine Latomia,[271] Tiberiane,[272] Umm Huyut (ancient name unknown),[273] Wadi Maghrabiya (ancient name unknown),[274] Persou/Mons Basanites,[275] and, possibly, Gebel Rokham/Atafla (ancient name unknown) in Wadi Mia,[276] to name a few, produced hard stones for statuary, sarcophagi, and architectural purposes. Mons Porphyrites provided ornamental imperial (usually, but not invariably) purple porphyry, while Domitiane and Tiberiane, the former near Mons Porphyrites and the latter near Mons Claudianus, produced quartz diorite. Mons Claudianus had tonalite gneiss, as did the nearby quarry of Umm Huyut; metagabbro came from Maghrabiya,[277] and both metagraywacke sandstone/siltstone and metaconglomerate came from Mons Basanites.[278] Gebel Rokham produced the only marble quarried from the Eastern Desert, and recent analysis of surface sherds suggests that it operated in Roman times.[279]

These stones were shipped all over the Roman world, which is evident from their appearance in edifices across the empire and from their survival in numerous Mediterranean shipwrecks.[280] Writers between the first century B.C.E. and the fourth century C.E., including Diodorus Siculus (3.12.1–3.14.6), Josephus (*BJ* 6.418), Aelius Aristeides (*Egyp-*

FIGURE 8-8

Mons Claudianus, view of main fort, baths, animal lines, and temple. Photo by S. E.Sidebotham.

tian Discourse 36.67), and Eusebius (*de Martyribus Palaestinae* 8.1 and 9.1), mention or imply that prisoners were sent to work the mines and quarries of Egypt.[281] Yet, the status of the labor forces at Mons Claudianus, Mons Porphyrites, and Domitiane was not servile; most or all of the work was conducted not by slaves or those condemned to the mines and quarries for various offences,[282] but rather by skilled free labor.[283] Ostraka from Domitiane indicate the presence of Jews receiving pay for their labor.[284] Individuals working in these desert outposts also received salaries that were, on average, substantially higher than what their peers in the Nile valley received, up to forty-seven drachmas per month according to documents from Mons Claudianus.[285]

The larger Roman-era quarries had attached settlements that were miniature cities. Some had, in addition to the male workforce and those protecting them, families of the residents. Women and children lived in some of these remote settings alongside their menfolk, as recorded in thousands of ostraka from some of these sites; in at least one instance at Mons Claudianus it seems that a school was established to educate the children living there.[286] Other identifiable buildings found in some of these larger quarry settlements, especially those at Mons Claudianus,[287] Mons Porphyrites,[288] and Mons Ophiates, included temples.[289] These facilities were well built and decorated and accompanied by dedicatory inscriptions. Surviving Greek texts indicate that a variety of Greco-Roman and Egyptian deities were worshipped, including Serapis and Isis. "Paneia"—for the most part ad hoc shrines at and along routes leading to and from the quarries, and dedicated to Pan and his Egyptian desert manifestation, Min—were also very popular.[290] Excavations have uncovered baths at Mons Claudianus[291] and at Mons Porphyrites.[292] These were constructed in typical Roman fashion, although smaller than those usually found in comparably sized communities in more water- and fuel-abundant areas. Many buildings providing these amenities, plus more mundane structures used for administrative, living, food-storage and -preparation, or working purposes, clustered close to large fortifications or settlements located in or near the quarries. Fortified installations were the administrative and defensive centers of quarrying operations; they may also have housed more important officials and some of the labor force.[293] Much of the quarrying cannot have been "for-profit"; rather, the output was destined for imperial building projects in Rome and elsewhere, which were completed without regard to cost.

Among over nine thousand ostraka from Mons Claudianus are numerous epistles indicating a lively trade in food, beer, wine, clothing, and prostitutes coming from the Nile valley via *praesidia* lining the roads; numerous business and personal transactions—especially requests for food—were handled through third parties who conveyed messages between the Nile valley and these desert enclaves.[294] Many letters are to or from military personnel stationed at the quarries.[295] A prime concern is acknowledging receipt of food rations for the month.[296] These desert outposts were, thus, a mélange of soldiers and civilians—many of the former hailing from outside Egypt and most of the latter from Egypt, with homes in the Nile valley. Evidence indicates that troops guarding the quarries came from garrisons stationed in the Nile valley.[297]

There are numerous examples of Eastern Desert stones serving the government's needs. Evidence of the importance and popularity of these beautiful hard stones can be seen in the Vatican Museum, which preserves two large and spectacularly decorated sarcophagi in purple porphyry from Mons Porphyrites: one of Helena, mother of Constantine the Great; and a second one of Constantia, daughter of the same emperor.[298] The famous Tetrarch statue group built into the corner of the Basilica of St. Mark in Venice, but taken originally perhaps from Constantinople or Nicomedia during the Fourth Crusade, was also carved from Mons Porphyrites purple porphyry.[299] Items made from this attractive stone have been found well beyond the boundaries of the Roman world; a vase and bowl made from Mons Porphyrites porphyry have been recorded from excavations at Begram, Afghanistan.[300]

Grandiorite/tonalite gneiss stones from Mons Claudianus are evident in columns decorating the front porch of the Pantheon and columns in the Basilica Ulpia, as well as from Hadrian's villa at Tivoli just outside Rome.[301] Mons Claudianus columns have also been found at Carthage, at Ephesus, and at Diocletian's palace at Split on the Adriatic coast of Croatia.[302]

Routes from the Quarries Judging by the sizes of the columns, column capitals, statues, sarcophagi, large basins, and other products made from Eastern Desert stones that survive around the empire and from examination of columns and other elements that were abandoned at the quarries themselves, it is clear that transporting stones from the quarries to their ultimate destinations was an engineering feat in itself. Columns, column capitals, basins, and other architectural elements now found abandoned at Mons Claudianus vary in size, but even the smallest was large and heavy; one of the most impressive columns, weighing an estimated 207 tons, with a length in excess of 18 m, still reclines broken and abandoned in one of the quarries.[303] An unfinished giant tub or basin 5.80 m long and 2.98 m wide in another hilltop quarry at Mons Claudianus also lies derelict.[304] Such huge monoliths would not have been quarried if some means of moving them had not been available. One can imagine the labor necessary to haul these stones to the Nile, thence by river to Alexandria, and from there via oceangoing ships for onward transport to their ultimate destinations around the Mediterranean.

There were two possible routes used to haul such giants to the Nile, which lay about 120 km west of Mons Claudianus.[305] Massive wooden wagons with numerous solidly constructed wheels drawn by large numbers of draft animals made the journeys.[306] The tracks these giant machines made in the desert floor can still be seen.[307] Surviving impressions on the desert surface suggest that the wagons were not of uniform size, but varied in their heft depending upon the cargoes they carried. Our surveys noted and measured some of these, as did earlier visitors G. W. Murray and Leo Tregenza. All noted these tracks in the flat sandy areas of the Naq al-Ter plain closer to the Nile in the vicinity of the *praesidia* at Deir al-Atrash and at al-Saqqia, the road station at Bir Salah, and the forts at al-Heita (figure 8-9) on the Abu Sha'ar/Mons Porphyrites–Nile road. Overall, gauges appear in several general ranges. The smallest is 2.13–2.40 m; the next grouping, 2.7–3.50 m; and the largest, 4.0 m.[308] The latter seems to represent a conveyance with three rows of wheels.[309] Wagons coming from Mons Porphyrites along this route were generally smaller than those leaving Mons Claudianus, given the relative sizes of the stones each quarry produced.

That portion of the route from the station at al-Saqqia onward to the Nile carried traffic from both Mons Claudianus and Mons Porphyrites, and it is in these areas that wagon ruts have been seen; but the Mons Claudianus traffic also had the option of a more southerly, shorter road. It is not clear why traffic from Mons Claudianus had two routes; it may have had to do with the weight of the wagons and their loads, or it may be that traffic going to the Nile with heavy loads used the more northerly route and lighter-weight traffic returning from the Nile to Mons Claudianus used the more southerly one. Neither the average rates of speed nor the number of travel days to reach the Nile are known. These would have been dictated by load dimensions and weights, the numbers and experience of the hauling teams, the size and health of the draft animals, time of year, and luck; if a wagon broke wheels on the Nile-bound journey, it could cause endless delays. Along routes from Mons Claudianus and Mons Ophiates one can still see discarded quarry stones, suggesting that serious accidents required abandonment of some or all of the cargo in the middle of the journey.

Between major quarries in the Eastern Desert—namely, Mons Claudianus and Mons

FIGURE 8-9
Lower fort at al-Heita on the Abu Sha'ar/Mons Porphyrites–Nile road. Note extensive use of mud brick in the towers and walls, and in the hilltop fort above. Photo by S. E.Sidebotham.

Porphyrites—and the Nile were numerous watering points to accommodate large numbers of pack and draft animals. These animal-watering points and tethering lines lay between the quarries and the Nile, and none have been detected between the quarries and the Red Sea coast, though the latter was substantially closer to both quarries than the Nile. This indicates that the Nile was the goal for those transporting the stones (see chapter 7).[310] The relatively huge loads leaving Mons Claudianus compared with those borne from Mons Porphyrites meant that the largest animal-watering points lay on routes leading to or from the former quarry. Initially, given the heat and water requirements, one scholar believes that quarrying operations took place mainly during the cooler months,[311] but excavations at Mons Claudianus and Mons Porphyrites and analysis of thousands of documents found at those sites indicate that quarrying and hauling operations took place year-round, though they were probably somewhat busier during the cooler months.[312]

Aside from problems entailed in the successful movement of stones from quarry to Nile, one can imagine the administrative and bureaucratic headaches entailed in the operation that allowed teams hauling the stone to use the water and revictualing points en route.

Wagons and carts were not the main means of conveyance for non-quarry-related activities in the Eastern Desert. Most traffic was on foot or employed camels, donkeys, or horses. Yet, early Roman ostraka from Bir Fawakhir along the Myos Hormos–Nile road record wagons used to deliver supplies to troops stationed there.[313] The offices of curator of wagons and curator of chariots appear on ostraka excavated at *praesidia* along the Myos Hormos–Nile road.[314] The Koptos Tariff also notes a fee of four drachmas levied on covered wagons that traveled one of the desert roads.[315]

Mines and Transport Roman-era mining in the Eastern Desert did not demand the huge wheeled transport or extensive watering points required for draft animals and people hauling consignments emanating from the larger quarries. The number of early Roman mines in the Eastern Desert was many times greater than the number of quarries. Mining concentrated on the extraction of metals such as gold;[316] precious and semiprecious stones such as beryls/emeralds from the Mons Smaragdus region (Wadis Sikait-Nugrus-Zabara-Umm Harba, etc.);[317] and amethysts from Wadi al-Hudi,[318] about 40 km east of Aswan, and, in both the Ptolemaic and early Roman periods, from an area southwest of Safaga in Wadi Abu Diyeiba.[319] These ores and gemstones could be removed using pack animals. This mineral exploitation existed, in most cases on a more modest scale, earlier in the Ptolemaic and later in the Islamic eras as well.

Although mines—especially gold, not so much beryl/emerald and amethyst—were more numerous in the Eastern Desert in the early Roman period than the quarries, they were generally also much smaller operations that, although labor-intensive, were much less so than the quarries. Unlike most quarries, the mines were "for-profit" operations. Perhaps their yield offset losses incurred by the imperial government from quarrying activities.

Most gold mined in the Eastern Desert was obtained by following veins of quartz through hard igneous rocks. Mines might be either open-pit-like affairs or tunnels that delved into mountainsides. Much initial gold-ore crushing took place on each site, as ubiquitous and numerous grinding stones attest. There were hundreds of gold-mining settlements ranging from tiny prospecting sites to huge operations requiring at least hundreds of people. Survey and excavation at the late Roman/early Byzantine gold-mining settlement at Bir Umm Fawakhir along the Myos Hormos–Nile road revealed accommodations for an estimated one thousand persons.[320]

Often the Romans continued to exploit mines that had been operating since Ptolemaic times if not earlier. Although Diodorus Siculus (3.12.1–3.14.6) discusses the servile status of those working the gold mines, undoubtedly as they existed in the early Ptolemaic era, we do not know the status, free or servile, of the gold miners in Roman times. In addition to working older mines, the Romans located and opened new gold-mining sites in the Eastern Desert until at least the sixth century C.E. One wonders what type of geological prospecting, hinted at in Pharaonic-era desert inscriptions[321] and Greek and Roman sources,[322] took place in the Roman period to locate and assess the potential of newly discovered auriferous sources.

Though not as well documented by excavations as the larger quarries, limited excavations at the late Roman gold-mining settlement at Bir Umm Fawakhir and at an early to late Roman beryl/emerald-mining community in Wadi Sikait, as well as surveys in other mining areas, provide information on their locations, numbers, sizes, and periods of use, as well as amenities available to their inhabitants.

Unlike the quarries, which required wagons and teams of animals to remove stones to the Nile, miners could transport ores and stones using pack animals, mainly camels and donkeys carrying the loads, no doubt, in panniers. Thus, the conveyance of mine products was relatively simple, but those responsible for transporting the gold-bearing ore or precious and semiprecious stones had security concerns for their cargoes that their quarry counterparts did not.

Other Settlements   In addition to mining and quarrying communities and military installations, there are at least twelve or thirteen settlements ranging in size from a few dozen to several hundred structures whose purposes cannot be precisely determined. Some are near ancient quarries and mines; one can be seen close to Mons Claudianus, and two near emerald mines at Sikait and Nugrus.[323] These enigmatic desert communities date from the fourth to sixth century c.e., are of very modest construction, and are mostly located close to, but not on or easily approached by, major desert roads.

In all cases but one the construction techniques are similar: small one-, two-, occasionally three-, and very rarely four-room structures made of cobbles and small boulders, with walls only about half a meter thick and not more than a meter or so high. Lack of adjacent tumble indicates that the walls were never originally much higher, suggesting that superstructures comprised perishable materials such as wooden beams and matting or tents. Those we have examined in detail include, from north to south, Umm Howeitat al-Bahri, Bir Gidami, Bir Handosi, Umm Heiran (near Sikait), Hitan Rayan, and Qariya Mustafa Amr Gama'a—the latter two near Berenike.[324] Only one of the settlements, that at Shenshef 21.3 km southwest of Berenike, is built with fine construction techniques—closely resembling those used in the mining settlement in Wadi Sikait—and comprises walls, some surviving to a height of several meters, built of quarried stone and preserving doors, windows, and niches.

Aside from Shenshef, these settlements may have been Christian hermit *(laura)* communities, though except for one site, our surveys have found no ancient crosses or other Christian signs associated with these places. Christian desert communities and monastic centers were popular in the fourth century and later in the Eastern Desert, and most were undoubtedly very humble places, like the settlements described here. Some locations, such as the cemetery near the Lykabettus quarries at Mons Porphyrites,[325] the building at Qattar just off the Abu Sha'ar-Kainepolis/Maximianopolis road,[326] and the late Roman fort converted to a monastic settlement at Abu Sha'ar,[327] are known Christian centers from surviving inscriptions and texts. Shenshef falls into a different category; it was a substantially wealthier community than the others and clearly had commercial contacts with Berenike. Its buildings comprise multiple-roomed structures, some quite large, with one or more courtyards. It likely did not serve a function similar to that of other desert settlements described here, though some Christians may have lived there.

CONCLUSION

The elaborate road system with its *praesidia* and *hydreumata,* mines, quarries, and other settlements of uncertain function, together with the Red Sea ports, dramatically illustrates the importance attached to the Eastern Desert and Red Sea coast by the Roman imperial and provincial governments, the military, civilian entrepreneurs, and others. At no other time in the history of the area aside from the present, with its concomitant tourist industry, was the population as great in cities along the Red Sea coast, and the economic importance of these cities as significant, as during the Roman occupation. The first, second, and early third centuries and the fourth to sixth centuries C.E. were ones of unparalleled activity and potential unimagined profitability for the government and private entrepreneurs who gambled their lives and fortunes on endeavors undertaken here. Judging by some of the more humble communities, not everyone ventured into the desert for financial profit. Some came for spiritual/religious purposes, or to escape legal or personal problems back home.

9

OTHER EMPORIA

Other ports operating throughout the Red Sea and Indian Ocean in Hellenistic and Roman times were important in the global economy (figure 9-1). Many were in contact either directly or indirectly with Berenike and with each other.

AMPELOME/AMPELONE

Though unlocated, Ampelome/Ampelone was likely founded by Ptolemy II along the Arabian Red Sea coast. Pliny (*NH* 6.32.159) reports that the colonists came from the Aegean city of Miletus, which was under Ptolemaic control at that time.[1]

LEUKE KOME

Leuke Kome/Albus Portus (White Village in Greek/Latin) was initially under Nabataean control. Strabo (*Geography* 16.4.23–24) and the *Periplus* (19) indicate that it was active in early Roman times, while Cosmas Indicopleustes (*Christian Topography* 2.62)[2] suggests that it continued to operate in the late Roman era. Though Leuke Kome has not been precisely located, a survey in the Kuraybah-'Aynunah area of northwestern Saudi Arabia found evidence of ancient activity there.[3] These remains are unexcavated.[4] The site, which includes Nabataean and early Roman potsherds, lies near the Strait of Tiran. Literary evidence does not indicate that Leuke Kome operated in earlier Hellenistic times.

Early Roman-era Leuke Kome played a key role in maritime commerce and overland

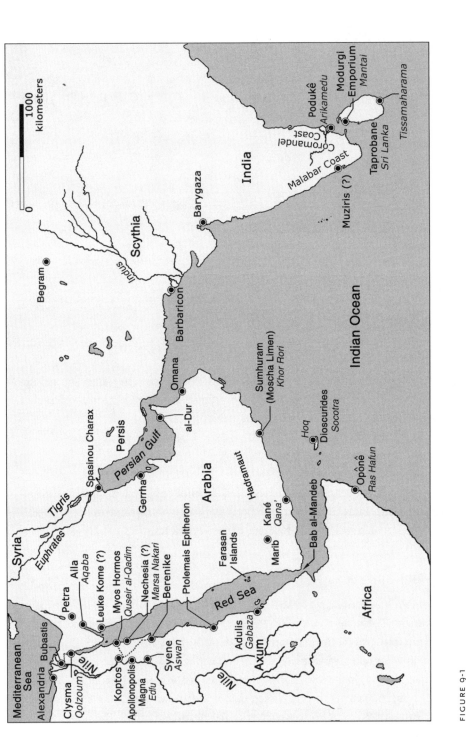

FIGURE 9-1

Map of the eastern Mediterranean, the Red Sea, the Persian Gulf, and the northwestern Indian Ocean, with major sites mentioned in the text. Drawing by M. Hense.

caravan trade passing en route to Petra. We are uncertain what contacts the port had with Ptolemaic emporia on Egypt's Red Sea coast. Relations between the Ptolemies and Nabataeans were sometimes poor, with the former accusing the latter of piratical activities,[5] suggesting that the Nabataeans operated from somewhere on the Red Sea, perhaps Leuke Kome.

Leuke Kome was prominent in the late first century B.C.E. (Strabo, *Geography* 16.4.22ff.), when a military expedition of ten thousand soldiers, launched in about 26/25 B.C.E. against Arabia Felix/Arabia Eudaimon, landed here, arriving from Arsinoë/Clysma. The troops comprised Roman legionaries stationed in Egypt and allied contingents from Judaea and Arabia Nabataea.[6] Thence the expedition marched south for six months, reaching Marib, capital of Sheba/Saba, in modern Yemen.[7] The army withdrew after an unsuccessful siege of Marib, its defeat due to nonhostile causes including disease and thirst. A fragment of a bilingual Greek-Latin inscription from Baraqish may be the tombstone of a Roman soldier who perished during that operation.[8] Retreating north, the expedition embarked for Myos Hormos. Since Strabo was a friend of the expedition commander, Aelius Gallus, his is the best surviving account—the only example of a Roman attack beyond imperial boundaries for commercial reasons. Pliny (*NH* 6.32.160), Josephus (*AJ* 15.317), and Dio Cassius (*Roman History* 53.29.3–8) also record the event. Augustus himself boasts of this expedition in the *Res Gestae* (5.26), which suggests that he viewed it as a political-diplomatic triumph.[9]

According to Strabo (*Geography* 16.4.23), a heavily used caravan route linked Leuke Kome to Petra.[10] The *Periplus* (19) also mentions this road and Leuke Kome. The *Periplus* says that freight arrived at Leuke Kome from Arabia in small ships and that a customs officer collected a 25 percent duty *(tetarte)* on imports. The harbor was guarded by a detachment of soldiers commanded by a *hekatontarches,* a centurion. There has been debate about the centurion's "nationality." Unfortunately, the term does not invariably denote that troops stationed here were Roman, since the Nabataean army also used this rank.[11] We cannot be certain what role Leuke Kome played in the Red Sea–Indian Ocean trade, though the port appears to have been in contact with Egyptian Red Sea entrepôts and with other harbors on the Arabian Red Sea coast. It may have continued to operate in the late Roman period, if one believes Cosmas. If so, the date of its ultimate demise remains unknown. Perhaps a settlement at Iotabê, which remains unidentified but was likely in the area of the Strait of Tiran, replaced Leuke Kome as a customs post/port beginning sometime in the fifth century; in any case, Iotabe appears to have operated for only about sixty years before it was abandoned.[12]

AILA/AELA/AELANA

Excavations at Aila (modern Aqaba), the northeasternmost- point on the Red Sea, have produced little indicating that it operated the Hellenistic period.[13] Nor does extant evidence suggest much activity here prior to Roman annexation in 106 C.E. or during the early Roman occupation. This is despite the fact that the Via Nova Traiana linked Aila in the early second century C.E. to more northerly settlements and, ultimately, to Bostra in southern Syria.[14] Excavations uncovered late Roman and Islamic settlements, including evidence of contact with other ports in the Red Sea, especially Berenike and Adulis, from the fourth century C.E. on. Writers who mention Aila in the early Roman period include Josephus (*AJ* 8.163), who records that the Ptolemies established a port named Berenike not far away. Strabo also mentions Aila (*Geography* 16.2.30) and the Gulf of Aila (16.4.18), as do Pliny the Elder (*NH* 5.12.65) and Claudius Ptolemy (*Geography* 5.16.1). But little archaeological evidence has been found indicating that Aila had much commercial interaction with areas in the Indian Ocean in early Roman times. Later authors also recount Aila's maritime contacts with India. Eusebius (*Onomasticon* 6.17–20 and 8.1) refers to ships sailing between Aila, Egypt, and India.[15] In 524/525 C.E. the *Martyrium Sancti Arethae* reports that fifteen ships sailed from Aila to assist in the Axumite war against the Himyarites in southern Arabia (see chapter 13).[16] Procopius (*History of the Wars* 1.19.3) also mentions Aila and describes ships sailing from the city (*History of the Wars* 1.19.24). The pilgrim Antonius of Placentia, passing through in 570 C.E., reports maritime traffic bringing a variety of spices from India to Aila.[17] Finds from Aila including Axumite/Adulis-made pottery, and Axumite coins indicate contacts with that African kingdom.[18] Yet, little or nothing of Indian origin has been documented. Parts of a city wall, a possible church, a kiln area for the manufacture of amphoras, and some other public and private buildings have been excavated, but nothing of the harbor has been found;[19] areas of early Islamic Aqaba have also been excavated.[20]

CLEOPATRIS/ARSINOË/CLYSMA (ISLAMIC QOLZOUM)

Cleopatris/Arsinoë/Clysma, later known as Qolzoum, is both adjacent to and beneath modern Suez. The Pithom stele mentions the port's foundation by Ptolemy II, who named it in honor of his sister and wife, Arsinoë.[21] Excavations produced little archaeological evidence from the Ptolemaic period.[22] Yet, despite its poor location vis-à-vis prevailing wind patterns, Cleopatris/Arsinoë/Clysma flourished in late Roman and Islamic times.[23] This was due in part to the termination of a canal at or near the city, which made transport of commodities by boat or barge between the Nile and the Red Sea relatively easy and inexpensive.[24]

Strabo (*Geography* 16.4.23 and 17.1.25–26) writes about the port, but the *Periplus* passes over it in silence. Claudius Ptolemy (*Geography* 4.5) lists it, and several ancient writers— including Lucian (*Alexander or the False Prophet* 44), in the later second century C.E.— refer to it. Lucian notes how easy it was to board a ship here bound for India. The Christian pilgrim Egeria passed through Clysma in the late fourth/early fifth century and noted the city's prominence as the port for India.[25] The *Martyrium Sancti Arethae* reports that Clysma sent twenty ships for the 524/525 C.E. campaign to southern Arabia noted earlier.[26] In the eleventh century Peter the Deacon (116) also mentioned the nun Egeria's passage through and comment on Clysma.[27] One scholar proposed that the city's prosperity was due in part to the redeployment of troops from the Myos Hormos–Nile road to Clysma beginning in the fourth century.[28] Unfortunately, little has been published about the excavations, and virtually nothing about "international" connections, that extant ancient written sources discuss. No ancient harbor has ever been uncovered. Fieldwork will begin again at Clysma in the future to document further the ancient port and its connection to the Nile canal.[29]

NILE–RED SEA CANAL

The history of the canal linking the Nile to the Red Sea at or near Arsinoë/Cleopatris/Clysma is incompletely understood. Logically, a Nile–Red Sea canal would have followed existing branches of the Nile in the Eastern Delta. The Pithom stele indicates that Ptolemy II excavated it[30] and suggests, given its find spot, that one of the canal's manifestations passed by Pithom (modern Tell al-Maskhuta). Today nothing recognizable survives of the Nile–Red Sea canal, although sections may have been visible until the early to mid 1980s.[31] In a densely inhabited, heavily cultivated, and damp environment such as the Nile Delta, one would not expect to find surviving evidence, though the layout of some of agricultural fields suggests the course of the canal. There are plans to continue survey work near the termination of the canal at Suez in the near future.[32]

There is disagreement about who constructed the earliest canal known here. Partly, this stems from the fact that rulers responsible for dredging or maintaining earlier canals were given credit for initial excavation, due to honest errors or flattery. We do not know the names or locations of most towns near which these canals passed, nor do we know the locations of the canals' termini throughout their long history, though we have an approximate idea.

The earliest possible reference to the canal can be found in the Middle Kingdom (1975–1640 B.C.E.)—the 12th Dynasty pharaoh Sesostris is mentioned in several ancient sources, including Strabo (*Geography* 17.1.25) and Pliny (*NH* 6.33.165)—and some have argued that it continued until the reign of Ramses III (1187–1156 B.C.E.);[33] not all scholars, however, accept this assertion.[34] Herodotus (2.158–159, 4.39, 4.42) reports that Necho II (610–595 B.C.E.) began excavating the canal but stopped as the result of an oracular warning. Herodotus (2.158) records that it required four days to negotiate the length of the canal, which was wide enough for two triremes to travel abreast. Diodorus Siculus (1.33.9) reports that Necho II began construction on the first Nile–Red Sea canal, which he never completed.[35] After the Achaemenid Persian conquest of Egypt in 525 B.C.E. several stelai found in the eastern Nile Delta record that Darius I (521–486 B.C.E.) continued Necho's canal, which he claims to have completed,[36] but Diodorus (1.33.9) writes that he did not. The Pithom stele indicates that a canal dug by Ptolemy II in 269 B.C.E. actually reached the Red Sea,[37] and Diodorus (1.33.11) agrees, adding that Philadephus's engineers did so using a system of locks. Archaeological surveying around and east of Tell al-Maskhuta noted twice as many Ptolemaic sites as Persian-era ones.[38] This may indicate that completion of the canal resulted in increased prosperity along and near its route.

The earliest written evidence of a Roman canal comes during the reign of Trajan,[39] but maintenance or reworking must have been carried out between the time of Ptolemy II's "construction" and Trajan's; a likely period would have been during the reign of Augustus or Tiberius. A survey noted even more early Roman sites than Ptolemaic ones east of Tell al-Maskhuta, indicating a peak of prosperity at that time; thereafter the number of sites declined.[40]

Pliny says (*NH* 6.33.165) that the canal was 65.5 Roman miles (96.8 km) long, 100 Roman feet (29.6 m) wide, and 30 Roman feet (8.88 m) deep. These dimensions must have varied with each new dredging. Authors referring to the canal include Herodotus (2.158–159; 4.39; 4.42), Aristotle (*Meteorologica* 1.14 352b25), Agatharchides (in Diodorus Siculus 1.33.7–12), Strabo (*Geography* 17.1.25–26), and Pliny the Elder (*NH* 6.33.165–166). Claudius Ptolemy (*Geography* 4.5) mentions the canal, and Lucian (*Alexander or the False Prophet* 44) perhaps alludes to it when he refers to the ease with which one could board a ship at Clysma bound for India. The late fourth-/early fifth-century Christian pilgrim Egeria also passed through Clysma several times, which suggests the prominence of the port for voyages to India in her day.[41] These later references to Clysma's importance may imply that a canal still existed and functioned from the late second century C.E. on and that it conveyed passengers and freight between the Nile and the Red Sea port. Papyri discuss repairs to the canal in 287 and 332 C.E.[42] and make references to a canal in the fifth and eighth centuries.[43] The ninth-century C.E. Arab writer al-Maqrizi indicates that the canal was navigable in his day and attributes one dredging of it to Hadrian.[44] These references in the third, fourth, fifth, eighth, and ninth centuries suggest that a canal was still in use then, but likely on a reduced scale. John, Bishop of Nikiu (*Chronicle* 72.19), notes Trajan's canal in the later seventh century, though he does not indicate whether it still functioned in his day.[45] Such canals existed, one assumes, aligned more or less along the courses of their predecessors—*viz.* following wherever possible one of the branches of the Nile—until they arrived at or near Arsinoë/Clysma/Cleopatris.[46] It seems, however, that only the Roman- and Islamic-era canals had termini on the Nile near Cairo. Recent work identified the Trajanic harbor and canal entrance. The latter was 40 m wide and lined with large ashlars.[47]

The creation of such a canal dramatically reduced transportation costs between the Nile valley and the Red Sea, which were relatively steep if conducted by overland caravan. As long as high-value merchandise or items of individually small size and light weight shipped in relatively large quantities were involved, overland transportation costs were not a serious impediment to their final cost to the consumer. If, however, one wished to carry, in quantity, necessities that were bulky but of low commercial value per unit, a canal would have been ideal for their movement.

Its long life, whether Pharaonic, Achaemenid Persian, Ptolemaic, Roman, or Arab Muslim, signals that everyone realized the great advantages that such a water communication route provided. That the canal terminated on the Nile, at or near Bubastis in Ptolemaic times and earlier according to Herodotus (2.158),[48] and, at least in Trajan's time, at Babylon south of Cairo, and not at one of the Nile branches headed toward Alexandria, suggests that one important function was to facilitate the transport of inexpensive bulk cargoes such as grain, wine, and textiles from the Arsinoite Nome and other adjacent regions to Clysma by barge or ship.[49] The Arsinoite Nome was one of Egypt's major grain, textile, and viticulture centers in the Ptolemaic and Roman periods and lay west of the Nile opposite Babylon.[50] According to the *Periplus* (6–8, 24, 28, 32, 39) all three of these prosaic items were imported to South Arabia and India from the Roman world. No doubt it was via the canal and by oceangoing merchantman departing from Clysma that many Red Sea ports obtained some of these commodities as well. Shipping goods via the canal was the most cost-effective way to transport them to both the more southerly sister ports in Egypt and to other, foreign destinations.[51]

On the other hand, evidence for trade coming from the east via the canal to the Nile is limited in the archaeological and textual record. Lack of material finds and references to imported items from the east might suggest that most cargoes merely passed through the canal for onward shipment to Alexandria. Yet, excavations indicate that Myos Hormos and Berenike also consumed some eastern imports; not all were destined for onward shipment (see chapter 12). Thus, one could reasonably expect evidence of consumption of imported eastern wares at Tell al-Maskhuta or elsewhere along the canal. That we have not found much indication of this suggests, possibly, that another answer should be sought.

Mariners may have hesitated tacking an additional 825 km or so from Berenike to Arsinoë against strong northerly winds, which would have added additional travel time and financial cost to the journey, not to mention a heightened possibility of shipwreck. Perhaps few ships bound for Egyptian Red Sea ports actually landed at Arsinoë to use the canal in Ptolemaic and early Roman times but opted, instead, to offload cargoes at more accessible southerly ports such as Myos Hormos and Berenike. By and large these imported cargoes were smaller, lighter-weight, more valuable imports per unit that could be more easily transported across the desert from Berenike or Myos Hormos. On the other hand, bulk exports, noted earlier and mentioned in the *Periplus*, and for which the canal was ideally suited, were better exported via the canal and Arsinoë to points farther south and east.

Later evidence suggests that the canal was not used perennially, but functioned only during the Nile's inundation season—from sometime in September to December/January.[52] Thus, use of the canal would not have been in sync with departure times of ships from the Red Sea ports for destinations in India.[53] The canal could have been used, however, by outbound traffic to the east coast of Africa outside the Bab al-Mandeb. One left the Red Sea ports between June and September if sailing to India and between November and April if sailing to the Indian Ocean coast of Africa (see chapter 4). Warehouses could have been used to store merchandise awaiting shipment from Clysma or other Egyptian

Red Sea ports to points in the Indian Ocean between the time that the Nile–Red Sea canal ceased operations each year and the period when the ships sailed from Egypt's Red Sea ports into the Indian Ocean.

OTHER PORTS

During the Hellenistic to late Roman periods there were scores if not hundreds of emporia of various sizes and importance scattered along the littorals of the Red Sea and Indian Ocean. Some were prominent, while others were obscure. Most are nameless and remain unlocated. Even the best known, like Berenike, have revealed only a fraction of the data that they can potentially provide.

ABU SHA'AR

The next site south that has been excavated is Abu Sha'ar, which for years some scholars identified with Myos Hormos,[54] one of two prominent early Roman ports on Egypt's Red Sea coast, together with Berenike, involved in maritime commerce with other areas of the Red Sea and Indian Ocean. Excavations at Abu Sha'ar refuted this identification; the site proved to be instead a late Roman fort (figure 8-7).[55] Remnants of Latin inscriptions found at the fort's western gate indicated its founding, or refounding, between 309 and 311 c.e.[56] The fragments list four Roman emperors reigning when the fort was built—Constantine I, Maximinus II, Licinius I, and Galerius—and the Roman governor, Aurelius Maximinus. They also record that the fort was on the *limes* (frontier administrative zone) garrisoned by a unit called the *Ala Nova Maximiana* (a mounted detachment of cavalry or camels) and that *mercatores* (merchants) were somehow affiliated with the installation.[57]

After abandonment by the military sometime in the late fourth century, Christian squatters moved in and used some of the fort's buildings. In the late fourth /early fifth centuries some Roman forts in the eastern part of the empire were abandoned,[58] and Arab *foederati* were increasingly deployed along portions of this frontier.[59] This was part of a major reorganization of frontier defenses. The military headquarters *(principia)* at Abu Sha'ar was converted into a church, as indicated by a fifth-century papyrus,[60] a rather formulaic inscription mentioning "Lord Jesus Christ" and dating to approximately the fourth to sixth century,[61] a polychrome cross in embroidered cloth (figure 9-2),[62] and other textiles[63] found in excavations of this structure. The recovery of bones wrapped in cloth and found in front of the apse of the *principia*/church suggests that this was also a *martyrium*, where the bones of some anonymous Christian martyr were displayed and worshipped— a common activity in the Coptic church in the fifth century.[64] A *dipinto* on the shoulder of an amphora found in the baths outside the fort records in Greek *mart*[— — —], a variation of the words *martyr, martyrium,* and their cognates.[65] This would be another confirmation of the presence of a martyr cult during the Christian occupation.

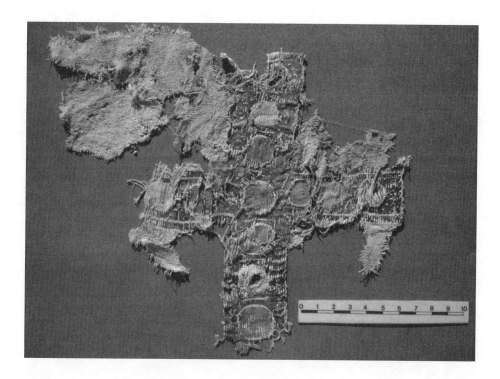

FIGURE 9-2

Abu Sha'ar, embroidered polychrome cloth decorated with a Christian cross. Scale = 10 cm.
Photo by S. E. Sidebotham.

During Christian use the fort's west gate collapsed, and that portal was little used thereafter. Subsequently, the north gate became the main entry into the "monastery."[66] The
walls of and arch over the north gate were covered in Christian inscriptions and graffiti.
These included two important texts in Greek. One noted Mary, Mother of God (*Theo-
tokos*),[67] while another recorded: "There is one God only, Christ."[68] A graffito inside the
fort had the epithet *Indicopleustes* (one who sails to India).[69] This may be evidence of contact between India and Abu Sha'ar, or it could refer to someone bragging about a trip
that never took place. It might also indicate somebody who "thought" he had been to India, but in late antiquity many were geographically ignorant and confused areas of modern Eritrea, Djibouti, Ethiopia, and the island of Socotra with India; the inhabitants in
these places looked similar in the eyes of Mediterranean peoples.[70] In any case, excavations revealed nothing of recognizably Indian provenance at the fort.

Abu Sha'ar fort never played much, if any, role in trade with the Indian Ocean, though
contacts with other Red Sea ports may have been more important. Abu Sha'ar's primary
role was as a military installation protecting this portion of the Eastern Desert, Red Sea
coast, and road system, with a subsequent secondary role as a monastery. In both capacities the site probably facilitated movement of people—later, Christian pilgrims—by sea

between the Nile valley and Upper Egypt on the one hand and Sinai and the holy places there on the other. Although investigations never found a port or harbor, Abu Sha'ar may have been a roadstead for maritime traffic between Egypt and Sinai.

PHILOTERAS

Between Clysma and Berenike ancient records report at least three other ports seemingly founded in the Ptolemaic period. One was Philoteras, and although several locations for it have been proposed, including an area south of Safaga and near the Middle Kingdom/ early New Kingdom anchorage in Wadi Gawasis, its location remains unknown.[71]

Strabo (*Geography* 16.4.5), Pomponius Mela (*De Chronographia* 3.80), Pliny the Elder (*NH* 6.33.168), and Claudius Ptolemy (*Geography* 4.5.8) drew much of their information about Philoteras from earlier Ptolemaic authors, but say little about it. Pliny calls it Philoterias or Aenum. Strabo (*Geography* 16.4.5) records that the general Satyros founded Philoteras and named it after the sister of Ptolemy II. Satyros may be the same man who offered a dedication to Arsinoë Philadelphus, sister and wife of Ptolemy II, at the Paneion at al-Kanaïs on the Berenike/Marsa Nakari–Apollonopolis Magna road.[72]

MYOS HORMOS

A prominent early Roman port was Myos Hormos, whose position scholars long debated[73] but that can now be identified with Quseir al-Qadim.[74] Diodorus Siculus (3.39–1–2), Strabo (*Geography* 16.4.5, 16.4.24, 16.4.45, 17.1.45), the *Periplus* (1, 19), Pliny the Elder (*NH* 6.33.168), and Claudius Ptolemy (*Geography* 4.5.8) mention Myos Hormos. The Nikanor Ostraka Archive[75] indicates that Myos Hormos was a competitor of Berenike. Headquartered at Koptos, several generations of the Nikanor family transported commodities between that Nile emporium and Berenike and Myos Hormos.

Ostraka, papyri, graffiti, and inscriptions from *praesidia* along the Myos Hormos– Nile road[76] suggest that Myos Hormos should be identified with Quseir al-Qadim. Myos Hormos is approximately 300 km north of Berenike and about 6–8 km north of the center of modern Quseir. Excavations document Roman activity here between the first and third centuries C.E.[77] Little aside from a coin and some sherds from the harbor attest Ptolemaic presence.[78] Strabo (*Geography* 17.1.45) writes that Myos Hormos was more important than Berenike in his day, but archaeological evidence from excavations in both ports does not bear him out.

Visible remains of Myos Hormos cover about ten hectares.[79] Archaeologists also identified Islamic use of the port. Excavators found structures including manufacturing, storage, domestic, and harbor facilities. Geological coring of the wadi south and west of the ruins indicates that the Roman harbor lay here. An early Roman wharf was made from thousands of recycled amphoras.[80] As the harbor silted up and the coastline prograded, the Romans may have cleared it to keep it accessible to maritime traffic. The remains of an artificial island in the silted-up harbor may be their dredge heap.[81] Unfortunately, they eventually lost the battle. During Islamic times in the late eleventh/twelfth through fifteenth centuries C.E., the emporium revived, and much of the city and harbor moved southward and eastward, closer to the advancing shoreline; the site was abandoned again in the fifteenth century.[82]

Artifacts, and floral and faunal evidence, indicate that Myos Hormos imported many items from the Mediterranean, the Red Sea, and the Indian Ocean regions in Roman times. Some imports were for local consumption; most were for onward transit. Indian-made sailcloth and textiles, fine Indian tableware and cooking pots, coconut, black peppercorns, and rice[83] (perhaps imported from Palestine, Syria, or Mesopotamia, where it was cultivated in early Roman times),[84] together with texts in Tamil-Brahmi, and perhaps Prakrit,[85] attest important contacts with India. Residents of Myos Hormos probably included Indians who resided there for mercantile purposes. Excavations at Myos Hormos also recorded pottery made in Axum and Adulis,[86] but Axum did not assume a prominent role in Red Sea–Indian Ocean commerce until the late third or early fourth century C.E., by which time Myos Hormos had been abandoned. Thousands of sherds of wine amphoras and glass indicate some items in demand in Arabia and India.

Excavations recorded Nabataean potsherds, ostraka, and graffiti.[87] Nabataean graffiti also appear along the Myos Hormos–Nile road.[88] A few sherds of Nabataean tableware were recovered at Berenike.[89] Thus, the slender evidence suggests limited contact between important Egyptian Red Sea ports and Nabataea in early Roman times.

Much of the third century was difficult politically and economically for many areas of the Roman world and the southern Red Sea; long-distance trade with other areas of the Red Sea and Indian Ocean decreased dramatically at this time. Perhaps the demise of Myos Hormos hinged on this factor; the steady silting of the harbor and progradation of the coastline must also have played a role in the port's abandonment. This silting phenomenon, common all along the Red Sea coast, also bedeviled Berenike throughout its history (see chapter 13).

Although recent research discounts it,[90] there is some evidence that beneath modern Quseir lay a Ptolemaic and possibly a late Roman settlement. Ptolemaic or Roman temple blocks were built into the walls of the Ottoman-French fort there[91] and in other buildings, suggesting that Quseir may have been occupied at those times. There are unsubstantiated reports of late Roman pottery,[92] which, if they are true, suggest that after Myos Hormos was abandoned in the third century, the port moved here to operate. Brocchi reported two sets of ruins in the nineteenth century, one at Quseir al-Qadim and the other at Quseir itself.[93] If Brocchi's observations are correct, an ancient settlement of unknown date lies beneath modern Quseir.

During the Ayyubid to Mamluk periods there was a revival of maritime activity at Quseir al-Qadim, as Myos Hormos was then called, with contacts extending as far as China.[94]

Quseir was important during Ottoman times and later played a minor role in the Napoleonic Wars.[95] It was also an important port for hajj pilgrims traveling between Egypt and Mecca via Jeddah until recently,[96] when Safaga, about 80 km north of Quseir, assumed that role.

MARSA NAKARI (NECHESIA?)

The last ancient port north of Berenike was at Marsa Nakari, which may be Nechesia, mentioned only by Claudius Ptolemy (*Geography* 4.5.8). Marsa Nakari was the smallest Ptolemaic-Roman Red Sea emporium in Egypt and was the only one, discounting Abu Sha'ar, with a defensive wall.[97] The town is about 150 km north of Berenike and approximately the same distance south of Myos Hormos.[98] Excavations revealed peak activity in the first and fourth to fifth centuries c.e.[99] A road linked Marsa Nakari to Apollonopolis Magna, with stops and gold mines near or along it dating from Ptolemaic times on.[100] This and the recovery of Ptolemaic artifacts from excavations[101] suggest that Marsa Nakari was functioning, if not founded, in the Ptolemaic period.

Along the Marsa Nakari–Apollonopolis Magna route are unfortified water stations, Ptolemaic- and Roman-era forts, and gold-mining settlements of Pharaonic, Ptolemaic, Roman, and Islamic date. Our surveys documented substantial evidence for both Ptolemaic and Roman use of the highway. We also discovered inscriptions at the small way station at Bir 'Iayyan. One text recorded the station's construction by Ptolemy II in 257 B.C.E., at a distance of 461 stades (97.7 km) from the Nile.[102] Thus, data from the road and from Marsa Nakari itself suggest that the site was probably originally a Ptolemaic foundation.

None of the finds, except some beads probably from Sri Lanka and India of late Roman date, indicate that Marsa Nakari was involved in commerce with the Indian Ocean basin. Regional coastal trade, its role as a safe haven for ships sailing between Myos Hormos and Berenike, and hinterland commercial contacts seem to have been Marsa Nakari's major raisons d'être.

An early Roman anhydrite quarry approximately 4 km west of Marsa Nakari was the source of much building stone used at the settlement.[103]

PTOLEMAIS (EPI)THERON

The Pithom stele[104] and Strabo (*Geography* 16.4.7) record that Ptolemy II founded Ptolemais (Epi)Theron to gather (*Geography* 16.4.4) and ship elephants north by sea, likely to Berenike. By early Roman times, however, the settlement had dwindled in importance. The *Periplus* (3) reports that small amounts of tortoiseshell, land tortoise, and ivory were available here. Pliny the Elder (*NH* 6.36.173) writes that Ptolemais Theron exported a great deal of ivory, rhinoceros horn, hippopotamus hides, tortoiseshell, apes, and slaves. Claudius Ptolemy (*Geography* 4.7) called it Ptolemais Venationum, but we cannot determine how important the settlement was in his day.

The location of Ptolemais (Epi)theron has never been pinpointed, though scholars have made attempts.[105] It was believed to be near Aqiq, along Sudan's Red Sea coast.[106] Yet, our survey found ruins at the village of Adobona suggesting that an ancient settlement, perhaps Ptolemais Theron, might be located there or nearby.[107] We identified architectural remains including fluted column drums near the village, but the sherds were Islamic. On the nearby island of Badhur we located cisterns and Muslim cemeteries, which we hypothesize were associated with the site near Adobona. Future survey work and excavation should clarify whether this is, indeed, Ptolemais (Epi)Theron.

ADULIS

Farther south along the coast was the emporium of Adulis (Gabaza) in modern Eritrea, whose remains lie in the Gulf of Zula/Annesley Bay. It was the port for the Kingdom of Axum, with its eponymous capital in Ethiopia today, and with which it was connected by a road requiring an eight-day journey in the time of the *Periplus* (4) and a twelve- to fifteen-day trip during the sixth century.[108] The *Periplus* (4, 6, 17, 24) indicates that Adulis operated at that time, that ivory and tortoiseshell were exports, and that Roman iron was one import. Pliny the Elder (*NH* 6.34.173) also discusses the port. Two of the latest references are by Cosmas Indicopleustes (*Christian Topography* 2.49, 2.54–56, 11.15, 11.17, 11.19)[109] and Stephanus of Byzantium.[110]

Fieldwork took place at Adulis beginning in the early nineteenth century.[111] Recent surveys discovered an earlier port, likely mentioned by the *Periplus* and Pliny the Elder,[112] and revealed more about the site from the fourth century C.E. on.[113] It seems that there were two ports at Adulis, one early in date and the other late Roman. Indeed, the Kingdom of Axum reached its floruit in international commerce beginning in the late third/early fourth century C.E.[114] Axumite coins and pottery have been found at Aila, Myos Hormos, and Berenike, and Axumite coins have been documented in Palestine, suggesting their transport by Christian pilgrims.[115] Axumite coins and pottery have also been found in southern Arabia and India.[116]

A military expedition launched by Axum against the Himyarite king Du Nuwas in 524–525 C.E. had the support of Justin I (518–527). The pretext was Du Nuwas's persecution of Christians, but there were also political and commercial considerations involving the Sassanians, Axumites, and Romans (see chapter 13).[117]

Justinian I (527–565 C.E.) proposed an alliance with the Christian coreligionist kingdoms of Axum and Himyar to fight the Sassanians; we are unsure, however, whatever became of his initiative.[118] Procopius, Cosmas Indicopleustes, and the recovery of Roman artifacts at Adulis and of Axumite finds at Berenike and, to a lesser extent, at Myos Hormos indicate trade contacts in early Roman times and increasing in the later period. Cosmas Indicopleustes spent time in Axum and was, apparently, present when the 524/525 expedition was launched. A fourth- to seventh-century C.E. shipwreck has been partially excavated near Adulis (see chapter 10).

Recently, two Roman military inscriptions were found on the Farasan islands, in the southern Red Sea. One, dated 143–144 C.E., records a vexillation of *Legio II Traiana Fortis* together with some auxiliary troops garrisoned there.[119] The Legio II was stationed in Egypt throughout this period, so any subunit of the parent legion would have arrived by sea undoubtedly from Berenike. The inscription does not mention the reason that Roman troops were located here, but monitoring maritime traffic and, perhaps, collecting tolls or taxes were undoubtedly primary assignments. The second inscription dates from about 120 C.E. and seems to record the presence of portions of the *Legio VI Ferrata*. This unit was stationed early in the second century in Syria and then briefly in Arabia and Palestine.[120]

Nabataean potsherds from one of the islands suggest the passage or presence of merchants from that desert kingdom.[121] Roman military units may have been stationed on other islands throughout the Red Sea whose identity has thus far been undetected. In 524/525 C.E. the *Martyrium Sancti Arethae* reports that the "Island of Farasan" sent seven ships to assist the Axumites in their war with the Himyarites noted earlier.[122] If true, this suggests that the islands were important in the early sixth century.

OPÔNÊ

Emporia in the Indian Ocean were involved in this maritime spice route. Ports in the Horn of Africa, such as Heïs and Damo, preserve imported artifacts of Roman origin.[123] One of the better-known harbors is Opônê (Ras Hafun), on the northeastern coast of Somalia. Neither Strabo nor Pliny mentions it, but the *Periplus* (13, 15)[124] and Claudius Ptolemy (4.7) do, and limited excavations have been carried out there. According to the *Periplus* (13), Opônê exported slaves, mostly to Egypt; cassia; aroma; perhaps matô; and tortoiseshell. Although we cannot distinguish any objects found at Berenike as deriving from Opônê, Roman ceramics have been excavated at one of the Opônê sites dating from the first century B.C.E.; these undoubtedly came from some port on Egypt's Red Sea coast, perhaps Berenike.[125] The other site at Opônê was in contact with the Persian Gulf and South Asia in the second and third centuries C.E. and then, in the third to the fifth centuries, only with the Persian Gulf.[126]

KANÉ/QANA' AND MOSCHA LIMEN/SUMHURAM/KHOR RORI

Two other ports are located on the southern coast of the Arabian Peninsula. One is Kané (modern Qana'), mentioned in the *Periplus* (27–28); and the other, about 800 km by sea to the east, is at Sumhuram, known as Moscha Limen (modern Khor Rori) and noted in the *Periplus* (32) as well. Both Kané and Moscha Limen seem to have been transshipment points for Roman products, including glass and fine wares, to points in the Persian Gulf, especially al-Dur, in the late first century B.C.E./first century C.E.[127]

The *Periplus* (27–28) mentions that Kané/Qana' belonged to the Kingdom of Hadramaut. At the time of the *Periplus* the port traded with Barygaza, Scythia, Omana, and Persis. Ships sailing between the Red Sea and India often stopped at Qana'; epigraphic evidence indicates the presence of a royal Hadramauti shipyard here.[128] Frankincense, an imperial monopoly, was brought to Qana' for storage in a warehouse from the island of Socotra, which was also under Hadramauti control. This was the major export from the city. Aloe was also exported and may have been transshipped to Qana' from Socotra. Qana' imported wheat from Egypt, wine, copper, tin, coral, embossed silverware, a great deal of money (coins?), horses, statuary, and fine clothing. Pliny (*NH* 6.26.104) and Claudius Ptolemy (*Geography* 6.7) also knew the port. There have been both land excavations[129] and underwater surveys of the harbor.[130] Excavations unearthed storage magazines; a temple, likely dedicated to the god Sayin; and a synagogue.[131] Also recovered were numerous Egyptian, Nubian, Black Sea, and Mediterranean-made amphoras, especially from Campania and from Kos, Laodicea (Syria), Spain, and Gaul; excavations also documented Eastern Sigillata wares and fine pottery made in Aswan, attesting a lively commerce with various Red Sea ports in Egypt in the first century C.E.[132] Indian and Nabataean ceramics were also recorded.[133] There were three main phases of occupation, with the most significant being the second to fifth/sixth centuries C.E.[134] In later times Qana' had little or no contact with India.[135]

About 800 km by sea east of Qana' along the southern coast of Arabia was the Hadramauti port of Moscha Limen (*Periplus* 32; Claudius Ptolemy *Geography* 6.7). This is ancient Sumhuram, modern Khor Rori. Excavations[136] of this fortified settlement unearthed residential areas, temples, and palaces.[137] Evidence indicates that Moscha Limen was founded in the third century B.C.E. and functioned until at least the fifth century C.E.[138] The harbor itself has not yet been found. The city flourished in the first century C.E.; finds include Roman amphoras and fine ware, some perhaps destined for onward shipment to the Persian Gulf.[139] A graffito carved on wall plaster depicts a two-masted sailing ship[140] similar to those appearing on coins minted by the Sātavāhanas between the second/first century B.C.E. and the second century C.E. This doodling may represent one of the ships that put into Sumhuram (see chapter 10).

SOCOTRA (DIOSCURIDA/DIOSCURIDES)

About 350–400 km south of Ras Fartak (South Arabia) and approximately 240 km eastnortheast of Cape Guardafui is the island of Socotra, known in Hellenistic and Roman times as Dioscurida/Dioscurides. Archaeological surveys identified cemeteries and settlements here.[141] A cave at Hoq, on the northeastern coast, produced ancient documents, including one written on a wooden tablet in Palmyrene, likely from the third century C.E. Other texts from this cave indicate the presence of Nabataeans, Indians, Ethiopians, and other "foreigners."[142] In antiquity Socotra was a crossroads for traffic between the Red Sea, India, and coastal sub-Saharan Africa south of the Horn.[143] These multilingual texts are, therefore, a reflection of Socotra's position on the trade routes.

Pliny the Elder (*NH* 6.32.153) and Claudius Ptolemy (*Geography* 6.7) mention the island. The *Periplus* (30–31) provides the most information, relating that the few inhabitants dwelt on the northern side of the island. These comprised Arabs, Indians, and some Greeks who engaged in maritime commerce. The island was poor, barren (no farm products, vines, or grain), and damp, with rivers, crocodiles, vipers, and huge lizards. The island exported tortoiseshell and Indian cinnabar. At the time of the *Periplus,* Socotra was under the control of Hadramaut, whose main city was at Qana'. Shippers from Muza (somewhere in southwestern Arabia, possibly beneath al-Mocha in Yemen), Limyrikê, and Barygaza (in western India) traded with the island sporadically, bringing rice, grain, cotton cloth, and female slaves.

Early Roman authors, including Dioscorides, who penned *Materia Medica* in about 65 c.e., note that the best-quality aloe came from Socotra. Aloe had a number of medical applications, one of which was as a laxative for both humans and animals.[144] Ammianus Marcellinus (23.6.47) referred to the island as Dioscurida and considered it, erroneously, a city on the Arabian coast. The latest ancient classical reference to Socotra comes in the sixth century, when Cosmas Indicopleustes (*Christian Topography* 3.65)[145] mentions that Christian clergy from Persia inhabited the island and that some of its residents, who were descendants of Ptolemaic colonists, spoke Greek.[146]

PORTS IN INDIA AND SRI LANKA

In India random discoveries and excavations have recovered quantities of Mediterranean-made objects including Roman denarii and aurei, fragments of transport amphoras, fine dinnerware, glass and terra-cotta oil lamps, and copper-alloy statuettes. Unfortunately, little or nothing organic shipped to India from the ancient Mediterranean survives. Numerous ports dotted the coasts of India, which were involved in local, regional, and long-distance commerce. The Romans seem to have been in direct contact with some emporia on the western[147] and southwestern coasts; there is some evidence that they also traded with ports on the east coast. Two ports of significance are Muziris and Podukê. The former was on the Kerala/Malabar (southwestern) coast, while the latter lay on the Coromandel (southeastern) coast. There were extensive contacts between the Roman world and Taprobane/Serendip (modern Sri Lanka), especially in late Roman times.[148]

Debate has long surrounded the location and identification of Muziris, mentioned in the *Periplus* (53 and 56) and by Pliny the Elder (*NH* 6.26.104) as a prominent port on the Kerala coast.[149] Claudius Ptolemy (*Geography* 7.1) also notes Muziris. Locating and identifying ancient sites in this region is problematical due to a change in sea level of up to 1 m over the past five thousand years, which has eroded or destroyed many coastal sites.[150] North of Cochin/Kochi the coastline has extended several kilometers westward, which would situate any ancient ports some distance inland.[151] Recently, excavations and surveys in the village of Pattanam have found evidence of a sizable settlement and large quantities of small finds, including thousands of beads,[152] copper-alloy and lead Chera coins,[153] and over three thousand Mediterranean-made amphora sherds.[154] Fragments of Roman glass pillar bowls and *terra sigillata* have also been recovered.[155] Remains of a wooden dugout boat almost 6 m long,[156] bollards made of teak,[157] and a wharf made of fired brick have been excavated.[158] The discovery of fragments of frankincense suggests contact with southern Arabia.[159] It is still too soon to make a positive identification of these remains with Muziris, but this site is the best candidate thus far proposed. The *Periplus* (56) states that ships took on pepper at Muziris destined for Western ports, and Tamil Sangam poems also note the trade in pepper here.[160] Other items exported from Muziris included malabathron, pearls, ivory, Chinese silk, Gangetic nard, gems, and tortoiseshell (*Periplus* 56). The Romans brought money, peridots (topazes?), clothing, multicolored textiles, sulfide of antimony, coral (presumably the western Mediterranean type), raw glass, copper, tin, lead, wine, realgar, orpiment, and grain (*Periplus* 56). The *Periplus* states that the latter commodity was for consumption by westerners residing in the port.

The *Peutinger Table* (see chapter 8) mentions a *templum augusti* at Muziris, which has spawned scholarly comments.[161] If there was a Temple of Augustus, it was probably dedicated to the reigning Roman emperor, whoever he might have been. Its existence might signal the presence of a Mediterranean population dwelling at the port at that time. Several scholars have suggested that there was a colony of foreigners (people from the Mediterranean and other regions west of India whom the Indians referred to as *Yavanas*) residing at Muziris, undoubtedly for commercial purposes.[162] There is a Tamil Sangam poem that mentions a *Yavana* settlement at Puhar,[163] and there must have been other locations in India with westerners in residence in the Roman period. There is also the argument that the erection of such a temple at Muziris was a diplomatic maneuver by indigenous peoples.[164] On the other hand, the term may be only a Roman misunderstanding for the name of a monument dedicated to some Indian deity.[165]

Undoubtedly the best-known emporium in India affiliated with long-distance maritime commerce with the Roman world and with Southeast Asia was one the *Periplus* (60) and Claudius Ptolemy (*Geography* 7.1) call "Poduca emporium"/Podukê (modern Arikamedu).[166] It lies about 3 km south of Pondicherry on India's Coromandel Coast, situated on the south bank of the Ariyankuppam River about 1 km west of the Bay of Bengal. Excavations conducted here revealed an important emporium. It was initially involved in local and regional commerce; indications are that the first contacts with the "western" world were possibly in the second or, more likely, first century B.C.E. and the Augustan era, extending, perhaps, into the fifth century C.E.[167] Fieldwork here recovered hundreds of Mediterranean-made amphora sherds from as far west as Spain and Gaul, the northern Adriatic, and the Aegean as well as fine Italian and eastern Mediterranean–made tableware and a few other objects of Mediterranean origin.[168] There was also a fragment of a storage jar from southern Arabia.[169] These objects from the Mediterranean and southern Arabia are not mentioned in extant written sources, probably for the same reason that ancient authors pass over in silence the export and use of Indian pottery found at Berenike, at Myos Hormos, and elsewhere in the "west." It was, in the case of the amphoras, what they contained that was traded; the containers themselves would not have been noteworthy, though for our purposes they are prime physical surviving evidence of this commercial contact. Fine Mediterranean tableware may have been used by "western" merchants resident at Podukê[170] or, possibly, by local elites,[171] and were so slight in number and value as to go unrecorded in the ancient sources.

In addition to contacts between Podukê and the Roman world in the late first century B.C.E./early first century C.E., there was also interaction with local and regional trade networks. We are uncertain whether Mediterranean goods were carried from ports on the Kerala coast, like Muziris, overland via the Pal(a)ghat Gap to Podukê, or whether items came by sea to Podukê from the Mediterranean.[172] Possibly both avenues were used. There may have been greatly reduced contacts with the Mediterranean in the second century C.E. In this case, one wonders whether Claudius Ptolemy's (*Geography* 7.1) reference to Podukê reflected that port's commercial importance at that time, or whether he merely made that assumption based on earlier sources that he consulted. Unfortunately, the climate has not preserved organic remains, aside from some bones, so we have less "eco-evidence" of trade with the west at Podukê than we have of trade with the east at Berenike. Excavations recovered a few fragments of later Roman amphoras,[173] suggesting extremely sporadic, probably indirect, contact with the Mediterranean world into about the fifth century C.E.

Evidence from Berenike, from some outlying settlements, from the mining community at Sikait, and from Marsa Nakari indicates contact with Sri Lanka in late antiquity. Large numbers of beads made in Sri Lanka have been found at these Egyptian sites, as well as sapphires, undoubtedly of Sri Lankan provenance, at Berenike and Shenshef (see chapter 12).[174] Based on excavation finds, it seems that Berenike's contacts with India were more extensive than with Sri Lanka.

First- to sixth-century sources including Strabo (*Geography* 2.1.14, 15.1.14–15), Pomponius Mela (*De Chorographia* 3.70), Pliny the Elder (*NH* 6.24.81, 6.24.84–85), the *Periplus* (59, 61), Claudius Ptolemy (*Geography* 7.4.11), and Cosmas Indicopleustes (*Christian Topography* throughout his book 11),[175] among others, write about Taprobane/Serendip (Sri Lanka).[176]

Pliny (*NH* 6.24.84–85) reports an embassy sent by the island's monarch to Rome to find out more about this Mediterranean civilization that minted coins shown to him by a freedman of a Roman tax collector named Annius Plocamus. Monsoon winds had carried the freedman to Taprobane. Two graffiti found along the Berenike–Koptos road mention Lysas, a freedman of Annius Plocamus. This could be the same man mentioned by Pliny. The Lysas graffiti date to 6 C.E., whereas Pliny places the Lysas story sometime in the reign of Claudius.[177] Either a great deal of time elapsed between the arrival of the freedman and the dispatch of the Sinhalese embassy to Rome, or we are perhaps dealing with a garbled version of the story in Pliny, who first heard the tale only when he initially started compiling his *Natural History,* during the reign of Claudius.[178] The location of the graffiti along the Berenike–Koptos road indicates that a freedman of Annius Plocamus conducted his activities via Berenike.

The *Periplus* (59 and 61) notes that Taprobane produced pearls and cotton/muslin garments. The island was also a source for semiprecious stones and turtle shells, some of the latter so large that they were used for the roofs of houses (Pliny, *NH* 6.24.91); such shells were likely more valued as an export item. Claudius Ptolemy (*Geography* 4.1) reports that Sri Lanka exported rice, honey, ginger, beryls (low-grade emeralds), amethysts, gold, silver, other metals, and elephants and tigers.[179]

Large numbers of coins, especially late Roman bronzes (fourth century C.E. and later) and their local imitations, have been found on the island. Unlike silver and gold specie from the west, we assume these small *aes* issues were not major items of interest in commerce.[180] One wonders what purpose these small Roman bronze coins served.

A well-known site in northern Sri Lanka is Mantai. Results of excavations have not been fully published. Settled initially in the Mesolithic period and then abandoned, Mantai was reoccupied sometime during the second half of the first millennium B.C.E. and continued in use until the tenth century C.E.[181] Ancient authors allude to the region around Mantai, while Claudius Ptolemy *Geography* (7.4) calls the site Modutti/Modurgi Emporium. Mantai was a major glass-bead manufacturing center, exporting as far afield as East Africa and Korea; pearls were also a major export item.[182]

Excavations in southern Sri Lanka at Tissamaharama, which functioned between the fourth/third century B.C.E. and the ninth century C.E., produced considerable evidence of contact with the Roman world.[183]

SAILING TIMES

Pliny (*NH* 6.26.104) writes that sailing times from the northern Red Sea emporia like Berenike to southern Arabian ports such as Qana' were about thirty days.[184] This likely represented a quick voyage not including stops and time spent in any intermediate ports. The monsoons then conveyed vessels to ports in western or southern India such as Muziris in a mere forty days or so.[185] The trip from northern Red Sea ports to Cape Guardafui took seventy-five to one hundred days if a ship was sailing in a leisurely fashion.[186] Returning to southern Arabia or the Bab al-Mandeb from India or Indian Ocean ports on the African coast was rather quick, but the journey up the Red Sea required more time than the outbound voyage in order to tack against strong winds above 18°–20° north latitude (see chapter 2). Sailing times to and from these locations were not that long. The year necessary to make a round-trip voyage between northern Red Sea ports and India or the two-year round trip to the Indian Ocean coast of Africa was due to mercantile activities and the long wait until the monsoon winds changed direction to allow the return. A priority for crews in foreign ports would have been repair and maintenance of their ships. They may also have engaged in commercial activities for personal gain. Of course, the primary mission of the merchants would have been trade.

CONCLUSION

Ptolemaic connections with other regions of the Red Sea and Indian Ocean were more extensive and regular than those of Pharaonic Egypt (see chapter 3). There is more ancient written testimony about Ptolemaic activities in the Red Sea than there is archaeological evidence. Yet, even the written sources reveal only a fraction of what could be learned about commercial and governmental activities in the last centuries B.C.E.

Evidence from or about ports in the Red Sea and Indian Ocean demonstrates that in Roman times these links were longer lasting and extended much farther afield than previously. Despite the relative abundance of data, however, many questions about these "international" contacts throughout the Red Sea and Indian Ocean remain—questions that can be better understood only through additional archaeological investigations.

10

MERCHANT SHIPS

Excavations have just begun in Berenike's harbor south-southeast of the Ptolemaic industrial area. Nevertheless, we can estimate dimensions of Ptolemaic and early Roman ships, perhaps including *elephantegoi* (see chapter 4), that landed here. Calculations, which are based on remains visible on the surface, may vary somewhat from the actual dimensions of piers and quays once these are excavated. The ends of the faces of the extant enclosing arm of the harbor are approximately 590 m apart, although about a 90 m portion toward its southwestern end has been partially destroyed or lies beneath sediments washed into the area. One well-preserved berth has an opening about 19–22 m wide, while its protective inner part measures about 60–61 m × approximately 36–37 m. Other visible spokes of the enclosing lunate-shaped harbor berm are more ruinous and less measurable in their current unexcavated state. These rough surface dimensions suggest that a ship less than 19–22 m wide with a length less than 60–61 m, possibly as little as 36–37 m, could fit in this space; this indicates a short ship compared to its breadth, one more difficult to sail but less likely to capsize. This is the type of vessel (see chapter 4) that would best carry a heavy but unstable (elephant) cargo. We do not know the original depth of water adjacent to this enclosure, but future excavation should reveal this and provide some idea of the potential displacement and draft of ships using this facility.

Other than estimation of sizes based upon examination of Berenike's harbor surface remains, we do not know the dimensions of ancient ships that plied the Red Sea. The size of a cedarwood bollard excavated in a first-/second-century c.e. level in the harbor suggests that it potentially accommodated medium- to larger-sized vessels. We have some indication of ancient ship dimensions from wrecks excavated in the Mediterranean and northern Europe dating from the fourth century B.C.E. to the seventh century C.E., and we can use these to estimate sizes of their Red Sea contemporaries. Studies of over twelve hundred ancient shipwrecks from the Mediterranean and northern Europe suggest three classes: vessels of about 75 tons or less (most common), ships of 75–200 tons, and those of 250 tons or more (least common).[1] The largest vessels, on average, seem to have sailed in the Mediterranean in the late first century B.C.E./first century C.E., which was also the period of greatest activity at Berenike.

Approximately seventy-nine Mediterranean wrecks whose lengths can be measured or estimated with some accuracy range from 10–12 m to 40–45 m.[2] Excluded from these examples are small riverboats, dugouts, and rafts, and large luxury barges found at Lake Nemi near Rome. Also not included are vessels that hauled an obelisk during the reign of Caligula and huge grain transports sailing from Egypt to Rome. In the mid second century C.E. Lucian (*Navigium/The Ship or the Wishes* 5–6) reports on the size of a ship called the *Isis* that docked at Piraeus after it had been blown off course while en route from Alexandria to Italy carrying grain. Its dimensions were exceptional: about 55 m × 13.72 m × 13.25 m; it probably carried twelve hundred to thirteen hundred tons.[3] It would be important to learn whether vessels of this size ever plied the Red Sea–Indian Ocean route.

Any of the seventy-nine Mediterranean ships noted earlier would easily fit into the berth at Berenike, suggesting that whatever vessels did dock here were potentially, on average, larger than those in the Mediterranean. About fifty additional ancient shipwrecks are found in the Mediterranean annually, putting the recent total at approximately two thousand to twenty-two hundred;[4] thus, the numbers presented here will be amplified in the future. To make the dangerous voyage carrying elephants or to engage in commerce with southern regions of the Red Sea or Indian Ocean required large and solidly constructed craft that could carry as much cargo as possible[5] and be able to cope with the intense winds in the region. A first-century C.E. papyrus at Yale University attests the strength of these northerly winds.[6]

Roman Berenike was in contact directly or indirectly with an extensive area stretching from Mauretania, elsewhere in North Africa, Spain, Gaul, Italy, the Aegean, Asia Minor, and Palestine to other areas of the Red Sea and South Asia (India, Sri Lanka) on a fairly regular basis (see chapters 6 and 12). Beads made in Jatim in eastern Java[7] and possibly in Vietnam and/or Thailand, or more likely Sri Lanka,[8] suggest occasional indirect contacts even farther afield; nothing recognizable from the Far East has been documented at Berenike, though such finds, especially Chinese silk, have appeared in Roman contexts from Palmyra and elsewhere in the Roman Near East.[9] Seldom does Berenike seem to have been in touch with the Persian Gulf, though six pearls, one individual and five others found on a gold-wire earring from our excavations, may have come from there.[10] Products imported to Berenike range from common trade goods and necessities to exotic, more expensive commodities.

Ships sailing the Red Sea in the Roman era would have had two basic functions: military and commercial. The existence of a Roman military fleet in the "Erythra Thalassa" during the reign of Trajan has been debated.[11] We cannot be certain in the context of the ancient source that reports this which body of water it refers to as the Erythra Thalassa; the Red Sea, Persian Gulf, and Indian Ocean could individually or collectively be labeled with this name.[12] We have no evidence that the Romans regularly operated a fleet on the Red Sea, though Roman military inscriptions from the Farasan Islands (see chapter 9) suggest the existence of a fleet, some of whose ships would have conveyed troops to that archipelago. The earliest extant evidence of a Roman fleet in the Red Sea leads us to the conclusion that it was constructed at Clysma to convey Aelius Gallus's army to Leuke Kome for the invasion of southern Arabia in 26/25 B.C.E. Strabo (*Geography* 16.4.23) reports that Gallus built 80 ships for the operation and subsequently increased this to 130. We do not know what happened to those vessels following the conclusion of that endeavor; they may have continued to sail in some military/coast guard capacity. Perhaps they formed the nucleus of or impetus for Trajan's fleet.

If ancient literary sources are correct, there were major differences in construction methods used by those sailing from Egypt on the one hand and by their Axumite, Indian, and Arab contemporaries on the other. Shipwreck excavations in the Mediterranean indicate that early Roman vessels were constructed by the so-called shell-first method. Hulls of large merchant vessels were built using timbers joined edge to edge with dowels and metal nails;[13] the hulls were then sheathed in pitch, and sometimes in lead, to retard the deleterious effects of boring marine organisms. The 95 kg of lead sheets excavated in Berenike's Ptolemaic industrial area suggest,[14] and Roman-era lead sheathing with nail holes found in excavations at Myos Hormos[15] demonstrates, that this practice was also used in the Red Sea. Once the shell was assembled, a skeleton of internal wooden ribs set perpendicular to the hull greatly strengthened the ship and bound it together.[16]

In the late Roman period a new method of ship construction, called the "skeleton-first," evolved, whereby first the internal ribs were assembled and then the hull ("shell") was built around it. Large timbers used in the skeleton strengthened the ship, and lower-quality planking for the hull could then be used; basically it was cheaper, easier, and faster to use this method than the earlier one. This building technique also allowed easier repairs to the hull.[17] The Mediterranean "shell-first" shipbuilding tradition evolved into the "skeleton-first" method over a lengthy period, and some ships—for example, two found off the coast of Turkey—exhibit a combination of both construction techniques.[18] It is very likely that these two traditions were also used in Roman-era ship construction at the various Red Sea ports in Egypt, though there is no archaeological evidence for this. Nor, unlike the situation in the Mediterranean, is there much direct evidence documenting the size of ships plying the Red Sea. These probably had varying dimensions; coastal lighters traveling regionally and those ships sailing the East African route may have been smaller and less solidly constructed than those merchantmen destined for Indian ports.[19] Casson speculates that the latter were large and solidly built.[20]

Excavations in winter 2010 in the southern harbor of Berenike documented early

Roman-era (first–second century C.E.) ship timbers made of cedar and joined in the mortise-and-tenon fashion typically found in the Mediterranean at that time. Some of these charred timbers measured up to 3.15 m long.[21] These represent the first remains ever scientifically documented of early Roman-era ship hulls from the Red Sea. Unfortunately, it cannot be determined at this point whether these timbers belonged to a military or merchant vessel, nor were there sufficient remains to ascertain the approximate length of the vessel or vessels from which they came. Accompanying them were numerous lengths of rope measuring 6.0–6.5 cm in diameter and up to 13 m long, clearly used in some maritime capacity.[22] We discussed earlier the average sizes of Mediterranean shipwrecks from Hellenistic to Roman times and later, and calculated that the Ptolemaic/early Roman harbor complex at Berenike could have accommodated even the largest of these vessels.

Periplus (27) describes rafts "of a local type" made of leather bags, presumably filled with air to allow them to float. Procopius (*History of the Wars* 1.19.23–26) notes that Axumites, Indians, and Arabs, in their shipbuilding methods, eschewed the use of nails, pitch, and lead sheathing, opting instead to bind wooden beams comprising the hull with cords or by sewing them.[23] This building method has a long tradition, and the oldest known plank boat in the world sewn together using *halfa* grass is associated with the burial of Cheops in the mid third millennium B.C.E.[24] Excavations at Myos Hormos recovered hull planking made of teak and sewn together using coconut coir; it had been recycled to cover an Islamic cist grave.[25]

This sewn-plank shipbuilding tradition persists today, but Procopius's belief (*History of the Wars* 1.19.24–25) that this method was used because of lack of iron with which to make nails due to a ban on its export from the Roman world is not likely. As the *Periplus* (15–16) suggests, the sewn-boat tradition predates the appearance of the Romans on the Red Sea or Indian Ocean.[26] Sewn boats may have had advantages over the traditional Roman type because they were less likely to break up on reefs.[27] There was a custom of making sewn boats in the lower Po River valley in Roman times and later.[28] Thus, it appears that vessels of all sizes and made from a variety of materials partook in the Red Sea and Indian Ocean commerce.[29]

There are depictions of single- and two-masted ships in India contemporary with our period of interest. These appear on coins of the Sātavāhanas/Andhras of the early centuries C.E. as well as in paintings in the Ajanta caves of about the sixth century C.E. It is impossible to discern from these images the sizes or construction methods of these vessels.[30]

No ancient (i.e., pre-1500 C.E.) ship's hull in the Red Sea has been scientifically excavated. The locations of numerous wrecks are known and have been for some time, especially to sport scuba divers.[31] These wrecks are not protected, so many of the remains and cargoes have been damaged or looted; what little we know about the ships and their contents comes from curios randomly gathered from the seafloor. This is not a representative sampling, especially when exact find spots have not been recorded.

Three known wrecks include one from the late first century B.C.E./first century C.E., a second from the first century C.E., and a third from the fourth to seventh century C.E. The earliest lies off Zabargad (St. John's) Island about 80 km southeast of Berenike.[32] No hull was found, and the site was dated from amphoras that the ship had been transporting. The vessel may have been on its way from Berenike, based upon the amphoras seen on the seabed.[33] The second wreck, found in water about 7–10 m deep, is north of Ras Benas at Fury Shoal; it is roughly contemporary with the Zabargad wreck,[34] but no hull has been found. The third wreck, incompletely excavated due to inclement sea conditions and political problems in Eritrea, dates from the fourth to seventh century C.E. It lies in only about 6 m of water off Black Assarca Island near Adulis.[35] The wreck's contents include Aila-made amphoras, so the ship must have sunk en route from that northern Red Sea port. A concentration of amphoras, no doubt indicating an ancient shipwreck, has been reported in about 10–12 m of water east of Ras Benas, but nothing more is known about this site.[36]

All these wrecks are well known to divers, are accessible in shallow water, and, if ever the authorities permit, should be examined by professional archaeologists soon, before they completely disappear. Many other wrecks no doubt await discovery and examination, which would provide firsthand evidence of their sizes and methods of construction—information that we can now glean only from ancient written records and modern practices. Given these lacunae, we must rely on ancient written descriptions and depictions and upon artifacts directly related to them to estimate their sizes.

We discussed Ptolemaic ships (including *elephantegoi*), shipping, and harbor facilities at Berenike in chapters 4 and 5 and, briefly, here and concluded that evidence bearing on these issues was fairly meager. Fortunately, for the early Roman period there are more data: mainly written, some pictorial, but very little archaeological. More questions remain than can be answered at present. Excavations in the early Roman trash dump north of the center of Berenike unearthed a large variety of finds in excellent states of preservation. The huge quantity and numerous types of refuse, from various public and private sources throughout the city, provide detailed evidence for daily life, industrial activity, Roman customs-house and shipping procedures, and the Roman military's involvement in freshwater procurement for the city. There are also parts of ships' rigging. Items from this trash, including papyri and ostraka, allow us to date its deposition to no later than the third quarter of the first century,[37] about the period of Pliny the Elder's *Natural History* and the composition of the *Periplus*.[38]

Excavations in this early Roman trash deposit recorded items used on board ships. Written documents also provide insights into these ships and what they were carrying. Contents of the papyri are usually private in nature and deal with bills of sale, receipts, personal letters, land registers, and so on, although one seems to bear on our subject and will be discussed later. The ostraka, on the other hand, are more public documents and more informative for our immediate purposes. Ones excavated in 2009–2010 deal with the Roman military's role in freshwater acquisition. It is too early to determine whether the water referenced in these documents was for use in the city alone or also was requisitioned for departing ships.[39] Other ostraka are archival and derive from Berenike's customs house, which makes them a window onto both what was passing through and on to departing ships, and what types of individuals were involved in this process. Unfortunately, the ostraka's contents reveal nothing about what inbound ships brought to Berenike. Some ostraka provide evidence for items loaded onto ships for crew consumption, including types of food and wine.[40] Other ostraka list items for export to Arabia and India. The latter export items—especially wine in terra-cotta containers, and perhaps also wine in leather bags *(marsippia)*—appear in larger numbers than those items designated for crew consumption;[41] the quality of wine drunk by the crews was probably poorer than that destined for the export market (see chapter 12). The second most common commodity appearing in the ostraka is olive oil, followed by beets, onions, and a medicinal herb; the latter were probably supplies for the crews.[42]

Other remains from the rubbish related to ships and shipping were brailing rings made of animal horn and wood.[43] These were tied to sails, and ropes were then fed through them to hoist and lower sails on the masts. A large piece of Indian-made sailcloth came from the trash (see chapter 12);[44] a parallel for the Berenike specimen was recovered at Myos Hormos.[45] Excavations also recorded items resembling lifting nets used to load or offload cargos, or they may have been carrying nets used with pack animals.[46] Similar types of nets have been found at Myos Hormos.[47] Excavations in the early Roman trash dump found pieces of leather that may be corners of reinforced sails, although they might have been used for tents or animal girths, as parallels from some *praesidia* along the Myos Hormos–Nile road suggest.[48] Similar items appeared at Mons Claudianus.[49] These same types of objects were also found at Didymoi on the Berenike–Koptos road;[50] clearly, in this instance they must be remnants of tents or animal girths. A similar leather object from Mons Porphyrites was, however, interpreted as a carrying loop for a water or wine bag.[51] Possibly this type of reinforced leather object had multiple uses, where ropes were attached under tension to other objects such as tents, sails, loops for carrying bags, and animal girths. Another papyrus from Berenike's trash is a list of items related to shipping, including bundles of rope, a mast belt, block-and-tackle equipment, branding irons, and a type of gum.[52]

Excavations at Myos Hormos found similar material from this same time period, including ropes, running rigging to raise and trim sails, sheaves (wooden pulley blocks), brailing rings made of wood and horn, lead hull sheathing, copper tacks,[53] and a fragment of mid-first-century C.E. Indian-made sailcloth.[54] That Indian-made sailcloth from the early Roman period has been found at both Berenike and Myos Hormos suggests that Indian-built or Indian-repaired or -supplied ships put in at these harbors. Whether these vessels were entirely made in India or were merely repaired or outfitted there, and whether they were owned and operated by Indians or "westerners," cannot be determined. Vesicular basalt ballast stones found at Myos Hormos likely derived from Qana' and Arabia Eudaimon (Aden) on the Indian Ocean coast of Yemen.[55] This indicates more contact with those regions than the rest of the archaeological record from Myos Hormos otherwise suggests.

The Koptos Tariff, roughly contemporary with the early Roman trash deposit at Berenike and the sailing-related finds from Myos Hormos, refers to the transport of a ship's mast to the Red Sea coast from the Nile.[56] An ostrakon from the *praesidium* at Krokodilô on the Myos Hormos–Koptos road sent by Artorius Priscillus to forts along the route bears on this issue. It says that wood destined for ships at Myos Hormos is being illicitly sold by "the wagoneers" and that this practice must cease![57] Shipbuilding/repair timbers were conveyed from the Nile valley by both wagon and camel.[58] Pliny the Elder (*NH* 13.19.63) reports that blackthorn wood growing near Thebes was used for making the ribs of ships. We do not know whether he is referring to Nile vessels or to those plying the Red Sea. The only possible association with a species of Pliny's description is acacia, a tree that grows in the Eastern Desert and one whose wood was used by peoples residing at Berenike. There is at present, however, no indication that the ship repair/shipbuilding industry at Berenike used acacia wood for maritime-related purposes. Possibly there was occasional ship construction at some Red Sea ports, though this could not have been a regular activity. There is evidence from as early as the Middle Kingdom that ship parts made in the Nile valley were hauled to Marsa Gawasis for assembly there to take part in expeditions to Punt.[59] Ships' timbers and other objects made of cedar, pine, oak, acacia, sycamore, mangrove, and ebony—deriving from Lebanon, the Nile valley, the Red Sea coast, and farther south—have been found at the Pharaonic roadsteads at Marsa Gawasis[60] and near 'Ain Sokhna (see chapter 3).[61] It is likely in both Ptolemaic and Roman times that ship "assembly" activities occurred at Red Sea ports, but we have no evidence for this. The most plausible place where ship assembly or building activities took place in the Ptolemaic-Roman period on the Red Sea was at Clysma, close to the terminus of the Nile–Red Sea canal (see chapter 9). The relatively cheap costs of transporting heavy or bulky items along the canal would have made such activities somewhat more cost-effective than if all ship parts had been hauled across the desert on pack animals or wagons. One should surmise, however, given long distances from the Nile and the relatively high cost of overland transport,[62] that most maritime-related "construction" activities probably involved ship repair rather than ship construction, certainly at Berenike. It is possible that timbers for shipbuilding, more likely repair, were conveyed to Berenike by sea from more northerly Red Sea ports, especially Clysma. It would be important to determine whether construction techniques, designs, and materials of ships sailing from the Egyptian Red Sea ports changed once the Romans understood and exploited the Indian Ocean monsoons. One would expect heavier timbers to be used in ship construction for vessels of all capacities, and for the size, shape, and number of sails to be adapted to the wind patterns and intensities of the monsoons.

Since no ancient shipwrecks have been scientifically excavated in the Red Sea, to understand the ships' appearance and the materials from which they were constructed, we must examine contemporary pictorial representations. One from Berenike is contemporary with the trash dumps, although from a different part of the site (figure 10-1). Other representations are graffiti at Mons Porphyrites. There is a graffito carved into wall plas-

FIGURE 10-1
Berenike, first-century C.E. graffito of a sailing
ship. Scale = 10 cm. Photo by S. E. Sidebotham.

ter at Khor Rori on the Indian Ocean coast of Oman,[63] and a stone relief of a sailing ship
in Palmyra.[64] There is also a representation from Hoq cave on Socotra and another from
the Ajanta caves in India.[65] One also appears on a sherd from the Coromandel port of
Alagankulam, south of Arikamedu.[66]

The ship graffito from Berenike dates from 50 to 70 C.E., contemporary with Pliny's
Natural History and with the latest phase of the early Roman trash dump at Berenike; it
also coincides with the date of the *Periplus*. Literary and archaeological evidence demonstrates that this was also the period of peak commercial maritime activity between the
Mediterranean world and Berenike on the one hand and the "east" on the other. The graffito
depicts a ship in harbor with sails furled. There are two lifts above, and two braces trail
down from the main yardarms and are tied off below. There is a pennant above the spin-
dle that waves in a strong wind, probably one of the northerlies that pervade the region.[67]
We cannot determine the size of the ship from this depiction, nor its method of construction, but if this is a representation of a long-distance merchantman involved in the
Red Sea–India trade, then it must have been quite solid and relatively large[68] to endure
the voyage and carry as much cargo and, thereby, make as much profit as possible. On
the other hand, if this vessel was involved in the relatively easy journey along the Red Sea
coast only or designed to venture to the Indian Ocean coast of Africa, it could have been
a smaller craft.[69] The graffito, unfortunately, does not permit more insight.

Depictions of four sailing ships remain at Mons Porphyrites. Although the quarries
here operated from the first into the fourth and possibly the fifth centuries C.E., we cannot be certain when the graffiti were drawn. Unfortunately, they are so schematic that

they are of no value in determining sizes, appearances, or the materials from which they were constructed. Nor can we be certain that they represent ships on the Red Sea; they might be Nile vessels. These graffiti appear on three of five freestanding rectilinear-shaped pilasters made of stones mortared together and covered with plaster. These pilasters stand on the western side of a well/cistern in the wadi north and below the main fort in Wadi Ma'amal. Although crudely rendered and difficult to date, two are probably postantique, while two others might be ancient but could also be more recent.[70] There is no way to determine whether numerous sickle- and square-shaped boats that appear as petroglyphs in the Eastern Desert sailed in the Red Sea or on the Nile; in any case, they predate by several millennia the period of our interest.[71]

The ship graffito at Khor Rori/Moscha Limen (see chapter 9)[72] is carved into wall plaster and represents an ancient two-masted sailing vessel.[73] Though Khor Rori was founded earlier, the zenith of activity there was in the first century c.e., continuing into the early third. The graffito likely dates from this period. The depiction is similar to that of two-masted ships found stamped on coins minted by the Sātavāhavana/Andhra dynasty sometime between the second/first century b.c.e. and the second century c.e. This doodling may well represent one of the vessels engaged in the India–Red Sea trade, but from it we can determine neither its size nor the methods or materials used in its construction.

Another ship, a single-masted vessel, appears on a relief fragment from a sarcophagus of a Palmyrene businessman dated 236 c.e.[74] Palmyra was active in trade between the Persian Gulf and the Mediterranean in the Roman period. Palmyrene, Greek, and Latin inscriptions from Palmyra provide important insights into this trade. Palmyrenes owned and leased ships in the Persian Gulf to engage in this trade, and they reached the island of Socotra, Egypt, and, undoubtedly, India (see chapter 11). This ship relief dates to an era of Palmyrene political, military, and economic prominence and may depict what one of these oceangoing merchantmen looked like.

The Hoq-cave ship graffito on Socotra has three sails and likely dates to the third century c.e. The representation in the Ajanta caves is probably from the sixth century c.e.[75] The graffito of a ship from Alagankulam appears on a first- to third-century c.e. potsherd and depicts what appears to be a large three-masted vessel.[76]

Though no Ptolemaic or Roman ships have been excavated in the Red Sea, our fieldwork at Berenike has documented evidence for materials used in ancient shipbuilding. Teak, a hardwood from South Asia, is quantitatively the most abundant wood species excavated at Berenike, and large teak planks and beams, some over 3 m long, are often used in architectural settings, including leveling courses to steady walls. Many of these planks have dowel holes cut into them and some have nails, indicating that their original purpose was not as wall supports. One piece over 3 m long with dozens of dowel holes was reused on the floor of the "Northern Shrine" devoted to an unidentified mystery cult (see chapters 12 and 13).[77] If the primary purpose of these timbers and planks had been as wall-leveling courses, there would have been no need for dowel holes or nails, which suggests that they originally had another use. Perhaps these planks or timbers came either

FIGURE 10-2
Berenike, cedar beams from the roof
of a structure near the Serapis temple.
Beams have been recycled from ships.
Photo by S. E. Sidebotham.

from large packing crates or, more likely, from the hulls or superstructures of ships.[78] The *Periplus* (36) reports that Omana (southeastern Arabian Peninsula) imported teak from India; this may have been used to build sewn boats called *madarate*.[79] The teak timbers with dowel holes and nails found in late Roman structures at Berenike suggest that ships were built in a western rather than an Indian shipbuilding tradition. Teak is durable and does not split, crack, shrink, or alter its shape. It is also easily worked and has great elasticity and strength.[80] This makes it ideal for use in boat and ship construction. Al-Mas'ūdi (ca. 888–957 C.E.) and Ibn-Jubayr (in the twelfth century) both mention ships built of teak in the sewn tradition sailing the Red Sea and Indian Ocean.[81] Excavations at Myos Hormos found two sets of timbers covering Islamic-era graves. One of these, likely the partial hull of a ship, was made of teak and sewn with coconut coir stitches and joined with wooden dowels.[82] The practice of recycling dismantled ships into architectural contexts had a long tradition in Egypt, from at least the Middle Kingdom (cf. Wadi Gawasis).[83]

If the interpretation that teak preserved in the late Roman structures at Berenike originally came from ships is correct, this raises many questions about where the ships from which they came were built, their sizes and appearances, and the reasons they ended up recycled here. We know that the voyage between the Red Sea ports and India was very difficult. Ships built in the west and arriving in India would have required some repairs, maintenance, and replacement of damaged or missing parts. Teak, locally available in

South India—the very areas that we know were major contact points for the Red Sea trade—would have been the perfect material to use in ship repair or shipbuilding. It is a very heavy and durable hardwood that can withstand a great deal of punishment of the type meted out by the monsoon winds and heavy seas these vessels negotiated on their journeys. Once the ships returned from India, their damaged sections would again have required repair or replacement. Since timber was a rare and valuable commodity in Berenike, it made sense to reuse it in architectural contexts in the city. That these teak timbers appear in late Roman edifices indicates that at that time, some ships were built, at least in part, of this durable wood. We do not know whether these timbers represent remains of late Roman ships or whether the ships from which they may have come were merely repaired in India or built there. There is no way to know what portions of these ships were made of teak and for whom these ships were repaired or built. Nor do we know whether teak might also have been used in ships in the early and middle Roman periods. Scientific excavation of a shipwreck in the Red Sea would help answer these questions.

Numerous cedarwood timbers, some at least as long as 2.33 m, with cuttings in them, lie on northeastern side of the Serapis temple (figure 10-2). They probably formed part of the roof of the temple or of adjacent structures. They, like the teak, seem to have been recycled from one or more ships. Use of Lebanese cedar in ship construction and as recycled material had a long tradition dating back to Pharaonic times in Egypt.[84]

Excavations north of the Serapis temple and near the church recovered large chunks of iron built into the walls. Most likely these were remains of anchors.[85]

The Ptolemaic industrial area (see chapter 5) is the only quarter of Berenike where Ptolemaic remains were not covered by Roman-occupation layers. Numerous iron and copper-alloy nails and tacks and lead sheets were manufactured here—all suitable for ship repair and refurbishment. This industrial zone was most active in the early to middle Ptolemaic period (mid third to second century B.C.E.), falling out of use, perhaps, along with the western portion of the southern harbor before late Ptolemaic or early Roman times due to severe silting. Counteracting the continuous silting up of the harbor must have required an enormous effort in maintenance, and by the time Strabo wrote, the westernmost portion of the harbor appears to have no longer been used. The central and eastern portions of the harbor, however, seem to have remained functional, at least in the early Roman period, since the basalt ballast found there is reported to be from Qana', in South Arabia,[86] and excavations at Qana' have noted that that emporium began its life only in the first century B.C.E. and experienced its zenith from the second to the fifth and sixth centuries C.E.[87] Thus, the ballast found on the surface of the harbor at Berenike can date to no earlier than the first century B.C.E.

11

COMMERCIAL NETWORKS AND TRADE COSTS

After the annexation of Egypt in 30 B.C.E. Berenike became an important player in a series of interconnected local, regional, and wider-ranging trade and communication systems within and beyond the Roman Empire. A brief examination of important routes in
the Mediterranean world and a lengthier discussion of the Red Sea–Indian Ocean network permit a better understanding of how Berenike fit into this European-African-Asian
trading system.

There were two major trade and communication webs in the Roman world; portions
of these were not mutually exclusive, but rather extensions of one another. First, there
were the land and water networks that linked the Roman Empire internally.[1] The second
main category comprised avenues that continued beyond the Roman Empire as extensions of internal lines of communication and commerce. There were five important
routes. These were the "Amber," "Salt/Slave," "Trans-Arabian Incense," "Silk," and "Maritime Spice" Routes (figure 11-1), examined briefly in chapter 1. The Amber Route linked
the Baltic and Scandinavia with the northern Adriatic port of Aquileia; along it amber
and other commodities passed to the Mediterranean world. The Salt/Slave Route thrust
into sub-Saharan Africa via ports on the Mediterranean coast of North Africa, like Carthage;
along it flowed commodities, salt and slaves being among the more important. The Trans-
Arabian Incense Route ran parallel to the western coast of the Arabian Peninsula, bind-
ing southern Arabia to ports on the southeastern Mediterranean seaboard and Persian
Gulf; this carried primarily incense. The "Silk Road" stretched from the Mediterranean
basin overland into central Asia and the Far East. The Silk Road crossed the greatest

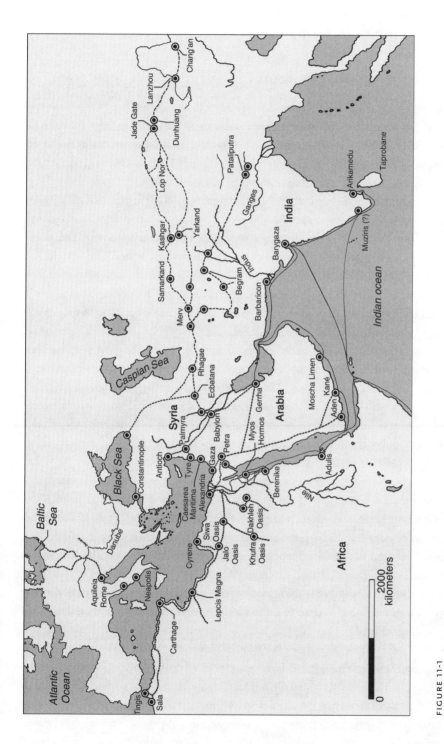

FIGURE 11-1

Map of the Amber Route, the Silk Road, the Salt-Slave Route, the Trans-Arabian Incense Route, and the Maritime Spice Route. Drawing by M. Hense.

distance of any terrestrial routes and was of great antiquity. The Maritime Spice Route,[2] of which Berenike was a part, was primarily by sea to the southeast and east into the Indian Ocean and, ultimately, to points beyond.

THE ROMAN EMPIRE'S INTERNAL ROUTES

Some of Rome's internal routes were long-lived and heavily used, especially on the Mediterranean littoral. Of particular importance were those carrying large volumes of basic necessities from primary production and distribution points to major nodes of consumption—necessities including grain shipped from Egypt, Sicily, and North Africa to feed not only Rome and later Constantinople,[3] but other urban centers as well.

Most Roman trade routes, whether water or land, were local or regional and, therefore, carried collectively the most merchandise over a prolonged period. Local and regional routes were most influenced by immediate prevailing needs and conditions and were, thus, frequently more subject to waxing and waning than water routes leading to major emporia, which required imports on a constant basis.[4] The creation, alteration, rise, decline, and demise of shorter routes depended upon supply and demand and, for agricultural and some manufactured products, on the climate and political and concomitant economic situations that promoted or retarded their use. Sometimes political and economic situations favoring or impeding trade affected the entire empire, or most of it, such as the prosperity of the first and most of the second centuries c.e. and the general political, military, and economic turmoil that slowed commercial activities throughout much of the third century c.e.—except, for example, in pockets of Britain and North Africa, which experienced relative economic well-being at that time.[5] Usually local or regional climatic, economic, and political conditions made a more immediate and profound impact on the degree of prosperity or malaise of a particular region.

Major cities were the largest and most important commercial points. First-tier *metropoleis* included Rome (through Puteoli, and later Ostia and Portus), Carthage, Alexandria, Constantinople, and Antioch (through Seleucia Pieria). The city of Rome in the early second century c.e. had a population estimated to be one million; the other four metropolitan centers had maximum populations of several hundred thousand, perhaps up to a quarter of a million to half a million.[6] Much bulk trade conducted to and from these urban centers was either within close proximity by land or over some greater distance by sea—in the case of Alexandria, also via the Nile; weather conditions and seasons dictated sailing schedules. Vegetius (*Epitoma rei militaris* 4.39.1–10) reports that long sea voyages between October/November and March/May in the Mediterranean were out of the question; it was extremely hazardous to undertake maritime activities during those months except in cases of dire, usually military, necessity because of foul weather and frequent storms that could quickly sink a ship.[7] Winter was also not harvest time and was, therefore, a slack period for shipment of some agricultural products such as grain and more perishable comestibles. Emporia along major lines of communication to and from these five cities benefited from their locations, acting as havens and revictualing points for ships and their crews traveling along the routes. Ports en route to these main emporia prospered partially because of the logistical support they offered ships involved in high-profile government-sanctioned and -subsidized long-distance trade in grain.

These ports en route, however, could not be sustained only by acting as transit points to or from larger entrepôts—especially in the winter, when sailing was minimal; the survival of smaller emporia, and others, most of which would not have been on any major maritime trade routes or, if so, may not have been major ports of call, depended upon their positions in the regional and local networks that were the backbone of the Roman economy. Their positions were important for two interconnected reasons: location on the sea; and, thereby, contact with other nearby ports, and communication with their hinterlands—inland communities within four or five days' travel time of the coast—on a more or less regular basis. These reasons were symbiotic.

DESERT CARAVAN CITIES: PETRA AND PALMYRA

The few exceptions to this rule of sea and riverine locations of most important urban areas in the Roman world include "caravan" cites such as Petra, capital of the Kingdom of Nabataea and after 106 c.e. part of the Roman province of Arabia; and Palmyra, which lay in the Syrian Desert between the Euphrates River and the Mediterranean (figure 11-2).

The earliest reference to the Nabataeans is in Assyrian annals of about 650 b.c.e.[8] The earliest western classical reference is Diodorus Siculus (2.48.1–5; 19.94.1–95.2),[9] who mentions the Nabataeans in a 312 b.c.e. context. Epigraphic studies suggest that the term "Nabataean" is not an ethnic one but a political label assigned to diverse groups, with different cultures, languages, and gods, residing within the Nabataean state.[10] Eventually the Nabataeans controlled portions of southern Syria, Israel, Jordan, Sinai, and northwestern Saudi Arabia.[11] They were major players along the Incense Route and, to a lesser extent, along the Silk Road and Maritime Spice Route. Their principal sources of revenue came from caravan trade as well as agriculture and animal husbandry.[12] The Nabataeans' major contact point with lands to the south lay on the Red Sea, in southern Arabia along overland caravan routes,[13] and, to a lesser extent, on the Persian Gulf.[14] They often led caravans, protected those conveying commodities, taxed them, and engaged in trade themselves, owning and operating ships in the Red Sea, Indian Ocean, and Persian Gulf.[15] We do not know how far south into the Arabian Peninsula Nabataean political hegemony reached or that of the Roman province of Arabia that supplanted it in 106 c.e.[16] Nabataean inscriptions and pottery found along routes to southern Arabia,[17] in South Arabia itself,[18] and in the Persian Gulf[19] attest their long-term interest in the commerce that passed along these desert tracks.

The Nabataeans also traded elsewhere in the Mediterranean world. Dedicatory inscriptions, over eighty-five graffiti in the Eastern Desert,[20] and ostraka[21] indicate their presence in Egypt, where they hauled cargoes between the Red Sea ports[22] and the Nile. Epigraphic

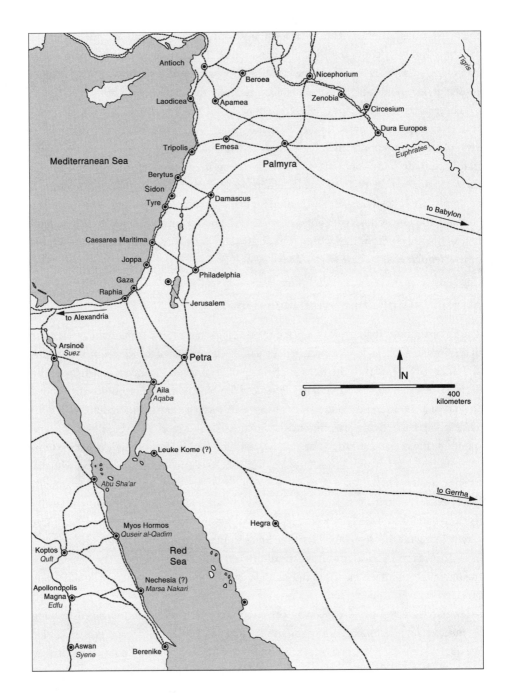

FIGURE 11-2

Map of trade routes associated with Petra and Palmyra. Drawing by M. Hense.

evidence highlights their presence throughout the eastern Mediterranean and Near East, including Gaza, Sidon, Beirut, Salamis in Cyprus, Rhodes, Kos, Miletus, Priene, Delos, Rhene Island near Delos, Tinos, Athens, Kourion (Cyprus), and Dura Europos.[23] Farther west, Nabataean inscriptions and artifacts of Nabataean provenance also appear in Puteoli.[24] Nabataean inscriptions and inscriptions in Latin, Latin-Nabataean, and Latin-Greek mentioning Nabataeans have also been found in Ostia and Rome[25] as well as Avenches/ Aventicum (Switzerland) (fragment of a Nabataean coin of Aretas IV) and Carnuntum/ Petronell (Austria).[26] Possible Nabataean sherds have been recorded from Sri Lanka.[27] The Nabataeans were also in contact with Palmyra.[28]

The other major caravan player in the eastern Roman Empire was Palmyra, known in Semitic languages as Tadmor/Thadamora. Located in the Syrian Desert northeast of Damascus, Palmyra prospered from its location vis-à-vis the water route leading to India through the Persian Gulf and along the "Silk Road." The Palmyrenes were sandwiched between the powerful Parthians, and later the Sassanians, and the Romans. Palmyra, the capital of these culturally hybrid peoples and the center through which passed Indian and Arabian merchandise on its way to Roman territory, first appears in Roman sources in 41 B.C.E., when Marc Antony raided the city.[29] Roman-era authors who wrote about the Palmyrenes included Josephus (*AJ* 8.154), Pliny the Elder (*NH* 5.21.88), and Appian (*Civil Wars* 5.1.9).[30] A municipal tariff issued in 137 C.E. by Palmyra reflects its rising political and economic importance.[31] The Palmyrenes under Odenathus came to prominence, however, in the third century C.E. as "protectors" of eastern portions of the Roman Empire from Sassanian attack at a time when the central Roman government could not defend the region itself.[32] Zenobia, widow of Odenathus, together with her younger son, Vaballathus, briefly set up her own empire, at Rome's expense, extending from Asia Minor to Egypt in 270 C.E.[33]

Evidence of Palmyrene presence and activities has been documented as far west as South Shields on Hadrian's Wall, where a tombstone was dedicated by the Palmyrene Barates to his British wife, Regina, probably in the later second century C.E.[34] There is a bilingual Latin-Palmyrene dedication to Malakbel (solar deity) and the gods of Palmyra in Rome of about 100 C.E. and a Palmyrene sanctuary in Rome just outside the Porta Portese of 236 C.E. dedicated to the Palmyrene gods Malakbel and 'Aglibol.[35] Palmyrene-style tombs were recorded on Kharg Island in the Persian Gulf.[36] Two Palmyrene grave stelai of the late second/early third century C.E. were found in Merv, Turkmenistan.[37] There is, however, some doubt that the Palmyrenes actually had a settlement in Merv. The grave stelai may derive from tombs in Palmyra as part of a collection formed in the nineteenth or early twentieth century.[38] The Palmyrenes may also have had a settlement at the mouth of the Indus River.[39] Another Palmyrene text appears on a wooden tablet in a cave on Socotra (see chapter 9). A third-century C.E. South Arabian inscription preserves an account of a Palmyrene (Tadmarite) embassy sent to the king of the Hadramaut.[40] Palmyrenes were soldiers and merchants at Nile cities including Koptos and Denderah, just north of Kainepolis/Maximianopolis, as early as the first century B.C.E.[41] They made dedications, restored three gates at Koptos, and had a cemetery and, possibly, a trade headquarters there.[42] They were also present at Berenike in the late second to third century c.e.[43]

The Palmyrenes also profited from caravan traffic, mainly that passing from the head of the Persian Gulf[44] via Spasinou Charax (Mesene)[45] up the Euphrates to the Mediterranean via Dura Europas and their caravan metropolis.[46] At Charax the Palmyrenes had a substantial commercial presence and owned or operated merchant ships sailing in the Gulf and beyond.[47] It was via Charax that goods traveled to and from other locations in the Persian Gulf and India. Palmyra's commercial interests were wide-ranging, and evidence of these has been found in Palmyra itself: Chinese-made silks were excavated at early Roman-era tombs near the city.[48] Clearly Palmyra's was a vibrant hybrid of Semitic, Hellenic, and Roman cultures.

Petra, Palmyra, and similar desert oasis settlements prospered primarily because of their dominating positions on or control of portions of ancient caravan routes along which were conveyed small, relatively lightweight (per unit) commodities of more than average value—usually aromatics and spices.[49] Yet, even these exceptional places also relied to some extent upon the agricultural wealth of their immediate surroundings.[50] In size, however, many Mediterranean ports dwarfed cities like Petra and Palmyra. Their spectacular rise to prominence was due to the extraordinary circumstances of location and opportunity.

COSTS OF TRANSPORT

Today large urban concentrations can exist and thrive far from an ocean, sea, or large river due to sophisticated terrestrial systems such as railroads and trucking and, to some extent, air cargo. However, this was not the case in antiquity in the "western" classical world. With few exceptions, most major urban centers in Greco-Roman times existed on or within about 24–33 km of the sea or along major navigable rivers; the latter settlements were few and not as large as those located on or near the Mediterranean. Some of the empire's major rivers, or portions of them, froze in winter, which also curtailed their use. Rich agricultural areas might also have sizable urban centers—a good example being Apamea, near the Orontes River in Syria.[51] Usually, however, major cities were heavily dependent for their prosperity upon commodities brought overland from their hinterlands within a few days' travel time at most, or from other nearby cities, or over waterborne communication routes ; the reasons for this are easily understood.

Reliable overland transport in bulk over distances greater than about 120–160 km, especially of basic commodities such as foodstuffs, building materials, and essential manufactured goods—though not of small-size, high-value commodities, as will be discussed in detail later—was relatively expensive.[52] There has been debate about the cost and efficiency of land versus water transport in antiquity. One school argues that transport by major river or sea was cheaper.[53] Others point out that this was not necessarily the case for many items traded overland.[54] Movement of commodities, especially over great distances, often involved a combination of both land and water transport, making any meaningful comparison of their respective costs impossible.[55] In addition, there were various reasons for transporting goods. Not all products were destined for commercial sale but might be tribute, military requisition, redistribution, and so on—factors that make direct comparison of land versus water transport difficult.[56] Whether a sea voyage was direct or involved numerous stops en route also dictated costs. The more stops there were, the higher the prices.[57] Land transport of some commodities in Egypt at certain times of year was very reasonable in cost and, during the Nile flood, would have been, in many cases, the only option.[58] In any event, transport by sea under optimal conditions was faster than by land. For example, according to Acts (27:1–3), St. Paul traveled by sea from Caesarea Maritima to Sidon in a day,[59] whereas we know that a comparable trip by land took three days.[60] We have other records of ships' speeds, which suggest an average of 70 nautical miles (130 km) per day.[61] Aelius Aristeides (*Orations* 48.66) claims to have traveled almost twice the average in a twenty-four-hour period.[62] Depending upon destination and time of year, travel and transport by sea could be substantially faster and cheaper.[63] Transport costs by sea varied even under the best conditions—based, in part, upon the size of the vessel, its cargo, and its destination. Roman-era shipwrecks in the Mediterranean provide some statistics on sizes of merchantmen (see chapter 10).[64] Although basic commodities imported from great distances—prime examples being pottery, bricks and roof tiles, less so heavy fancy building stone—can be found in inland areas far from their sources of origin, these did not make up the majority of manufactured items used in those remote locations and may represent the residue of consumer goods used primarily by elites who could afford the cost of imported versus locally made products.

One explanation for cost issues should be sought in examination of the seasonality of transport. Since sea travel was drastically reduced from October to March/May, it may be that land transport was not only cheaper then, but also the only reliable option for conveying commodities any distance. Though it may not have been necessary to ship some cargoes during the sailing hiatus, others would have been required on a regular basis throughout the year regardless of weather and irrespective of the cost and difficulty of shipping them.

Other factors to consider when evaluating costs of land versus water transport are expenses associated with shipbuilding, and ship repair and maintenance. Few if any ancient statistics survive, but costs must have been considerable. Regular sailing in the Mediterranean, in the Indian Ocean during the monsoons, or in the Red Sea inflicted varying degrees of damage on ships. Chapter 10 suggests that expenses to maintain these vessels were significant and persistent. Ship-repair materials found at Wadi Gawasis— and recycled teak and cedar timbers, lead sheathing, nails and tacks, and other ship-related materials found at Berenike and Myos Hormos—illustrate that costs of ship repair and maintenance must have been substantial. The passage of ships' masts along Eastern Desert roads, indicated in the Koptos Tariff, appears to have been commonplace in Roman times. These items and the labor costs associated with their installation on ships are expenses that would have exceeded those sustained when building and maintaining wagons and carts or buying and maintaining pack and draft animals—costs that are likely not reflected in documents such as Diocletian's Edict of Maximum Prices, issued in 301 C.E. Such expenses, which are not mentioned in extant ancient sources and are, therefore, effectively hidden from modern scrutiny, dramatically affected transport costs, especially on short and medium-haul voyages.

Land and water transport often complemented one another and should not be viewed solely as competitive. Seasons and weather greatly affected transport costs, especially by sea, as noted earlier. For example, it likely cost the same to transport wheat by ship from Alexandria to Rome, about 2,015 km, as it did to haul the same cargo approximately 160 km overland by the most efficient means possible.[65] Recently scholars have questioned this long-held premise, suggesting that factors such as land-transport costs incurred to move wheat to and from ships[66] do not make for a clear-cut argument.[67] This scholarly disagreement might best be seen from the point of view of costs incurred based upon seasonality of travel in the Mediterranean basin.

We have few Roman-era documents from the Eastern Desert that provide transport costs. Excavations in *praesidia* along the Myos Hormos–Nile road uncovered about twenty-four hundred ostraka, but only one provides a snapshot of local transport costs, and it does not deal with Rome's "international" eastern trade but reflects, instead, local transport from station to station of small quantities of items. We do not know, in many cases, whether cost of transport is included in the cost of the item to be transported. This particular text records little about costs incurred for conveying goods by camel caravan between the Nile and the Red Sea, which were likely very different.[68] One ostrakon records the conveyance of a jar of *hallec,* fish sauce, probably from Myos Hormos to the *praesidium* at Maximianon, a distance of about 65 km, for the sum of one drachma.[69] We do not know what other cargo might also have been carried along with this jar, nor do we know the type of transport—pack animal or wagon—that may have been used. A highly skilled laborer at Mons Claudianus in this period earned forty-seven drachmas a month.[70] Thus, an outlay of one drachma for the transport of a commodity to be consumed over some period of time was not excessive.

Throughout the Roman period no major innovations in modes of transport that led to dramatic cost savings took place. Thus, we can assume that ratios of land- versus water-conveyance costs held steady for most of antiquity, with sea-transport costs in winter being prohibitively expensive, but highly competitive for destinations on or close to the sea during the sailing season. It is, therefore, little wonder that the ancient "western" world's substantial urban centers were located on or quite close to major water-transportation routes; these were economically affordable lifelines throughout much of the year, without which large cities simply could not exist.

During those periods when sailing was minimized, ships venturing any distance did so only if compelled by serious circumstances, such as wars or food crises. Maritime transport costs in this scenario must have been extremely high, whereas those by land, except in the foulest weather or during periods of great political turmoil, would probably have remained fairly constant throughout the year. Thus, although not as competitive during the sailing season, land transport would have been very attractive during the late fall, winter, and early spring periods, when sailing costs would have increased dramatically. In some instances any price comparisons between land and water transport are pointless, since most rural areas of the empire could be reached only by land transport and would have been solely dependent on it.

A good illustration of the cost-effectiveness of sea transport during the sailing season was the importation of Egyptian wheat from Alexandria by sea to cities on the coast of Syria, when Syria itself produced wheat.[71] This demonstrates that beyond a particular distance for specific, usually bulk agricultural, commodities at certain times of year, overland transportation costs were higher, and, where possible, cheaper waterborne conveyance was preferred, assuming that points of departure and arrival were well served by harbors.

The "Edict of Maximum Prices" lists ceilings on the amounts paid for goods and services throughout the Roman world.[72] This is the most important economic record we have from classical antiquity, for it shows the Roman government attempting—unsuccessfully, because it did not control the primary means of production or distribution and could not rely on a stable and trusted fiduciary monetized economic system—to curb spiraling inflation. Many scholars believe that the section of the edict dealing with transport indicates that it was substantially cheaper to ship bulk commodities by water than by land, certainly during the sailing season.[73]

Lack of a large-scale manufacturing base and dearth of a significant element of the population with buying power to afford many manufactured goods to spur larger output and, thereby, decrease prices also affected costs of products and transportation. Thus, by necessity the Greco-Roman world was closely tied to the sea and major rivers for much of its trade of basic goods over long distances. For the most part inland settlements had to rely on nearby sources. Due to an economy that was primarily nonindustrialized and essentially agrarian, with rudimentary preindustrial terrestrial transport systems that could produce and usually economically convey commodities probably no father than four or five days' travel time distant, the populations of these inland centers had to remain relatively small compared with their maritime and riverine counterparts. Yet, the Roman Empire was primarily an agrarian-based economy, where most people lived in the countryside in small communities. Those living more than about 160 km from the nearest coast or navigable river lacked contact on a continuing and extensive basis with riverine ports or those on the Mediterranean. These hinterland denizens were, perforce, more dependent upon locally produced consumables of all types than their larger riverine and maritime counterparts.

There is debate about the degree of economic unification of the Roman world.[74] Given the situations noted earlier in this chapter, most people living in the Roman Empire obtained essential products—especially food, clothing, and building materials—in close proximity to their homes. Imports of merchandise from great distances and at some cost included marble and other fancy stone for building; items as prosaic as roof tiles or pottery might be transported across great distances for use on the other side of the empire.[75] Many of these latter types of commodities traveled as secondary cargoes aboard ships carrying primarily other goods, mainly agricultural (grains, wine, oil), the odd nooks and crannies in their holds stuffed with products that could have acted as ballast, filling what would otherwise have been wasted space; at least some additional profit, however slight, could be gleaned from such filler cargoes.[76] The discovery of well-traveled mundane commodities deep in the hinterlands may represent purchase and usage by the elites of those areas and does not necessarily epitomize a widespread phenomenon of extensive and sustained long-distance trade in those commodities for the general populace.

Pliny the Elder (*NH* 12.32.64–65) records 688 denarii for a camel load of aromatics carried for a 65-day journey of 1,487.5 Roman miles[77] (2,199.25 km) from southern Arabia to Gaza, but this represents commodities with a high price-to-weight ratio shipped over extremely long distances and subject to numerous expenses along the way.[78] Pliny's description, therefore, does not represent the typical situation in the Mediterranean world. Strabo (*Geography* 16.4.4) estimates that it was a 70- to 110-day journey overland from southern Arabia to Aila/Aela on the Red Sea.[79]

BANKS, LENDERS, AND BORROWERS

As sophisticated as some of the ancient business transactions seem to have been, the banking system in the Greek and Roman world was surprisingly rudimentary when it came to loans for risky commercial maritime ventures; banks—especially in Egypt—seem to have functioned more to facilitate payment of taxes.[80] In general, it seems that some businessmen either singly or in groups, depending upon the size of the loan and the risk involved, acted as banks, as did some temples. These groups seem to have provided most capital required to undertake dangerous voyages in the Red Sea and Indian Ocean.

Purchasing and transporting merchandise required outlays of funds. The long and dangerous voyages to the Indian Ocean demanded brave individuals aboard the ships themselves and money lenders with a high tolerance for risk. Though we have no specific statistics for money lending for such journeys in the Red Sea and Indian Ocean in the Ptolemaic and Roman era, we know that in the Mediterranean in the late Roman/early Byzantine period, bottomry loans, as we briefly discuss later in the chapter, were at rates ranging from about 12 to 30 percent or more.[81] We might speculate that high-risk trips in the Red Sea and Indian Ocean with a good probability of shipwreck incurred much higher rates and undoubtedly derived from multiple sources. Ad hoc groups of investors, which were likely not long lasting, might pool their financial capital for a specific voyage. Once the trip had been completed, many of these associations would be dissolved. Any recouping of the principal loaned and the interest earned on that loan came only after the safe arrival and sale of the cargo. We have to assume that some funds were also provided to the skipper and the crew at their departure to tide them over in foreign ports until their return to Egypt. These were undoubtedly deducted from their final pay. But how were crews paid, and at what rates?

Although no documents survive from the Red Sea–Indian Ocean trade itself that deal with shipping costs and salaries of crews, several examples survive related to ship and boat trade along the Nile in the early Ptolemaic period, and perhaps they can provide some idea of what captains and crews of the "international" Red Sea–Indian Ocean commerce in Roman times were paid. Ptolemaic documents pertaining to Nile shipping indicate that after expenses the skipper appears to have received one-half the profits, which he probably shared with the crew.[82] If this was the case in Roman times in the Red Sea–Indian Ocean trade as well, one can see how attractive one of these long and extremely hazardous voyages, if successful, would be for captain and crew. Let us consider an approximately 6,930,000-drachma cargo mentioned in a mid-second-century c.e. papyrus now located in Vienna.[83] This important document traces a consignment of Gangetic nard (used to flavor wine, to anoint the dead, for perfumes and medicines, and in cooking),[84] ivory, and fabrics by a ship named the *Hermapollon* from Muziris, on India's Kerala coast,[85] to a Red Sea port in Egypt, whose identity on the manifest does not survive. The consignment was then conveyed by camel under guard across the desert to Koptos and subsequently downriver to Alexandria, where the *tetarte*, a 25 percent ad valorem tax, was levied by government officials. Estimation of the amount of *tetarte* to be paid was probably calculated on cargoes at their ports of disembarkation, but the actual amount was likely paid to officials only (since it often involved large sums of money) at Koptos or Alexandria.[86] We cannot know whether this staggering sum of nearly 7 million drachmas was the typical value of such cargoes, but this amount would have been sufficient to construct an aqueduct for the city of Alexandria Troas in Asia Minor during the reign of Hadrian.[87] It is highly unlikely that this particular consignment, weighing about 3.5 tons, filled the entire hold of the *Hermapollon;* it must have been merely one of a number of cargoes belonging to different business interests.[88] The practice of mixed cargoes of merchandise belonging to different entrepreneurs is well attested in Roman maritime commerce in the Mediterranean.[89] This may also have been the practice in Roman maritime commercial activities in the Red Sea and Indian Ocean. An ordinary merchantman in the Mediterranean could convey cargo many times the size of that appearing in the papyrus (see chapter 10),[90] suggesting that the consignment in our document made up only part of the *Hermapollon*'s cargo. We can only imagine what the remaining freight of the *Hermapollon* might have been and its value.

Although we will never know the volume or value of this trade in any particular year, calculations based on information in the "Muziris" papyrus provide an approximate idea of the cost of merchandise imported to the Red Sea ports of Egypt. Since no ancient ships have been excavated in the Red Sea, let us take examples from the Mediterranean as models for our projections. Examination of approximately twelve hundred ancient shipwrecks in the Mediterranean up to the late 1980s/early 1990s indicates that the most common

Roman merchantman had a capacity of about 75 tons.[91] The next most common category was ships with capacities of 75 to 200 tons. The largest, and least common, variety had a capacity of 250 tons and more.[92]

The 75-ton-capacity vessel could carry more than twenty-one consignments, each weighing 3.5 tons (the weight of the Muziris papyrus cargo), with room to spare. If each consignment had a value of approximately 7 million drachmas, then such a vessel could potentially carry a total cargo valued at about 147 million drachmas. Some ships plying the Egypt–Arabia–India route would have been substantially larger, some smaller, and not all consignments would have had this value; some would have been less, others more valuable. Strabo records (*Geography* 2.5.12) in his day that about 120 ships per annum were involved in this trade. The peak of this commerce, based upon archaeological evidence from Myos Hormos and Berenike, seems to have been during the Claudian-Neronian-Flavian periods (41–96) through the reign of Trajan (98–117) and perhaps somewhat later; we can, thus, conservatively estimate that perhaps 150 or more ships a year were involved in this lucrative commerce at that time.

If we take Strabo's figure of 120 ships, the 75-ton-capacity figure for a merchantman, and the 147-million-drachma value of a cargo, the result is an estimated (probably minimum) annual value of imports in the first and early second centuries C.E. of 17.64 billion drachmas. Larger and more numerous ships and cargoes would, of course, greatly increase this figure. When one considers that the average monthly salary of a skilled workman along the Nile in the first to second century C.E. was approximately 25 drachmas and that his skilled counterpart in an Eastern Desert quarry received 47 drachmas a month,[93] the estimated buying power of one year's worth of these combined cargoes of Eastern merchandise at 17.64 billion drachmas truly becomes evident. The government collected 25 percent ad valorem taxes on this, and levied fees for using the ports, the desert roads, and so on. The income the provincial and Roman imperial governments garnered from indirect involvement in and promotion of this commerce was staggering and clearly worth the efforts expended to build and maintain roads and forts protecting this commerce, and to underwrite the cost of the garrisons.

Another document found in a tower tomb in Umm Bilqis at Palmyra records even more impressive sums involved in the caravan trade passing through that desert emporium and the resulting revenues generated for the government.[94] It is impossible to ascertain what percentage of the tax revenues of the Roman state these figures from Egypt and Syria represent. One must assume, however, that they are not unusual, suggesting that profits in this international commerce were substantial and that tax revenues accruing to the government were considerable.

For the cargo aboard the *Hermapollon* detailed on the Vienna papyrus, subtracting expenses—which would probably have included ship repairs (let us guess 25 percent of roughly 7 million, or 1.75 million, drachmas), the 25 percent ad valorem *(tetarte)* tax (another approximately 1.75 million), and transdesert and Nile River transport costs that would have been levied—there would have been roughly 3.2–3.3 million drachmas left. In this scenario half of the 3.2–3.3 million drachmas left over would go to the investors/ship owners (about 1.6–1.65 million) and, if our Ptolemaic model is correct, the balance of roughly 1.6–1.65 million to the skipper and his crew—a truly amazing amount of money if our estimate is correct, one that would have afforded any of the crew members a long and prosperous retirement. It is unlikely, however, that a captain and his crew would become ancient millionaires after one or two years of work, no matter how dangerous. Evidence from Ptolemaic Nile shipping practices may provide a more likely answer. Sometimes both skippers and crews might work for a fixed annual wage paid upon successful completion of a voyage.[95] This is likely the arrangement most often used in the risky, high-stakes international commerce between the Red Sea and Indian Ocean in Roman times. Perhaps a bonus was paid upon successful completion of a voyage. Skippers and crews might also supplement their pay with commercial activities of their own in the ports they visited during such voyages.

An inscription from the second or early third century c.e. refers to women as owners of a "fleet" in the Red Sea.[96] Aelia Isidora and Aelia Olympias made a dedication to Leto at the temple at Medamoud (northeast of Thebes and south of Koptos), and in it they refer to themselves as *naukleroi* (ship owners) and *emporoi* (merchants). We do not know how many ships their "fleet" comprised, their sizes, or whether they merely sailed up and down the Red Sea coast among the various ports or also ventured farther south into the Indian Ocean. How these women financed their operations is also a mystery.

Bottomry loans were made by individuals or groups that pooled their capital to make high-risk, high-interest loans to ship owners or merchants making the voyages. These were usually for a single venture. Money was proffered, with collateral being the very ships themselves (i.e., their bottoms or hulls, hence the term) that carried the cargoes for which the loans were secured. Interest rates in general would be considered usurious by today's standards and never seem to have been below about 12 percent, with rates of 30 percent or more being not uncommon.[97] We can imagine that rates on bottomry loans or other loans intended for ships and merchandise braving the Indian Ocean trade may have been substantially higher. The risk was considered so great that there was, until the reign of Justinian I (527–565), no attempt to regulate rates charged for this type of loan. In 528 Justinian fixed such loans at 12 percent per year. This lasted only a short time, since he was successfully petitioned to rescind this law.[98] The extremely high risk incurred by those loaning money to shippers was such that low interest rates would have led to a drastic decline in those willing to make loans, to the detriment of commerce in general. If a ship sank, the lender lost his investment. If the journey was successful, the lenders recouped their investment plus interest from the proceeds of the sale of the cargoes.

It is clear that immense profits were made and that cargoes comprised a variety of products. The government could not miss the opportunity to reap income from those engaged in this trade by levying tolls and taxes to fatten its coffers. In the Ptolemaic period customs excises could amount to 25 to 50 percent.[99] In Roman times these were in the range of a 25 percent ad valorem *tetarte* levied on cargoes carried by those vessels,[100] and a toll to cross the desert, with rates varying depending upon one's profession; prostitutes paid many times that of anybody else: 108 drachmas.[101] There were also costs of the caravans—including rental of donkeys and camels—and, probably (as perhaps recorded in the Koptos Tariff), costs for use of *praesidia* and their wells, and for protection provided by their garrisons.

Although we have no way of knowing the extent of legitimate profits the government and civilians engaged in this commerce made except to surmise that they must have been substantial, we have evidence and can also conjecture that there was a lively underground economy associated with this trade. Our excavations found possible evidence of this among Roman auxiliary soldiers in one shrine in Berenike; there an auxiliary archer from Palmyra named Marcus Aurelius Mokimos made an elaborate dedication that must have cost far more than he could afford on his military stipend alone. His military pay was likely insufficient, and he must have augmented that meager income with the profits from some of the tempting entrepreneurial activities available at the port, this added wealth then being reflected in his dedication (see chapters 6, 12, and 13).[102]

TRADE BEYOND BERENIKE AND ROME'S BORDERS

We discussed briefly other international trade routes emanating from the Roman world in chapter 1. Our interest is with coastal sub-Saharan Africa,[103] Arabia, South Asia, and, to a much lesser extent, China, Korea, and Southeast Asia. From these distant lands peoples in the Mediterranean basin acquired commodities the most high profile of which included spices, aromatics, woods, exotic animals, textiles including silk, and precious and semiprecious stones. One wonders how some of these items found their way to the Mediterranean; for example, Calpurnius Siculus (*Eclogues* 7.65–66) tells us that by the reign of Nero (54–68 C.E.), people in the city of Rome had seen polar bears, found only in the northern arctic regions, chasing seals in a pool.[104]

As noted previously, the Mediterranean basin's contacts with Arabia, India, and points east and south were fairly circumscribed and sporadic until the Roman Empire had expanded to include all of coastal Mediterranean North Africa and large portions of the Middle East. As the latter area came under Roman control during the first century B.C.E. and through the first and early second centuries C.E., the western termini of the overland and maritime trade routes on the eastern coast of the Mediterranean that linked the "western world" with lands to the east also fell into Roman hands. Once this happened and possibilities for enhanced contacts and commercial rewards were understood, west–east trade—that is, between the Mediterranean basin on the one hand and lands south and east of it on the other—and communication increased dramatically.

12

TRADE IN ROMAN BERENIKE

Evidence for Berenike's commercial contacts in the Roman period is far better than for the Ptolemaic. Berenike's peak era of trade was the first century c.e.; it may have continued into the second century, but not into the latter part, when a smallpox or measles epidemic, starting probably in spring 166, likely devastated the port's inhabitants, as it did much of Egypt and the Roman Empire as a whole.[1] There was a modest recovery during the late second/early third century c.e., as Palmyrene dedications to the Roman Imperial cult and Hierobol (see chapters 6 and 13) suggest.[2] We know far less about the remainder of the third century, since excavations have recovered little from that period except some sherds and a few coins.[3] The third century witnessed sustained political and economic turmoil throughout much of the Roman Empire including Egypt—a situation not conducive to commercial activities. Toward the end of the third century problems along the Nile, including several rebellions, the possible destruction or at least temporary abandonment of Koptos, and militarization of areas of Upper Egypt (the Thebaid) and the Eastern Desert, would have stymied trade.[4] Wars among states in southern Arabia and between Abyssinia and southern Arabia throughout the third century also adversely impacted "international" maritime commerce emanating from Berenike and other Red Sea ports.[5] Beginning in the middle of the fourth century, however, Berenike experienced a major renaissance, which lasted until sometime in the fifth century. Toward the end of the fifth and the early part of the sixth century Berenike was in decline and was abandoned by the middle of the sixth century for reasons outlined in chapter 13.

There are two major sources of information about items traded at or passing through

Berenike in Roman times. First, there are hundreds of ostraka and dozens of papyri excavated from the early Roman trash dump north of the city; second, there are the physical remains of the items themselves. A third source concerning products and prices is the plethora of ancient authors who wrote about this commerce.[6] The artifacts and ecofacts found in excavations at Berenike fall into two major categories: items destined for export from the Roman world to other regions of the Red Sea and Indian Ocean, and those that were imported. The latter includes merchandise used by residents of Berenike and items intended for other points in Egypt and the Mediterranean. It is not possible to identify precisely many ports with which Berenike traded at any time in the Roman period, but we can determine which regions Berenike dealt with and in this way ascertain which ports in those regions most likely traded with Berenike. In this regard we are far more enlightened than we are about Berenike's contacts in Ptolemaic times—except in connection with the elephant-hunting ports of the Red Sea, as noted in chapter 4. The reason for our lack of precision is, as was the case in the Ptolemaic era, dearth of specificity in ancient written sources. Our general ignorance of precisely where many of the ecofacts and artifacts recovered in excavations at Berenike were produced also equivocates the answers. It is virtually impossible to discern with 100 percent accuracy specific points of origin. As more written records are recovered, read, and analyzed, and as the discipline of archaeology becomes more sophisticated and more "scientific" tools are brought to bear in studying the ecofacts and artifacts, we will be in a better position to make these determinations more accurately. As other Red Sea and Indian Ocean ports are found, identified, excavated, and studied, we will also be better able to answer these questions.

Turning to the physical evidence from Berenike, we are on solid ground indeed, our only limitation being items that have not survived and those that remain to be dug up. We cannot, in most instances, determine whether items imported to Berenike were destined for consumption at the port itself or were intended for transshipment through the city to onward destinations within the Roman Empire. Nor can we establish whether many Mediterranean-made amphora sherds found in our excavations were destined for onward export to Arabia, India, and elsewhere; undoubtedly Berenike's inhabitants consumed the contents of some of these jars.

Another question is which of the items found in the excavations, and clearly imported from afar, were truly commercial objects and which were personal items of ships' crewmembers or passengers or conveyed by crew or passengers for use by friends or family residing at Berenike. This, though difficult to determine, is not impossible in all cases. Many commodities may have reached Berenike via intermediate points and not directly from the original sources of production or distribution.

A major handicap is the extremely small area of Berenike itself that we have excavated. Despite the embarrassment of riches uncovered thus far, one must keep in mind that only about 2 percent of the surface area of the site has been excavated, and much less than that vertically. Knowledge of regions and specific ports with which Berenike communicated will grow as fieldwork continues.

Let us examine this issue as best we can given the caveats noted here. One can analyze extant literary sources that record items imported to and exported from the Roman Empire, often with no more specificity than to say that they came to Egypt from southern Arabia, southern India, and so on via the Red Sea. None of these sources notes, however, that a particular product arrived from a specific eastern port—only the *Periplus* does that to a limited extent, and, of course, only for its time period (about 40–70 C.E.)[7]—through the Egyptian Red Sea ports including Berenike.

We can combine literary with archaeological evidence to establish which regions Berenike did business with and attempt to identify, as best we can, which ports Berenike most likely had as trading partners. There are two categories: those areas contacted by sea, and those reached by land. The former category is the larger and more "international" of the two.

ARCHAEOLOGICAL EVIDENCE

The easiest way to understand Berenike's commercial web in the Roman period is to begin with evidence of the most easterly regions in contact with our port and then move west across the Indian Ocean and Red Sea. We found a large polychrome bead—unfortunately, a surface find. Closest parallels indicate its provenance as Jatim, East Java, dating to no earlier than the fifth century C.E.[8] We do not know how this bead arrived at Berenike, nor can we determine whether it was a trade item or a personal possession. Only one has so far been documented, suggesting that it is unusual and not indicative of regular contacts with that distant island.

Beads have been found from excavated Roman contexts at Berenike that were likely made in either Vietnam or Thailand (although they may be from Sri Lanka).[9] There are no extant ancient literary accounts that mention trade between the Roman world and those locations, though the *Periplus* (56, 60, 63) and Claudius Ptolemy (*Geography* 7.3) recognized the existence of those distant lands, which they called Sinae (China) and Chryse Chersonesus (the Southeast Asian/Malay peninsula).[10] Also, objects of Mediterranean manufacture including lamps, intaglios, and coins have been found in Thailand, Vietnam, and elsewhere in Southeast Asia.[11] It is uncertain how Mediterranean artistic influences[12] and Roman artifacts found in China, Korea, and elsewhere in eastern and northeastern Asia arrived at those destinations—likely by sea via Southeast Asia, as ancient Chinese sources suggest.[13] It is doubtful that any Mediterranean contact via Berenike with lands east of India was direct; more likely it was via middlemen, especially those from the Indian subcontinent, who traded with both the Mediterranean west and Southeast Asia and central and northwestern Asia on a regular basis.[14] There were, however, several Roman "embassies" that arrived in China in the second and third centuries that we discuss later in this chapter.

The Berenike excavations produced many botanical remains and artifacts originating from the Indian subcontinent and the northwestern Indian Ocean.[15] Roman writers and

Tamil Sangam poets of about the first three centuries C.E.[16] discuss many of these, so their recovery is not surprising—merely confirmation that the ancient authors were well informed. Our excavations have shown, in many cases, that items noted in ancient literature were traded long after they were mentioned—something not known to us prior to our fieldwork.

More interesting are excavated items that pass unmentioned in extant written sources as commercial merchandise. We can only speculate why the ancient writers failed to note these objects. Perhaps not all finds excavated at Berenike that clearly came from South Asia and the northwestern Indian Ocean were trade goods, but rather items used by Indians or others from South Asia who lived at Berenike or elsewhere in the Mediterranean world. Several classical Greco-Roman authors mention that "foreigners," including Indians, resided in Mediterranean lands.[17] Dio Chrysostom (*Discourse* 32.40), in the first to early second century C.E., noted the presence of foreigners from many distant lands, including India, in the audience of a theater at Alexandria. The recovery of Indian and Arabian pottery, graffiti, and other items from Berenike, Myos Hormos, and other Roman portions of the Red Sea and Mediterranean world (e.g., Safaitic or Thamudic graffiti at Pompeii) indicates their presence.[18] Two recently recovered South Arabian graffiti, one from Myos Hormos and the second from Berenike, depict similar monograms or ligatured letters, suggesting activities of the same South Arabian merchant or trading firm at both ports.[19] Equally, ancient authors may have highlighted only the exotic, more expensive, and more unusual imports and did not feel compelled to list the more prosaic or lesser-used trade goods, which will be discussed later in this chapter. The high-profile items may be broadly defined as edible[20] and inedible products.

PEPPER

The most noteworthy import to Berenike was black pepper, a product of southern India and known from both Roman and South Indian literary sources (especially Tamil Sangam poems) as a commodity in great demand in the Mediterranean. There were other types of pepper exported to the west including long pepper and white pepper. Black pepper was cultivated in southwestern India and the Western Ghat Mountains and was shipped from nearby ports along the Kerala coast (southwestern coast of India) like Muziris and Nelkynda.[21] White pepper is merely black pepper that has ripened.[22] Long pepper was cultivated in northern India and was shipped to the Mediterranean from Barygaza on the northwest coast.[23] Yet, although excavations recovered other items at Berenike, including some matting and semiprecious stones, that likely came via Barygaza, we have not yet identified any long pepper. Nor have excavations at Myos Hormos recovered any long pepper. The high price recorded for long pepper (fifteen denarii per pound) by Pliny (*NH* 12.14.28), which was almost four times that for black pepper (four denarii per pound), may have led to a preference by Mediterranean peoples for black pepper. White pepper was seven denarii per pound. Pliny's figures are probably reliable for the city of Rome.[24]

The dearth of long-pepper finds from the Roman world may, however, have more to do with the difficulty of transporting the product than with its price. Long pepper is highly susceptible to mold and quick to spoil—all major problems on a long sea voyage. This more than anything may account for the dearth of long pepper and relative abundance of black pepper from excavations at Berenike. Pepper was bought, sold, and shipped as peppercorns and not ground; grinding took place in the kitchen.[25]

Based on finds from shipwrecks, we know that pepper had been imported to the Mediterranean basin since at least the second millennium B.C.E.[26] Pliny the Elder (*NH* 12.14.28) discusses different types of pepper. Judging, however, by the prices he records for them, and the plethora of ancient references, other varieties do not seem to have been as popular as black pepper because they were more expensive. One denarius was approximately one and a half days' pay for a Roman legionary only a few years after Pliny wrote,[27] and that was considered good pay; the average person was probably not going to purchase black pepper by the pound but in substantially smaller weights. Thus, pepper's price was not excessive, nor was pepper beyond the means of any except the most destitute. A late first-/early second-century C.E. writing tablet from Vindolanda near Hadrian's Wall records the purchase of pepper, seemingly by one or more people of relatively low socioeconomic status.[28] That such a document containing references to pepper was found at a military outpost on the periphery of the Roman world suggests that pepper was widely available and reasonably priced throughout the empire only a few decades after Pliny wrote. The price of pepper—we assume the black variety—seems to have dropped during the following centuries, suggesting that it was viewed increasingly as a staple.[29] Neither pepper nor frankincense appears in a late second-/early third-century rescript by Aelius Marcianus—preserved in the sixth-century *Digest of Justinian* (39.4.16)—that lists imports from India, Arabia, and elsewhere in the "east" that are subject to import duty *(vectigalia)*.[30] This silence in an important fiscal document suggests that these items were considered basic commodities and that the Roman government by that time ceased to levy tolls or taxes on their importation.[31]

South Indian literature, mainly Tamil Sangam poetry, alludes to westerners (including Persians and Roman subjects), whom they called *Yavanas*, arriving by ship to South India,[32] especially to Muziris, to collect the black pepper (*Ahananuru* 149, 7–11). Roman sources are replete with references to black pepper's value and uses. It was an important commodity in the maritime trade between southern India and Rome; Tamil Sangam poems refer to it as black gold because it was exchanged for *Yavana* gold.[33] The profits realized by distributors in the Mediterranean world were also substantial. This led, according to Pliny the Elder (*NH* 12.14.28–29), to its occasional adulteration with Alexandrian mustard and other cheaper substances in order to increase profits.[34]

Pepper was a far more important commodity in antiquity in the west than it is today. It was a critical ingredient in many medicines, as Celsus *(De Medicina)* and other medical writers make clear. Pepper was also used extensively in funerary and religious rituals, as is evident at Berenike and as is recounted in ancient authors. Pepper also had various culinary applications, as Roman cookbooks, especially that of Apicius in the first century C.E., indicate.[35] The discovery of pepper shakers in archaeological contexts in the Roman world points to its domestic use.[36] Ground pepper might be mixed with wine for taste.[37] From the reign of Domitian (81–96 C.E.) a large pepper warehouse, the *horrea piperataria*, existed in Rome, partially visible today beneath the later Basilica Nova/Basilica of Maxentius/Basilica of Constantine erected in the fourth century C.E.[38] The sixth-century historian Zosimus (*New History* 5.41.4)[39] records that three thousand pounds of pepper were used as a partial bribe to Alaric and his barbarians in 408 C.E. to dissuade them from sacking Rome. It was only a temporary solution, for Alaric sacked the city two years later anyway. Cosmas Indicopleustes (*Christian Topography* 11.10) writes about pepper in the sixth century C.E. and provides a drawing of a pepper tree.[40] Thus, pepper had a long and important history throughout Roman history.

Prior to 1999, excavations at Berenike recovered thousands of black peppercorns from many areas and from all periods of the Roman occupation.[41] Pepper has also been found at other Roman-era sites in the Eastern Desert, including Myos Hormos, Mons Claudianus, and Shenshef southwest of Berenike (see chapter 13).[42] The quantities at Berenike, however, surpassed the number of peppercorns found in excavations anywhere else in the Roman world.[43] We did not know whether these chance finds were random losses, dropped while passing through the port, or if they had actually been lost while in use by residents of Berenike itself. Excavators recovered the peppercorns in many different contexts: in trash, inside buildings, and outside buildings.

Then in 1999 excavations in the first-century C.E. courtyard floor of the Serapis temple revealed two large round-bottomed terra-cotta storage containers made in India that had been used so often that the resulting wear holes in one of them required patching (figure 12-1).[44] One jar preserved most of its original wooden lid. Unfortunately, that one was empty. The jar next to it, however, and lacking a lid, held 7.55 kg of black peppercorns.[45] This large cache, found in the precinct of the temple, had been destined for use there. Exactly how it was to be used is unclear, but excavations in another area of Berenike identified as a religious center, which we labeled "Shrine of the Palmyrenes," accommodated multiple cults ranging from the late second/early third to the late fourth/early fifth century C.E. This sacred structure also preserved large numbers of peppercorns, suggesting that they had been used in religious ceremonies.

This Shrine of the Palmyrenes catered to the Roman imperial cult dedicated, according a Greek inscription, to Caracalla and his mother, Julia Domna, and dated to September 8, 215 C.E.[46] This same building also contained a cult area for the Palmyrene god Hierobol/Yarhibol, recounted in a bilingual inscription dating between about 180 and 212 C.E.,[47] and indications are that the Egyptian deity Harpocrates may also have been worshipped here.[48] Excavations in this confined area produced about two hundred charred peppercorns.[49] These numbers suggest not random losses, but their specific use in some aspect of one or more of the cults whose rituals were practiced here.[50] On the other hand, excavations recovered no peppercorns in a late Roman cult center (the "Northern Shrine")

north of the Serapis temple, where some type of mystery religion was practiced at the turn of the fourth to fifth century C.E.[51] It is not clear why the early Roman phases of the Serapis temple and the earlier and later phases of the Roman imperial cult Shrine of the Palmyrenes should preserve large numbers of peppercorns, which were clearly used in some aspect of those cults, whereas no peppercorns appeared in the Northern Shrine. Clearly, pepper figured in some but not all pagan religious rituals in the city, probably burned as offerings. Excavations of a fifth-century church[52] also recovered no peppercorns, suggesting that their use in sacred rituals did not extend to Christianity, at least in Berenike.

OTHER DISCOVERIES DERIVING FROM INDIA

Other items excavated at Berenike came from India or the Indian Ocean basin, and though ancient authors record some, others are not mentioned by either the ancient classical western sources or the Tamil Sangam poets. These included botanical remains both edible and inedible as well as artifacts of various kinds.

SORGHUM AND RICE

The cultivation of sorghum originated in East Africa and then appeared in India.[53] It is uncertain where the sorghum found at Berenike, some of which seems to have been cultivated at or near the city itself, originated. It may have had an Indian provenance, or the practice of its cultivation may have migrated directly northward from sub-Saharan Africa.

Excavations at Berenike also retrieved rice from both early and late Roman levels.[54] Initial studies concluded that the rice had been imported from India, where the earliest evidence of its cultivation is sometime in the latter half of the third millennium B.C.E., with a large increase in its use in the second millennium B.C.E.[55] Asiatic rice seems to have reached the Near East, where it was cultivated in Hellenistic times.[56] Surprisingly, Chinese sources refer to rice cultivation in the Middle East during the Former Han era (206 B.C.E.–25 C.E.).[57] Strabo (*Geography* 15.1.18) confirms surviving Chinese accounts and indicates that rice was cultivated in Palestine, Syria, and Mesopotamia in the first century C.E.; so the rice found at Berenike might have come from there.[58] Rice has also been found in an early first-century C.E. context in Roman Germany.[59] It is also reported to have been cultivated in the Po Valley.[60]

The types of foods most people ate in antiquity remained fairly constant. Thus, they are good indicators of ethnicity and cultural and social identity due the conservative nature of most ancient peoples' diets.[61] Therefore, we might reasonably conclude that Indians or others from South Asia residing at Berenike were the rice eaters; it is unlikely that westerners living at Berenike were the consumers. Perhaps they ate rice from numerous Indian-made plates and bowls that we have recovered from the excavations.

COCONUTS

Excavations found coconut husks at all levels throughout the Roman occupation of Berenike, indicating that these were not randomly washed up on shore as flotsam by the tides but purposely brought into the city.[62] Perhaps Indian Ocean natives residing in Berenike consumed these coconuts and their milk and oil; or some of the husks, at least, may represent discarded remains of food eaten by crews aboard ships that had just arrived at Berenike from the Indian Ocean. Coconuts played an important role in Indian culture, as inscriptions there indicate.[63] They had a wide variety of uses as food and drink, and for making household utensils such as pots; one could also make charcoal from the husks, and its fiber (coir) was used to make ropes, carpets, mattresses, and so on.[64] One would assume that if they were eaten at sea, their husks would then have been thrown overboard and would not, in all likelihood, be brought to Berenike to be discarded there. Coconut, easily conveyed, preserved, and stored, would have been ideal for long ocean voyages; experiments have shown that the water or milk from unripe coconuts is a source of vitamin C.[65] Perhaps the ancients realized that consumption of the juice and meat of this nut could prevent scurvy long before the British Navy served limes to its sailors.

In the late second/early third century C.E. Philostratus (*Life of Apollonius of Tyana* 3.5) talks about nuts found as curiosities in temples. He could be referring to coconuts in Indian cult practices[66] or to their presence in Mediterranean temples. Cosmas Indicopleustes (*Christian Topography* 11.15)[67] writes about coconuts in the sixth century C.E., but he does not indicate that they were imported to the west. In fact, no ancient "western" author reports coconut as a trade item, and it may be that it was not but was used instead by ships' crews or residents of the port who originally hailed from the Indian Ocean littoral, where the fruit is plentiful and is an important and omnipresent food and industrial commodity. Sātavāhana inscriptions from centuries bracketing the turn of the Christian era refer to coconut-tree plantations in India.[68] Coconut fiber might also be spun to make coir string used in ship construction.[69] One fragment of coconut husk from Berenike was deliberately holed as if it had been used as a tool or for decoration.[70]

OTHER FOODS

Dozens of mung beans have been recorded from excavations at Berenike. Mung beans, cultivated in India and Southeast Asia, have a high nutritional value; their close relative in the west is the cowpea. The mung beans recovered at Berenike are the first discovered in any archaeological context from either Europe or Africa.[71]

Amla or Indian gooseberry is a subtropical fruit, and its remains have also been recorded from our excavations. The thick outer wall of this fruit is high in vitamin C and is today canned, pickled, or dried.[72] It is likely that such specialty foods were consumed by South Asian residents of Berenike in the Roman period.

Sesame seeds imported from India have also been recovered at Berenike,[73] as have dates from either Arabia or India.[74] The Berenike excavations have found remains of the so-called Ethiopian pea—the only archaeological context known thus far.[75] Other types of spices originating from somewhere in East Africa have also been recorded from Berenike.[76]

Other foods were also imported from Europe, the Mediterranean, the Fayum, or the Nile valley, including walnuts, hazelnuts, almonds, stone-pine nuts, peaches, cherry plums, domestic plums, apples, olives and grapes, doam nuts, and *nabaq*.[77]

Excavations also documented the shells and bones of a number of foods imported to Berenike. Aside from any meat or fowl brought in from the Nile valley, two items especially attract attention. One is the remains of Nile catfish bones in early Ptolemaic and early to late Roman periods at Berenike. The fish was probably transported dried or otherwise cured; this was an extremely popular food in the Nile valley from Paleolithic times on, and was also exported to other areas of the Mediterranean over a long period.[78]

Another high-profile item was the edible land snail (escargot), also imported from the

Mediterranean (southern France and northern Italy); this was also found from early and late Roman contexts at Berenike and has also been excavated in early Roman levels at Mons Claudianus.[79] Clearly, some elements of the population at Berenike ate very well indeed.

OTHER BOTANICAL FINDS

The Berenike excavations recovered samples of Job's tear, a grass seed from northeastern India closely related to maize; inhabitants in India today use the plant as a minor cereal and animal fodder, and to brew beer and wine.[80] The four specimens found at Berenike had been pierced to make beads, as was also the practice in northeastern India.[81]

The excavation of highly toxic red and black seeds called rosary peas (*Abrus precatorius* L.)[82] also tells us something about the trade with either India or East Africa. Although until quite recently used to weigh gold in shops in India and elsewhere in the Indian Ocean basin, it is, and was, also mixed with frankincense and myrrh.[83] Its recovery in the excavations may be indirect evidence that these aromatics passed through Berenike; certainly this would have been expected, since ancient authors describe how these solidified tree resins were major import items from southern Arabia and the Horn of Africa region through Egypt's Red Sea ports. Other evidence for consumption of aromatics at Berenike includes the find of stone altars in both the so-called Shrine of the Palmyrenes and the Northern Shrine (see chapter 13). Both have burned residues of some type of incense. Hundreds of wooden bowls found in religious contexts in the Shrine of the Palmyrenes and at least two on the courtyard floor of the early Roman Serapis temple also preserved charred remains in their interiors, suggesting the presence and use of incense or peppercorns in these religious contexts.[84] Only in 2009 did we record the first direct evidence of the importation of frankincense to Berenike, and that is discussed later, in the section on imported wood.

Frankincense and myrrh were consumed in prodigious amounts for funerary, religious, and medicinal purposes in the Mediterranean world throughout antiquity and in ever-increasing amounts in Roman times, as numerous contemporary authors tell us.[85] Pliny notes (*NH* 12.41.83) the huge quantities of perfumes (incense) consumed in funeral rites and declares that Arabia did not produce enough each year to keep pace with the demand. He uses the funerals of the Emperor Nero's wife, Poppaea (*NH* 12.41.83), and that of a popular charioteer named Felix (*NH* 7.53.186) as examples of extravagant uses of imported aromatics burned to honor the deceased.[86]

Another plant that may point to trade with Arabia or sub-Saharan East Africa is the balsam tree, the fruits and seeds of which were recovered at Berenike.[87] Balsam was important for the production of aromatics. It is not certain that the samples recovered from Berenike are from Arabia or East Africa, since balsam also grows in the Gebel Elba area near the Egyptian-Sudanese border.[88]

Another product found at Berenike of sub-Saharan origin and attesting contacts with those regions, likely by sea, was a seed of the baobab tree.[89]

Other prosaic finds from the Berenike excavations include Indian pottery, fine dinnerware, more mundane coarse wares used for cooking, and larger containers for conveying commodities.[90] Such crockery has also been found in excavations at one of the fort gates at Vetus Hydreuma, the first stop on the road linking Berenike to the Nile;[91] at Myos Hormos;[92] and at Koptos.[93] Indian pottery may also have been found at Petra.[94] Indian fine pottery especially noted at Berenike is the so-called rouletted ware, which appears to have been made in the Ganges River delta.[95] This likely arrived at Berenike and other points along the Red Sea coast via ports in northwestern India such as Barygaza, or was transshipped via Muziris or one of the other, more southerly emporia along the Kerala coast. Ancient authors would not have mentioned Indian-made pottery, since it probably was not an actual item to be traded to "foreigners" in the west, but was to be used by crews on ships or by Indians resident in Western lands. Indian-made containers would not be referenced, either, since these were not commercially important items, but used merely to convey the desired merchandise, most likely long since consumed and, therefore, leaving no trace.

Excavations at Berenike have recovered not only Indian ceramics,[96] but also pottery from the African Kingdom of Axum, made probably both at or near Axum itself as well as at its Red Sea port of Adulis.[97] Excavations at Berenike have recovered a few scraps of pottery that appear to be from the Persian Gulf,[98] but there was, throughout the Roman era, relatively little direct contact between the Red Sea and the Gulf.[99] In fact, the *Periplus* indicates little or no contact between the two regions.[100] From late Roman contexts excavations have unearthed sherds of handmade jars that derive from factories in southern Arabia.[101] Of course, these jars could have arrived at Berenike much earlier. Enigmatically, Myos Hormos and Aila have more evidence of contact with southern Arabia, especially in the latter case from the fourth century c.e. on, than has been demonstrated at Berenike.[102] Fieldwork at Berenike has also recorded pottery that has yet to be identified; it may come from farther down on the Indian Ocean coast of Africa.

Excavations at Berenike have found sherds of fine tableware (mainly *terra sigillata*) made in Italy and Gaul as well as from the eastern Mediterranean.[103] Stamps in the shape of small human feet *(planta pedis)*, ovals, squares, or rectangles are frequently impressed in the inside bottom of these wares—stamps that contain the abbreviated names of the owners of the workshops that made them. Thus, we can date the fragments of this ancient dinnerware and trace them back to the workshops that produced them. This provides a useful insight into Berenike's commercial network in the Mediterranean, at least in early Roman times.

Far more prevalent, however, are the myriad fragments of amphoras. Though many of these were made in Egypt, including Aswan and the Lake Mareotis areas, along the Nile valley, and elsewhere, numerous others came from all parts of the Mediterranean world, including Mauretania, Baetica, Tarraconensis, Cadiz, southern Gaul, North Africa (Tripolitania), Italy (Campania), the Aegean Sea (Rhodes and Knidos), Asia Minor (Ephesus and Cilicia), and possibly Cyprus, Gaza, and Aila on the Red Sea.[104] Identifying their provenances and dates provides data about Berenike's Mediterranean and Red Sea trading partners and how these changed during the approximately five and a half centuries of Roman presence at the port. Some amphoras were recycled to contain other types of commodities, so we cannot always be certain that the jars had only a single initial use or, on the other hand, multiple uses over a longer period of time.

Fieldwork recovered more amphoras than any other type of ceramic vessel, indicating that trade and commerce were paramount at Berenike. In early Roman times amphoras derived from the western Mediterranean, including northwestern Africa, Spain, Gaul, the central North African coast, Italy, and points in the eastern Mediterranean and the Aegean. During the late Roman renaissance at the port beginning in the middle of the fourth century (see chapter 13), the vast majority, if not all, of the amphoras were from central North Africa and southern Asia Minor/Cyprus (the late Roman Amphora 1/LRA1: see chapter 13), Aila, and the Nile valley. Clearly, commercial contacts between Berenike and the Mediterranean shrank dramatically from the fourth century C.E. on from what they had been in the early Roman period. At that time Berenike seems to have had little contact with Italy or the western Mediterranean; virtually all of her communications with the Mediterranean in late Roman times were with the eastern portion. This is not what was taking place within the Mediterranean itself at that same period; there is ample evidence of extensive trade between the eastern and western portions of the empire in late Roman times, especially in the fourth and fifth centuries.[105] We are not certain why this dichotomy in trade patterns in the Mediterranean versus Berenike exists or what it implies about commerce at Berenike in late Roman times.

These amphoras carried predominantly wines in all periods of the Roman occupation of Berenike. The majority of the customs passes written on ostraka from the first-century C.E. trash dump mention wine to be loaded onto ships in the harbor.[106] The most common type of wine was identified in terms of *italika* (mentioned in forty-two ostraka), which may indicate that this was Italian wine rather than just a type of amphora, perhaps made in Italy, that might have been recycled to contain Egyptian brands.[107] Four ostraka specify that the wine was from Italy, and it was transported in different types of containers described by the general term *keramika* and by a designation that seems to describe a specifically shaped vessel, the *kiliopomata* (a container also used for pickled onions and vinegar).[108] *Ladikena*, ceramic vessels presumably containing wine from Laodicea in Syria (an important wine-producing center), appear in twenty-three ostraka. Some of the exported wine may have been shipped in bags, presumably made of leather, called *marsippia*,[109] as well as in ceramic amphoras. The Roman army seems to have made fairly regular use of leather bags to store and ship water[110] and likely wine as well. Mention in the ostraka of "Ptolemaic" wine may indicate its origin from Egyptian vineyards.

Mediterranean-made wines were important export items from Egypt according to the *Periplus* (6, 7, 17, 24, 28, 39, 49, 56). Mediterranean and Aegean wines mentioned in the *Periplus* and in ostraka from the early Roman trash dump at Berenike, which is roughly contemporary with the *Periplus,* were exported from Berenike; some were undoubtedly consumed at the port as well. In fact, judging from the shape of the recovered amphora fragments, wine seems to have been a major commodity at Berenike, undoubtedly for local consumption as well as for export.[111] "Italian," "Aminaean" (produced in Campania, Sicily, Spain, and Syria),[112] Rhodian, Ephesian, Kolophonian (Asia Minor), and Laodicean (especially Syrian) wines[113] were popular exports according to the early Roman Berenike ostraka, and some of these are, coincidentally, also mentioned in the *Periplus* as popular Mediterranean items in demand at Arabian and Indian emporia.[114] At the turn of the Christian era Strabo (*Geography* 16.2.9) notes the export of Laodicean wine, which he observes was abundant, to Alexandria. Thus, it is likely that at least some of that vintage was available for traders to ship to Arabian and Indian customers via the Red Sea ports.[115] There is also some evidence for the export of wine from Euboea via Berenike.[116] It would appear, however, that Italian wines were the most popular export items to the "east" via the Red Sea ports, followed by vintages from Syria (Laodicea) and Asia Minor.[117] It is interesting that the Indians imported wine from the Mediterranean apparently in some quantity when Philostratus (*Life of Apollonia of Tyana* 3.5) in the late second/early third century C.E. tells us that the Indians themselves produced wines with a fine bouquet. Perhaps this later reference to Indian-produced wines reflects a conscious effort on the part of some entrepreneurs in the subcontinent to manufacture wine domestically—a practice that may have developed sometime between the first century, a peak period in the lucrative wine trade from the Mediterranean to India, and the late second/early third centuries C.E., when Philostratus wrote.

Certain wines listed in Roman sources as exports to Arabia and India—some of the amphora fragments carrying those wines have been found in excavations in India—were not particularly renowned in the Mediterranean. Those with a high salt content such as brands from Kos were less likely to spoil on the long journey from the Mediterranean to some port in Arabia or India than the more delicate and costly vintages from Chios, Thasos, and Lesbos.[118] Koan and pseudo-Koan wines may have been selected for sale or trade in preference to other varieties mainly because of these saline-preservative qualities. Columella advises the use of salt as a preservative in making most wine (*De Re Rustica* 12.21.2–6, cf. 12.25.1–3). Pliny the Elder (*NH* 14.10.77–79) also implies the use of salt or seawater in recipes for making Koan wine; Pliny also notes (*NH* 14.10.79) that Rhodian wine resembles that of Kos. The *Periplus* suggests that Indians and Arabs were among the keenest consumers of Mediterranean wines. Quintus Curtius Rufus (8.9.30), writing at about the time of the reign of Claudius, indicates that the "Indian" king consumed wine and that it was popular with all the Indian people; presumably Rufus is referring to vintages imported from the Mediterranean. Thus far, between twenty-six and fifty sites in India have preserved remains of Mediterranean-made amphoras, many of which carried wine—suggesting how popular this commodity was in the subcontinent.[119]

It may be possible to discern what wine was destined for trade and what part was ships' rations. Quantities mentioned in the ostraka for *italika* of wine vary from one to sixteen. With the exception of two cases,[120] the quantities are even numbers, which would correspond to well-balanced pack-animal loads using panniers. Laodicean wine occurs less frequently in the ostraka, but is transported in larger quantities, up to thirty *ladikena*, or—as is the case in Berenike Ostrakon 39—twenty-eight *ladikena* and twenty *koilopomata* of Italian wine.[121] The Ptolemaic wine mentioned is possibly the same as the "Ptolemaic monthly provisions" listed in Berenike Ostrakon 20, which also lists ten Rhodian monthly provisions.[122] It may be that Egyptian wine was given as provisions for the crew whereas the Italian and Laodicean wines were export products—a suggestion corroborated by the *Periplus*.[123] It is uncertain who imbibed these wines, though Indian chieftains were likely among the clientele.[124] This consumption may have been practiced because of personal preference or for prestige purposes. There is also a hint that "Indians" consumed wine on religious occasions (cf. Strabo 15.1.53), making the uses of some imported Mediterranean wines interesting when compared with the uses of Roman imports of frankincense and myrrh from Arabia and the Horn of Africa for religious purposes.

Numerous Egyptian-made amphoras have been recovered in the Berenike excavations, and, since wine was likely an important cash crop in Egypt[125] and was readily available, it would have been ideal for crew consumption aboard outbound ships. Wine and vinegar for crew consumption also had practical medicinal value, since both are antiscorbutic[126] and would have prevented scurvy on long voyages. The *ladikena* amphora, however, could also be reused for Egyptian wine, as can be inferred from the much abbreviated text of Berenike Ostrakon 88, which specifies that a *ladikena* filled with local wine should be allowed to pass into the harbor area.[127] The most frequently used type of wine amphora is the Dressel 2–4, a form that was produced in several areas[128] and designated its contents as "good-quality wine." From its clay fabric and its distribution, it is often possible to determine whether the amphora (and its initial contents) originated in Laodicaea (Syria) or elsewhere.[129]

Olive oil is also mentioned in customs passes from the early Roman trash dump. It is usually transported in *hemikadia* vessels, but one ostrakon records seven *italika* of oil, indicating use of a recycled wine amphora.[130] This may have been destined for consumption by westerners residing in Arabia and India.

Fish products, including pungent sauces such as *hallec* and *garum*, were popular in the Mediterranean.[131] Although not mentioned in the Berenike ostraka, Mediterranean-made jars found at Arikamedu designed to transport *garum*[132] indicate that this product was also exported, though probably in small quantities for consumption likely by westerners residing there. *Garum, hallec*, or a variant was also consumed at Berenike, as the find of some of the condiment itself tells us.[133]

GLASS

The *Periplus* (6, 7, 17, 39, 49, 56) mentions raw glass, finished glass, and glass stones (perhaps beads) as export items to India, Arabia, and other locations and says that some glass was actually manufactured in Upper Egypt at Diospolis (Thebes) (*Periplus* 6).[134] Some Chinese writers also record glass exported from the Roman world;[135] Roman, Sassanian, and

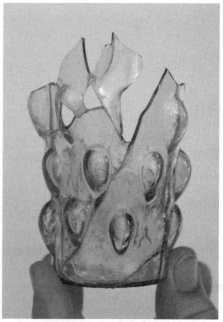

Berenike, examples of fine glass from the excavations. Scale = 10 cm. Photos by S. E. Sidebotham.

Islamic glass imports have been recovered from excavations in China,[136] and several outstanding examples of polychrome painted goblets and a beaker, a pillar, and *millefiori* bowls, "honeycombed" glass vessels, openwork trailing decorated containers, and glass preserved in other unusual designs have been recorded from excavations at Begram, Afghanistan.[137] Excavations at Berenike have recovered many hundreds if not thousands of sherds of glass.[138] Whereas some of these represent cheap, likely not export-quality items, probably used by residents of the port, other glass is of very high caliber. This includes outstanding examples of intricately incised and facet-cut glass, cameo glass, mosaic glass, *millefiori,* and painted glass (figures 12-2a and 12b).[139] One striking vessel comprises many fragments of a polychrome painted glass bowl depicting fish and a dolphin.[140] Though some fancy glassware may have been used by a segment of the port's wealthier residents, other examples found in our excavations must have been destined for export. This seems to have been the case also at Myos Hormos.[141] Excavations at Arikamedu and Pattanam (India) documented fragments of glass including remains of pillar bowls of Roman manufacture; many sherds of this type of bowl have also been found at Berenike and at sites in the Persian Gulf, and, as noted earlier, some have been found that come from Afghanistan.[142] Reconstructed fragments of an almond-bossed glass beaker recovered in 2009 at Berenike (figure 12-2b) have close parallels with a vessel found in the Getty Museum in Malibu, California,[143] and with another example excavated at al-Dur in the Persian Gulf.[144]

COMMON ROCKS, MARBLE, PRECIOUS AND
SEMIPRECIOUS STONES, BEADS, AND PEARLS

There was a surprising array of stones imported to Berenike. One of these, unmentioned by any extant ancient written source, is vesicular basalt, which likely came from Qana' in southern Arabia,[145] and perhaps from elsewhere as well. Other likely sources of vesicular basalt were the coast of Saudi Arabia, southern Sudan and Ethiopia, and some Red Sea islands.[146] The vesicular basalt found at Berenike had, in all likelihood, served as ships' ballast that had been discarded in the Ptolemaic-early Roman harbor area (see chapter 10).[147] Some vesicular basalt was also found recycled in the walls of several early Roman buildings at Berenike.[148] Vesicular basalt grinding stones for grain have also been found in excavations at Berenike.[149] Since we know from an ostrakon—not, however, found at Berenike—that there was an early Roman granary at Berenike,[150] recycling of this useful stone for grinding grain into flour would be expected. Surveys recovered similar vesicular basalt grinding stones at Shenshef,[151] about 21 km southwest of Berenike; unfortunately, no tests have been performed to determine their provenance.

Also documented were small, thinly cut and shaped flat marble slabs, polished on both sides, which were likely used as floor and/or wall decoration in either public or religious structures or in the homes of wealthy entrepreneurs or government officials. The pale gray samples come from the Proconnesian quarries in the Propontis (Sea of Marmara) in Asia Minor.[152] This quarry had been very active throughout the Roman era and earlier, and its products, including architectural elements and sarcophagi, have been found all over the ancient Mediterranean world,[153] and elsewhere in the Red Sea at least as far south as Adulis.[154]

Peridot also appears in the excavations, undoubtedly obtained from nearby St. John's Island (Geziret Zabargad; ancient Topazus/Ophiodes), which lies about 80 km southeast of Berenike.[155] Peridot, probably exported from St. John's Island via Berenike, was a commodity shipped to ports in India according to a number of ancient authors including the *Periplus* (39, 49, 56).[156]

Numerous fragments of emeralds/beryls found at Berenike come from the mines in Mons Smaragdus, what are today the Sikait/Nugrus/Gebel Zabara/Umm Kabu areas northwest of the port.[157] These regions were the only sources for the stone available in the ancient Mediterranean world.[158] In fact, emeralds/beryls were the most common precious/semiprecious stones found in excavations at Berenike. Yet, the quality was relatively poor, and the Egyptian variety was likely not exported to India, which produced its own beryls/aquamarines/emeralds (Pliny, *NH* 37.20.76–78);[159] in the late Roman period Egyptian "emeralds" were exported to the Axumites[160] and, perhaps, elsewhere. These emeralds appear in contemporary Roman jewelry and in representations of jewelry worn by adult female figures painted on the Fayum mummy portraits of the first few centuries C.E.[161]

The Berenike excavations have also recorded obsidian, the closest sources of which are southwestern Saudi Arabia, Djibouti, and Ethiopia or the Aegean/eastern Mediterranean.[162] These were used as jewelry or cutting blades.[163] Excavations in 2009 in the southwestern harbor produced flakes and what appear to be obsidian blades or scrapers. These were found in connection with a possible small-scale industrial area or industrial dump, and the date of the strata in which they were discovered and the circumstances of their find suggest that they may have been used in small-scale industry at Berenike in the first to second century C.E.

Fieldwork recovered two sapphires, both in late Roman contexts: one fragmentary piece at Berenike; and a fine specimen in excavations at Shenshef, cut to fit into jewelry. These would have come from Sri Lanka directly or via a port in southern India.[164] Sri Lanka was especially active in trade with Berenike in late Roman times, as the discovery of many beads, noted later in this chapter, indicates.

Excavations at Berenike have found a single small unworked fragment of lapis lazuli; the only known ancient source for this stone in the Old World in antiquity was in the Kokscha Valley in Afghanistan.[165]

Excavations recovered a rim fragment of a plate made of travertine. Analysis suggests that it is probably Arabian *lygdos* derived from quarries near Marib or Sirwah (Yemen). Pliny and other ancient authors discuss this type of stone, and examination shows that the quarries from which it derived were active in the ancient pre-Islamic kingdom of Saba in the last centuries B.C.E. and the first century C.E.[166]

A beautiful gold-wire earring with five small pearls on it has also been documented from excavations at Berenike.[167] The closest stylistic parallels appear on second-/early third-century C.E. Fayum mummy portraits.[168] Excavations also recovered one loose pearl.[169] This single specimen and those on the Berenike earring were likely imported from the Persian Gulf,[170] as was the case in Pliny's day (*NH* 12.41.84), or from the Gulf of Mannar between India and Sri Lanka (ancient Taprobane/Serendip),[171] as the *Periplus* (35, 56, 63) indicates.[172] Quintus Curtius Rufus (8.9.19) comments on valuable Indian pearls, and ancient Indian writers also note the importance of the pearl industry to the southern parts of the subcontinent in Roman times.[173] Pliny, citing the third-century B.C.E. ambassador and writer Megasthenes (see chapter 4), claims (*NH* 6.24.81) that Sri Lanka produced more large pearls than India and that these were highly prized on the island (*NH* 6.24.89).

There seems to have been very little direct commercial contact between the Persian Gulf and northern Red Sea ports throughout the Roman era. This seems to be borne out by statements in the *Periplus,* or lack thereof; the main entrpôts for those sailing from the Red Sea were on India's west coast, with those on the Indian Ocean coast of Africa a distant second.[174] The Persian Gulf and the east coast of India figure little in the *Periplus.* The Romans never controlled the Persian Gulf, except a small segment of the northern portion for an extremely brief period toward the end of the reign of Trajan (in 115–117 C.E.). The Gulf fell within the sphere of influence of the Parthians and later the Sassanians,[175] both major political rivals and military adversaries of the Romans, though items of Roman Mediterranean provenance have, of course, been found in the region.[176]

Not all rocks and semiprecious/precious stones found at Berenike were imported for use there or for onward transit to other points in the Mediterranean basin. Some were likely intended for export to Arabia, Africa, and India from Berenike. The *Periplus* (10) lists precious stones as export commodities without being more specific. Realgar (from gold mines in the Eastern Desert), specimens of which have been found in our excavations, as well as amethyst, red jasper, green malachite, and turquoise, were also exported.[177] These were available from the Eastern Desert or from Sinai and would have been exported from Berenike or Myos Hormos or both.

Of the thousands of beads recovered in excavations at Berenike, a large percentage were made in western and southern India,[178] and Sri Lanka. In late Roman Berenike over half the beads recovered were manufactured in Sri Lanka.[179] From India came beads made of garnet, quartz crystal, and milky quartz. The carnelian, sard, and agate beads found in such abundance in our excavations were also imported. Sard and agate came from India, whereas carnelian likely derived from Sri Lanka.[180] There were also beads made of glass and gold foil.[181] Large numbers of glass beads were made at Arikamedu on the Coromandel Coast; also from the late Roman period we found tiny glass beads in yellow, green, blue, purple, red, orange, black, and violet, which were produced in Sri Lanka, likely at Mantai.[182] Despite large numbers of beads found at Berenike, Sikait, and Marsa Nakari that are imports from India and Sri Lanka, no ancient author or document mentions a trade in beads between the Red Sea ports of Egypt and South Asia.

Many pieces of roughed-out onyx and, to a lesser extent, sardonyx blanks have been excavated at Berenike.[183] These likely came from Barygaza in northwest India according to the *Periplus* (48 and 49) and were used to make cameos.[184] Similar cameo blanks have been recovered from excavations at Kamrej (ancient Kammoni, mentioned in the *Periplus* (43); Kamanes, in Claudius Ptolemy, *Geography* 7.1) on the Tapi River southeast of Barygaza.[185] It is the lighter, uppermost surface of the onyx/sardonyx that was carved to create the cameo against a background of darker stone beneath it.[186] Excavations at Arikamedu documented similar cameo blanks,[187] as have recent excavations at Pattanam on the Kerala coast.[188] It seems that the roughed-out blanks were sent west from India and the finished products created in one of the Mediterranean workshops.

Red coral *(Corallium rubrum),* found throughout the western Mediterranean, parts of the Adriatic, and the Aegean as well as in the Atlantic just outside the Strait of Gibraltar,[189] was extremely popular among Indian women according to Pliny the Elder (*NH* 32.11.21–24),[190] and the *Periplus* (28, 39, 49, 56) lists coral as an export item from the Red Sea ports. The *Kauṭilīya Arthaśāstra* (2.11.42), an economic, political, military, and legal treatise broadly dated between the late fourth century B.C.E. and the third century C.E.,[191] also mentions red coral imported from the Mediterranean world and indicates that it came from Alexandria.[192] Red coral was also a significant import to Sri Lanka and was transshipped via South Asia to Southeast Asia as well.[193] The best red coral came from the western Mediterranean (Pliny, *NH* 32.11.21), and, in addition to its beauty, Indian women believed that it had apotropaic powers (*NH* 32.11.23). Coral also had various medicinal applications, as Pliny points out (*NH* 32.11.24), making it not just a luxury item but also a "necessity." Large quantities of unworked red coral recovered at Berenike appear, however, to be a local Red Sea variety and not the highly prized Mediterranean type. Pliny (*NH* 32.11.21) was aware that red coral, inferior to that from the western Mediterranean, could also be obtained from the Red Sea and the Persian Gulf. At Berenike fieldwork has recovered only five beads made of the Mediterranean variety of coral that Pliny extols;[194] we cannot be certain, however, whether these few specimens were for use at Berenike or were destined for export to Indian markets. This is not surprising, for if the Mediterranean species was as valuable to Indian women as Pliny claims, every effort would have been made to insure its safe transit through and voyage to those eastern consumers. Even Chinese sources extol red coral imported from Ta-Chin (the "west," likely the Roman Empire). Indeed, several Chinese sources report that red coral was artificially cultivated. They describe how iron nets were set into the sea, through which the coral grew. When it reached a certain height and became red in appearance, the iron nets were pulled up along with the coral.[195] No extant Roman author describes this process.

IMPORTED TIMBER AND WOOD FROM THE INDIAN OCEAN BASIN
TEAK

Another import to the Mediterranean world via Berenike goes unmentioned in the *Periplus*, Pliny, and other ancient authors dealing with trade between India and the West. Excavations at Berenike have found quantitatively more teakwood, imported from South Asia, than any other species.[196] Even the locally available tamarisk, mangrove, and acacia appear less frequently. The teak is found most often recycled as large beams constructed into walls of late Roman structures, especially in areas immediately north of the Serapis temple, the Shrine of the Palmyrenes. and the Northern Shrine. One beam in the Northern Shrine was over three meters long. All teak beams found in Berenike's walls have small rectangular dowel holes cut along their lengths, and some have nails embedded in them. It is unlikely that this valuable hardwood was initially intended for leveling functions in walls, and the dowel holes and nails would not have been needed if this had, indeed, been their original purpose. These lengths of timber were perhaps originally parts of large packing crates or, more likely, portions of ships.[197] The British have also found teak in their excavations at Myos Hormos.[198] There is evidence that some Arabs used teak when building their sewn boats in the early Roman period.[199] Teak (see chapter 10) was a durable, easily worked timber used for shipbuilding for centuries by Arabs in the southern Red Sea and Indian Ocean.[200] Once merchant ships arrived at Berenike from India, they would have required repair and maintenance after their rough voyages. In such a wood-poor environment as the Eastern Desert, those repairing and refurbishing these merchantmen would have recycled the timbers from the ships. Hence, these beams ended up in the walls of the late Roman city.

Teak was also used to construct at least part of the gate of the large *praesidium* in Wadi Kalalat, about 8.5 km west-southwest of Berenike. Some of the charcoal examined from excavations at Shenshef also indicated the use of teak.[201] There was a long Egyptian tradition, dating from at least the Middle Kingdom, of dismantling ships and recycling the timbers for architectural and other purposes.[202]

SANDALWOOD

Sandalwood may also have been found at Berenike.[203] The *Kauṭilīya Arthaśāstra* (2.11.43–55)[204] lists sixteen kinds of sandalwood from India, though eastern Indonesia, Sri Lanka, Malaysia, and, less likely, Taiwan may have been the source for some of the sandalwood found in the Mediterranean.[205]

BAMBOO

Bamboo was important in India;[206] there were guilds of bamboo workers in western India in ancient times.[207] This exotic wood has turned up in small quantities in excavations at Berenike in both early and late Roman levels.[208] Analysis of some woven mats found in Berenike's early Roman trash dump indicates that they were made of bamboo and produced in a weaving pattern typical of northwestern India and surrounding areas today.[209] These mats may have provided those aboard ships sailing from India with some protection from sun and wind. These mats may also be the remains of sails.[210] Their appearance need not imply direct contacts between Berenike and northwestern India, whose major ports were Barbarikon and Barygaza. It could be that these mats were traded up and down the length of the western coast of India and were brought aboard a ship sailing from one of the more southerly ports along the Kerala coast, an area frequented by those trading from the Red Sea. Though no Greco-Roman writers report bamboo as an import from India, the *Kauṭilīya Arthaśāstra* indicates that it was exported from the Western Deccan areas of India during the rule of the Sātavāhanas in the early centuries C.E.[211] The *Arthaśāstra*, however, does not specify that bamboo was exported to the Roman world.

The same may be true of the cameo blanks and other semiprecious stones from western and northwestern India that have been found at Berenike as well as the only Indian coin thus far recovered in the excavations. A silver coin of King Rudrasena III of the Kshatrapas of western India dating to 362 C.E. was found in Berenike's fifth-century church[212] (see chapter 13); it likely arrived via one of the southern Indian ports of call.

BOSWELLIA

The most recent discovery of a new type of wood from Berenike came during fieldwork in 2009. Excavations in the early Roman trash and in the harbor area produced pieces of

FIGURE 12-3
Berenike, wooden *pyxis* lid of ca. 400 C.E.
depicting Aphrodite *anodyomene* inside a
Greco-Egyptian-style temple. Scale = 5 cm.
Photo by S. E.Sidebotham.

Boswellia wood.[213] That genus of tree, which produces frankincense, was in Roman times found only in the Horn of Africa region and in southern Arabia. Close examination of one large fragment revealed small droplets of the sap that was so eagerly sought and consumed throughout the ancient world.

WOOD FROM EUROPE AND THE MEDITERRANEAN

Quantities of other wood species imported from Europe and the Mediterranean have also turned up in the Berenike excavations. These include Jerusalem pine, umbrella pine, some type of coniferous timber, willow, beech, oak, and cork.[214] These appear in a number of shapes and sizes as a variety of objects including planks, parts of furniture, bowl fragments, and jar and amphora stoppers.[215] Some of the cork amphora stoppers are surprisingly well preserved and have also been found at Myos Hormos[216] as well as on numerous shipwrecks in the Mediterranean dating from the sixth century B.C.E. to the late twelfth/early thirteenth century C.E.[217] Several Roman authors mention the use of cork jar stoppers, including Cato the Elder (*De Re Rustica* 120) and Horace (*Odes* 3.8.10). In the Roman world cork derived from trees cultivated in the Iberian Peninsula, Sicily, Sardinia, Morocco, Algeria, and western parts of Tunisia.[218] Other wooden objects from the Berenike excavations were more aesthetically pleasing. For example, there is the wooden lid of a strikingly attractive jewelry box *(pyxis)* decorated with a crouching figure of Aphrodite wringing her hair *(anadyomene)* within a Greco-Egyptian style temple. This charming example of wood carving dates to about 400 C.E. (figure 12-3).[219] Unfortunately, the species of wood used to make this lid could not be determined.

CEDAR

Analysis of large wooden beams found adjacent to the northern face of the Serapis temple revealed that they were made of cedar.[220] Originally from Lebanon, these substantial beams, one measuring at least 2.33 m long (figure 10-2),[221] likely derived from a late Roman context, though various dowel holes and tooling marks suggest that these had been recycled from some earlier context that cannot be determined with certainty. Given the sizes of some of the beams and the tool marks on them, an original maritime-related context would not be unexpected—perhaps beams from a dismantled ship. Cedarwood had a long tradition of use in ship construction in Egypt, dating back to at least the Middle Kingdom.[222] There was also a tradition in Egypt of recycling dismantled ships timbers into architectural contexts (see chapter 3).[223] The location of these beams hinted that they served as roofing either for portions of the Serapis temple or for part of the courtyard that abutted the temple to the north.

Excavations in 2009–2010 in the harbor located south of the Ptolemaic industrial zone revealed cedar ship timbers and a bollard. The bollard could have accommodated small to medium-sized vessels in the harbor in the first to second century C.E.[224]

SYRIAN FIR

Excavations in 2009 made another addition to the corpus of imported materials to Berenike. In the same harbor trench that produced the large cedar bollard we recorded two blocks of a resinous material. One weighed about 190 grams and the other approximately 339 grams. An impression of leather, wood, or more likely matting left on the larger piece hinted at the container in which it may originally have been shipped or stored. Examination determined that these resinous lumps were from a Cilician fir tree *(Abies cilicica)*,[225] which in antiquity grew in Syria and Asia Minor and which can still be found today in Lebanon. The resin was used for mummification and medicine. The oil and resin from the tree are antiseptic and diuretic and can be used to treat wrinkles and to extract worms and are also reported to promote hair growth. Samples have been found in Old Kingdom tombs; a jar labeled "fir resin" was recovered in the tomb of Tutankhamen.[226]

CLOTH, GARMENTS, AND MATTING

The *Periplus* (6–8, 24, 28, 39, 49, 56) mentions that textiles of all kinds and qualities (including linen from Egypt) were also exported from the Egyptian Red Sea ports, though these likely came by sea from farther north, perhaps from Clysma via the Nile–Red Sea canal (see chapter 9).[227] Quantities of Indian-made textiles were also imported, and many have been found at Berenike.

SAILS

Indian-made cloth also appears at Berenike. The largest fragment (see chapter 10) was made in a weaving pattern not found in the Mediterranean, Egypt, or the Red Sea and has been identified as Indian.[228] Cotton webbing woven in a similar manner as the sail was likely used to reinforce sails.[229] These were not trade items, but used aboard ships conveying merchandise from the east. Excavators found the tattered sail remnants in the first century C.E. Roman trash dump, discarded after apparent heavy use. There is, of course, no way to know whether the ship it came from was Indian, Roman, or, of some other origin. Such a distinction would be nearly impossible to make. The fragment of a sail with a weave pattern and date similar to those of the Berenike example (first century C.E.) was recently excavated at Myos Hormos; it was also identified as Indian-made. That specimen still had a brailing ring attached to it.[230]

COTTON TEXTILES

The *Periplus* (6, 14, 31, 32, 36, 39, 48, 49, 51, 56, 59, 63) reports that Roman Egypt imported a variety of textiles, including cotton cloth and garments, and even silk, from Arabia, Persia, and India. In India there were, of course, weavers and guilds of textile workers, as well as royal textile factories that employed slaves.[231]

Excavations at Berenike and Myos Hormos recovered a substantial number of fragments of cotton textiles from all periods of the Roman occupation.[232] Cotton, originally cultivated in India, was grown in Roman Egypt by at least the second century C.E.[233] The only method currently known to determine the provenance of cotton textiles found thus far is to study the weaving patterns; those used in Egypt and the Mediterranean world were very different from those employed in ancient India.[234] One fragment of "resist-dyed" cotton from a fifth-century C.E. trash deposit in Berenike's late Roman commercial-residential quarter (see chapter 13) looks exactly like two scraps found along the Silk Road in western China.[235] An analogous fragment was also documented from the 2001 excavation season.[236] Similar designs appear in paintings depicting wall hangings and other decorations, generally dated to the fifth century C.E., in the Ajanta Caves in India.[237] The striking similarities among these textiles from China, Berenike, and the Ajanta Cave paintings suggest that the cloth was likely mass-produced in India for a domestic market, and for export to the Roman world, to central Asia and China, and likely also to southeast Asia,[238] where the humid climate is not conducive to the preservation of organic remains. The project excavated at least nine fragments of similar resist-dyed cotton cloth of Indian origin from late Roman levels at Berenike;[239] these also had parallels in some of the Ajanta Cave paintings.[240] Excavations also recovered Indian-made cotton sleeping mats.[241]

No silk has been found at Berenike, though Chinese-made silk or silk imitating Chinese styles has been recovered at Palmyra[242] and Indian-made silk has been excavated at Dura Europas.[243] The Chinese believed that the Romans had their own silk production.[244]

COINS

A few Ptolemaic silver coins have been recorded from excavations at Berenike, but no Roman silver or gold coins have been recovered; numerous Roman billon tetradrachms from the Alexandria mint have been documented.[245] Approximately 41 percent of all identifiable coins found at Berenike between 1994 and 2001 date from Augustus through the Flavian period, with the bulk of those from the reigns of Claudius, Nero, and the Flavians. Second- and third-century issues account for only about 9 percent of the total, while coins from the second quarter of the fourth into the late fourth and the early fifth centuries make up about 34 percent of the total.[246] Thus, the corpus of base-metal and billon Roman coins from Berenike, especially of Claudius, Nero, and the Flavians, suggests economic prosperity at that time and later in the fourth century.

An important export from the Roman world to Arabia and especially to India was coins, particularly aurei and denarii.[247] The *Periplus* (8, 24, 39, 49, 56, 67 [?]) indicates this in several passages. These coins were in demand, and thousands have been found in India since 1786,[248] in Arabia, and a few in Sri Lanka. Denarii and aurei were preferred, especially those of Augustus and Tiberius, to a lesser extent of later first- and second-century Roman rulers; but large numbers of smaller-denomination late Roman (mainly fourth- and to a lesser extent fifth-century C.E.) *aes* coins and their local Sinhalese imitations have also been found in southern India and Sri Lanka.[249] A few have been found along the Indian Ocean littoral of East Africa.[250] Later, Byzantine-style coins (mined after 498 C.E.) have also been recovered in these regions.[251]

Scholars have long noted the presence of large numbers of Augustan and Tiberian denarii in India. Many have attributed this phenomenon to the prominence, if not zenith, of the Rome–India trade at that time. Others believe that many of these coins probably arrived in the subcontinent later in the first century, preferred by merchants because of the superiority of their fineness and weight over later first-century (post-Neronian) and subsequent issues.

These arguments are based upon numismatic evidence alone, which includes comparative studies of hoard compositions in both the Roman world and India. Yet, newly compiled data from archaeological work in Egypt should now be considered in this discussion. Data from the Red Sea coast and Eastern Desert shed light on the question of the dates of arrival of Augustan and Tiberian denarii to the subcontinent. Numismatic and epigraphic (especially ostraka) evidence from excavations at Berenike, and epigraphic evidence from *praesidia* along the Berenike–Koptos and Myos Hormos–Koptos roads and from Koptos itself (see chapter 8), however, suggest that the floruit of this commerce was in the Claudian, Neronian, and Flavian eras (41–96 C.E.) and into the early second century.

The preponderance of the pre-Neronian denarii (especially those of Augustus—his Gaius and Lucius Caesars reverse from the Lugdunum mint—and Tiberius's PONTIF MAXIM reverse, all of which were 98 percent silver) while so few Neronian, Flavian, or Trajanic denarii are documented in the Indian corpus, during the very period when all the other nonnumismatic evidence from outside the subcontinent suggests the zenith of the commerce between the Mediterranean world and South Asia, must indicate that many of the earlier coins entered the region in the second half of the first century and later. At some point these favored Augustan and Tiberian silver issues would have become difficult to acquire in the Mediterranean world as they were removed from circulation and hoarded there for their bullion. Had the denarius itself been used only as currency in the India trade, the issues from Nero on would have been as suitable as the earlier ones. However, these later issues were not favored. Because the weight and fineness of the post-Neronian denarii made them not as desirable to Indian entrepreneurs, there was a shift to using Roman gold aurei in the trade. These retained their fineness of 99 percent well into the third century. Yet with the aurei, those heavier issues of Augustus, Tiberius, and Domitian were also preferred in the India trade. This suggests that they, too, were viewed by the Indian entrepreneurs primarily as bullion. It is interesting to note that the weight of the aureus declined after Nero but was briefly increased by Domitian (ruled 81–96)—viz. during the very period when all the evidence taken in toto suggests a floruit in this trade between the Mediterranean world and the subcontinent. Perhaps the brief increase in the weight of the aureus by Domitian had some association with the expansion of the India trade at that time.

Though one cannot deny the possibility that some Augustan and Tiberian denarii and aurei arrived in India in the late first century B.C.E. and the early decades of the first century C.E.—that is, soon after they were minted—data from the Eastern Desert and Red Sea ports suggest that this trade peaked in the Flavian period and later and that, likely, a large number if not preponderance of the Augustan and Tiberian silver and gold coins found in India arrived at that time.

BALANCE OF TRADE

Controversy surrounds the purpose of Roman coins found especially in India, but elsewhere as well. Some argue that they may be evidence of purchase and that, therefore, their presence in India is indicative of a "balance-of-trade deficit" unfavorable to Rome.[252] Some authors, like Pliny (*NH* 6.26.101 and 12.41.84),[253] seem to suggest this. In the former passage Pliny indicates that India absorbed not less than 50 million sesterces (12.5

million denarii) per year sending goods to the Roman world, which sold for one hundred times their original cost. In the latter passage he says that India, China, and Arabia took 100 million sesterces (25 million denarii) each year in this trade. Tacitus (*Annals* 3.52–53) writes that the emperor Tiberius (14–37 C.E.) proposed stringent antiluxury legislation to curb Rome's wealth from being diverted to hostile nations to purchase jewels for Roman women. Yet, these passages and other comments by Roman authors about the influx of foreign, especially Indian and other "eastern," wares into the empire cannot be taken at face value and must be seen as literary devices that used imported luxury items as topoi for moralizing comments about the decadence of contemporary society.[254]

At a purely economic level, one must question whether Roman gold and silver coins found in India and elsewhere support Pliny's and Tacitus's laments and those of other writers. Caution should be exercised in giving too much credence to such hyperbolic statements. The presence of Roman aurei and denarii in South Asia not only may be evidence of buy-sell commercial transactions, but may have a variety of other meanings. Some coins may have been traded as bullion, as suggested earlier,[255] just like other commodities made of precious metals. One Nikanor ostrakon dated 62 C.E. refers to a shipment of bullion to Myos Hormos,[256] likely for export to some other emporium in the Red Sea or Indian Ocean. An early second-century papyrus deals with the price of silver bullion at Koptos, perhaps also destined for the "eastern" trade.[257] Since many Roman silver coins found in India seem to have been deliberately defaced, perhaps as a test of their purity, one might argue that they served precisely this purpose. We are uncertain whether defacement took place before the coins left Roman territory or after their arrival in India. Often, but not invariably, a slash mark or small punch marks appear on the obverse of Roman coins found in India. Since some early Indian coins were punch-marked, we might surmise that at least the punch marks appearing on the Roman coins were probably made in India.[258] These marks appeared on the coins as indications that they had been tested for their weight and fineness—all signs that they were treated as bullion. Alternatively, a recent theory holds that the slash marks were symbolic cancellations of the authority of the busts of the Roman emperors who issued them; the defacement had political implications rather than purely economic ones.[259]

Although some scholars aver that Roman coins found in India, taken in conjunction with concerns expressed by several ancient Roman writers, indicate a balance-of-trade deficit unfavorable to Rome, others believe that a more nuanced explanation is in order. There is little hint that the ancients understood the concept of "balance of trade," and since few reliable statistics survive from the ancient world dealing with quantities conveyed in this commerce,[260] there is no way to determine who the "winners" and "losers" may have been. The coins may, in fact, have served a variety of roles. They may have functioned as temple offerings in some cases (a redistributive function), for exchange purposes (as coinage or bullion), for symbolic purposes (a status symbol), or in a reciprocal, gift-giving type of role.[261] Most of the first-century Roman silver and gold coins have been found in hoards, most notably in the Coimbatore/Palaghat Pass areas joining the Kerala/

Malabar coast to the Coromandel littoral.[262] These hoards may reflect the political instability of the region rather than trade between southern India and the Roman world. Hoards were usually buried in times of political and military turmoil, at least in the ancient Mediterranean world; perhaps wars among the three major South Indian states reflected in Tamil poems were the cause of the burial (and nonretrieval) of these coins.[263]

Thus, the presence of Roman coins in India does not necessarily indicate any balance-of-trade deficit, nor does it invariably signal that merchandise was purchased in every case. In fact, the *Periplus* (49) mentions that Roman coins could be exchanged at a profit at Barygaza. The ratio of gold to silver in Rome was one to twelve until 64 C.E., during the reign of Nero, when it was modified to approximately one to eleven. Then during the reign of Vespasian, in about 70 C.E., the ratio was one to ten, approximately that in India.[264] Thus Roman coins minted before 64 C.E. and even before 70 C.E. were profitable to exchange at Barygaza for Indian silver. That numerous Roman coins found in India date to the period before Nero's reform of 64 C.E. suggests that many of them may have been involved in exchanges years after the *Periplus* was written and decades or more after the coins were minted. In other words, those trading Roman coins in the later first, second, or subsequent centuries may have gathered or otherwise hoarded the earlier (pre-64 or pre-70 C.E.) Roman-issue coins of finer purity and traded these in India not only at Barygaza, but perhaps also at other emporia. These "Roman" merchants, far from losing money in this trade, in fact stood to make a profit if they exchanged their denarii elsewhere in India for local silver at as advantageous a rate as they received at Barygaza. Thus, the presence, in some cases, of Roman coins in India may indicate that the Romans enjoyed a "balance-of-trade surplus" rather than a deficit, if one wants to employ this modern concept. It is, of course, likely that other Indian ports in periods following the composition of the *Periplus* (about 40–60 C.E.) also engaged in such coin-exchange activities.

During the reign of Diocletian (284–305) prices for some commodities, including imports from the "east," as recorded in the *Edict of Maximum Prices* (301 C.E.) (see chapter 11), were cheaper than they had been in Pliny the Elder's day;[265] others were more expensive. Drops in prices may have been due to the importation of greater quantities. Lower prices for some imported commodities in late Roman times may also have been the result of a decrease in demand. Of course, a combination of increased imports and decreasing demand may also have been responsible for declining prices.

We can draw conclusions from an examination of three frequently imported commodities: frankincense, myrrh, and black pepper. Pliny the Elder (*NH* 12.32.65) records that frankincense sold for 3 to 6 denarii per pound. In the *Edict of Maximum Prices* (36.56) the finest frankincense sold for 100 denarii per pound. Yet, in terms of the buying power of daily wages, frankincense was cheaper in the early fourth century than it had been in the first. A Roman legionary earned about 1 denarius in one and a half days in the late first century C.E.,[266] and it would, therefore, have taken him four and a half to nine days to earn 3 to 6 denarii to buy a pound of frankincense at Pliny's prices. A papyrus of 301 C.E. suggests that a Roman soldier's pay was 21,800 denarii per annum[267] (viz. just under 60 denarii a day); it would have taken him less than two days to buy a pound of frankincense. Pliny (*NH* 12.35.70) records that stacte myrrh sold for 3 to 50 denarii a pound or four and a half to seventy-five days' pay for a legionary at contemporary rates of pay. In the time of the *Edict*, troglodytic myrrh sold for 400 denarii a pound,[268] or about seven days' pay for a Roman soldier. Black pepper was another commodity frequently mentioned by ancient authors. In contrast to frankincense and myrrh, black pepper's cost (adjusted for inflation) appears to have been higher in the fourth century than in the first. Pliny (*NH* 12.14.28) notes that it fetched 4 denarii per pound, or six days' pay for a Roman legionary. It was 800 denarii per pound in the *Edict*,[269] or about fourteen days' pay for a contemporary Roman soldier.

Egypt was a closed economic unit within the Roman world until the late third century C.E., and regular-issue Roman coins were not allowed to circulate there until the late 290s.[270] Thus, it is not clear how regular-issue Roman gold and silver coins were transported through Egypt to the Red Sea ports for export to India and Arabia. None of the excavations at Myos Hormos, Berenike, Marsa Nakari, or Cleopatris have documented Roman denarii or aurei—the silver and gold coins in demand in India and elsewhere. This suggests that coins destined for export markets were kept under lock and key and carefully loaded onto ships, which carried them to Arabia and India. Whoever may have actually transported the aurei and denarii from Alexandria to the Red Sea ports, the Roman government must have played a role in guaranteeing that these coins destined for international trade did not end up loose in Egypt. The government seems to have done a good job, for very few regular-issue Roman denarii and aurei struck before the big reform in the late 290s C.E. have been found in excavations anywhere in Egypt.[271]

Entrepreneurs in the Roman world seem not to have been interested in receiving payment for their merchandise in foreign coins. Only one bronze Axumite coin and one silver Indian coin have been found in ten seasons of excavations at Berenike. The *aes* coin depicts Aphilas, the last pre-Christian king of Axum (reign about 270/290 to before 330 C.E.).[272] The silver one was issued by the Kshatrapa king Rudrasena III (Svami Rudrasena, ruled 348–390 C.E.).[273] No foreign coins have turned up in excavations at Myos Hormos, at Marsa Nakari or, it seems, at Clysma. This suggests that Mediterranean entrepreneurs preferred payment from their Arabian, Indian, and other foreign counterparts in local commodities that they could sell at a substantial profit in their domestic markets. It may also indicate that exchange rates for these foreign coins into Roman gold and silver coins both overseas and within the limits of the Roman world were very disadvantageous—a further disincentive for their acceptance by "western" entrepreneurs.

Some Axumite coins have been found at Aila and in Palestine, where they were undoubtedly lost or left by Christian pilgrims visiting the Holy Land from that African kingdom.[274] A large hoard of late Roman/Byzantine mixed with Axumite gold coins was found in Yemen,[275] and individual specimens have been recorded elsewhere in southern Arabia and India.[276] A hoard of twenty-seven Axumite coins together with fourteen Roman gold solidi and two Gupta coins was found in Mangalore on the west coast of India;[277] at least one imitation, possibly of an Axumite coin, has also been found on the subcontinent.[278] An Axumite coin and one imitation have also been documented from excavations at Tissamaharama, Sri Lanka.[279] Kushana gold coins have turned up on the road linking Axum to the Red Sea coast, indicating the two-way nature of the commerce.[280]

Overall this Red Sea–Indian Ocean commerce seems to have been very freewheeling and one that undoubtedly included barter, which Pausanias (3.12.4) in the second century C.E. also suggests,[281] as well as purchase. Roman coins could also represent gift exchange or other types of transactions among Indians rather than between Romans/westerners and Indians. Roman silver and gold coins would have been important to South India, since some kingdoms in the region at this time were consolidating and expenses incurred in maintaining the monarchs and the states were increasing.[282] The foreign coins would have facilitated this trend.

Compared with numbers discovered in southern India, few Roman coins have been found in excavated or other securely documented archaeological contexts in northern India, southern Arabia, or the Kingdom of Axum—all of which were important trading partners for Rome. Is this dearth an accident, or were the imported Roman coins melted down? Or was the trade conducted mainly by barter? Perhaps a combination of all of these factors explains the relative infrequency of Roman coins found in regions of virtually all of the Roman Empire's southern and eastern trading partners. Even the numbers of Roman coins from southern India (less than ten thousand at last count) are relatively small when one considers the apparent intensity and duration of this trade over several centuries.

One could argue that throughout the history of this international commerce there were winners and losers at all points along the trade routes. No one party would have suffered substantial losses all the time; otherwise, he would simply have gotten out of the business. As in all commercial activities, those involved at every stage of the transaction took their cut, with perhaps the actual shippers who were carrying the cargoes receiving the lion's share of the profit considering they were the ones taking the greatest risks. In any case, the Roman world's Red Sea–Indian Ocean commerce probably made up a small percentage of all Roman annual production of goods and services, and it is unlikely that this trade would have resulted in a notable drain on the empire's silver and gold coins, the use of which—despite the immense profits involved—it played at best a secondary role overall.

PRIMARILY A TRADE IN "LUXURIES"?

There was a tiny portion of the Roman Empire's population for whom cost was no object; this small group had immense, but not necessarily sustained, buying power. There were also items deemed important and, therefore, required by many regardless of cost. Many scholars over the past century or so have proclaimed this "eastern" commerce in the Roman era as one primarily of luxuries—imports from distant lands. In many cases their characterization is viewed from a modern perspective, not an ancient one. Additionally, there are several aspects of this characterization that should be examined, and in so doing this designation should be at least seriously reconsidered and modified, if not abandoned. First, Roman sources are fairly explicit in stating that many of the frequently mentioned and, one assumes, therefore, oft-traded commodities included frankincense, myrrh, and pepper. A careful examination of the plethora of extant ancient writings indicates, as noted earlier, that these commodities had close associations with religious and burial rites and with medical and pharmacological applications. For ancient peoples except the most destitute, religious, funerary, and medical applications would hardly have been considered luxuries, but rather, necessities.

Furthermore, the costs noted earlier for many frequently consumed aromatics indicates that they did not have "luxury" prices but were, rather, affordable in small amounts for most and, in fact, became, in general, cheaper between the first and fourth centuries C.E. This implies that the amounts/volumes were large enough and that prices were reasonable and, indeed, that the volumes increased, or purchases decreased, leading to a further reduction in prices throughout the first to early fourth century. If prices for these three commodities had been "luxury" ones, then one would have to assume that the quantities in which they were imported would have been relatively small. The frequency with which frankincense, myrrh, and pepper are mentioned by numerous ancient writers in food recipes, in medical prescriptions, and in religious and funerary contexts suggests, however, that they were familiar commodities and were regularly used by a substantial number of people. What kept this trade lucrative was not the rarity of most of the items involved, with prohibitively high prices, which would have kept volumes at a minimum, but instead reasonably priced commodities sold on a relatively vast scale. Merchants knew that this latter approach was a more secure way of creating and maintaining markets and, therefore, more or less steady, healthy profits over a long period of time. The robustness of the market for these items over a rather long period of time may also suggest something of the buying power of many living in the ancient Mediterranean world. Perhaps some reconsideration of this aspect of the ancient Roman economy is in order as well.

Another question, apparently not entertained by earlier scholars, is what type of trade this was from the perspective of non-Mediterranean peoples: Indians, Arabs, and others. There is ample evidence that some items imported from the Mediterranean were as highly prized by Indian consumers, and likely Arabs and others as well, as "exotic" imports made by Mediterranean inhabitants. Mediterranean wines and red coral top the list as imports that Indians highly prized, but what socioeconomic groups in India valued and consumed these products? We know also that at least some Roman coins imported to India were used in jewelry decorations—viz. viewed not as bullion or currency, but as highly valued objects because of their "exotic" origins, beauty, and great value (owing to their metal content).

Indian perceptions of the nature of commerce with the west are unknown. We cannot be certain whether they viewed items they imported from the Mediterranean basin, elsewhere in Africa, and Arabia (frankincense and myrrh) as luxuries, or as more prosaic objects used in non-luxury-consumption contexts. Different segments of Indian society would, depending upon their buying power, have had varying views on the luxury versus mundane status of such imported commodities. For example, the *Periplus* (49) and Q. C. Rufus (8.9.30) indicate that Arabian and Indian monarchs/nobility consumed Mediterranean wines,[283] as does Tamil-Sangam poetry roughly dated to the first few centuries C.E.[284] Yet, the plethora of Mediterranean-made amphora fragments identified from dozens of sites in the subcontinent (noted earlier) suggests that wine consumption was much more widespread than extant western literary texts suggest. We do not know what any non-Mediterranean consumers paid for such items, since that information is nowhere recorded in extant sources. In fact, we do not know precisely what any of the Mediterranean objects sold or bartered in Arabia or South Asia fetched in exchange. We have only the moralizing passages of Greek and Roman authors, few if any of whom engaged firsthand in the commerce about which they wrote and which they viewed from only a "western" perspective. This dearth of important data must leave the question of the predominantly "luxury" status of this commerce—from either the Mediterranean or non-Mediterranean, and nonliterary, perspective—either unanswered or, more likely, subject to a great deal of skepticism. The argument here is that this commerce was not one the volume of which was predominantly measured in "luxury" products. Given the range of commodities recorded in all the sources, this commerce was one that included items from the most prosaic to the most "exotic," but concluding that this was primarily a trade based on luxuries and one that was disadvantageous economically to the Roman world cannot be supported by the extant literary and archaeological evidence.

HOW GOVERNMENTS AND RULERS
CONTROLLED AND PROFITED FROM TRADE

There is circumstantial as well as more compelling evidence that states bordering the Red Sea and Indian Ocean whose subjects were involved in the lucrative international trade along the Maritime Spice Route sought, to some extent, to control, engage in, and profit from it directly themselves and not simply indirectly through levying taxes, tolls, and other forms of fiscal control. The evidence comes from ancient authors, from ostraka and papyri as well as other "epigraphic" sources, and from archaeological remains of an architectural nature.

It is inconceivable that the rulers or governments of any of the ports involved in this lucrative commerce would not have attempted at some level to control, monitor, tax, or engage in this trade themselves at the ports as well as via the overland caravan tracks that linked the ports to other regions. The temptation to make large profits was simply too great.

The *Periplus* (1, 4, 21, 32, 35, 52) notes three types of specially designated ports of trade. One is termed *hormos apodedeigmenos*, the second *emporion enthesmon*, and the third *emporion nomimon*. Scholars have pondered the meanings of these terms, but no consensus has been reached.[285] Each term suggests some special status, with the implication being some type of monitoring or control by authorities. Elsewhere the *Periplus* (27) notes how all frankincense grown in the region was brought to the South Arabian port of Qana' both overland and by raft. Though the *Periplus* does not apply any of these designations to Qana', the fact that all frankincense in the region had to pass through the city strongly suggests that the political powers were closely regulating its sale and probably taxing it in the process; perhaps there was some royal monopoly. Similar situations existed at other ports in southern Arabia.[286]

Elsewhere archaeologists have discovered special roads cut through mountains in southern Arabia that forced caravans onto specific routes; one example at Aqabat Najd Marqad, the pass called Mablaqah, under the control of the Qatabanian kingdom, linked Wadi Baihān with Wadi Harib.[287] What better way to control, tax, and monitor the transportation system carrying frankincense and myrrh along the caravan tracks leading north to consumers in the Mediterranean world than to direct caravans along specified roads that could be easily monitored by government authorities?

The *Periplus* (52) notes that strong measures were taken by some rulers in India to have foreigners' ships comply with local laws by bringing "Greek" (i.e., Roman) ships that strayed into some ports "under guard" to Barygaza.[288] Buddhist writings known as the *Jātakas* indicate that one Indian prince engaged in commercial activities himself.[289] The Tamil-Brahmi graffito scratched on a Roman amphora fragment from a mid-first-century C.E. context at Berenike records a Tamil chieftain named Korran.[290] Perhaps he engaged in the lucrative commerce because his political position entitled him to do so, as the case of the prince noted earlier suggests. The *Kauṭilīya Arthaśāstra* (4.2.36) mentions "administered" trade—viz. trade under state supervision, which set prices for commodities and allowed a certain percentage to go to private entrepreneurs.[291] Indian rulers regularly invested in craftsmen's guilds by making donations, with interest going to Buddhist monasteries. Rulers also built rest houses on trade routes, and monasteries acted as staging posts. Traders and artisans also made frequent and large donations to monasteries.[292] All these activities would have promoted commerce and benefited the states and rulers in whose territories these activities took place. The extent to which such international commerce was instrumental in the creation or consolidation of states along the Red Sea–Indian Ocean littorals has received a great deal of attention[293] but is not within the scope of our study.

There is also evidence for government control from the Roman world of both a de jure and de facto nature and, directly and indirectly, for government involvement in this international trade. The ostraka from Berenike, many of which come from the customs house, rarely list titles of anybody except those in the military. In documents directly connected with this trade (for example, the ostraka bearing personal names of those moving goods through the customs house at Berenike), it is military personnel who seem to be the presiding authorities.

The Koptos Tariff and the three inscriptions carved between 11 C.E. and 18 C.E., late in the reign of Augustus and early in that of Tiberius, placing mines and quarries under government control, and the levying of the 25 percent *(tetarte)* ad valorem tax on imported trade items are some indications of the Roman government's interest in making money—including from this high-profile and extremely lucrative commerce. The late second/early third-century rescript of Aelius Marcianus, preserved in the sixth century in the *Digest of Justinian* (39.4.16),[294] plus inscriptions indicating that the Roman government, through *publicanii*, also levied a *tetarte* on goods imported from the east via Syria,[295] strongly suggest more than passing interest in this trade by the Roman emperors. In the Egyptian Eastern Desert, the extensive infrastructure of roads, signal and watch towers, *hydreumata*, and *praesidia* and their garrisons—part of whose responsibility was to provide escorts for certain individuals, groups, and civilian merchant caravans[296]—points, at a minimum, to keen Roman government interest in monitoring trade and merchants, and making a profit by taxing them.

But did Roman government officials or the emperor himself actually engage in this commerce? Roman emperors were certainly interested in acquiring revenue, as is evident from an early date when Augustus and Tiberius consolidated their hold over the mines and quarries in the Eastern Desert and elsewhere in the Roman world. This was discussed briefly earlier in this chapter and more extensively in chapter 8. The names of imperial freedmen and Roman soldiers and auxiliaries appear in contexts that suggest something beyond an official interest. There are hints that at least some in the Roman government, including officials at the very highest levels, including imperial freedmen and soldiers, were eager to acquire profits for themselves directly from this commerce—either legally or otherwise.

A degree of corruption must have existed, though this can only be deduced and not directly proven in the case of the Red Sea–Indian Ocean commerce. Many would have been unable to resist. Certainly any soldier stationed along the Eastern Desert roads—as ostraka recently excavated from Krokodilô attest[297]—or in any of the ports would have been tempted to supplement his meager income by some means. The dedication of an inscription to the Roman imperial cult of 215 c.e. and an accompanying bronze statue made by Marcus Aurelius Mokimos, a simple archer in a Roman auxiliary unit from Palmyra, must have been well beyond his means were his salary his only source of income. He and some of his companions, well placed in their missions of patrolling the Eastern Desert roads and protecting caravans and stationed at Berenike, would have been hard-pressed to resist the temptations of engaging in extortion or black marketeering. The relatively lavish dedication of the inscription and statue is, very likely, evidence of both their piety and their avarice.[298]

DIPLOMATIC CONTACTS AND CULTURAL EXCHANGE
EMBASSIES

We discussed in chapter 4 the exchange of embassies and diplomatic missions in the third century b.c.e. between Hellenistic states in the Aegean and eastern Mediterranean on the one hand and the court of Aśoka, a king of the Mauryan dynasty in India, on the other. These diplomatic contacts seem to have increased and expanded geographically after the Roman annexation of Egypt in 30 B.C.E. and especially after the emperor Augustus's sanctioned attack on southern Arabia in 26/25 B.C.E. (See chapter 9 under "Leuke Kome.")

Roman authors refer to the arrival of embassies from China, India, Arabia, and other eastern lands throughout the first few centuries C.E. and until the reign of Justinian I (527–565 C.E.)[299] and beyond,[300] in the seventh century, after the period of our interest.[301] Yet, we do not know the nature of these contacts or their frequency, nor do we know what issues were topics of discussion. Surely commercial considerations must have figured in some of the contacts. The zenith of Roman knowledge of "Thina" and the "Seres," as they called China and the Chinese, was in the late first century B.C.E./first and second centuries C.E.[302] Chinese records also report Roman embassies arriving in China in 166 C.E.,[303] in 226,[304] and in 285.[305] Although extant Roman sources are silent about all three of these "embassies"—in fact, about any diplomatic efforts they initiated—Chinese writers are not.[306] The Chinese claim that the missions arrived by sea, the 166 one via Vietnam.[307] They record that the embassy told the Chinese court that they had been sent by the Roman emperor An-Tun. If the embassy took some years to arrive, it may have originally been dispatched during the reign of Antoninus Pius (138–161) or Marcus Aurelius (161–180). Both bore the name Antoninus (An-Tun in Chinese). This was the only mission recorded during the (Later) Han period, when the emperor Huan was on the throne (158–166). Chinese documents also note their efforts—some perhaps diplomatic, some commercial, some undoubtedly a combination of both—to reach the eastern portions of the Roman world, undoubtedly by sea or via the terrestrial Silk Roads of central Asia.[308] Embassies traveling between the Roman Empire on the one hand and southern India, and perhaps areas of western India and Sri Lanka, on the other would have gone by sea via one of the major Egyptian Red Sea ports, either Berenike or Myos Hormos. If Chinese sources can be trusted, the Roman missions (whether genuinely diplomatic or merely merchants posing as diplomats) would also have departed Roman territory likely via one of the Red Sea ports, probably Berenike.

CULTURAL EXCHANGES

Evidence for cultural exchanges between the Mediterranean basin via Egypt and the Persian Gulf on the one hand and India and other "eastern" lands on the other was at least as important as trafficking in commodities. There was influence between the west and the east in art, language, religion, philosophy, medicine, and astrology.[309] In art, the hybrid appearance of "Gandharan" sculpture from northwestern India in early and later Hellenistic times has long been known and studied. That, however, was an influence that arrived via the overland connection and continued with Greco-Indian kingdoms in the region for centuries following the death of Alexander the Great.[310]

We are interested in exchanges by sea. Surprisingly, there seems to be little borrowing of Latin by Sanskrit except for the loanword *denarius*,[311] the Roman silver coin much in demand in the trade with India. Greek, however, is a different story. Greek arrived in two different periods in India. The first followed Alexander's conquests when successor Hellenistic states in modern northwestern India-Pakistan and Afghanistan continued to use the language on inscriptions and coin legends. The second period was in the late first century B.C.E. and subsequently with the arrival via the Red Sea of westerners, especially from the hellenophone regions of the eastern Mediterranean and Egypt. These contacts tended to be with the southern areas of the Indian subcontinent and, to a limited extent, with the western and northwestern parts of the Indian littoral. There must have been many entrepreneurs and political figures who were multilingual in Greek and one or more of the southern Indian tongues. Actual borrowing of Greek vocabulary into Indian languages was more significant than acquisition of Latin loanwords.

There is some indication that commercial activities between India and the west benefited Indian monastic communities in the form of dedications made possible from profits in this trade or loans made by monasteries to those engaged in commercial activities, but there is no evidence that these monasteries themselves engaged in commerce with the Mediterranean region.[312] Indian guilds, on the other hand, were very active in commercial activities, as ancient evidence both literary and archaeological indicates; many objects of Mediterranean origin have been excavated at guild sites in India.[313] There is also evidence that some westerners traveling to India, most likely for commercial reasons, made donations to and dedications at some Indian religious sites. Thus, we should not be surprised to find religious and philosophical influences flowing in one or both directions.

There were, for example, surprising similarities between the cults of Isis and Osiris, which were extremely popular in Egypt from an early date and throughout the eastern Mediterranean and Italy in Hellenistic and Roman times, and those of the Indian deities Īśvara and Īsī, respectively.[314] In fact, it was at Koptos, the pivotal point on the Nile for the transdesert routes arriving from the Egyptian Red Sea ports, that Isis learned of Osiris's death, and her cult was quite popular at that Nile emporium. We should not, then, be surprised that many entrepreneurs and ships' crews coming from the Nile valley would have been from the Koptos area, and adherents of these popular Egyptian cults would naturally have carried their beliefs with them on their journeys to India. By the same token, Indians traveling to Egypt would have been exposed to the Isis-Osiris cults and might have transported these, transforming them upon returning to India.[315] Scholars have noted the similarities between these two disparate Indian and "western" cults since at least the late eighteenth century.

Iconographically and functionally there were close affiliations between Isis and Pattinī, a deity popular with Sinhalese and Tamils in Sri Lanka: Pattinī's husband, like that of Isis, was killed and resurrected. In southern India her cult was syncretized with those of Draupadī, Bhagavatī, and Kālī. Isis and Pattinī shared the seemingly contradictory positions of being at the same time both virgins and mothers. Castration figures are prominent in myths surrounding both deities, as are hidden chambers suggesting the mystery qualities of the cults. The earliest evidence for Pattinī comes from a Tamil epic composed probably in the first few centuries C.E.—the period of intensive maritime contact between Roman Egypt and India.[316]

Christianity, too, would have arrived in India from Mesopotamia and Persia, likely via the Persian Gulf, and ancient sources remark on numerous Persian and Syrian Christian clerics and churches established in southern India and Sri Lanka.[317] It is also likely, however, that Christianity made the journey across the maritime trade routes from Egypt, probably in a fashion similar to the transmission of the Isis and Osiris cults. Whether actively carried there by a proselytizing St. Thomas or St. Bartholomew or infused gradually over the centuries by a variety of nameless "westerners" and "Indians," Christianity began in the early to middle first century C.E. to arrive in the subcontinent. In the second century C.E. Lucian of Samosata (*Toxaris, or Friendship* 34) noted an Egyptian named Demetrius who left twenty thousand drachmas to a friend and went to India to join the Brahmans. Elsewhere Lucian (*Runaways* 7) wrote that Indian holy men (called *gymnosophists* by the Greeks) would cremate themselves with no outward change in their expressions. Pantaenus, who taught at Alexandria in about 180 to 190 C.E., may have been an important purveyor of the new faith to the subcontinent. In the fourth century, Eusebius (*Ecclesiastical History* 5.10.2) noted the presence of Christianity in India and observed (5.10.3) that Pantaenus was one of its agents. The *Acts of St. Thomas* of the third century hints at Christian communities in India and beyond.[318] Eusebius (*Ecclesiastical History* 5.10.3) wrote that Pantaenus saw Indian Christians in possession of the Gospel of Matthew and that the Apostle Bartholomew had preached to them and had left the writings of Matthew with them, written in Hebrew. Philostratos writes in his *Life of Apollonius of Tyana* (3.14) that he knew of sages in India using Greek religious rites and notes the presence of statues of some Greek deities including Athena Polias, Apollo of Delos, and Dionysus of Limnae and of Amyclae, as well as others. Indian philosophy may be detected in some of the works of Clement of Alexandria in the late second/early third centuries C.E.[319]

In the fourth to fifth century Palladius *(Account on the Life of the Brahmans)* provides an interesting story—but secondhand, purportedly from an Egyptian jurist captured in northwestern India who learned the language and provided Palladius with his information—of the educated men of India, lauding their learning and wisdom.[320] We cannot measure what, if any, impact Brahman or any Indian religious or philosophical traditions had on the west at that time.

Cosmas Indicopleustes (*Christian Topography* 3.65, 11.14)[321] notes the presence of Christianity in South Asia, in Taprobane (Sri Lanka), along the Malabar/Kerala coast of India itself, and in northwestern India. Some papyri also attest the spread of Christianity to India, especially in the second and subsequent centuries. Koptos was an important center of Christian activity in Egypt from an early date. That Nile emporium was the seat of a bishop in the mid fourth century and was represented episcopally at the Council of Ephesus in 431.[322] Thus, transmission of Christianity by traders to India from the Koptos area and by Indians visiting Egypt was also likely.[323]

An important Chinese inscription indicates that Nestorian Christianity reached China by at least the seventh century,[324] while Islam, Judaism, and Manichaeism were evident there by the time of the Tang Dynasty (618–907).[325]

Similarities between Christ and the Hindu deity Krishna have long been noted. Iconographically and mythologically the parallels are striking. Krishna was born in a cowshed, Jesus in a manger; a local king (Kamsá) decreed that all male children in his realm be put to death (as did Herod in Judaea: cf. Matt. 2:16–18), and the motif of the deity at its mother's breast was popular (as it was also with Isis and Horus) in stories related to both Krishna and Christ. The impact of Christian doctrine on any Indian religions, however, is not evident and remains to be established. The real impact of Christianity on India was the transmission of the religion itself rather than any influences it may have had on indigenous Indian cults.[326] Influences appear to have been more at the individual than the institutional level. Yet, one of the greatest religious impacts, Buddhism, was carried by merchants and others from India to Southeast Asia.[327] Though it was known to some in the Roman world by at least the second century c.e., Buddhism had relatively little impact there; Clement of Alexandria in the late second/early third century c.e. does, however, mention Buddha by name (*Stromateis* 1.71.6).[328]

Some Roman authors indicate their knowledge of and great respect for some Indian religions and figures, but there are no demonstrable examples of Indian religious influences on the religions of the Mediterranean in the Roman era.[329] Philosophically earlier, the Buddhist concept of the transmigration of souls (reincarnation) and a similar notion among Pythagorean thinkers in the earlier Archaic and Classical Greek periods may be evidence of influence;[330] certainly Philostratos (*Life of Apollonius of Tyana* 8.7.4) thought so. This concept, however, may also have developed independently in both Buddhist India and in the Archaic and Classical Greek west at about the same time. The philosophical idea of a hierarchical organization of societies as seen in Plato's *Republic* is similar to that in Vedic-Upanisadic philosophy, but whether this idea was transmitted from one region to the other or developed independently in Greece and India is not known.[331]

Literary and plot comparisons and contrasts have been made between the *Iliad* and the *Mahābhārata,* though no certain influence of one on the other can be determined with certainty.[332] A similar situation arises when comparing Bharata's *Nātyaśāstra* and Aristotle's *Poetics* regarding their respective attitudes toward drama.[333]

More practically, India exported to the western world via Egypt a variety of plants and botanical products that were used for medicinal, religious, and culinary purposes.[334] Along with the products seem to have come some Indian pharmacological ideas on their practical application, which were borrowed by westerners. Indian ideas on the causes of diseases and theories on the balance of "humors" of the human body were very similar to those held by physicians in the Mediterranean.[335] Aromatics have particular prominence in the works of western scholars in the Roman era such as Celsus, Scribonius Largus in the mid first century c.e., and Dioscorides, whose book *Materia Medica* is contemporary with Pliny's *Natural History* and with the latest phase of our early Roman trash dump at

Berenike. Dioscorides' book is probably the most important work on pharmaceutics written in antiquity. Other important western authors who discuss imported Indian aromatics used in medical prescriptions include Galen, personal physician to the emperors Marcus Aurelius (161–180 C.E.) and Commodus (180–192). The writings of these men predate the earliest know Indian medical treatises: the *Caraka Samhitā*, compiled sometime at the end of the second century C.E.; the *Susruta Samhitā*, put together sometime in the fourth century C.E.; and the so-called Bower Manuscript, also compiled sometime in the fourth century C.E. Though these Indian texts postdate the western "classical" ones, they surely preserve ancient Indian medical knowledge of great antiquity undoubtedly purveyed orally to westerners, who then wrote it down. Nard, bdellium, and costus, varieties of aloe,[336] and various types of pepper were mixed with other products to provide remedies for a wide variety of ailments. Their therapeutic properties would have been known to Indians and would have been enthusiastically embraced by peoples in the west. All these commodities figure large in the writings of those dealing with items exported from India to the Mediterranean world via Egypt. The remarkable number of Roman-era references to these "exotic" plants used for medicinal purposes indicates that their importation, whatever the cost, was considered a necessity. Not all medical knowledge flowed one way. There is evidence that the idea of dissection of the human body for medical purposes arrived in India from the "west."[337]

Other examples of cultural transmission include Indian borrowing of astronomy and astrology from the west. An astrological text from Alexandria was translated into Sanskrit as the *Yavanajātaka* in 149 C.E. Signs of the zodiac are remarkably similar between India and the west. The idea of the seven-day planetary week also made its way from the west to India, as did the concept of a twenty-four-hour day, first conceived by Hipparchos in the second century B.C.E.[338]

13

LATE ROMAN BERENIKE AND ITS DEMISE

Following a brief flurry at Berenike in the late second/early third centuries, there was a hiatus with little archaeological documentation for much activity until about the mid fourth century C.E. Evidence for continued occupation in this period includes a papyrus of 163 C.E. requisitioning a camel from Fayum for imperial service on the Berenike caravan route.[1] There were additions to the Serapis temple during the joint reigns of Marcus Aurelius and Lucius Verus in 161–169;[2] and our project recovered a Greek inscription mentioning the Roman imperial cult dated to 215 C.E.[3] as well as a Palymrene-Greek bilingual text dedicated to Hierobol/Yarhibol of about 180–212 C.E.[4] Excavations recorded pottery and a few coins dating from about the middle of the third century, indicating, perhaps, that Berenike had not been completely abandoned at that time.[5] Exactly what was going on, however, is uncertain. Involvement in commerce seems to be the only reason anyone would live here. Presumably trade continued on a greatly reduced scale, as suggested by the story of Firmus, reportedly a pretender to the Roman throne in the late third century, who supposedly profited from trade between Roman Egypt and southern India (*Historia Augusta, Firmus* 3.3–6).[6] The general turmoil of the third/early fourth centuries had, however, an extremely deleterious impact upon commerce, especially that requiring long-distance travel.[7]

This period of about a century was filled with angst throughout much of the Roman world. Political and economic turmoil, civil war, and plagues and famines within the empire, combined with almost unremitting pressure on Rome's northern borders by Germanic tribes and on her eastern frontier by the Parthians and then the Sassanians, led to a downward spiral of civic building activity, except for fortifications, throughout much of the Mediterranean world. This seems also to have been the case at Berenike. Locally, regionally, and in some cities along the Nile this was a period of rebellion against Roman authority. The destruction of Koptos by Galerius in 293–294 due to a revolt must have had a negative impact on Berenike as well.[8] In addition, it was a time of increased banditry by those fleeing into the deserts to avoid burdensome taxes and duties. There was also an upsurge in nomadic raids and depredations against communities along the Nile and, undoubtedly, against desert outposts and the Red Sea ports. It is, however, difficult if not impossible to differentiate between banditry and nomadic *razzias*. Much of the third century also saw turmoil in southern areas of the Red Sea, with a war between the Abyssinians and the South Arabs and among several South Arabian states themselves.[9] All this upheaval would have drastically reduced commerce across the Eastern Desert and in the Red Sea.

There is little archaeological evidence that Berenike functioned during these forlorn years, though just enough to indicate that the city was not completely abandoned. Locally, the presence of a Roman military unit in Berenike that had been formerly stationed in Syria reflects this period of turmoil. The *Ala Heracliana*, a group of Palmyrene archers (see chapter 5), was transferred from Palmyra to Arabia and Egypt by Commodus in 185.[10] Caracalla stationed a *numerus* (five hundred cavalry or camel-mounted troops) at Koptos to protect the trade routes through the Eastern Desert. A bilingual Greek-Palmyrene inscription from Berenike with a dedication to good fortune and to the Palmyrene god Yarhibol/ Hierobol augments the meager evidence from this period.[11] A *chiliarch* (commander of a unit of one thousand men) is mentioned on the inscription, suggesting the possible size of Berenike's garrison and the surrounding forts or along the road to Koptos at that time. A second inscription, dedicated by the archer Marcus Aurelius Mokimos, son of Abdaeus, both distinctly Palmyrene names, bears a date in the month Thoth of the 24th year of Caracalla, which equates to 8 September 215 C.E. (see chapters 5 and 6).[12] Clearly, the early third century C.E. witnessed some activity at Berenike, and presumably this continued into the second half of the third century C.E., when Zenobia of Palmyra conquered Egypt for a brief period.[13] By the late third/early fourth centuries C.E., however, the once thriving harbor where people of many nationalities had earlier been drawn by the promise of gain and profit had lost its attraction.

By the mid fourth century there are many indications that good times had returned, and that commerce in the Red Sea and Indian Ocean in general, and in the Red Sea and at Berenike in particular, had a substantial renaissance.[14] In contrast to documents for early Roman trade at Berenike, little information for this period derives from textual sources. Apart from a few literary accounts—such as Epiphanius, who notes that Mani (215–277, founder of Manichaeism) gained his wealth by trade through Berenike,[15] and the comment that two ships were sent from Berenike in 524–525 C.E. to assist the Axumites in a war against the Himyarites[16]—most information comes from the archaeological record. This second period of prosperity lasted at Berenike throughout the rest of the fourth and into the fifth century, but seems to have waned later in the fifth and given way to stagnation and eventual abandonment of the city before the middle of the sixth century C.E.

Late Roman Berenike provides most of the evidence for the physical appearance of the city at any point in its history. Though quantities and varieties of pottery, coins, and other artifacts, and floral and faunal remains, are substantial from this time, they are not as impressive as those from the early Roman period. Mint marks on coins and analysis of pottery and amphoras found at the site indicate that contacts with the western Mediterranean at this time were greatly reduced from what they had been in the early Roman era. Most communication seems to have been with the eastern Mediterranean basin, with the Nile valley, and, to a lesser extent, with other Red Sea ports. This is in marked contrast to activities in the Mediterranean itself at this time, which point to a vibrant trade across the entire breadth of that basin.[17] We are uncertain at this point why such a dichotomy existed.

The Kingdom of Axum, a rising power from the late third/early fourth century C.E., had contacts with the Egyptian Red Sea harbors. Excavations at Berenike in the fifth-century church recovered a coin of Aphilas, the last pre-Christian king of Axum (reigned c. 270/290 to before 330 C.E.).[18] The Kingdom of Axum in modern Ethiopia and Eritrea, and the Kingdom of Himyar in southern Arabia, both controlling important incense-producing regions or transportation routes from them, were key players in the trade at this time. These two kingdoms bordered on and controlled the southern Red Sea coast. There are, in fact, etymological reasons to surmise that a Himyarite ruler may have founded the Axumite kingdom.[19]

Contacts between the "east" and Berenike carried on and were, perhaps, even extended in the mid to late fourth and fifth centuries. Trade was especially brisk between Berenike and Sri Lanka and India.[20] This may reflect an expansion of the communication network in the Indian Ocean basin rather than increased initiative by the Romans. If Indian harbors where ships from Egypt landed had a variety of commodities available, and the home market was willing to pay the price, the Indian merchants would find a receptive clientele for goods that were gathered through internal trade in their large international ports. Chapter 6 explored briefly whether Indians resided in early Roman Berenike. For the late Roman period there is slightly different evidence, but it is likely that at this time, too, South Asians visited and possibly stayed for periods of time in the emporium. Indian-made cooking pots have been found in late Roman contexts. Excavations of a Roman trash dump in the late Roman commercial-residential quarter[21] documented several examples of a type of belt, perhaps a camel girth. These present an enigma, which may indicate that there were Indians residing in Berenike. In some cases made from plant fibers, but also fabricated from goat hair, the preferred local material in Berenike for camel girths, these belts were made by a method known as "sewn string" or "ply split braiding." This technique, first noted at Berenike in 1995,[22] occurs frequently in late Roman contexts.[23] So far there are no known parallels in Egypt in either the archaeological or the ethnographic record. The best known parallel in the Eastern Hemisphere for the "ply split braiding" technique is found today in the Thar Desert (in Rajasthan) and in Gujurat in northwestern India, and in adjacent areas of Afghanistan and Pakistan.[24] We might consider the occurrence of this technique, executed in local Berenike materials, as another indication that Indians, perhaps from the northwestern part of the subcontinent, were present in Berenike in late Roman times and that they manufactured these objects.

There was a massive urban-renewal project beginning about the middle of the fourth century c.e. at Berenike. The eastern side of the city especially experienced a construction boom with the erection of several temples, a commercial-residential quarter, warehouses, and a large Christian ecclesiastical complex. Much of this was built atop a gigantic fill comprising thousands of tons of broken early and late Roman potsherds, mainly amphoras. These had been deliberately placed to form a foundation for the buildings subsequently erected upon it.[25] Inhabitants of Myos Hormos used a similar technique; there, in addition, thousands of whole amphoras were employed to extend usable working space into the sea, albeit in early Roman times.[26] This method of construction can be found elsewhere in the empire.[27] Previously we described the problems of harbor silting and the resulting "migration" of the city over the centuries ever eastward toward the retreating coastline. This huge pottery fill was intended to elevate areas previously either underwater or at the beach's edge and make them usable for construction purposes. Atop this massive fill, and elsewhere in sectors west of the filled area, the newly erected late Roman-era structures had walls comprising fossilized fist-sized and larger coral heads, and occasionally larger shells, stacked using their rough edges and mud mortar as bonding material. This method of coral construction is well known along the East African coast of the Red Sea and Indian Ocean[28] and can also be seen at Aidhab, an early Islamic hajj port about 260 km south of Berenike. Steps, doorjambs, and other critical architectural joins were made of gypsum/anhydrite ashlars, often recycled from earlier edifices. Roofs comprised long wooden beams of palm trees covered with smaller branches and, we assume, mud or clay.[29]

This was a tradition that persisted; the architecture of Islamic buildings along the Red Sea and the East African coast shows a preponderance of the use of coral. The Islamic city of Quseir, about 8 km south of Myos Hormos, was built of quarried coral.[30] These buildings probably date back to the fifteenth and sixteenth centuries, but construction methods are very different from those at Berenike; the coral at Quseir was quarried in rectangular blocks measuring approximately 60 cm × 40 cm × 40 cm.[31] A building style more closely related to that at Berenike, making use of fossilized coral heads, can be seen in historical buildings on the East African coast at the great mosques of Gedi in Kenya, and Kilwa in Tanzania.[32] In the case of Berenike, occasionally recycled teakwood beams were used as leveling courses in the coral-head walls (see chapters 10 and 12). By contrast, in Aidhab the same technique was used as at Quseir: fossilized coral beds were quarried for regularly formed building blocks.[33] Aidhab can be considered the successor of Berenike, taking over as southern harbor in Egypt when Berenike went out of use. Fossilized coral heads found in the environs of Berenike are irregularly wedge-shaped, and the building methods used in the ancient emporium had to be adapted to that. Most evidence of coral architecture at Berenike comes from the mid to late fourth- and fifth-century expansion of the port.

The size of the buildings and the layout of the streets, evident even in the unexcavated areas of Berenike, provide some idea of the function of different parts of the community. Excavations, however, provide more precise identifications of the buildings of fourth- and fifth-century c.e. Berenike.

The easiest way to examine construction activities at Berenike in this period is to progress across the site from the west toward the east. At the northwestern corner of the town adjacent to the main road that led toward the Nile valley, excavations have begun to uncover the remains of a fourth- to fifth-century c.e. necropolis.[34] It is only from the late Roman period that a formal cemetery at Berenike has been identified. Two types of interments appear here. One reflects a group of adults who had a fair amount of wealth. They were buried in graves made of coral-head walls and interred in wooden coffins that have almost completely deteriorated. From the bronze nails and corner pieces it is possible to reconstruct the size and, to a certain extent, the value of these coffins made of wood—an extremely scarce and costly commodity in Berenike. These tombs had been badly robbed, the bones unceremoniously thrown out or into the corners of the tombs at some date that our excavations could not determine.

The other burials here were cist graves, simple holes cut into the ground; excavations found two of these. One contained the body of a two-year-old girl and the other of an adolescent. Both individuals had less wealth than those in the more grandiose graves nearby, but their burials were not robbed and remained intact, either through oversight of the robbers or in the knowledge that they contained little or nothing of value to the looters. The two-year-old girl had been wrapped in a burial shroud, but only remains of this could be seen over her tiny skull, which had been covered by a large potsherd. Grieving survivors had placed beads, perhaps a bracelet or necklace, in the grave to accompany her into the afterlife. The adolescent had no grave goods with him.

Apart from this formal necropolis at the entrance to the city, surveys around Berenike located an enormous field of ring-cairn tombs. These were also late Roman, roughly contemporary with the "northwest" cemetery. At least 640 of these ring-cairn tombs have been mapped just west and southwest of the city, on hills and slightly raised limestone platforms of fossilized coral reefs.[35] These graves comprised dry stone walling with local desert stones collected from the mountains at a distance of at least 8 km to the west and had the form of a doughnut, with an outside diameter of approximately 1.50 m and an inside diameter of 0.75 m. The bottom of a typical ring-cairn tomb had a rectangular pit dug in the bedrock, which was then lined, or covered, with flat stone slabs. Often the ring-cairn tombs formed clusters of three or more, using parts of the walls of the neighboring tombs. They had mostly been badly robbed, with some potsherds and bones scattered about. Associated sherds dated mostly to the late fourth to fifth centuries c.e.[36] Many questions remain about these burials. For example, it is not clear whether the clustered ring-cairn tombs represented family groups. Similar ring-cairn tombs can be found throughout the southern part of the Eastern Desert, near settlements such as Hitan Rayan and Shenshef.[37] The ring-cairn tombs are usually located on elevated areas overlooking a wadi, likely in an attempt to protect them from occasional floodwaters that pass through.

The late Roman burials present many questions. It is not clear why there is a late Roman-era cemetery at the northwestern edge of Berenike and a much larger contemporary ring-cairn necropolis west and southwest of the city. Even more enigmatic, no formal burials from the early Roman era have been found that are associated with the city. As will be examined later, the population in the late Roman period differed markedly from that in the early Roman era. It may be that the military was one determining factor in the organization and habitation of early Roman Berenike. The fourth and especially the fifth centuries C.E. show a city that was inhabited by commercially organized merchants and transport companies. The town had pagan and Christian groups living and worshipping alongside each other. Especially in the fifth and early sixth centuries the role of people who were originally desert dwellers seems to have increased dramatically at Berenike. The variation in burial customs seems to indicate a very fundamental change in how the population of Berenike in its two periods of Roman-era prosperity viewed their town. Early Roman Berenike was Nile-focused, and organized by outsiders arriving from Koptos, Alexandria, and other areas outside Egypt. Many deceased persons were likely transported to their hometowns in the Nile valley for burial. That a tax on transporting dead bodies was levied, at least in the first century C.E. according to the Koptos Tariff, indicates that this was not a rare occurrence.[38] By contrast, it seems that the population of fourth- to fifth-century Berenike considered the town as home, a place to remain and to bury their dead. It is difficult to decide whether the difference between the cemetery along the entrance road northwest of Berenike and the hundreds of ring-cairn tombs reflects a variation in status, wealth, or ethnic background. Applying these terms is fraught with difficulties because of the plethora of elements that determine a person's status. The tombs west and southwest of the city may indicate that these people were originally desert dwellers who made their fortunes in Berenike and ended their days amid relative wealth and comfort at the port but who wanted, when buried, to remind those left behind of their origins. The general lack of grave goods in the burials adjacent to the road northwest of the city may, on the other hand, reflect not so much a difference in wealth or status as a difference in religion. Christian burials were not provided with grave goods for use in the afterlife. Yet, since these latter graves have been robbed, we do not know whether they originally contained funerary objects or not.

Moving eastward across the site, there is little evidence that the early Roman trash dump continued in use in late Roman times, aside from one intrusive burial.[39] The late Roman period witnessed trash deposited within or outside and adjacent to abandoned buildings in the town. Activities continued in the Shrine of the Palmyrenes, where excavations recovered the Roman imperial cult inscription of Mokimos and the associated bronze statue

fragments. Stratigraphic evidence suggests reuse of the bronze simulacrum and affiliated Mokimos inscription in the fourth/fifth century. Excavations could not determine
when the bilingual Greek-Palmyrene inscription and putative associated bronze statue of
Yarhibol noted earlier fell out of use. Chapter 6 noted that excavations in the Shrine of
the Palmyrenes also documented over one hundred wooden bowls,[40] similar to those found
on the early Roman courtyard floor of the Serapis temple, and a small stone sphinx reused
as part of a later wall of the building[41] These were associated with the later phases of the
shrine, likely in the fourth and fifth centuries.[42]

Immediately north of the Serapis temple and above the early Roman-era courtyard
floor where excavations found the Indian jar with peppercorns was a small-scale manufacturing area in late Roman times. We are uncertain, however, whether these endeavors
were associated with nearby religious activities, since it is not known whether the Serapis
temple continued in use into the fourth and fifth centuries.

About 80 meters north of the Serapis temple, near the northern inlet of the city, was
a pagan-cult center that was active only in the later fourth/early fifth centuries.[43] This so-
called Northern Shrine went through two rapid phases of use at that time. Cult activities
took place in an enclosure made of fossilized coral heads, perhaps barrel vaulted, with a
single small entrance on the east. Internal lighting came minimally from the portal and
terra-cotta oil lamps. Amphora toes may have been reused as torches or may have been
recycled as incense burners.[44] Ancient mystery cults often held their rites in enclosed
spaces to shield activities from prying eyes of the uninitiated. Such circumstances required
artificial illumination. The amount of smoke produced by such burning suggests that the
small door alone would not have been an adequate exhaust for the fumes; it is likely that
one or more openings in the roof or walls would have been necessary, but these have left
no trace in the archaeological record.

Excavations recorded evidence for cult activities: a round columnar-shaped altar with
burning on top, four rectilinear-shaped stone temple pools typical of religious centers in
ancient Egypt and Nubia,[45] a painted ostrich egg, and a small bronze statuette—among
other items.[46] Excavators documented stone seats parallel to the interior northern and
southern walls of this narrow building. One of the stones atop the northern row of seats
was a broken and reused relief depicting a figure standing on a raised dais with a second
figure standing below and to the left.[47] The effigy on the dais may represent a cult statue
and the other a priest or devotee. There is no way to determine whether the relief came
from this shrine or elsewhere, because excavations in most buildings of Berenike's later
occupation have recovered reused stones.[48] The interior of the Northern Shrine also preserved teak timbers, one over 3 m long, possibly recycled from a ship (see chapters 10
and 12). Initiates into such "mysteries" were frequently sworn to secrecy and moved up
a hierarchical ladder over time. Circumstantial evidence suggests that Mithras, whose initiates were male only, might have been worshipped here. Mithras was popular among the
Roman military and entrepreneurs—the very people who gravitated to and lived in
Berenike in Roman times. Yet, examination of the shrine's contents does not support this

interpretation, and Mithraism was not a prominent cult in Egypt, even during the early Roman period, when the role of the military was much more prominent than in the era in which the shrine operated.[49] Thus, the shrine was likely dedicated to another deity.

Excavations in winter 2010, on what appeared to be either a small island or dredge heap in the southern harbor at Berenike south of the early-middle Ptolemaic industrial zone, documented another late Roman-era temple, which had at least two major phases of use.[50] Temple walls comprised stacked extinct coral heads with some gypsum/anhydrite ashlars; a single narrow portal pierced the short southern wall. A pair of benches inside and parallel to the eastern and western temple walls resembled those found in the Northern Shrine. Temple contents included a reused inscription in Greek from the first year of Trajan's reign (98 C.E.) dedicated to Isis, Tyche, and perhaps Serapis. Also documented were painted ostrich eggshell fragments, one of which bore a pentagram; the bottom of a terra-cotta lamp also preserved a graffito of a pentagram. The pentagram, a symbol of the Dog Star that marked the beginning of Egyptian New Year, was closely affiliated with Isis. About fifty cowry shells (used for prognostication), two rectangular-shaped stone altars, a columnar-shaped altar, miniature stone temple pools, a terra-cotta incense burner, a small terra-cotta jar filled with lunate-shaped silver decorations likely deriving from a door or chest, remnants of wooden bowls (similar to those found in other religious contexts at Berenike), a pair of thin decorated bronze handles and a bronze *patera/phiale* with remnants of an attached iron tripod made up some of the other finds from the interior of the sanctuary. Sherds suggested activity here from the late fourth in the sixth century C.E.[51]

The location of an Isis temple in the harbor was most appropriate given her connection with magic and prognostication, which would have been popular with those about to embark on or return from dangerous voyages in the Red Sea and Indian Ocean. The close association of Isis with the opening of the sailing season, celebrated annually in the Mediterranean as the *Navagium Isidis/Ploiaphesia*,[52] would have been particularly apt at Berenike for those engaged in perilous voyages in the Erythra Thalassa.

Isis was very popular in the Ptolemaic and Roman periods throughout Egypt and the wider Mediterranean. She was frequently syncretized with other Egyptian and Greco-Roman deities including those concerned with sailing and the protection of sailors. She was also carried to India and perhaps identified with one of the deities there (see chapter 12). Such a cult center dedicated to Isis at Berenike would not be surprising and would, in fact, be expected. She was worshipped in the city, as an inscription from the early second century C.E. reused in a domestic context in a late Roman building indicates.[53] Furthermore, textual sources note that Isis was extremely important to the Blemmyes, a nomadic group of desert dwellers.[54] Her cult and a few others continued to operate despite the Edict of Theodosius I, which ordered all Egypt to convert to Christianity in 391 C.E. and decreed closure of all pagan shrines.[55] Justinian I (reigned 527–565) finally brought worship in the temple of Isis and other Blemmye shrines at Philae to an end when he ordered his general Narses to tear down the sanctuaries, arrest the priests, and transport the cult statues to Constantinople.[56] Graffiti of the period commemorate the conversion of the Temple of Isis at Philae into a church.[57]

The Pharaonic-era Medjay may have been the forerunners of the Blemmyes.[58] Earlier authors, starting in the third century B.C.E., noted where the Blemmyes lived, and later Roman-era descriptions of the Blemmyes are less than flattering.[59] Generally considered marauders, they created misery for the Romans and forced Diocletian to withdraw the border of Roman Egypt from Qasr Ibrim to Aswan, 300 km to the north.[60] Yet, a fifth-century C.E. letter written in Greek appears to be a message from Phonen, king of the Blemmyes, to Abourni, king of the Noubades. In this extraordinary epistle Phonen indicates that he wishes to avoid war with his Noubade neighbors.[61] The Blemmyes are usually equated with the Bega, a desert-dwelling tribe, or conglomeration of tribes, living between the Nile valley and the Red Sea at roughly 15°–24° north latitude and frequently identified with the present-day "tribes" of the Beja, encompassing the Hadendowa, Beni Amer, Habab, Bishareen, and ʻAbabda.[62] The problems of identifying the ethnicity or identity of peoples from the archaeological record are complex. Outsiders compiled most extant textual sources on the Blemmyes and wrote their histories from second- or thirdhand accounts. It is clear from descriptions that the Blemmyes were "the other"—the enemy. Pliny's description is the most fanciful; he reports that they were a race without a head, and with ears and eyes on their chest (*NH* 5.8.46). Closer studies of textual sources and archaeological evidence suggest that identification of the Blemmyes with the Bega/Beja as one nomadic "tribe" is too simplistic. The Bega/Beja was likely a series of allegiances among several groups of Nile valley inhabitants in the Dodekaschoinos and those living in the Eastern Desert and along the Red Sea shore of southeastern Egypt and northeastern Sudan.[63] Because so little is known about these people, they should be labeled "Eastern Desert dwellers."

We do not know whether the Northern Shrine continued in use until very late in the history of Berenike. Although Egypt had been decreed Christian in 391 C.E., it is not certain that imperial fiats had any immediate impact on Berenike. Archaeological evidence does not indicate whether the Serapis temple ceased to function at that time or had closed earlier. It is probable that the official temples would have been closed, although smaller shrines may have continued to operate on a low-key basis. On the other hand, Wilkinson's discovery of a miniature stone double temple-pool offering in the first room of the Serapis temple suggests that it was used until near the end of Berenike's existence.[64] It is possible that at the fringes of the late Roman/Byzantine Empire, especially those where desert nomads were prominent, pagan cults continued to be celebrated. It appears that Berenike was, indeed, a very tolerant place, characterized by acceptance of different cultures and creeds, since a large Christian ecclesiastical center functioned at that time.[65] Perhaps the only indication of discontinued use of a pagan cult center is the Shrine of the Palmyrenes, dedicated in the early third century to Yarhibol and the imperial cult of Caracalla and Julia Domna. Here we excavated about one-third of a bronze statue plastered crudely into a stone socle. Intentional mutilation of this *simulacrum* took place by ripping the top part off and folding and piercing a bronze sheet of the front with a sharp iron tool.[66]

Berenike offers a unique opportunity to study cult practices of the late Roman period. In contrast to large temples in the Nile valley, which were reused as churches, as Roman military camps, or as settlements or were cleared early in the history of Egyptology, all shrines at Berenike preserve traces of religious activities. All of Berenike's shrines, except the church, contained miniature stone temple-pool offerings. In the Serapis temple, as mentioned earlier, Wilkinson early in the nineteenth century found a double temple pool with stairs. The Northern Shrine had four temple-pool offerings, whereas the Shrine of the Palmyrenes had one. This type of offering, probably used for water libations, occurred throughout Egypt, especially in Nubia.[67]

More noteworthy are traces of wooden bowls in all non-Christian shrines. Several earlier visitors cleared the Serapis temple (see chapter 2), and none mentions the occurrence of brown circles in the sand. Meredith reports that Wilkinson found much wood (perhaps the doors) and "some pieces of wood of the same form which I also found for the same purpose in the temples of the Nile" without elaborating on either form or purpose.[68] Wilkinson makes no mention of circular shapes or wooden bowls. On the early Roman surface of the forecourt of the Serapis temple, however, excavations documented remains of wooden bowls,[69] just north of the large storage jar containing black peppercorns (see chapter 12). The Northern Shrine also had remains of wooden bowls,[70] while the Shrine of the Palmyrenes preserved more than one hundred brown circles in the sand and provided some indications of how these bowls, now completely decayed, may have been used.[71] Sectioning showed the outline of the bowl with a layer of sand at the bottom and charred material on top. These bowls were in positions suggesting that they had fallen off shelves or had been stacked on the floor. Excavators recovered one atop a small stone incense burner. The bowls seem to be ready-made offerings; all the dedicant had to do was sprinkle incense on top of the glowing charcoal and place the bowl before the deity's image.[72] Black pepper may have been an ingredient of the incense mixture. Little of the black material remained, however, and it was too decayed to enable further analysis.

East of the cult centers and the Serapis temple, but west of the seaside limits of the ancient city, excavations unearthed multiple-storied buildings complete with staircases (figure 13-1). Some of the inner walls made of fossilized coral heads were built in a specific fashion, dubbed *Opus Berenikeum*, comprising square boxes built of gypsum ashlars to provide sturdy frameworks, which were filled in with coral heads. The outer walls of the buildings comprised double rows of coral heads, both rows facing outward, with a smaller-coral-head core filling. In several cases woven-grass matting appeared between the courses to provide better coherency. Quoins of gypsum or anhydrite ashlars were common as well. This part of the city was a late Roman commercial and residential area, built mostly in the mid to late fourth/early fifth centuries, modifying early Roman house plans

FIGURE 13-1
Berenike, typical building of the late Roman commercial-residential quarter (Trenches BE99-28/BE00-38). Scale = 1 m. Photo by S. E. Sidebotham.

but adhering more or less to the earlier street plan. Evidence suggests that ground floors and courtyards of buildings in this part of the city were for business or commercial activities, while the upper story or stories were domestic-residential areas. Finds of utilitarian cooking and coarse wares as well as fine dinnerware—the kind of pottery typical of a domestic setting in kitchen or dining areas—provided the interpretative evidence. These items came crashing down from the upper stories of several buildings as the structures decayed, deteriorated, and collapsed after the city had been abandoned.[73]

These multiple-storied structures also had niches built into their walls (figure 5-1). Where excavated, these niches were usually lined with wood and had wooden shelves. A single stone staircase made of large ashlars, perhaps reused from earlier structures, was tucked into a corner of the ground floor of all but one of these buildings and led upstairs to now-missing second-story domestic areas. This multistoried layout was typical of structures in ancient Egypt and throughout the Mediterranean world: shops and other commercial/business activities were conducted on the ground floor, while upper stories were private and used for domestic and residential activities.[74] It may be that guild members who were engaged in the sale of aromatics resided and conducted other business in this part of the city, dealing, as do Middle Eastern *aswaq* (markets) today, with similar wares found in a single location within a shopping district or city quarter.

Beneath large amounts of collapsed walls mixed with fragments of upper-floor domestic cooking wares was evidence of commercial activities. Small metal scales and tiny weights indicate that relatively small items were traded or sold in these ground-floor areas. Excavation of small single entrances into each building, together with the recovery of bronze faceplates to door-locking mechanisms, points to heightened security concerns—something necessary if items handled in these areas were of great value, perhaps precious or semiprecious stones, or spices and aromatics.

Weighing scales played an important role in the perfume industry, which made extensive use of aromatics and spices. In about 895, during the reign of the Emperor Leo VI (886–911), there was a Roman law recorded in the *Ordinances* (from *The Book of the Eparch* 10.5) laid out for the eparch of Constantinople that was very explicit: perfumers had to use scales and weights when buying wares—which would, of course, have included expensive aromatics such as frankincense and myrrh.[75] There is every reason to think this was also the case in earlier times, and perhaps the scales recovered in this area of Berenike served a similar purpose in the fourth and fifth centuries. Even though *The Book of the Eparch* dates to approximately five centuries after the late Roman buildings at Berenike and their contents, its stipulations may reflect the legal situation in the earlier period as well. The *Ordinances* stipulate that perfumers could not purchase wares purveyed by grocers or sold by steelyard (i.e., heavy scales), but could only buy articles sold on scales (smaller than steelyards).[76] The small, delicate scales from our excavations may be similar to ones alluded to in *The Book of the Eparch*, and if so, their appearance may indicate that commerce in aromatics and spices took place in these precincts. That might imply another difference from activities in Berenike in the early Roman period, when precious articles were shipped to and handled from the Nile valley warehouses by commercial companies rather than by local salesmen in Berenike itself. Of course, since virtually nothing of the early Roman city has been excavated, this conclusion may be premature.

One of the houses in this part of town expanded its activities into the adjacent street, and an interesting trade it was: Berenike had its own antiques market, or junkyard, where two-hundred- to three-hundred-year-old stone architectural elements were stored or perhaps traded or sold, such as column drums and capitals. Part of the street in front of the entrance to a fourth-/fifth-century courtyard and house was taken up by these stone objects. The house itself was built of coral heads, with many reused blocks: ashlars, some inscribed, taken from earlier buildings, lay on the courtyard floor. Two column capitals, which had been reused from some earlier structure, flanked a broad, short staircase that led up from the courtyard into the central interior of the house.[77] Out of the tumble came two worked-gypsum blocks, probably reused as windowsills or quoins—a regular occurrence in this quarter of the city. They contained two nearly identical dedicatory inscriptions to Zeus made by a woman named Philotera and dated to Nero's reign (see chapter 6).[78] It is uncertain how these slabs and columns ended up here. Several scenarios are possible, including one that proposes that some of Berenike's larger pagan temples were closed in the late fourth century and that these texts were taken at that time. But that is not consistent with the evidence from the Shrine of the Palmyrenes and especially the Northern Shrine, which continued to function then. Unless these shrines were sealed and abandoned, it is difficult to explain the arrangement as discovered by our excavations, with offering tables intact and in situ. It seems more likely that the Philotera dedications were removed during renovation of one of the shrines. This same late Roman building with the Zeus inscriptions also produced part of an inscription from the early second century dedicated to Isis and made by a man whose name is lost but whose father was Papiris. The dedicant was a secretary and interpreter.[79] One would expect to find many people with multilingual talents in cosmopolitan Berenike.

East of this late Roman commercial-domestic quarter, which was built in a uniform fashion, was a less homogenous area with larger buildings stretched out toward the sea. The plans, sizes, and functions of these edifices differ. A high circular mound revealed impressive foundations of a large structure.[80] The remains may indicate a towerlike feature, with support walls that braced a substantial superstructure. This may have been a lighthouse, paired with a circular feature on the peninsula on the south side of the harbor inlet. Such a coupled arrangement is a Roman harbor model that was typical for the Mediterranean[81] and may have been used at Berenike as well. J. G. Wilkinson's plans of Berenike sketched in 1826, and the earliest ones drawn of the site, indicate an artificial mound on the eastern end of a peninsula that enclosed Berenike's southern harbor. This area is, today, extremely hazardous due to the presence of land mines and cannot be examined, but the mound would have been an excellent location for a small temple, altar, or edifice associated with coordination or monitoring of ship movements into and out of the southern harbor. Where documented in Roman Mediterranean ports, such structures were visible to those approaching from the sea on the port (left) side. Frequently, these monuments were paired with a counterpart, often a lighthouse, on the starboard (right) side as one approached the harbor entrance[82]—precisely the location of the mound with massive walls.

In the fifth century this putative tower or lighthouse stood about two streets back from the edge of town, but before the mid-fourth-century and later urban extension, the tower may have stood at the edge of the contemporary harbor, later extended with the huge fill of potsherds noted earlier to accommodate buildings that postdated the construction and use of the putative lighthouse. Unfortunately, none of the excavated objects associated with this structure provided any indication of what function it once served, which is not surprising if it had been abandoned two centuries before and used as a quarry for building materials. The amount of tumble around the base of the building was impressive but, when calculated to wall dimensions, would not amount to a height that we expect considering the massive foundations. One of the putative foundation cells contained the body of an adult male about thirty to forty years old, his head bent back in an unnatural angle. He may have died accidentally or may have been murdered; we could not determine which.

The town's mid to late fourth-century extension, built on the mixed early and late Roman pottery dump, witnessed construction of two rows of large buildings east and south of the putative lighthouse. The buildings closest to the sea, at the far eastern and southern rim of the town, were ample in size. At the northeastern edge of the settlement a large building stood out ("Building F"). The plan and overall appearance of this structure suggest that it was probably a temple with a surrounding *temenos* wall; its entrance faced southeast. Recovery of fragments of fourth-century c.e. glass lanterns may suggest a temple, but numerous plaster jar stoppers do not reinforce this suggestion. If during one of its two building phases this edifice was a temple, it had lost that function by the time Berenike was abandoned. It may have been a more general public building (customs office?), or perhaps it was a former public building in disrepair that had been reused as a convenient space where goods were repacked; this would explain the occurrence of amphora stoppers. The relatively small amount of tumble from this area may point to a partial dilapidation and subsequent reuse of the complex.[83]

A second edifice, southeast of Building F, exhibited at least three construction phases. The building seems to have been partly demolished and rebuilt on a different plan within a very short period of time during Berenike's late Roman renaissance.[84] Since excavations halted here prematurely, the structure's purpose could not be determined.

Evidence from this northeastern corner of the city suggests that it was not as prosperous as other areas of Berenike. The dilapidated state of this part of town may be related to continuous harbor silting. Below the area between the *temenos* and Building F proper, excavations recorded traces of a seawall and small wooden poles or bollards (see chapter 5). Perhaps the poles/bollards were where small boats tied up adjacent to the seawall. During the early Roman period one of Berenike's harbors may have been north of town, with another to the south. Or perhaps the pressure of traffic was intense enough to employ every part of the shoreline. Clearly, by the fifth century c.e. the northern inlet had silted up or had filled with windblown sand and was no longer in use as a harbor.

By contrast, the extreme southeastern side of town seems to have operated in tandem with a harbor during the late Roman period. A warehouse dating to about 400 c.e. had a room with completely intact Aila-made amphoras (figures 13-2a and 13-2b).[85] The difference between activities here and those in the northeastern part of town is striking. Logically, a warehouse would have been located near the harbor, where items such as the amphoras stored here were either loaded onto or brought off ships. There is no way to know the status of the amphoras documented in the warehouse. They were found empty, without their original stoppers. Their contents are unknown, nor can one conclude whether they were destined for consumption at Berenike. They may have been waiting to be refilled, temporarily stored here with their original contents, or waiting to be otherwise recycled at Berenike for onward export. Reuse of amphoras was not uncommon, although for the early Roman period it is clear that reuse was neither haphazard nor informal: customers expected certain contents in specific types of containers.[86]

The largest building complex on site, at the eastern edge of town, is an ecclesiastical structure (figure 13-3). Excavated from 1996 to 2001, the building slowly revealed its function.[87] The first area excavated, in the southwestern part of the complex, documented part

FIGURES 13-2A
AND 13-2B
Berenike, late Roman
warehouse containing
Aila-made amphoras, on
the southeastern part of
the site (Trench BE95-5).
Scale = 50 cm. Photos
by S.E.Sidebotham.

FIGURE 13-3
Berenike, view of the Christian ecclesiastical complex, looking southeast. Scale = 1 m.
Photo by S. E. Sidebotham.

of a room with gypsum ashlar benches along all sides. Another area was a partly unroofed kitchen, with many layers filled with fish bones. A pot of *garum* stood in one corner. Continued excavation showed that the northern side of the building had domestic features, with cooking and small-scale industrial areas, while the southern side was swept clean, nicely floored at its eastern end, and better maintained in many ways. Excavation of the entire southern area of the building showed that the room with benches was an antechamber to a pillared hall that ran the entire west–east length of the building. Traces of wood on the western face of the section walls suggested the presence at one time of a structure that screened off the eastern end of the building. Remains of a bronze cross, probably a decorative handle that broke off a fancy oil lamp found separately, provided the first clue to the function of the building. Two other oil lamps made of terra-cotta were decorated with crosses, and a third had a salutation in raised relief in Sahidic Coptic, which read: "Jesus, forgive me."[88]

 We have not determined whether the complex, which was clearly divided into an ecclesiastical component and living quarters, also had sleeping accommodations. The northern, messy side of the building may have been living quarters for the church's caretakers, or, alternatively, a communal monastic area. Continued excavation here should provide the answer. Egyptian monasticism was mostly based on weekly communal services of monks who lived like hermits in the desert. Usually these monks resided in caves, natural or artificial, and sometimes in Pharaonic-period tombs. Abandoned parts of the settlement may have provided enough isolation to allow a monastic existence. This type of monasticism, based on the life of St. Antony, is very different from the Pachomian form, which is the model for medieval European cenobitic monasticism. With the growth of early Christianity in Egypt it is also conceivable that traders and sailors seeking reassurance before, or coming to offer thanks following, their hazardous maritime travels were numerous and required a large church. The small room with benches might have been reserved for novices, who were not yet full members of the Christian community. Equally, since churches and monasteries in late Roman times engaged in commerce and, in Egypt at least, were the largest landowners in the province,[89] the church at Berenike, the grandest single religious structure thus far found at the site and more substantial than even the Serapis temple, may have owed its size and relative sumptuousness to profits reaped from participation in late Roman commerce with the east. This may have included ownership of a commercial fleet.[90]

Analysis of many ecofacts and artifacts excavated from late Roman levels at Berenike indicates a robust trade with other areas of the Red Sea and Indian Ocean at that time. These include the recovery of the late third-/early fourth-century coin from the Kingdom of Axum, depicting King Aphilas, mentioned earlier. Also documented was a silver coin, dated 362 C.E., of the western Indian ruler Rudrasena III.[91] Both these coins came from the church.

BERENIKE'S HINTERLAND IN THE LATE ROMAN ERA

Enigmatically, of the ten forts forming a defensive ring around Berenike in the early Roman period, only one or two, at Vetus Hydreuma/Wadi Abu Greiya about 25 km northwest of the city, still operated in late Roman times. This seems odd given that the late Roman period witnessed a great revival in Berenike's economic fortunes. Instead, archaeological surveys around Berenike recorded several unfortified late Roman settlements. These included Qariya Mustafa 'Amr Gama'a in Wadi Umm Atlee,[92] Shenshef,[93] and Hitan Rayan.[94] There was also a smaller settlement at Qariya Ali Mohammed Husein (figure 5-6),[95] not far from Berenike. All four of these settlements, which range from just a few buildings in the case of Qariya Ali Mohammed Husein to several hundred in the case of Shenshef, were mainly of the late fourth/fifth and sixth centuries C.E., and the raisons d'être of none of the four have ever been precisely determined. Our detailed surveys of all four sites and limited excavations at Shenshef do, however, allow us to make some observations.

The location of Shenshef has long been known, though its function continues to remain a mystery to those who have studied this ancient desert settlement, which lies 21.3 km southwest of Berenike. J. G. Wilkinson visited the remains and discussed them in his unpublished field notes.[96] H. Barth visited the site in late October 1846,[97] and J. Ball[98] J. Rai-

Shenshef, view of one of the larger and better-preserved houses. Photo by S. E. Sidebotham.

mondi,[99] and G. W. Murray subsequently also saw it.[100] None knew the purpose of this large and well-built late Roman settlement comprising several hundred structures and hundreds of tombs (figure 13-4); a late first-century B.C.E./early first-century C.E. fort crowns the top of a nearby mountain overlooking the main settlement.[101] Murray speculated that Shenshef might have been a retreat for some residents of Berenike each autumn or a warehouse for precious commodities destined for trade through Berenike.[102] The residents of Shenshef were in touch with Berenike and, based upon our study of the rubbish excavated at the site, some of them, at least, had an opulent lifestyle. In addition to peppercorns,[103] sorghum,[104] teak,[105] beads,[106] and other imports from South Asia via Berenike, we also recovered a stunning cut sapphire from the trash dump—an excellent example of an import from Serendip/Taprobane (Sri Lanka).[107] Imported for consumption from the Mediterranean were walnuts, olives, almonds, and umbrella pine. Red Sea shells and fish were, however, poorly represented at the site; faunal remains indicated a population heavily dependent on herding goats and sheep. The pottery excavated at Shenshef is very similar to that from Berenike and includes imports that arrived by sea via Berenike.[108]

The smaller and more humble communities in Wadi Umm Atlee and at Hitan Rayan were also in contact with Berenike, as the recovery of large quantities of amphora sherds from so-called Late Roman Amphora I containers, likely made in southern Asia Minor or northern Cyprus, indicate. These vessels probably arrived by sea via Berenike; it is highly unlikely that they came overland from the Nile. Both of these settlements, each comprising over one hundred surviving structures, may have been Christian hermit communities.

We have found a number like them throughout the Eastern Desert similar both in location (removed from larger settlements and roads), dates, and methods of construction; and in types of pottery they contain.[109] Although only about 9 km apart as the crow flies, Hitan Rayan and Shenshef were connected to each other by a twisting mountain route about 11–12 km long dotted with small quarries, huts, graves, cairns, and cleared and built-up road segments; there were alternate routes in several locations. The thoroughfare accommodated human pedestrian and animal traffic, but not wagons due to some extremely steep sections.[110]

Other settlements within the 40 km radius of Berenike included the five forts at Vetus Hydreuma[111] and the fort in Wadi Lahma, most of which had ceramic evidence of early Roman and, in one or two cases, Ptolemaic activity.[112] The area inland from Berenike is honeycombed with roads and tracks of various sizes and dates, one of these being a back road to Vetus Hydreuma that passed near the small late Roman settlement of Qariya Ali Mohammed Husein; a side route from here led to Hitan Rayan.[113] There was also, father along this back route between Berenike and Vetus Hydreuma, a large late Roman-era cemetery at Taw al-Kefare.[114] This road continued through Wadi Abu Dab and had, carved along some adjacent rock faces, pictographs of indeterminate date.[115]

Ten military installations guarded approaches to Berenike, and those closest to the city also supplied it with water in early Roman times.[116] It is surprising to find no early Roman-era settlements in the environs of the port except the *praesidia* at Siket and the two in Wadi Kalalat as well as several at Vetus Hydreuma; with few exceptions, all the communities and most of the graves and cemeteries that we have investigated have been late Roman. Our survey found one small, possibly early Roman cemetery less than a kilometer east of the entrance to Hitan Rayan; we have no idea what population center it might have served, since Hitan Rayan itself is a late Roman settlement.

LATE ROMAN BERENIKE'S LONG-DISTANCE COMMERCE

The relations that late Roman Berenike had with Axum, the new power in the southern Red Sea region, bear some scrutiny. From the late third/early fourth century on, Axum, centered in Eritrea and Ethiopia, became a major player in maritime trade with other areas of the Red Sea and Indian Ocean, and this is confirmed by the finds of Axumite coins and pottery throughout the Red Sea and Indian Ocean (see chapters 6 and 12). In fact, the first minting of Axumite coins[117] coincides with the rise of Axum as a major trading power in the late third century. Some imitations of Axumite coins have been documented in India and the eastern Roman Empire.[118] Though Axumite coins have not been found outside the Kingdom of Axum in great numbers, the fact that someone, likely in Egypt, felt the need to imitate or counterfeit them suggests something about the commercial and political importance of that state in the late Roman era.

One would expect to see the prominent Axumite role in this commerce represented at Berenike. Apart from one coin, excavations have also recovered quantities of Axumite pottery, but the numbers are surprisingly small.[119] The rise of Axum sometime in the late third century c.e. coincided with the demise of the Meroitic Empire. There has been some speculation that the king of Axum may actually have originally come from Himyar in southern Arabia, across the Red Sea.[120] This would have created a very strong power block, because Axum and Himyar together could dominate the production and trade of Somali and South Arabian frankincense and myrrh.[121] They would also have controlled the Bab al-Mandeb, the narrow strait joining the Red Sea to the Indian Ocean. In the early sixth century, however, the relations between the rulers of South Arabia and the Ethiopian highlands were not cordial.

Many objects reflective of long-distance maritime commerce for a large import market or for personal use by residents appear in late Roman contexts at Berenike (see chapter 12). Pepper, semiprecious stones, especially beads, and other objects occur with regularity, suggesting the robust level of economic prosperity at Berenike and in the Eastern Roman Empire as a whole at that time. Toward the late fifth/early sixth centuries c.e., however, the prosperity waned. Parts of the town were abandoned and used as trash dumps, which provide useful information about the items people used and discarded, their diets, and the availability of goods, as well as changing preferences. In contrast to early Roman times, diets in the late fifth/early sixth centuries c.e. lacked much variation. Pork, beef, chicken, and Nile fish were not, as in early Roman times, consumed regularly; sheep and goat provided most animal protein. Surprisingly, the percentage of game consumed, such as gazelle or ibex, did not rise between the early and late Roman periods. Even the variety in Red Sea fish consumed dwindled, let alone the availability of such delicacies as escargot.[122] The material culture shows a perceivable shift as well: a larger percentage of rope, for instance, was made of goat hair and even of uncured leather, while papyrus rope seems to occur less frequently.[123] In general, in late Roman Berenike there was a greater emphasis on local resources, which could be produced or obtained in or near the settlement. Changes in consumption patterns between early and late Roman Berenike are important indicators of shifts in populations residing there. The dwindling role of the Nile valley as a source for staple foods and other provisions and their replacement with products of local fishermen and herdsmen seem to represent the latest phase in an ongoing development. Berenike in late antiquity probably was a place of permanent residence rather than an outpost where a person simply fulfilled his service or sought a fortune for a number of years before departing. The population in the latest phase was much more desert oriented than the earlier inhabitants of the town.

In this light, it is important to compare water provisions in the late Roman period with earlier times. Chapters 7 and 8 noted that it was mainly the Roman military that provided water, as illustrated by the establishment and refurbishment of *praesidia* near early Roman Berenike and along the Berenike–Koptos road, and as reflected in the ostraka recorded in 2009–2010. Installations near Berenike (in Wadi Kalalat and Siket) seem to have fallen out of use by late Roman times, though some along the road leading to Koptos continued

in operation. It remains to be determined where late Roman Berenike obtained its drinking water. Self-reliance was more important to denizens of the port at this time than it
had been in earlier centuries. Because local production became increasingly important
in the latest phase of Berenike's existence, likely there was more emphasis on small garden plots and desert cultivation. Desert irrigation throughout antiquity made use of existing wells and cisterns, and occasionally springs or, less often, *qulut* and *hafayir* (see
chapter 7).

BERENIKE'S DEMISE

Excavations at Berenike, especially study of pottery from the latest strata, document that
the town was abandoned sometime in the first half of the sixth century C.E. The Ptolemaic industrial quarter had long since been neglected as such by late antiquity; at some
unknown date a few human skeletons were hastily discarded in this area. Two had no
heads and no grave goods, nor was there any evidence that they had received proper burials;[124] they appear to have been discarded in what must have been an area outside the city
at that time. Evidence of a rough grave cut for one of these bodies showed that it did not
lose its head after being deposited: the pit provides a snug fit around the neck stump and
shoulders. The foot of one appeared to have been gnawed, perhaps by scavengers, after
it had been dumped here. It is not clear why these persons were buried without heads.
One can only assume either that they died as the result of some gruesome accident or,
perhaps more likely, had been executed by decapitation and tossed out here. A third body
was discarded in a fetal position in one of the broken Ptolemaic waterproof tanks.[125] Another, complete skeleton was also found in this area.[126] The remains of a forty- to fifty-
year-old female, whose pelvis had been modestly covered by a large broken potsherd, lay
deposited atop an early Ptolemaic brick-making facility.[127]

There is scant evidence of human activity at Berenike in the very latest period of its
existence. A few poorly built walls made of chunks of coral and large seashells and taking the appearance in plan of bananas indicate that they were probably windbreaks behind which transient visitors could shelter from the strong prevailing north winds. Some
of these "banana" walls had the remains of temporary cooking fires that had been set on
their leeward sides. From the nature of the fires that were kindled and the size and method
of construction of the windbreaks, nobody permanently resided in the city in its latest
period of occupation.

Trash dumps accumulating in and around abandoned buildings within the city testify
to Berenike's slow decline. Obviously, there was no single cause for the port's demise;
rather, its end was likely due to a combination of factors. The continued silting of the
southern harbor in this late period may have reached a point at which few large ships
could approach without beaching on a sandbar or hitting bottom in the shallow water. In
order to maintain a harbor at the mouth of a wadi, regular and costly upkeep was required.

Maintaining a population at Berenike necessitated at least some continued import of food and raw materials along the desert roads. This would have been expensive and would have been worthwhile only if profits from commerce outweighed these costs.

It is unclear how far increased influence of the nomadic population of the Eastern Desert affected Berenike's commercial operations. With the weakening of the government's grip on trade, already apparent when comparing early and late Roman Berenike, the merchants may have become overly dependent on their desert guides and "protectors." Textual sources mention the increased power of the Blemmyes in the area.[128] The Blemmyes may be a designation of individuals and groups that do not comprise all desert nomads, and could represent a specific group that had its actual power base along the Nile.[129] Olympiodorus, an Egyptian from Thebes, writes in the fifth century (*History* 35.2) that the Blemmyes were in charge of the emerald mines of Mons Smaragdus, and the region around Berenike.[130]

Sometime in the sixth century, perhaps during the reign of Justinian I (527–565), Stephanus of Byzantium listed Berenike Trog(l)odytike.[131] The latest dated ancient reference we have to Berenike appears in 524/525 C.E. in the *Martyrium Sancti Arethae* (27–29). It indicates that Timothy, bishop of Alexandria, at the behest of Emperor Justin I (518–527), ordered troops and ships sent to assist the Axumites.[132] The Axumite king Elesbaan/Kaleb was urged into a war against the Kingdom of Himyar in reaction to the burning of a group of Christian Arabs in the South Arabian city of Najran in 523 C.E.[133] It is noteworthy that an inscription from Marib written in the Old Ethiopic language and script also seems to refer to this invasion.[134] Twenty ships were to be sent from the harbor of Clysma, seven from the island of Iotabê, seven from the island of Farasan, five from Aila, two from Berenike, and nine from "India."[135] We have no idea if the troops or ships were ever sent. The indication "India" most probably points to a region closer to Axum, because by the sixth century, and certainly earlier, geographical knowledge in the Mediterranean world had deteriorated such that there was confusion of India with areas of Ethiopia and the Horn of Africa.[136] What is most striking, however, is the fact that Clysma, which was in early Roman times a desolate, minor harbor, was, by this time, asked to send ten times more ships than Berenike. If this reflects the relative commercial activities of the respective harbors at that time, it is an indication that Berenike's heydays had long passed.

Berenike was not overwhelmed by some sudden catastrophe but died a slow and natural death. We are not certain at this point what caused the port's demise, but we have some hypotheses. By the late fifth/early sixth centuries the Axumites and Arabs at the southern end of the Red Sea dominated the maritime trade.[137] Evidence of the growing commercial muscle of Axum is apparent in late Roman Berenike, where our excavations recovered Axumite pottery and a coin. At least one Axumite graffito from this era is known from the Berenike–Nile road.[138] Of course, this competition had the potential to impact negatively on the prosperity of Berenike, though we do not know that it did.

Procopius (*History of the Wars* 2.22.1–23.21; 2.24.8, 12) reports that a severe plague, likely bubonic (*Yersinia pestis*), swept up from Africa, or perhaps India or Arabia, into the Mediterranean in the first half of the sixth century; it is first recorded at Pelusium in the summer of 541.[139] It proved to be extremely virulent, causing devastation not only in Egypt, but in many regions of the Roman Empire and western Europe, for more than two hundred years thereafter.[140] At its height in Constantinople in the summer of 542 this pestilence carried away upward of five thousand to sixteen thousand people every day.[141] An inscription from Marib dated 543 indicates that this same plague also seems to have struck the Arabian Peninsula with devastating results.[142] Its most likely entry points into Egypt were the Red Sea ports. Perhaps the overwhelming effects of this disease also added to Berenike's woes; one might speculate that this, in addition to the silting of the harbors and competition from South Arabian, Axumite, and other middlemen, led to Berenike's ultimate downfall.[143] Whatever the cause of the city's final abandonment, by about 550 Berenike had become a ghost town, visited thereafter only by occasional transient travelers.

The end of Berenike did not, however, spell the end of other ports at the northern end of the Red Sea. Ironically, despite their adverse locations vis-à-vis the strong northerly winds, not only Aila continued to operate in this late period,[144] but also Clysma/Cleopatris/Arsinoë.[145] A Roman customs post and commercial center on the island of Iotabê, as yet unlocated, but somewhere at the northern end of the Red Sea, operated for about sixty years, which coincided approximately with the final years of activity at Berenike.[146] Farther south on the Red Sea coast Adulis, the port of the Kingdom of Axum, flourished.[147] In the Indian Ocean by the fifth century and into the seventh century C.E., Kané/Qana' on the southern coast of Arabia still operated; its commercial links at that time were, however, apparently strongest with the East African coast rather than the Red Sea.[148] There is evidence for the presence of both Christians and Jews in Qana' in the fourth to sixth centuries (see chapter 9).[149] Of course several kingdoms in southern Arabia continued to flourish in this period in late antiquity just prior to the rise of Islam,[150] and some must have had ports on the Red Sea and Indian Ocean coasts; these, however, remain to be identified.

Berenike was not abandoned suddenly, but apparently it was too far away from the new centers of habitation to tap as a quarry for wooden beams or stone blocks. In fact, the site has been surprisingly undisturbed since its desertion. Many archaeological sites in Egypt display ample evidence of looting, but Berenike has been allowed to crumble quietly and fill up with windblown sand. What modern looting has occurred here has been since the enforced closure of our excavations after the 2001 season. The result is a site that is, for the most part, a treasure trove of information on Indian and other "non-Roman" material culture, information that has not survived in the wet conditions of the Indian Ocean littoral. Excavations at late Roman Berenike have revealed something about the desert dwellers who temporarily settled here; such people rarely leave a trace in other archaeological contexts. Research at Berenike has documented something about the ordinary Roman soldiers and Egyptian camel drivers whose lives otherwise escape detection in the government annals and ancient authors of the era.

Trade with India was still lucrative at that time, but those who profited were increas-

ingly not the late Roman/Byzantine state treasury or Roman merchants and ship owners or officials, but rather the Persians, Axumites, Himyarites, and denizens of South Asia.
The economic power block of Himyar-Axum replaced the Roman one for control of the
Red Sea–Indian Ocean trade. After Berenike a new harbor came into existence about
260 km to the south at Aidhab. Aidhab was the first hajj harbor of Egypt and became
especially important during the Crusades, when the land route through Clysma and the
Sinai was cut off to Muslims. At that time North African pilgrims traveled up the Nile to
Qus or Sus (Aswan), crossed the desert—usually via Wadi Allaqi—to Aidhab, and then
traveled by sea to Jeddah.[151] After its decline, the pilgrims to Mekka departed primarily
from Quseir.[152]

NOTES

1. INTRODUCTION

1. Frank (1991); Frank (1993); Frank and Gills (1993).
2. Hopkirk (1980) [numerous editions and publishers] and Hopkirk (1993) popularize earlier research on the Silk Road; Wriggins (1996); Wheeler (1955): 154–171, 181–182; Miller (1969): 119–141; Pigulewskaja (1969): 150–171; Raschke (1974a); Raschke (1974b); Raschke (1978): especially 610–630; Ferguson (1978): 586–587; Franck and Brownstone (1986); Herbert (1997), Debaine-Francfort and Idriss (2000), Baumer (2002) and Lawton (2004); Knauer (1998) for camels on the Silk Road. *Les Annales archéologiques arabes syriennes* 42 (1996) for specialized research on the western ends of the Silk Road; Boulnois (2004); Whitfield (1999); Foltz (1999); Bernard (2005); Liu and Shaffer (2007); Olson (1979): Roman-Parthian relations; Wang (2004) for coinage along the Silk Road; *SRAA* is a journal dedicated to Silk Road studies; Mutschler and Mittag (2008).
3. Groom (1981): 165–213; Salles (1988); Saud et al. (1996); De Maigret (1997); Jasmin (2005); De Maigret (2004); Beeston (2005): 53, 54 (fig. 2), 59; Crone (1987): 3–50; Kitchen (2001); Macdonald (1994); Goren (2000).
4. Wheeler (1955): 126–153; Charlesworth (1974): 57–73 and 97–111; Raschke (1978); Sidebotham (1986); Young (2001); Peacock and Williams (2007); Teggart (1939) and Gungwu (1998) for the Chinese end of the route.
5. Wheeler (1955): 95–111; Heine (1983); Desanges (1999); Roe (2005–2006).
6. Wheeler (1955): 13–14, 23, 92, 177; Spekke (1976): 47–71 for the Amber Route, 14–46 for classical authors dealing with amber; Fraquet (1987): 19–23 for Amber Route in the Roman Empire; Grimaldi (1996): 47–61 on Baltic amber; Plisson (2005): 70 for amber from Sicily, Romania, and Burma; Dubin (1995): 73, 101.

7. Sidebotham and Wendrich (1995, 1996, 1998a, 1998b; 1999, 2000a, 2001–2002, 2007a); Bagnall et al. (2000); Bagnall et al. (2005); Cappers (2006); Sidebotham et al. (2008).

8. Sidebotham (1986): 164–165 and notes 229–230; Young (2001): 71–72; Harker (2008); Cuvigny (2003b): 346–357; Lewis (1938) = Lewis (1995); MacMullen (1966): 255–268 for brigandage in general; Butcher (2003): 409–410 and note on 462; Wolff (1999): 398; Shaw (2004) in general.

9. Hogarth (1896); Raschke (1978): 649 and 893 (note 961); Bernand (1984a): 199–208 (no. 67) with bibliography, translation, and commentary (= *OGIS* 674 = *IGRR* I.1183); Sidebotham (1986): 35, 53, 67, 80–81; Young (2001): 48–50; Burkhalter-Arce (2002); Cuvigny (2003a): 273–274.

10. Huntingford (1980): 143–157.

11. Glover (1969): 132–175; Parker (2008): 21–28.

12. Diodorus Siculus; Quintus Curtius Rufus; Plutarch, *Life of Alexander the Great, On the Fortune or Virtue of Alexander,* and *Moralia;* Arrian, *Anabasis* and *Alexander and Indica.*

13. Pearson (1960).

14. Scullard (1974): 120–145; Casson (1993); Burstein (1996).

15. Wheeler (1955): 115; Sidebotham (1986): 182–186.

2. GEOGRAPHY, CLIMATE, ANCIENT AUTHORS, AND MODERN VISITORS

1. Meredith (1957a); Murray and Warmington (1967): 24; Bagnall and Rathbone (2004): 290–292; Sidebotham et al. (2008): 159–165.

2. Meigs (1966): 65.

3. Whitewright (2007a): 84–85; Siddall et al. (2004): 421–422.

4. Meigs (1966): 63; Searight (2007): 121.

5. Searight (2007): 121.

6. Meigs (1966): 63.

7. *Western Arabia* (1946): 61.

8. *Western Arabia* (1946): 60–61; Meigs (1966): 63–64; Braithwaite (1987): 25; Searight (2007): 121 reports depths of 1,500 fathoms (2,830 m).

9. Meigs (1966): 63.

10. Ormond and Edwards (1987): 280, 284–286.

11. Peppard (2009).

12. Tibbetts (1961): 326; Edwards (1987): 49 and 51; *Red Sea and Gulf of Aden Pilot* (1980): 19, 24, maps on 29 (1.135a) and 31 (1.135b).

13. Sampsell (2003): 154; Midant-Reynes (2000): 20–21.

14. Sampsell (2003): 156.

15. Osman and Sidebotham (2000): 19.

16. Meigs (1966): 64 reports 0.2 inches; Butzer and Hansen (1968): 423 report 4 mm per annum at Quseir; Edwards (1987): 56–57; Reddé (2003b): 40; Zitterkopf and Sidebotham (1989): 164.

17. Personal observations of Sidebotham; Murray (1968): 47–48.

18. Maxfield (2001a): 143.

19. Sidebotham and Wendrich (1998b): 95; Sidebotham and Wendrich (2001–2002): 48.

20. Aldsworth et al. (1995); Meredith (1957a): 56–59; Murray and Warmington (1967); Belzoni, (1820): 331 estimated about 1,600 feet N–S × about 2,000 feet E–W.

21. Harrell (1996): 102–103, 106, 108; Harrell (1998): 125, 128–129.

22. Butzer and Hansen (1968): 423.

23. Harrell (1996): 124–125.

24. *Western Arabia* (1946): 74; Murray (1968): 45.

25. Purser et al. (1987): 247–267; Blue (2006a).

26. Plaziat et al. (1995): 15–16; Harrell (1996): 102–104; Siddall et al. (2003); Blue (2006a): 43.

27. Liverani (2003). Bellwald and al-Huneid (2003); Nehmé (2003): 162–163.

28. Van Neer and Ervynck (1999a): 333–337.

29. Van Neer and Ervynck (1999a): 337.

30. Cappers (2006): 45–48, 140–143.

31. Sidebotham, personal experiences; Gauthier-Pilters and Dagg (1981): 170; Schmidt-Nielsen (1964): 9; Zitterkopf and Sidebotham (1989): 164.

32. Bernand (1972a); Bernand (1972b); Bülow-Jacobsen et al. (1995); Fournet (1995); De Romanis (1996a): 203–217, 241–259; De Romanis (1996b); Cuvigny et al. (1999); Cuvigny et al. (2000).

33. Edwards (1987): 48–49; Harrell (1996): 103.

34. Head (1987a).

35. Raschke (1978): 939 (note 1152); Huntingford (1980): 146–147; Sidebotham (1986): 6 and note 30 (for inscription *OGIS* 132 of 130 B.C.); *Periplus* 53, Pliny, *NH* 6.26.101.

36. Wilford (2002): 6–46 and 152–153.

37. Wilford (2002): 155–162.

38. Kortenbeutel (1931): 8–13 for earlier sources.

39. Fraser (1972a): 173–174; Retsö (2003): 295–300; Seland (2006): 41; Burstein (2008a): 137–139.

40. Burstein (1989): 13–41.

41. Seland (2006): 41; dates of composition are disputed, on which see Pierce (2007): 33, note 1.

42. Pierce (2007).

43. Kammerer (1929): for classical and Arab writers dealing with the Red Sea.

44. Dihle (1965): 80–84; Jameson (1968); Sidebotham (1986): 120–130; Buschmann (1991); Marek (1993); Marek (1994); Potts (1994); Luther (1999); von Wissmann (1978); Bianchetti (2002): 290 and note 42; Retsö (2003): 402–403; Retsö (2000): location of Arabia Eudaimon/Arabia Felix changed throughout antiquity. At one time it designated eastern Arabia, at another all of the Arabian Peninsula, and, by the fourth century C.E., southwestern Arabia.

45. Sidebotham (1986): 129–130, 172 for Augustan-era embassies.

46. Sidebotham (1986): 139–140 and notes; Millar (1998): 120–121; Whittaker (2002): 89; Ruffing (2002): 364; Kramer (2003); Belfiore (2004): 245–266.

47. Sidebotham (1986): 130–133; Whittaker (2002): 89.

48. Sidebotham (1986): 138–141, 177–178; Parker (2008): 209–214, 219–221.

49. Sidebotham (1986): 139–140; Retsö (2003): 403–407.

50. Jackson (1988): 56–85.

51. Scarborough (1982).

52. A second- or third-century date for the *Periplus* is no longer a serious consideration. Dihle (1965): 9–35 (first century C.E.); cf. Wheeler (1955): 115–125 (first century C.E.); Mathew (1975): 154–163 after composition of Pliny's *Natural History* (77 C.E.) and before Ptolemy's *Geography* (about mid–second century C.E.); Casson (1989): 5–7 (40–70 C.E.); Belfiore (2004): 77–82 (second half first century C.E.), 91–92 for other bibliography on the date; Eggermont (1968): ca. 30 C.E.; Raschke (1978): 663–666 (first century C.E.); Leslie and Gardiner (1996): 13 and note 30 (first century C.E.); Ehlers (1985): 77–78 (40–70 C.E.); Groom (1995): 180, 182, 187, 190 (ca. 45 C.E.); Fussman (1991): 36, 38 (30–50 C.E.) = Fussman (1997): 66 (ca. 40 C.E.); Tibi (1996): 237 (ca. 100 C.E.); Robin (1991): 25, 29 (40-after 78 C.E.) = Robin (1997): 59 (first century C.E.); Shitomi (1976): 37–38 (60–70 C.E.); Bianchetti (2002): 281 and note 9 (second half first century C.E.); Sidebotham (1986): 187–188; Retsö (2003): 421–422 (late first century C.E.); Seland (2010): 13–15 (mid–first century C.E.); Fraser (1972a): 174.

53. Pliny (*NH* 6.35.181 and 12.8.19) does not mention the marshy area; Raschke (1978): 647 and 874–875 notes 917–918; also Sherk (1974): 559–560; El-Sheikh (1992): 158–160.

54. Seland (2006): 39–41.

55. Casson (1989): 11–12, 283–291; Desanges (1996); Mazzarino (1997); Tchernia (1997b); De Romanis (1997a); Ehlers (1985).

56. Strabo, *Geography* 2.3.4; *Periplus* (57); Fraser (1972a): 174; Desanges (1978): 151–173 (on Eudoxus of Cyzicus), 303–305; Puskás (1987): 144–146.

57. "Western" discovery of the monsoons varies from about 116 B.C.E. to ca. 40 C.E.: Wheeler (1955): 126–130; Thiel (1967): 12, 17ff.; Fraser (1972a): 174, 182–183; Shitomi (1976); Desanges (1978): 158–159, 303–305; Raschke (1978): 660–662 and 968–976 (notes 1271–1319); Casson (1980); Ehlers (1985); Puskás (1987): 144–146; Casson (1989): 11–12, 283–291; Desanges (1996); De Romanis (1997a); Mazzarino (1997); Tchernia (1997b); Bianchetti (2002): 282 and note 11; Tripati and Raut (2006) for monsoon from east coast of India to Sri Lanka and Southeast Asia.

58. Miller (1969): 242–275 for overview of ancient geographers; Ball (1942) for ancient geographers on Egypt.

59. Wheatley (1961): 138–176.

60. Dilke (1985): 77–81; Wilford (2002): 31; Seland (2006): 41–42; Desanges (1978): 330–335.

61. Kortenbeutel (1931): 11–12; Thrower (1996): 23; Dilke (1985): 72–75, 77, 81; Wilford (2002): 30, 34, 37. Perhaps Marinus of Tyre and Maës Titianus were the same person. Carey (1956) on Maës Titianus.

62. Wilford (2002): 30. 34–39.

63. Miller (1969): 271–276; Thrower (1996): 23–24; Faller (2000): 112–115.

64. Cosmas citations from Wolska-Conus (1968–1973); Dilke (1985): 171–172; Wilford (2002): 43; Miller (1969): 166–169 and Pigulewskaja (1969): 110–129; Seland (2006): 42.

65. Wolska-Conus (1973): 348–349; McCrindle (1897): 358–373.

66. Starkey and El Daly (2000).

67. Kammerer (1936): 124–126.

68. D'Anville (1766): 231–233.

69. Belzoni (1820): 330–335; Siliotti (2001); Mayes (2003); Manley and Rée (2001): 84–99.

70. Wilkinson (1835): 418.

71. D'Athanasi (1836): 33–34; Manley and Rée (2001): 88, 89, 110–113, 115, 117–119, 121–122, 143–146, 159, 165–166, 201, 202, 220, 221, 224, 234, 242, 256, 268, 274, 286, and 292.

72. Wellsted (1836): 96–100; Wellsted (1838): 334–339.

73. Barth (1859): 2, 13, 15–16.

74. Schweinfurth (1922): 131–132.

75. Golénischeff (1890): 75–96.

76. Purdy (1886): 431.

77. Colston (1886): 512.

78. Floyer (1893a): 3, 4, 8, 10–13, 17, 20, 49, 57–59, 88–89, 117, 131, 142, 149, photo opposite p. 10; Floyer (1893b): 413–414.

79. Daressy (1922): 169–184; Bernand (1977): 177–191.

80. Raimondi (1923b): 53–76. Purdy (1886): 431 possibility of railroad between Berenike and Berber on the Nile.

81. Bent and Bent (1900): 291–292, 296.

82. Ball (1912): 1, 29, 65.

83. Murray (1925): 143; Murray (1926b); Murray (1968): 49–58.

84. Figari (1864); Barron and Hume (1902); Hume (1907); Ball (1912); Barthoux (1922); Hume (1925); Ball (1931): 696–697, 717, 724, 725, 734; Hume (1934); Hume (1935); Hume (1937); Little and Attia (1943).

3. PRE-ROMAN INFRASTRUCTURE IN THE EASTERN DESERT

1. Peden (2001); cf. Wengrow (2006): 111–114.

2. Moeyersons et al. (2002): 837–851; Wengrow (2006): 27, 54 (for burials).

3. Červíček (1974); Close (1999); Fuchs (1988): 17, 19–20; Fuchs (1989); Holmes (1999); Redford and Redford (1989); Rohl (2000); Winkler (1938); Midant-Reynes (2000): 27, 37, 99; Friedman and Hobbs (2002); Huyge (2002).

4. Wengrow (2006): 14, 27, 34, 51, 55, 80, 255.

5. Winkler (1938): 24–25, 27, 28–29, 30, 31–32, pl. XXIII (3), pls. XXV–XXXII; Červíček (1974): 156–157, Abb. 23, Abb. 44, Abb. 69, Abb. 161, Abb. 164 (?), Abb. 191–193, Abb. 202(?), Abb. 216 li., Abb. 216 re., Abb. 221, Abb. 222 li., Abb. 222 re., Abb. 245, Abb. 314–315, Abb. 318–319, Abb. 322–323, Abb. 326(?), Abb. 332 (?), Abb. 336, Abb. 391, Abb. 481(?), Abb. 482, Abb. 484(?), Abb. 496–497; Redford and Redford (1989): 12–13 (figs. 10–11), 14–15 (figs. 13–14); Rohl (2000): 17 (no. 10), 41 (no. 17), 43 (no. 6, fig. 6), 46 (no. 16, fig. 11), 46 (no. 20), 46 (no. 22), 49 (no. 4, fig. 3), 74 (no. 2, fig. 1), 74 (no. 3, fig. 2), 74 (no. 5, fig. 4), 74 (no. 7), 75 (no. 1, fig. 1), 75 (no. 2, fig. 2), 78 (no. 9, fig. 8: on p. 76), 81 (no. 2), 89 (no. 5, fig. 3), 90 (no. 2, fig. 2: late in date), 91 (no. 5, fig. 2), 95 (no. 4, fig. 3), 103 (no. 9, fig. 8), 103 (no. 11, fig. 10), 105 (no. 13, fig. 12), 105 (No.14), 105 (no. 20), 105 (no. 23, fig. 17), 108 (no. 2, fig. 4), 111 (no. 6), 111 (no. 7, fig. 3: on p. 110), 111 (no. 11),

113 (no. 3, fig. 3), 115 (no. 4, fig. 4), possibly 115 (no. 5), 115 (no. 7, fig. 5), 115 (no. 8, fig. 6), 117 (no. 3, fig. 3), 118 (site ER-2: no. 2, fig. 2), 118 (site AW-2: no. 1), 119 (site PL-2: no. 3), 123 (no. 1, fig. 1), 136 (no. 11), 136 (no. 18), 138 (no. 2), 138 (no. 4), possibly 138 (no. 6), 138 (no. 8, fig. 2 on p. 139), 138 (no. 9), 138 (no. 10), 143 (no. 8, fig. 4), 143 (no. 10, fig. 6), 146 (no. 1, fig. 4), 146 (no. 2, fig. 5), 148 (no. 15).

6. Rock art at al-Hosh (near al-Kab) pre-dates the early 7th millennium BP (mid 6th millennium cal. BCE), Huyge (2000–2001); Huyge et al. (2001).

7. Hobbs and Goodman (1995): 9.

8. Huyge (1998), but cf. Muzzolini (1999); Huyge (1999).

9. Winkler (1938): 5 (site 8A), 5 (site 10), 5 (sites 12 and 12A-C), 6 (site 21?), 7 (site 24H), 8 (site 25), 8 (site 25A?), 8 (site 25B?), 8 (site 28?), 9 (site 35?); Červíček (1974): 156–157, Abb. 23, Abb. 44, Abb. 69, Abb. 161, Abb. 164 (?), Abb. 191–193, , Abb. 202(?), Abb. 216 li., Abb. 216 re., Abb. 221, Abb. 222 li., Abb. 222 re., Abb. 245, Abb. 314–315, Abb. 318–319, Abb. 322–323, Abb. 326(?), Abb. 332 (?), Abb. 336, Abb. 391, Abb. 481(?), Abb. 482, Abb. 484(?), Abb. 496–497; Vinson (1994); Muzzolini (1995); Fuchs (1989): 143–144 (fig. 25), 145–146 (fig. 28), 145 (fig. 29), 151; Redford and Redford (1989): 11–12 (figs. 7–8), 12–13 (figs. 10–11), 14–15 (figs. 13–14).

10. Winkler (1938): 22, 25, 27, 30, 35–39, plate IX (no. 2), plate XII (no. 1), plate XIII (no. 3), plate XIV (nos. 1–2), plate XV (no. 1), , plate XIX (no. 3), plate XXII (nos. 1–2), plate XXIII (nos. 1–2), pls. XXXIII–XLI; Červíček (1974): 98–138 (in general), Abb. 19, Abb. 26(?)—Abb. 41–42, Abb. 52–55, Abb. 66, Abb. 71–76, Abb. 80–84, Abb. 88 (?), , Abb. 93–94, Abb. 118(?), Abb. 120–121, Abb. 143, Abb. 147(?), Abb. 155, Abb. 225(?), Abb. 227, Abb. 241, Abb. 244, Abb. 263–265, Abb. 267–270, Abb. 274–279, Abb. 286, Abb. 289–290, Abb. 294 (?), Abb. 302–304, Abb. 308–311, Abb. 322(?), Abb. 335, Abb. 343–344, Abb. 345(?), Abb. 359–361, Abb. 363–364, Abb. 381, Abb. 383, Abb. 395, Abb. 404, Abb. 414, Abb. 418, Abb. 420, Abb. 428, Abb. 461–464, , Abb. 472, Abb. 474, Abb. 483(?), Abb. 487–488(?), Abb. 494, Abb. 502, Abb. 506–508, Tafel 1 (nos. 1–2), Tafel 2 (no. 3), Tafel 6 (no. 12), Tafel 7 (no. 14), Tafel 14 (no. 27); Redford and Redford (1989): 10–11 (fig. 5), 10–11 (fig. 6), 14–15 (figs. 13–14), 19–20 (figs. 26–27), 26 (fig. 40), 26–27 (figs. 41–42), 26, 28 (fig. 43), 28–29 (figs. 44–45), 35–36 (figs. 63–64), 36–37 (figs. 65–66), 37–38 (fig. 69); Rohl (2000): 5–9, 177–186; Redford and Redford (1989): 10–11 (fig. 6), 19–20 (figs. 26–27), 26 (fig. 40), 26–27 (figs. 41–42), 26, 28 (fig. 43), 28–29 (figs. 44–45), 35–36 (figs. 63–64), 36–37 (figs. 65–66), 37–38 (fig. 69); Rohl (2000): 5–9, 177–186 and passim; Midant-Reynes (2000): 231; Fuchs (1989); Wengrow (2006): 112–114; Van Rengen et al. (2006): 17–18, 22, 23.

11. Peden (2001); Van Rengen et al. (2006): 17–23.

12. Wengrow (2006): 211.

13. All Pharaonic dates are based on Baines and Málek (2000).

14. MacKay (1915): 38–40; Murray (1955): 171–174; Garbrecht (1999); Fahlbusch (2004).

15. Fahlbusch (2004).

16. Wengrow (2006): 147.

17. Murray (1955): 175; Breasted (2001a): 208–210 (nos. 427–433).

18. Murray (1955): 175; Breasted (2001a): 213 (no. 442).

19. Peden (2001): 124–126; Hikade (2006).

20. Castel and Goyon (1980); Castel and Soukiassian (1985); Castel et al. (1989); Castel et al. (1999); Régen and Soukiassian (2008).
21. Harrell and Lewan (2002).
22. Harrell and Brown (1992a); Harrell and Brown (1992b); Ballet et al. (2000): 152 and fig. 48 for a color photo of the Turin papyrus.
23. Winkler (1938).
24. Cherry (2000); Rohl (2000): 10–11.
25. Dates of rock varnish provide *termini ante quem,* dates at which the drawings certainly existed, rather than absolute dates of drawings themselves: Redford and Redford (1989): 7; Huyge et al. (2001); Wengrow (2006): 111–112 for caveats in dating rock art.
26. Couyat and Montet (1912); Goyon (1957).
27. Breasted (2001d): 225–226 (no. 466); Harrell and Brown (1992a); Harrell and Brown (1992b); Hikade (2001): 36–46 for Old and Middle Kingdom, 196–212 and 274 for Ramses IV; Hikade (2006) for New Kingdom.
28. Breasted (2001d): 226 (no. 446).
29. Aufrère (1991a): 80–81.
30. Klemm and Klemm (1993): 355–411.
31. Harrell and Brown (1992b): 8.
32. Couyat and Montet (1912); Goyon (1957); Peden (2004): 345; Bernand (1972a); Meyer (1999b).
33. Goyon (1957); Meyer (1999b); Kitchen (2004): 25, 27.
34. Kitchen (1993): 603–605; Kitchen (2004): 28–30; Dixon (2004): 34; Chami (2004): 95.
35. Phillips (1997b); Wicker (1998); Kitchen (2004): 28 and bibliography.
36. Frost (1996); Vandersleyen (1996); Bard and Fattovich (2007); Bard et al. (2007); Fattovich and Manzo (2008); Bard and Fattovich (2010).
37. Fattovich (2005); Fattovich and Bard (2006); Ward and Zazzaro (2007); Gerish et al. (2007); Carannante et al. (2007): 190–195; Bard et al. (2007); Bard and Fattovich (2010).
38. Shaw (2000): 322; Fattovich (2005): 15; Bard and Fattovich (2007): 22–23; Abd el-Raziq et al. (2002); Abd el-Raziq et al. (2004); Abd el-Raziq et al. (2006); Lacaze and Camino (2008) for analogous site at Rod al-Khawaga.
39. Aston et al. (2000); Castel et al. (1998); Lucas and Harris (1989): 202–203, 208–209 for Sinai.
40. Vercoutter (1959); Klemm and Klemm (1994); Klemm et al. (2001); Klemm et al. (2002).
41. Shaw and Jameson (1993); Shaw (1999b).
42. Rothe and Rapp (1995).
43. Harrell (2002); Partridge (1996).
44. Shaw (1986): 195–198; Shaw (1987): 160–162; Shaw (1994): 110–113.
45. Klemm et al. (1984): 211, 213 (Abb. 2); Bloxam and Storemyr (2005): 38–40.
46. Klemm et al. (1984): 211; cf. Shaw (1986); 196 (fig. 10.4); Shaw (1987): 162 (fig. 13.2).
47. Bulliet (1975): 113–117; Midant-Reynes and Braunstein-Silvestre (1977); Rowley-Conwy (1988); Shaw (1979); Shaw (1995); Wilson (1984): 4–14; Midant-Reynes (2000): 37; Adams (2007): 49–56; Graf (2007): 443, and Butcher (1995–1996) for two-humped Bactrian camels in Roman Arabia. Redford and Redford (1989): 26–27 (figs. 41–42) for a Bactrian camel graffito in Egypt's Eastern Desert.

48. Partridge (1996): 138–140; Schmidt-Nielsen (1964): 85–92; Cuvigny (2005a): 349.

49. Kuper (2001); Kuper (2003).

50. Sidebotham et al. (1991): 598–599 (table 1), 600.

51. Harrell and Brown (1992a); Harrell and Brown (1992b).

52. Harrell and Brown (1992a); Harrell and Brown (1992b).

53. Breasted (2001c): 78–87; Brand (2000): 279–282 (nos. 3.127–3.128).

54. Bonneau (1993): 61–62; Seidbotham and Zitterkopf (1995): 45, 49 (fig. 16); for use of the terms *hydreuma/hydreumata* in ancient sources, see: Strabo, *Geography* 16.4.14; *Periplus* 25–26; Pliny, *NH* 6.26.102–103 (Berenike–Nile road); *O. Bodl.* 111.245 (first century C.E.); Ptolemy, *Geography* 1.10.2; *OGIS* 701.12 (Egypt, second century C.E.); Bagnall et al. (2001); De Romanis (2003): 119–121.

55. Breasted (2001c): 78–87.

56. Tresson (1922); Ballet et al. (2000): 152, 153 (fig. 113); Breasted (2001c): 117–123.

57. Gates (2005).

58. Adams (2001a): 141–142.

59. Bagnall (1985).

60. Bulliet (1975); Midant-Reynes and Braunstein-Silvestre (1977); Rowley-Conwy (1988); Shaw (1979); Shaw (1995); Wilson (1984): 4–14; Midant-Reynes (2000): 37; Adams (2007): 49–56.

61. Partridge (1996): 138–140.

62. Adams(2001b): 173–174, 176; Goldsworthy (1996): 293–294; Maxfield (2001a); Peacock (1997d).

63. Sidebotham and Zitterkopf (1995): 45–48; Sidebotham and Zitterkopf (1996): 357–371; Sidebotham (1997a): 385–387.

64. Sidebotham (1997a): 388–390; Sidebotham (1999c): 364–368.

65. Thissen (1979): most Demotic graffiti in Wadi Hammamat are undated, but (p. 90) he believes they are Ptolemaic; Fournet (2003): 429–430 for Roman-era Demotic; Peden (2001): 285; Brun: (2003b): 188–191, 205 (fig. 178); Winkler (1938): 9 (site 34), 10; Fournet (1995) for Ptolemaic graffiti in Greek (at Abu Kwei, not Wadi Hammamat); Wilfong (2000): 26, 81 (fig. 52) for Ptolemy III hieroglyphs in temple at Fawakhir; Bernand (1972a) for Roman-era graffiti;

66. Bülow-Jacobsen (2003a): 56; Reddé and Brun (2003): 133; Brun (2003b): 191, 199.

67. Personal communication from D. P. S. Peacock and R. S. Tomber.

68. Weigall (1913): 61, plate X nos. 21–24; Whitcomb (1996): 760, note 748; Le Quesne (2004): 145 and note 3, 148 (fig. 62); Le Quesne (2007): 166–167.

69. Bagnall et al. (1996).

70. Bernand (1972b): 46–54 (no. 10) = Yoyotte and Charvet (1997): 254 (Ba, no. 210).

71. Bagnall et al. (1996): 320; Bernand (1972b); Sidebotham (1997a): 389–390; Sidebotham (1999c): 364–368.

72. Bernand (1972b): 44–46 (no. 9 bis) = Yoyotte and Charvet (1997): 253 (Ac, no. 259).

73. Bernand (1977): 253–261 (no. 86) = Yoyotte and Charvet (1997): 254 (Ca, no. 286) = *OGIS* 132.

74. Gates (2005).

4. PTOLEMAIC DIPLOMATIC-MILITARY-COMMERCIAL ACTIVITIES

1. Fraser (1972a): 175; Ogden (2000): 161–168; Aston et al. (2000): 15 (table 2.2), 50–52; Lucas and Harris (1989): 388–389. Meredith (1957b) and Bernand (1977): 136–140 (nos. 59–62) for Ptolemaic inscriptions at Abu Diyeiba; Harrell and Sidebotham (2004); Harrell et al. (2006); Mueller (2006b): 47–49, 151–157.

2. Fraser (1972a): 180; Fraser (1972b): 388, notes 380–385.

3. Orrieux (1983); Orrieux (1985); Pestman (1980); Pestman (1981a); Retsö (2003): 300–301.

4. Edgar (1931): 7 [*P. Cairo Zen.* 4.59536 dated to 261 B.C.E. (year 25), written before Zeno went to Palestine and refers to "Minaean frankincense"]; cf. *PSI* 6 628 and Edgar (1925): 16–17 [*P. Cairo Zen.* 1.59009]; Hoyland (2001): 41; Orrieux (1983): 42; Pestman (1981a): 153, 172, 200.

5. Westermann (1924): 250–251.

6. Orrieux (1983): 63 (*P. Cairo Zen.* 59040), 89–90 (*PSI* 332).

7. Fraser (1972a): 175; Fraser (1972b): 295 note 335; Fantasia (1997).

8. Athenaeus, *Deipnosophistae* 5.201; Rice (1983).

9. Beeston (1984); Sayed (1984); Seipel (1998): 293, 295 note 164; Groom (2005): 108.

10. Beeston (2005): 55.

11. Berghaus (1991): 108; Karttunen (1995): 90.

12. Fraser (1972a): 141 and 175; Fraser (1972b): 248 note 65 and 295 note 335.

13. Personal communication from S. M. Burstein.

14. Fraser (1972a): 175; (Fraser 1972b): 295 note 334.

15. Préaux (1978): 377–378; Préaux (1979): 364 and note 4; Wilcken (1963): 92–94; Wilhelm (1937): 148–150.

16. Kitchen (1993): 603–605; Phillips (1997b): 423–425; Fattovich (1999): 637; Nibbi (1981): 99–150; Shaw (2000): 322, 324; Meeks (2003); Harvey (2003); Sayed (2003); Kitchen (2004); Kitchen (2005): 11–12, 13.

17. Fraser (1972a): 150.

18. Bingen (1978): 8ff.

19. Graf and Sidebotham (2003); Hoyland (2001): 21–26; Sidebotham (1986): 6.

20. Desanges (1978): 264.

21. Tarn (1929): 13, 15–16, 21, 22; *OGIS* 132 (130 B.C.E.); Diodorus Siculus 3.43.4–5 and Strabo, *Geography* 16.4.18 on piracy; Fraser (1972a): 177.

22. Hölbl (2001): 204.

23. *OGIS* 132.

24. Pliny the Elder, *NH* 6.26.101; Sidebotham (1986): 6 and note 30; Sidebotham (1991b): 23, 37 note 74.

25. *P. Cairo Zen.* 59001, 59009 and *PSI* 628; Sidebotham (1986): 6 and note 31.

26. Sidebotham (1986): 6.

27. See Chapter 2, note 57.

28. Fraser (1972a): 182–183; Shitomi (1976); Casson (1989): 11–12, 283–291; Desanges (1996); De Romanis (1997a); Mazzarino (1997); Tchernia (1995); Tchernia (1997a).

29. Casson (1989): 283–291; Casson (1991): 8–11; Bianchetti (2002): 280–281.

30. Bernand (1969): 306–311, no. 352; 311–314, no. 353; 319–321, no.356; Mooren (1972): 127, 132; Otto and Bengtson (1938): 1–22; Fraser (1972a): 182; Thomas (1975): 121–122. *SB* 2264 and 8036 for this official.

31. Thapar (1992): 3; Allchin (1995a); Allchin (1995b).

32. Sircar (1957): 51–55, especially 54; Benveniste (1964); Das (2006): 98–153 (and 130–133 for Mauryan-Ptolemaic trade): does not take into account recent excavations; Thapar (1997a): 303–305: Mauryan chronology is subject to debate.

33. Cunningham (1961): 84–88, 125–126. Gokhale (1966): 34, 52, 79; Fraser (1972a): 180–181; Raschke (1974a); McEvilley (2002): 368–369; Rostovtzeff (1932b): 743.

34. Łajtar (1999).

35. Fraser (1972a): 141; Hultzsch (1904): 403; Rostovtzeff (1986): 1248; Raschke (1979): 69 and notes 10–11; Thiel (1967): 53–55; Krishnamurthy (2000): 1–56 for "Classical Greek," Seleucid and other western "Hellenistic" coins found in India; Karttunen (1995): 90.

36. Humphrey and Hugh-Jones (1992).

37. Van Beek (1958): 141, note 144.

38. Crone (1987): 3–50; Kitchen (2001); Potts (1988): 127–162; Beeston (2005): 53, 54 (fig. 2), 56, 59; Groom (1981): 165–213; Salles (1988); Saud et al. (1996); De Maigret (1997); MacDonald (1997); Jasmin (2005); De Maigret (2004).

39. The date of the earliest domestication of the camel in Arabia is debated: Bulliet (1975); Rice (1983): 92–93 and note 167; Ripinsky (1975); Ripinsky (1983); Zeuner (1963): 341–343; Retsö (1991); Saud et al. (1996).

40. Maraqten (1996): 215–216; Singer (2007): 14.

41. Pliny the Elder, *NH* 12.32.64. *NH* 12.32.65 refers to exorbitant costs of overland caravan transport.

42. Crone (1987).

43. Speidel (1992a): 88 (table 1), 93 (table 3); Herz (2007): 308–313.

44. Winkler (1938): 4 (site 6), 5 (site 8a), 5 (site 12), 6 (site 15), 6 (site 16), 6 (site 17), 6 (site 18), 6 (site 18a), 7 (site 24H), 8 (site 25a), 8 (site 26), 8 (site 27), 9 (site 38), plate XIV (1), plate XX (1) = (in detail) plate XXI (2), plate XXVII (2–3); Redford and Redford (1989): 5, 13–14 (fig. 12), 14–15 (figs. 13–14), 28–29 (figs. 44–45); Rohl (2000): 17 (no. 1), 27 (no. 3), possibly 30 (no. 7, fig. 6), possibly 49 (no. 3), 51 (no. 5), 58 (no. 9, fig. 4), 58 (no. 2), 62–63 (no. 11, fig. 9), 74 (no. 5, fig. 4), 105 (no. 19), possibly 107 (no. 3, fig. 3), 111 (no. 2), 127 (no. 3, fig. 3 on p. 126), 129 (no. 6, fig. 4), 129 (no. 10), 143 (no. 8, fig. 4 on p. 142), 143 (no. 10, fig. 6), 148 (no. 11, fig. 7); Fuchs (1989): 130.

45. Morkot (1998): 148–150; Scullard (1974): 260–261; Lobban and de Liedekerke (2003).

46. Burstein (1996).

47. Burstein (1996): 803.

48. Reinach (1892); Wellmann (1905); Scullard (1974): 64–65; For Indian views see *Kauṭilīya Arthaśāstra* 2.31.1–2.32.22 (on care and training of elephants), 10.4.14 and 10.5.54 (use of elephants in battle) [= Kangle (1986a): 174–179, 444, 449].

49. Toynbee (1973): 33; for Aristotle's description of (Indian) elephants and the (possible) sources of his information, see Bigwood (1993).

50. Toynbee (1973): 32 Darius did not deploy elephants at Gaugamela; Scullard (1974): 64–67 citing Arrian, Quintus Curtius Rufus, Diodorus Siculus.
51. Scullard (1974): 66.
52. Casson (1993b): 247; Scullard (1974): 67–71; Arrian, *Anabasis of Alexander* 5.9.1, 5.10.2, 5.11.4, 5.17.3–5.
53. Scullard (1974): 73–76.
54. Pliny the Elder, *NH* 8.9.27; Scullard (1974): 104.
55. Scullard (1974): 104–105.
56. Toynbee (1973): 348 note 13.
57. Krebs (1965): 97.
58. Pliny the Elder (*NH* 8.9.27) also makes this claim in general. Diodorus Siculus (17.88.3) and Quintus Curtius Rufus (8.14.30) say that Porus's elephants trampled both friend and foe.
59. Scullard (1974): 140.
60. Carthage, Pyrrhus of Epirus, and Juba of Mauretania.
61. Vieillefond (1970): 60.
62. Vieillefond (1970): 166–170 (= *Cestorum Fragmenta* 1.18).
63. Scullard (1974): plates XIII–XVI; Holt (2003).
64. Scullard (1974): plates VIIa–b, VIIIa–b, IXa–b and Xa–b; Venit (2002): 175–179 (especially 178, fig. 155) for tomb paintings of African fauna, including an elephant from tombs at Marisa (Idumaea) dating from the third to the first century B.C.E..
65. Markoe (2003): 13; Joukowsky (2003): 218–219 and figs. 236–237.
66. Joukowsky (2003): 220–222.
67. Scullard (1974): 79–81; Casson (1993): 247.
68. Scullard (1974): 95; Diodorus Siculus 19.82.3–4 and 19.84.4.
69. Rice (1983): 91, cf. 91 note 161.
70. Scullard (1974): 103.
71. Adams (2008).
72. Parker (2002a): 52.
73. Scullard (1974): 126–133; Hofmann (1975); Huntingford (1980): 166–172; Hölbl (2001): 55–58; Burstein (2008a).
74. Sidebotham saw the *dipinto*, unpublished; Sidebotham and Zitterkopf (1996): 372, 376 (fig. 21–20).
75. Sidebotham et al. (2004): 152–153.
76. Bernand (1972b): 44–46 (no. 9bis) and pl. 54.41–42; Sidebotham and Zitterkopf (1995): 49 (fig. 17); Keenan et al. (2000a): atlas sheet 80 and Keenan et al. (2000b): 1173 for location of al-Kanaïs.
77. Personal communication from S. M. Burstein.
78. Personal communication from Gábor Lassányi; Luft (2006) believes that at least one of the elephant pictographs here is early Neolithic in date.
79. Herbert et al. (2003) for Koptos.
80. Bagnall (1976b): 35 and note 93; Sidebotham (1997a): 387–388.
81. Winkler (1938): 4 (site 6), 5 (site 8a), 5 (site 12), 6 (site 15), 6 (site 16), 6 (site 17), 6 (site 18), 6 (site 18a), 7 (site 24H), 8 (site 25a), 8 (site 26), 8 (site 27), 9 (site 38), plate XIV (1), plate XX (1) = (in detail) plate XXI (2), plate XXVII (2–3); Červíček (1974): 171–172, Abb.

29–30, Abb. 70, Abb. 109, Abb. 110(?), Abb. 132(?), Abb. 134(?), Abb. 229, Abb. 252(?), Abb. 253, Abb. 282(?), Abb. 466(?), Abb. 505; Redford and Redford (1989): 5, 13–14 (fig. 12), 14–15 (figs. 13–14), 28–29 (figs. 44–45); Rohl (2000): 17 (no.1), 27 (no.3), possibly 30 (no.7, fig. 6), possibly 49 (no.3), 51 (no.5), 58 (no.9, fig. 4), 58 (no.2), 62–63 (no.11, fig. 9), 74 (no.5, fig. 4), 105 (no.19), possibly 107 (no.3, fig. 3), 111 (no.2), 127 (no.3, fig. 3 on p. 126), 129 (no.6, fig. 4), 129 (no.10), 143 (no.8, fig. 4 on p. 142), 143 (no.10, fig. 6), 148 (no.11, fig. 7).

82. Naville (1885): 18, line 24; Sethe (1904): 101.13–102.8; Fraser (1972a): 177; Fraser (1972b): 298–299 notes 346–347.

83. Athenaeus (*Deipnosophistai* 5.200 and 5.202) for elephants; 5.197–203 (for the procession in general) drawing on Kallixeinos of Rhodes; Rice (1983): 4–5.

84. Rice (1983): 90–91.

85. Wolska-Conus (1968): 370–373; Huntingford (1980): 166–167; Desanges (1978): 345–346; cf. Fauvelle-Aymar (2009).

86. *OGIS* 54 in Bagnall and Derow (2004): 51–53 (no. 26); Bagnall and Derow (1981): 49–50 (no. 26); Burstein (1985): 125–126 (no. 99).

87. Klemm et al. (2002): 219; Klemm et al. (2001): 654–655 do not believe the Ptolemies controlled the Wadi Allaqi; Castiglioni and Vercoutter (2001): 55; Burstein (2008a).

88. Klemm and Klemm (1994): 206–211; Klemm et al. (2001): 654–656; Klemm et al. (2002): 218–219 and 227 (fig. 6).

89. Morkot (1998): 152; Diodorus Siculus, *Bibliotheke* 3.26.1–2.27.4; Pliny the Elder, *NH* 6.35.191 and 8.8.26.

90. Hölbl (2001): 25, 153–154, 306–307 the Ptolemaic army comprised Greek, Macedonian, and Egyptian troops.

91. Scullard (1974): 120–145 for Ptolemies and Seleucids; 146–147 for Carthage; Casson (1993b); Desanges et al. (1993); Mueller (2006b): 154–155; Bengston (1955) for Ptolemaic elephant hunting in Jewish literature, especially the Maccabees.

92. Rostovtzeff (1908): 302.

93. Personal communication from M. Horton.

94. Fraser (1972b): 308–309 notes 370–374; Desanges (1978): 297–298 for organization of elephant hunts.

95. Yoyotte and Charvet (1997): 253 = Bernand (1977): 193–198 (no. 77) and 244–245 (no. 84).

96. Fraser (1972a): 179.

97. Fraser (1972a): 178–179; Scullard (1974): 126–128 and note 70; Mueller (2006b): 154–155 (table 4.1) for list and ancient references.

98. Treidler (1959); Fraser (1972a): 178; Fraser (1972b): 304 note 359; Hinkel (1992): 313–314; Mueller (2006b): 153–154.

99. Thapar (1997a): 16–18; Velissaropoulos (1991): 266–271 for Megasthenes; Tola and Dragonetti (1991): 125–128 for other diplomatic exchanges between Seleucids and Mauryans.

100. Thapar (1997a): 57–70, 87–90.

101. Scullard (1974): 97–98; Trautmann (1982) for Mauryan military use of elephants.

102. Scullard (1974): 97; Casson (1993): 248 and note 3; Tola and Dragonetti (1991): 125–128 for Seleucids and Mauryans, 128–130 for Ptolemies and Mauryans.

103. Burstein (1989): 174.
104. Scullard (1974): 25.
105. Burstein (1989): 174–175.
106. Rice (1983): 92 and note 165.
107. Burstein (1989): 8, note 1.
108. Casson (1993): 253 note 25.
109. Pliny the Elder, *NH* 8.9.27, for sizes of African and Indian pachyderms.
110. Scullard (1974): 145.
111. Krebs (1965): 101 estimates that the Ptolemies had 400 elephants in 280–250 B.C.E..
112. Scullard (1974): 136 disagrees.
113. Arrian 5.15.4 records the greatest number of any surviving ancient account at just over 200; Diodorus Siculus (17.87.2) reports 130; Quintus Curtius Rufus (8.13.6) says 85; Polyaenus (*Stratagems of War* 4.3.22) does not specify the number of elephants.
114. Toynbee (1973): 35 and 347 note 3; Scullard (1974): 33.
115. Wilcken (1963): 532–533 (no. 451) = *P. Eleph.* 28; Preaux (1979): 36; Scullard (1974): 137.
116. *P. Eleph.* 28: Wilcken (1963): 532–533 (no. 451) = Bagnall and Derow (2004): 201–202 (no. 223) = Bagnall and Derow (1981): 167 (no. 101).
117. Desanges (1970): 31–32, 38.
118. Herodotus (6.48 and 6.95), Thucydides (2.56.1 and 4.42.1), Aristophanes (*Knights* line 599), Livy (44.28.7); Pliny the Elder (*NH* 7.56.209); Aulus Gellius (*Attic Nights* 10.25.5); Arrian (*Anabasis* 2.19.1); fourth-century B.C. inscription [in Kirchner (1927): 231–234, inscription no. 1623, line 14]; Casson (1986b): 93–94; Morrison, Coates and Rankov (2000): 227–228 and 230; Guasti (2007): 143.
119. Naville (1885): 18 line 24.
120. Burstein (1989): 141 and note 3.
121. Casson (1993): 253–254.
122. Wilcken (1963): 534–535 (no. 452); Mueller (2006b): 152–153 for English translation.
123. Krebs (1965): 96–101.
124. Casson (1993): 253.
125. Personal communication from L. Casson.
126. Sidebotham and Wendrich (2001–2002): 41 for elephant tooth; Van Neer and Ervynck (1999a): 332, 348 for ivory.
127. Wilson (1983): 15, 34–39.
128. Scullard (1974): 252, 254 and plate XIXb; Carandini, Ricci and de Vos (1982): 216 (121) for bull, 219 (fig. 123) and plate XXIX for elephant; Guasti (2007): 141–142.
129. Carandini et al. (1982): 209 (fig. 115), 211 (fig. 116) and plate XXVIII.
130. Carandini et al. (1982): 213 (fig. 118), 214 (fig. 119) and plate XXIX.
131. J. E. M. F. Bos and H. Planjer: unpublished ms. "An Elephant Carrier in Cairo?"
132. Blake (1936): 183–184 and plate 46.3; Guasti (2007): 142 (and note 27) and fig. 4.
133. Wilcken (1963): 533–535 (no. 452)[cf. Mueller (2006b): 151–154]; Sidebotham and Wendrich (2001–2002): 25–27.
134. Head (1987a); Blue (2006a).
135. Naville (1885): 18 line 24; Roeder (1959): 125–126.

136. Paice (1992): 229 cites Strabo, *Geography* 7.319 (7.6.1–2), which has nothing to do with Egypt or the canal.

137. Wilcken (1963): 534–535 (no. 452).

138. Bülow-Jacobsen (2003a): 56; Reddé and Brun (2003): 133; Brun (2003b): 191.

139. Wilcken (1963): 533–535 (no. 452) = *Papyri Petrie* II, 40; Scullard (1974): 132 and note 72.

140. Van't Dack and Hauben (1978).

141. Benedict (1936): 159–176; Krebs (1965): 97.

142. Casson (1989): 284; Whitewright (2007a): 78–81.

143. Scullard (1974): 62–63; Rice (1983): 91, note 160; Casson (1993): 248.

144. Scullard (1974): 62–63; Pliny the Elder, *NH* 8.9.27; Appian, *Syrian Wars* 6.31.

145. Scullard (1974): 62.

146. Rostovtzeff (1908): 304; Hofmann (1975): 104–111; Hölbl (2001): 56; Van't Dack and Hauben (1978): 64 and note 38; for Ptolemy IV see Yoyotte and Charvet (1997): 253 (Aa, no. 77) = Bernand (1977): 193–198 (no. 77); Burstein (1989): 10–11.

147. Sidebotham (1986): 4.

148. Scullard (1974): 178–235; 250–254 and plates XVII–XX and XXIV.

149. Scullard (1974): 179, 184–185 (Livy 31.36.4 on Cynoscephalae), (Livy 44.41.5 on Pydna). Polybius 18.23.7 and 18.25.7 on Cynoscephalae.

150. Scullard (1974): 190–191. Appian, *Hispania/Wars in Spain* (9.46).

151. Guasti (2007): 142 for later use of Puteoli as disembarkation point for elephants, though unclear whether these animals were to be displayed in Puteoli, its environs, or Rome.

152. Scullard (1974): 197; Dio Cassius 43.3.4; Appian, *Civil Wars* 2.96.

153. Toynbee (1973): 37; Meiggs (1982): 330; Juvenal, *Satires* 12.102–104 and Aelian, *On the Characteristics of Animals* 2.11; *ILS* 1578 [= Dessau (1892): 338] tombstone of Tiberius Claudius Speclatorus, procurator of elephants at Laurentum.

154. Jennison (1937): 65; Pliny the Elder, *NH* 8.1.1–8.13.35; Aelian, *On the Characteristics of Animals* 2.11; two reliefs of African elephants dated ca. 79–96 C.E. in the Getty Museum (accession numbers 71.AA.463.1 and 71.AA.463.2).

155. Scullard (1974): 205–206 and notes 149–150.

156. Wolska-Conus (1973): 350–351; *Christian Topography* 11.22–23 [Wolska-Conus (1973): 352–355].

5. PTOLEMAIC AND EARLY ROMAN BERENIKE AND ENVIRONS

1. Harrell (1996): 108–109.

2. Hölbl (2001): 257–271.

3. Hölbl (2005): 18–20, 26 (Abb. 34–35), 27 (Abb. 36) for overview; Sidebotham and Zych (2010): 15 and figs. 21 and 22.

4. Mueller (2006b): 109–114.

5. Cohen (2006): 320–325.

6. Sidebotham (2000b): 74–77; Sidebotham (2008): 313–314 and fig. 14.

7. Sidebotham (2000): 74–75; Harrell (2007): 167–168; Sidebotham (2008a): 313–314 and fig. 14.

8. Sidebotham (1996a): 25, 27, 29, 30–31; Sidebotham (2008a) 313–314 and fig. 15.

9. Herbich (2007).

10. Peacock et al. (2007): 59; personal communication from J. A. Harrell.

11. Bradford (2000): 44; Bradford (2001); Whittaker (2002): 38; Blue (2002): 145 and 148 (fig. 8); Blue (2006a): 47; Blue and Peacock (2006): 70–74; Blue (2006b): 83; Thomas (2006b): 90, 94; Peacock and Blue (2006a): 175.

12. Peña (2007): 170–174, 254 for examples of amphora reuse in architectural contexts.

13. Tuck (1997).

14. Sidebotham (1986): 52.

15. Tait (1930): 110–125 (nos. 220–304). There are four more in the Bodleian and *O. Brüss* 7; Rostovtzeff (1931); Fuks (1951); Meredith (1952): 104; Raschke (1978): 644 (and 847, note 801); Ruffing (1993); Cuvigny (2003a): 274–275 for bibliography.

16. First suggested by Sidebotham (1986): 52–53.

17. Sidebotham (2007a): 202 (table 8–6); Sidebotham (in preparation b).

18. Sidebotham (1986): 27–29, 52–53; Turner (1989): 10, 123 (table 2), 124 (table 3).

19. Bernand (1972a), nos. 41–43 and 45–47; nos. 38, 44, 48–49 possibly Tiberian; from Paneion at al-Boueib: nos. 143–145 and possibly 142 and 146; Sidebotham (1986): 55.

20. From Mons Porphyrites (July 23, 18 C.E.): Van Rengen (1995): 240–245; Van Rengen (2001): 60–62; from Wadi Umm Wikala/Semna (May 26, 11 C.E.): Bernand (1977): 118–128 (no. 51); Sidebotham et al. (2001): 138–141; From Wadi Hammamat (October 2, 18 C.E.): Bernand (1972a): 80–92 (no. 41) with bibliography.

21. Meredith (1957a): 60, 63, 65.

22. Kennedy (1985); Bagnall et al. (2000): 7; personal communication from R. S. Bagnall; Bagnall et al. (2001) for inscriptions on the road; Bernand (1972a): 38–39 (no. 2) for Laqeita; recent inscription of Domitian from Umm Balad: personal communication from H. Cuvigny.

23. Alston (1995): 71–79, 83–86, 99–100; Leadbetter (2000); Leadbetter (2002): 85, 86; Barnes (1976): 180–182; Cuvigny (2003b): 346–352

24. Cuvigny (2003b): 346 and note 135.

25. Alston (1995): 83–84; Cuvigny (2003b): 346–352. MacMullen (1966): 255–268 and Shaw (1984): 3–52 in general.

26. Robin (1997): 53

27. Diodorus Siculus 3.43.4–5; Strabo, *Geography* 6.4.18; *OGIS* 132 (130 B.C.E.); Sidebotham (1986): 6.

28. Thapar (1992); De Romanis (1997c): 88–92

29. Conrad (1981): 68–69; Duncan Jones (1996): 108–136; Scheidal (2002); Bagnall (2002): 114–120; Nutton (2004): 24.

30. Sidebotham (1996a): 82–93; Sidebotham (1998b): 20–45; Sidebotham (2000b): 44–73.

31. Hense (1999): 222.

32. Price (1984).

33. Ballet et al. (2000); Herbert et al. (2003).

34. Raschke (1978): 644 and 850–851 (notes 821–822); Bernand (1984a): 238–241 (no. 85); Speidel (1984).

35. Bernand (1984a): 238–241 (no. 85); Speidel (1984); Dijkstra and Verhoogt (1999): 215.

6. INHABITANTS OF BERENIKE IN ROMAN TIMES

1. Sidebotham and Wendrich (1998b): 88 for the lower estimate, 88–89 for discussion.
2. Sidebotham and Zych (2010): 11 and figs. 6–8.
3. Tait (1930): 110–125 (nos. 220–304) plus four in the Bodleian and *O. Brüss* 7; Rostovtzeff (1931) for a review of Tait; Fuks (1951); Meredith (1952): 104; Raschke (1978): 644 and 847 (note 801); Ruffing (1993); cf. Cuvigny (2003a): 274–275 for bibliography.
4. Cuvigny (2003a); Bülow-Jacobsen (2003b); Cuvigny (2005b).
5. Bagnall et al. (2005): 59–64 (nos. 145–152); Bagnall et al. (2000).
6. Bagnall et al. (2005): 52.
7. Bagnall et al. (2000): 50–55 (nos. 53, 55–67), 61 (no. 86); Bagnall et al. (2005): 11, 52.
8. Bagnall et al. (2005): 91–92 (no. 212).
9. Clarysse and Thompson (2006): 332–341, especially 333, 336 (table 8.8) and 337 (fig. 8.1).
10. Bagnall et al. (2000): 24–32; Bagnall et al. (2005): 9–14.
11. *O. Petrie* nos. 252 and 271 = Tait (1930): 116, 120; Raschke (1978): 644 and 848 (notes 805–806), 646 and 859 (notes 870–871).
12. Smallwood (1967): 54 (no. 156), 113–118 (no. 391) and Smallwood (1976): 258, 290, 317, 365, 391 note no. 8 on Tiberius Julius Alexander; Raschke (1978): 644 and 848–849 (note 807), 646 and 859 (note 872); Barzanò (1988); Alston (2002): 98–99, 226, 227, 235.
13. Orrieux (1983); Orrieux (1985); Pestman (1980a); Pestman (1980b); Pestman (1981a); Pestman (1981b)
14. Bowman (1986): 56–88.
15. Bagnall et al. (2005): 92 (line 2)
16. Bagnall et al. (2005): 91–92 (no. 212); Fuks (1951).
17. Tait (1930): 124 (*O. Petrie* 292); Bagnall et al. (2000): 68–69 (no. 106).
18. Bagnall et al. (2005): 86 (no. 202).
19. Communication from R. S. Bagnall and R. Ast.
20. Bagnall et al. (2005): 95–96 (no. 222).
21. Bagnall et al. (2005): 47–48 (no. 132).
22. Bagnall et al. (2005): 33–37 (no. 125).
23. Drexhage (1991): 280–286 for donkey costs elsewhere in Egypt; Oates (1988); Litinas (1999).
24. Winkler (1938): 7 (site 24B)(M318), pl. VIII.2.
25. Meredith (1954): 283–284; Bernand (1977): 160–165 (with bibliography); De Romanis (1996a): 203–217, 243–259 with bibliography; De Romanis (1996b); Sidebotham and Zitterkopf (1996): 358–359 (pls. 21–1, 21–2).
26. Bernand (1977): 161–162 (no. 64); De Romanis (1996a): 211.
27. Winkler (1938): 7 (Site 24B), 10, pl. VIII, no. 2; Bernand (1977): 162–164 (no. 65); Raschke (1978): 644 and 849–850 (notes 808–819); Sidebotham (1986): 32–33; De Romanis (1996a): 211–212 for additional bibliography; Bianchetti (2002): 290.
28. Bernand (1977): 162–164 (no. 65); Raschke (1978): 644; Sidebotham (1986): 32–33; De Romanis (1996a): 211–212 for additional bibliography.
29. D'Arms (1974): 107–109; D'Arms (1981): 166; Rathbone (1983): 88, 96 (notes 23 and 27).
30. Bernand (1977): 164–165 (no. 66); De Romanis (1996a): 213.

31. Bernand (1977): 165 (no. 67) believes Primus was a freedman of Sextus Mevus Celer; De Romanis (1996a): 214.

32. De Romanis (1996a): 210–217.

33. Littmann and Meredith (1954b) = Bernand et al. (1991): 74.

34. Meyer (1995a): 200; Meyer (1995b): 47–49; At Bir Umm Fawakhir: Cuvigny (2003a): 284; Fournet (2003): 428 for Thamudic graffiti at Krokodilô and Semitic names written in Greek, 429 for South Arabic and Aramaic graffiti.

35. Tomber (2008): 76.

36. Thomas (2001b).

37. Bagnall et al., (2005): 98–102 (nos. 228–250).

38. Sundelin (1996) : 300–302 (entry c., fig. 16-1, pl. 16–2); Dieleman (1998): 272 (no. 19), 273 (figs. 13–5 and 13–6); Cashman et al. (1999): 287, 293 (no. 8); Bos and Helms (2000): 292–293 (no. 18 and pl. 12–16); Bos (2007): 263 (no. 8 and pl. 14–10), possibly 265 (no. 13 and pl. 14–14); Thomas (2001b): 67–70, 101–106.

39. Thomas (2001b): Possibly 116 bottom right.

40. Thomas (2001b): 73.

41. Sidebotham (1986): 91; Thomas (2001b): 72–73.

42. Jones (1997).

43. Dijkstra and Verhoogt (1999).

44. Verhoogt (1998): 193–196.

45. Bagnall et al. (2001); Bagnall et al. (2005): 96–97.

46. Bagnall et al. (2005): 103–104 (nos. 251–253).

47. Personal observations of R. S. Tomber and the author; Tomber (2008): 75, fig. 13 left; Tomber, Graf and Healey (forthcoming); Sidebotham and Zych (2010): 12 and figs. 9 and 10.

48. Verhoogt (1998): 193–196, 198; Dijkstra and Verhoogt (1999); Possibly Bagnall et al. (2005): 105 (no. 254).

49. Bernand, Drewes and Schneider (1991): 357–358 (no. 268) for Axumite text from Berenike-Nile roads.

50. Gragg (1996).

51. Tomber (2008): 43 for this ubiquitous type.

52. Mahadevan (1996); Mahadevan (2003): 43, 49, 56 (fig. 1.21 B and C), 61 (nos. 8–9), 93, 146–147, 163, 164, 235.

53. Thomas and Masser (2006): 136, 137, 138, 140 for Myos Hormos.

54. Begley and Tomber (1999); Tomber and Begley (2000).

55. Wendrich (2007): 236.

56. Bagnall et al. (2005): 52.

57. Roth (1999): 26–30; Leguilloux (2003): 552–558.

58. Van Neer and Ervynck (1999a): 329, 339.

59. Van Neer and Ervynck (1999a): 327, 328, 339.

60. Referred to as "piglets," H. Cuvigny, personal communication; Cuvigny (2003f): 374–389; Maxfield (2005): 202, 205. For the Koptos Tariff: Hogarth (1896): 27–33; for bibliography until the late 1970s: Raschke (1978): 649 and 893 (note 961); Bernand (1984a): 199–208 (no. 67) for bibliography, translation, and commentary (= *OGIS* 674 = *IGRR*

I.1183); Sidebotham (1986): 35, 53, 67, 80–81; Young (2001): 48–50; Burkhalter-Arce (2002); Cuvigny (2003a): 273–274.

61. Barnard (1998): 389, 390 (table 18–1), 395 and table 18–9 and pl. 18–10.
62. Sidebotham and Wendrich (2001–2002): 35 and fig. 23.
63. Barnard (1998): 390 (table 18–1), 396 and pl. 18–11.
64. Barnard (1998): 389, 390 (tables 18–1 and 18–2), 391 (table 18–3, pl. 18–4), 392 and fig. 18–5, 393 (pl. 18–6); Sidebotham (1998b): 107, 108 (pl. 3–84); Sidebotham and Wendrich (2001–2002): 35, 36 (fig. 25).
65. Francis (2000); Francis (2004); Francis (2007).
66. Wild and Wild (1998): 224, 225, 226, 236; Wild and Wild (2000): 256–262.
67. Hayes (1995); Nicholson (1998); Nicholson (1999); Nicholson (2000a); Nicholson (2000b); Nicholson and Price (2007).
68. Bagnall et al. (2005): 41–43 (no. 129).
69. Bagnall et al. (2005): 21–22 (nos. 118–119).
70. Holtheide (1980); Hobson (1983); Sidebotham (1986): 87.
71. *O. Petrie* nos. 244 and 257 in Tait (1930): 114 and 117.
72. Cockle (1992); Cockle (1997); Cribiore (1996).
73. Van Beek (1989).
74. Young (2001): 49–50.
75. Van Neer and Ervynck (1998): 367 for Berenike; Hamilton-Dyer (2001): 260, 261 (table 9.6), 262, 265 (table 9.10), 266, 304 (fig. 9.12) for consumption of donkeys, horses, camels at Mons Claudianus.
76. Van Neer and Lentacker (1996): 340 (table 20–2), 343 (table 20–4), 345 (table 20–5), 346; Van Neer and Ervynck (1998): 364 (table 17–8), 383; Van Neer and Ervynck (1999a): 346 (table 18–9), 348.
77. Sidebotham (1998b): 75; Van Neer and Ervynck (1998): 363; Sidebotham (1999b): 30, 41; Sidebotham and Wendrich (1998b): 452; cf. Curtis (1991).
78. Van Neer and Ervynck (1999a): 329, 339.
79. Bagnall et al. (2005): 43–45 (no. 130).
80. Cappers (2006): 90.
81. Sidebotham and Wendrich (2001–2002): 30 and fig. 10; Cappers (2006): 114–119; Tomber (2008): 76.
82. Cappers (2006): 96 (lentils), 95 = 96 (chick peas), 98 (white lupin), 131 (bitter vetch), 131–132 (fava beans).
83. Cappers (2006): 84–85 for coriander; Cappers (2006): 86–87 for cumin.
84. Cappers (1998a): 319–324; (Cappers 1998b): 76–80; Cappers (2006): 45–48, 140–143; Sidebotham (1994a): 157; Oleson (2000a) in general.
85. Cappers (1996): 332–336.
86. For gardens at Berenike: Cappers (1998a): 319–321; Cappers (2006): 140–143; for desert gardens elsewhere: Van der Veen (1998); Cuvigny (2003f): 383 (at Persou on Myos Hormos-Nile road); Bülow-Jacobsen (2003b): 419, 420–421, 423–424 (appendix): at Persou; Sidebotham (1994a): 157; Sidebotham (1994b): 267 for Abu Sha'ar.
87. Cuvigny (1997a).
88. Hughes (1994).

89. Manderscheid (2000) for synopsis.

90. Nicholson (2000a): 203–205; Sidebotham (2000b): 146; Sidebotham and Wendrich (2000b): 415–416.

91. Hölbl (2005): 18–20, 26 (Abb. 34–35), 27 (Abb. 36).

92. Meredith (1957a): 62, 70.

93. Meredith (1957a): 68.

94. Daressy, quoted by Meredith (1957a): 60–61.

95. Meredith (1957a): 61, 69.

96. Meredith (1957a): 60.

97. Aufrère (1991a): 142; Aufrère (1991b): 544, 549 note 534; Meredith (1957a): 60.

98. Aufrère (1991a): 124.

99. Pinch (1993): 156.

100. Aufrère (1991b): 594–595.

101. Witt (1971): 178–183.

102. Aufrère (1991a): 142.

103. Sidebotham (2007b): 75.

104. Sidebotham (1999b): 67, 70–71 (and table 2–38), 72 (and pl. 2–39), 73 (and pl. 2–40), 74, 78.

105. Sidebotham (1999b): 59, 60–61 (no. 10), 62, 78 (pl. 2–43), 79; Hölbl (2005): 19 paraphrasing us.

106. Bagnall et al. (2005): 27–28 (no. 121).

107. Bagnall et al. (2005): 21–22 (nos. 118–119).

108. Bagnall et al. (2005): 22.

109. Dijkstra and Verhoogt (1999).

110. Bagnall et al. (2001); Bagnall et al. (2005): 23–27 (no. 120).

111. Cuvigny (2003b): 302–305.

112. Bagnall et al. (2001); Bagnall et al. (2005): 23–27 (no. 120).

7. WATER IN THE DESERT AND THE PORTS

1. Sidebotham (2003) for earlier overview.

2. Ballet et al.(2000): 160 and fig. 117; Scala (2002).

3. Sidebotham et al. (2008).

4. Personal experiences of the author; Schmidt-Nielsen (1964): 9; Gauthier-Pilters and Dagg (1981): 170; Zitterkopf and Sidebotham (1989): 164.

5. Cuvigny (2005a).

6. Cuvigny (2005a): 348–349.

7. Bernand (1972a); Bernand (1972b); Bülow-Jacobsen et al. (1995); Fournet (1995); De Romanis (1996a): 203–217, 241–259; De Romanis (1996b); Cuvigny et al. (1999); Cuvigny et al. (2000).

8. Casson (1989): 283–291.

9. Casson (1989): 283–291.

10. Peña (1989): 130 and n. 19.

11. Personal communication from D. P. S. Peacock; Bernand (1972a); Bernand (1972b);

Bülow-Jacobsen et al. (1995); Fournet (1995); De Romanis (1996a): 203–217, 241–259; De Romanis (1996b); Cuvigny et al. (1999); Van Rengen (2007).

12. Sidebotham et al. (2004a); Foster et al. (2007).

13. Schmidt-Nielsen (1964): 81–93; Bagnall (1985): 3–5 and note 10; Rowley-Conwy (1988); Hobbs (1989): 34–37; Hamilton-Dyer (1998): 122, 124; Hamilton-Dyer (2001): 255.

14. Schmidt-Nielsen (1964): 85–92.

15. Schmidt-Nielsen (1964): 85–92; Gauthier-Pilters and Dagg (1981): 50–58.

16. Murray (1968): 70–71.

17. Murray (1968): 70.

18. Murray (1968): 70; cf. Groom (1981): 174.

19. Nicholson (1985): 161.

20. Schmidt-Nielsen (1964): 88.

21. Adams (2007): 54.

22. Gauthier-Pilters and Dagg (1981): 109–110; Groom (1981): 159–160; Maxfield (2001a): 159 suggests 173 kg.

23. Figari (1865): 457; Weigall (1913): 25, 36; Bülow-Jacobsen (2003b): 406–408; Maxfield (2001a): 160; Maxfield (1996): 11–12 (and note 4) estimates a baggage camel's speed at 4 km per hour.

24. Weigall (1913): 26.

25. White (1984): 129; Maxfield (2001a): 159 suggests 45 kg; Adams (2007): 57–58 suggests up to 150 kg.

26. Schmidt-Nielsen (1964): 81–93; Hobbs (1989): 34–37; Bagnall (1985): 4–5 and n. 10.

27. Cuvigny (2005a): 349.

28. Meigs (1966): 64; Reddé (2003b): 40; Zitterkopf and Sidebotham (1989): 164.

29. Bagnall (2005): 189; Cappers (2006): 38.

30. Ball (1912): 242–250 for a table; Babiker (2001): 61–62.

31. Ball (1912): 25–26 and pl. III, 240–241.

32. Seen by Sidebotham and Zitterkopf; Barron and Hume (1902): 17–18; Hume (1925): 110–111 and pl. XCVa, fig. 171a.

33. Personal experiences of S. E. Sidebotham and R. E. Zitterkopf.

34. Hume (1925): 110–111.

35. Murray (1926b) also notes these; Aldsworth and Barnard (1998): 428–429.

36. Head (1987b): 16.

37. Klunzinger (1878): 230–237.

38. Chesneau (1900): 419.

39. Chesneau (1900): 419.

40. Krzywinski (2007): 51 and 52 (fig. 4).

41. Klunzinger (1878): 230–237.

42. Hodge (2000): 22–27 for discussion.

43. Hume (1925): 111–112 and pl. XCV, figs. 170–171, pl. XCVI, fig. 172.

44. Hume (1925): 111.

45. Bellefonds (n.d.): 264 and pl. 13; Hume (1907): 25–26; Kurtz and Bellefonds (2000): 173–174 (fig. 15).

46. Hume (1907): 16–17, 26, 32; Sidebotham et al. (2004b).

47. Sidebotham et al. (2004b): 157–158.
48. Welsby (2003): 72–73.
49. Barker et al. (1996a) and Barker et al. (1996b) for ancient irrigation in Libya.
50. Hinkel (1991); Welsby (2003): 73–75 and 76 (fig. 7.6); Näser (2010).
51. Babiker (2001): 70–71; cf. Krzywinski (2001a): 83–95.
52. Welsby (2003): 73–75, 76 (fig. 7.6).
53. Krzywinski (2007): 51, 53, 54 (fig. 6) also notes this; Hinkel (1991): 45 (Abb. 12) for table, sketch plans, dimensions of larger *hafayir.*
54. Sidebotham (1994b): 267.
55. Hobbs (1989): 45.
56. Sidebotham and H. Barnard surveyed this in summer 1996; de la Roque (1922): 119–122 for description and sketches.
57. Sidebotham and Zitterkopf (1995): 44 (fig. 6).
58. Krzywinski (2007): 49, 50 (fig. 23), 51, 53.
59. Babiker (2001): 67.
60. Klunzinger (1878): 230–237.
61. Murray (1955).
62. Hume (1925): 116–138.
63. Sidebotham and Zitterkopf (1996): 384, 388.
64. Reddé and Golvin (1986–1987): 12–14, figs. 7–9; Zitterkopf and Sidebotham (1989): 172, fig. 3d, 177; Keenan et al. (2000): 1174.
65. Reddé (2003b): 40.
66. Maxfield (1997a): 122–134.
67. Copeland and Handley (2001).
68. For Mons Claudianus: Maxfield (1997a): 98–99; Peacock (1997a): 141–145 ("the *hydreuma*"); Maxfield (1997b): 170–173 ("wadi walls"/"water supply"); for Mons Porphyrites: Maxfield (2001c).
69. Maxfield (2001c): 47–56.
70. Sidebotham (1990); Maxfield (2001c): 49, 54–55.
71. Peacock et al. (2001a): 15 (fig. 2.4, no. 3), 17.
72. Maxfield (2001c): 42–47 for the "north well."
73. Maxfield and Peacock (2001a): 202–209.
74. Peacock and Maxfield (1997).
75. Maxfield (1997a): 85.
76. Sidebotham (2003): 97.
77. Sidebotham et al. (1991): 582–583.
78. Meredith (1952): 102, 103, fig. 4; Reddé and Golvin (1986–1987): 37 and fig. 31.
79. Murray (1925): 148; Meredith and Tregenza (1949): 115–124; Meredith (1952): 101–102 and 101, note 4, 106; Tregenza (1955): 39–49.
80. Sidebotham and Zitterkopf (1997): 228, 229, 235, fig. 9.
81. Zitterkopf and Sidebotham (1989): 172: fig. 3b, 175–176.
82. Zitterkopf and Sidebotham (1989): 173, fig. 4a, 178; Reddé (2003): 42.
83. Lepsius (1853): 278.
84. Meyer and Heidorn (1998).

85. Brun (2003a): 92; Al-Resseeni et al. (1998) for (analogous) hajj routes and stations be-
    tween Egypt and Syria on the one hand, and Mecca and Medina on the other.

86. Reddé (2003b): 42.

87. Bülow-Jacobsen (2008): 311.

88. Cf. Vegetius, *Epitoma Rei Militaris* IV.10.

89. Zitterkopf and Sidebotham (1989): 166; Sidebotham et al. (1991): 619.

90. Cuvigny (2005b): 33–46; Fournet (2003): 490–492; Brun et al. (2003): 226–227; Holm-
    berg (1933); Pflaum (1940); Casson (1974): 182–190; Chevallier (1997): 276–278;
    Mitchell (1976).

91. Cuvigny (2003b): 332–333; Bülow-Jacobsen (2003b): 408–409.

92. Cuvigny (2003b): 332–333.

93. Kennedy and Riley (1990): 194–212; Isaac (1992): 186–208.

94. Bernand (1984a): 178–184, no. 56; Kennedy (1985); De Romanis (1996a): 219–224;
    Lesquier (1918): 417–458; Guéraud (1942); Maxfield (2000): 424–434; Alston (1995):
    81–82, 97–98, 194–201; Sidebotham and Wendrich (2001–2002): 43–48; Bagnall et
    al. (2001).

95. De Romanis (2003); Cuvigny (2005b): 36–37 (note 10), 90–91 (no. 47); 96 (no. 49).

96. Valbelle and Carrez-Maratray (2000): 60.

97. Bruyère (1966): 64–75.

98. Bruyère (1966): 66–72.

99. Sidebotham (1995b): 87–93; Sidebotham and Zitterkopf (1996): 384–391; Sidebotham
    et al. (2000a); Sidebotham (2000e): 359–366.

100. Whitcomb and Johnson (1979); Whitcomb and Johnson (1982a); Whitcomb and John-
     son (1982b); Whitcomb (1996); Whitcomb (1999); Whitcomb and Johnson (1981); Whit-
     comb and Johnson (1981–1982); Peacock et al. (1999); Peacock et al. (2000); Peacock
     et al. (2001b); Peacock et al. (2002); Peacock et al. (2003); Peacock and Blue (2006c).

101. Bonneau (1993): 56–61; De Romanis (2003): 120–121; Cuvigny (2003a): 267–273 for
     reservoir with *saqqiya*.

102. Peña (2007): 134–135 and fig. 6.2 for depiction of barrel/cask in a mule cart.

103. Prickett (1979): 300–304; Whitcomb (1982).

104. Van Rengen (1999); Murphy (2000); Van Rengen et al. (2006).

105. Earl and Glazier (2002): 89, 93 (fig. 65), 94 (fig. 66); Earl and Glazier (2006b): 27 (fig.
     2.39), 31 (fig. 2.44), 32–33.

106. Peacock (2006a): 12.

107. Sidebotham and Zitterkopf (1996): 384–392; Sidebotham (2000e): 359–366.

108. Bagnall et al. (2005): 79–80 (no. 191).

109. Bülow-Jacobsen (1992a); Winterbottom (2001): 330–331, 350, fig. 10.17, no. 62; cf.
     Volken (2008).

110. Phillips (1997a); Phillips (2007): 391, 394 (fig. 17.5, bottom).

111. Cuvigny (2003a): 271–272.

112. Sidebotham et al. (2002): 190, 192, 200, 204, 206, 207, 211 (fig. 18, no. 31), 213, 215,
     216 (fig. 22, no. 55), 220 (and table 2), 221; Peña (2007): 133–138 for LRA1 amphorae
     and recycling of amphorae as water jars.

113. Sidebotham et al.(2002): 190.

114. Personal communication from R. S. Tomber.

115. Kuper (2001); Kuper (2003).

116. Sidebotham et al. (1991): 598–599 (table 1), 600.

117. Zitterkopf and Sidebotham (1989): 164.

118. Sidebotham et al.(2001): 152–153. 169–170.

119. Sidebotham et al. (2001): 169.

120. Sidbotham (1997a): 388–390; Sidebotham (1999c): 364–368.

121. Brun (2003d): 83.

122. Maxfield (1997a): 56.

123. Kennedy (1995).

124. Scaife (1935): plan VIII; Sidebotham et al. (1991): 580–582; Cuvigny (2002–2003).

125. Peacock (1997c).

126. Sidebotham et al. (1991): 578–580; Maxfield and Peacock (2001a): 215–238.

127. Sidebotham and Zitterkopf (1995): 49, fig. 16.

128. Sidebotham and Zitterkopf (1995): 48, fig. 15.

129. Sidebotham and Zitterkopf (1995): 45, fig. 7.

130. Sidebotham and Zitterkopf (1995): 46, fig. 10.

131. Sidebotham and Zitterkopf (1995): 45, 47, fig. 11.

132. Sidebotham and Zitterkopf (1995): 45, 48, fig. 15.

133. MS. G. Wilkinson XXXVIII.39 Page 58, courtesy Bodleian Library, Oxford.

134. Sidebotham (1999c): 364–368.

135. Sidebotham (1999c): 364–368.

136. Bagnall et al. (1996): 319.

137. Bagnall et al. (2001).

138. De Romanis (2003): 119 and note 14 believes otherwise, but his citations of Pliny the Elder, *NH*, say nothing about the subject.

139. Sidebotham and Zitterkopf (1996): 384–391; Sidebotham (2000e): 359–366; Sidebotham et al. (2000b).

140. Bagnall et al. (2001).

141. Bagnall et al.(2001).

142. Bernand (1972a): 38–39 (no. 2).

143. Personal communication from H. Cuvigny; Bülow-Jacobsen (2008): 311.

144. Sidebotham et al. (2000a); Bagnall (2000); Cuvigny (2005b): 30 (no. 30, line 24) for possible appearance of Similis's name.

145. Sidebotham et al. (2000a): 395–397 for larger *praesidium;* Haeckl (2007): 347 for smaller installation.

146. Haeckl (2007).

147. Meredith (1953b): 105; Bernand (1984b): 80–81 (no. 29) with cross references = Bernand (1977): 167–177 (no. 69); Sidebotham et al. (2004): 20–21; Cuvigny (2003a): 271; Foster et al. (2007): 331, 333 (pls. 18–66, 67 and 68).

148. Personal communication from R. S. Bagnall.

149. *OGIS* 764; Hogarth (1896): 27–33; Lewis (1983): 141; Bernand (1984a): 199–208 (no. 67); Sidebotham (1986): 80–81; Young (2001): 48–50, 63, 67, 209; Burkhalter-Arce (2003); Cuvigny (2003a): 273–274.

150. Cuvigny (2003a): 273 for bodies; Cuvigny (2003f): 374–375, 383–388 for prostitutes.
151. Bülow-Jacobsen et al. (1995).
152. Bülow-Jacobsen and Cuvigny (2007): 12.
153. Bülow-Jacobsen and Cuvigny (2007): 13–17.
154. Bülow-Jacobsen and Cuvigny (2007): 16.
155. Bülow-Jacobsen and Cuvigny (2007): 16.
156. De Romanis (2003): 117–122; Cuvigny (2003d); Cuvigny (2003e); Cuvigny (2005b).
157. Sidebotham and Zitterkopf (1997): 228, 236–237, figs. 11–12.
158. Reddé and Brun (2003): 104; Reddé (2003a): 246–247.
159. Reddé (2003a): 246–247.
160. Sidebotham (1994a): 138, 144.
161. Sidebotham (1994b): fig. 14, 268, 272; Sidebotham (1994b): 267–268; figs. 3, 13–14.
162. Sidebotham (1994b): 267–268; figs. 3, 13–14.
163. Sidebotham (1994b): 266.
164. Sidebotham (1994b): 265 and figs. 2 and 10.
165. Sidebotham (1994b): 263, 266 and fig. 2.
166. Bagnall and Sheridan (1994b): 116–119.
167. Sidebotham (1994b): 263–266, figs. 2, 5–12.
168. Sidebotham and Zitterkopf (1997); Sidebotham and Zitterkopf (1998); Sidebotham et al. (2000b); Sidebotham and Zitterkopf (2005); Sidebotham et al. (in preparation).
169. Sidebotham (1994b): 265, 267; Sidebotham et al. (in preparation).
170. Sidebotham et al. (1991): 584–587.
171. Sidebotham and Zitterkopf (1997): 226 and 235 (fig. 9, D).
172. Personal observation of author.
173. Personal observation of author.
174. Sidebotham et al. (1991): 591–594.
175. Sidebotham et al. (2000a): 380, fig. 17–1, 381.
176. Tregenza (1949): 130–133 refers to it as Tal'et El-Zerqa; Reddé and Golvin (1986–1987): 38 and note 21; Sidebotham (2000d): 1161 and Sidebotham (2000c): map sheet 78.
177. Reddé and Brun (2003): 104; Reddé (2003a): 246.
178. Peacock (1997b).
179. Maxfield (1997b): 171–172.
180. Prickett (1979): 272; Maxfield (1997b): 172–173; Peacock (2006b): 32 (fig. 2.45) and 33.
181. Welsby (2003): 72–73.
182. Meredith (1958): 14, fig. 5, reproduces MS.G. Wilkinson XLV D.8, Bodleian Library, Oxford.
183. Bagnall et al. (2001); Bernand (1972a): 38–39 (no. 2).
184. Prickett (1979): 272–273.
185. Sidebotham et al. (1991): 584, Fig, 13J, 585.
186. Sidebotham et al. (1991): 591, fig. 20F, 594.
187. Personal observations of Sidebotham and Zitterkopf.
188. Personal observations of Sidebotham and Zitterkopf.
189. Oleson (2000b): 225; Wilson (2002): 7–9; Sidebotham et al. (2008): 322 (fig. 13.10).
190. Oleson (1984): 131–171.

191. Oleson (2000a): 201–204; Oleson (2000b): 225–229.

192. Personal observations of author in 1997.

193. See Sidebotham et al. (2008): 323 (fig. 13.11).

194. Maxfield (2001c): 51, 53, 55.

195. Oleson (1984): 180 (entry no. 5).

196. Oleson (1984): 131–171; Vitruvius (*De Architectura* 10.4.1–10.6.4, 10.7.1–5) discusses other water-lifting devices and pumps.

197. Cuvigny (2003f): 389–391.

198. Sidebotham et al. (1991): 588–591.

199. Sidebotham (1994a): 157 and note 47; Hobbs (1989): 45–46; Hobbs (1995): 9, 11, 16, 143, 178–188; Newton et al. (2005) for *qanats;* Mattingly and Wilson (2003) for *qanats/ foggaras;* Oleson (2000a) in general; Zalat and Gilbert (2008): 19–55 for current practices near Mt. Sinai.

200. Van der Veen (1998); Van der Venn and Hamilton-Dyer (1998): 114; Van der Venn (2001).

201. Sidebotham (1994a): 157; Sidebotham (1994b): 267.

202. Cappers (1998a): 319–324; Cappers (1998b): 76–80.

203. Meyer (1995a): 199, 223; Meyer (1995b): 37, 41, 47, 61, 75–78; Meyer and Omar (1995): 491, 493, fig. 2; 496–497; Meyer (1997); Meyer et al. (2000).

204. Brun (2003e): 97; Cuvigny (2003f): 380–383; Bülow-Jacobsen (2003b): 416, 419; Leguilloux (2003): 567–568; cf. Cuvigny (2007).

205. Van der Venn (2001): 219.

206. Sidebotham (1994b): 267.

207. Sidebotham et al. (2004a): 14–15 and 16 (fig. 25).

208. Wilkinson (1998): 23–24 (vines); Farrar (2000): 36–37; Carroll (2003): 92, 95.

209. Belzoni (1820): 315–316.

210. For St. Antony's Monastery: Wilkinson (1832): 31 and Meinardus (1989): 19; for St. Paul's Monastery: Wilkinson (1832): 34–35 and Meinardus (1989): 40; Zalat and Gilbert (2008): 19–55 near St. Catherine's Monastery in Sinai.

211. Hirschfeld (1992): 200, 204.

212. Walters (1974): 220; Bagnall (1993): 289–293; Mango (1996): 149; Kingsley and Decker (2001): 9; Wipszycka (1972): 34–63, 121–153; Alston (2002): 304–305; Wipszycka (2007): 335–336; Török (2005): 86 accumulation of property by churches began second half fourth century; Tomber (2008): 168–170.

213. Hobbs (1989): 45; Krzywinski (2001a): 105; Krzywinski (2007): 49.

214. For Ma'aze and 'Ababda: personal observations of Sidebotham and Zitterkopf; Sidebotham (1994a): 157 and note 47; Wilkinson (1832): 31, 34–35; Hobbs (1989): 45–46; Van der Venn (1998); Cappers (2006): 45–48; Kinglake (1982): 232–233 for Sinai; Murray (1955); Perevolotsky (1981): 331–357; Hobbs (1995): 9, 11, 16, 77, 143, 178–188; Zalat and Gilbert (2008): 19–55 for Bedouin practices in Sinai; Newton et al. (2005) and Mattingly and Wilson (2003) for *qanats;* Oleson (2000a) in general.

215. For glass working: Nicholson (1998): 280; for metal working: Sidebotham (2000b): 10–11, 23–24; Hense (1995): 56, 56 (fig. 26), 57; Hense (1996): 225–226; Hense (1998): 220; Hense (1999): 230; Hense (2000): 202; Hense (2007): 218.

216. Russell (1981): additions of Rufinus (13.7–8); Meyer (1950/1998): section 53; Chitty (1966): 90 and note 62.

217. Wilson (2000): 142–143.

218. Meyer (1995a); Meyer (1995b); Meyer and Omar (1995); Meyer (1997); Meyer (1998); Meyer (1999); Meyer et al. (2000).

219. Shepherd (1993): 255–257.

220. Hume (1937): 689–778; Vercoutter (1959); Lucas and Harris (1989): 224–234; Klemm and Klemm (1994); Wilson (2000): 135–142; Klemm et al. (2002); Meyer (1998).

221. Sidebotham and Wendrich (2001–2002): 26–27; Sidebotham and Zych (2010): 10, 11 (fig. 4).

222. Hodges (1989): 66.

223. Hodges (1989): 82; Wilson (2000): 142–143.

224. Blue and Walsh (2001); Whittaker et al. (2006): 78, 80; Thomas and Masser (2006): 135, 138.

225. Cuvigny (2005a): 314.

226. Manderscheid (2000) and Redon (2009): 424–433 and 444–445 (table 1 with bibliog.) for synopsis.

227. Redon (2009): 427 (n. 160); other probable baths (not positively identified) include Barramiya and Aphrodito.

228. Sidebotham (1994b): 270–272, figs. 20–23; Sidebotham et al. (2008): 55 (fig. 3.6 no. 9), 56, 324, 325 (figs. 13.12–13); Redon (2009) 424, 427–428, 431, 433, 448 (fig. 7), 450 (fig. 12a).

229. Maxfield (1997a): 122–134; Redon (2009): 424–425, 427, 429, 431–433, 449 (fig. 11), 450 (fig. 12b).

230. Brun (2003c): 61; Reddé and Brun (2003): 106–107, 163–166 (figs. 103–113); Reddé (2003a): 247; Sidebotham et al. (2008): 326 and fig. 13.14; Redon (2009): 424–425, 432–433, 447 (fig. 3), 450 (fig. 12f).

231. Reddé (2003a): 247; personal communication from H. Cuvigny; Redon (2009): 424–425, 433, 450 (fig. 12g).

232. Copeland and Handley (2001): 19–23; Redon (2009): 424–425, 449 (fig. 8), 450 (fig. 12c).

233. Redon (2009): 424–425, 433.

234. Redon (2009): 424–425, 433, 447 (fig. 4).

235. Nicholson (2000a): 203–205; Sidebotham (2000b): 146; Sidebotham and Wendrich (2000b): 415.

236. Nicholson (2000a): 203–205; Sidebotham and Wendrich (2000b): 416.

237. Bülow-Jacobsen (2001): 121 (*O. Did. Inv.* 329 [letter from Longinus to Numerius] = *O. Did.* 343: in Cuvigny [forthcoming]).

238. Maxfield (2000): 429; Maxfield (2001a): 161–163 on Eastern Desert animal lines.

239. Peacock (1997c); Harrell and Lazzarini (2002).

240. Sidebotham (1996b): 186–189; Harrell et al. (1999): 289–292.

241. Maxfield (1997a): 91, fig. 2.55; 92, fig. 2.56; Maxfield and Peacock (2001a): 208 (fig. 5.26), 209.

242. Maxfield and Peacock (2001a): 202–209.

243.   Maxfield and Peacock (2001a): 215–239; Maxfield (2007): 26–30.
244.   Sidebotham et al. (1991): 582–583; Maxfield and Peacock (2001b): 208 (fig. 5.26).
245.   Sidebotham et al. (1991): 584–587; Maxfield and Peacock (2001a): 208 (fig. 5.26); Maxfield (2001a): 161, 162 (table 7.4), 163 (fig. 7.5).
246.   Sidebotham et al. (1991): 587; Maxfield and Peacock (2001a): 208 (fig. 5.26); Maxfield (2001a): 161, 162 (table 7.4), 163 (fig. 7.5) .
247.   Sidebotham et al. (1991): 588–591; Maxfield and Peacock (2001a): 208 (fig. 5.26); Maxfield (2001a): 161, 162 (table 7.4).
248.   Sidebotham et al. (1991): 591–594; Maxfield and Peacock (2001a): 208 (fig. 5.26).
249.   Sidebotham et al. (1991): 595.
250.   Sidebotham et al. (1991): 576–578; Maxfield (2007): 80 (fig. 3.44), 81 for a plan of this small *praesidium*.
251.   Sidebotham (1996): 181–183 and pl. XVI.1.
252.   Sidebotham, (1996): 183–185.
253.   Meredith (1952): 102 and n. 2, 103 fig. 4; Reddé and Golvin (1986–1987): 37, fig. 31 [reproduces J. G. Wilkinson (M.S. LXV, D. 35)]; Maxfield (2001a): 161, 162 (table 7.4), 163 (fig. 7.5). In June 1999 our survey drew a plan of the site; publication forthcoming.
254.   Maxfield (1997a): 86–93; Hamilton-Dyer (1998): 122, 124; Van der Veen and Hamilton-Dyer (1998): 103–104; 105; Hamilton-Dyer (2001): 255, 262, 264.
255.   Bagnall et al. (1996): 319–320; Sidebotham (1997a): 388–390; Sidebotham (1999c): 364–368.
256.   Maxfield (1997a): 91, fig. 2.55; Maxfield and Peacock (2001a): 208 (fig. 5.26).
257.   Harrell (2004b); Sidebotham et al. (2004): 27 and figs. 63–65.
258.   Sidebotham et al. (2004a): 9 and fig. 5, 10 (fig. 6).
259.   Sidebotham et al. (2004a): 9 (fig. 5), 10 (fig. 6).
260.   Hughes (1994).
261.   Cuvigny (1997a).
262.   Hughes (1994): 123.
263.   Hughes (1994): 123–124; Callataÿ (2005) for more on air pollution.
264.   Shazly and Hassan (1972); Gamili et al. (1999/2000): 236, 237.
265.   Especially Hughes (1994).
266.   Bagnall et al. (2001); Bagnall et al. (2005): 23–27 (no. 120).
267.   Bülow-Jacobsen and Cuvigny (2007): 12.
268.   Three inscriptions—one of Augustus (May 26, 11 C.E.) and two of Tiberius (July 23 and October 2, 18 C.E.)—indicate tighter Roman government control over exploitation of the mineral wealth: Wadi Umm Wikala/Semna [Bernand (1977): 118–128 (no. 51)]; Sidebotham et al. (2001): 138–141 (11 C.E.); Wadi Hammamat [Bernand (1972a): 80–92 (no. 41) with bibliography (18 C.E.)] and Mons Porphyrites (18 C.E.) [Van Rengen (1995); Van Rengen (2001)].
269.   Sidebotham (1986): 9.
270.   Sidebotham (1986): 48–71, 116–141; Young (2001): 38–74.
271.   Sidebotham (1986): 141–162; Sidebotham and Zitterkopf (1997); Sidebotham and Zitterkopf (1998); Sidebotham et al. (2000b); Bagnall (2000); Young (2001): 74–79.
272.   Bagnall (2000).

273. Cuvigny (2006): 410.

274. Cuvigny (2003d); Cuvigny (2003e); Cuvigny (2005b).

275. Sidebotham (1986): 162–166; Verhoogt (1998): 193–196; Dijkstra and Verhoogt (1999); Young (2001): 80–85.

276. Sidebotham and Wendrich (1998b); Meyer et al. (2000); Sidebotham and Wendrich (2001–2002); Young (2001): 86–88.

8. NILE–RED SEA ROADS

1. Starr (1982): 117; Hughes (1994): 116; Hopkins (1988): 759–760: 56,000 miles of paved highways and 200,000 miles of secondary and tertiary roads; Leslie and Gardinder (1996): 52, 60, 62, 70 for Chinese awareness of Roman roads.

2. Statius (*Silvae* 4.3.40ff.) describes a typical Roman road; Radke (1971): 22–31.

3. Lesquier (1918): 377–383; Bagnall (1976b): 27; Maxfield (2005): 201; Reddé (2002).

4. Extensive/growing bibliography on Eastern Desert roads: Lesquier (1918); Couyat (1910a); Couyat (1910b); Murray (1925); Meredith (1952); Meredith (1953b); Sidebotham (1986); Sidebotham et al. (1991); Young (2001); Reddé (2002); Sidebotham (2002a); Cuvigny (2003d); Cuvigny (2003e); Cuvigny (2005b); Sidebotham and Wendrich (1995, 1996, 1998a, 1998b 1999, 2000a, 2001–2002, 2007a); Sidebotham et al. (2008).

5. Osman and Sidebotham (2000): 19; Sidebotham (2002a): 423–424; Talbert (2000): map sheets 77, 78, 80, and 81. This supersedes Meredith (1958); Sidebotham and Zitterkopf (1995); Sidebotham and Zitterkopf (1996); Sidebotham (1997a); Sidebotham (1997b).

6. Sidebotham, Zitterkopf (1997); Sidebotham and Ziterkopf (1998); Sidebotham et al. (2000b); Sidebotham and Zitterkopf (2005); Sidebotham et al. (in preparation).

7. Sidebotham et al. (1991).

8. Murray (1925): 148; Sidebotham et al. (1991): 620; Peacock (1997d): 264–266.

9. Zitterkopf and Sidebotham (1989); Brun (2002); Cuvigny (2003d) Cuvigny (2003e); Cuvigny (2005b).

10. Sidebotham (1997a): 388–390; Sidebotham (1999c): 364–368; Keenan et al. (2000a); Keenan et al. (2000b); Sidebotham (2002): 427–428.

11. Murray (1925): 143–145; Meredith (1953b): 98–101; Sidebotham and Zitterkopf (1995); Sidebotham (2002a); Sidebotham and Zitterkopf (1996): 357–371; Sidebotham (1998c); Sidebotham (1999c): 349–354.

12. Murray (1925): 145; Meredith (1953b): 99; Sidebotham and Zitterkopf (1995); Sidebotham (1997a): 385–387; Sidebotham and Zitterkopf (1996): 357–371; Sidebotham (1998c); Sidebotham (1999c): 349–354.

13. Starr (1982): 117 for some use of criminals and POWs.

14. Sidebotham et al. (in preparation).

15. Graf (1995b) for southern Via Nova Traiana; Bauzou (1998a-h); Kennedy (2000): 88, 89.

16. Sidebotham and Zitterkopf (1996): 372–382.

17. Sidebotham et al. (2004b): 152–153.

18. Sidebotham et al. (2001).

19. Klemm et al. (1984): Tafel 11b; cf. Wagner (1987): 140–154.

20. Hester et al. (1970).

21. Butcher (2003): 127–134, especially 128, associated bibliography on 448; Kennedy and Riley (1990): 78–94; Chevallier (1997): 247.

22. Kildahl (1979): 258; Raven (1984): 71; Mattingly (1994): 61; Chevallier (1997): 250, 252–261.

23. Isaac and Roll (1982); Fischer et al. (1996); Chevallier (1997): 250.

24. Graf (1997a): 125; Via Nova Traiana linked Bostra with Aila/Aqaba and was paved throughout: Graf (1997b): 273; Chevallier (1997): 245–250 (Syria and Arabia).

25. Ulpian, *Corpus Iuris Civilis, Digestum* 43.11.1.2; Laurence (1999): 67 (provides incorrect citation of Ulpian).

26. Author's observations during colonnaded-street survey in Petra, Jordan, in summer 2008.

27. Sidebotham (1991c); Peacock and Maxfield (2001a): 8.

28. Sidebotham (1991c): 184, Abb. 17 for photo of the now missing section.

29. Sidebotham (1991c): 185, Abb. 22; Sidebotham et al. (1991): 600.

30. Sidebotham (1991c); Sidebotham (1989); Habachi (1960): 223, 224, 225, 225–227 (figs. 5–8), 231, 232 for Pharaonic paved roads in the Aswan quarry region.

31. Seen by Sidebotham and Barnard in summer 1997.

32. Peacock (2006a): 9–10 for region of Myos Hormos.

33. Sidebotham et al. (2000b): 122.

34. Sidebotham et al. (1991): 600.

35. Sidebotham (1999c): 351–354.

36. Sidebotham (1999c): 351 and 354.

37. Sidebotham (2000e): 372–373 (table 16–19).

38. Radke (1971): 22–23; Pekáry (1968): 22–36.

39. Cuvigny (2003b): 318, 333; Bagnall (1985): 2–4; Adams (1995).

40. Chevallier (1997): 108–110 for discussion.

41. Sidebotham and Zitterkopf (1997): 225; Sidebotham (2002a): 424.

42. Sidebotham (2002a): 424–425.

43. Sherk (1974): 556–558; White (1984): 92–97, 99, 203; Chevallier (1997): 275–276; Radke (1971); Casson (1974): 163–175.

44. Van Rengen (1995): 240–245; Van Rengen (2001): 60–62; Bernand (1977): 118–128 (no. 51); Bernand (1972a): 80–92 (no. 41); Sidebotham et al. (2001): 138–142.

45. Cuvigny (2003a): 278, 279; Cuvigny (2003b): 321–325.

46. Cuvigny (2003b): 302–305; expanded in Bülow-Jacobsen and Cuvigny (2007): 28–33.

47. Cuvigny (2003b): 297–301.

48. For Romans, there was no clear distinction between *skopelos* and *burgus*. Sometimes *burgus* was a fortified tower to defend communities [Austin and Rankov (1995): 27, 66], implying that a *burgus* was larger than a *skopelos*. Sometimes the distinction is not clear; the terms seem interchangeable [Austin and Rankov (1995): 193].

49. Bagnall (1976b): 25–26; Clarysse (1984): 1024; Jaritz and Rodziewicz (1993): 118–119; Brun et al. (2003); Maxfield (2000): 416.

50. Zitterkopf and Sidebotham (1989): 180–188; Brun et al. (2003).

51. Zitterkopf and Sidebotham (1989): 181, for towers on this road: 180–188; Brun et al. (2003): 207–210; Sidebotham et al. (2008): 227, Pls. 4.18–19.

52. Peacock (2006a): 11; Prickett (1979): 298 (pl. 84: map) and 311 for more on Qasr Hadie; Zitterkopf and Sidebotham (1989): 159 (fig. 2) and 174; Sidebotham and Zitterkopf (1998): 353; Sidebotham et al. (2000b): 117–118; Sidebotham et al. (in preparation).

53. Bagnall (1977): 70; for discussion of *skopelarioi:* Bagnall (1976b): 25–26.

54. Bagnall (1976b): 62–65 (nos. 24–26); Bagnall (1977): 71, 77; Brun et al. (2003): 216–228; Hennig (2006) for guards [ὀρ(ε)οφύλακες] along Western Desert roads.

55. Maxfield (2005): 203–204; Cuvigny (1997b): 141–156 (no. 304).

56. Zitterkopf and Sidebotham (1989): 180–188; Brun et al. (2003); Sidebotham et al. (2008): 227, pls. 4.18–19.

57. Woolliscroft (2001): 22, 24, 26, 28, 35, 44, 45, 48, 159, 162, 163, 166 (no. 42) citing Vegetius, 170 (no. 52), who cites Julius Africanus (*Kestoi* 77) [this latter citation is incorrect]; Brun et al. (2003): 210–214.

58. Van't Dack (1962): 340–341; Brun et al. (2003): 225; Speidel (1988a) 789–791 = Speidel (1992b): 262–263, 266.

59. Zitterkopf and Sidebotham (1989): 186; Brun et al. (2003): 215 and 226.

60. Woolliscroft (2001): 21–30, less likely 36–46.

61. Woolliscroft (2001): 167–168.

62. Austin and Rankov (1995): 66.

63. Woolliscroft (2001): 49; Brun et al. (2003): 225: do not know any ancient documents referring to optical signaling.

64. Zitterkopf and Sidebotham (1989): 184–189 and Sidebotham et al. (1991): 622.

65. Graf (2005): 158, 159.

66. Woolliscroft (2001): 166–167 citing Frontinus (*Strategemata* 3.13.8) and Pliny the Elder (*NH* 10.53.110) for carrier pigeons. Varro *De re rustica* 3.7.7: theatergoers release homing pigeons [Guiraud (1997): 20–21]; Jennison (1937): 103–104.

67. Keegan (2003): 27–28.

68. Woolliscroft (2001): 21, 46–48.

69. Woolliscroft (2001): 46–48.

70. Brun et al. (2003) provide no estimated transmission time; Peacock (2006a) 11.

71. Cuvigny (2005b): 6.

72. Cuvigny (2005b): 188–192 (nos. 121–128).

73. Prickett (1979): 319; Reddé and Golvin (1986–1987): 58.

74. Sidebotham (2002a): 425, 435 (fig. 4).

75. Reddé and Brun (2003): 77.

76. Couyat (1910a): 533–536 (and figs. 2–3): two statues (of Apollo and Venus?) from the Fawakhir region; Guéraud (1942): 141; Meyer et al. (2000); Reddé and Brun (2003): 80. Gold mining at Bir Umm Fawakhir: Meyer (1995a); Meyer (1995b); Meyer and Badr el-Din (1995); Meyer, and Heidorn (1998); Meyer et al. (2000); Meyer et al. (2003); Brun (2003b): 204.

77. Peden (2001): 285; Brun: (2003b): 188–191; Winkler (1938): 9 (site 34), 10; Thissen (1979): bulk of Demotic ostraka in Wadi Hammamat are undated, but (p. 90) most were prob-

ably written in the Ptolemaic era; Fournet (2003): 429–430: ostrakon in Demotic and five Roman-era *dipinti* on amphora sherds.

78. Wilfong (2000): 26, 81 (fig. 52); Brun (2003b) 188–191, 205 (fig. 178).

79. Reddé and Brun (2003): 113, 173 (fig. 134).

80. Brun (2003b): 190–191; Cuvigny (2003a): 277.

81. Bülow-Jacobsen (2003a): 56; Reddé and Brun (2003): 133; Brun (2003b): 191.

82. Sidebotham (1986): 53–54; Tomber (2008): 60.

83. Weigall (1913): 60–61; Pricket (1979): 296; Whitcomb (1996): 760; Le Quesne (2004): 145, 148 (fig. 62); Le Quesne (2007): 166–167.

84. Whitcomb (1999); Le Quesne (2004): 145 for transfer from Quseir al-Qadim to Quseir in the sixteenth century; Le Quesne (2007): 22.

85. Klunzinger (1878): 318–327.

86. Le Quesne (2004): 26–29, 148, 153–155; Le Quesne (2007): 312–315.

87. Zitterkopf and Sidebotham (1989): 173 (fig. 4a), 178; Reddé and Brun (2003): 92, 94 and 150 (fig. 59).

88. Abu Sha'ar-Nile road: Sidebotham et al. (1991): 596 (fig. 25), 598–599 (table 1); for the Via Nova Hadriana near Myos Hormos: Prickett (1979): 298, pl. 84, p. 311; Sidebotham and Zitterkopf (1998): 353; tower immediately south of Myos Hormos: Sidebotham et al. (2000b): 117–118; Peacock (2006a): 7–14 for environs of Myos Hormos.

89. Roll (1995): 1166.

90. Sidebotham and Zitterkopf (1997): 224 (table), 227; Sidebotham et al. (2000b): 116 (table 1).

91. Sidebotham and Zitterkopf (1997): 224 (table), 227, 236 (fig. 10); Sidebotham et al. (2000b): 116 (table 1).

92. Sidebotham (2002a): 425, and note 18.

93. Sidebotham (1999c): 365–366, 367 (table 19–12).

94. Peacock and Maxfield (2001): 4 (fig. 1.3); Maxfield and Peacock (2001b): 105; Peacock and Phillips (2001): 132 (fig. 4.1).

95. Peacock and Maxfield (2001): 4 (fig. 1.3); Peacock and Phillips (2001): 132 (fig. 4.1), 135, 136 (fig. 4.7).

96. Peacock and Maxfield (2001): 4 (fig. 1.3); Peacock and Phillips (2001): 132 (fig. 4.1), 152, 153 (fig. 4.38).

97. Sidebotham et al. (2004a): 9, 10 (fig. 8).

98. Discovered by our survey June 18, 1993.

99. Sidebotham et al. (2004a): 26 (fig. 60).

100. Sidebotham et al. (2004a): 25 and 26 (fig. 60).

101. Sidebotham and Zitterkopf (1996): 401–403.

102. Sidebotham et al. (2004a): 25, 26 (fig. 59).

103. Sidebotham observed and photographed these.

104. Sidebotham (2002a): 426–428.

105. Couyat (1910a): 537 table for hill of ruins/rubbish and brick wells; Zitterkopf and Sidebotham (1989): 179; Lepsius (1853): 277 for five wells and two dilapidated buildings; Lesquier (1918): 445, 450, 452; Murray (1925): 144 notes "Palms, well, heap of ruins." Reinach (1910): 117–119; Weigall (1913): 31–32: inscription in Greek from Laqeita of

emperor Tiberius Claudius; Bernand (1972a): 37–38 (no. 1) found in cistern: Claudian; Bernand (1972a): 38–39 (no. 2), found in well: Flavian; see Alston (1995): 194; Cuvigny (1996b): 98–99.

106. Sidebotham and Zitterkopf (1997): 227; Sidebotham et al. (2000b): 115, 119–121 (illustrations).
107. Sidebotham and Zitterkopf (1997): 227; Sidebotham et al. (2000b): 115.
108. Chevallier (1997): 61.
109. Graf (1995a); Graf (1997b): 272.
110. Radke (1971): 31–39; Chevallier (1997): 61–81; Laurence (1999): 47–48, 52, 54–55, 65–66; Fasolo (2003): 46–52.
111. Isaac (1992): 305–306; Roll (1995): 1168; Chevallier (1997): 63.
112. Chevallier (1997): 249; Butcher (2003): 60.
113. Fischer, Isaac and Roll (1996): 25–29.
114. Al-Thenayian (1999): 155–156 and for Abbasid milestones.
115. Hester et al. (1970): 385–389; *CIL* III Suppl. 6633, 14148^2, 14148^3; Monneret de Villard (1941): 34; Eide et al. (1998): 921–924 (no. 220) for commentary on *CIL* III Suppl.14148^2 dated ca. 103–107 C.E.
116. Drower (1995): 123 (large tablets at four-mile intervals [= *schoenus*], smaller upright blocks at one-mile intervals [1,000 cubits]); Adams (2001a): 141.
117. Hester et al. (1970): 385–389 and pls. 99–100.
118. Bagnall (1976b): 37.
119. Bagnall (1976b): 35; cf. Sidebotham (1986): 58; Sidebotham and Zitterkopf (1995).
120. De Romanis (1996a): 215 (no. 17); Cuvigny (2003c): 12 and note 46.
121. Sidebotham et al. (2000b): 122–126; Sidebotham (2002a): 425–426.
122. Sidebotham et al. (2000b): 124–126.
123. Pekáry (1968): 96; Starr (1982): 117; Chevallier (1997): 275.
124. Hopkins (1988): 760.
125. Speidel (1992a): 88 (table 1), 93 (table 3); Herz (2007): 308–313.
126. Starr, (1982): 117; for private vs. public roads: Laurence (1999): 59–62.
127. Maxfield (2000): 434.
128. Maxfield (2001a): 151, 152 (table 7.2).
129. Lesquier (1918): 417–458; Bagnall (1976b); Speidel (1982); Speidel (1984); Speidel (1988a) = Speidel (1992b); Maxfield (2000); Cuvigny (2003d); Cuvigny (2003e); Cuvigny (2005b); Maxfield (2005).
130. Reinach (1911a): 49–64.
131. Fink (1971): No. 63 (pp. 217–227, especially line 32); Isaac (1992): 115–116; Adams (1995) for desert supply; Austin and Rankov (1995): 177–180; Birley (2002): 94–95; Gichon (1989): 155–170.
132. Dennis (1985): vii proposes about 550 C.E.; Cosentino (2000).
133. Austin and Rankov (1995): 5, 27; Dennis (1985): 123 (section 42 lines 24–28); Zuckerman (1990); Lee (1999).
134. Fink (1971): 228–233 (no. 64). The figures total 535 men, not 505 as Fink (232) records.
135. Clarysse (1984): 1021–1026.
136. Clarysse (1984): 1021–1026.

137. Cuvigny (2003b): 326–330; Bagnall (1977); Bagnall (1982).

138. El-Saghir et al. (1986): vi, 20–21, 99, 122.

139. El-Saghir et al. (1986): vi, 20–21, 99, 122; Sidebotham (1994a): 142-143, 157-158; Bagnall and Sheridan (1994a): 159-163.

140. Cuvigny (2005b): 187–188 (no. 120).

141. Bingen et al. (1997): 50–51 (no. 227).

142. Bingen et al. (1997): 115–118 (no. 279), 215–217 (nos. 375–376) and 220 (no. 380).

143. Brun et al. (2003): 227; Maxfield (2005): 204.

144. Cuvigny (2003b): 344.

145. Bülow-Jacobsen (2003b): 404.

146. Carrié (1999).

147. Kolb (1997): especially 536; Carrié (1999); Pflaum (1940); Casson (1974): 184 and 351 for notes; Chevallier (1997): 276–278; Kolb (2001); Holmberg (1933); Casson (1974): 182–190; Mitchell (1976).

148. Cuvigny (2003b): 332.

149. Cuvigny (2003b): 326–327.

150. Teixidor (1984): 23–31; Drexhage (1988); Stoneman (1992): 59–63; Gawlikowski (1994); Hartmann (2001).

151. Hogarth (1896): 27–33; for bibliography until the late 1970s see Raschke (1978): 649 and 893 (note 961); Bernand (1984a): 199–208 (no. 67) with bibliography, translation, and commentary (= OGIS 674 = IGRR I.1183); Sidebotham (1986): 35, 53, 67, 80–81; Young (2001): 48–50; with translation; Burkhalter-Arce (2002); Cuvigny (2003a): 273–274.

152. Cuvigny (2003a): 288; Cuvigny (2003b): 296–297, 324–327.

153. Bülow-Jacobsen (2003b): 413.

154. For Koptos inscription: IGRR I.1169 = OGIS 639 see Reinach (1911b): 58, 79 = Bernand (1984a): 238–241 (no. 85) = Hogarth (1896): 33–34 (no. 55) and pl. XXVIII, no. 6] with commentary; for dated Berenike text: Verhoogt (1998): 193–196; Cuvigny (2003b): 338; Maxfield (2000): 426.

155. Dijkstra and Verhoogt (1999) for bilingual Palmyrene-Greek text.

156. Dabrowa (1991); Gebhardt (2002): 276–285 for Palmyrene caravan trade, 285–291 for Palmyrene auxiliary troops.

157. Reinach (1913): 46–50; Bernand (1984a): 262–263 (no. 103), 238–241 (no. 85) for Koptos; 146–148 (no. 39) for Tentyris; Ballet et al. (2000): 134–136 (and figs. 43–44, cat. 100–104) for Koptos.

158. Drexhage (1988): passim; Stoneman (1992): 31–50, 59–63; Gawlikowski (1994).

159. Drexhage (1988); Stoneman (1992): 45, 46–48; Gawlikowski (1994).

160. Bernand (1984a): 146–148 (no. 39); Cuvigny (2003a): 276 for mention of archers on the Myos Hormos–Koptos road.

161. Littmann and Meredith (1953): nos. 34, 36a, and 37 on camel drivers; Littmann and Meredith (1954a): no. 75 for a plasterer; no. 81 for a priest and no. 61 for a patcher of clothes; Briquel-Chatonnet and Nehmé (1998); Toll (1994); Graf and Sidebotham (2003): 68, 72; Cuvigny (2003a): 276 (at Qasr al-Banat).

162. Sidebotham (1986): 95–96 for Palmyrene activities in Egypt; 94–95 for Nabataeans.

163. Kennedy (1985); Sidebotham (1986): 65; Isaac (1992): 200; Cuvigny (2003a): 267–273; Maxfield (2000): 419, 425–426.

164. Bernand (1984a): 178–184 (no. 56); Kennedy (1985); Isaac (1992): 200; De Romanis (1996a): 219–224; Cuvigny (2003a): 267–273.

165. Bagnall et al. (2001); Cuvigny (2001) for report on Didymoi excavations; Meredith (1954) for Aphrodito.

166. Bernand (1972a): 38–39 (no. 2).

167. Cuvigny (2002–2003); cf. Bülow-Jacobsen (2008).

168. Bagnall (2000).

169. Cuvigny (2006).

170. Fink (1971): 228–233 (no. 64); Speidel (1988b).

171. Bernand (1984a): 178–184 (no. 56); Kennedy (1985); Sidebotham (1986): 65; Isaac (1992): 200; De Romanis (1996a): 219–224; Maxfield (2000): 425–426; Cuvigny (2003a): 267–273.

172. Bülow-Jacobsen (2003b): 405–406; cf. *P. Lond.* 2.328 = Kenyon (1898): 74–76.

173. Harrauer and Sijpesteijn (1985); Casson (1986a); Thür (1987); Thür (1988); Casson (1990); Belfiore (2004): 235–244.

174. Bülow-Jacobsen (2003b): 406–408.

175. Cuvigny (2002–2003); Maxfield (1996): 17 for *dromedarii* in the Eastern Desert; Bülow-Jacobsen (2003b): 405–406; Fink (1971): 228–233 (No. 64) for August 156 C.E. papyrus from Contrapollonopolis Magna, lists a unit of the *Cohors I Augusta Praetoria Lusitanorum Equitata:* 3 decurions, 6 centurions, 145 cavalry, 18 camel riders, and 363 infantry. Figures total 535 men and not 505 as Fink (232) records; Dabrowa (1991) for *dromedarii* in general.

176. Bowman (1978): 34.

177. Shaw (1979/1995); Demougeot (1960): especially for Tunisia-Algeria; Midant-Reynes and Braunstein-Silvestre (1977); Wilson (1984): 9–10; Adams (2007): 49–56.

178. Figari (1865): 457; Weigall (1913): 25, 36; Bülow-Jacobsen (2003b): 406–408; Maxfield (1996): 11–12 (and note 4) estimates a baggage camel's speed at 4 km per hour; Maxfield (2001a): 160.

179. Potts (1988): 155–157.

180. Gauthier-Pilters and Dagg (1981): 109.

181. Gauthier-Pilters and Dagg (1981): 109–110.

182. Maxfield (2001a): 159.

183. Wilson (1984): 164, 166.

184. Whittaker (2002) for perception of ancient maps.

185. Brodersen (2001).

186. Salway (2001) in general.

187. Sherk (1974): 559.

188. Chevallier (1997): 61.

189. De Romanis (1996a): 215 (no. 17); Cuvigny (2003c): 12 and note 46.

190. See chapter 2, note 52.

191. Casson (1989).

192. Thrower (1996): 23–24; Chevallier (1997): 60.

193. Stevenson (1991): 100–101.

194. Stevenson (1991): 107.

195. Claudius Ptolemy, *Geography* 6.7, for Arabia Felix [= Stevenson (1991): 137–140], 6.16 for Serica [= Stevenson (1991): 145–146], 7.1–7.4 for India, Sinae, Taprobane [= Stevenson (1991): 149–159].

196. Janvier (1984).

197. Thrower (1991): 24; Wilford (2002): 30.

198. *Tabula Peutingeriana* (1976): segment VIII; Cunz (1990): 23; Dilke (1985): 125; Dilke (1985): 112–120 for *Peutinger Table;* Brodersen (1995); Chevallier (1997): 53–56; Salway (2001): 22–32, 43–47; Salway (2004); Talbert (2004); Brodersen (2003); Talbert (2010).

199. Brun (2003b).

200. Sidebotham (1986): 59–61.

201. Cunz (1990): 23; Dilke (1985): 125–128 for *Antonine Itinerary;* Chevallier (1997): 56–59.

202. Cunz (1990): 23.

203. Pinder and Parthy (1860): 58–59 ; Dilke (1985): 112–113 and 174–176 for *Ravenna Cosmography;* Dillemann and Janvier (1997): 157–167 on Egypt, 161f. on Red Sea coast, 164f. on Berenike–Koptos road; Ball (1942): 138–158 for *Antonine Itinerary* and *Peutinger Table;* Chevallier (1997): 60.

204. Adopted and modified from Sidebotham (1986): 60.

205. Whittaker (2002): 85–86.

206. Bagnall (1976b): 35; Sidebotham and Zitterkopf (1995): 41, 50; Sidebotham (1997a): 386–388.

207. Leadbetter (2000); Leadbetter (2002); Bowman (1976): 159–160; Bowman (1978); Barnes (1976): 180–182; Bowman (1986): 44–45; Alston (1999) for late second-century Boukoloi revolt in Lower Egypt.

208. Helm (1984): 226.

209. Leadbetter (2000): 84; Leadbetter (2002): 85–89.

210. Robin (1997): 53.

211. Thomas (1976); Bowman (1978): 27.

212. Bagnall (2000); Bagnall et al. (2001).

213. Reddé and Brun (2003): 75–76, 141 (fig. 27) for Qasr al-Banat; 80 for al-Muweih; 92–93, 152 (fig. 65) for Bir al-Hammamat.

214. Bagnall et al. (2001); cf. Cuvigny (2001).

215. Cuvigny (2006).

216. Maxfield (2000): 427.

217. Maxfield (2000): 427; Maxfield (2001a): 163, 164 (fig. 7.6).

218. Peacock (1992).

219. Zitterkopf (1998); Maxfield (2001a): 161, 162 (table 7.4).

220. Sidebotham et al. (2001): 144 (fig. 3c), 157 (fig. 11).

221. Abu Sha'ar al-Bahri, Quei, Fawakhir, Laqeita and Sheikh Salem; Leadbetter (2000): 85 and notes 21–22 for late Roman fort at Koptos, no longer visible, but assumed to be on eastern bank of Nile.

222. Maxfield (2000): 433; compare Abraq: Sidebotham (1995b): 99–100: ca. 161.5 m E–W by ca. 98.25 m N–S; Sidebotham and Zitterkopf (1996): 372, 373–374 (figs. 21–17 and 21–18).

223. Lewis (1938) = Lewis (1995); Alston (1995): 81–86; Sidebotham (1986): 164–165 and notes 229–230; for brigandage in general see MacMullen (1966): 255–268; McGing (1998); Adams (2007): 20–21; Butcher (2003): 409–410 and note on 462; Cuvigny (2003b): 346–359; Cuvigny (2005b): 135–154 (no. 87); De Romanis (2003); Wolff (1999) 398; Shaw (1984) and Shaw (2004) in general.

224. Alston (1995): 81-86, 83 and 224 (note 102) for Xenophon of Ephesus; Xenophon, *Ephesiaca* IV.1 [= Reardon (1989): 154-155]; O'Sullivan (1995): 1-9 for name, date, and provenance of Xenophon.

225. Bülow-Jacobsen (2003a): 52–53; Maxfield (2007): 52 (fig. 3.22) and 53 for possible *aedes* in *praesidia* along the Myos Hormos-Nile road.

226. Kaper (1998): 146–147; Carrié (2001); Peacock (2001b); Peacock (2001c); Maxfield (2001b); Traunecker (2002); also Reddé (2003a): 248–251; Cuvigny (2005b): 188–189 (nos. 121–128); Hölbl (2005): 9–34; Maxfield (2007): 52 (fig. 3.22) and 53: Sidebotham et al. (2008): 111–150.

227. Sidebotham (1994b): 268.

228. For small *praesidium* in Wadi Kalalat: Sidebotham (1995b): 87, 88 (fig. 49) and Haeckl (2007): 345 (fig. 19–1); for large *praesidium* in Wadi Kalalat: Sidebotham et al. (2000a): 387–391; for small *praesidium* at Siket: Sidebotham (2000e): 359–365 and Pintozzi (2007): 359 (fig. 20–2).

229. In general Sidebotham et al. (1989); Sidebotham (1991a); Sidebotham (1991b); Sidebotham (1991d); Sidebotham (1992a); Sidebotham (1992b); Sidebotham (1993); Sidebotham (1994a); Sidebotham (1994b); Sidebotham (1997b); Bagnall and Sheridan (1994a); Bagnall and Sheridan (1994b); Van Neer and Wendrich (1994); Van Neer and Sidebotham (2002); Mulvin and Sidebotham (2004); Jørgensen (2006).

230. Sidebotham (1994b): fig. 4 between 264 and 265 for latest fort plan.

231. Sidebotham et al. (2000a): 380 (fig. 17–1) for latest plan.

232. Observations of Sidebotham and Zitterkopf, unpublished plan.

233. Sidebotham et al. (2000a).

234. Reddé and Brun (2003): 87, 98; Cuvigny (2003f): 382; Leguilloux (2003): 551, 552–553, 554, 556, 557, 558, 569–570, 574, 575 (tables 1, 2 and 3) for Krokodilô and Maximianon, 578 (table 7), 578 (table 8), 579 (table 9), 584 (figs. 250–251), 585 (figs. 252–253), 586 (figs. 254–256), 587 (fig. 257).

235. Reddé and Brun (2003): 106–107 (figs. 103–108 on pp, 163–165); Reddé (2003a): 247; Redon (2009): 424–425, 433, 447 (fig. 4).

236. Reddé and Brun (2003): 105, 106; Reddé (2003a): 248.

237. Sidebotham (1994b): 270–272 and figs. 20–23 for bath.

238. Ptolemaic-Roman forts on high ground: al-Heita, Shenshef, three at Vetus Hydreuma/ Wadi Abu Greiya, above Abu Gerida, Abraq, Wadi al-Hudi.

239. Lewis (1938) = Lewis (1995); Sidebotham (1986): 164–165 and notes 229–230; for brigandage in general see MacMullen (1966): 255–268; McGing (1998); Butcher (2003): 409–410 and note on 462.

240. Isaac (1992): 186–187.

241. Mitthof (2001): 295–296.

242. Adams (1995): 121–124.

243. Kennedy (1985); Isaac (1992): 200; De Romanis (1996): 219–224; Sidebotham (1986): 65 and note 53.

244. Adams (1995): 121–124.

245. Sidebotham (1994a): 157; Sidebotham et al. (1989): 143, for earlier estimates that are too high.

246. Cuvigny (2003b): 307–309.

247. Cuvigny (2005b): 3, 179 (no. 117).

248. Maxfield (1996): 18.

249. Cuvigny (2005a): 344; Maxfield (2000): 432.

250. Cuvigny (2003b): 309–310.

251. Cuvigny (2003b): 333; Maxfield (1996): 17.

252. Cuvigny (2002–2003) unpublished report (inv. no. 952).

253. Maxfield (2000): 413.

254. Cuvigny (2003d); Cuvigny (2003e); De Romanis (2003): 117–122; Cuvigny (2005b): 35–37 (no. 6), 89–95 (no. 47), 96–97 (no. 49).

255. Maxfield (2000): 432.

256. André and Filliozat (1980): 54 (section 103).

257. Murray (1925): 114, note 5; Maxfield (2000): 432–433.

258. Cuvigny (2003f): 361–373.

259. Maxfield (2005): 203.

260. Cuvigny (2003b): 312.

261. Maxfield (2000): 431 citing *ILS* 9142.

262. Maxfield (1996): 16 and Maxfield (2000): 431, both citing *P. Mich.* III, 203.

263. Speidel (1988b); Cuvigny (2003b): 312.

264. Leguilloux (2003): 573–574, 575 (tables 1–2), 582 (table 14), 584 (figs. 250–251), 588 (fig. 263), 564–565 for Mons Claudianus; Hamilton-Dyer (2001): 283–292, 309 (figs. 9.31–9.37), 310 (figs. 9.38–9.47).

265. For Berenike: Harrell (1996): 112; Harrell (1998): 142–143; Wendrich et al. (2003): 54 (table 1), 57; Seeger and Sidebotham (2005): 20 for Marsa Nakari.

266. Bagnall and Harrell (2003): 231.

267. Maxfield (2001a): 148; Gregarek (2002): 208–209 for use of colored stones from Augustus to Hadrian.

268. Maxfield et al. (2001b); Peacock and Maxfield (2007); Klemm and Klemm (2008): 269–280.

269. Peacock and Maxfield (1997); Klemm and Klemm (2008): 280–290.

270. Sidebotham et al. (2001); Klemm and Klemm (2008): 291–294.

271. Sidebotham et al. (1991): 580–582.

272. Peacock (1997c); Harrell and Lazzarini (2002); Klemm and Klemm (2008): 290–291.

273. Sidebotham (1996b): 186–189; Harrell et al. (1995): 289–292; Klemm and Klemm (2008): 291.

274. Sidebotham (1996b): 189–190; Harrell et al. (1995): 285–289; Klemm and Klemm (2008): 294.

275. Brown and Harrell (1995): 221, 225 (table), 229 (fig. 8); Harrell et al. (2002); Klemm and Klemm (2008): 297–311.

276. Alford (1901–1902): 14–15; Lucas and Harris (1989): 414–415; Harrell (2002): 240; Brown and Harrell (1995): 225, 231 and fig. 9; Barthoux (1922): 33; Klemm and Klemm (1993): 427-429 and 444 (Farbtafel 6.1); Klemm and Klemm (2008): 312–314; Hume (1934): 171-172 and pls. XLVI #3-4, XLVII.

277. Harrell et al. (1999): 285–289; Klemm and Klemm (2008): 294.

278. Sidebotham et al. (2001): 140, note 13; Harrell (2002): 238–240; Harrell et al. (2002).

279. Brown and Harrell (1995): 225, 228, 230, 231, 231 (fig. 9), 231 (table 4); Klemm and Klemm (2008): 312–314; Ball (1912): 349: marble near Qash Amir, west of Gebel Elba, but no indication of quarrying.

280. Parker (1992): 19.

281. Peacock and Maxfield (2001): 5–6; Maxfield (2001a): 154; Maxfield and Peacock (2007): 427.

282. Millar (1984); Shepherd (1993): 59–68; Thompson (2003): 142–143.

283. Cuvigny (1996a); Maxfield (2001a): 154–155; Thompson (2003): 137–139; Maxfield and Peacock (2007): 427–429.

284. Cuvigny (2002–2003): 7.

285. Cuvigny (1996a).

286. Cockle (1992); Cockle (1997); Cribiore (1996).

287. Maxfield (1997a): 101–116 for Zeus Helios Great Serapis temple at Mons Claudianus; Hölbl (2005): 9–34 for larger temples in the region.

288. Peacock (2001b) for Isis temple at Mons Porphyrites; Peacock (2001c) for Serapis temple; Maxfield (2001b) for Isis Myrionomos temple.

289. Sidebotham et al. (2001): 154–156 (inscription on 138–141).

290. Bernand (1972b) Bernand (1977); Hughes (1994): 48; Aufrère (1998): 9–10, 12–14; Traunecker (2003): 358, 360–361, 371–372, 373.

291. Maxfield (1997a): 122–134.

292. Copeland and Handley (1998); Copeland and Handley (2001); Bailey (2007): 255–256 for "bath-flasks" at Mons Porphyrites.

293. Thompson (2003): 139.

294. Bülow-Jacobsen (1992b); Bülow-Jacobsen (1997a); Bülow-Jacobsen (1997b); Bingen (1997a); Bingen (1997b); Van der Venn (2001): 219; Bülow-Jacobsen (2003b): 419–423; for prostitutes in the Koptos Tariff: Bernand (1984a): 201 (no. 67), lines 16–17; Young (2001): 49.

295. For letters to/from military personnel: Van Rengen (1997); Kayser (1997).

296. Cuvigny (2000); Van der Venn (2001): 219; Van Rengen (2007): 408.

297. Maxfield (2001a): 151, 152 (table 7.2).

298. Bandinelli (1971): 281 and pls. 369–370.

299. Bandinelli (1971): 278 and 280 (pl. 256); Delbrueck (1932) for other examples.

300. Hiebert and Cambon (2008): 201 (figs. 215–216).

301. Maxfield (2001a): 156 (table 7.3), 157.

302. Peacock et al. (1997): 330–334; Adams (2001b): 171; Maxfield (2001a): 156.

303. Peacock (1997b): 180–181 (figs. 6.2–6.3) and 212–214; Maxfield (2001a): 158.

304. Peacock (1997b): 205 (fig. 6.20), 215; measurements by Sidebotham.

305. Peacock (1997d): 261, 264–266.

306. Peacock (1997d): 261–264; Maxfield (2001a): 164–165; Adams (2001b): 173, 174, 176.
307. Sidebotham et al. (1991): 597–598, 600; Sidebotham (1996b): 183; Maxfield (2001a): 164–165.
308. Sidebotham et al. (1991): 597–598, 600; Sidebotham (1996b): 183; Peacock (1997d): 261–265 and 271 (figs. 7.13 and 7.14); Maxfield (2001a): 164–165.
309. Sidebotham (1996b): 183; Peacock (1997d): 261–263 and 271 (figs. 7.13–7.14).
310. Sidebotham (1986): 63–64; Sidebotham et al. (1991): 572–573.
311. Peña (1989): especially 129–130 and note 19.
312. Maxfield (2001a): 157.
313. Guéraud (1942); Adams (1995): 119; Bülow-Jacobsen (2003b): 408–409.
314. Cuvigny (2003b): 318; Fournet (2003): 477.
315. Bernand (1984a): 201 (no. 67) lines 27–28, paid 4 drachmas; Young (2001): 49–50; Burkhalter-Arce (2002).
316. Klemm and Klemm (1994); Klemm et al. (2001); Klemm et al. (2002); Meyer and Heidorn (1998); Meyer et al. (2000).
317. MacAlister (1900); Shaw (1999a); Shaw (2002): 249–250; Shaw et al. (1999); Sidebotham et al. (2004a); Harrell, (2004a); Hölbl (2003); Foster et al. (2007).
318. Lucas and Harris (1989): 388–389; Shaw (1994); Shaw and Jameson (1993); Shaw (1999b).
319. Meredith (1957b); Bernand (1977): 136–140 (nos. 59–62); Shaw (2002): 249; Harrell and Sidebotham (2004); Harrell et al. (2006).
320. Meyer et al. (2000): 15–17.
321. Yoyotte (1975): 52–53; Eichler (1993): 188–192; Fischer (1985); Klemm et al. (1995). Reference to a Pharaonic-era prospector recorded at Ain Sokhna (personal communication from P. Tallet).
322. Healy (1988): 780, 784; Harrell (2002): 242.
323. Sidebotham et al. (2004a): 23 and fig. 49 for Umm Hieran and 25–26 for Nugrus West.
324. Sidebotham et al. (2002) for all but Umm Heiran; Sidebotham et al. (2004a): 23 and fig. 49 for Umm Heiran; Earl and Glazier (2002): 89–93 for a similar settlement at Nakheil; Earl and Glazier (2006b): 29–32; Peacock and Blue (2006a): 177; Monneret de Villard (1935): 29–61 and Ricke et al. for similar settlements in Nubia; Ricke et al. (1967): 33–37; in general: Grossmann (2002): 50–54. Sidebotham (1995b): 96–98 and Aldsworth and Barnard (1996) for Hitan Rayan; Murray (1926): 167 mentions a settlement in "Umm Etli," must = Wadi Umm Atlee; cf. Luft (2010).
325. Sidebotham et al. (1991): 576; Peacock et al. (2001): 127–128.
326. Sidebotham et al. (1991): 583–584.
327. Sidebotham (1993); Sidebotham (1994a): 136–141; Bagnall and Sheridan (1994a): 164–166.

9. OTHER EMPORIA

1. Tarn (1929): 21–22; Fraser (1972a): 177; Fraser (1972b): 301–302, note 352; Cohen (2006): 44–45, 307, 329 note 3, 400.
2. Wolska-Conus (1968): 376–377.

3. Ingraham et al. (1981): 76–77; Sidebotham (1986): 124–126; Gatier and Salles (1988a); Cohen (2006): 329–330.

4. Casson (1989): 143–145 for discussion of *Periplus* 19; Ingraham et al. (1981): 76–77; Sidebotham (1986): 124–126; Gatier and Salles (1988a); Ruffing (2002): 370; Cuvigny (2003c): 28–30; Cohen (2006): 329–330.

5. Tarn (1929): 13, 15–16, 21, 22.

6. Jameson (1968); von Wissmann (1978); Sidebotham (1986): 120–130; Buschmann (1991); Marek (1993); Luther (1999).

7. Beeston (1979): 11 believes the expedition reached al-'Abr, not Marib; Nicolet (1991): 85, 89 (note 4); Dueck (2000): 87.

8. Costa (1977); Marek (1994).

9. See Chapter 2; Sidebotham (1986): 120–130.

10. Millar (1998): 124–125.

11. Young (1997); Millar (1998): 124–125; Young (2001): 95–96; Bowsher (1989): on the Nabataean army in general.

12. Mayerson (1992) = Mayerson (1994b); cf. Ward (2007): 163–164.

13. Personal communication from S. T. Parker.

14. Parker (2002b): 423; Millar (1998): 125.

15. Millar (1998): 125.

16. Kobishchanov (1979): 78; *Martyrium Sancti Arethae* (27, 28, 29); Vasiliev (1950): 294–295; Rubin (1989); Eide et al. (1998): 1185–1188 (no. 327); Kirwan (1972): 171; Shahîd (1971): 212–214; Shahîd (1989): 360–376 on Christianity at Najran; Eide et al. (1998): 1187–1188 (no. 327); Fauvelle-Aymar (2009): 135.

17. Vasiliev (1950): 364–365; Wilkinson (1977) 88 (40. v 186).

18. Tomber (2005d): 42–47 for pottery; Whitcomb (1994): 16–18 for coins.

19. Parker (1996b); Parker (1998); Parker (2000); Parker (2002b); cf. Ward (2007): 163, 166.

20. Whitcomb (1989a); Whitcomb (1989b); Whitcomb (1994); Whitcomb (1995); Whitcomb (1990): debate on fort date: Diocletianic or early Islamic.

21. Roeder (1959): 124–125; Desanges (1978): 267.

22. Bruyère (1966): 49–52; Bourdon (1925); Desanges (1978): 267; Sidebotham (1991): 15–17; Mayerson (1996); Cooper (2005); Cohen, (2006): 308–309 and 327–329.

23. Bourdon (1925); Bruyère (1966); Sidebotham (1991): 15–17; Mayerson (1996); Cooper (2005); Cohen, (2006): 308–309, 327–329.

24. Sidebotham (1991b): 16–17.

25. Gingras (1970): 60 and 179–180 (notes 88–90); Wilkinson (1971): 205–206; cf. Ward (2007): 162–163.

26. Kobishchanov (1979): 78; Vasiliev (1950): 294–295 (on the campaign), 364–365 (on late antique Clysma); *Martyrium Sancti Arethae* (27, 28, 29); Rubin (1989); Eide et al. (1998): 1185–1188 (no. 327); Kirwan (1972): 171; Shahîd (1971): 46–47, 212–214 on campaign in general; Shahîd (1989): 360–376 on Christianity at Najran; Eide et al. (1998): 1187–1188 (no. 327).

27. (CCSL 175, 101; Vasiliev [1950]: 364); Wilkinson (1971).

28. De Romanis (2002): 24–26; Brun (2003b): 202.

29. Personal communication from J. P. Cooper; Cooper (2005).

30. Roeder (1959): 122; Fraser (1972a): 177; Desanges (1978): 263–264.

31. Redmount (1986): 20; Redmount (1995): 132–135.

32. Personal communication from J. P. Cooper; Cooper (2005).

33. Posener (1938): 261–262, 266, 268, 269, 270.

34. Sayed (1993); Wikander (2000a): 324–325.

35. Lloyd (1977): 142–145; Tuplin (1991): 238, 239, 242.

36. Scheil (1930); Kortenbeutel (1931): 19–20; Posener (1936): 48–87; Posener (1938): 271–273; Hinz (1975); Shea (1977); Tuplin (1991): 238–240, 242–248; Paice (1992): 227; Redmount (1995): 127–128 (on Darius I); Cataudella (2002); Cooper (forthcoming): in general.

37. Naville (1885): 16–20; Roeder (1959): 122; Fraser (1972a): 177; Fraser (1972b): 298–299 (notes 346–347); Desanges (1978): 263–264.

38. Paice (1992): 230, 234 (table 1).

39. Naville (1885): 16–19; Bourdon (1925); Sidebotham (1991): 16–17 and notes; Bonneau (1993): 7 (and note 32); De Romanis (2002); Cooper (2005).

40. Paice (1992): 230.

41. *Itinerarium Egeria* chapters 6 and 7 = (Gingras 1970): 60 and 179–180 (notes 88–90); Wilkinson (1971): 205–206.

42. For the late third century see Boak and Youtie (1960): 313–317 (no. 81) = *SB* V, 7676; for the fourth century (332 C.E.) see *P. Oxy.* 12.1426.

43. For 423 C.E.: *PSI* 87; *PSI* 689 (420/421, 423 C.E.); for 710 C.E.: *P. Lond.* 1346; Sijpesteijn (1963): 73 for the ninth century.

44. Maclaren (1825); Sidebotham (1986): 67–68 and notes 62–63; Paice (1992): especially 234 (table 1); Cataudella (2002).

45. Charles (1916): 55–56 (= section 72.19).

46. Posener (1938): 258–273; Oertel (1964): 18–52; Bourdon (1925); Sijpesteijn (1963) and Sijpesteijn (1965) for Trajan.

47. Sheehan (forthcoming).

48. Fraser (1972a): 177 and Fraser (1972b): 298–299 and notes 346–347.

49. Sidebotham (1991b): 17.

50. Bagnall (1993): 82–83 for textiles; Bagnall (2005): 195 for wine.

51. Sidebotham (1991b): 16–17.

52. Cooper (forthcoming).

53. Cooper (forthcoming).

54. Sidebotham et al. (1989): 132–133; Whitcomb (1996): 766 (table); Cuvigny (2003c): 24–27.

55. Sidebotham et al. (1989); Sidebotham (1991a); Sidebotham (1991b); Sidebotham (1991d); Sidebotham (1992a); Sidebotham (1992b); Sidebotham (1993); Sidebotham (1994a); Sidebotham (1994b); Sidebotham (1997b); Bagnall and Sheridan (1994a); Bagnall and Sheridan (1994b); Wendrich and Van Neer (1994); Van Neer and Sidebotham (2002); Mulvin and Sidebotham (2004); Jørgensen (2006).

56. Bagnall and Sheridan (1994a): 159.

57. Sidebotham (1994a): 142–143; Bagnall and Sheridan (1994a): 159–163.

58. Sidebotham (1994a): 156–158; Butcher (2003): 409; Parker (2006a): 558–562; intimated

by Kaegi (1992): 59–60, 79, 87; Török (2005): 84 for St. Antony in an abandoned fort on the edge of the desert; Hirschfeld (1992): 18, 47–54, 215 for Christian reuse of abandoned forts in Judaea.

59. Shahîd (1984): 499–510; Shahîd (1989): 477–479, 506–507.
60. Bagnall and Sheridan (1994a): 164–166.
61. Bagnall and Sheridan (1994a): 163–164.
62. Sidebotham (1994a): 141 and 141 (fig. 6).
63. Jørgensen (2006).
64. Kamil (1990): 78; Mayerson (1976); Pietersma and Comstock (1987).
65. Bagnall and Sheridan (1994b): 110–111.
66. Sidebotham (1994a): 144; Sidebotham (1993).
67. Bagnall and Sheridan (1994b): 114–115.
68. Sidebotham (1993): 6; Bagnall and Sheridan (1994b): 112–113.
69. Bagnall and Sheridan (1994b): 112.
70. Sidebotham (1986): 41 and notes 81–82; Mayerson (1993) = Mayerson (1994a); Comes (1966); Desanges (1969); Warmington (1974): 139–140; Schneider (2004): especially 15–35.
71. Couyat (1910a): 527, 531–532 (mislocated at Abu Sha'ar al-Qibli); Ball (1942): 183–185; Meredith (1958): 4 (fig. 1), 9 (fig. 4) and map sheet; Sidebotham (1991b): 19; Murray (1925): 142; Fraser (1972a): 177–178 and note 348/354; Cohen (2006): 339–341; Mueller (2006b): 152; Kortenbeutel (1931): 23–24; Desanges (1978): 268; Burstein (2008a): 142 "about seventy miles south of the entrance to the Gulf of Suez."
72. Bernand (1972b): 41–44 (no. 9).
73. Couyat (1910a): 527–528, 532; Cuvigny (2003c): 24–27; Whitcomb (1996); Peacock (1993); Bülow-Jacobsen et al. (1994); Cuvigny (2003c): 24–27; Cohen (2006): 332–338; Desanges (1978): 268–270.
74. Desanges (1978): 269–270; Peacock (1993); Cuvigny (2005b) for Myos Hormos and/or the Myos Hormos road: 11–27 (no. 1), 28–29 (no. 2), 29–30 (no. 3), 77–85 (no. 41), 85–86 (no. 42), 86 (no. 43), 86–88 (no. 44), 89 (no. 46), 89–95 (no. 47), 97 (no. 50), 98–101 (no. 51), 102–103 (no. 53), 104–105 (no. 56), 105 (no. 57), 110–111 (no. 61), 111–112 (no. 62), 132–133 (no. 84), 135–154 (no. 87); Peacock and Blue (2006c).
75. Tait (1930): 110–125 (nos. 220–304) plus four ostraka in the Bodleian Library and O. Brüss. 7; Fuks (1951); Ruffing (1993); Cuvigny (2003a): 274–275.
76. Cuvigny (2003a).
77. Whitcomb and Johnson (1979); Whitcomb and Johnson (1981); Whitcomb and Johnson (1981–1982); Whitcomb and Johnson (1982a); Whitcomb and Johnson (1982b); Vogelsang-Eastwood (1989); Whitcomb (1996); Whitcomb (1999); Meyer (1992); Hiebert (1991); Peacock et al. (1999; 2000; 2001b; 2002; 2003); Peacock and Blue (2006c); Alston (2002): 341.
78. Contra Brun (2003b): 188–191; earlier excavations recovered a worn coin of Ptolemy III; Tomber (2008): 60.
79. Peacock and Blue (2006b): 2; Whitcomb (1996): 756 and note 35.
80. Blue and Peacock (2006): 70–73; Peacock and Blue (2006a): 175; Tomber (2008): 60; Peña (2007): 170–174, 181–192, 254 for other examples.
81. Whitcomb (1979b): 43; Blue (2006a): 53.

82. Peacock and Blue (2006b): 4, 6; cf. Guo (2004).

83. Van der Venn (2003): 209; Van der Venn (2004).

84. Cappers (1998a): 305–306; Cappers (1999a): 56; Zohary and Hopf (2000): 91; rice was also cultivated in the Po Valley.

85. Johnson and Whitcomb (1979): 86j, 87 (pl. 27j); Johnson (1982): 258 (pl. 610), 263–264; Whitcomb (1996): 749 and note 11; Salomon (1991); Salomon (1993): 593.

86. Tomber (2005d): 46–47 = Tomber (2007a).

87. Whitcomb (1996): 749; Hammond (1979); Toll (1994); Thomas (2006a): 153.

88. Fournet (2003): 428 and note 5.

89. Hayes (1995): 38; Hayes (1996): 150.

90. Peacock (2006a): 14–15.

91. Le Quesne (2004): 145 and note 3; Le Quesne (2007): 48, 50, 165–168; Weigall (1913): 81; Murray (1925): 142; Desanges (1978): 270.

92. Personal communication from Michael Jones (Cairo).

93. Brocchi (1841): 125.

94. Whitcomb (1979a): 108; Carswell (1982); Bridgman et al. (2006); Phillips et al. (2006).

95. Le Quesne (2004): 152–153; Le Quesne (2007).

96. Klunzinger (1878): 318–327; Brocchi (1841): 122.

97. Couyat (1910a): 528, 538 identified "Chouni," near Safaga, with Nechesia; Murray (1925): 142–143; Seeger (2001); Seeger and Sidebotham (2005).

98. Cohen (2006): 338–339.

99. Seeger (2001); Seeger and Sidebotham (2005); Sidebotham et al. (2008): 166, 167 (fig. 7.15).

100. Sidebotham (1997a): 388–390; Sidebotham (1999c): 364–368.

101. Seeger (2001): 81 and 87 (fig. 11); Seeger and Sidebotham (2005).

102. Bagnall et al. (1996).

103. Seeger and Sidebotham (2005): 20; unpublished report by J. A. Harrell.

104. Sethe (1904): URK II: 101.13–102.8; Roeder (1959): 125–126.

105. Crowfoot (1911): 531–534; Desanges (1978): 272–275.

106. Crowfoot (1911): 529–534; Kortenbeutel (1931): 26–27; Desanges (1978): 250–251, 272–273; Hinkel (1992): 313–315; Burstein (1996): 800 and note 6; Insoll (2003): 91; Mueller (2006a); Peacock et al. (2007b): 136–137; Burstein (2008a): 142–143.

107. Seeger et al. (2006).

108. Munro-Hay (1982): 116; Phillips (2003): 437 citing Procopius, *History of the Wars* 1.19.22, for a twelve-day journey and Wilson (1994): 28 (citing Nonnosos section 2b) for a fifteen-day journey; Phillipson (2009): for Axum as an emporium.

109. Wolska-Conus (1968): 358–359, 364–369; Wolska-Conus (1973): 346–351.

110. Billerbeck (2006): 56–57.

111. Paribeni (1907); Munro-Hay (1982): 107 for earlier work; Kirwan (1972); Desanges (1978): 276–278; Ruffing (2002): 369 and note 50; Peacock et al. (2007a): 12–17.

112. Geresus et al. (2005); Peacock and Blue (2007); Peacock et al. (2007a): 2–4, 7–9, 31–32, 37, 57–64, 79–84, 125–134.

113. Habtemichael et al. (2004); Geresus et al. (2005); Peacock and Blue (2007); Peacock et al. (2007a): 4–5, 10–12, 58, 85–86, 95–96, 103–104, 112, 125–134.

114. Munro-Hay (1982); Munro-Hay (1993): 614–621; Munro-Hay (1996); Raunig (2004): 87–91 (for bibliography); Manzo (2005); Peacock and Blue (2007); cf. Seland (2010): 34–39.

115. Hahn (2000): 285–286; Tomber (2005d): 43 and 45; Tomber (2008): 163; Sidebotham (2007a): 209 (no. 114), 210 (pl. 8–14): for Axumite coin at Berenike; Tomber (2007a): for Axumite sherds at Berenike; Whitcomb (1994): 16–18 for Axumite coins from Aila; Munro-Hay (1991): 180–195 for Axumite coinage.

116. Munro-Hay (1996); Tomber (2005d): 43, 45–47; Hahn (2000): 285, 287–288 and note 25; Munro-Hay (1989).

117. *Martyrium Sancti Arethae* (27, 28, 29): see Shahîd (1971): 212–214; Cosmas Indicopleustes, *Christian Topography* 2.56 also records this [cf. Wolska-Conus (1968): 368–369)]; cf. Vasiliev (1950): 294–295; Rubin (1989); Eide et al. (1998): 1185–1188 (no. 327); Kobishchanov (1979): 91–108 for Axumite–South Arabian Wars in 517–537 c.e.; Kobishchanov (1979): 99–103 for the 524/525 campaign; Fauvelle-Aymar (2009): 135 for dates.

118. McCrindle (1897): vi–vii with notes; Kobishchanov (1979): 78–79; Munro-Hay (1982): 116–117.

119. Phillips et al. (2004): 239–250; Villeneuve et al. (2004a): 419–429; Villeneuve et al. (2004b): 143–190; cf. Villeneuve (2005–2006): 290–296.

120. Villeneuve (2005–2006): 289–290.

121. Schmid (2007): 65 (no. 6).

122. Kobishchanov (1979): 78.

123. Chittick (1976): 123–124 for Damo; Chittick (1980a): 364 for Heïs and Damo; Desanges et al. (1993); Rutten (2007): 12, 13 (fig. 5), 14;. Chami (1999) for Mediterranean beads in Tanzania.

124. Casson (1989): 130–135, 138–139; Chittick (1976): 120, 123, 133. Chittick (1980a): 364–365 for Ras Hafun.

125. Chittick (1980a): 364–365; Casson, (1989): 132 for bibliography; Smith and Wright (1988); cf. Seland (2010): 40.

126. Smith and Wright (1988).

127. Rutten (2007): 8, 18, 19, 20.

128. Beeston (2005): 58, 62 (note 11).

129. Sedov (1992); Sedov (1996); Sedov (1997); Sedov (2007); Mouton et al. (2006); Mouton et al. (2008); Salles and Sedov 2010; cf. Seland (2010): 26–29.

130. Davidde (1997a): 354–355; Davidde (1997b): 86–87; Davidde (1998): 8; Davidde et al. (2004).

131. Sedov (2005): 162–165 for temple and 165, 166 (fig. 77), 169–171 for synagogue; synagogue: Bowersock (1993) = Bowersock (1994); Sedov (2007): 74, 88 (fig. 4.15), 92, 99 (fig. 4.24), 103 for temple and synagogue.

132. Ballet (1998): 47–50; Sedov (2007): especially 77–78 for Mediterranean amphoras at Qana'; Davidde et al. (2004); Rutten (2007): 12, 13 (fig. 5), 14, 18, 20: Roman fine wares.

133. Sedov (2007): 78; Salles and Sedov (2010): 201, 205, 525 (pl. 97).

134. Davidde et al. (2004); Sedov (2007).

135. Sedov (1996); Mango (1996): 154–155.

136. Avanzini (2002); Avanzini and Sedov (2005): 11–17; Avanzini (2007); Avanzini (2008); cf. Seland (2010): 29–31.

137. Sedov (2005): 171–184 for Sumhuram; Avanzini (2007): 25.

138. Avanzini (2007): 23, 25–26.

139. Rutten (2007): 12, 13 (fig. 5), 14, 18, 20.

140. Avanzini (2007): 27, 28 (fig. 4).

141. Raschke (1978): 645 and 853 (note 839); Shinnie (1960); Doe (1992): 41–112; Naumkin and Sedov (1993); Weeks et al. (2002); Cohen (2006): 325–326; Tomber (2008): 108–109; Beyhl (1998); cf. Seland (2010): 44–46.

142. Dridi (2002); Dridi and Gorea (2003); Lévêque (2002); Robin and Gorea (2002); Villeneuve (2002); Villeneuve (2003); Strauch and Bukharin (2004).

143. Shinnie (1960); Doe (1992); Naumkin and Sedov (1993) = Naumkin and Sedov (1995); Weeks et al. (2002).

144. Scarborough (1982): 138–141; Groom (2005): 110.

145. Wolska-Conus (1968): 502–505; McCrindle (1897): 119; Müller (2001) for literary sources on Socotra.

146. Bengtson (1955): 155–156.

147. Margabandhu (1965).

148. Sidebotham (1986): 32–33; Mango (1996): 156–157; Faller (2000): 135–188; Ehlers (1985); Pigulewskaja (1969): 141–149 for ports on the west coast of India in late Roman/Byzantine times.

149. Casson (1989): 14–17 and 23–33.

150. Ray (1986): 57; Rajan (1996): 99–100: on sea-level variations from 36,000 years B.P.

151. Narayana and Priju (2006).

152. Personal observations of Sidebotham.

153. Personal observations of Sidebotham.

154. Gurukkal and Whittaker (2001); Shajan et al. (2004); Selvakumar et al. (2005); Tomber (2005b); Shajan et al. (2005); Cherian et al. (2007): 6–7; personal communication; personal observations of Sidebotham. Contra Cherian et al. (2007): 7, there are no Nabataean sherds from the excavations (personal communication R. S. Tomber).

155. Cherian et al. (2007): 7; Personal observations of Sidebotham.

156. Cherian et al. (2007): 6.

157. Cherian et al. (2007) 5–6; personal communication about wood species.

158. Personal communication from V. Selvakumar; paper presented at Ravenna in July 2007 by Cherian and Shajan; Cherian et al. (2007): 5 and fig. 3 for wharf.

159. Personal communication from Shajan, excavation codirector.

160. Sidebotham (1986): 23–24; Hart and Heifetz (1999): 195–196 (poem no. 343 lines 1–4); *Ahananuri* (149, 7–11) in Suresh (2007): 2.

161. Francis (2002): 156 (Temple of Agastya?, a local deity); Metzler (1989); Ray (1994): 66; Ruffing (2002): 371 and note 62; Bianchetti (2002): 289 and note 38; Ruffing (2002): 371 and note 62; Tomber (2008): 30, 148.

162. Ray (1986): 193; Ray (1988); Casson (1989): 24 and note 22 with bibliography; Thosar (1991): for *Yavanas* elsewhere in India; Zvelebil (1973): 34–35 and notes 1–2; Tomber (2008): 26–29.

163. *Silappadhikaram* (5–10) in Puskás (1987): 153–154 and Suresh (2007): 3.

164. Metzler (1989): 197–200.

165. Metzler (1989); Ray (1994): 66; Ruffing (2002): 371 and note 62; Francis (2002): 156 (Temple of Agastya?, a local deity); Tomber (2008): 30, 148.

166. Casson (1989): 47, 89 and 228–229; Stevenson (1991): 150.

167. Tomber (2008): 136–137; Will (2004b): 326–329 for earliest amphoras dated second century b.c.e.

168. Wheeler et al. (1946): 17–125; Will (1996b); Slane (1996); Will (2004b); Tomber (2004a): 401; Tomber (2005c): 229–230; Suresh (2004): 99–111; Rutten (2007): 13 (and fig. 5), 14, 16 (copies of *sigillata* shapes), 20; Tomber (2008): 139, 149.

169. Tomber (2008): 137.

170. Begley et al. (1996); Begley et al. (2004); Gupta (1995–1996) for overview of stratigraphic interpretations of Wheeler et al. and the Casals; Tchernia (1998): 447–456 and 458–463; Ray (1993): 486 and 489.

171. Slane (1996); Tomber (2008): 13, 14, 43, 45, 115–116, 134, 136, 150, 151, 161 (table 2), 139, 146 (in Sri Lanka); Rutten (2007): 20.

172. Suresh (2004): 30–31, 38, 82 (note 8), 136 (and note 19), 142, 153–154.

173. Will (1996b): 320, 348–349 (no. 78); Will (2004b): 328; Tchernia (1986): 152–153.

174. Francis (2000): 222–223, 225 and Francis (2007) for beads; Harrell (1998): 144 and Harrell (1999): 114 for sapphires; Wendrich et al. (2003): 62 = Wendrich et al. (2006): 43.

175. Wolska-Conus (1973): 314–357.

176. De Romanis (1988); Rosenberger (1996); Bopearachchi (1996); Faller (2000): 135–188 for late antique authors on Taprobane.

177. Meredith (1953a); Miller (1969): 15–16; De Romanis (1996a): 211–212; De Romanis (1997b): 201–206; Faller (2000): 60–64, 237–239 (B.5–B.8); cf. now Abeydeera (2009) for possible epigraphic evidence from Sri Lanka.

178. Sidebotham (1986): 32–33 and note 57; De Romanis (1996a): 247–250.

179. Sidebotham (1986): 32–33 and notes; Stevenson (1991): 158.

180. Codrington (1924): 31–48 and pl. II nos. 26 to about 43; Dihle (1978): 571–573; Raschke (1978); Bopearachchi (1996): 67–72. Bopearachchi (1992): 112–117 for Sinhalese imitations of late Roman bronze coins; Tomber (2008): 145.

181. Begley (1967); Silva (1985); Carswell (1991): 198.

182. Carswell (1991): 200.

183. Weisshaar and Wijeyapala (2000); Hannibal-Deraniyagala (2000); Schenk (2000); for urbanization of the island: Coningham and Allchin (1995).

184. Casson (1989): 285.

185. Casson (1989): 289.

186. Casson (1989): 286.

10. MERCHANT SHIPS

1. Houston (1988); Parker (1992): 26; Pomey and Tchernia (1980/1981); Kingsley (2009a).

2. Casson (1971): 214–216; Parker (1992): 49–50, 58, 59, 64, 102–103, 117, 133, 141–142, 143, 154–155, 156, 163, 165–166, 167, 168–169, 178–179, 188, 193, 197, 203–204, 217, 231–233, 236–238, 245–250, 253, 255–256, 262–266, 279–281, 299–301, 303, 308–309, 316–317, 329–330, 332–334, 340, 342–343, 345, 361, 370, 372–375, 396, 408, 412–416, 426, 429–430, 434–435, 443–444, 454–455.

3. Casson (1971): 186–189; Casson (1974): 158–159; Casson (1994): 123–124.

4. Gibbins (2001): 273; Kingsley (2009b).

5. Also argued by Casson (1989): 35, 291.

6. Peppard (2009): dated June 5, 97 C.E.

7. Francis (2007): 254–255; Lankton (2003): 70–72 and 79–81;

8. Francis (2000): 222.

9. Loewe (1971); Thorley (1971): 71–80; Raschke (1978): 587–588; Al-As'ad et al. (1995); Stauffer (1995); Stauffer (1996); Lyovushkina (1995/96).

10. Francis (2000): 223; or from the Gulf of Mannar between India and Sri Lanka..

11. Sidebotham (1986): 71.

12. Sidebotham (1986): 182–186.

13. Casson (1971): 201–213; Casson (1991): 27–28, 173–175; Casson (1994): 101–126, 146.

14. Sidebotham and Wendrich (2001–2002): 26; Sidebotham (2007b): 36–37.

15. Casson (1971): 195, 209–210, 214–215 (table); Casson (1994): 34 (fig. 29), 35, 106, 120 (fig. 91), 121, 139 (fig. 105), 140; Sidebotham (2008a): 307.

16. Greene (1986): 20–23; Casson (1994).

17. Greene (1986): 23; Casson (1994).

18. Bass (1982): 311–312.

19. Casson (1989): 34–35.

20. Casson (1989): 35; Whitewright (2007a): 83–84.

21. Sidebotham and Zych (2010): 19–21.

22. Sidebotham and Zych (2010): 20 (figs. 44–45), 21 and figs. 49–50.

23. Deloche (1996); McGrail (1996); Kentley (1996); Chittick (1976): 127 and note 10 for sewn boats in Somalia; for synopsis of shipping in ancient India see Srinivas (1998); Bag (1988); Chauhan (1998); Rajan (1998); Venkatesan (1998).

24. McGrail (1996): 228.

25. Blue (2002): 149; Macklin (2006): 158.

26. Chittick (1976): 127; Chittick (1980b); Varadarajan (2005); Deloche (1996); McGrail (1996); Manguin (1996) for stitched planked hulled vessels in Southeast Asia; Kentley (1999); Swamy (1999): 125 (5a), 137, 139–140 (5a), 141.

27. Munro-Hay (1982): 117.

28. Parker (1992): 138 (no. 293), 457–458 (nos. 1248–1249).

29. Casson, (1989): 117–118, 203–204, 229–230.

30. Deloche (1996): 199–224; Ray (1986): 42–43, 120 (fig. 4.2), 150, 155–156 for more on Sātavāhana coins; De Romanis (2006): 73–74 and notes for images of ships on Indian coins.

31. Haldane (1996).

32. Wainwright (1946).

33. Verri (1994); Peña (2007): 71–82 for amphoras from shipwrecks.

34. Ghisotti (1996); Stoll et al. (1999): 188–189.

35. Pedersen (2000).

36. Reported to Sidebotham by the Egyptian dive master at the Lahami Beach Resort Hotel in August 2007.

37. Sidebotham (1998b): 109 on these dumps; Sidebotham (1999b): 46–57; Sidebotham (2000b): 100–107 and Sidebotham (2007b): 44–54. There was Ptolemaic material beneath and intrusive late Roman material from these dumps.

38. See chapter 2 note 52.

39. Personal communication from R. S. Bagnall; Sidebotham and Zych (2010): 11.

40. Bagnall et al. (2000): 21–24; Bagnall et al. (2005): 60–61, 64–65.

41. Bagnall et al. (2005): 64 for a list; Roth (1999): 122, 201, 203; Volken (2008) for Roman army water bags.

42. Bagnall et al. (2000): 14, 15, 21–24.

43. Sidebotham and Wendrich (1998b): 91 and fig. 12; Vermeeren (2000): 341 and 342; Wild and Wild (2000): 268 (pl. 11–10); more were documented in the 2009 excavation season.

44. Wild and Wild (2000): 265, 266–269, 272; Wild and Wild (2001); Wild (2004): 61–63; Wild and Wild (2005): 13–14.

45. Whitewright (2003): 71 and 73 fig. 59; Whitewright (2007a): 81 (fig. 6:6), 83.

46. Sidebotham and Wendrich (2001–2002): 43 and fig. 45; Veldmeijer and Van Roode (2004).

47. Richardson (2002): 79.

48. Brun and Leguilloux (2003): 540 (no. 3), 541–542 (nos. 13–15), 544 (no. 3), 545 (nos. 13–14), 546 (no. 15).

49. Winterbottom (2001): 335–336 and 351 (fig. 10.19).

50. Leguilloux (2006): 80–82, 85 (figs. 56–57), 150 (Of-028, Of-029), 151 (Of-036, Of-037, Of-045, Of-054), 152 (Of-062), 209 (Planche 42).

51. Phillips (2007): 391, 394 (fig. 17.5, bottom).

52. Bagnall et al. (2005): 45–47 (no. 131).

53. Thomas and Whitewright (2001); Thomas et al. (2002); Blue (2002): 149; Earl and Glazier (2006a): 42; Blue (2006a): 59; Whittaker et al. (2006): 80 and 81; Whittaker (2006): 85; Thomas (2006b): 90; Thomas and Masser (2006): 131, 135, 137, 138, 139; Van Rengen and Thomas (2006): 147, 149, 153, 154; Whitewright (2007a): 83–84; Whitewright (2007b).

54. Whitewright (2003): 71 and 73 fig. 59; Whitewright (2007a): 81 (fig. 6:6), 83; Whitewright (2007b): 285–286, 289–290.

55. Peacock et al. (2007b): 59.

56. Hogarth (1896); Raschke (1978): 649 and 893 (note 961) for bibliography until the late 1970s; Bernand (1984a): 199–208 (no. 67) for bibliography, translation, commentary (= *OGIS* 674 = *IGRR* I.1183); Sidebotham (1986): 35, 53, 67, 80–81; Young (2001): 48–50; Burkhalter-Arce (2002); Cuvigny (2003a): 273–274.

57. Cuvigny (2005b): 77, 81 and 94 (no. 41).

58. Cuvigny (2005b): 77, 81 and 94 (no. 41).

59. Sayed (1983): 29–30; Vandersleyen (1996): 107–115; Bard et al. (2007); Kitchen (2005): 11.

60. Fattovich (2005); Fattovich and Bard (2006); Bard et al. (2007); Bard and Fattovich (2007).

61. Abd el-Raziq et al. (2002): 112; Abd el-Raziq et al. (2006): 5–6.

62. Tuck (1997): 11 and notes.

63. Avanzini (2007): 27, 28 (fig. 4).

64. Schmidt-Colinet (1995): 81 (Abb. 126).

65. Dridi (2002): 584–585, figs. 12–13.

66. Tchernia (1998): 455–457 and 463 (fig. 7); Mahadevan (2003): 46, 154 (fig. 4.3), 155–156; Sridhar (2005): 67–70, 72 (fig. 7), 73, 122 (nos. 23–24), 125 (top); Coningham et al. (2006): 298 (sf. 10548) for ship graffito on a sherd from Anuradhapura, Sri Lanka.

67. Sidebotham (1996a): 53; Sidebotham (1996d).

68. Casson (1989): 34–35; Bianchetti (2002): 283 and note 13.

69. Casson (1989): 34.

70. Sidebotham (1990); Maxfield (2001c): 54 (fig. 255) and 55.

71. Winkler (1938): 22, 25, 27, 30, 35–39, pl. IX (no. 2), pl. XII (no. 1), pl. XIII (no. 3), pl. XIV (nos. 1–2), pl. XV (no. 1), pl. XIX (no. 3), pl. XXII (nos. 1–2), pl. XXIII (nos. 1–2), pls. XXXIII–XLI; Rohl (2000): 5–9, 177–186 and passim; Midant-Reynes (2000): 231; Fuchs (1989); Redford and Redford (1989): 10–11 (fig. 5), 10–11 (fig. 6), 14–15 (figs. 13–14), 19–20 (figs. 26–27), 26 (fig. 40), 26–27 (figs. 41–42), 26, 28 (fig. 43), 28–29 (figs. 44–45), 35–36 (figs. 63–64), 36–37 (figs. 65–66), 37–38 (fig. 69); Červíček (1974): 98–138 (in general), Abb. 19, Abb. 26(?), Abb. 41–42, Abb. 52–55, Abb. 66, Abb. 71–76, Abb. 80–84, Abb. 88 (?), Abb. 93–94, Abb. 118(?), Abb. 120–121, Abb. 143, Abb. 147(?), Abb. 155, Abb. 225(?), Abb. 227, Abb. 241, Abb. 244, Abb. 263–265, Abb. 267–270, Abb. 274–279, Abb. 286, Abb. 289–290, Abb. 294 (?), Abb. 302–304, Abb. 308–311, Abb. 322(?), Abb. 335, Abb. 343–344, Abb. 345(?), Abb. 359–361, Abb. 363–364, Abb. 381, Abb. 383, Abb. 395, Abb. 404, Abb. 414, Abb. 418, Abb. 420, Abb. 428, Abb. 461–464, , Abb. 472, Abb. 474, Abb. 483(?), Abb. 487–488(?), Abb. 494, Abb. 502, Abb. 506–508, Tafel 1 (nos. 1–2), Tafel 2 (no. 3), Tafel 6 (no. 12), Tafel 7 (no. 14), Tafel 14 (no. 27); Rohl (2000): 5–9, 177–186; Wengrow (2006): 112–114; Van Rengen et al. (2006): 17–18, 22, 23.

72. *Periplus* 32; Casson (1989): 170–173; Bonacossi (2002): 48–49.

73. Avanzini (2007): 27, 28 (fig. 4).

74. Schmidt-Colinet (1995): 81 (Abb. 126).

75. Dridi (2002): 584–585, figs. 12–13.

76. Tchernia (1998): 455–457 and 463 (fig. 7); Mahadevan (2003): 46, 154 (fig. 4.3), 155–156; Sridhar (2005): 67–70, 72 (fig. 7), 73, 122 (nos. 23–24), 125 (top); Coningham et al. (2006): 298 (sf. 10548) for ship graffito on a sherd from Anuradhapura, Sri Lanka.

77. Sidebotham (2000b): 134–144; Sidebotham (2007b): 82–83; Abraham (2007): 290.

78. Vermeeren (1999b): 319; Vermeeren (2000): 340–341.

79. Groom (1995): 189.

80. Hourani (1995): 89–90.

81. Hourani: (1995) 90, 92–93; Worrall (2009): for a Tang-dynasty/Abbasid-era (ninth century) shipwreck using the sewn-plank tradition excavated near Belitung, Indonesia.

82. Blue (2002): 149.

83. Ward and Zazzaro (2007): 135, 139, 142–143, 145.

84. Ward and Zazzaro (2007): 135–150.

85. Personal communication from A. M. Hense. The anchor in the Trench 10 wall had a cross section of 7 cm × 14 cm. There was another fragment in trench BE01–50.014 with a cross section of 55 cm × 65 cm.

86. Peacock et al. (2007b): 59; J. A. Harrell, personal communication; Sidebotham and Zych (2010): 12–13 and fig. 13.

87. Davidde et al. (2004); Sedov (2007).

11. COMMERCIAL NETWORKS AND TRADE COSTS

1. Rostovtzeff (1979); Finley (1985); Jones (1974); Garnsey et al. (1983); Casson (1984a); Greene (1986); Fulford (1987); Garnsey and Saller (1987); Duncan-Jones (1982); Duncan-Jones (1990); Duncan-Jones (1994); Parkins and Smith (1998).

2. Raschke (1978) with extensive bibliography; Sidebotham (1986); Young (2001); Peacock and Williams (2007).

3. Garnsey (1983); Casson (1984b); Garnsey and Saller (1987): 83–103; Meijer and van Nijf (1992): 98–102.

4. Greene (1986): 17–35.

5. Millar (1967): 169–181 for Africa; Frere (1987): 245–247, 272–273, Washer (1998): 123–125 and Todd (1999): 166–170 for Britain.

6. Duncan-Jones (1982): 259–287.

7. Best times May to September, but March to November still possible: Casson (1971): 270–273; Casson (1994): 123; Roth (1999): 190–191.

8. Pritchard (1969): 298–300; cf. Graf (1990).

9. Bowersock (1983): 76–89.

10. Healy (1989): the Nabataeans were Arabs; Graf (1990); MacDonald (1991): Nabataeans were not a Bedouin state.

11. Hammond (1973); Negev (1977); Negev (1986); Taylor (2002); Markoe (2003b).

12. Sidebotham (1996c); Gawlikowski (1997); Markoe (2003b).

13. Groom (1981): 165–213; Macdonald (1994); Saud et al. (1996); Goren (2000); Salles (1988); De Maigret (1997); Jasmin (2005); De Maigret (2004); Beeston (2005): 53, 54 (Fig. 2), 59; Crone (1987): 3–50; Kitchen (2001).

14. Gatier and Salles (1988b); Macdonald (1994): 134 and note 18; Wiesehöfer (1998): 16, 18.

15. References to Nabataean "piracy" indicate a maritime presence in the Red Sea: Tarn (1929): 13, 15–16, 21, 22; *OGIS* 132 (of 130 B.C.E.); Diodorus Siculus 3.43.4–5; Strabo, *Geography* 16.4.18.

16. Sartre (1981); Bowersock (1983): 90–99; Gatier and Salles (1988b).

17. al-Ansary (1982): 22, 63 (nos. 2–6); al-Kabawi et al. (1989): 43, 47–48; Mildenberg (1995); Mildenberg (1996); Groom (1981): 165–188; MacDonald (1994); Schmid (2007): 62–65; Hashim (2007): 102–122 for Nabataean pottery from Saudi Arabia.

18. MacDonald (1994); Schmid (2007): 65 (in Marib, Qana', and Khor Rori); Gerlach (2005): 39, fig. 8 for bilingual Sabaean-Nabataean inscription. Date in caption of seventh to sixth century B.C.E. is incorrect.

19. MacDonald (1994): 134; Sartre (2005): 268; Schmid (2007): 64 (Failaka/Ikaros, Kuwait).

20. Clermont-Ganneau (1919); Winkler (1938): 4 (site no. 1), 4 (site no. 6), 5 (site no. 12D),

7 (site no. 24B), 7 (site no. 24N), 10; Tregenza and Walker (1949); Littmann and Meredith (1953); Littmann and Meredith (1954a); Jomier (1954); Hammond (1979); Briquel-Chatonnet and Nehmé (1998); Reddé and Brun (2003): 80; Cuvigny (2003a): 276; Fournet (2003): 428; Zayadine (1990): 151–153; Ruffing (2002): 373–374; Sartre (2005): 268; Fiema and Jones (1990); Schmid (2007): 66 for Nabataean sherds at Myos Hormos and Berenike.

21. Toll (1994).

22. Schmid (2007): 66 for Nabataean sherds at Myos Hormos and Berenike.

23. Roche (1996): 75 (no. 1: Gaza), 75–77 (nos. 2–3: Sidon), 77 (no. 4: Antioch), 77 (no. 5: Cyprus), 78 (nos. 6–7: Rhodes), 78–80 (no. 8: Cos), 80–83 (no. 9: Miletus), 83 (no. 10: Priene), 83–85 (no. 11: Delos), 85 (no. 12: Rhene Island), 85–86 (no. 13: Tinos), 86 (no. 14: Athens, references to Nabataean rhetoricians); Roller (1998): 225, 226–228, 234; cf. Graf and Sidebotham (2003): 71; Schmid (2007): 71–73, 74.

24. Renan (1873): 380; Dubois (1907): 99–101, 161–162, 268; Meshorer (1975): 61; Ostrow (1977): 210, 226 (note 31); De Romanis (1993): 64–65 (Nabataean god Dusares at Puteoli); Roche (1996): 86–89 (nos. 15–17: Puteoli); Schmid (2007): 74–75.

25. Roche (1996): 89–95 (nos. 18–22: Rome); Bowersock (1997); Noy (2000): 239–240; Graf and Sidebotham (2003): 71; Schmid (2007): 74–75.

26. Roche (1996): 95 (no. 23: Nabataean coin); Schmid (2007): 72–73.

27. Schmid (2007): 66; Cherian et al. (2007): 7 is not Nabataean (personal communication from R. S. Tomber).

28. Teixidor (1973); Zayadine (1996).

29. Stoneman (1992) 20; Appian, *Civil Wars* 5.1.9.

30. Millar (1998): 121, 123, 130–131, 137.

31. Matthews (1984); Stoneman (1992): 57–59; Healy (1996): 34 and note 5.

32. Butcher (2003): 58–60; de Blois (1975); Stoneman (1992); Gawlikowski (1958); Potter (1996); Dignas and Winter (2007): 155–164.

33. Palmyrenes in Egypt: Clermont-Ganneau (1903); Schwartz (1953); Graf (1989); Stoneman (1992): 158–161 and 178–179; Butcher (2003): 58–60.

34. Colledge (1976): 231–232.

35. Colledge (1976): 231; Noy (2000): 177–179, 240, 242–245 for Palmyrenes in Rome.

36. Bin Seray (1996): 20 and note 40; Butcher (2003): 185.

37. Masson (1967).

38. Cussini (1998).

39. Stoneman (1992): 45.

40. Graf (1989): 147–148; Jamme (1963): 44–45 (no. 931); Steiner (2004): 277 note 3.

41. Schwartz (1953); Bingen (1984); Speidel (1984).

42. Bernand (1984a) 262–263 (no. 103), 238–241 (no. 85) [= *IGRR* I.1169 = *OGIS* 639]; Reinach (1911b): 58, 79 = Hogarth (1896): 33–34 (no. 55) and Pl. XXVIII, no. 6 [Palmyrene archer], 189–190 (no. 62) merchant from Aden, 193–195 (no. 65) merchant from Aden; Palmyrene grave stelai at Koptos: Reinach (1913): 46–50; Dijkstra and Verhoogt (1999): 215–216; Ballet et al. (2000): 134–136 (and figs. 43–44, cat. 100–104).

43. Sidebotham and Wendrich (1998a): 93–94; Verhoogt (1998): 193–196; Dijkstra and Verhoogt (1999).

44. Matthews (1984): 164–168; Gawlikowski (1988); Bin Seray (1996); Potts (1997); Ruffing (2002): 363–364.

45. Gawlikowski (1988): 167; Bin Seray (1996); Seyhrig (1936); Potts (1997); Gawlikowski (1994); Colombo (1995); Ruffing (2002): 363 and notes.

46. Seyhrig (1936); Browning (1979), Teixidor (1984): especially 31–42; Schmidt-Colinet (1995); *Les Annales Archéologiques Arabes Syriennes* 42 (1996). Palmyrene ships in Persian Gulf: Butcher, (2003): 185; Drexhage (1982); Mattingly (1995); Al-As'ad (1996); Will (1996a); Gawlikowski (1996); Frézouls (1996); Zuhdi (1996); Bin Seray (1996); Healy (1996); Butcher (2003): 184–186; Potts (2009): 41–42.

47. Ruffing (2002): 363 and note 15, 365 and note 29.

48. Stauffer (1995); Stauffer (1996); Butcher (2003): 185 (Fig. 72), 186 (and note on 451), 301.

49. Butcher (2003): 184–186; Markoe (2003b).

50. Butcher (2003): 156–157.

51. Butcher (2003): 156–157; Decker (2009): 172–173.

52. Duncan-Jones (1982): 1–2, 366–369 contra Butcher (2003): 183–184.

53. Jones (1964): 841–842; Duncan-Jones (1982): 366–369; Horden and Purcell (2000): 151; Temin (2001): 176, 188–189; Yeo (1946): 230–233, 236.

54. Greene (1986): 39–43; Butcher (2003): 183–184; cf. Laurence (1999): 95–108; Paterson (2001): 373; Decker (2009): 246–257.

55. Arnaud (2007): 325.

56. Whitewright (2007a): 86.

57. Arnaud (2007): 334.

58. Adams (2007): 1–13, 19–20.

59. Haenchen (1971): 698.

60. Butcher (2003): 132.

61. Salway (2004): 46; Casson (1971): 281–296 and Duncan-Jones (1990): 7–29 on distances, lengths of voyages, and speeds of vessels in the Mediterranean; Whitewright (2007a): 84; Arnaud (2007) for sailing speeds in the Mediterranean.

62. Salway (2004): 46.

63. Casson (1971): 281–296 and Duncan-Jones (1990): 7–29; Whitewright (2007a): 84; Arnaud (2007).

64. Casson (1971): 214–216; Parker (1992): 49–50, 58, 59, 64, 102–103, 117, 133, 141–142, 143, 154–155, 156, 163, 165–166, 167, 168–169, 178–179, 188, 193, 197, 203–204, 217, 231–233, 236–238, 245–250, 253, 255–256, 262–266, 279–281, 299–301, 303, 308–309, 316–317, 329–330, 332–334, 340, 342–343, 345, 361, 370, 372–375, 396, 408, 412–416, 426, 429–430, 434–435, 443–444, 454–455.

65. Meijer and Nijf (1992): 152–158; Laurence (1998): 134.

66. Laurence (1998): 134.

67. Paterson (2001): 370, 373.

68. *P. Lond.* 2.328 = Kenyon (1898): 74–76; Adams (2007): 129 (and note 32), 147 (and note 43), 151 (and note 61), 202 (and note 22), 215 (and note 80), 234 (and note 49).

69. Reddé and Brun (2003): 100 for distance; Bülow-Jacobsen (2003b): 423 for cost.

70. Cuvigny (1996a): 140–141.

71. Butcher (2003): 166.

72. Graser (1940a); Graser (1940b); Crawford and Reynolds (1979); Arnaud (2007).
73. Yeo (1946): 221; Duncan-Jones (1990): 25 (in general 7–29); Casson (1974): 189; Meijer and van Nijf (1992): 136–148 for land, 149–151 for river and 152–158 for sea; Laurence (1998): 129–136; Tuck (1997): 11 and note 22.
74. Most recently Bowman and Wilson (2009).
75. Paterson (2001): 370.
76. Pucci (1983); Greene (1986): 156–167; Gill (1991); Butcher (2003): 186–187.
77. Beeston (2005): 56; Chevallier (1997): 61: 1478.5 meters = 1 Roman mile:
78. Beeston (1979): 9 and note 12, manuscript may be corrupt; al-Ghabbān (2007): especially 11 (Fig. 2) and 13–23 for a northern portion of this route.
79. Beeston (1979): 9; Beeston (2005): 56.
80. Thompson (1988) for overview of (mainly Greek) banking; Andreau (1999) for Roman banking; Capponi (2005): 166–167 for connection between banks and tax collecting in Egypt.
81. Jones (1964): 350, 868–869 and 1361–1362 (notes 107–109); Casson (1984): 45 notes rates of 22.5 to 30 percent for four- to five-month loans, 67.5 to 90.5 percent per annum, in fourth-century B.C.E. Athens; Ashburner (1976): ccix–ccxxiii.
82. Casson (2004): 98.
83. Harrauer and Sijpesteijn (1985): 73–79; Sijpesteijn (1987): 5; Thür (1987); Thür (1988); Casson (1990) = Casson (2001); De Romanis (1998); Rathbone (2000); Belfiore (2004): 235–244.
84. Dalby (2000): 86–88.
85. See note 83; Gurukkal and Whittaker (2001); Shajan et al. (2004); Shajan et al. (2005); Selvakumar et al. (2005); Cherian et al. (2007).
86. Cuvigny (2005b): 14–16.
87. Casson (1990): 205 note 29.
88. Casson (1993a): 73.
89. Houston (1988): 558; Tomber (1993): 145–146.
90. Casson (1986b): 172; Casson (1990): 205 note 29; Parker (1992): 26.
91. Parker (1992): 26; Parker (1996a); Kingsley (2009a); Wilson (2009): 219–229.
92. Parker (1992): 26.
93. Cuvigny (1996a).
94. De Romanis (2006): 62–66; Hillers and Cussini (1996): 304 (no. 2634) for the Palmyrene text; Gawlikowski (1986).
95. Casson (2004): 100.
96. Sidebotham, (1986): 86–88 and notes.
97. Hatzfeld (1919): 206–212.
98. Jones (1964): 350, 866–869.
99. Sidebotham (1986): 5–6.
100. Sidebotham (1986): 105: tax on ships using Nile ports is certain; one on merchantmen docking at Red Sea emporia is likely.
101. Koptos Tariff of 90 C.E. (*OGIS* 674 = *IGRR* I.1183) see Sidebotham (1986): 35, 53, 67, 80–81 and Young (2001): 48–50, with translation; cf. Burkhalter-Arce (2002); Cuvigny (2003f): 383–388 for prostitutes in camps along the Myos Hormos–Nile road.

102. Cf. Kaegi (1981): 133–135, 300–301 on greed and corruption among soldiers in the later Roman and early Byzantine period.

103. See synopsis in Chami (2004).

104. Toynbee (1973): 94 Calpurnius Siculus lived in either the first or third century C.E. Keene (1887): 153 and notes. Cf. the early second-century C.E. writer Juvenal (*Satires* 3.238).

12. TRADE IN ROMAN BERENIKE

1. Conrad (1981): 68–69; Duncan-Jones (1996); Scheidel (2001): 95; Scheidel (2002); Bagnall (2002); Nutton (2004): 24.

2. Verhoogt (1998): 193–196; Dijkstra and Verhoogt (1999).

3. Sidebotham (2007a): 202 (table 8–6); Sidebotham (forthcoming): no mid-third-century coins appeared from the 2001 excavations.

4. Barnes (1976): 174, 180–182; Leadbetter (2000); Leadbetter (2002).

5. Robin (1997): 53.

6. André and Filliozat (1986) for authors writing in Latin about India.

7. See chapter 2 note 52.

8. Francis (2007): 254–255; Sidebotham and Wendrich (2001–2002): 42 and fig. 43; Lankton (2003): 70–72, 79–81.

9. Francis (2000): 222.

10. Casson (1989): 235–236; Faller (2000): 88–94 on the Seres (Chinese).

11. Wheeler (1955): 172–176; Raschke (1978): 674, 675, 1048–1049 (notes 1640–1645), 1052 (note 1672); Plisson (2005): 71.

12. Parlasca (1980).

13. Leslie and Gardiner (1996): 13 (and note 28), 157, 164, 165, 170, 227; Raschke (1978): 643 and note 765; Umehara (1926); Okamura (2002) for examples of Roman glass found in China and Korea; Brill (1991/92) Chinese word for transparent glass (*boli*) may derived from Greek.

14. Hall (1985): 1–47; Ray (1999); De Romanis and Tchernia (1997); Mitchiner (1991); Wicks (1991); Hall (1991); Glover (1996); Basa (1999); Soebadio (1999); Ardika (1999); Plisson (2005): 68.

15. Abraham (2007); Sidebotham (2008b).

16. Zvelebil (1973).

17. Mahadevan (2003): 43, 49, 56 (fig. 1.21B and C), 61 (nos. 8–9), 93, 146–147 (no. 84), 163, 164 and 235.

18. Winkler (1938): 4 (site no. 1) Himyarite, 4 (site no. 6) Himyarite, 5 (site no. 8) Thamudic, 7 (Site no. 24B) Himyarite, 7 (site no. 24 I) Himyarite, 10; Beeston (2005): 55; Tomber (2004b): 353, fig. 2, from Myos Hormos = Tomber (2008): 75 (fig. 13), 78; Noy (2000) for the city of Rome; Calzini Gysens (1990) believes the graffiti from Pompeii are Safaitic, but D.F. Graf reports (personal communication) that they may be Thamudic. 2009 excavations recovered South Arabian sherds, which preserved graffiti in South Arabian letters; Tomber et al. (forthcoming).

19. Tomber (2004b): 353 (fig. 2) = Tomber (2008): 75 (fig. 13), 78 and unpublished graffito (note 18 above).

20. Dalby (2003).

21. Cappers (1998a): 311; Miller (1969): 80–83; Casson (1989): 220; Waard (1989); Parker (2008): 151–152.

22. Dalby (2000): 91.

23. Cappers (1998a): 311; Miller (1969): 80–83; Dalby (2000): 89; Hyman and Hyman (1980): 50–52; Gokhale (1987) for Barygaza.

24. Duncan-Jones (1997): 150–151, 154, 156.

25. Solomon (1995): 116.

26. Parker (2002a): 43; Parker (2008): 151.

27. Speidel (1992a): 88 (table 1), 93 (table 3); Herz (2007): 308–313.

28. Bowman et al. (1994): 135–141 (no. 184), especially line 4.

29. Mrozek (1982).

30. Jolowicz and Nicholas (1972): 394 for Aelius Marcianus; Mommsen and Krueger (1985): 407 for the *Digest of Justinian* 39.4.16; Tomber (2008): 24; Parker (2008): 149–150.

31. Groom, (1981): 155.

32. Sidebotham (1986): 23–24; Meile (1940); Zvelebil (1973); Ray (1988) = Ray (2005b); Suresh (2004): 16–17, 23–24, 138–139; Suresh (2007): 2–4; Parker (2008): 173 and note 72.

33. Thapar (1992): 12–13.

34. Cappers (2006): 113–114; Apicius, *De re coquinaria* 1.1; McGovern (2003): 309; Dalby (2000): 90.

35. Apicius, *De re coquinaria:* passim; cf. Solomon (1995); Vehling (1936); Hower and Rosenbaum (1958).

36. Parker (2002a): 45.

37. Apicius, *De re coquinaria* 1.1; McGovern (2003): 309; Dalby (2000): 90.

38. Miller (1969): 25 and 83; Nash (1968): 485–487; Richardson (1992): 194–195; Meijer and van Nijf (1992): 129; Rickman (1971) 104–106.

39. Jones (1964): 185–186; Ridley (1982): xi–xii.

40. Wolska-Conus (1973): 334–335.

41. Cappers (1998a): 312–313; Cappers (1999a): 54–56; Cappers (2006): 111–117, 164.

42. Van der Venn (2001): 199 (for Mons Claudianus); Cappers (2006): 117–118 (fig. 4.59).

43. Bianchetti (2002): 281 and note 6 for tiny amounts of peppercorns from Roman Britain (Bath), Germany (Oberaden, Straubing and Hanau) and Gaul (Biesheim-Kunheim); Cappers (2006): 118 (fig. 4.59), 119; Schwinden (1983); Knörzer (1966); Kuncan (1984); Küster (1995): 137 and 138 (Tab. 36) for peppercorns from Straubing on the Danube; Kreutz (1995): 70; Jacomet and Schibler (2001): 65–66 and fig. 12 (Biesheim-Kunheim on the Rhine); Reddé et al. (2005): 255 (Oedenburg on the Rhine).

44. Sidebotham and Wendrich (2001–2002): 30 and fig. 10; Cappers (2006): 114, 116 (fig. 4.58); Sidebotham (2007b): 73 (pl. 4–37), 74–75 and pls. 4–38 to 4–40; Tomber (2008): 76, 77 (fig. 14).

45. Sidebotham and Wendrich (2001–2002): 30 and fig. 10; Wendrich et al. (2003): 68 (table 2), 69 = Wendrich et al. (2006): 31 (table 2.2), 45–46, 49 (fig. 2.3f); Cappers (2006): 114, 116 (fig. 4.58); Sidebotham (2007b): 74.

46. Verhoogt (1998): 193–196 and 198; Sidebotham and Wendrich (1998a): 93.

47. Dijkstra and Verhoogt (1999).
48. Sidebotham (2000b): 60 and fig. 2–36.
49. Sidebotham (2000b): 66.
50. Cappers (2006): 114–116.
51. Sidebotham (2000b): 134–144; Sidebotham (2007b): 77–89; Sidebotham and Wendrich (1998a): 94–95; Sidebotham and Wendrich (2001–2002): 30–31.
52. Sidebotham and Wendrich (2001–2002): 32–34.
53. Cappers (1998a): 309; cf. Rowley-Conwy et al. (1999); Plisson (2005): 70.
54. Cappers (1999a): 56–57, 66 (fig. 2); Cappers (1996): 322 (table 19–2), 327, 330; Cappers (1998a): 289, 295 (table 15–3); 303 (table 15–6), 305–306; Cappers (1999b): 302 (table 16–1); Cappers (2000): 306; Cappers (2006): 104–105; Vergara and De Datta (1989).
55. Zohary and Hopf (2000): 91.
56. Zohary and Hopf (2000): 91.
57. Leslie and Gardiner (1996): 34, 37.
58. Cappers (1998a): 305–306; Cappers (1999a): 56–57.
59. Capers (1998a): 306; Cappers (1999a): 57; Knörzer (1966); Wendrich et al. (2003): 64 (table 2), 72 = Wendrich et al. (2006): 25 (table 2.2), 46, 48 (fig. 2.3c), 51.
60. Zohary and Hopf (2000): 91.
61. Wilkins (1995a): 2; Wilkins (1995b): 242–244; Butcher (2003): 171; Morley (2007): 47.
62. Cappers (1998a): 313–317; Cappers (1999a): 57; Wendrich et al. (2003): 67 (table 2), 70, 71 = Wendrich et al. (2006): 30 (table 2.2), 46, 47, 49 (fig. 2.3e), 50; Cappers (2006): 73–79.
63. Ray (1986): 100.
64. Ohler (1989): 90; Plisson (2005): 69.
65. Miller (1971): 16–17; Ziethen and Klingenberg (2002): 382 and note 17.
66. Wendrich et al. (2003): 71.
67. Wolska-Conus (1973): 344 (note 15[1]) and 390 (fig. 7); McCrindle (1897): 362.
68. Ray (1986): 92.
69. Chittick (1980b): 301; Blue (2002): 149.
70. Cappers (1999a): 66 (fig. 3); Cappers (2006): 76 (fig. 4.30).
71. Cappers (1999a): 58; Wendrich et al. (2003): 64 (table 2), 70; Cappers (2006): 132–133, 164.
72. Cappers (1999a): 57–58; Wendrich et al. (2003): 70; Cappers (2006): 108–109, 164 (*Phyllanthus emblica* L.).
73. Wendrich et al. (2003): 65 (table 2) = Wendrich et al. (2006): 27 (table 2.2); Philostratus, *Life of Apollonius of Tyana* 3.5 for sesame seeds from India; Cappers (2006): 124–125; Bedigian (2003): 24; Plisson (2005): 69.
74. Wendrich et al. (2003): 67 (table 2) = Wendrich et al. (2006): 29 (table 2.2).
75. Wendrich et al. (2003): 69 and 70 = Wendrich et al. (2006): 45.
76. Wendrich et al. (2003): 67 (table 2) = Wendrich et al. (2006): 30 (table 2.2).
77. Wendrich et al. (2003): 66 (table 2) = Wendrich et al. (2006): 28–30 (table 2.2); Cappers (2006).
78. Van Neer and Ervynck (1999a): 329, 339.
79. Van Neer and Ervynck (1999a): 327, 328, 339.

80. Arora (1977): 358–366.
81. Arora (1977): 362, 365; Cappers (1996): 331–332; Cappers (1998a): 289, 303 (table 15–6), 311; Cappers (1999a): 58–59; Wendrich et al. (2003): 64 (table 2), 70; Cappers (2006): 79–80.
82. *Abrus Pricatorius* L. is *gunja* in Sanskrit, *kunnikkuru* in Malayalam, and *kunrimani* in Tamil (personal communication from V. Selvakumar).
83. Cappers (1999a): 64; Wendrich et al. (2003): 68 (table 2) = Wendrich et al. (2006): 31 (table 2.2, mistakenly has the provenance as "East Africa?"); Cappers (2003): 201; Cappers (2006): 54–55.
84. Sidebotham (2007b): 75.
85. Miller (1969) 1–29; Martinetz et al. (1989): 125–139 for frankincense; 141–151 for myrrh; Groom (1981): 1–21, 136–137, 143–164; Donato and Seefried (1989): 38–39, 40 (fig. 16); Tucker (1986); Rossignani (1997) for frankincense from a Roman burial in Milan; De Romanis (1997d) for aromatics in archaic Rome; Zaccagnino (1997) for incense in the Greek world; Invernizzi (1997) for altars and braziers to burn aromatics.
86. Sidebotham (1986): 37.
87. Cappers (1996): 306–308; Donato and Seefried (1989): 25.
88. Cappers (1996): 308.
89. Cappers (2003): 201; Cappers (2006): 58–89.
90. Begley and Tomber (1999); Tomber and Begley (2000); Tomber (2000a); Tomber (2002): 27–29; Tomber (2004a): 396.
91. Personal observation by Sidebotham; personal communication from R. S. Tomber.
92. Tomber (2000a); Tomber (2000b); Tomber (2001); Tomber (2002): 27–29; Tomber (2004a): 395.
93. Tomber (2002): 29.
94. Gogte (1999); Butcher (2003): 96. Identification of pottery from Petra as Indian is debated.
95. Tomber (2008): 44–45.
96. Tomber (2000a); Tomber (2002); Begley and Tomber (1999); Tomber and Begley (2000).
97. Tomber (2007a); Tomber (2005a): 99–100 for first attested Axumite sherd from India; Gupta (2007): 116.
98. Tomber (2008): 79–80; and Kennet (2004).
99. Whitehouse and Williamson (1973); Winter (1987); Salles (1988); Potts (1990); Salles (1992); Salles (1993); Potts (1996); Potts (1997); Tomber (2008): 109–116.
100. Casson (1989): 19, 178–180; Groom (1994): 199; Salles (1995/2005); Tomber (2008): 109–116.
101. Tomber (2004a).
102. Tomber (2004b).
103. Hayes (1995): 35; Wild (forthcoming).
104. Wendrich et al. (2003): 72–79 = Wendrich et al. (2006): 32–35 (table 2.3), 51–55.
105. Kingsley (2001): 53–57; Ward-Perkins (2001).
106. Bagnall et al. (2000): 15–21; Bagnall et al. (2005): 8–9, 63–65, 76–77.
107. Bagnall et al. (2000): 14–24.

108. Bagnall et al. (2000): 41–42 (no. 18), 46–47 (no. 39), 51 (no. 54) and 60 (no. 84).

109. Bagnall et al. (2005): 66–69, 70, 71–72, 73–74 (nos. 158–163, 165–166, 169–171, 173–175, 177–178, 182).

110. Roth (1999): 122, 201, 203; Volken (2008).

111. Tomber (2005b); Wendrich et al. (2003): 72–79 = Wendrich et al. (2006): 32–33 (table 2.3), 51–55.

112. Wendrich et al. (2003): 77 = Wendrich et al. (2006): 52, 53, 55; Rathbone (1983): 82, 85, 92, 95 (note 9), 96 (note 11) Tchernia (1986): 152–153 for Mediterranean wine exports to India; Tomber (2004a): 401; Will (2004a); Will (2004b); Williams (2004); Tomber (2008): 42, 56, 149–150, 156–157.

113. Rathbone (1983): 84, 85, 86, 95 (note 9), 96 (note 11) for Laodicean wines.

114. Rathbone (1983): 84–87; Ballet (1998): 42–50; Tomber (1998); Ruffing (1999); Bagnall et al. (1999); Bagnall et al. (2000); Ruffing (2001): 66–67, 66 note 56, 79; Bagnall et al. (2005): 8–9, 60, 63, 65, 76–78.

115. Rathbone (1983): 86.

116. Bagnall et al. (2005): 9 and 77–78 (no. 188).

117. Ruffing (2001): 79.

118. Will (2004a): 436; Will (2004b): 330–331.

119. Casson (1989): 229; Ray (1994): 67–71 estimates twenty-six sites; Tchernia (1997a): 238 says over thirty sites; Gupta (personal communication) approximately fifty-five sites (with seven other possible, or perhaps producing imitations of amphoras); Gupta et al. (2000); Williams (2004): 447, 448 (fig. 5) estimates fifty-five sites; Tomber (2005c): 224; Tomber (2007b): 972 Mediterranean amphoras from at least thirty-one sites in India; Suresh (2004): 99 suggests amphora finds from about forty sites in India; Tomber (2008): 126–127, 166–167.

120. Bagnall et al. (2000): 37 (no. 2) lists one *italika*; 52–53 (no. 59) has three *italika*.

121. Bagnall et al. (2000): 46–47.

122. Bagnall et al. (2000): 42.

123. Bagnall et al. (2000): 16–21.

124. Q.C. Rufus (8.9.30); *Periplus* 49; Parker (2008): 312.

125. Rathbone (1997): 198.

126. Roth (1999): 37.

127. Bagnall et al. (2000): 18–19, 62.

128. Tomber (2008): 43.

129. Wendrich et al. (2006): 51–53.

130. Bagnall et al. (2000): 38 (no. 4).

131. Curtis (1991) for Egypt: 131–141, 141–147 for Syria, Palestine and the Near East.

132. Will (1996b): 317, 319, 340–345 (nos. 61–68); Will (2004b): 328, 382 (no. 273).

133. Sidebotham (1998b): 76, 77 (pl. 3–61); Van Neer and Ervynck (1998): 381; Sidebotham and Wendrich (1998b): 447, 452.

134. Stern (1991); Meyer (1992): 45, 48, 56; Suresh (2004): 134–137.

135. Leslie and Gardiner (1996): 212–214; Brill (1991/92) Chinese word for transparent glass (*boli*) may have derived from Greek.

136. Kinoshita (2009).

137. Hiebert and Cambon (2008): 168–175, 197–200.

138. Hayes (1995): 38, 40 (fig. 16); Wendrich (1996): 134 (table 5–6); 135 (table 5–7); 131 and table 5–4; 136, 137, 141; Nicholson (1998); Nicholson (1999); Nicholson (2000a); Nicholson (2000b); Nicholson and Price (2007).

139. Hayes (1995): 38, 40 (fig. 16); Nicholson (1998); Nicholson (1999); Nicholson (2000a); Nicholson (2000b); Nicholson and Price (2007).

140. Nicholson and Price (2007).

141. Meyer (1992): 10, 56–74.

142. Francis (2004): 518; Pillar bowl fragments from Pattanam/Muziris: personal observations of Sidebotham; Suresh (2004): 135 from Bahrain, Begram, Taxila and in Andhra, India at Daranikota; Potts (1997): 98, 99 (fig. 2), 100 (fig. 3), 102 (fig. 5) from Bahrain and al-Dur; Wheeler (1955): 158 and 159 (fig. 19) and Whitehouse (1989a) from Begram.

143. Getty Museum accession number 85.AF.90 ("A.D. 1–100").

144. Potts (1997): 98, 99 (fig. 2a).

145. Peacock et al. (2007b): 59; J. A. Harrell, personal communication.

146. Harrell (1996): 109; Zarins (1996); personal communication from D.P.S. Peacock; Peacock et al. (2007b).

147. Parker (1992): 28, 40 (ballast stones/amphoras: 6th-5th c. B.C.E.), 74 (second c. B.C.E.?), 85 (third c. C.E.?), 103 (ca. 100–50 B.C.E.?), 105 (ca. 110–90 B.C.E.?), 107 (piles of ballast/amphoras only: unknown date), 109 (ca. 1200 B.C.E.), 122 (ca. 36 B.C.E.), 133(?)(ca. 100 B.C.E.), 134 (ca. 40–60 C.E.), 137 (5th-6th c. C.E.), 143 (ca. 15–20 C.E.), 149 (ca. 100 B.C.E.), 158 (ca. 1350–1400 C.E.), 162 (ca. 2200 B.C.E.), 167 (2nd c. B.C.E.), 173 (ca. 140–100 B.C.E.), 189 (6th-5th c. B.C.E.), 208 (ca. 1–25 C.E.), 220 (6th c. C.E.), 232 (ca. 310–300 B.C.E.), 236 (3rd-4th c. C.E.), 237 (3rd c. C.E.), 248 (ca. 430–390 B.C.E.), 258 (1st c. B.C.E.?), 261 (2nd c. B.C.E.), 263–264 (ca. 250–175 B.C.E.), 270 (ca. 50 B.C.E.-110 C.E.?), 274 (ca. 1404 C.E. and ca. 200–250 C.E.), 275 (medieval), 276 (2nd-3rd c. C.E.), 284 (ca. 150–1 B.C.E.), 324 (3rd c. C.E.), 335 (6th c. C.E.?), 343 (ca. 160–200 C.E.), 344 (medieval?), 360 (ca. 225–150 B.C.E.?), 378 (Roman era), 396 (ca. 300–280 B.C.E.), 398 (ca. 1025 C.E.), 402 (ca. 1600 B.C.E.), 440(?) (ca. 1325 B.C.E.) for ballast types.

148. Especially in Trench 12 in an early Roman stratum beneath the church built atop it.

149. Harrell (2007a): 173.

150. Tait (1930): 122 (*O. Petrie* 285): Adams (1995): 122.

151. Harrell (1998): 139–140.

152. Harrell (1996): 111; Harrell (1998): 142; Wendrich et al. (2003): 54 (table 1) = Wendrich et al. (2006): 21 (table 2.1).

153. Dodge and Ward-Perkins (1992): 31–37, 61–105, 115–119, 121–127, 130–139, 144–151; Butcher (2003): 206, 209.

154. Peacock et al. (2007a): 114–115.

155. Harrell (1996): 112; Harrell (1998): 144; Harrell (1999): 115–116; Strabo, *Geography* 16.4.6, calls the island Ophiodes (Snaky); Pliny, *NH* 37.32.108–109, calls the island Topazos/Topazus; Ball (1912): 28 (under mining leases) and Moon et al. (1923); Wainwright (1946) J. A. Harrell recently conducted a survey of the island.

156. Wendrich et al. (2003): 54 (table 1), 56 = Wendrich et al. (2006): 21 (table 2.1).

157. Harrell (1996): 112; Harrell (1998): 142–143; Sidebotham et al. (2004a) and Foster et al. (2007) for more on Mons Smaragdus.

158. Harrell (2004a): 69–70; Sinkankas (1989): 445–455.

159. Wendrich et al. (2003): 57 = Wendrich et al. (2006): 21 (table 2.1); Rajan (1997): 8 beryl, aquamarines, sapphires, and corundum from the Coimbatore region; De Romanis (1997c): 96–97 and notes; Suresh (2004): 31, 82 (note 8), 136, 144, 146; Chakrabati (2006): 345 gemstones from the Coimbatore region; Pliny, *NH* 37.20.79, recounts Indian counterfeiting of beryls by staining rock crystal; Kangle (1986a): 99 (*Kauṭilīya Arthaśāstra* 2.11.29).

160. Mango (1996): 153.

161. Walker and Bierbrier (1997): 57–58 (no. 33), 58–59 (no. 34), 61–62 (no. 37), 64–65 (no. 41), 72–73 (no. 49), 73–74 (no. 51), 99–100 (no. 91), 100–101 (no. 93); Doxiadis (2000): 26 (no. 21), 28 (no. 24), 29 (no. 25), probably 31 (no. 29), 57 (no. 40), 58 (no. 41), 59 (nos. 43–44), 74 (no. 64), 75 (nos. 65–66), probably 107 (no. 76), 111 (no. 81), 165 (no. 102); Schenke (2001): 281–289.

162. Harrell (1996): 112; Harrell (1998): 145; Harrell (1999): 115; Zarins (1996) for earlier trade in obsidian; Peacock et al. (2007b): 54–57, 59, 63; De Romanis (1996a): 225–239; *Periplus* (5) reports its importation to Berenike from Eritrea.

163. Wendrich et al. (2003): 59 = Wendrich et al. (2006): 22 (table 2.1).

164. Harrell (1998): 144; Harrell (1999): 114; Wendrich et al. (2003): 62 = Wendrich et al. (2006): 23 (table 2.1).

165. Harrell (1998): 144–145; Harrell (1999): 111; Wendrich et al. (2003): 54 (table 1), 60 = Wendrich et al. (2006): 22 (table. 2.1).

166. Harrell (2007b).

167. Sidebotham (1999b): 81; Sidebotham and Wendrich (2002): 30 and fig. 11.

168. Walker and Bierbrier (1997): 166–167 (no. 195); cf. 58–59 (no. 34); 59–60 (no. 35), 111–112 (no. 106); Doxiadis (2000): 28–29 (no. 25), 106–107 (no. 76), 110–111 (no. 83).

169. Francis (2000): 223.

170. Casson (1989): 178; Potts (1997): 93.

171. Francis (2000): 223; Faller (2000): 41–88 for ancient sources on Taprobane including Strabo, the *Periplus*, Pomponius Mela, and Pliny the Elder.

172. Donkin (1998): 1–3 for ancient Indian sources on pearls, 3–5 for Greek-Roman sources on pearls, 43 (map 11), 45 (map 12), 54 (map 13), 61 (map 14), 62 (map 15); Landman et al. (2001): 64–69 in Roman-Byzantine times, 103–106 in West Asia/Near East, 106–107 in Africa, 107–108 in South Asia.

173. Kangle (1986a): 97–98 (*Kauṭilīya Arthaśāstra* 2.11.4, 6, 7, 17, 20, 21, 27); De Romanis (1997c): 113–116.

174. Casson (1989): 21–22.

175. Daryaee (2009): 136–140 for Sassanian "international" trade, especially via the Persian Gulf.

176. Potts (1996); Whitehouse (1996); Salles (1995/2005); Potts (1997); Howgego and Potts (1992), all coins are surface finds including an aureus of Tiberius and fourth century C.E. Roman *aes* issues; Papadopoulos (1994).

177. Harrell (1999): 115–118.
178. Ray (1986): 132 for beads made in the Deccan; Francis (2000): 221–223, 224–225.
179. Francis (2000): 222.
180. Wendrich et al. (2003): 55 (table 1), 61 = Wendrich et al. (2006): 22 (table 2.1); Plisson (2005): 70–71 for other sources in the Indus, Egypt, Afghanistan, Yemen, Nubia, Sinai, Madagascar, Romania, and the Czech Republic.
181. Francis (2000): 216–217; Francis (2007): 253, 255.
182. Francis (2000): 221–223; Francis (2004): 450–504, 525–530.
183. Harrell (1998): 143–144; Harrell (1999): 112.
184. Harrell (1999): 111–112; Wendrich et al. (2003): 55 (table 1) = Wendrich et al. (2006): 22 (table 2.1).
185. Gupta et al. (2004): 32.
186. Boardman (2001): 379–382 on carving-drilling techniques.
187. Francis (2004): 492 (fig. 7.31) for Arikamedu; J.A. Harrell indicates that the samples are onyx and not agate (personal communication).
188. Personal observations of Sidebotham.
189. Harmelin (2000): 15 (fig. 4) for map locating origins of red coral.
190. Pliny the Elder, *NH* 32.11.21–23; *Periplus* 39, 49, 56, and *Kauṭilīya Arthaśāstra* 2.11.2–27 = Kangle (1986a): 97–98; De Romanis (2000), the entire volume provides background on Mediterranean red coral.
191. Kangle (1986b): 59–115; Gupta (2007): 113; Mabbet (1964); Seland (2006): 46–47.
192. Ray (1986): 131; De Romanis (2000); Kangle (1986a): 100 for *Kauṭilīya Arthaśāstra* 2.11.42.
193. De Romanis (1997b): 189–191.
194. Francis (2000): 213.
195. Leslie and Gardiner (1996): 87, 96, 110–111, 114, 210, 217, 228–230, 269.
196. Vermeeren (2000): 340; Cappers (1999a): 59; Ray (1986): 122.
197. Vermeeren (1999b): 319; Vermeeren (2000): 340–341.
198. Blue (2002): 149.
199. Groom (1995): 189 (*Periplus* 36).
200. Hourani (1995): 89–93; Ray (1986): 116; Tripati et al. (2005).
201. Vermeeren (1999a): 201.
202. Ward and Zazzaro (2007): 135, 139, 142, 143, 145.
203. Vermeeren (2000): 318, 321, 329, 340–342, specimens may be myrtle.
204. Kangle (1986a): 101.
205. Ray (1986): 122; Plisson (2005): 69.
206. Ray (1986): 122.
207. Ray (1986): 112.
208. Sidebotham (2000b): 141; Vermeeren (2000): 321, 325, 328, 340–342; Sidebotham and Wendrich (2000b): 418; Cappers (2006): 164.
209. Wendrich (2007): 228, 233 (table 12–2), 236, 250; Collingwood (1998): 18.
210. Chittick (1980b): 297, 298.
211. Ray (1986): 134; Leslie and Gardiner (1996): 246–248 for baby on raft with similarities to stories of Moses, and Romulus and Remus.

212. Sidebotham and Wendrich (2001–2002): 4; Sidebotham (2007a): 201, 209 (no. 115), 210 (pl. 8–15).

213. Identification by project botanist; for literature on frankincense: Miller (1969): 102–104, 107; Groom (1981); Crone (1987): 51–53.

214. Vermeeren (1998); Vermeeren (1999a); Vermeeren (2000).

215. Vermeeren (1998); Vermeeren (1999a); Vermeeren (2000).

216. Thomas (2001a): 53; Thomas (2002): 64; Beckmann (1846): 322–323; Thomas and Tomber (2006): 242–243 record no cork stoppers from Mons Claudianus.

217. Lloris (1970): 72–73; Parker (1992): 50 (no. 28: 100–80 B.C.E.), 70 (no. 96: late second c. B.C.E.), 101 (no. 183: ca. 540 B.C.E.), 107 (no. 200: ca. 100 B.C.E. (?)), 141 (no. 304: ca. 175–150 B.C.E.), 167 (no. 373: late second c. B.C.E.), 177 (no. 398: early fourth c. c.E. (?)), 192 (no. 451: ca. 600–590 B.C.E.), 193 (no. 453: ca. 200–225 C.E.), 202 (no. 476: ca. 120–100 B.C.E. (?)), 221 (no. 530: ca. 100–25 B.C.E.), 222 (no. 531: ca. 200–140 B.C.E. (?)), 241 (no. 593: late third-early second c. B.C.E.), 249 (no. 616: 70–50 B.C.E.), 264 (no. 663: ca. 1150–1200 C.E.), 301 (no. 783: ca. 300–350 C.E. (?)), 307 (no. 801: ca. 15–25 C.E.), 313 (no. 819: ca. 50 B.C.E.), 314 (no. 821: tenth c. c.E.), 330 (no. 874: ca. 400 C.E.), 331 (no. 876: mid-second c. C.E.), 380 (no. 1020: ca. 110–80 B.C.E. (?)), 391 (no. 1055: 365–380 C.E.), 394 (no. 1060: ca. 100–50 B.C.E.), 396 (no. 1065: ca. 300–280 B.C.E.), 408 (no. 1100: ca. 320–340 C.E. (?)), 422 (no. 1142: ca. 310–260 B.C.E. (?)), 431 (no. 1169: late fourth-early third c. B.C.E. (?)), 433 (no. 1174: ca. 20–10 B.C.E.), 439 (no. 1192: ca. 50 B.C.E.-25 C.E.).

218. Thomas (2001a): 51.

219. Haeckl (1999).

220. Personal communication from I. Zych and J. Zieliński.

221. Personal communication from I. Zych.

222. Ward and Zazzaro (2007): 135–150.

223. Ward and Zazzaro (2007): 135, 139, 142–143, 145 for Wadi/Mersa Gawasis; Macklin (2006): 158 and Peacock and Blue (2006a): 177 for Islamic era at Quseir al-Qadim.

224. Sidebotham and Zych (2010): 19–21.

225. Sidebotham and Zych (2010): 21.

226. Manniche (1999): 64–65.

227. *Periplus* 48, 49 and Sidebotham (1986): 25 and note 34; Sidebotham (1991b): 16–17 for use of canal to export textiles from Egypt.

228. Wild (1997); Wild and Wild (2000): 265–269, 271–273; Wild and Wild (2001); Wild (2002): 9–10; Wild and Wild (2005): 13–14; Wild (2004): 61–63; Wild and Wild (2008): 230–231.

229. Wild (2002): 13; Wild and Wild (2008): 230–231.

230. Whitewright (2003): 71, 73 (fig. 59); Whitewright (2007a): 81 (fig. 6:6), 83–84.

231. Ray (1986): 112–113.

232. Wild (2002): 10, 12 (table 3), 13; Wild and Wild (2005); Wild (2006): 179, 180 (fig. 4), 181, 183, 183 (fig. 7), 184; Thomas (2007): 155–156; Wild and Wild (2008); Kerkhoven and Koopmans (1989); also Wild (1997); Wild (2004); Wild and Wild (1996); Wild and Wild (1998); Wild and Wild (2000); Wild and Wild (2001); Vogelsang-Eastwood (1989) for resist-dyed textiles from Myos Hormos/Quseir al-Qadim.

233. Wild (1997): 89; Wild et al. (2007); Thomas (2007): 156 and note 57; Wild et al. (2008): 145–149; Potts (1997): 93 cotton may have been cultivated in Bahrain in Seleucid times; Parker (2008): 156–157; Gopal (1961): 60–61 on Indian cotton.

234. Wild (1997): 287–298.

235. In 1998 Sidebotham saw a fragment in the Urumchi Museum from Baschu northeast of Kashgar; Debaine-Francfort and Idriss (2000): 80 (no. 22) another fragment from Karadong (ancient Keriya), in Desrosiers, Debaine-Francfort, and Idriss (2001): 51 and fig. 6.4 (= colour pl. III).

236. Sidebotham (forthcoming a): Trench BE01–47.012.

237. Behl (1998): 184, 187.

238. Kerlogue (2005): 132–134; Ray (2005a).

239. Wild (2006): 184.

240. Behl (1998): 131 and 134 (blue check cushion), 143 (lotus), 160–161 (vegetation type).

241. Wild (2006): 180 (fig. 4) and 181.

242. Stauffer (1995): 66–71; Stauffer (1996); Sidebotham (1986): 39 and note 74 on silk imports to the Roman world; Parker (2008): 156; Lyovushkina (1995/96).

243. Ray (1986): 113; Gopal (1961): 61–63 and Parker (2008): 156 on Indian silk industry.

244. Leslie and Gardiner (1996): 225–228.

245. Sidebotham (1998a); Sidebotham (1999a); Sidebotham (2000a); Sidebotham (2007a); Sidebotham (in preparation a); Sidebotham and Seeger (1996).

246. Sidebotham (2007a): 202 (table 8–6); similar percentages for coins from the 2001 season: Sidebotham (in preparation a).

247. For Roman coins in India/Sri Lanka: Sewell (1904); Rodewald (1976); Sidebotham (1986): 27–32; Turner (1989); Berghaus (1992) for review of Turner; Berghaus (1989); Turner and Cribb (1996); Berghaus (1991); Gupta (1991); Ray (1991); MacDowall (1991); Walser (2001); Suresh (2004): 26–88; Walburg (2008); Tomber (2008): 30–37.

248. Turner (1989); Suresh (2004): 26–88. Berghaus (1992): 226 and pls. 27–28.

249. Walburg (1991); Mango (1996): 156 note 59; Bopearachchi (1992): 112–117; Bopearachchi (2006): 13, 18.

250. Chittick (1966): issues of Carus (282–284) and Constans (335–337) and Heraclius (610–641).

251. Mango (1996): 150 (fig. 9), 156 and note 59; Chittick (1966) and Meyer (2007): 60 for an issue of Heraclius (610–641).

252. Miller (1969): 216–217.

253. Sidebotham (1986): 38–39.

254. Parker (2008): 105–106, 147–202.

255. Wheeler (1955): 140–142; Raschke (1978): 644, 669; cf. Sidebotham (1986): 18–19, 28, 30, 31, 38–39; Turner (1989): 16, 19, 32; Tomber (2008): 34; MacDowall (2004a) and MacDowall (2004b) for discussion.

256. *O. Petrie* 290 in Tait (1930): 123.

257. *P. Giess.* 47: Sidebotham (1986): 18–19.

258. Turner (1989): 32–36.

259. Hall (1999): 434.

260. Sidebotham (1986): 13–47; Walser (2001).

261. Renfrew (1975): 53; De Romanis (2006): 69–82.

262. Puskás (1987): 154.

263. Meyer (2007): 61–62.

264. MacDowall (1996): 92; MacDowall (2004b): 43.

265. Graser (1940a); Graser (1940b); Mrozek (1982); Desanges (1984): 357; Arnaud (2007): 321, Edict prices were arbitrary and not applied realistically across the entire empire; Tomber (2008): 161–162 implies this; Rathbone (2009): 317.

266. Speidel (1992a): 88 (table 1), 93 (table 3); Duncan-Jones (1994): 34 (table 3.2); Herz (2007): 308–313.

267. Rathbone (2009): 317.

268. Rathbone (2009): 317.

269. Personal communication from M.H. Crawford; Rathbone (2009): 317.

270. Duncan-Jones (1994): 90.

271. Duncan-Jones (1994): 91–92.

272. Sidebotham and Wendrich (2001–2002): 41 and fig. 40; Sidebotham and Wendrich (2002): 30 (fig. 9); Sidebotham (2007a): 201, 209 (no. 114), 210 (pl. 8–14).

273. Sidebotham and Wendrich (2001–2002): 41 and fig. 40; Sidebotham and Wendrich (2002): 30 (fig. 10); Sidebotham (2007a): 201, 209 (no. 115), 210 (pl. 8–15).

274. Whitcomb (1994): 16–18; Munro-Hay (1991): 180–195 for Axumite coins in general.

275. Munro-Hay (1989).

276. Tomber (2008): 105 for three Axumite coins from southern Arabia.

277. Hahn (2000): 287 and note 21.

278. Hahn (2000): 288 and note 25.

279. Tomber (2008): 147; Walburg (2008): 54.

280. Munro-Hay (1996): 413–414.

281. Thapar (1992): 6–7; Humphrey and Hugh-Jones (1992); Walser (2001).

282. Thapar (1992): 15.

283. Parker (2008): 312.

284. Hart and Heifetz (1999): 43 (poem no. 56, lines 18–20).

285. Palmer (1951); Casson (1989): 271–277; Peacock et al. (2007a): 126.

286. Seland (2005).

287. Doe (1971): 215 and plates 112–113; Groom (1981): 181–182.

288. Thapar (1992): 12 attributes these actions to hostilities between Sakas and Sātavāhanas, but it may have been undertaken to insure compliance with local laws, customs, and toll procedures.

289. Ray (1986): 109.

290. Mahadevan (1996); Mahadevan (2003): 43, 49, 56 (fig. 1.21 B and C), 61 (nos. 8–9), 93, 146–147, 163, 164, 235.

291. Kangle (1986a): 262; Ray (1986): 106.

292. Thapar (1992): 10–11.

293. Seland (2006); Seland (2010).

294. Jolowicz and Nicholas (1972): 394; Mommsen and Krueger (1985): 407 for *Digest of Justinian* 39.4.16; Groom (1981): 155; Tomber (2008): 24; Parker (2008): 149–150.

295. Sidebotham (1986): 110 and note 148.

296. Maxfield (2000): 407; Harrauer and Sijpesteijn (1985): the so-called Muziris papyrus: 130 (recto, column 2, lines 2–4), 133; Cuvigny (2003b): 326–327; Cuvigny (2005b): 7, 77, 80 (*O. Krok.* 41, lines 35–60), 85 (*O. Krok.* 42, lines 9–13), 87 (*O. Krok.* 44, lines 4–7).

297. Cuvigny (2005b): 168–171 (no. 99).

298. Kaegi (1981): 133–135, 300–301 for greed and corruption among soldiers in the later Roman/Byzantine era.

299. Priaulx (1860); Priaulx (1861); Priaulx (1862); Priaulx (1863); Cimino and Scialpi (1974): 8–13; Sidebotham (1986): 129–130; Noy (2000): 101 and note 127 for classical references.

300. Ferguson (1978): 594–596; Raschke (1978): 645; Mango (1996): 157, 159.

301. Ferguson (1978): 598–599; Leslie and Gardiner (1996): 158–159.

302. Leslie and Gardiner (1996): 121–126.

303. Leslie and Gardiner (1996): 51, 62, 100, 111, 153–158, 161, 164, 169, 182.

304. Leslie and Gardiner (1996): 100, 158–159.

305. Leslie and Gardiner (1996): 82, 159–160.

306. Leslie and Gardiner (1996).

307. Leslie and Gardiner (1996): 154.

308. Hirth (1975): 173–178 for 166 C.E., 306 for 226 C.E. and 271–274 for 284 C.E.; Ferguson (1978): 591–599; Graf (1996); Teggart (1939); Leslie and Gardiner (1996); Pulleyblank (1999) for review.

309. Chapekar (1977): 36–42 for anatomy; 42–46 for medicine; 46–49 for math; 73–81 on philosophy; Fynes (1991) and Parker (2008); Filliozat (1949).

310. Chapekar (1977): 20–31; Whitehouse (1989b): most Roman artifacts arrived in Begram by sea via India; McEvilley (2002): 372–376, 378–379, 388–390; Tomber (2008): 123 for Gandhara, 123–124 for Begram.

311. Fynes (1991): 107.

312. Ray (1986): 86–89; Schopen (1994): 527–554; Ray (2005a): 21.

313. Ray (1986): 129–132.

314. Thapar (1992): 20 is unconvinced about this association.

315. Extensive bibliography on Isis: Dunand (1973a); Dunand (1973b); Dunand (1973c); Budischovsky (1977); Dunand (1979).

316. Obeyesekere (1984): 451–482; 530–552; Fynes (1991): 154–179.

317. Wiesehöfer (1998): 19–20.

318. Butcher (2003): 376.

319. Dihle (1964): 60–71; McEvilley (2002): 76–77 on Christianity.

320. Muckensturm-Poulle (2005).

321. Wolska-Conus (1968): 502–505; Wolska-Conus (1973): 342–345; McCrindle (1897): 118–119, 365.

322. Leadbetter (2000): 84 and notes 17–18.

323. Amélineau (1893): 62–64, 213–215; Van der Vliet (2002); Farquhar (1926); Farquhar (1927); Frend (1968); Fynes (1991): 180–208; McEvilley (2002): 259–260, 269–270 for philosophical/religious exchanges; Parker (2008): 300 (citing *P. Oxy.* 1380), 301–307.

324. Leslie and Gardiner (1996): 115, 230.

325. Leslie and Gardiner (1996): 230.

326. Fynes (1991): 180–208; Frend (1968): 306–311.

327. Thapar (1992): 20.

328. Ferguson (1991): 76.

329. McEvilley (2002); Parker (2008): 251–307.

330. Puskás (1987): 142–143; McEvilley (2002): 16, 18, 139, 149 (note 92), 179, 321, 415, 488 (note 56), 505, 565 (note 12).

331. Puskás (1987): 143.

332. Pande (1991b).

333. Pande (1991a)

334. Schmidt (1979); Miller (1969).

335. Bussagli (1951) summarizes Filliozat (1949) and Benveniste (1945).

336. Scarborough (1982).

337. Fynes (1991): 209–255.

338. Fynes (1991): 256–267.

13. LATE ROMAN BERENIKE AND ITS DEMISE

1. *P. Lond.* 2.328 = Kenyon (1898): xxxi, 74–76; Adams (2007): 129 (and note 32), 147 (and note 43), 151 (and note 61), 202 (and note 22), 215 (and note 80), 234 (and note 49).

2. Meredith (1957a): 61, 69.

3. Verhoogt (1998): 193–196.

4. Dijkstra and Verhoogt (1999).

5. Sidebotham (1999a): 192–193; Sidebotham (2000a): 171 (table 4–4), 172 (nos. 2–3), 173 (pl. 4–6), 175 (pl. 4–7); Sidebotham (2007a): 200 (table 8–2), 201 (table 8–3), 202 (table 8–6), 206 (nos. 39–40), 209 (no. 114), 210 (pl. 8–14); Sidebotham and Seeger (1996): 179, 180 (table 7–1), 181 (table 7–4), 182,-183, 190 (pl. 7–9e-f), 191 (pl. 7–10e-f), 194 (nos. 68–69).

6. Barnes (1978): especially 11–22 and Syme (1983): especially 1–11, 98–108, 209–223 on reliability of (*Scriptores*) *Historia Augusta* for this period in Roman history.

7. Desanges (1978): 340–348.

8. Bowman (1978): 27; Bowman (1986): 44–45.

9. Robin (1997): 53.

10. Dijkstra and Verhoogt (1999): 215; Demougeot (1960): 243–244.

11. Dijkstra and Verhoogt (1999).

12. Verhoogt (1998): 193–196.

13. Graf (1989): 143–144, 146–147.

14. Desanges (1978): 353–360; Faller (2000): 135–188 for late Roman literary sources (Ammianus Marcellinus and lesser-known authors) dealing with Sri Lanka.

15. Mayerson (1993): 174 = Mayerson (1994a): 366.

16. *Martyrium Sancti Arethae* (27, 28, 29); Vasiliev (1950): 294–295; Desanges (1978): 194–196; Rubin (1989); Eide et al. (1998): 1185–1188 (no. 327).

17. Mango (1996): 141–145, 148–151 for examples from Judaea; Mediterranean: Kingsley

(2001): 53, 54, 57; Kingsley and Decker (2001): 10; Mango (2001): 87; Ward-Perkins (2001): 170; Butcher (2003): 188; Martin (2008): 108–109 for Ostia; Decker (2009).

18. Sidebotham and Wendrich (2002): 30, Figs. 9–10; Sidebotham (2007a): 209 (no. 114), 210 (pl. 8–14).

19. Kirwan (1972): 176.

20. Sidebotham (2002b): 230–231, 234; Sidebotham and Wendrich (1998b): 90–93; Sidebotham and Wendrich (2001–2002): 25–28, 41–43; Sidebotham and Wendrich (2007b): 374; Tomber (2007a); Tomber (2008): 161–170.

21. Sidebotham (2000b): 120–134; Peña (2007): 282–283 for trash dumping inside structures in late Roman times.

22. Wild and Wild (1996): 253–254.

23. Wendrich (1999): 279; Wendrich (2000): 248–250.

24. Collingwood (1998): 18.

25. Sidebotham (2002b): 220; Sidebotham (2007b): 148; Peña (2007): 181–192.

26. Blue (2006a): 49; Blue and Peacock (2006): 70–74; Peacock and Blue (2006a): 175–176; Blue (2006b): 83; Thomas (2006b): 90;

27. Adam (1994): 153, 183 for other uses of amphoras in wall and dome construction; Peña (2007): 181–188, especially 187–188, 254.

28. Fischer (1984).

29. Sidebotham (2007b): 94 (Pls. 4–64 and 4–65), 96 for fallen roof beams.

30. Le Quesne (2007): 155 for blocks in Ottoman/Napoleonic fort at Quseir.

31. Personal observation of the author.

32. Fischer (1984): 107–159, especially 110 and pls. on 118 (Gedi) and 142 (top: Kilwa).

33. Couyat (1911); Murray (1926a); Gibb (1960); Tibbetts (1961); Garcin (1972); Ghosh (1992): 174–178 and 371 (notes); Peacock and Peacock (2008).

34. Sidebotham and Wendrich (2001–2002): 35–36; Sidebotham (2002b): 235.

35. Barnard (1998): 397–401; Sidebotham and Wendrich (2001–2002): 35.

36. Barnard (1998): 397–401.

37. Aldsworth and Barnard (1996): 437–440 and Barnard (1998): 397–398 for Hitan Rayan; Barnard (1998): 397–398 and Aldsworth and Barnard (1998): 429 for Shenshef [Ball (1912): 31, 113 and pl. IV, bottom]; Sidebotham and Wendrich (2001–2002): 35.

38. Burkhalter-Arce (2002); Sijpesteijn (1987): 25 and notes 57–58; Wallace (1938/1969): 273–275, 274 and note 100 for funeral processions: going to the desert for burial and returning rather than going into the desert, retrieving the deceased, and returning; Sidebotham and Wendrich (2007b): 374.

39. Trench BE01–48.032/033 publication in preparation.

40. Sidebotham (1999b): 67, 70–71 (and table 2–38), 72 (and pl. 2–39), 73 (and pl. 2–40), 74, 78; Sidebotham and Wendrich (2001–2002): 30.

41. Sidebotham (1999b): 59, 60–61 (no. 10), 62, 78 (pl. 2–43), 79.

42. Sidebotham (2000b): 63–65; Hölbl (2005): 9–34 in general for larger temples.

43. Sidebotham (2002b): 236.

44. Peña (2007): 144.

45. Ricke et al. (1967): 13–15 and Abb. 24–26, Tafel 7D, 31 and Abb. 45, Tafel 10; Kuenz (1981); Ballet et al. (2000): 131 (cat. 98).

46. Sidebotham (2000b): 134–144; Hense (2000): 195–197.

47. Sidebotham (2007b): 84 and pl. 4–53, fig. 4–54.

48. Sidebotham (1998b): 63; Sidebotham (2000b): 145–147.

49. Daniels (1975); Şerban and Băluţă (1979); Clauss (2000): 34–37.

50. Sidebotham and Zych (2010): 15–19.

51. Sidebotham and Zych (2010): 15–19.

52. Sidebotham and Zych (2010): 15–19.

53. Bagnall et al. (2005): 27–28 (no. 121).

54. Eide et al. (1998): 1177–1181 (no. 324); Barnard (2005): 27 (table 1B, nos. 260, 261, 272).

55. Pharr (1952): 472–476 (*Cod. Theo.* 16.10.1–16.10.23) and 482–483 (*Constitutiones Sir-mondianae* 12); Eide et al. (1998): 1177–1181 (no. 324).

56. *Procopius, History of the Wars* 1.19.35–37; Alston (2002): 272–273, 283–285; Török (2005): 99 and note 314.

57. Eide et al. (1998): 1177–1181 (no. 324); Török (2005): 87 for converting pagan temples to churches in Egypt.

58. Updegraff (1988): 52–55; Barnard (2005); Lassányi (2005).

59. Updegraff (1988): 62–67; Barnard (2005): 34.

60. Eide et al. (1998): 1188–1193 (no. 328) = Procopius, *History of the Wars* 1.19.27–37; Up-degraff (1988): 72–76.

61. Skeat (1977); Eide et al. (1998): 1158–1165 (no. 319).

62. Kirwan (1972): 173; Barnard (2005).

63. Barnard (2005); Burstein (2008b).

64. Meredith (1957a): 65.

65. Török (2005): 89–92 for Christian-pagan and Christian-Christian "heresy" in late Roman Egypt.

66. Hense (1999): 222–223.

67. Ricke et al. (1967): 13–15 and Abb. 24–26, Tafel 7D, 31 and Abb. 45, Tafel 10; Kuenz (1981).

68. Meredith (1957a): 70.

69. Sidebotham (2007b): 75.

70. Sidebotham (2000b): 140; Sidebotham (2007b): 79 (pl. 4–46), 80, 83.

71. Sidebotham (1999b): 70–74; Sidebotham (2000b): 64–65, 72.

72. Sidebotham (1999b): 70–74; Sidebotham (2000b): 140; Sidebotham (2007b): 79 (pl. 4–46), 80, 83.

73. Sidebotham (2002b): 220–230.

74. Sidebotham and Wendrich (2001–2002): 39–40; Sidebotham (2007b): 112; Freshfield (1938): Chapter 10, part 5; Alston (2002): 53, 55.

75. Freshfield (1938): 31.

76. Freshfield (1938): Chapter 10, part 5.

77. Sidebotham (2007b): Trench 37: 120–133.

78. Bagnall et al. (2005): 21–22 (nos. 118–119).

79. Bagnall et al. (2005): 27–28 (no. 121).

80. Sidebotham (1998b): 79–96.

81. Tuck (1997): 102–104, 117, 182; Tuck (2008): 330–332, 337, 339 for Ostia, Portus, and Lepcis Magna.

82. Tuck (1997): 102–104, 117, 182.

83. Trench BE95–4; Mahadevan (1996); Sundelin (1996); Sidebotham (1996a): 53–76 for Trench BE95/96–7; Sidebotham (1999b): 80–87 for Trench BE97/98–17; Sidebotham (2000b): 73–88.

84. Sidebotham (2007b): 139–146 for Trench BE99–26.

85. Trench BE95/96/97–5: Hense (1999): 219–222; Sidebotham (1996a): 76–82; Sidebotham (1998b): 13–20; Sidebotham (1999b): 5–13; Tomber (1999): 124–136.

86. Wendrich et al. (2006): 52 = Wendrich et al. (2003): 73; Peña (2007): 64–66.

87. Trenches 8, 12, 22, 30 and 39: see Barnard and Wendrich (2007): 5–7 (table 2–1), 13 (fig. 2–7); Sidebotham et al. (in preparation).

88. Sidebotham (2000b): 43 (fig. 2–27), 44; Sidebotham and Wendrich (1998b): 93; Bagnall et al. (2005): 102

89. Walters (1974): 220; Bagnall (1993): 289–293; Mango (1996): 149; Kingsley and Decker (2001): 9; Wipszycka (1972): 34–63, 121–153; Alston (2002): 304–305; Wipszycka (2007): 335–336; Török (2005): 86 for accumulation of property by churches beginning second half fourth century; Tomber (2008): 168–170.

90. Tomber (2008): 169 for ownership of fleet by Church at Alexandria in the seventh century.

91. Sidebotham (2007a): 200, 202 (table 8–6), 209 (no. 115), 210 (pl. 8–15).

92. Sidebotham and Wendrich (2000b): 368–371; Sidebotham and Wendrich (2001–2002): 47; Sidebotham et al. (2002): 213–225; likely Murray (1926b): 167.

93. Sidebotham (1995b): 93–96; Sidebotham and Zitterkopf (1996): 391–397; Aldsworth and Barnard (1998); Gould (1999); Aldsworth (1999); Cappers (1999c); Vermeeren (1999c); Van Neer and Ervynck (1999b); Tomber (2008): 76, 83–87 (table 1), 165; Colston (1887): 583–584; Ball (1912): 113–114; Daressy (1922): 175 and notes below for theories about the site's purpose.

94. Sidebotham (1995b): 96–98; Aldsworth and Barnard (1996); Sidebotham et al. (2002): 206–213, 218–225.

95. Sidebotham (1999c): 360–364.

96. Wilkinson's unpublished manuscripts refer to Shenshef.

97. Barth (1859): 17–18.

98. Ball (1912): 31, pl. IV (bottom), 113–114.

99. Raimondi (1923b): fig. 20 (between 64–65).

100. Murray (1926b); Murray (1968): 53–54.

101. Sidebotham (1995b): 93–96; Aldsworth and Barnard (1998); Gould (1999); Aldsworth (1999); Cappers (1999c); Vermeeren (1999c); Van Neer and Ervynck (1999b).

102. Raimondi (1923b): fig. 20 (between 64–65); Murray (1925): 143; Murray (1926): 167; Murray (1968): 53–54; Sidebotham (1995b): 93–96.

103. Cappers (1999c): 422, 425.

104. Cappers (1999c): 422, 423. 425.

105. Vermeeren (1999c): 427–428.

106. Gould (1999): 375.

107. Harrell (1999): 114; Wendrich et al. (2003): 62 = Wendrich et al. (2006): 43.

108. Gould (1999): 378.

109. For Hitan Rayan see also Sidebotham (1995b): 96–98; Aldsworth and Barnard (1996); Sidebotham et al. (2002) in general; Murray (1926b): 167 mentions a settlement in "Umm Etli," which must be Wadi Umm Atlee; for similar settlements in Nubia see Monneret de Villard (1935): 29–31, 42, 56, 58–61; Ricke et al. (1967): 33–37; Ghica et al. (2008); cf. Luft (2010).

110. Sidebotham and Zitterkopf (1996): 401–403.

111. See Sidebotham (2002a): 417.

112. Sidebotham and Zitterkopf (1995): 40 (fig. 2), 44 (fig. 5), 45; Keenan et al. (2000a); Keenan et al. (2000b): 1174.

113. Sidebotham (1999c): 360–364.

114. Sidebotham (1999c): 355–358.

115. Sidebotham (1999c): 356, 358.

116. Forts from south to north: the hilltop fort at Shenshef, the two forts in Wadi Kalalat, the one at Siket, the five at Vetus Hydreuma (in Wadi Abu Greiya), and the one in Wadi Lahami: for GPS coordinates see: Sidebotham and Wendrich (2001–2002): 38, note 5.

117. Tomber (2008): 163.

118. Tomber (2008): 140, 147, 163.

119. Tomber (2007a); Tomber (2008): 88–93, 161–166 (and table 3 on 166).

120. Kirwan (1972): 176.

121. Kirwan (1972).

122. Van Neer and Ervynck (1998): 353; Van Neer and Ervynck (1999a): 327, 328, 339.

123. Wendrich (1995); Wendrich and Veldmeijer (1996); Veldmeijer (1998); Wendrich (1998); Wendrich (1999); Wendrich (2000); Wendrich (2007).

124. Sidebotham and Wendrich (2001–2002): 36 and fig. 28.

125. Sidebotham and Wendrich (2001–2002): 25–26 and fig. 26; Sidebotham (2007b): 35–36 and pl. 4-4.

126. Sidebotham and Wendrich (2001–2002): 36 and fig. 27; Sidebotham (2007b): 35–36 and pl. 4-4.

127. Sidebotham (1998b): 107–108 (pl. 3–84); Barnard (1998); Sidebotham and Wendrich (2001–2002): 35–36 and fig. 25; Sidebotham and Wendrich (2007b): 372 on late Roman burials.

128. Desanges (1978): 364–365; Eide et al. (1998): 1055–1057 (no. 279), 1057–1059 (no. 280), 1060–1063 (no. 282), 1063–1065 (no. 283), 1065–1066 (no. 284), 1079–1081 (no. 293), 1083–1087 (no. 295), 1107–1109 (no. 301), 1110–1112 (no. 302), 1115–1121 (no. 305), 1125–1126 (no. 308), 1126–1128 (no. 309), 1134–1138 (no. 313), 1138–1141 (no. 314), 1147–1153 (no. 317), 1153–1158 (no. 318), 1158–1165 (no. 319), 1175–1176 (no. 323), 1177–1181 (no. 324), 1182–1185 (no. 326), 1188–1193 (no. 328), 1193–1194 (no. 329), 1196–1216 (nos. 331–343); Barnard (2008).

129. Barnard (2005).

130. Blockley (1983): 200–201.

131. Billerbeck (2006): 338–339.

132. *Martyrium Sancti Arethae* (27, 28, 29): see Pigulewskaja (1969): 194–196; Shahîd (1971): 212–214; Cosmas Indicopleustes, *Christian Topography* 2.56 also records this event [Wolska-Conus (1968): 368–369)]; Vasiliev (1950): 294–295; Rubin (1989); Eide

et al. (1998): 1185–1188 (no. 327); Kobishchanov (1979): 91–108 in general for the 517–537 wars; Kobishchanov (1979): 99–103 for the 524–525 campaign.

133. Kirwan (1972): 171; Shahîd (1971): 46–47; Shahîd (1988): 46–47, 88; Desanges (1978): 272–307; Shahîd (1989): 360–376 for Christianity at Najran; Eide et al. (1998): 1187–1188 (no. 327).

134. Robin (2005): 15 (fig. 6), 16; Hoyland (2001): 51–54.

135. *Martyrium Sancti Arethrae* (29); Mayerson (1996): 123.

136. Comes (1966); Desanges (1969); Mayerson (1993) = Mayerson (1994a); Warmington (1974): 139–140; Schneider (2004): especially 15–35; for confusion of parts of Africa with India in the time of Diocletian on tombstone of soldier Aurelius Gaius: *AÉ* (1981): 207–209 (no. 777) and Drew-Bear (1981): 97 (line 13), 117–118; Dihle (1965): 65–79 for a history of the name "Aethiopia." Desanges (1993) for location of "Western" Ethiopians.

137. Kobishchanov (1979): 171–182 for overview of Axumite trade; Munro-Hay (1982); Munro-Hay (1991): 172–176 for overview of Axumite commerce; Munro-Hay (1996); Tomber (2007a); Tomber (2008): 164–167.

138. Bernand et al. (1991): 357–358 (no. 268).

139. Little (2007): 3; Morony (2007): 63; McCormick (2007): 303–304.

140. Keys (1999): 17–24; Scheidel (2001): 100; Nutton (2004): 25 and note 54; Bratton (1981); Conrad (1981): 83–119; Sidebotham and Wendrich (2001–2002): 48; Little (2007): 3; Rosen (2007) for a popular account.

141. Rosen (2007): 210–211; Morony (2007): 72 and note 101.

142. Robin (2005): 16; Morony (2007): 63.

143. Pigulewskaja (1969): 175–271.

144. Parker (1996b); Parker (1997); Parker (1998); Parker (2000); Parker (2002b).

145. Bourdon (1925); Bruyère (1966); Cooper (2005), Cooper (forthcoming).

146. Mayerson (1992) = Mayerson (1994b).

147. Kobishchanov (1979): 64–117, 171–189; Munro-Hay (1982); Munro-Hay (1991); Munro-Hay (1996); Peacock et al. (2007a).

148. Sedov (1996); Sedov (1997); Sedov (2007); Mouton et al. (2006); Salles and Sedov (2010); Davidde (1997a); Davidde (1997b); Davidde (1998); Sedov (2005): 162–165 for the temple at Qana' and 165, 166 (fig. 77), 169–171 for the synagogue; also for the synagogue at Qana' see Bowersock (1993) = Bowersock (1994); Sedov (2007): 74, 88 (fig. 4.15), 92, 99 (fig. 4.24), 103, for the temple and the synagogue; Ballet (1998): 47–50; Sedov (2007): especially 77–78 for Mediterranean amphoras found at Qana'; Davidde et al. (2004).

149. Sedov (1996); Mango (1996): 154–155; Sedov (2007); Salles and Sedov (2010).

150. Crone (1987): 40–50; Sedov (2007); Potts (2008).

151. Couyat (1911); Murray (1926a); Gibb (1960); Tibbetts (1961): 322–324; Garcin (1972); Ghosh (1992): 174–178 and 371 (notes); Peacock and Peacock (2008).

152. Le Quesne (2007): 26–27, 274, 296, 312–315. This northward trend continued; at present Safaga, 80 km north of Quseir, is the major harbor for Egyptian hajjis, who cannot afford to fly to Saudi Arabia.

BIBLIOGRAPHY

Abd el-Raziq, M., et al. 2006. Ayn Soukhna et la Mer Rouge. *Égypte, Afrique & Orient* 41, 3–6.

Abd el-Raziq, M., et al. 2002. *Les inscriptions d'Ayn Soukhna*. Cairo.

Abd el-Raziq, M., et al. 2004. Les mines de cuivre d'Ayn Soukhna. *Archéologia* 414, 10–21.

Abeydeera, A. 1998. The Geographical Perceptions of India and Ceylon in the *Periplus Maris Erythraei* and in Ptolemy's *Geography. Terrae Incognitae* 30, 1–25.

———. 2009. Raki's Mission to Romanukharattha: New Evidence in Favor of Pliny's Account of Taprobanê, *N.H.* 6.84–91. *HABIS* 40, 145–165.

Abraham, S. A. 2007. South Asian Perspective. In Sidebotham and Wendrich 2007a, 285–294.

Adam, J.-P. 1994. *Roman Building Materials and Techniques*. Bloomington and Indianapolis.

Adam, J.-P., et al. 2003. Al-Zarqâ' (Maximianon). In Cuvigny 2003d, 100–126.

Adams, C. E. P. 1995. Supplying the Roman Army: *O. Petr.* 245. *ZPE* 109, 119–124.

———. 2001a. "There and Back Again": Getting Around in Roman Egypt. In Adams and Laurence 2001, 138–166.

———. 2001b. Who Bore the Burden? The Organization of Stone Transport in Roman Egypt. In Mattingly, D. J., and Salmon, J. (eds.), *Economies beyond Agriculture in the Classical World*. Pp. 171–192. London and New York.

———. 2007. *Land Transport in Roman Egypt: A Study of Economics and Administration in a Roman Province*. Oxford.

Adams, C. E. P., and Laurence, R. (eds.). 2001. *Travel and Geography in the Roman Empire*. London and New York.

Adams, G. W. 2008. The Unbalanced Relationship between Ptolemy II and Pyrrhus of Epirus. In McKechnie and Guillaume 2008, 91–102.

Aldsworth, F. G. 1999. The Buildings at Shenshef. In Sidebotham and Wendrich 1999, 385–418.

Aldsworth, F. G., and Barnard, H. 1996. Survey of Hitan Rayan. In Sidebotham and Wendrich 1996, 411–440.

———. 1998. Survey of Shenshef. In Sidebotham and Wendrich 1998a, 427–443.

Aldsworth, F. G., et al. 1995. The Town Site: Survey, Plan and Description. In Sidebotham and Wendrich 1995, 13–20.

Alford, C. J. 1901–1902. Gold Mining in Egypt. *TIMM*, 11th session, 10, 2–28.

Allchin, F. R. 1995a. Mauryan Architecture and Art. In Allchin, F. R., *The Archaeology of Early Historic South Asia: The Emergence of Cities and States*. Pp. 222–273. Cambridge.

———.1995b. The Mauryan State and Empire. In Allchin, F. R., *The Archaeology of Early Historic South Asia: The Emergence of Cities and States*. Pp. 187–221. Cambridge.

Alston, R. 1995. *Soldier and Society in Roman Egypt: A Social History*. London and New York.

———. 1999. The Revolt of the Boukoloi: Geography, History and Myth. In Hopwood, K. (ed.), *Organised Crime in Antiquity*. Pp. 129–153. London and Swansea, UK.

———. 2002. *The City in Roman and Byzantine Egypt*. London and New York.

Amélineau, E. 1893. *La Géographie de l'Égypte à l'époque Copte*. Paris.

André, J., and Filliozat, J. 1980. *Pliny l'Ancien: Histoire Naturelle. Livre VI, 2ᵉ parte (L'Asie centrale et orientale, l'Inde)*. Paris.

———. 1986. *L'Inde vue de Rome: Textes latins de l'antiquité relatifs à l'Inde*. Paris.

Andreau, J. 1999. *Banking and Business in the Roman World*. Cambridge.

Les Annales Archéologiques arabes syriennes 42 (1996): *Special Issue Documenting the Activities of the International Colloquium Palmyra and the Silk Road*. Damascus.

L'Année Épigraphique. 1981. Paris.

Al-Ansary, A. R. 1982. *Qaryat al-Faw: A Portrait of Pre-Islamic Civilisation in Saudi Arabia*. Riyadh and New York.

Aperghis, M. 2001. Population-Production-Taxation-Coinage: A Model for the Seleukid Economy. In Archibald et al. 2001, 69–102.

Archibald, Z. H., et al. (eds.). 2001. *Hellenistic Economies*. London and New York.

Ardika, I. W. 1999. Ancient Trade Relation between India and Indonesia. In Behera, K. S. (ed.), *Maritime Heritage of India*. Pp. 80–89. New Delhi.

Arnaud, P. 2007. Diocletian's Prices Edict: The Prices of Seaborne Transport and the Average Duration of Maritime Travel. *JRA* 20 (1), 321–336.

Arora, R. K. 1977. Job's-tears (*Croix lacryma-jobi*)—a Minor Food and Fodder Crop of Northeastern India. *Economic Botany*, 358–366.

Al-As'ad, K. 1996. Caravan Roads of Palmyra. In *Les Annales Archéologiques arabes syriennes* (1996), 123–124.

Al-As'ad, K., et al. 1995. Die Textilen aus Palmyra: Ein internationales und interdisziplinäres Projekt. In Schmidt-Colinet, A. (ed.), *Palmyra Kulturbegegnung im Grenzbereich*. Pp. 54–56. Mainz.

Ashburner, W. (ed.). 1976. *ΝΟΜΟΣ ΡΟΔΙΩΝ ΝΑΥΤΙΚΟΣ The Rhodian Sea-Law*. Reprint. Aalen.

Aston, B. G., et al. 2000. Stone. In Nicholson, P. T., and Shaw, I. (eds.), *Ancient Egyptian Materials and Technology*. Pp. 5–77. Cambridge.

Aufrère, S. 1991a. *L'univers minéral dans la pensée égyptienne*. Vol. 1. Cairo.

———. 1991b. *L'univers minéral dans la pensée égyptienne.* Vol. 2. Cairo.

Aufrère, S. H. 1998. Religious Prospects of the Mine in the Eastern Desert in Ptolemaic and Roman Times. In Kaper 1998a, 5–19.

Austin, N. J. E., and Rankov, N. B. 1995. *Exploratio: Political and Military Intelligence in the Roman World from the Second Punic War to the Battle of Adrianople.* London and New York.

Avanzini, A. (ed.). 1997. *I Profumi d'Arabia: Atti del convegno.* Rome.

———. (ed.). 2002. *Khor Rori Report 1.* Pisa.

———. 2007. Sumhuram: A Hadrami Port on the Indian Ocean. In Seland 2007, 23–31.

———. (ed.). 2008. *A Port in Arabia between Rome and the Indian Ocean (3rd C. B.C.–5th C. A.D.).* Khor Rori Report 2. Rome.

Avanzini, A., and Sedov, A. 2005. The Stratigraphy of Sumhuram: New Evidence. *PSAS* 35, 11–17.

Babiker, M. 2001. Water in the Desert. In Krzywinski, K., and Pierce, R. H. (eds.), *Deserting the Desert a Threatened Cultural Landscape between the Nile and the Sea.* Pp. 61–74. Bergen.

Bag, A. K. 1988. Ships and Ship-building Technology in Ancient and Medieval India. In Rao 1988, 8–11.

Bagnall, R. S. 1976a. *The Administration of the Ptolemaic Possessions outside Egypt.* Leiden.

———. 1976b. *The Florida Ostraka, Documents from the Roman Army in Upper Egypt.* Durham, NC.

———. 1977. Army and Police in Roman Upper Egypt. *JARCE* 14, 67–86.

———. 1982. Upper and Lower Guard Posts. *Cd'É* 57 (113), 125–128.

———. 1985. The Camel, the Wagon and the Donkey in Later Roman Egypt. *BASP* 22, 1–6.

———. 1993. *Egypt in Late Antiquity.* Princeton, NJ.

———. 2000. Inscriptions from Wadi Kalalat. In Sidebotham and Wendrich 2000a, 403–412.

———. 2002. The Effects of the Plague: Model and Evidence. *JRA* 15, 114–120.

———. 2005. Evidence and Models for the Economy of Roman Egypt. In Manning, J. G., and Morris, I. (eds.), *The Ancient Economy Evidence and Models.* Pp. 187–204. Stanford, CA.

Bagnall, R. S, and Derow, P. 1981. *Greek Historical Documents: The Hellenistic Period.* Atlanta.

———. 2004. *The Hellenistic Period Historical Sources in Translation.* New ed. Malden, MA, and Oxford.

Bagnall, R. S., and Harrell, J. A. 2003. Knekites. *Cd'É* 78 (155–156), 229–235.

Bagnall, R. S., and Sheridan, J. A. 1994a. Greek and Latin Documents from 'Abu Sha'ar, 1990–1991. *JARCE* 31, 159–168.

———. 1994b. Greek and Latin Documents from 'Abu Sha'ar, 1992–1993. *BASP* 31, 109–120.

Bagnall, R. S., et al. 1996. A Ptolemaic Inscription from Bir 'Iayyan. *Cd'É* 71 (142), 317–330.

Bagnall, R. S., et al. 1999. The Ostraka. In Sidebotham and Wendrich 1999, 201–205.

Bagnall, R. S., et al. 2000. *Documents from Berenike.* Vol. 1. *Greek Ostraka from the 1996–1998 Seasons.* Brussels.

Bagnall, R. S., et al. 2001. Security and Water on the Eastern Desert Roads: The Prefect Iulius Ursus and the Construction of *Praesidia* under Vespasian. *JRA* 14, 325–333.

Bagnall, R. S., et al. 2005. *Documents from Berenike.* Vol. 2. *Texts from the 1999–2001 Seasons.* Brussels.

Bagnall, R. S., and Rathbone, D. W. (eds.). 2004. *Egypt from Alexander to the Early Christians: An Archaeological and Historical Guide.* London and Los Angeles.

Bailey, D. 2007. Glass. In Peacock and Maxfield 2007, 233–266.

Baines, J., and Málek, J. 2000. *Cultural Atlas of Ancient Egypt*. New York.

Ball, J. 1912. *The Geography and Geology of South-Eastern Egypt*. Cairo.

———. 1942. *Egypt in the Classical Geographers*. Cairo.

Ball, S. H. 1931. Historical Notes on Gem Mining. *Economic Geology and the Bulletin of the Society of Economic Geologists* 26, 681–738.

Ballet, P. 1998. Cultures matérielles des déserts d'Égypte sous le Haut et le Bas-Empire. Productions et échanges. In Kaper 1998a, 31–54.

Ballet, P., et al. 2000. *Coptos. L'Égypte antique aux portes du désert. Lyon, musée des Beaux-Arts 3 février–7 mai 2000*. Lyon and Paris.

Bandinelli, R. B. 1971. *Rome, the Late Empire: Roman Art, A.D. 200–400*. New York.

Bard, K. A., and Fattovich, R. (eds.). 2007a. *Harbor of the Pharaohs to the Land of Punt: Archaeological Investigations at Mersa/Wadi Gawasis, Egypt, 2001–2005*. Naples.

———. 2007b. Introduction. In Bard and Fattovich 2007a, 17–27.

———. 2010. Spatial Use of the Twelfth Dynasty Harbor at Mersa/Wadi Gawasis for the Seafaring Expeditions to Punt. *Journal of Ancient Egyptian Interconnections* 2 (3), 1–13.

Bard, K. A. and Shubert, S. B. (eds.). 1999. *Encyclopedia of the Archaeology of Ancient Egypt*. London and New York.

Bard, K. A., et al. 2007. Sea Port to Punt: New Evidence from Marsā Gawāsīs, Red Sea (Egypt). In Starkey, J., Starkey, P., and Wilkinson, T. (eds.), *Natural Resources and Cultural Connections of the Red Sea*. Pp. 143–148. Oxford.

Barker, G., et al. 1996a. *Farming the Desert: UNESCO Libyan Valleys Archaeological Survey*. Vol. 1. *Synthesis*. Paris and Tripoli.

Barker, G., et al. 1996b. *Farming the Desert: The UNESCO Libyan Valleys Archaeological Survey*. Vol. 2. *Gazetteer and Pottery*. Paris and Tripoli.

Barnard, H. 1998. Human Bones and Burials. In Sidebotham and Wendrich 1998a, 389–401.

———. 2005. Sire, il n'y à pas de Blemmyes. A Re-Evaluation of Historical and Archaeological Data. In Starkey, J. C. M. (ed.), *People of the Red Sea: Proceedings of Red Sea Project II Held in the British Museum October 2004*. Pp. 23–40. Oxford.

———. 2006. Eastern Desert Ware: Fine Pottery from an Arid Wasteland. *EA* 28, 29–30.

———. 2008. *Eastern Desert-Ware: Traces of the Inhabitants of the Eastern Deserts in Egypt and Sudan during the 4th–6th Centuries C.E.* Leiden.

Barnard, H. and Wendrich, W. Z. 2007. Survey of Berenike. In Sidebotham and Wendrich 2007a, 4–21.

Barnes, T. D. 1976. Imperial Campaigns, A.D. 285–311. *Phoenix* 30 (2), 174–193.

———. 1978. *The Sources of the Historia Augusta*. Brussels.

Barron, T., and Hume, W. F. 1902. *Topography and Geology of the Eastern Desert of Egypt Central Portion*. Cairo.

Barth, H. 1859. Reise von Assuān über Berenike nach Kossēr im October und November 1846. *ZAE* 7, 1–31.

Barthoux, J. 1922. *Chronologie et Description des roches ignées du désert Arabique*. Cairo.

Barzanò, A. 1988. Tiberio Giulio Alessandro, Prefetto d'Egitto (66/70). *ANRW* 2.10.1, 518–580.

Basa, K. K. 1999. Early Trade in the Indian Ocean: Perspectives on Indo-South-east Asian Maritime Contacts (*c.* 400 B.C.–A.D. 500). In Behera, K. S. (ed.), *Maritime Heritage of India*. Pp. 29–71. New Delhi.

Bass, G. F. 1982. Conclusions. In Bass, G. F., et al., *Yassi Ada*. Vol. 1. *A Seventh Century Byzantine Shipwreck*. Pp. 311–319. College Station, TX.

Baumer, C. 2002. *Die Südliche Seidenstraße Inseln in Sandmeer Versunkene Kulturen der Wüste Taklamakan*. Mainz.

Bauzou, T. 1998a. Les Bornes milliaires de la *Via Nova:* Évolution du IIe au IVe siècle. In Humbert, and Desreumaux 1998, 145–152.

———. 1998b. La Branche de Mafraq (Site de Al-Fudain). In Humbert and Desreumaux 1998, 129–132.

———. 1998c. Les Inscriptions relevées sur les Bornes milliaires du secteur septentrional de la *Via Nova*. In Humbert and Desreumaux 1998, 153–233.

———. 1998d. Le Segment septentrional de la *Via Nova* et la Table de Peutinger. In Humbert and Desreumaux 1998, 141–143.

———. 1998e. Le Système des tours associées à la *Via Nova*. In Humbert and Desreumaux 1998, 135–140.

———. 1998f. La Valeur des Milles romains sur la *Via Nova:* Étude métrologique. In Humbert, and Desreumaux 1998, 133–134.

———. 1998g. Les Vestiges de la *Via Nova* entre Busrā et ʿAmman. In Humbert and Desreumaux 1998, 109–127.

———. 1998h. La *Via Nova:* Introduction. In Humbert and Desreumaux 1998, 105–107.

Beckmann, J. 1846. *A History of Inventions, Discoveries, and Origins*. Vol. 1. 4th ed. London.

Bedigian, D. 2003. Sesame in Africa: Origin and Dispersals. In Neumann, K., et al. (eds.), *Food, Fuel and Fields: Progress in African Archaeobotany*. Pp. 17–36. Cologne.

Beeston, A. F. L. 1979. Some Observations on Greek and Latin Data Relating to South Arabia. *BSOAS* 42, 7–12.

———. 1984. Further Remarks on the Zaydil Sarcophagus Text. *PSAS* 14, 100–102.

———. 2005. The Arabian Aromatics Trade in Antiquity. In Macdonald, M. C. A., and Phillips, C. S. (eds.). *A. F. L. Beeston and the Arabian Seminar and Other Papers Including a Personal Reminiscence by W. W. Müller*. Pp. 53–64. Oxford.

Behl, B. K. 1998. *The Ajanta Caves: Artistic Wonder of Ancient Buddhist India*. New York.

Benveniste, E. 1945. La doctrine médicale des Indo-Européens. *RHR* 130, 5–12.

Begley, V. 1967. Archaeological Exploration in Northern Ceylon. *Expedition* 9 (4), 21–29.

Begley, V., and Tomber, R. S. 1999. Indian Pottery Sherds. In Sidebotham and Wendrich 1999, 161–181.

Begley, V., et al. 1996. *The Ancient Port of Arikamedu: New Excavations and Researches 1989–1992*. Vol. 1. Pondicherry, India.

Begley, V., et al. 2004. *The Ancient Port of Arikamedu: New Excavations and Researches 1989–1992*. Vol. 2. Paris.

Behl, B. K. 1998. *The Ajanta Caves: Artistic Wonder of Ancient Buddhist India*. New York.

Belfiore, S. 2004. *Il Periplo del Mare Eritreo di anonimo del I sec. d. C. e altri testi sul commercio fra Roma e l'Oriente attraverso l'Oceano Indiano e la Via della Seta*. Rome.

Bellefonds, P. L. de. N.d. *L'Etbaye pays habité par les Arabes Bicharieh: Géographie, ethnologie, mines d'or*. Paris.

Bellwald, U., and al-Huneid, M. 2003. *The Petra Siq. Nabataean Hydrology Uncovered*. Amman, Jordan.

Belzoni, G. 1820. *Narrative of the Operations and Recent Discoveries within the Pyramids, Temples, Tombs, and Excavations, in Egypt and Nubia; and of a Journey to the Coast of the Red Sea, in Search of the Ancient Berenice; and Another to the Oasis of Jupiter Ammon*. London.

Bender Jørgensen, L. 2006. The Late Roman Fort at Abū Sha'ār, Egypt: Textiles in Their Archaeological Context. In Schrenk, S. (ed.), *Textiles In Situ: Their Find Spots in Egypt and Neighbouring Countries in the First Millennium C.E.*. Pp. 161–173. Bern, Switzerland.

Benedict, F. G. 1936. *The Physiology of the Elephant*. Washington, DC.

Bengston, H. 1955. Kosmas Indikopleustes und die Ptolemäer. *Historia* 4 (2/3), 151–156.

Bent, T., and Bent, M. T. 1900. *Southern Arabia*. London.

Benveniste, E. 1945. La doctrine médicale des Indo-Européens. *RHR* 130, 5–12.

———. 1964. Édits d'Aśoka en traduction grecque. *JA* 252, 137–157.

Berghaus, P. 1989. Funde severischer Goldmünzen in Indien. In Drexhage, H.-J., and Sünskes, J. (eds.), *Migratio et Commutatio Studien zur alten Geschichte und deren Nachleben. Thomas Pekáry zum 60. Geburtstag am 13. September 1989 dargebraucht von Freunden, Kollegen und Schülern*. Pp. 93–101. St. Katharinen, Germany.

———. 1991. Roman Coins from India and Their Imitations. In Jha, A. K. (ed.), *Coinage, Trade and the Economy, January 8th–11th, 1991. 3rd International Colloquium*. Pp. 108–121. Maharashtra.

———. 1992. Zu den römischen Fundmünzen aus Indien. *Schweizerische Numismatische Rundschau* 71, 226–247 and plates 27–28.

Bernand, A. 1969. *Les Inscriptions grecques de Philae: Époque ptolémaique*. Paris.

———. 1972a. *De Koptos à Kosseir*. Leiden.

———. 1972b. *Le Paneion d'El-Kanaïs: Les inscriptions grecques*. Leiden.

———. 1977. *Pan du désert*. Leiden.

———. 1984a. *Les portes du désert: Recueil des inscriptions grecques d'Antinooupolis, Tentyris, Koptos, Apollonopolis Parva et Apollonopolis Magna*. Paris.

Bernand, E. 1984b. Epigraphie grecque et architecture égyptienne. In Walter, H. (ed.), *Hommages à Lucien Lerat*. Pp. 73–89. Besançon and Paris.

Bernand, E., et al. 1991. *Recueil des Inscriptions de l'Éthiopie des périodes Pré-Axoumite et Axoumite. Vol. 1. Les Documents (Académie des Inscriptions et Belles-Lettres)*. Paris.

Bernard, P. 2005. De l'Euphrate à la Chine avec la caravane de Maès Titianos (c. 100 ap. n.è.). *CRAI* fasc. 3, 929–969.

Beyhl, F. E. 1998. Anmerkungen zum Drachenblut und zu den Namen der Insel Soqotra. *ZDMG* 148, 35–82.

Bianchetti, S. 2002. Die Seerouten nach Indien in hellenistischer und römischer Zeit. In Olshausen, E., and Sonnabend, H. (eds.), *Stuttgarter Kolloquium zur historischen Geographie des Altertums 7, 1999. Zu Wasser und zu Land. Verkehrswege in der antiken Welt*. Pp. 280–292. Stuttgart.

Bigwood, J. M. 1993. Aristotle and the Elephant Again. *AJP* 114 (4), 537–555.

Billerbeck, M. 2006. *Stephani Byzantii Ethnica Volumen I: Α-Γ. Corpus Fontium Historiae Byzantinae. Consilio Societatis Internationalis Studiis Byzantinis Provehendis Destinatae Editum. Volumen XLIII/1*. Berlin and New York.

Bin Seray, H. M. 1996. Spasinou Charax and Its Commercial Relations with the East through the Arab Gulf. *Aram* 8, 15–23.

Bingen, J. 1978. *Le Papyrus Revenue Laws—Tradition grecque et Adaptation hellénistique*. Opladen.

———. 1984. Une dédicace de marchands palmyréniens à Coptos. *Cd'É* 59, 355–358.

———. 1997a. Lettres privées (279–303). In Bingen et al. 1997, 113–140.

———. 1997b. Lettres privées provenant de Raïma (255–278). In Bingen et al. 1997, 81–112.

Bingen, J., et al. 1992. *Mons Claudianus. Ostraca Graeca et Latina I (O. Claud. 1 à 190)*. Cairo.

Bingen, J., et al. 1997. *Mons Claudianus ostraca graeca et Latina II (O. Claud. 191 à 416)*. Cairo.

Birley, A. 2002. *Garrison Life at Vindolanda: A Band of Brothers*. The Mill, Brimscombe Port, Stroud, UK.

Blake, M. E. 1936. Roman Mosaics of the Second Century in Italy. *MAAR* 13, 67–214.

Blockley, R. C. 1983. *The Fragmentary Classicizing Historians of the Later Roman Empire: Eunapius, Olympiodorus, Priscus and Malchus*. Vol. 2. *Text, Translation and Historiographical Notes*. Liverpool.

Bloxam, E., and Storemyr, P. 2005. The Quarries of Gebel Gulab and Gebel Tingar, Aswan. *EA* 26, 37–40.

Blue, L. 2002. Myos Hormos/Quseir al-Qadīm. A Roman and Islamic Port on the Red Sea Coast of Egypt: A Maritime Perspective. *PSAS* 32, 139–150.

———. 2006a. The Sedimentary History of the Harbour Area. In Peacock and Blue 2006c, 43–61.

———. 2006b. Trench 12. In Peacock and Blue 2006c, 81–84.

Blue, L., and Peacock, D. 2006. Trench 7A. In Peacock and Blue 2006c, 68–74.

Blue, L., and Walsh, M. 2001. Trench 10. In Peacock, D. P. S., et al. (eds.), *Myos Hormos—Quseir al-Qadim: A Roman and Islamic Port Site. Interim Report 2001*. Pp. 25–29. Southampton, UK. Unpublished.

Boak, A. E. R., and Youtie, H. C. (eds.). 1960. *The Archive of Aurelius Isidorus in the Egyptian Museum, Cairo, and the University of Michigan (P. Cair. Isidor.)*. Ann Arbor, MI.

Boardman, J. 2001. *Greek Gems and Finger Rings Early Bronze Age to Late Classical*. New expanded edition. London.

Bonacossi, D. M. 2002. Excavations at Khor Rori: The 1997 and 1998 Campaigns. In Avanzini, A. (ed.), *Khor Rori Report*. Pp. 29–69. Pisa.

Bonneau, D. 1993. *Le Régime Administratif de l'eau du Nil dans l'Égypte grecque, romaine et byzantine*. Leiden, New York, and Cologne.

Bopearachchi, O. 1992. Le commerce maritime entre Rome et Sri Lanka d'après les données numismatiques. *RÉA* 1–2, 107–121.

———. 1996. Seafaring in the Indian Ocean. Archaeological Evidence from Sri Lanka. In Ray and Salles 1996, 59–77.

———. 2006. Coins. In Coningham, R. (ed.), *Anuradhapura: The British-Sri Lankan Excavations at Anuradhapura Salgaha Watta 2*. Vol. 2. *The Artifacts*. Pp. 7–26. Oxford.

Bopearachchi, O., and Pieper, W. 1998. *Ancient coins from Sri Lanka*. Turnhout.

Bos, J. E. M. F. 2007. Jar Stoppers, Seals, and Lids, 1999 Season. In Sidebotham and Wendrich 2007a, 258–269.

Bos, J. E. M. F., and Helms, C. C. 2000. Jar Stoppers and Seals. In Sidebotham and Wendrich 2000a, 275–303.

Bouché-Leclercq, A. 1978. *Histoire des Lagides*. Reprint. Aalen, Germany.

Boulnois, L. 2004. *Silk Road, Monks, Warriors and Merchants on the Silk Road*. Geneva.

Bourdon, C. 1925. *Anciens canaux, anciens sites et portes de Suez*. Cairo.

Bowersock, G. W. 1983. *Roman Arabia*. Cambridge, MA, and London.

———. 1993. The New Greek Inscription from South Yemen. In Langdon, J. S., et al. (eds.), *TO ΕΛΛΗΝΙΚΟΝ. Studies in Honor of Speros Vryonis, Jr.* Vol. 1. *Hellenic Antiquity and Byzantium*. Pp. 3–8. New Rochelle, NY.

———. 1994. The New Greek Inscription from South Yemen. In Bowersock, G. W. (ed.), *Studies on the Eastern Roman Empire: Social, Economic and Administrative History, Religion, Historiography*. Pp. 285–290. Goldbach, Germany.

———. 1997. Comentarii Breviores: Nabataeans on the Capitoline. *Hyperboreus* 3 (2), 347–352.

Bowman, A. K. 1976. Papyri and Roman Imperial History, 1960–1975. *JRS* 66, 153–173.

———. 1978. The Military Occupation of Upper Egypt in the Reign of Diocletian. *BASP* 15, 25–38.

———. 1986. *Egypt after the Pharaohs 332 B.C.–A.D. 642: From Alexander to the Arab Conquest*. Berkeley and Los Angeles.

———. 1994. *Life and Letters on the Roman Frontier: Vindolanda and Its People*. London.

Bowman, A. K., and Wilson, A. (eds.). 2009. *Quantifying the Roman Economy: Methods and Problems*. Oxford.

Bowman, A. K., et al. 1994. *The Vindolanda Writing-Tablets (Tabulae Vindolandenses II)*. London.

Bowsher, J. M. C. 1989. The Nabataean Army. In French, D. H., and Lightfoot, C. S. (eds.), *The Eastern Frontier of the Roman Empire: Proceedings of a Colloquium Held at Ankara in September 1988*. Pp. 19–30. Oxford.

Bradford, N. 2000. The Harbour Area Excavations. In Peacock, D. P. S., et al. (eds.), *Myos Hormos—Quseir al-Qadim: A Roman and Islamic Port Site on the Red Sea Coast of Egypt. Interim Report 2000*. Pp. 43–45. Southampton, UK. Unpublished.

———. 2001. Pit 10000 Harbour Area. In Peacock, D. P. S., et al. (eds.). *Myos Hormos—Quseir al-Qadim: A Roman and Islamic Port Site on the Red Sea Coast of Egypt. Interim Report 2001*. Pp. 31–34. Southampton, UK. Unpublished.

Braithwaite, C. J. R. 1987. Geology and Palaeogeography of the Red Sea Region. In Edwards and Head 1987, 22–44.

Brand, P. J. 2000. *The Monuments of Seti I. Epigraphic, Historical and Art Historical Analysis*. Leiden, Boston, and Cologne.

Bratton, T. L. 1981. The Identity of the Plague of Justinian. *Transactions and Studies of the College of Physicians of Philadelphia*, ser. 5,3, 113–124, and 174–180.

Breasted, J. H. 2001a. *Ancient Records of Egypt*. Vol. 1. *The First through Seventeenth Dynasties*. Urbana and Chicago.

———. 2001b. *Ancient Records of Egypt*. Vol. 2. *The Eighteenth Dynasty*. Urbana and Chicago.

———. 2001c. *Ancient Records of Egypt*. Vol. 3. *The Nineteenth Dynasty*. Urbana and Chicago.

———. 2001d. *Ancient Records of Egypt*. Vol. 4. *The Twentieth through the Twenty-sixth Dynasties*. Urbana and Chicago.

Bridgman, R., et al. 2006. The Islamic Harbour. In Peacock and Blue 2006c, 95–115.

Brier, B., and Wilkinson, C. 2005. A Preliminary Study on the Accuracy of Mummy Portraits. *ZÄS* 132, Heft 2, 107–111 and Tafeln XXIII–XXIX.

Brill, R. H. 1991/92. Some Thoughts on the Origin of the Chinese Word "BOLI." *SRAA* 2, 129–136.

Briquel-Chatonnet, F., and Nehmé, L. 1998. Graffitti nabatéens d'al-Muwayah et de Bi'r al-Hammâmât (Égypte), *Semitica* 47, 81–88.

Brocchi, G. B. 1841. *Giornale delle osservazioni fatte ne' viaggi in Egitto, nella Siria e nella Nubia* vol. 2. Bassano.

Brodersen, K. 1995. *Terra Cognita: Studien zur römischen Raumerfassung.* Hildesheim, Germany; Zürich and New York.

———. 2001. The Presentation of Geographical Knowledge for Travel and Transport in the Roman World *Itineraria non tantum adnotata sed etiam picta.* In Adams and Laurence 2001, 7–21.

———. 2003. Die Tabula Peutingeriana: Gehalt und Gestalt einer "alten Karte" und ihrer antiken Vorlagen. In Unverhau, D. (ed.), *Geschichtsdeutung auf alten Karten: Archäologie und Geschichte.* Pp. 289–297. Wiesbaden.

Brown, L. 1982. *The Indian Christians of St. Thomas: An Account of the Ancient Syrian Church of Malabar.* Cambridge and New York.

Brown, V. M., and Harrell, J. A. 1995. Topographical and petrological survey of ancient Roman quarries in the Eastern Desert of Egypt. In Maniatis, Y., et al. (eds.). *The Study of Marble and Other Stones used in Antiquity. ASMOSIA III Athens: Transactions of the 3rd International Symposium of the Association for the Study of Marble and Other Stones used in Antiquity.* Pp. 221–234. London.

Browning, I. 1979. *Palmyra.* Park Ridge, NJ.

Brun, J.-P. 2002. *Hodos Myoshormitikè:* l'équipment de la route de Coptos et la mer Rouge aux époques ptolémaïque et romaine. *Topoi supplément* 3, 395–414.

———. 2003a. Bi'r al-Hammâmât. In Cuvigny 2003d, 91–94.

———. 2003b. Chronologie de l'équipement de la route à l'époque gréco-romaine. In Cuvigny 2003d, 187–205.

———. 2003c. Méthodes et conditions de fouille des fortins et des dépotoirs ou les affres d'un Gallo-Romain en Égypte. In Cuvigny 2003d, 61–71.

———. 2003d. Al-Muwayh (Krokodilô). In Cuvigny 2003d, 77–91.

———. 2003e. Le Village dans les carrières du Wâdî Hammâmât (Persou I). In Cuvigny 2003d, 95–97.

Brun, J.-P., and Leguilloux, M. 2003. Les objets en cuir. In Cuvigny 2003e, 539–547.

Brun, J.-P., et al. 2003. Le mystère des tours et la question des *skopeloi.* In Cuvigny 2003d, 207–234.

Bruyère, B. 1966. *Fouilles de Clysma-Qolzoum (Suez). 1930–1932.* Cairo.

Budischovsky, M.-C. 1977. *La diffusion des cultes Isiaques autour de la mer Adriatique.* Vol. 1. *Inscriptions et monuments.* Leiden.

Bülow-Jacobsen, A. 1992a. The Archive of Successus (124–136). In Bingen et al. 1992, 111–121.

———. 1992b. The Private Letters (137–171). In Bingen et al. 1992, 123–157.

———. 1997a. The Correspondance of Dioscorus and Others (224–242). In Bingen et al. 1997, 43–68.

———. 1997b. The Correspondance of Petenephotes (243–254). In Bingen et al. 1997, 69–80.

———. 2001. Drinking and Cheating in the Desert. In Gagos, T., and Bagnall, R. S. (eds.), *Essays and Texts in Honor of J. David Thomas.* Pp. 119–123. Oakville, CT.

———. 2003a. Toponyms and *Proskynemata*. In Cuvigny 2003d, 51–59.

———. 2003b. The traffic on the road and the provisioning of the stations. In Cuvigny 2003e, 399–426.

———. 2008. An Ostracon from the Quarry at Umm Balad. In Hoogendijk, F. A. J. and Muhs, B. P. (eds.) (with indexes by M. J. Bakker). *Sixty-Five Papyrological Texts Presented to Klass A. Worp on the Occasion of his 65th Birthday (P. L. Bat. 33)*. Pp. 311–315. Leiden-Boston.

Bülow-Jacobsen, A., and Cuvigny, H. 2007. Sulpicius Serenus, *procurator Augusti*, et la titulature des préfets de Bérénice. *Chiron* 37, 11–33.

Bülow-Jacobsen, A., et al. 1994. The Identification of Myos Hormos. New Papyrological Evidence. *BIFAO* 94, 27–42.

Bülow-Jacobsen, A., et al. 1995. Les inscriptions d' Al-Muwayh. *BIFAO* 95, 103–124.

Bukharin, M. D. 2005–2006. Romans in the Southern Red Sea. *Arabia* 3, 135–140.

Bulliet, R. W. 1975. *The Camel and the Wheel*. Cambridge, MA.

Burkhalter-Arce, F. 2002. Le 'Tarif de Coptos'. La Douane de Coptos, les fermiers de l'*apostolion* et le préfet du désert de Bérénice. In Boussac, M. F. (ed.), *Topoi supplément* 3, 199–233.

Burstein, S. M. (trans., ed.). 1985. *The Hellenistic Age from the Battle of Ipsos to the Death of Kleopatra VII*. Cambridge.

———. (trans., ed.). 1989. *Agatharchides of Cnidus on the Erythraean Sea*. London.

———. 1996. Ivory and Ptolemaic Exploration of the Red Sea: The Missing Factor. *Topoi* 6 (2), 799–807.

———. 2000. Exploration and Ethnography in Ptolemaic Egypt. *AW* 31 (1), 31–37.

———. 2008a. Elephants for Ptolemy II: Ptolemaic Policy in Nubia in the Third Century B.C. In McKechnie and Guillaume 2008, 135–147.

———. 2008b. Trogodytes = Blemmyes = Beja? The Misuse of Ancient Ethnography. In Barnard, H., and Wendrich, W. (eds.). *The Archaeology of Mobility: Old World and New World Nomadism*. Pp. 250–263. Los Angeles.

Buschmann, K. 1991. Motiv und Ziel des Aelius-Gallus-Zuges nach Südarabien. *WO* 22, 85–93.

Bussagli, M. 1951. Recent Research on Ancient Indian Medicine. *EW* 2, 147–150.

Butcher, K. 1995–1996. Bactrian camels in Roman Arabia. *Berytus* 42, 113–116.

———. 2003. *Roman Syria and the Near East*. London.

Butzer, K. W., and Hansen, C. L. 1968. *Desert and River in Nubia: Geomorphology and Prehistoric Environments at the Aswan Reservoir*. Madison, WI.

Callataÿ, D. de. 2005. The Graeco-Roman Economy in the Super Long-run: Lead, Copper, and Shipwrecks. *JRA* 18, 361–372.

Calzini Gysens, J. 1990. Safaitic Graffiti from Pompeii. *PSAS* 20, 1–7.

Cappers, R. T. J. 1996. Archaeobotanical Remains. In Sidebotham and Wendrich 1996, 319–336.

———. 1998a. Archaeobotanical Remains. In Sidebotham and Wendrich 1998a, 289–330.

———. 1998b. A Botanical Contribution to the Analysis of Subsistence and Trade at Berenike (Red Sea Coast of Egypt). In Kaper 1998a, 75–86.

———. 1999a. Archaeobotanical Evidence of Roman Trade with India. In Ray, H. P. (ed.), *Archaeology of Seafaring: The Indian Ocean in the Ancient Period*. Pp. 51–69. Delhi.

———. 1999b. The Archaeobotanical Remains. In Sidebotham and Wendrich 1999, 299–305.

———. 1999c. The Archaeobotanical Remains from Shenshef. In Sidebotham and Wendrich 1999, 419–426.

———. 2000. Archaeobotanical Remains. In Sidebotham and Wendrich 2000a, 305–310.

———. 2003. Exotic Imports of the Roman Empire: An Exploratory Study of Potential Vegetal Products from Asia. In Neumann, K., et al. (eds.), *Food, Fuel and Fields: Progress in African Archaeobotany*. Pp. 197–206. Cologne.

———. 2006. *Roman Foodprints at Berenike: Archaeobotanical Evidence of Subsistence and Trade in the Eastern Desert of Egypt*. Los Angeles.

Capponi, L. 2005. *Augustan Egypt: The Creation of a Roman Province*. New York and London.

Carandini, A., et al. 1982. *Filosofiana, the Villa of Piazza Armerina: The Image of a Roman Aristocrat in the Time of Constantine*. Palermo.

Carannante, A., et al. 2007. Other Finds. In Bard and Fattovich 2007a, 189–215.

Carrié, J.-M. 1999. Cursus Publicus. In Bowersock, G. W., et al. (eds.), *Late Antiquity: A Guide to the Postclassical World*. Pp. 402–403. Cambridge, MA, and London.

———. 2001. Le temple de Sérapis. In Maxfield and Peacock 2001b, 127–155.

Carroll, M. 2003. *Earthly Paradises: Ancient Gardens in History and Archaeology*. Los Angeles.

Carswell, J. 1982. Imported Far Eastern Wares. In Whitcomb, D. S., and Johnson, J. H. (eds.), *Quseir al-Qadim 1980 Preliminary Report*. Pp. 194–195. Malibu, CA.

———. 1991. The Port of Mantai, Sri Lanka. In Begley, V., and De Puma, R. D. (eds.), *Rome and India: The Ancient Sea Trade*. Pp. 197–203. Madison, WI.

Cary, M. 1956. Maës, Qui et Titianus. *CQ*, n.s., 6 (3–4), 130–134.

Cashman, V. L., et al. 1999. Jar Stoppers. In Sidebotham and Wendrich 1999, 285–297.

Casson, L. 1971. *Ships and Seamanship in the Ancient World*. Princeton, NJ.

———. 1974. *Travel in the Ancient World*. London.

———. 1980. Rome's Trade with the East: The Sea Voyage to Africa and India. *TAPA* 110, 21–36.

———. 1984a. *Ancient Trade and Society*. Detroit.

———. 1984b. The Role of the State in Rome's Grain Trade. In Casson 1984a, 96–116.

———. 1986a. P. Vindob. 40822 and the Shipping of Goods from India. *BASP* 23, 73–79.

———. 1986b. *Ships and Seamanship in the Ancient World*. 2nd ed. Princeton, NJ.

———. 1988a. Piracy. In Grant, M., and Kitzinger, R. (eds.), *Civilization of the Ancient Mediterranean: Greece and Rome*. Vol. 2. Pp. 837–844. New York.

———. 1988b. Transportation. In Grant, M., and Kitzinger, R. (eds.). *Civilization of the Ancient Mediterranean: Greece and Rome*. Vol. 1. Pp. 353–365. New York.

———. 1989. *The Periplus Maris Erythraei: Text with Introduction, Translation, and Commentary*. Princeton, NJ.

———. 1990. New Light on Maritime Loans: P. Vindob G 40822. *ZPE* 84, 195–206.

———. 1991. *The Ancient Mariners, Seafarers and Sea Fighters of the Mediterranean in Ancient Times*. 2nd ed. Princeton, NJ.

———. 1993a. Graeco-Roman Trade in the Indian Ocean. In Vryonis, S. (ed.), *The Greeks and the Sea*. Pp. 67–76. New Rochelle, NY.

———. 1993b. Ptolemy II and the Hunting of African Elephants. *TAPA* 123, 247–260.

———. 1994. *Ships and Seafaring in Ancient Times*. Austin, TX.

———. 2001. New Light on Maritime Loans: P. Vindob G 40822. In Chakravarti, R. (ed.), *Trade in Early India*. Pp. 228–243. New Delhi.

———. 2004. "I've Already Sold My Tunic": Nile Skippers and Their Problems in the Mid-Third Century B.C. In Hocker, F., and Ward, C. (eds.), *The Philosophy of Shipbuilding*. Pp. 95–102. College Station, TX.

Castel, G., and Goyon, J.-C. 1980. Installations rupestres du moyen et du nouvel empire au Gebel Zeit (prés de Râs Dib) sur la mer rouge. *MDAIK* 36, 299–318.

Castel, G., and Soukiassian, G. 1985. Dépôt de stèles dans le sanctuaire du Nouvel Empire au Gebel Zeit. *BIFAO* 85, 285–293.

Castel, G., et al. 1989. *Gebel el-Zeit 1: Les mines de galena (Égypte, IIème millénaire av. J.-C.)*. Cairo.

Castel, G., et al. 1998. Les mines du ouadi Um Balad désert Oriental. *BIFAO* 98, 57–87.

Castel, G., et al. 1999. Gebel Zeit. In Bard and Shubert 1999, 334–338.

Castiglioni, A., and Vercoutter, J. 1995. *Das Goldland der Pharaonen*. Mainz.

Cataudella, M. R. 2002. Quante vie d'acqua fra il Mediterraneo e la Persia? In Olshausen, E., and Sonnabend, H. (eds.), *Stuttgarter Kolloquium zur historischen Geographie des Altertums 7, 1999. Zu Wasser und zu Land. Verkehrswege in der antiken Welt*. Pp. 48–59. Stuttgart.

Červíček, P. 1974. *Felsbilder des Nord-Etbai, Oberägyptens und Unternubiens*. Wiesbaden.

Chakrabati, D. K. 2006. *The Oxford Companion to Indian Archaeology: The Archaeological Foundations of Ancient India Stone Age to A.D. 13th Century*. Oxford.

Chami, F. A. 1999. Roman Beads from the Rufiji Delta, Tanzania: First Incontrovertible Archaeological Link with the *Periplus*. *CA* 40 (2), 237–241.

———. 2004. The Egypto-Graeco-Romans and Panchaea/Azania: Sailing in the Erythraean Sea. In Lunde and Porter 2004, 93–103.

Chapekar, N. M. 1977. *Ancient India and Greece: A Study of Their Cultural Contacts*. Delhi.

Charles, R. H. 1916. *The Chronicle of John, Bishop of Nikiu, Translated from Zotenberg's Ethiopic Text*. London.

Charlesworth, M. P. 1974. *Trade-Routes and Commerce in the Roman Empire*. Chicago.

Chauhan, R. R. S. 1988. Some Interesting Findings of Sunken and Wrecked Ships in the Indian Ocean during Ancient and Medieval Periods. In Rao 1988, 14–16.

Chauveau, M. 2000. *Egypt in the Age of Cleopatra: History and Society under the Ptolemies*. Ithaca, NY, and London.

Cherian, P. J., et al. 2007. The Muziris Heritage Project: Excavations at Pattanam—2007. *JIOA* 4, 1–10.

Cherry, P. 2000. The World's Oldest Maps? A Preliminary Study of the Abstract Rock-art Lines. In Rohl, D. (ed.), *The Followers of Horus: Eastern Desert Survey Report*, 1, 166–168. Abington, Oxon., UK.

Chesneau, M. 1900. Les mines d'émeraude de l'Étbaï septentrional: Le Géographie. *BSG* 2 (2), 417–419.

Chevallier, R. 1997. *Les voies romaines*. Paris.

Chittick, N. 1966. Six Early Coins from Near Tanga. *Azania* 1, 156–157.

———. 1976. An Archaeological Reconnaissance in the Horn: The British-Somali Expedition, 1975. *Azania* 11, 117–133.

———. 1980a. Pre-Islamic Trade and Ports of the Horn. In Leakey, R. E., and Ogot, B. A. (eds.),

Proceedings of the 8th Panafrican Congress of Prehistory and Quaternary Studies: Nairobi, 5 to 10 September 1977. Pp. 364–366. Nairobi.

———. 1980b. Sewn Boats in the Western Indian Ocean, and a Survival in Somalia. *International Journal of Nautical Archaeology and Underwater Exploration* 9 (4), 297–309.

Chitty, D. J. 1966. *The Desert a City.* Crestwood, NY.

Cimino, R. M., and Scialpi, F. 1974. *India and Italy (Exhibition Organized in Collaboration with the Archaeological Survey of India and the Indian Council for Cultural Relations).* Rome.

Clarysse, W. 1984. A Roman Army Unit Near Thebes. In *Atti del XVII Congresso internazionale di papirologia.* Pp. 1021–1026. Naples.

Clarysse, W., and Thompson, D. J. 2006. *Counting the People in Hellenistic Egypt.* Vol. 2. *Historical Studies.* Cambridge.

Clauss, M. 2000. *The Roman Cult of Mithras: The God and His Mysteries.* New York.

Clermont-Ganneau, C. 1903. Inscription gréco-palmyrénienne d'Égypte. *RAO* 5, 300–306.

———. 1919. Les Nabatéens en Égypte. *RHR* 80, 1–29.

Close, A. E. 1999. Paleolithic Tools. In Bard and Shubert 1999, 597–604.

Cockle, W. E. H. 1992. Writing and Reading Exercises (179–190). In Bingen et al. 1992, 169–176.

———. 1997. School Exercises. Verse and Prose (409–416). In Bingen et al. 1997, 249–276.

Codrington, H. W. 1924. *Ceylon Coins and Currency.* Colombo, Ceylon (Sri Lanka).

Cohen, G. M. 2006. *The Hellenistic Settlements in Syria, the Red Sea Basin, and North Africa.* Berkeley, Los Angeles, and London.

Coleman, R. G. 1993. *Geologic Evolution of the Red Sea.* Oxford and New York.

Colledge, M. A. R. 1976. *The Art of Palmyra.* London.

Collingwood, P. 1998. *The Techniques of Ply-Split Braiding.* London.

Colombo, V. 1995. Nabataeans and Palmyrenes: An Analysis of the Tell El-Shuqafiyye Inscriptions. *Aram* 7, 183–187.

Colston, R. E. 1886. Les Expéditions égyptiennes en Afrique. Journal d'un Voyage du Caire à Kéneh, Bérénice et Berber et retour par le désert de Korosko. *BSkGÉ* 2nd ser., no. 9, 489–568.

———. 1887. Les Expéditions égyptiennes en Afrique. Documents. Rapport géologique sur le région située entre Bérénice et Berber. *BSkGÉ,* 2nd ser., no. 11, 573–597.

Comes, H. 1966. Did Cosmas Come to India? *Indica* 3, 7–24.

Coningham, R. A. E., and Allchin, F. R. 1995. The Rise of Cities in Sri Lanka. In Allchin, R., et al. *The Archaeology of Early Historic South Asia: The Emergence of Cities and States.* Pp. 152–183. Cambridge.

Coningham, R., Ford, L., Cheshire, S. and Young, R. 2006. Unglazed Ceramics. In Coningham, R. (ed.), *Anuradhapura: The British–Sri Lankan Excavations at Anuradhapura Salgaha Watta 2.* Vol. 2. *The Artifacts.* Pp. 127–331. Oxford.

Conrad, L. I. 1981. The Plague in the Early Medieval Near East. PhD diss., Princeton University. Princeton, NJ.

Cooper, J. P. 2005. *The Nile–Red Sea Canal in Antiquity: A Consideration of the Evidence for Its Existence, Duration and Route.* MA thesis, University of Southampton. Southampton, UK.

———. Forthcoming. Nile-Red Sea Canals: Chronology, Location, Seasonality and Function. In *Proceedings of the Fourth International Conference on the Peoples of the Red Sea Region. 25th–26th September 2008.* Southampton, UK.

Copeland, P. 2006. Trench 2B. In Peacock and Blue 2006c, 116–127.

Copeland, P., and Handley, F. 1998. The "Bath House," Wadi Abu Ma'amel. In Peacock, D. P. S., and Maxfield, V. (eds.), *The Roman Imperial Porphyry Quarries: Gebel Dokhan, Egypt. Interim Report 1998*. Pp. 6–8. Southampton, UK. Unpublished.

———. 2001. The Bathhouse. In Maxfield and Peacock 2001b, 19–23.

Cosentino, S. 2000. The Syrianos's "Strategikon": A 9th Century Source? *Byzantinistica* 2, 243–280.

Costa, P. M. 1977. A Latin-Greek Inscription from the Jawf of Yemen. *PSAS* 7, 69–72.

Couyat, J. 1910a. Ports gréco-romains de la mer Rouge, et grandes routes du Désert Arabique. *CRAI*, 525–542.

———. 1910b. La route de Myos-Hormos et les carrières de porphyry rouge. *BIFAO* 7, 15–33.

———. 1911. Les routes d'Aidhab. *BIFAO* 8, 135–143.

Couyat, J., and Montet, P. 1912. *Les inscriptions hiéroglyphiques et hiératiques du Ouâdi Hammâmât*. Cairo.

Crawford, M., and Reynolds, J. 1979. Aezani Copy of the Prices Edict. *ZPE* 34, 163–210.

Cribiore, R. 1996. *Writing, Teachers, and Students in Graeco-Roman Egypt*. Atlanta.

Crone, P. 1987. *Meccan Trade and the Rise of Islam*. Princeton, NJ.

Crowfoot, J. W. 1911. Some Ports of the Anglo-Egyptian Sudan. *GJ* 37, 523–550.

Cunningham, A. 1961. *Corpus Inscriptionum Indicarum*. Vol. 1. *Inscriptions of Aśoka*. Varanasi, India.

Cunz, O. (ed.). 1990. *Itineraria Romana Volumen Prius Itineraria Antonini Augusti et Burdigalense*. Stuttgart.

Curtis, R. I. 1991. *Garum and Salsamenta: Production and Commerce in Materia Medica*. Leiden, New York, Copenhagen, and Cologne.

Cussini, E. 1998. Review of Schmidt-Colinet, A. (ed.), *Palmyra: Kulturbegegnung im Grenzbereich Mainz, 1995. JAOS* 118 (1), 142–143.

Cuvigny, H. 1996a. The Amount of Wages Paid to the Quarry-Workers at Mons Claudianus. *JRS* 86, 139–145.

———. 1996b. Ulpius Himerus, procurateur imperial I. Pan 53. *BIFAO* 96, 91–101.

———. 1997a. La mort et la maladie (191–223). In Bingen et al. 1997, 19–41.

———. 1997b. Tableaux de service (304–308). In Bingen et al. 1997, 141–163.

———. 2000. *Mons Claudianus ostraca graeca et latina III. Les reçus pour avances à la familia O. Claud. 417 à 631*. Cairo.

———. 2001. Un soldat de la *cohors I Lusitanorum* à Didymoi: Du nouveau sur l'inscription *I. Kanaïs* 59bis. *BIFAO* 101, 153–157.

———. 2002–2003. Umm Balad, saison décembre 2002–Janvier 2003. Unpublished report for the Egyptian Supreme Council of Antiquities.

———. 2003a. Les documents écrits de la route de Myos Hormos à l'époque gréco-romaine (inscriptions, graffiti, papyrus, ostraca). In Cuvigny 2003e, 265–294.

———. 2003b. Le functionnement du réseau. In Cuvigny 2003e, 295–359.

———. 2003c. Introduction. In Cuvigny 2003d, 1–35.

———. (ed.). 2003d. *La route de Myos Hormos. L'armée romaine dans le désert Oriental d'Égypte. Praesidia du désert de Bérénice* I (FIFAO 48/1). Cairo.

———. (ed.). 2003e. *La route de Myos Hormos. L'armée romaine dans le désert Oriental d'Égypte. Praesidia du désert de Bérénice* I (*FIFAO* 48/2). Cairo.

———. 2003f. La société civile des *praesidia*. In Cuvigny 2003e, 361–397.

———. 2005a. L'organigramme du personnel d'une carrière impériale d'après un ostracon du Mons Claudianus. *Chiron* 35, 309–353.

———. 2005b. *Ostraca de Krokodilô: La correspondance militaire et sa circulation. O. Krok.* 1–151. *Praesidia du désert de Bérénice* II. Cairo.

———. 2006. Désert Oriental: Le *praesidium* de Iovis-Dios. *BIFAO* 106, 409–412.

———. 2007. Les noms du chou dans les ostraca grecs du désert Oriental d'Égypte κράμβη, κραμβίον, καυλίον. *BIFAO* 107, 89–96.

———. (ed.). Forthcoming. *Didymoi: Une garnison romaine dans le désert Oriental d'Égypte.* Vol. 2. *Les Textes.* Cairo.

Cuvigny, H., et al. 1999. Inscriptions rupestres vues et revues dans le désert de Bérénice. *BIFAO* 99, 133–193.

Cuvigny, H., et al. 2000. Le paneion d'Al-Bawayb revisité. *BIFAO* 100, 243–266.

Dabrowa, E. 1991. *Dromedarii* in the Roman Army: A Note. In Maxfield, V. A., and Dobson, M. J. (eds.), *Roman Frontier Studies 1989: Proceedings of the XVth International Congress of Roman Frontier Studies.* Pp. 364–366. Exeter, UK.

Dalby, A. 2000. *Dangerous Tastes: The Story of Spices.* London.

———. 2003. *Food in the Ancient World from A to Z.* London and New York.

Daniels, C. M. 1975. The Role of the Roman Army in the Spread and Practice of Mithraism. In Hinnells, J. R. (ed.), *Mithraic Studies: Proceedings of the First International Congress of Mithraic Studies.*Vol. 2. Pp. 249–274. Manchester, UK, and Totowa, NJ.

D'Anville, J. B. B. 1766. *Mémoires sur l'Égypte ancienne et moderne, suivis d'une description du golf Arabique ou de la mer Rouge.* Paris.

Daressy, G. 1922. Bérénice et Abraq. *ASAE* 22, 169–184.

D'Arms, J. H. 1974. Puteoli in the Second Century of the Roman Empire: A Social and Economic Study. *JRS* 64, 104–124.

———. 1981. *Commerce and Social Standing in Ancient Rome.* Cambridge, MA.

Daryaee, T. 2009. *Sasanian Persia: The Rise and Fall of an Empire.* London and New York.

Das, G. P. 2006. *India–West Asia Trade in Ancient Times (6th Century B.C. to 3rd Century A.D.).* New Delhi.

D'Athanasi, G. 1836. *A Brief Account of the Researches and Discoveries in Upper Egypt, Made under the Direction of Henry Salt, Esq.* London.

Davidde, B. 1997a. I porti dell'Arabia Felix: Un nuovo campo di indagine per la ricerca dell'archeologia subacquea. In Associazione italiana archeologia subacquei (ed.), *Atti del convegno nazionale di archeologia subacquea: Anzio, 30–31 maggio e 1° giugno 1996.* Pp. 351–355. Bari.

———. 1997b. Qanà: Alla ricerca del porto perduto. *Archeologia viva* 63, 86–87.

———. 1998. Progetto Qanà. *L'archeologo subacqueo* 2, 8.

Davidde, B., et al. 2004. New Data on the Commercial Trade of the Harbour of Kanē through the Typological and Petrographic Study of the Pottery. *PSAS* 34, 85–100.

Debaine-Francfort, C., and Idriss, A. (eds.). 2000. *Keriya mémoires d'un fleuve. Archéologie et Civilisation des oasis du Taklamakan. Mission archéologique franco-chinoise au Xinjiang.* Paris.

De Blois, L. 1975. Odaenathus and the Roman-Persian War of 252–64 A.D. *Talanta* 6, 7–23.

Decker, M. 2009. *Tilling the Hateful Earth: Agricultural Production and Trade in the Late Antique East*. Oxford.

de la Roque, F. Bisson. 1922. Voyage au Djebel Shaïb. *BSRGÉ* 11, 113–140.

Delbrueck, R. 1932. *Antike Porphyrwerk*. Berlin and Leipzig.

Deloche, J. 1996. Iconographic Evidence on the Development of Boat and Ship Structures in India (2nd cent. B.C.–15th cent. A.D.): A New Approach. In Ray and Salles 1996, 199–224.

De Maigret, A. 1997. The Frankincense Road from Najrān to Ma'ān: A Hypothetical Itinerary. In Avanzini 1997, 315–331.

————. 2004. La route caravanière de l'encens dans l'Arabie préislamique: Élements d'information sur son itinéraire et sa chronologie. *CY* 11, 36–46.

Demougeot, E. 1960. Le Chameau et l'Afrique du Nord romaine. *AESC* 15, 209–247.

Dennis, G. T. 1985. *Three Byzantine Military Treatises*. Washington, DC.

De Romanis, F. 1988. Romanukharaṭṭha e Taprobane: Sui rapporti Roma-Ceylon nel I sec. d. C. *Helikon* 28, 5–58.

————. 1993. Puteoli e l'Oriente. In Zens, F., and Jodice, M. (eds.), *Puteoli*. Pp. 61–72. Naples.

————. 1996a. *Cassia, cinnamomo, ossidiana: Uomini e merci tra oceano Indiano e Mediterraneo*. Rome.

————. 1996b. Graffiti greci da Wadi Menīh al-Hēr: Un vestorius tra Coptos e Berenice. *Topoi* 6 (2), 731–745.

————. 1997a. Hypalos: Distanze e venti tra Arabia e India nella Scienza ellenistica. *Topoi* 7 (2), 671–692.

————. 1997b. Romanukharaṭṭha and Taprobane: Relations between Rome and Sri Lanka in the First Century A.D. In De Romanis and Tchernia 1997, 161–237.

————. 1997c. Rome and the *Nótia* of India: Relations between Rome and Southern India from 30 B.C. to the Flavian Period. In De Romanis and Tchernia 1997, 80–160.

————. 1997d. Tus e murra: Aromi sudarabici nella Roma arcaica. In Avanzinni 1997. Pp. 221–230.

————. 1998. Commercio, Metrologia, Fiscalità su P. Vindob. G 40.822 verso. *MÉFRA* 110, 11–57.

————. 2000. Esportazioni di corallo mediterraneo in India nell'età ellenistico-romana. In Morel et al. (eds.), *Corallo di ieri—Corallo di oggi: Atti del Convegno, Ravello, Villa Rufolo, 13–15 dicembre 1996*. Pp. 211–216. Bari.

————. 2002. Τραϊανὸς ποταμός: Mediterraneo e Mare Rosso da Traiano a Maometto. In Villari, R. (ed.), *Controllo degli stretti e insediamenti militari nel Mediterraneo*. Pp. 21–70. Rome.

————. 2003. Between the Nile and the Red Sea: Imperial trade and Barbarians. In Liverani 2003, 117–122.

————. 2006. *Aurei* after the Trade: Western Taxes and Eastern Gifts. In De Romanis, F., and Sorda, S. (eds.), *Dal Denarius al Dinar L'Oriente e la Moneta romana*. Istituto italiano di Numismatica. *Atti dell'Incontro di Studio Roma 16–18 settembre 2004*. Pp. 55–82. Rome.

De Romanis, F., and Tchernia, A. 1997. (eds.). *Crossings: Early Mediterranean Contacts with India*. New Delhi.

Desanges, J. 1969. D'Axoum à l'Assam, aux portes de la Chine: Le Voyage du "Scholasticus de Thèbes" (entre 360 et 500 après J.-C.). *Historia* 18 (5), 627–639.

———. 1970. Les Chasseurs d'éléphants d'Abou Simbel. In *Actes du Quatre-Vint-Douzième Congrès National des Sociétés Savantes Strasbourg et Colmar 1967 Section d'Archéologie*. Pp. 31–50. Paris.

———. 1978. *Recherches sur l'Activité des Méditerranéens aux confines de l'Afrique (VIe siècle avant J.-C.–IVe siècle après J.-C.)*. Rome.

———. 1984. Rome et les riverains de la mer Rouge au IIIe siècle de notre ère: Aperçus récents et nouveaux problèmes. In Reddé, M. (ed.), *Toujours Afrique Apporte fait Nouveau (Scripta Minora)*. Pp. 345–358. Paris.

———. 1993. Diodore de Sicile et les Éthiopiens d'Occident. *CRAI*, 527–541.

———. 1996. Sur la mer Hippale, au souffle du vent Hippale. *Topoi* 6 (2), 665–670.

———. 1999. Aperçus sur les contacts transsahariens d'après les sources classiques. In Desanges, J. (ed.), *Toujours Afrique Apporte fait Nouveau (Scripta Minora)*. Pp. 239–247. Paris.

Desanges, J., et al. 1993. *Sur les routes antiques de l'Azanie et de l'Inde, Les Fonds Révoil du Musée de l'Homme (Heïs et Damo, en Somalie)*. Paris.

Desrosiers, S., Debaine-Francfort, C., and Idriss, A. 2001. Two Resist-Dyed Cottons Recently Found at KaraDong, Xinjiang (Third Century A.D.). In Rogers, P.W., et al. (eds.), *The Roman Textile Industry and Its Influence: A Birthday Tribute to John Peter Wild*. Pp. 48–55. Oxford.

Dessau, H. (ed.). 1892. *Inscriptiones Latinae Selectae*. Vol. 1. Berlin.

Dieleman, J. 1998. Amphora Stoppers. In Sidebotham and Wendrich 1998a, 265–277.

Dignas, B., and Winter, E. 2007. *Rome and Persia in Late Antiquity: Neighbours and Rivals*. Cambridge and New York.

Dihle, A. 1964. Indische Philosophen bei Clemens Alexandrinus. In Stuiber, A., and Hermann, A. (eds.), *Mullus: Festschrift Theodor Klauser*. Pp. 60–70. Münster and Westfälen.

———. 1965. *Umstrittene Daten: Untersuchungen zum Auftreten der Griechen am Roten Meer*. Cologne and Opladen.

———. 1978. Die entdeckungsgeschichtlichen Voraussetzungen des Indienhandels der römischen Kaiserzeit. *ANRW* 2.9.2, 546–580.

Dijkstra, M., and Verhoogt, A. M. F. W. 1999. The Greek-Palmyrene Inscription. In Sidebotham and Wendrich 1999, 207–218.

Dilke, O. A. W. 1985. *Greek and Roman Maps*. Ithaca, NY.

Dillemann, L., and Janvier, Y. 1997. *La Cosmographie du Ravennate*. Brussels.

Dittenberger, W. 1903. *Orientis Graeci Inscriptiones Selectae*. Vol. 1. Hildesheim, Germany.

Dixon, D. M. 2004. Pharaonic Egypt and the Red Sea Arms Trade. In Lunde and Porter 2004, 33–41.

Dodge, H., and Ward-Perkins, B. 1992. *Marble in Antiquity: Collected Papers of J. B. Ward-Perkins*. London.

Doe, B. 1971. *Southern Arabia*. New York, St. Louis, and San Francisco.

———. 1992. *Socotra. Island of Tranquillity*. London.

Donato, G., and Seefried, M. 1989. *The Fragrant Past: Perfumes of Cleopatra and Julius Caesar. Emory University Museum of Art and Archaeology Atlanta April 5–June 25, 1989*. Rome.

Donkin, R. A. 1998. *Beyond Price: Pearls and Pearl-Fishing Origins to the Age of Discovery*. Philadelphia.

Doxiadis, E. 2000. *The Mysterious Fayum Mummy Portraits: Faces from Ancient Egypt*. Cairo.

Drew-Bear, T. 1981. Les voyages d'Aurélius Gaius, soldat de Dioclétien. In Fahd, T. (ed.), *La Géographie administrative et politique d'Alexandre à Mahomet. Actes du Colloque de Strasbourg 14–16 juin 1979.* Pp. 93–141. Leiden.

Drexhage, H.-J. 1991. *Preise, Mieten/Pachten, Kosten und Löhne im römischen Ägypten bis zum Regierungsantritt Diokletians: Vorarbeiten zu einer Wirtschaftsgeschichte des römischen Ägypten.* Vol. 1. St. Katharinen, Germany.

Drexhage, R. 1982. Der Handel Palmyras in römischer Zeit. *MBAH* 1 (1), 17–34.

———. 1988. *Untersuchungen zum römischen Osthandel.* Bonn.

Dridi, H. 2002. Indiens et Proche-Orientaux dans une grotte de Suquṭrā (Yémen). *JA* 290 (2), 565–610.

Dridi, H., and Gorea, M. 2003. Le Voyage d'Abgar à Suqutra. *Archaeologia* 396, 48–57.

Drower, M. S. 1995. *Flinders Petrie: A Life in Archaeology.* Madison, WI.

Dubin, L. S. 1995. *The History of Beads from 30,000 B.C. to the Present.* London.

Dubois, C. 1907. *Pouzzoles antique (histoire et topographie).* Paris.

Dueck, D. 2000. *Strabo of Amasia: A Greek Man of Letters in Augustan Rome.* London and New York.

Dunand, F. 1973a. *Le culte d'Isis dans le basin oriental de la Méditerranée.* Vol. 1. *Le culte d'Isis et les Ptolémées.* Leiden.

———. 1973b. *Le culte d'Isis dans le basin oriental de la Méditerranée.* Vol. 2. *Le culte d'Isis en Grèce.* Leiden.

———. 1973c. *Le culte d'Isis dans le basin oriental de la Méditerranée.* Vol. 3. *Le culte d'Isis en Asie Mineure clergé et ritual des sanctuaries Isiaques.* Leiden.

———. 1979. *Religion populaire en Égypte romaine les terres cuites isiaques du Musée du Caire.* Leiden.

Duncan-Jones, R. 1982. *The Economy of the Roman Empire: Quantitative Studies.* Cambridge.

———. 1990. *Structure and Scale in the Roman Economy.* Cambridge.

———. 1994. *Money and Government in the Roman Empire.* Cambridge.

———. 1996. The Impact of the Antonine Plague. *JRA* 9, 108–136.

———. 1997. Numerical Distortion in Roman Writers. In Andreau, J., et al. (eds.), *Économie antique Prix et formation des prix dans les economies antiques.* Pp. 147–159. Saint-Bertrand-de-Comminges and Toulouse.

Dunn, M. 2000. *The Emergence of Monasticism: From the Desert Fathers to the Early Middle Ages.* Oxford.

Earl, G., and Glazier, D. 2002. Survey at Bir Nakheil. In Peacock, D. et al. (eds.), *Myos Hormos— Quseir al-Qadim: A Roman and Islamic Port Site. Interim Report 2002.* Pp. 89–94. Southampton, UK. Unpublished.

———. 2006a. Site Survey. In Peacock and Blue 2006c, 34–42.

———. 2006b. Survey at Bi'r an-Nakhil. In Peacock and Blue 2006c, 26–33.

Edgar, C. C. (ed.). 1925. *Zenon Papyri.* Vol. 1. Cairo.

———. (ed.). 1931. *Zenon Papyri.* Vol. 4. Cairo.

Edwards, F. J. 1987. Climate and Oceanography. In Edwards and Head 1987, 45–69.

Edwards, F. J., and Head, S. M. (eds.). 1987. *Key Environments, Red Sea.* Oxford and New York.

Eggermont, P. H. L. 1968. The Date of the *Periplus Maris Erythraei.* In Basham, A. L. (ed.), *Pa-*

pers on the Date of Kaniṣka Submitted to the Conference on the Date of Kaniṣka, London, 20–22 April, 1960. Pp. 94–96. Leiden.

Ehlers, W.-W. 1985. Mit dem Südwestmonsun nach Ceylon: Eine Interpretation der Iambul-Exzerpte Diodorus. *Würzburger Jahrbücher für die Altertumswissenschaft* 11, 73–84.

Eichler, E. 1993. *Untersuchungen zum Expeditionswesen des ägyptischen Alten Reiches.* Wiesbaden.

Eide, T., Hägg, T., Pierce, R. H., and Török, L. (eds.). 1998. *Fontes Historiae Nubiorum, Textual Sources for the History of the Middle Nile Region between the Eighth Century B.C. and the Sixth Century A.D.* Vol. 3. *From the First to the Sixth Century A.D.* Bergen, Norway.

Ellis, W. M. 1994. *Ptolemy of Egypt.* London and New York.

Fahlbusch, H. 2004. The Saad el-Kafara—The Oldest High Dam of the World. In Bienert, H. D., and Häser, J. (eds.), *Men of Dikes and Canals: The Archaeology of Water in the Middle East. International Symposium Held at Petra, Wadi Musa (H.K. of Jordan) 15–20 June, 1999.* Pp. 365–378. Rahden and Westfälen.

Faller, S. 2000. *Taprobane im Wandel der Zeit: Das Śrî-Laṅkâ-Bild in Griechischen und Lateinischen Quellen zwischen Alexanderzug und Spätantike.* Stuttgart.

Fantasia, U. 1997. L'Egitto tolemaico e la terra degli aromata. In Avanzini 1997, 395–412.

Farquhar, J. N. 1926. The Apostle Thomas in North India. *BJRL* 10, 80–111.

———. 1927. The Apostle Thomas in South India. *BJRL* 11, 20–50.

Farrar, L. 2000. *Ancient Roman Gardens.* Phoenix Mill, Thrupp, Stroud, Gloucestershire.

Fasolo, M. 2003. *La Via Egnatia.* Vol. 1. *Da Apollonia e Dyrrachium ad Herakleia Lynkestidos.* Rome.

Fattovich, R. 1999. Punt. In Bard and Shubert 1999, 636–637.

———. 2005. Marsā Gawāsīs: A Pharaonic Coastal Settlement by the Red Sea in Egypt. In Starkey, J. C. M. (ed.), *People of the Red Sea. Proceedings of the Red Sea Project II Held in the British Museum October 2004.* Pp. 15–22. Oxford.

Fattovich, R., and Bard, K. A. 2006. À la recherché de Pount: Mersa Gaouasis et la navigation ègyptienne dans la mer Rouge. *Égypte, Afrique et Orient* 41, 7–30.

Fattovich, R., and Manzo, A. 2008. The Location of Punt: New Evidence from Marsa/Wadi Gawasis (Egypt). Paper Delivered at the Conference: Red Sea IV. Connected Hinterlands. The Fourth International Conference on the Peoples of the Red Sea Region. 25–26 September 2008. Southampton, UK.

Fauvelle-Aymar, F.-X. 2009. Les inscriptions d'Adoulis (Érythrée): Fragments d'un royaume d'influence hellénistique et gréco-romaine sur le côte africaine de la mer Rouge. *BIFAO* 109, 135–160.

Ferguson, J. 1978. China and Rome. *ANRW* 2.9.2, 581–603.

———. 1991. (trans). *Clement of Alexandria Stromateis Books One to Three.* Washington, DC.

Festugière, A. J. (ed.). 1974. *Léontios de Néapolis. Vie de Syméon le Fou et de Jean de Chypre.* Paris.

Fiema, Z. T., and Jones, R. N. 1990. The Nabataean King-List Revised: Further Observations on the Second Nabataean Inscription from Tell Esh-Shuqafiya, Egypt. *ADAJ* 34, 239–248.

Figari, A. 1864. *Studii scientifici sull'Egitto e sue adiacenze compressa la penisola dell'Arabia Petrea con accompagnamento di carta geografico-geologica.* Vol. 1. Lucca.

———. 1865. *Studii scientifici sull'Egitto e sue adiacenze compressa la penisola dell'Arabia Petrea con accompagnamento di carta geografico-geologica.* Vol. 2. Lucca.

Filliozat, J. 1949. *La Doctrine classique de la médecine indienne: Ses origins et ses parallèles grecs.* Paris.

Fink, R. O. 1971. *Roman Military Records on Papyrus.* Cleveland, OH.

Finley, M. I. 1985. *The Ancient Economy.* London.

Fischer, H. G. 1985. More about the *Smntjw. GM* 84, 25–32.

Fischer, M., et al. 1996. *Roman Roads in Judaea.* Vol. 2. *The Jaffa-Jerusalem Roads.* Oxford.

Fischer, R. 1984. *Korallenstädte in Africa: Die vorkoloniale Geschichte der Ostküste.* Oberdorf.

Floyer, E. A. 1887. Notes on a Sketch Map of Two Routes in the Eastern Desert of Egypt. *PRGS* 9, (11), 659–681.

———. 1892. The Mines of the Northern Etbai or of Northern Aethiopia. *JRAS* 24, 811–833.

———. 1893a. *Étude sur le Nord Etbai entre le Nil et la mer rouge.* Cairo.

———. 1893b. Further routes in the Eastern Desert. *GJ* 1 (5), 408–431.

Foltz, R. C. 1999. *Religions of the Silk Road: Overland Trade and Cultural Exchange from Antiquity to the Fifteenth Century.* New York.

Foster, B. C., et al. 2007. Survey of the Emerald Mines at Wadi Sikait 2000/2001 Seasons. In Sidebotham and Wendrich 2007a, 304–343.

Fournet, J.-L. 1995. Les inscriptions grecques d' Abū Kū' et de la route Quft-Qusayr. *BIFAO* 95, 173–233.

———. 2003. Langues, écritures et culture dans les *praesidia.* In Cuvigny 2003e, 427–500.

Francis, Jr., P. 2000. Human Ornaments. In Sidebotham and Wendrich 2000a, 211–225.

———. 2002. Early Historic South India and the International Maritime Trade. *Man and Environment* 27 (1), 153–160.

———. 2004. Beads and Selected Small Finds from the 1989–92 Excavations. In Begley, V., et al., *The Ancient Port of Arikamedu: New Excavations and Researches 1989–1992.* Vol. 2. Pp. 447–604. Paris and Pondicherry, India.

———. 2007. Personal Adornments. In Sidebotham and Wendrich 2007a, pp. 251–257.

Franck, I. M., and Brownstone, D. M. 1986. *The Silk Road: A History.* New York and Oxford.

Frank, A. G. 1991. A Plea for World System History. *JWH* 2, 1–28.

———. 1993. Bronze Age World System Cycles. *CA* 34 (4), 383–429.

Frank, A. G., and Gills, B. K. 1993. *The World System: Five Hundred Years or Five Thousand?* London.

Fraquet, H. 1987. *Amber.* London and Boston.

Fraser, P. M. 1972a. *Ptolemaic Alexandria.* Vol. 1. Oxford.

———. 1972b. *Ptolemaic Alexandria.* Vol. 2. Oxford.

Frend, W. H. C. 1968. Some Cultural Links between India and the West in the Early Christian Centuries. *Theoria and Theory* 2 (4), 306–331.

Frere, S. 1987. *Britannia: A History of Roman Britain.* 3rd ed. London and New York.

Freshfield, E. H. 1938. *Roman Law in the Later Roman Empire. Byzantine Guilds Professional and Commercial. Ordinances of Leo VI c. 895 from the Book of the Eparch.* Cambridge.

Frézouls, E. 1996. Palmyre et les conditions politiques du développement de son activité commerciale. In *Les Annales Archéologiques arabes syriennes: Revue d'Archéologie et d'Histoire* 42, 147–155.

Friedman, R., and Hobbs, J. J. 2002. A "Tasian" Tomb in Egypt's Eastern Desert. In Friedman, R. (ed.), *Egypt and Nubia: Gifts of the Desert.* Pp. 178–191. London.

Frost, H. 1996. "Ports" Cairns and Anchors: A Pharaonic Outlet on the Red Sea. *Topoi* 6 (2), 869–902.

Fuchs, G. 1988. Die arabische Wüste (Ägypten) und ihre historische Bedeutung von der Vorgeschichte bis in die Römerziet. *AntW* 19 (4), 15–30.

———. 1989. Rock Engravings in the Wadi el-Barramiya, Eastern Desert of Egypt. *African Archaeology Review* 7, 127–153.

Fuks, A. 1951. Notes on the Archive of Nicanor. *JJP* 5, 207–216.

Fulford, M. 1987. Economic Interdependence among Urban Communities of the Roman Mediterranean. *WA* 19, 58–75.

Fuller, D. 2003. Further Evidence on the Prehistory of Sesame. *Asian Agri-History* 7 (2), 127–137.

Fussman, G. 1991. Le *Périple* et l'histoire politique de l'Inde. *JA* 279, (1–2), 31–38.

———. 1997. The *Periplus* and the Political History of India. In De Romanis and Tchernia 1997, 66–71.

Fynes, R. C. C. 1991. *Cultural Transmissions between Roman Egypt and Western India.* PhD diss., University of Oxford.

El-Gamili, M. M., et al. 1999/2000. Wadi Sikeit, the Ancient Emerald Mine Sites, Egypt A Geo-Archaeological Investigation. *ASAE* 75, 229–244 and plates I–IV.

Garbrecht, G. 1999. Wadi Geradi Dam. In Bard and Shubert 1999, 864–866.

Garcin, J.-C. 1972. Jean-Léon l'Africain et 'Aydab. *Annales Islamologiques* 11, 189–192.

Garnsey, P. 1983. Grain for Rome. In Garnsey, P., et al. (eds.), *Trade in the Ancient Economy.* Pp. 118–130. Berkeley and Los Angeles.

Garnsey, P., and Saller, R. 1987. *The Roman Empire Economy, Society and Culture.* Berkeley and Los Angeles.

Garnsey, P., et al. 1983. *Trade in the Ancient Economy.* Berkeley and Los Angeles.

Gates, J. E. 2005. *Traveling the Desert Edge: The Ptolemaic Roadways and Regional Economy of Egypt's Eastern Desert in the Fourth through First Centuries B.C.E.* PhD diss., University of Michigan. Ann Arbor.

Gatier, P.-L., and Salles, J.-F. 1988a. Appendice L'Emplacement de Leuké Komé. In Salles 1988, 186–187.

———. 1988b. Aux frontières méridionales du domaine nabatéen. In Salles 1988, 173–185.

Gauthier-Pilters, H., and Dagg, A. I. 1981. *The Camel: Its Evolution, Ecology, Behavior and Relationship to Man.* Chicago.

Gawlikowski, M. 1958. Les princes de Palmyre. *Syria* 62, 251–261.

———. 1986. Les comptes d'un homme d'affaires dans une tour funéraire à Palmyre. *Semitica* 36, 87–99.

———. 1988. Le commerce de Palmyre sur terre et sur eau. In Salles 1988, 163–172.

———. 1994. Palmyra as a Trading Centre. *Iraq* 56, 27–33.

———. 1996. Palmyra and Its Cavaran Trade. In *Les Annales Archéologiques arabes syriennes: Revue d'Archéologie et d'Histoire* 42, 139–145.

———. 1997. The Syrian Desert under the Romans. In Alcock, S. (ed.), *The Early Roman Empire in the East.* Pp. 37–54. Oxford.

Gebhardt, A. 2002. *Imperiale Politik und provinziale Entwicklung: Untersuchungen zum Verhältnis von Kaiser, Herr und Städten im Syrien der vorseverischen Zeit.* Berlin.

Geresus, Y., et al. 2005. *The Eritro-British Project at Adulis: Interim Report*. Asmara, Eritrea, and Southampton, UK. Unpublished.

Gerisch, R., et al. 2007. Finds: Other Wood and Wood Identification. In Bard and Fattovich 2007a, 165–188.

Gerlach, I. 2005. Sirwah: New Research at the Sabaean City and Oasis. In Gunter, A. C. (ed.), *Caravan Kingdoms: Yemen and the Ancient Incense Trade*. Pp. 34–41. Washington, DC.

Al-Ghabbān, M. A. B. I. 2007. Le Darb al-Bakra: Decouverté d'une nouvelle branche sur le route commerciale antique, entre al-Ḥijr (Arabie S'Aūdite) et Pétra (Jordanie). *CRAI*, 9–24.

Ghica, V., et al. 2008. Les ermitages d'Abū Darağ revisités. *BIFAO* 108, 115–163.

Ghisotti, A. 1996. The Amphorae at Fury Shoal. In Manferto, V., and Accomazzo, L., *Diving Guide to the Red Sea Wrecks*. Pp. 92–95. Shrewsbury, UK.

Ghosh, A. 1992. *In an Antique Land*. Delhi.

Gibb, H. A. R. 1960. 'Aydhāb. In Gibb, H. A. R., et al. (eds.), *Encyclopedia of Islam*. Vol. 1. A-B. P. 782. Leiden and London.

Gibbins, D. 2001. Shipwrecks and Hellenistic Trade. In Archibald et al. 2001, 273–312.

Gichon, M. 1989. Military Intelligence in the Roman Army. In Herzig, H., and Frei-Stolba, R. (eds.), *Labor Omnibus Unus. Gerold Walser zum 70. Geburtstag Dargebracht von Freunden, Kollegen und Schulern*. Pp. 155–170. Stuttgart.

Gill, D. W. J. 1991. Pots and Trade: Spacefillers or *Objets d'Art*. *JHS* 111, 29–47.

Gingras, G. E. (trans.). 1970. *Itinerarium Egeria. Egeria: Diary of a Pilgrimage*. New York and Paramus, NJ.

Glover, I. C. 1996. The Archaeological Evidence for Early Trade between South and Southeast Asia. In Reade, J. (ed.), *The Indian Ocean in Antiquity*. Pp. 365–400. London and New York.

Glover, T. R. 1969. *Herodotus*. Reprint. New York.

Gogte, V. D. 1999. Petra, the *Periplus* and Ancient Indo-Arabian Maritime Trade. *ADAJ* 43, 299–304.

Gokhale, B. G. 1966. *Aśoka Maurya*. New York.

———. 1987. Bharukaccha/Barygaza. In Pollet, G. (ed.), *India and the Ancient World: History, Trade and Culture before A.D. 650*. Pp. 67–79. Leuven.

Goldsworthy, A. K. 1996. *The Roman Army at War, 100 B.C.–A.D. 200*. Oxford.

Golénischeff, W. 1890. Une excursion à Bérénice. *Recueil de Travaux relatifs à la philologie et à l'árchéologie égyptiennes et assyriennes* 13, 75–96.

Gopal, L. 1961. Textiles in Ancient India. *JESHO* 4 (1), 53–69.

Goren, A. 2000. Les Nabatéens et la route de l'encense. In Lemaire, A. (ed.), *Les routes du Proche-Orient: Des séjours d'Abraham aux caravanes de l'encens*. Pp. 107–115. Paris.

Gould, D. A. 1999. The Excavations at Shenshef. In Sidebotham and Wendrich 1999, 371–383.

Goyon, G. 1957. *Nouvelles inscriptions rupestres du Wadi Hammâmât*. Paris.

Graf, D. F. 1989. Zenobia and the Arabs. In French, D. H., and Lightfoot, C. S. (eds.). *The Eastern Frontier of the Roman Empire. Proceedings of a Colloquium Held at Ankara in September 1988*. Pp. 143–167. Oxford.

———. 1990. The Origin of the Nabataeans. *Aram* 2 (1–2), 45–75.

———. 1995a. Milestones with Uninscribed Painted Latin Texts. *SHAJ* 5, 417–425.

———. 1995b. The *Via Nova Traiana* in Arabia Petraea. In Humphrey, J. H. (ed.), *The Roman and Byzantine Near East: Some Recent Archaeological Research*. Pp. 241–265. Ann Arbor, MI.

———. 1996. The Roman East from the Chinese Perspective. In *Les Annales Archéologiques arabes syriennes Revue d' Archéologie et d'Histoire* 42, 199–216.

———. 1997a. The Via Militaris and the Limes Arabicus. In Groenman-van Waateringe, W., et al. (eds.), *Roman Frontier Studies 1995. Proceedings of the XVIth International Congress of Roman Frontier Studies.* Pp. 123–133. Oxford.

———. 1997b. The *Via Militaris* in Arabia. *DOP* 51, 271–281.

———. 2004. Nabataean Identity and Ethnicity: The Epigraphic Perspective. *SHAJ* 8, 145–154.

———. 2005. Rome and China: Some Frontier Comparisons. In Visy, Z. (ed.), *Limes XIX. Proceedings of the XIXth International Congress of Roman Frontier Studies Held in Pécs, Hungary, September 2003.* Pp. 157–165. Pécs.

———. 2007. Two-Humped Camel Drachms: Trajanic Propaganda or Reality? *SHAJ* 9, 439–450.

Graf, D. F., and Sidebotham, S. E. 2003. Nabataean Trade. In Markoe 2003b. Pp. 65–73.

Gragg, G. 1996. South Arabian/Axumite Dipinto. In Sidebotham and Wendrich 1996, 209–211.

Graser, E. R. 1940a. The Edict of Diocletian on Maximum Prices. In Frank, T. (ed.), *An Economic Survey of Ancient Rome.* Vol. 5. Pp. 307–421. Baltimore.

———. 1940b. The Significance of Two New Fragments of the Edict of Diocletian. *TAPA* 71, 157–174.

Greene, K. 1986. *The Archaeology of the Roman Economy.* Berkeley and Los Angeles.

Gregarek, H. 2002. Roman Imperial Sculpture of Colored Marbles. In Herrmann, Jr., J. J., et al. (eds.), *ASMOSIA 5 Interdisciplinary Studies on Ancient Stone. Proceedings of the Fifth International Conference of the Association for the Study of Marble and Other Stones in Antiquity, Museum of Fine Arts, Boston, 1998.* Pp. 206–214. London.

Grimaldi, D. A. 1996. *Amber: Window to the Past.* New York.

Groom, N. 1981. *Frankincense and Myrrh: A Study of the Arabian Incense Trade.* London, New York, and Beirut.

———. 1994. Oman and the Emirates in Ptolemy's Map. *AAE* 5, 198–214.

———. 1995. The *Periplus*, Pliny and Arabia. *AAE* 6, 180–195.

———. 2005. Trade, Incense, and Perfume. In Gunter, A. C. (ed.), *Caravan Kingdoms: Yemen and the Ancient Incense Trade.* Pp. 104–113. Washington, DC.

Grossmann, P. 2002. *Christliche Architektur in Ägypten.* Leiden, Boston, and Cologne.

Grundmann, G., and Morteani, G. 2008. Multi-stage Emerald Formation during Pan-African Regional Metamorphism: The Zabara, Sikait, Umm Kabo Deposits, South Eastern Desert of Egypt. *JAES* 50, 168–187.

Guasti, L. 2007. Animali per Roma. In Papi, E. (ed.), *Supplying Rome and the Empire: The Proceedings of an International Seminar Held in Siena—Certosa di Pontignano on May 2–4, 2004, on Rome, the Provinces, Production and Distribution.* Pp. 138–152. Portsmouth, RI.

Guéraud, O. 1942. Ostraka grecs et latins de l'Wâdi Fawâkhir. *BIFAO* 41, 141–196.

Guiraud, C. 1997. *Économie rurale/Varron, livre III.* Paris.

Gungwu, W. 1998. *The Nanhai Trade: The Early History of Chinese Trade in the South China Sea.* Singapore.

Guo, L. 2004. *Commerce, Culture, and Community in a Red Sea Port in the Thirteenth Century: The Arabic Documents from Quseir.* Leiden and Boston.

Gupta, P. L. 1991. Coins in Rome's Indian Trade. In Jha, A. K. (ed.), *Coinage, Trade and the Economy January 8th–11th, 1991, 3rd International Colloquium.* Pp. 122–137. Maharashtra, India.

Gupta, S. 1995–1996. Beyond Arikamedu: Macro Stratigraphy of the Iron Age-Early Historic Transition and Roman Contact in South India. *Purātattva* 26, 50–61.

———. 2007. Frankincense in the "Triangular" Indo-Arabian-Roman Aromatics Trade. In Peacock, D., and Williams, D. (eds.), *Food for the Gods: New Light on the Ancient Incense Trade.* Pp. 112–121. Oxford.

Gupta, S. P., et al. 2000. Dressel 2–4 Amphorae and Roman Trade with India: The Evidence from Nevasa. *JSAS* 16, 7–18.

Gupta, S. P., et al. 2004. On the Fast Track of the Periplus: Excavations at Kamrej—2003. *JIOA* 1, 9–33.

Gurukkal, R., and Whittaker, C. R. 2001. In Search of Muziris. *JRA* 14 (1), 334–350.

Guzzo, M. G. A. 2000. Épigraphie nabatéenne. In Lemaire, A. (ed.), *Les routes du Proche-Orient: Des Séjours d'Abraham aux caravanes de l'encens.* Pp. 93–105, 128. Paris.

Habachi, L. 1960. Notes on the Unfinished Obelisk of Aswan and Another Smaller One in Gharb Aswan. In Struve, V. V. (ed.), *Drevnii Egipet.* Pp. 216–236. Moscow.

Habtemichael, D., et al. 2004. (eds). *The Eritro British Project at Adulis, Interim Report 2004.* Asmara, Eritrea, and Southampton, UK. Unpublished.

Haeckl, A. E. 1999. The Wooden "Aphrodite" Panel. In Sidebotham and Wendrich 1999, 243–255.

———. 2007. Excavations at the Smaller *Praesidium* in Wadi Kalalat. In Sidebotham and Wendrich 2007a, 344–357.

Haenchen, E. 1971. *The Acts of the Apostles: A Commentary.* Philadelphia.

Haerinck, E. 1998. International Contacts in the Southern Persian Gulf in the Late 1st Century B.C./1st Century A.D.: Numismatic Evidence from Ed-Dur (Emirate of Umm al-Qaiwain, U.A.E.). *Iranica Antiqua* 33, 273–302.

Hahn, W. 2000. Axumite Numismatics: A Critical Survey of Recent Research. *RN* 155, 281–311.

Haldane, C. 1996. Archaeology in the Red Sea. *Topoi* 6 (2), 853–868.

Hall, K. R. 1985. *Maritime Trade and State Development in Early Southeast Asia.* Honolulu.

———. 1991. Coinage, Trade, and Economy in Early South India and Southeast Asia. In Jha, A. K. (ed.), *Coinage, Trade and Economy January 8th–11th, 1991, 3rd International Colloquium.* Pp. 99–107. Maharashtra, India.

———. 1999. Coinage, Trade and Economy in Early South India and Its Southeast Asian Neighbours. *IESHR* 36, 431–459.

Hamilton-Dyer, S. 1998. Roman Egypt: Provisioning the Settlements of the Eastern Desert, with Particular Reference to the Quarry Settlement of Mons Claudianus. In Mills, C. M., and Coles, G. (eds.), *Life on the Edge: Human Settlement and Marginality.* Symposia of the Association for Environmental Archaeology 13. Pp. 121–126. Oxford.

———. 2001. The Faunal Remains. In Maxfield, V. A., and Peacock, D. P. S. (eds.), *Survey and Excavations Mons Claudianus 1987–1993.* Vol. 2. *Excavations: Part 1 (FIFAO 43).* Pp. 249–310. Cairo.

Hammond, P. C. 1973. *The Nabataeans—Their History, Culture and Archaeology.* Gothenburg.

———. 1979. Nabataean Epigraphy. In Whitcomb, D. S., and Johnson, J. H. (eds.), *Quseir al-Qadim 1978 Report.* Pp. 245–247. Cairo and Princeton, NJ.

Hannibal-Deraniyagala, A. S. 2000. Beads from Tissamaharama, Sri Lanka. In Taddei, M., and de Marco, G. (eds.), *South Asian Archaeology 1997. Proceedings of the Fourteenth International Conference of the European Association of South Asian Archaeologists, Held in the Istituto Italiano per l'Africa e l'Oriente, Palazzo Brancaccio, Rome, 7–14 July 1997.* Vol. 2. Pp. 647–651. Rome.

Harker, A. 2008. *Loyalty and Dissidence in Roman Egypt: The Case of the Acta Alexandrinorum.* Cambridge.

Harmelin, J. G. 2000. Le corail rouge de Méditerranée: Quelques aspects de sa biologie et de son écologie. In Morel, J.-P., et al. (eds.), *Corallo di ieri—Corallo di oggi, Atti del Convegno, Ravello, Villa Rufolo, 13–15 dicembre 1996.* Pp. 11–20. Bari.

Harmless, W. 2004. *Desert Christians: An Introduction to the Literature of Early Monasticism.* Oxford.

Harrauer, H., and Sijpesteijn, P. J. 1985. Ein neues Dokument zu Roms Indienhandel, P. Vindob. G 40822. *Anzeiger der Österreichischen Akademie der Wissenschaften, phil. hist. Kl.* 122, 124–155.

Harrell, J. A. 1996. Geology. In Sidebotham and Wendrich 1996, 99–126.

———. 1998. Geology. In Sidebotham and Wendrich 1998a, 121–148.

———. 1999. Geology. In Sidebotham and Wendrich 1999, 107–121.

———. 2002. Pharaonic Stone Quarries in the Egyptian Deserts. In Friedman, R. (ed.), *Egypt and Nubia Gifts of the Desert.* Pp. 232–243. London.

———. 2004a. Archaeological Geology of the World's First Emerald Mine. *Geoscience Canada* 31 (2), 69–76.

———. 2004b. A Stone Vessel Quarry at Gebel Umm Naqqat. *EA* 24, 34–36.

———. 2007a. Geology. In Sidebotham and Wendrich 2007a, 166–174.

———. 2007b. The *Lygdos* of *Arabia Felix. Marmora* 3, 9–20.

Harrell, J. A., and Brown, V. M. 1992a. The Oldest Surviving Topographical Map from Ancient Egypt: (Turin Papyri 1879, 1899, and 1969). *JARCE* 29, 81–105.

———. 1992b. The World's Oldest Surviving Geological Map: The 1150 B.C. Turin Papyrus from Egypt. *Journal of Geology* 100, 3–18.

Harrell, J. A., and Lazzarini, L. 2002. A New Variety of *granite bianco e nero* from Wadi Barud, Egypt. In Herrmann, Jr., J. J., et al. (eds.), *ASMOSIA 5: Interdisciplinary Studies on Ancient Stone.* Pp. 47–51. London.

Harrell, J. A., and Lewan, M. D. 2002. Sources of Mummy Bitumen in Ancient Egypt and Palestine. *Archaeometry* 44 (2), 285–293.

Harrell, J. A., and Sidebotham, S. E. 2004. Wadi Abu Diyeiba: An Amethyst Quarry in Egypt's Eastern Desert. *Minerva* 15 (6), 12–14.

Harrell, J. A., et al. 1999. Two Newly Discovered Roman Quarries in the Eastern Desert of Egypt. In Schvoerer, M. (ed.), *Archeomateriaux, marbres et autre roches—Actes de la Conférence internationale ASMOSIA IV, 9–13 Octobre 1995.* Pp. 285–292. Bordeaux.

Harrell, J. A., et al. 2002. Breccia verde antica—Source, Petrology and Ancient Uses. In Lazzarini, L. (ed.), *Interdisciplinary Studies on Ancient Stone—ASMOSIA VI, Proceedings of the Sixth International Conference of the Association for the Study of Marble and Other Stones in Antiquity, Venice, June 15–18, 2000*. Pp. 207–218. Padova.

Harrell, J. A., et al. 2006. The Ptolemaic to Early Roman Amethyst Quarry at Abu Diyeiba in Egypt's Eastern Desert. *BIFAO* 106, 127–162.

Harris, W. V., and Ruffini, G. 2004. *Ancient Alexandria between Egypt and Greece*. Leiden.

Hart, G. L., and Heifetz, H. (trans. and eds.). 1999. *The Four Hundred Songs of War and Wisdom:. An Anthology of Poems from Classical Tamil. The Puṟanāṉūṟu*. New York.

Hartmann, U. 2001. *Das palmyrenische Teilreich (Oriens et Occidens 2)*. Stuttgart.

Harvey, S. P. 2003. Interpreting Punt: Geographic, Cultural and Artistic Landscapes. In O'Connor, D., and Quirke, S. (eds.), *Mysterious Lands*. Pp. 81–91. London.

Hashim, S. A. 2007. *Pre-Islamic Ceramics in Saudi Arabia: The Chronological and Typological Study of the Ceramics Technology and Craft Production Discovered in Saudi Arabia, from the Neolithic Period until the Dawn of Islam*. Riyadh.

Hatzfeld, J. 1919. *Les Trafiquants italiens dans l'Orient héllenique*. Paris.

Hayes, J. W. 1995. Summary of Pottery and Glass Finds. In Sidebotham and Wendrich 1995, 33–40.

———. 1996. The Pottery. In Sidebotham and Wendrich 1996, 147–178.

Head, S. M. 1987a. Corals and Coral Reefs of the Red Sea. In Edwards and Head 1987, 128–151.

———. 1987b. Introduction. In Edwards and Head 1987, 1–21.

Healy, J. F. 1988. Mines and Quarries. In Grant, M., and Kitzinger, R. (eds.), *Civilization of the Ancient Mediterranean: Greece and Rome*. Vol. 2. Pp. 779–793. New York.

———. 1989. Were the Nabataeans Arabs? *Aram* 1, 38–44.

———. 1996. Palmyra and the Arabian Gulf Trade. *Aram* 8, 33–37.

Heine, P. 1983. Transsaharahandelswege in antiker und frühislamischer Zeit. *MBAH* 2 (1), 92–99.

Helm, R. 1984. *Hieronymi Chronicon, Eusebius Werke*. Vol. 7. 3rd ed. Berlin.

Hennig, D. 2006. Oreophylakes in Ägypten. *Chiron* 36, 1–10.

Hense, A. M. 1995. Metal Finds. In Sidebotham and Wendrich 1995, 49–57.

———. 1996. Metal Finds. In Sidebotham and Wendrich 1996, 213–227.

———. 1998. The Metal Finds. In Sidebotham and Wendrich 1998a, 199–220.

———. 1999. The Metal Finds. In Sidebotham and Wendrich 1999, 219–230.

———. 2000. Metal Finds. In Sidebotham and Wendrich 2000a, 191–202.

———. 2007. Metal Finds. In Sidebotham and Wendrich 2007a, 211–219.

Herbert, K. 1997. The Silk Road: The Link Between the Classical World and Ancient China. *CB* 73 (2), 119–124.

Herbert, S. C., et al. 2003. *Kelsey Museum of the University of Michigan–University of Assiut Excavations at Coptos (Qift) in Upper Egypt, 1987–1992*. Portsmouth, RI.

Herbich, T. M. 2007. Magnetic Survey. In Sidebotham and Wendrich 2007a, 22–29.

Herz, P. 2007. Finances and Costs of the Roman Army. In Erdkamp, P. (ed.), *A Companion to the Roman Army*. Pp. 306–322. Malden, MA, and Oxford.

Hester, J. J., et al. 1970. New Evidence of Early Roads in Nubia. *AJA* 74 (4), 385–389.

Hiebert, F. T. 1991. Commercial Organization of the Egyptian Port of Quseir al-Qadim: Evidence from the Analysis of the Wooden Objects. *Archéologie Islamique* 2, 127–159.

Hiebert, F. T., and Cambon, P. (eds.). 2008. *Afghanistan: Hidden Treasures from the National Museum, Kabul.* Washington, DC.

Hikade, T. 2001. *Das Expeditionswesen im ägyptischen Neuen Reich: Ein Beitrag zu Rohstoffversorgung und Außenhandel.* Heidelberg.

———. 2006. Expeditions to the Wadi Hammamat during the New Kingdom. *JEA* 92, 53–168.

Hillers, D. R., and Cussini, E. 1996. *Palmyrene Aramaic Texts.* Baltimore and London.

Hinkel, F. W. 1992. *The Archaeological Map of the Sudan.* Vol. 6. *The Area of the Red Sea Coast and Northern Ethiopian Frontier.* Berlin.

Hinkel, M. 1991. Hafire im antiken Sudan. *ZÄS* 118 (1), 32–48.

Hinz, W. 1975. Darius und der Suezkanal. *Archäologische Mitteilungen aus Iran* 8, 115–121.

Hirschfeld, Y. 1992. *The Judean Desert Monasteries in the Byzantine Period.* New Haven, CT, and London.

Hirth, F. 1975. *China and the Roman Orient: Researches into Their Ancient and Medieval Relations as Represented in Old Chinese Records.* Reprint. Chicago.

Hobbs, J. J. 1989. *Bedouin Life in the Egyptian Wilderness.* Austin, TX.

———. 1995. *Mount Sinai.* Austin, TX.

Hobbs, J. J., and Goodman, S. M. 1995. Leopard-Hunting Scenes in Dated Rock Paintings from the Northern Eastern Desert of Egypt. *Sahara* 7, 7–16.

Hobson, D. 1983. Women as Property Owners in Roman Egypt. *TAPA* 113, 311–321.

Hodge, A. Trevor. 2000. Collection of Water. In Wikander, Ö. (ed.), *Handbook of Ancient Water Technology.* Pp. 21–28. Leiden, Boston, and Cologne.

Hodges, H. 1989. *Artifacts: An Introduction to Early Materials and Technology.* London.

Hölbl, G. 2001. *A History of the Ptolemaic Empire.* London and New York.

———. 2003. Luoghi di culto nel Wadi Sikait, deserto orientale, Egitto. In Basile, C., and Di Natale, A. (eds.), *Atti del VII Convegno nazionale di Egittologia e Papirologia, Siracusa, 29 novembre–2 dicembre 2001.* Pp. 23–56. Siracusa.

———. 2005. *Altägypten im römischen Reich: Der römische Pharao und seine Tempel.* Vol. 3. *Heiligtümer und religiöses Leben in den ägyptischen Wüsten und Oasen.* Mainz.

Hofmann, I. 1975. *Wege und Möglichkeiten eines indischen Einflusses auf die meroitische Kultur.* Bonn.

Hogarth, D. G. 1896. The Classical Inscriptions. In Petrie, W. M. F., *Koptos.* Pp. 27–33. London.

Hohlfelder, R. L. (ed.). 2008. *The Maritime World of Ancient Rome. Proceedings of "The Maritime World of Ancient Rome" Conference Held at the American Academy in Rome 27–29 March 2003.* Ann Arbor, MI.

Holmberg, E. J. 1933. *Zur Geschichte der Cursus Publicus.* Uppsala.

Holmes, D. L. 1999. Neolithic and Predynastic Stone Tools. In Bard and Shubert 1999, 564–568.

Holt, F. L. 2003. *Alexander the Great and the Mystery of the Elephant Medallions.* Berkeley, Los Angeles, and London.

Holtheide, B. 1980. MATRONA STOLATA–FEMINA STOLATA. *ZPE* 38, 127–134.

Hopkins, K. 1988. Roman Trade, Industry and Labor. In Grant, M., and Kitzinger, R. (eds.), *Civilization of the Ancient Mediterranean: Greece and Rome.* Vol. 2. Pp. 753–778. New York.

Hopkirk, K. 1993. *Central Asia: A Traveller's Companion.* London.

Hopkirk, P. 1980. *Foreign Devils on the Silk Road: The Search for the Lost Cities and Treasures of Chinese Central Asia.* London.

Horden, P., and Purcell, N. 2000. *The Corrupting Sea.* Oxford.

Hourani, G. F. 1995. *Arab Seafaring in the Indian Ocean in Ancient and Early Medieval Times.* Revised and expanded ed. by J. Carswell. Princeton, NJ.

Houston, G. W. 1988. Ports in Perspective: Some Comparative Materials on Roman Merchant Ships and Ports. *AJA* 92 (4), 553–564.

Hower, B., and Rosenbaum, E. 1958. *The Roman Cookery Book.* London and New York.

Howgego, C., and Potts, D. T. 1992. Greek and Roman Coins from Eastern Arabia. *AAE* 3, 183–189.

Hoyland, R. G. 2001. *Arabia and the Arabs: From the Bronze Age to the Coming of Islam.* London and New York.

Hughes, J. D. 1994. *Pan's Travail: Environmental Problems of the Ancient Greeks and Romans.* Baltimore and London.

Hultzsch, E. 1904. Remarks on a Papyrus from Oxyrhynchus: An English Version, with Some Corrections, of a German Article Which Appeared in the Berlin "Hermes," Vol. XXXIX, p. 307ff. *JRAS,* 399–405.

Humbert, J.-B., and Desreumaux, A. (eds.). 1998. *Fouilles de Khirbet es-Samra en Jordanie.* Vol. 1. *La voie romaine, le cemetière, les documents épigraphiques (École biblique et archéologique française de Jérusalem centre d'études des religions du Livre CNRS).* Turnhout, Belgium.

Hume, W. F. 1907. *A Preliminary Report of the Geology of the Eastern Desert of Egypt between the Latitude of 22° N and 25° N.* Cairo.

———. 1925. *Geology of Egypt.* Vol. 1. *The Surface Features of Egypt, Their Determining Causes and Relation to Geological Structure.* Cairo.

———. 1934. *Geology of Egypt.* Vol. 2. *The Fundamental Pre-Cambrian Rocks of Egypt and the Sudan; their Distribution, Age, and Character.* Part 1. *The Metamorphic Rocks.* Cairo.

———. 1935. *Geology of Egypt.* Vol. 2. *The Fundamental Pre-Cambrian Rocks of Egypt and the Sudan; their Distribution, Age and Character.* Part 2. *The Later Plutonic and Minor Intrusive Rocks.* Cairo.

———. 1937. *Geology of Egypt.* Vol. 2. *The Fundamental Pre-Cambrian Rocks of Egypt and the Sudan; their Distribution, Age and Character.* Part 3. *The Minerals of Economic Value.* Cairo.

Humphrey, C., and Hugh-Jones, S. 1992. *Barter, Exchange and Value.* Cambridge.

Huntingford, G. W. B. 1980. *Periplus of the Erythraean Sea.* London.

Huyge, D. 1998. Possible Representations of Palaeolithic Fish-Traps in Upper Egyptian Rock Art. *RAR* 15 (1), 3–11.

———. 1999. El-Hosh Revisited. *RAR* 16 (1), 51–52.

———. 2000–2001. Rock Art Research in Upper Egypt: The Environs of El-Hosh. Report on the Work Done in 1998. *ASAE* 76, 45–52.

———. 2002. Cosmology, Ideology and Personal Religious Practice in Ancient Egyptian Rock Art. In Friedman, R. (ed.), *Egypt and Nubia Gifts of the Desert.* Pp. 192–206. London.

Huyge, D., et al. 2001. Dating Egypt's Oldest "Art"': AMS [14]C Age Determinations of Rock Varnishes Covering Petroglyphs at El-Hosh (Upper Egypt). *Antiquity* 75 (287), 68–72.

Hyman, P., and Hyman, M. 1980. Long Pepper: A Short History. *Petits propos culinaires* 6, 50–52.

Ingraham, M. L., et al. 1981. Saudi Arabian Comprehensive Survey Program: C. Preliminary

Report on a Reconnaissance Survey of the Northwestern Province (with a Note on a Brief Survey of the Northern Province). *Atlal* 5, 58–84.

Insoll, T. 2003. *The Archaeology of Islam in Sub-Saharan Africa.* Cambridge.

Invernizzi, A. 1997. Coppe e bracieri da incenso nell'oriente classico. In Avanzini 1997, 121–146.

Isaac, B. 1992. *The Limits of Empire: The Roman Army in the East.* Rev. ed. Oxford.

Isaac, B., and Roll, I. 1982. *Roman Roads in Judaea.* Vol. 1. *The Legio-Scythopolis Road.* Oxford.

Jackson, R. 1988. *Doctors and Diseases in the Roman Empire.* Norman, OK.

Jackson, R. B. 2002. *At Empire's Edge: Exploring Rome's Egyptian Frontier.* New Haven, CT, and London.

Jacomet, S., and Schibler, J. 2001. Les contributions de l'archéobotanique et de l'archéozoologie à la connaissance de l'agriculture et de l'alimentation du site romain de Biesheim-Kunheim. In Plouin, S., et al. (eds.), *La frontière romaine sur le Rhin supérieur: À propos des fouilles récentes de Biesheim-Kunheim. Exposition présentée au Musée gallo-romain de Biesheim du 31 août au 20 octobre 2001.* Pp. 60–68. Biesheim, France.

Jameson, S. 1968. Chronology of the Campaigns of Aelius Gallus and C. Petronius. *JRS* 58, 71–84.

Jamme, A. 1963. *The Al-'Uqlah Texts. (Documents Sud-Arabe, III).* Washington, DC.

Janvier, Y. 1984. Rome et l'Orient lontain: Le problème des sères. Réexamen d'une question de géographie antique. *Ktema* 9, 261–303.

Jaritz, H., and Rodziewicz, M. 1993. The Investigation of the Ancient Wall Extending from Aswan to Philae. Second Preliminary Report. With a Contribution on the Pottery from the Watch-Tower at Tell Asmar. *MDAIK* 49, 107–127.

Jasmin, M. 2005. Les conditions d'émergence de la route de l'encens à la fin du IIᵉ millénaire avant notre ère. *Syria* 82, 49–62.

Jennison, G. 1937. *Animals for Show and Pleasure in Ancient Rome.* Manchester, UK.

Johnson, J. H. 1982. Inscriptional Material. In Whitcomb, D. S., and Johnson, J. H. (eds.), *Quseir al-Qadim 1980 Preliminary Report.* Pp. 263–266. Malibu, CA.

Johnson, W. R., and Whitcomb, D. S. 1979. Pottery: Roman Pottery–Islamic Pottery. In Whitcomb, D. S., and Johnson, J. H. (eds.), *Quseir al-Qadim 1978 Preliminary Report.* Pp. 67–103. Cairo and Princeton, NJ.

Jolowicz, H. F., and Nicholas, B. 1972. *Historical Introduction to the Study of Roman Law.* 3rd ed. Cambridge.

Jomier, J. 1954. Les graffiti "sinaïtiques" du Wadi Abou Daradj. *RB* 61, 419–424.

Jones, A. H. M. 1964. *The Later Roman Empire, 284–602: A Social, Economic and Administrative Survey.* Norman, OK.

———. 1974. *The Roman Economy: Studies in Ancient Economic and Administrative History.* Totowa, NJ.

Jones, S. 1997. *The Archaeology of Ethnicity.* New York.

Jørgensen, L. B. 2006. The Late Roman Fort at Abū Sha'ār, Egypt: Textiles in Their Archaeological Context. In *Textiles in Situ: Their Find Spots in Egypt and Neighbouring Countries in the First Millennium C.E..* Pp. 161–173. Bern, Switzerland.

Joukowsky, M. S. 2003. The Great Temple. In Markoe, G. (ed.), *Petra Rediscovered: Lost City of the Nabataeans.* Pp. 214–222. New York and Cincinnati.

al-Kabawi, A., et al. 1989. Preliminary Report on the Fourth Season of Comprehensive Rock Art and Epigraphic Survey of Northern Saudi Arabia 1408 A.H./1987 A.D. *Atlal* 12 (2), 41–51.

Kaegi, W. E. 1981. *Byzantine Military Unrest, 471–843: An Interpretation.* Amsterdam.

———. 1992. *Byzantium and the Early Islamic Conquests.* Cambridge.

Kamil, J. 1990. *Coptic Egypt History and Guide.* Rev. ed. Cairo.

Kammerer, A. 1929. *La mer rouge, l'Abyssinie et l'Arabie depuis l'Antiquité: Essai d'Histoire et de Géographie historique.* Vol. 1. *Les Pays de la mer érythrée jusqu'a la fin du moyen âge.* Cairo.

———. 1936. *Le Routier de Dom Joam de Castro: L'Exploration de la mer Rouge par les Portugais en 1541.* Paris.

Kangle, R. P. 1986a. *The Kauṭilīya Arthaśāstra.* Part 2. *An English Translation with Critical and Explanatory Notes.* Reprint. Delhi.

———. 1986b. *The Kauṭilīya Arthaśāstra.* Part 3. *A Study.* Reprint. Delhi.

Kaper, O. E. (ed.). 1998a. *Life on the Fringe. Living in the Southern Egyptian Deserts during the Roman and early Byzantine Periods. Proceedings of a Colloquium Held on the Occasion of the 25th Anniversary of the Netherlands Institute for Archaeology and Arabic Studies in Cairo 9–12 December 1996.* Leiden.

Kaper, O. E. 1998b. Temple Building in the Egyptian Deserts during the Roman Period. In Kaper 1998a, pp. 139–158.

Karttunen, K. 1995. Early Roman Trade with South Asia. *Arctos* 29, 81–91.

Kayser, F. 1997. Listes de Soldats (388–408). In Bingen et al. 1997, 229–247.

Keegan, J. 2003. *Intelligence in War: Knowledge of the Enemy from Napoleon to Al-Qaeda.* New York.

Keenan, J., et al. 2000a. Map Sheet 80 Coptos-Berenice. In R. J. A. Talbert, (ed.), *Barrington Atlas of the Greek and Roman World.* Princeton, NJ.

Keenan, J., et al. 2000b. Map 80 Coptos-Berenice. In R. J. A. Talbert, (ed.), *Barrington Atlas of the Greek and Roman World: Map-by-Map Directory.* Vol. 2. Pp. 1170–1180. Princeton, NJ.

Keene, C. H. 1887. *The Eclogues of Calpurnius Siculus and M. Aurelius Olympius Nemesianus with Introduction, Commentary, and Appendix.* London.

Kennedy, D. 1985. The Composition of a Military Work Party in Roman Egypt (*ILS* 2483: Coptos). *JEA* 71, 156–160.

———. 1995. Water Supply and Use in the Southern Hauran, Jordan. *JFA* 22(3), 275–290.

———. 2000. *The Roman Army in Jordan: A Handbook Prepared on the Occasion of the XVIIIth International Congress of Roman Frontier Studies, Amman, Jordan, 2–11 September 2000.* London.

Kennedy, D. L., and Riley, D. 1990. *Rome's Desert Frontier from the Air.* Austin, TX.

Kennet, D. 2004. *Sasanian and Islamic Pottery from Ras al-Khaimah: Classification, Chronology, and Analysis of Trade in the Western Indian Ocean.* Oxford.

Kenoyer, J. M. 1986. The Indus Bead Industry: Contributions to Bead Technology. *Ornament* 10 (1), 18–23.

Kentley, E. 1996. The Sewn Boats of India's East Coast. In Ray and Salles 1996, 247- 260.

———. 1999. The Sewn Boats of Orissa. In Behera, K. S. (ed.), *Maritime Heritage of India.* Pp. 188–195. New Delhi.

Kenyon, F. G. 1898. *Greek Papyri in the British Museum. Catalogue, with Texts.* Vol. 2. London.

Kerkhoven, G. J., and Koopmans, A. 1989. Goosypium hirsutum L. In Westphal, E., and Jansen,

P. C. M. (eds.), *Plant Resources of South-East Asia: A Selection*. Pp. 145–150. Wageningen, Netherlands.

Kerlogue, F. 2005. Textiles of Jambi (Sumatra) and the Indian Ocean Trade. In Barnes, R. (ed.), *Textiles in Indian Ocean Societies*. Pp. 130–149. London and New York.

Keys, D. 1999. *Catastrophe: An Investigation into the Origins of the Modern World*. New York.

Kildahl, P. A. 1979. Roman Roads in North Africa. In Powell, Jr., M. A., and Sack, R. H. (eds.), *Studies in Honor of Tom B. Jones*. Pp. 257–275. Neukirchen and Vluyn, Germany.

Kinglake, A. 1982. *Eothen*. Reprint. Oxford and New York.

Kingsley, S. 2001. The Economic Impact of the Palestinian Wine Trade in Late Antiquity. In Kingsley and Decker 2001a, 44–68.

———. 2009a. Great Voyages, Great Ocean-Going Ships? In Mango 2009, 323–326.

———. 2009b. Mapping Trade by Shipwrecks. In Mango 2009, 31–36.

Kingsley, S., and Decker, M. (eds.). 2001a. *Economy and Exchange in the Eastern Mediterranean during Late Antiquity: Proceedings of a Conference at Sommerville College, Oxford, 29th May, 1999*. Oxford.

———. 2001b. New Rome, New Theories on Inter-Regional Exchange. An Introduction to the East Mediterranean Economy in Late Antiquity. In Kingsley and Decker 2001a, 1–27.

Kinoshita, H. 2009. Foreign Glass Excavated in China, from the 4th to the 12th Centuries. In Mango 2009, 253–261.

Kirchner, J. 1927. (ed.). *Inscriptiones Graecae*. 2nd ed. Berlin.

Kirwan, L. P. 1972. The Christian Topography and the Kingdom of Axum. *GJ*, 166–177.

Kitchen, K. A. 1993. The Land of Punt. In Shaw, T., et al. (eds.), *The Archaeology of Africa: Food, Metals and Towns*. Pp. 587–608. London and New York.

———. 2001. Economics in Ancient Arabia from Alexander to the Augustans. In Archibald et al. 2001, 157–173.

———. 2004. The Elusive Land of Punt Revisited. In Lunde and Porter 2004, 25–31.

———. 2005. Ancient Peoples West of the Red Sea in Pre-Classical Antiquity. In Starkey, J. C. M. (ed.), *People of the Red Sea. Proceedings of Red Sea Project II Held in the British Museum October 2004*. Pp. 7–14. Oxford.

Klemm, D. D., et al. 1984. Die pharaonischen Steinbrüche des Silifizierten Sandsteins in Ägypten und die Herkunft der Memnon-Kolosse. *MDAIK* 40, 207–220.

Klemm, D. D., et al. 2001. Gold of the Pharaohs: 6000 Years of Gold Mining in Egypt and Nubia. *JAES* 33 (3–4), 643–659.

Klemm, D. D., et al. 2002. Ancient Gold Mining in the Eastern Desert of Egypt and the Nubian Desert of Sudan. In Friedman, R. (ed.), *Egypt and Nubia: Gifts of the Desert*. Pp. 215–231 and plates 113–130. London.

Klemm, R., and Klemm, D. D. 1993. *Steine und Steinbrüche im alten Ägypten*. Berlin.

———. 1994. Chronologischer Abriß der antiken Goldgewinnung in der Ostwüste Ägyptens. *MDAIK* 50, 189–222.

———. 2008. *Stones and Quarries in Ancient Egypt*. London.

Klemm, R., et al. 1995. Evolution of Methods for Prospection, Mining and Processing of Gold in Egypt. In Esmael, F. A. (ed.), *Proceedings of the First International Conference on Ancient Egyptian Mining and Metallurgy and Conservation of Metallic Artifacts. Cairo, Egypt, 10–12 April 1995*. Pp. 341–354. Cairo.

Klunzinger, C. B. 1878. *Upper Egypt: Its Peoples and Its Products*. London.

Knauer, E. R. 1998. *The Camel's Load in Life and Death: Iconography and Ideology of Chinese Figurines from Han to Tang and Their Relevance to Trade along the Silk Routes*. Zurich.

Knörzer, K.-H. 1966. Über Funde römischer Importfrüchte in Novaesium (Neuß/Th.). *Bonner Jahrbücher*, 433–443.

Kobishchanov, Y. M. 1979. *Axum*. University Park, PA, and London.

Kolb, A. 1997. Der *Cursus Publicus* in Ägypten. In *Akten des 21. Internationalen Papyrologenkongresses, Berlin 13–19.8.1995*. Pp. 533–540. Stuttgart and Leipzig.

———. 2001. Transport and Communication in the Roman State: *The Cursus Publicus*. In Adams and Laurence 2001, 95–105.

Kortenbeutel, H. 1931. *Der ägyptischer Süd- und Osthandel in der Politik der Ptolemäer und römischen Kaiser*. Berlin and Charlottenburg.

Kozawa, Y., et al. 1988. Development of the Elephant Molar and the Evolution of Its Enamel Structure. In Russell, D. E., et al. (eds.), *Teeth Revisited: Proceedings of the VIIth International Symposium on Dental Morphology*. Pp. 125–131. Paris.

Kramer, N. 2003. Das Itinerar Σταθμοὶ Παρθικοί des Isidor von Charax: Beschreibung eines Handelsweges? *Klio* 85 (1), 120–130.

Krebs, W. 1965. Einige Transportprobleme der antiken Schiffahrt. *Das Altertum* 11, 86–101.

Kreutz, A. 1995. Landwirtschaft und ihre ökologischen Grundlagen in den Jahrhunderten um Christi Geburt: Zum Stand der naturwissenschaftlichen Untersuchungen in Hessen. *Berichte der Komission für Archäologische Landesforschung in Hessen* 3, 59–91.

Krishnamurthy, R. 2000. *Non-Roman Ancient Foreign Coins from Karur in India*. Chennai, India.

Krzywinski, J. 2001b. *Etbai, det gode land Nomadkulturen mellom Nilen og Rødehavet*. Bergen.

———. 2007. Water Harvesting in the Eastern Desert of Egypt. In Seland 2007, 45–57.

Krzywinski, K. 2001a. A Desert Landscape in Transformation: The Fossil Pollen Records of the ED. In Krzywinski, K., and Price, R. H. (eds.), *Deserting the Desert: A Threatened Cultural Landscape between the Nile and the Sea*. Pp. 99–108. Bergen.

Kuenz, C. 1981. Bassins et Tables d'Offrandes. *BIFAO* 81, 243–282.

Küster, H. 1995. *Postglaziale Vegetationsgeschichte Südbayerns Geobotanische Studien zur Prähistorischen Landschaftskunde*. Berlin.

Kuncan, D. 1984. Der erste römerzeitliche Pfefferfund-nachgewesen im Legionslager Oberaden (Stadt Bergkamen). *Ausgraben und Funde im Westfälen-Lippe* 2, 51–56.

Kuper, R. 2001. By Donkey Train to Kufra?—How Mr Meri Went West. *Antiquity* 75 (290), 801–802.

———. 2003. The Abu Ballas Trail: Pharaonic Advances into the Libyan Desert. In Hawass, Z., and Brock, L. P. (eds.), *Egyptology at the Dawn of the Twenty-first Century. Proceedings of the Eighth International Congress of Egyptologists Cairo, 2000*. Vol. 2. *History, Religion*. Pp. 372–376. Cairo and New York.

Kurtz, M., and Bellefonds, P. L. de. 2000. A la découverte des mines d'or du désert nubien: L. M. A. de Bellefonds en Etbaye, 1831–1832. In Starkey, J., and El-Daly, O. (eds.), *Desert Travellers from Herodotus to T. E. Lawrence*. Durham, UK.

Lacaze, G., and Camino, L. 2008. *Mémoires de Suez. François Bissey et René Chabot-Morisseau à la découverte du désert oriental d'Égypte (1945–1956)*. Pau, France.

Łajtar, A. 1999. Die Kontakte zwischen Ägypten und dem Horn von Afrika im 2. JH. v. CH."
JJP 29, 51–66.

Landman, N. H., et al. 2001. *Pearls: A Natural History.* New York.

Lankton, J. W. 2003. *A Bead Timeline.* Vol. 1. *Prehistory to 1200 C.E. A Resource for Identification, Classification and Dating.* Washington, DC.

Lassányi, G. 2005. The Blemmyes and the Frontier Defence in Egypt in Late Antiquity. Some Archaeological Notes. In Visy, Z. (ed.), *Limes XIX. Proceedings of the XIXth International Congress of Roman Frontier Studies Held in Pécs, Hungary, September 2003.* Pp. 785–792. Pécs.

Laurence, R. 1998. Land Transport in Roman Italy: Costs, Practice and the Economy. In Parkins, H., and Smith, C. (eds), *Trade, Traders and the Ancient City.* London and New York.

——. 1999. *The Roads of Roman Italy: Mobility and Cultural Change.* London and New York.

Lawton, J. 2004. *Silk, Scents and Spice.* Paris.

Leadbetter, B. 2000. Galerius and the Revolt of the Thebaid in 293/4. *Antichthon* 34, 83–95.

——. 2002. Galerius and the Eastern Frontier. In Freeman, P., et al. (eds.), *Limes XVIII. Proceedings of the XVIIIth International Congress of Roman Frontier Studies Held in Amman, Jordan (September 2000).* Vol. 1. Pp. 85–89. Oxford.

Lee, A. D. 1999. Espionage. In Bowersock, G. W., et al. (eds.), *Late Antiquity: A Guide to the Postclassical World.* Pp. 430–432. Cambridge, MA, and London.

Leguilloux, M. 2003. Les animaux et l'alimentation d'après la faune: Les restes de l'alimentation carnée des fortins de Krokodilô et Maximianon. In Cuvigny 2003e, 549–588.

——. 2006. *Les objects en cuir de Didymoi. Praesidium de la route caravanière Coptos-Bérénice. Praesidia du désert de Bérénice III (FIFAO).* Cairo.

Lepsius, R. 1853. *Letters from Egypt, Ethiopia, and the Peninsula of Sinai.* London.

Le Quesne, C. 2004. Quseir Fort and the Archaeology of the Hajj. In Lunde and Porter 2004, 145–156.

——. 2007. *Quseir: An Ottoman and Napoleonic Fortress on the Red Sea Coast of Egypt.* Cairo.

Leslie, D. D., and Gardiner, K. H. J. 1996. *The Roman Empire in Chinese Sources.* Rome.

Lesquier, J. 1918. *L'Armée romaine d'Égypte d'Auguste à Dioclétien.* Cairo.

Lévêque, R. 2002. Découvertes lors du tournage d'un documentaire sur Socotra. *Regards, Spéléo Info* 42, 8–10.

Lewis, N. 1938. ΜΕΡΙΣΜΟΣ ΑΝΑΚΕΧΩΡΗΚΟΤΩΝ: An Aspect of the Roman Oppression in Egypt. *JEA* 23, 63–75.

——. 1954. On Official Corruption in Roman Egypt: The Edict of Vergillius Capito. *TAPA* 98, 153–158.

——. 1983. *Life in Egypt under Roman Rule.* Oxford.

——. 1995. Μερισμὸς ἀνακεχωρηκότων: An Aspect of the Roman Oppression in Egypt. In Lewis, N. (ed.), *On Government and Law in Roman Egypt: Collected Papers of Naphtali Lewis.* Pp. 1–13. Atlanta.

Litinas, N. 1999. P. Lond. III 1128: Sale of a Donkey. *ZPE* 124, 195–204.

Little, L. K. 2007. Life and Afterlife of the First Pandemic. In Little L. K. (ed.), *Plague and the End of Antiquity: The Pandemic of 541–570.* Pp. 3–32. Cambridge.

Little, O. H., and Attia, M. I. 1943. *The Development of Aswan District with Notes on the Minerals of South-Eastern Egypt.* Giza.

Littmann, E., and Meredith, D. 1953. Nabataean Inscriptions from Egypt. *BSOAS* 15, 1–28.

———. 1954a. Nabataean Inscriptions from Egypt–II. *BSOAS* 16, 211–246.

———. 1954b. An Old Ethiopic Inscription from the Berenice Road. *JRAS* 3rd ser., 119–123.

Liu, X., and Shaffer, L. N. 2007. *Connections Across Eurasia: Transportation, Communication, and Cultural Exchange on the Silk Roads.* New York.

Liverani, M. (ed.). 2003. *Arid Lands in Roman Times: Papers from the International Conference (Rome July 9th-10th 2001).* Florence.

Lloris, M. B. 1970. *Las Anforas romanas en España.* Zaragoza.

Lloyd, A. B. 1977. Necho and the Red Sea: Some Considerations. *JEA* 63, 142–155.

Lobban, R. A., and de Liedekerke, V. 2003. Elephants in Ancient Egypt and Nubia. *Cahiers Caribéens d'Égyptologie* 5, 59–78.

Loewe, M. 1971. Spices and Silk: Aspects of World Trade in the First Seven Centuries of the Christian Era. *JRAS,* 166–179.

Lorton, D. 1971. The Supposed Expedition of Ptolemy II to Persia. *JEA* 57, 160–164.

Lucas, A., and Harris, J. R. 1989. *Ancient Egyptian Materials and Industries.* 4th rev. ed. London.

Luft, U. 2006. Zu der Datierung der Elefantendarstellungen in Bi'ir Minih (Ostwüste). *Acta Antiqua Academiae Scientiarum Hungaricae* 46 (1–2), 173–180.

Luft, U. 2010. *Bi'r Minayh. Report on the Survey 1998–2004. (Studia Aegyptiaca Series Maior III).* Budapest.

Lunde, P., and Porter, A. (eds.). 2004. *Trade and Travel in the Red Sea Region: Proceedings of Red Sea Project I Held at the British Museum October 2002.* Oxford.

Luther, A. 1999. *Medo nectis catenas?* Die Expedition des Aelius Gallus im Rahmen der augusteischen Parther politik. *Orbis Terrarum* 5, 157–182.

Lyovushkina, S. V. 1995/96. On the History of Sericulture in Central Asia. *SRAA* 4, 143–150.

Mabbet, I. W. 1964. The Date of the Arthaśāstra. *JAOS* 84 (2), 162–169.

MacAlister, D. A. 1900. The Emerald Mines of Northern Etbai. *GJ* 16, 537–549.

MacDonald, M. C. A. 1991. Was the Nabataean Kingdom a "Bedouin State"? *ZDPV* 107, 102–119.

———. 1994. A Dated Nabataean Inscription from Southern Arabia. In Nebes, N. (ed.), *Arabia Felix Beiträge zur Sprache und Kultur des vorislamischen Arabien. Festschrift Walter W. Müller zum 60. Geburtstag.* Pp. 132–141. Wiesbaden.

———. 1997. Trade Routes and Trade Goods at the Northern End of the "Incense Road" in the First Millennium B.C. In Avanzini 1997, 333–349.

MacDowall, D. W. 1991. Indian Imports of Roman Silver Coins. In Jha, A. K. (ed.), *Coinage, Trade and the Economy, January 8th-11th, 1991. 3rd International Colloquium.* Pp. 145–163. Maharashtra, India.

———. 1996. The Evidence of the Gazetteer of Roman Artefacts in India. In Ray and Salles 1996, 79–95.

———. 2004a. Foreign Coins Found in India. In View of the Monetary Systems Operating in the Countries of Their Origin. In Macdowall, D. W., and Jha, A. (eds.), *Foreign Coins Found in the Indian Subcontinent 8th-10th January, 1995. 4th International Colloquium.* Pp. 9–14. Maharashtra, India.

———. 2004b. The Indo-Roman Metal Trade. In Macdowall, D. W. and Jha, A. (eds.), *Foreign Coins Found in the Indian Subcontinent 8th-10th January, 1995. 4th International Colloquium.* Pp. 39–44. Maharashtra, India.

MacKay, E. 1915. Old Kingdom Dam in Wadi Gerrawy. In Petrie, W. M. F., and MacKay, E. (eds.), *Heliopolis, Kafr Ammar and Shurafa*. Pp. 38–40. London.

Macklin, A. 2006. Trench 1A, with a Note on the Ostrich Egg by Dionisius Agius. In Peacock and Blue 2006c, 157–160.

Maclaren, C. 1825. Account of the Ancient Canal from the Nile to the Red Sea. *Edinburgh Philosophical Journal* 13 (26), 274–291.

MacMullen, R. 1966. *Enemies of the Roman Order: Treason, Unrest, and Alienation in the Empire*. Cambridge, MA.

Magdelaine, C. 2000. Le corail dans la littérature médicale de l'Antiquité gréco-romaine au Moyen-Êge. In Morel, J.-P., et al. (eds.), *Corallo di ieri, Corallo di oggi: Atti del Convegno Ravello, Villa Rufolo, 13–15 dicembre 1996*. Pp. 239–253. Bari.

Mahadevan, I. 1996. Tamil-Brāhmi Graffito. In Sidebotham and Wendrich 1996, 205–208.

———. 2003. *Early Tamil Epigraphy: From the Earliest Times to the Sixth Century A.D.* Cambridge, MA.

Manderscheid, H. 2000. The Water Management of Greek and Roman Baths. In Wikander, Ö. (ed.), *Handbook of Ancient Water Technology*. Pp. 484–535. Leiden, Boston, and Cologne.

Mango, M. M. 1996. Byzantine Maritime Trade with the East (4th–7th centuries.). *Aram* 8, 139–163.

———. 2001. Beyond the Amphora: Non-Ceramic Evidence for Late Antique Industry and Trade. In Kingsley and Decker 2001a, 87–106.

———. (ed). 2009. *Byzantine Trade, 4th-12th Ccenturies. The Archaeology of Local, Regional and International Exchange. Papers of the Thirty-eighth Spring Symposium of Byzantine Studies, St. John's College, University of Oxford, March 2004*. Abington, Oxon., UK.

Manguin, P.-Y. 1996. Southeast Asian Shipping in the Indian Ocean during the First Millennium A.D. In Ray and Salles 1996, 181–198.

Manley, D. and Rée, P. 2001. *Henry Salt, Artist, Traveller, Diplomat, Egyptologist*. London.

Manniche, L. 1999. *An Ancient Egyptian Herbal*. Revised reprint ed. London.

Manzo, A. 2005. Aksumite Trade and the Red Sea Exchange Network: A View from Bieta Giyorgis (Aksum). In Starkey, J. C. M. (ed.), *People of the Red Sea: Proceedings of Red Sea Project II Held in the British Museum October 2004*. Pp. 51–66. Oxford.

Manzo, A., and Perlingieri, C. 2007. Finds: Pottery. In Bard and Fattovich 2007a, 101–134.

Maraqten, M. 1996. Dangerous Trade Routes: On the Plundering of Caravans in the Pre-Islamic Near East. *Aram* 8, 213–236.

Marek, C. 1993. Die Expedition des Aelius Gallus nach Arabien Jahre 25 v. Chr. *Chiron* 23, 121–156.

———. 1994. Der römische Inschriftenstein von Barāqiš. In Nebes, N. (ed.), *Arabia Felix. Beiträge zur Sprache und Kultur des vorislamischen Arabien. Festschrift Walter W. Müller zum 60. Geburtstag*. Pp. 178–190. Wiesbaden.

Margabandhu, C. 1965. Trade Contacts between Western India and the Graeco-Roman World in the Early Centuries of the Christian Era. *JESHO* 8 (3), 316–322.

Markoe, G. 2003a. Introduction. In Markoe 2003b, 13–18.

———. (ed.). 2003b. *Petra: Rediscovered Lost City of the Nabataeans*. New York and Cincinnati.

Marquaille, C. 2008. The Foreign Policy of Ptolemy II. In McKechnie and Guillaume 2008, 39–64.

Martin, A. 2008. Imports at Ostia in the Imperial Period and Late Antiquity: The Amphora Evidence from the DAI-AAR Excavations. In Hohlfelder 2008, 105–118.

Martinetz, D., et al. 1989. *Weihrauch und Myrrhe: Kulturgeschichte und wirtschaftliche Bedeutung Botanik, Chemie, Medizin.* Stuttgart.

Masson, M. E. 1967. Two Palmyrene Stelae from the Merv Oasis. *East and West* 17, 239–247.

Mathew, G. 1975. The Dating and the Significance of the *Periplus of the Erythrean Sea.* In Chittick, H. N., and Rotberg, R. I. (eds.), *East Africa and the Orient: Cultural Syntheses in Pre-Colonial Times.* Pp. 147–163. New York and London.

Matthews, J. F. 1984. The Tax Law of Palmyra. *JRS* 74, 157–180.

Mattingly, D. J. 1994. *Tripolitania.* Ann Arbor, MI.

Mattingly, D. J., and Wilson, A. 2003. Farming the Sahara: The Garamantian Contribution in Southern Libya. In Liverani 2003, 37–50.

Mattingly, G. L. 1995. The Palmyrene Luxury Trade and Revelation 18:12–13: A Neglected Analogue. *Aram* 7, 217–231.

Maxfield, V. A. 1996. The Eastern Desert Forts and the Army in Egypt during the Principate. In Bailey, D. M. (ed.), *Archaeological Research in Roman Egypt: The Proceedings of the Seventeenth Classical Colloquium of the Department of Greek and Roman Antiquities, British Museum, Held on 1–4 December, 1993.* Pp. 9–19. Ann Arbor, MI.

———. 1997a. The Central Complex: A Description of the Visible Remains. In Peacock, D. P. S., and Maxfield, V. A. (eds.), *Survey and Excavation Mons Claudianus 1987–1993.* Vol. 1. *Topography and Quarries (FIFAO 37).* Pp. 17–138. Cairo.

———. 1997b. Wadi Walls. In Peacock, D. P. S., and Maxfield, V. A. (eds.), *Survey and Excavation Mons Claudianus 1987–1993.* Vol. 1. *Topography and Quarries (FIFAO 37).* Pp. 163–173. Cairo.

———. 2000. The Deployment of the Roman Auxilia in Upper Egypt and the Eastern Desert during the Principate. In Alföldy, G., et al. *(eds.), Kaiser, Heer und Gesellschaft in der römischen Kaiserzeit Gedenkschrift für Eric Birley.* Pp. 407–442. Stuttgart.

———. 2001a. Stone Quarrying in the Eastern Desert with Particular Reference to Mons Claudianus and Mons Porphyrites. In Mattingly, D. J., and Salmon, J. (eds.), *Economies beyond Agriculture in the Classical World.* Pp. 143–170. London and New York.

———. 2001b. The Temple of Isis Myrionomos. In Maxfield and Peacock 2001b, 39–42.

———. 2001c. The Water Supply. In Maxfield and Peacock 2001b, 42–56.

———. 2005. Organisation of a Desert Limes: The Case of Egypt. In Visy, Z. (ed.), *Limes XIX. Proceedings of the XIXth International Congress of Roman Frontier Studies Held in Pécs, Hungary, September 2003.* Pp. 201–210. Pécs.

———. 2007. Excavations at Badia. In Peacock and Maxfield 2007, 25–81. London.

Maxfield, V. A., and Peacock, D. P. S. 2001a. Infrastructure. In Maxfield and Peacock 2001b, 193–239.

———. 2001b. *The Roman Imperial Quarries Survey and Excavation at Mons Porphyrites 1994–1998.* Vol. 1. *Topography and Quarries.* London.

———. 2007. Discussion and Conclusion. In Peacock and Maxfield 2007, 413–431.

Maxfield, V. A., et al. 2001a. The Quarry Villages. In Maxfield and Peacock 2001b, 57–129.

Mayerson, P. 1976. An Inscription in the Monastery of St. Catherine and the Martyr Tradition. *DOP* 30, 375–379.

————. 1992. The Island of Iotabê in the Byzantine Sources: A Reprise. *BASOR* 287, 1–4.

————. 1993. A Confusion of Indias: Asian India and African India in the Byzantine Sources. *JAOS* 113, 169–174.

————. 1994a. A Confusion of Indias: Asian India and African India in the Byzantine Sources. In Mayerson 1994c, 361–366.

————. 1994b. The Island of Iotabê in the Byzantine Sources: A Reprise. In Mayerson 1994c, 352–355.

————. 1994c. *Monks, Martyrs, Soldiers and Saracens: Papers on the Near East in Late Antiquity (1962–1993).* Jerusalem and New York.

————. 1996. The Port of Clysma (Suez) in Transition from Roman to Arab Rule. *JNES* 55, 119–126.

Mayes, S. 2003. *The Great Belzoni: The Circus Strongman Who Discovered Egypt's Ancient Treasures.* London and New York.

Mazzarino, S. 1997. On the Name of the *Hipalus (Hippalus)* Wind in Pliny. In De Romanis and Tchernia 1997, 72–79.

McCormick, M. 2007. Toward a Molecular History of the Justinianic Pandemic. In Little, L. K. (ed.), *Plague and the End of Antiquity: The Pandemic of 541–570.* Pp. 290–312. Cambridge.

McCrindle, J. W. 1897. *The Christian Topography of Cosmas, an Egyptian Monk.* London.

McEvilley, T. 2002. *The Shape of Ancient Thought: Comparative Studies in Greek and Indian Philosophies.* New York.

McGing, B. C. 1998. Bandits, Real and Imagined, in Greco-Roman Egypt. *BASP* 35, 159–183.

McGovern, P. E. 2003. *Ancient Wine: The Search for the Origins of Viniculture.* Princeton, NJ.

McGrail, S. 1996. The Study of Boats with Stitched Planking. In Ray and Salles 1996, 225–238.

McKechnie, P., and Guillaume, P. (eds.). 2008. *Ptolemy II Philadelphus and His World.* Leiden and Boston.

Meeks, D. 2003. Locating Punt. In O'Connor, D., and Quirke, S. (eds.), *Mysterious Lands.* Pp. 53–80. London.

Meiggs, R. 1982. *Trees and Timber in the Ancient Mediterranean World.* Oxford.

Meigs, P. 1966. *Geography of Coastal Deserts.* Paris.

Meijer, F., and van Nijf, O. 1992. *Trade, Transport and Society in the Ancient World: A Sourcebook.* London and New York.

Meile, P. 1940. Les yavanas dans l'Inde tamoule. *JA* 232, 87–123.

Meinardus, O. F. A. 1989. *Monks and Monasteries of the Egyptian Deserts.* Rev. ed. Cairo.

Meredith, D. 1952. The Roman Remains in the Eastern Desert of Egypt. *JEA* 38, 94–111.

————. 1953a. Annius Plocamus: Two Inscriptions from the Berenice Road. *JRS* 43, 38–40.

————. 1953b. The Roman Remains in the Eastern Desert of Egypt (continued). *JEA* 39, 95–106.

————. 1954. Inscriptions from the Berenice Road. *Cd'É* 57, 281–287.

————. 1957a. Berenice Troglodytica. *JEA* 43, 56–70.

————. 1957b. Inscriptions from the Amethyst Mines at Abu Diyeiba (Eastern Desert of Egypt). In *Eos Commentarii Societatis Philologae Polonorum,* vol. 48, fasc. 2, *Symbolae Raphaeli Taubenschlag Dedicatae* II. Pp. 117–119. Bratislava and Warsaw.

————. 1958. *Tabula Imperii Romani, Coptos Sheet N. G. 36.* London.

Meredith, D., and Tregenza, L. A. 1949. Notes on Roman Roads and Stations in the Eastern Desert I. *BFAFU* 11 (1), 97–126.

Meshorer, Y. 1975. *Nabataean Coins. QEDEM* 3. Jerusalem.

Metzler, D. 1989. Kaiserkult ausserhalb der Reichsgrenzen und römischer Fernhandel. In Drexhage, H., and Suenskes, J. (eds.), *Migratio et Commutatio: Studien zur alten Geschichte und deren Nachleben. Thomas Pekáry zum 60. Geburtstag am 13. September 1989 dargebracht von Freunden, Kollegen und Schülern.* Pp. 196–200. St. Katharinen, Germany.

Meyer, C., 1992. *Glass from Quseir al-Qadim and the Indian Ocean Trade.* Chicago.

———. 1995a. A Byzantine Gold Mining Town in the Eastern Desert of Egypt: Bir Umm Fawakhir, 1992–1993. *JRA* 8, 192–224.

———. 1995b. Gold, Granite and Water: The Bir Umm Fawakhir Survey Project 1992. *AASOR* 52, 37–92.

———. 1997. Bir Umm Fawakhir: Insights into Ancient Egyptian Mining. *JMMM*, 64–67.

———. 1999a. Bir Umm Fawakhir. In Bard and Shubert 1999, 175–177.

———. 1999b. Wadi Hammamat. In Bard and Shubert 1999, 868–871.

Meyer, C., and Badr el-Din, Omar M. 1995. The Geological Context of Bir Umm Fawakhir. *Proceedings of the Egyptian-Italian Seminar on Geosciences and Archaeology in Mediterranean Countries (Cairo 28th–30th November 1993).* Pp. 491–501. Cairo.

Meyer, C., and Heidorn, L. 1998. Three Seasons at Bîr Umm Fawâkhîr in the Central Eastern Desert. In Kaper 1998a, 197–212.

Meyer, C., et al. 2000. *Bir Umm Fawakhir Survey Project 1993: A Byzantine Gold-Mining Town in Egypt.* Chicago.

Meyer, C., et al. 2003. Ancient Gold Extraction at Bir Umm Fawakhir. *JARCE* 40, 13–53.

Meyer, J. C. 2007. Roman Coins as a Source for Roman Trading Activities in the Indian Ocean. In Seland 2007, 59–67.

Meyer, R. T. 1950/1998. *St. Athanasius: The Life of St. Antony.* New York and Ramsey, NJ.

Midant-Reynes, B. 2000. *The Prehistory of Egypt: From the First Egyptians to the First Pharaohs.* Oxford.

Midant-Reynes, B., and Braunstein-Silvestre, F. 1977. Le chameau en Égypte. *Orientalia* 46, 337–362.

Mildenberg, L. 1995. Petra on the Frankincense Road? *Transeuphratène* 10, 69–72.

———. 1996. Petra on the Frankincense Road—Again? *Aram* 8, 55–65.

Millar, F. 1967. *The Roman Empire and Its Neighbours.* New York.

———. 1984. Condemnation to Hard Labour in the Roman Empire, from the Julio-Claudians to Constantine. *PBSR* 52, 124–147.

———. 1998. Caravan Cities: The Roman Near East and Long-Distance Trade by Land. In Austin, M., et al. *(eds.), Modus Operandi: Essays in Honour of Geoffrey Rickman.* Pp. 119–137. London.

Miller, C. D. 1971. *Food Values of Breadfruit, Taro Leaves, Coconut and Sugar Cane.* Honolulu and New York.

Miller, J. I. 1969. *The Spice Trade of the Roman Empire, 29 B.C. to A.D. 641.* Oxford.

Mitchell, S. 1976. Requisitioned Transport in the Roman Empire: A New Inscription from Pisidia. *JRS* 66, 106–131.

Mitchiner, M. 1991. Early Trade between India and Mainland Southeast Asia as Reflected by

Coinage. In Jha, A. K. (ed.), *Coinage, Trade and Economy: January 8th–11th, 1991. 3rd International Colloquium.* Pp. 62–83. Maharashtra, India.

Mitthof, F. 2001. *Annona Militaris: Die Heeresversorgung im spätantiken Ägypten. Ein Beitrag zur Verwaltung-und Heeresgeschichte des römischen Reiches im 3. bis 6. Jh. N. Chr.* Vol. 2. Florence.

Moeyersons, J., et al. 2002. Dry Cave Deposits and Their Palaeoenvironmental Significance during the Last 115ka, Sodmein Cave, Red Sea Mountains, Egypt. *Quaternary Science Reviews* 21 (7), 837–851.

Mommsen, T., and Krueger, P. 1985. *The Digest of Justinian.* Vol. 3. Philadelphia.

Monneret de Villard, U. 1935. *Mission archéologique de Nubie 1929–1934. La Nubia medioevale.* Vol. 1. *Inventario dei Monumenti.* Cairo.

———. 1941. *La Nubia romana.* Rome.

Moon, F. W., et al. 1923. *Preliminary Geological Report on Saint John's Island (Red Sea).* Cairo.

Mooren, L. 1972. The Date of *SB* V 8036 and the Development of the Ptolemaic Maritime Trade with India. *Ancient Society* 3, 127–133.

Morkot, R. 1998. "There Are No Elephants in Dóngola": Notes on Nubian Ivory. *Cahier de recherches de l'Institut de papyrologie et d'égyptologie de Lille* 17 (3), 147–154.

Morley, N. 2007. *Trade in Classical Antiquity.* Cambridge.

Morony, M. G. 2007. "For Whom Does the Writer Write?": The First Bubonic Pandemic according to Syriac Sources. In Little L. K. (ed.), *Plague and the End of Antiquity: The Pandemic of 541–570.* Pp. 59–86. Cambridge.

Morrison, J. S., et al. 2000. *The Athenian Trireme: The History and Reconstruction of an Ancient Greek Warship.* 2nd rev. ed. Cambridge.

Mouton, M., et al. 2006. La port sudarabique de Qâni': Paléogéographie et organisation urbaine. *CRAI,* 777–808.

Mouton, M., et al. 2008. A New Map of Qâni' (Yemen). *AAE* 19, 198–209.

Mrozek, S. 1982. Zum Handel von einigen Gewürzen und Wohlgerüchen in der spätrömischen Zeit. *MBAH* 1 (2), 15–21.

Muckensturm-Poulle, C. 2005. Palladius's Brahmans. In Boussac, M.-F., and Salles, J.- F. (eds.), *Athens, Aden, Arikamedu: Essays on the Interrelations between India, Arabia and the Eastern Mediterranean.* Pp. 157–166. New Delhi and Lyon.

Mueller, K. 2006a. Did Ptolemais Theron Have a Wall? Hellenistic Settlement on the Red Sea Coast in the Pithom Stela and Strabo's *Geography. ZÄS* 133 (2), 164–174.

———. 2006b. *Settlements of the Ptolemies: City Foundations and New Settlement in the Hellenistic World.* Leuven, Paris and Dudley, MA.

Müller, W. W. 2001. Antike und mittelalterliche Quellen als Zeugnisse über Soqotra, eine einstmals christliche Insel. *Oriens Christianus* 85, 139–161.

Mulvin, L., and Sidebotham, S. E. 2004. The Gameboards from Abu Sha'ar (Red Sea Coast), Egypt. *Antiquity* 78, 602–617.

Munro-Hay, S. C. H. 1982. The Foreign Trade of the Aksumite Port of Adulis. *Azania* 17, 107–125.

———. 1989. The al-Madhāriba Hoard of Gold Aksumite and Late Roman Coins. *NC,* 83–100.

———. 1991. *Aksum: An African Civilisation of Late Antiquity.* Edinburgh.

———. 1993. State Development and Urbanism in Northern Ethiopia. In Shaw, T., et al. (eds.), *The Archaeology of Africa: Food, Metals and Towns.* Pp. 609–621. London and New York.

———. 1996. Aksumite Overseas Interests. In Reade, J. (ed.), *The Indian Ocean in Antiquity*. Pp. 403–416. London and New York.

Murphy, D. 2000. Rock Art. In Peacock, D., et al. (eds.), *Myos Hormos—Quseir al-Qadim: A Roman and Islamic Port Site. Interim Report 2000*. Pp. 79–82. Southampton, UK. Unpublished.

Murray, G. W. 1925. The Roman Roads and Stations in the Eastern Desert of Egypt. *JEA*, 11, 138–150.

———. 1926a. Aidhab. *GJ* 68, 235–240.

———. 1926b. Notes on the Ruins of Hitân Shenshef, near Berenice. *JEA* 12, 166–167.

———. 1955. Water from the Desert: Some Ancient Egyptian Achievements. *GJ* 121, 171–181.

———. 1968. *Dare Me to the Desert*. South Brunswick, NJ, and New York.

Murray, G. W., and Warmington, E. H. 1967. Trogodytica: The Red Sea Littoral in Ptolemaic Times. *GJ* 133, 24–33.

Mutschler, F.-H., and Mittag, A. (eds.). 2008. *Conceiving the Empire: China and Rome Compared*. Oxford.

Muzzolini, A. 1995. Sur "Leopard-Hunting Scenes in Dated Rock Paintings from the Northern Eastern Desert of Egypt" par J. J. Hobbs et S. M. Goodman. *Sahara* 7, 126–127.

———. 1999. On Huyge's Possible Representations of Fish-Traps in Upper Egyptian Rock Art. *RAR* 16 (1), 50–51.

Narayana, A. C., and Priju, C. P. 2006. Evolution of Coastal Landforms and Sedimentary Environments of the Late Quaternary Period along Central Kerala, Southwest Coast of India. *Journal of Coastal Research*, special issue 39, 1898–1902.

Näser, C. 2010. The Great Hafir at Musawwarat El-Sufra. Work of the Archaeological Mission of Humbolt University Berlin. *Polish Archaeology in the Mediterranean Supplement Series* 2.2, 69–76.

Nash, E. 1968. *Pictorial Dictionary of Ancient Rome*. Vol. 1. Rev. ed. London.

Naumkin, V. V., and Sedov, A. V. 1993. Monuments of Socotra. *Topoi* 3 (2), 569–623.

Naville, E. 1885. *The Store-City of Pithom and the Route of the Exodus*. London.

Negev, A. 1977. The Nabataeans and the Provincia Arabia. *ANRW* 2.8, 520–686.

———. 1986. *Nabataean Archaeology Today*. New York.

Nehmé, L. 2003. The Petra Survey Project. In Markoe, G. (ed.), *Petra Rediscovered: Lost City of the Nabataeans*. Pp. 145–163. New York and Cincinnati.

Newton, C., et al. 2005. Un jardin d'oasis d'époque romaine à 'Ayn-Manâwir (Kharga, Égypte). *BIFAO* 105, 167–195.

Nibbi, A. 1976. Remarks on the Two Stelae of the Wadi Gasus. *JEA* 62, 45–56.

———. 1981. *Ancient Egypt and Some Egyptian Neighbours*. Park Ridge, NJ.

Nicholson, M. J., 1985. The Water Requirements of Livestock in Africa. *Outlook on Agriculture* 14 (4), 156–164.

Nicholson, P. T. 1998. The Glass. In Sidebotham and Wendrich 1998a, 279–288.

———. 1999. The Glass. In Sidebotham and Wendrich 1999, 231–241.

———. 2000a. The Glass. In Sidebotham and Wendrich 2000a, 203–209.

———. 2000b. Roman Glass from Berenike (Egypt): Some New Work. *Annales du 14ᵉ Congrès de l'Association internationale pour l'Histoire de Verre. Italia/Venezia-Milano 1998*. Pp. 151–155. Ad Lochem, Netherlands.

Nicholson, P. T., and Price, J. 2007. Glass Fish Vessel. In Sidebotham and Wendrich 2007a, 220–224.

Nicolet, C. 1991. *Space, Geography and Politics in the Early Roman Empire*. Ann Arbor, MI.

Noy, D. 2000. *Foreigners at Rome: Citizens and Strangers*. London and Swansea, UK.

Nutton, V. 2004. *Ancient Medicine*. London and New York.

Oates, J. F. 1988. Sale of a Donkey. *BASP* 25, 129–135.

Obeyesekere, G. 1984. *The Cult of the Goddess Pattini*. Chicago and London.

Oertel, F. 1964. Das Problem des antiken Suezkanals. In Repgen, K., and Skalweit, S. (eds.), *Spiegel der Geschichte. Festgabe für Max Braubach zum 10. April 1964*. Pp. 18–52. Münster and Westfälen.

Ogden, J. 2000. Metals. In Nicholson, P. T., and Shaw, I. (eds.), *Ancient Egyptian Materials and Technology*. Pp. 148–176. Cambridge.

Ohler, J. G. 1989. Cocos nucifera L. In Westphal, E., and Jansen, P. C. M. (eds.), *Plant Resources of South-East Asia: A Selection*. Pp. 90–95. Wageningen, Netherlands.

Okamura, L. 2002. Gold Crowns and Roman Glass in Kyŏngju, Samguk Silla. Paper delivered at the Eleventh International Conference of the World History Association, co-sponsored by the Korean Historical Association on occasion of its fiftieth anniversary, Seoul National University, Seoul, South Korea, 15–18 August.

Oleson, J. P. 1984. *Greek and Roman Mechanical Water-Lifting Devices: The History of a Technology*. Toronto, Buffalo, and London.

———. 2000a. Irrigation. In Wikander, Ö. (ed.), *Handbook of Ancient Water Technology*. Pp. 183–215. Leiden, Boston, and Cologne.

———. 2000b. Water-Lifting. In Wikander, Ö. (ed.), *Handbook of Ancient Water Technology*. Pp. 217–302. Leiden, Boston, and Cologne.

Olson, R. A. 1979. Parthia, China and Rome: Perspectives along the Great Silk Route. In Powell, Jr., M. A., and Sack, R. H. (eds.), *Studies in Honor of Tom B. Jones*. Pp. 329–339. Neukirchen and Vluyn, Germany.

Ormond, R. F. G., and Edwards, A. J. 1987. Red Sea Fishes. In Edwards and Head 1987, 251–287.

Orrieux, C. 1983. *Les Papyrus de Zenon: L'horizon d'un grec en Egypte au IIIᵉ siècle avant J. C.* Paris.

———. 1985. *Zénon de Caunos, parépidèmos, et le destin grec*. Paris and Besançon.

Osman, R. A. K., and Sidebotham, S. E. 2000. Geomorphology and Archaeology of the Central Eastern Desert of Egypt. *Sahara* 12, 7–30.

Ostrow, S. E. 1977. *Problems in the Topography of Roman Puteoli*. PhD diss., University of Michigan. Ann Arbor.

O'Sullivan, J. N. 1995. *Xenophon of Ephesus: His Compositional Technique and the Birth of the Novel*. Berlin and New York.

Otto, W., and Bengtson, H. 1938. *Zur Geschichte des Niedergangs des Ptolemäerreiches: Ein Beitrag zur Regierungszeit des 8. und des 9. Ptolemäers*. Munich.

Paice, P. 1992. The Punt Relief, the Pithom Stele, and the *Periplus of the Erythraean Sea*. In Harrak, A. (ed.), *Contacts between Cultures: West Asia and North Africa*. Vol. 1. Pp. 227–235. Lewiston, NY.

Palmer, J. A. B. 1951. Periplus Maris Erythraei ἐμπόριον νόμιμον and Other Expressions. *CQ* n. s. 1, 156–158.

Pande, A. 1991a. Bharata and Aristotle. In Arora, U. P. (ed.), *Graeco-Indica: India's Cultural*

Contacts with the Greek World (In Memory of Demetrius Galanos (1760–1833). A Greek Sanskritist of Benares). Pp. 197–205. New Delhi.

Pande, G. C. 1991b. The Iliad and the Mahābhārata. In Arora, U. P. (ed.), *Graeco-Indica: India's
Cultural Contacts with the Greek World (In Memory of Demetrius Galanos (1760–1833). A Greek
Sanskritist of Benares)*. Pp. 192–196. New Delhi.

Papadopoulos, J. K. 1994. A Western Mediterranean Amphora Fragment from ed-Dur. *AAE*
5, 276–279.

PSI. 1912. *Papiri greci e latini*. Florence.

Paribeni, R. 1907. Ricerche nel luogo dell'antica Adulis. *Monumenti Antichi, Reale Accademia
dei Lincei* 18 (3), 437–572.

Parker, A. J. 1992. *Ancient Shipwrecks of the Mediterranean and the Roman Provinces*. Oxford.

———. 1996a. Sea Transport and Trade in the Ancient Mediterranean. In Rice, E. E. (ed.), *The
Sea and History*. Pp. 97–109. Thrupp Stroud, Gloucestershire.

Parker, G. R. 2001. Porous Connections: The Mediterranean and the Red Sea. *Thesis Eleven* 67,
59–79.

———. 2002a. *Ex Oriente Luxuria:* Indian Commodities and Roman Experience. *JESHO* 45
(1), 40–95.

———. 2008. *The Making of Roman India*. Cambridge and New York.

Parker, S. T. 1996b. The Roman 'Aqaba Project: The 1994 Campaign. *ADAJ* 40, 231–257.

———. 1997. Preliminary Report on the 1994 Season of the Roman 'Aqaba Project. *BASOR*
305, 19–44.

———. 1998. The Roman 'Aqaba Project: The 1996 Campaign. *ADAJ* 42, 375–394.

———. 2000. The Roman Aqaba Project: The 1997 and 1998 Campaigns. *ADAJ* 44, 373–394.

———. 2002b. The Roman 'Aqaba Project: The 2000 Campaign. *ADAJ* 46, 409–428.

———. 2006a. History of the Roman Frontier East of the Dead Sea. In Parker 2006c, 517–575.

———. (ed.). 2006b. *The Roman Frontier in Central Jordan: Final Report on the Limes Arabicus
Project, 1980–1989*. Vol. 1. Washington, DC.

———. (ed.). 2006c. *The Roman Frontier in Central Jordan: Final Report on the Limes Arabicus
Project, 1980–1989*. Vol. 2. Washington, DC.

Parkins, H., and Smith, C. 1998. (eds.). *Trade, Traders and the Ancient City*. London and New
York.

Parlasca, K. 1980. Griechisches und Römisches im altern China. *Allgemeine und vergleichende
Archäologie Beiträge* 2, 297–308.

Partridge, R. 1996. *Transport in Ancient Egypt*. London.

Paterson, J. 2001. Hellenistic Economies: The Case for Rome. In Archibald et al. 2001, 367–378.

Peacock, D. P. S. 1992. *Rome in the Desert: A Symbol of Power*. An Inaugural Lecture Delivered
at the University on 3rd December 1992, Southampton, UK.

———. 1993. The Site of Myos Hormos: A View from Space. *JRA* 6, 226–232.

———. 1997a. The Hydreuma. In Peacock and Maxfield 1997, 139–148.

———. 1997b. The Quarries. In Peacock and Maxfield 1997, 175–255.

———. 1997c. The Quarries and Settlement of Tiberiane (Wadi Barud). In Peacock and
Maxfield 1997, 273–283.

———. 1997d. Transportation and Routes to the Nile. In Peacock and Maxfield 1997, 257–271.

———. 1997e. Wadi Umm Diqal. In Peacock and Maxfield 1997, 149–162.

————. 2001a. Myos Hormos—Quseir al-Qadim: A Roman and Islamic Port Site Interim Report, 2001. Southampton, UK. Unpublished.

————. 2001b. The Temple of Isis. In Maxfield and Peacock 2001b, 23–24.

————. 2001c. The Temple of Serapis. In Maxfield and Peacock 2001b, 36–38.

————. 2006a. Regional Survey. In Peacock and Blue 2006c, 7–16.

————. 2006b. The Wadi Walls. In Peacock and Blue 2006c, 33.

Peacock, D. P. S., and Blue, L. 2006a. Discussion and Conclusion. In Peacock and Blue 2006c, 174–177.

————. 2006b. Introduction. In Peacock and Blue 2006c, 1–6.

————. (eds.). 2006c. *Myos Hormos—Quseir al-Qadim. Roman and Islamic Ports on the Red Sea.* Vol. 1. *Survey and Excavations, 1999–2003.* Oxford.

————. 2007. Incense and the Port of Adulis. In Peacock, D., and Williams, D. (eds.), *Food for the Gods: New Light on the Ancient Incense Trade.* Pp. 135–140. Oxford.

Peacock, D. P. S., and Maxfield, V. A. 1994. *The Roman Imperial Porphyry Quarries: Gebel Dokhân, Egypt. Interim Report, 1994.* Unpublished.

————. 1995. *The Roman Imperial Porphyry Quarries: Gebel Dokhân, Egypt. Interim Report, 1995.* Unpublished.

————. 1996. *The Roman Imperial Porphyry Quarries: Gebel Dokhân, Egypt. Interim Report, 1996.* Unpublished.

————. (eds.). 1997. *Survey and Excavation Mons Claudianus, 1987–1993.* Vol. 1. *Topography and Quarries.* Cairo.

————. 2001. Introduction. In Maxfield and Peacock 2001b, 1–9.

————. (eds.). 2007. *The Roman Imperial Quarries Survey and Excavation at Mons Porphyrites, 1994–1998.* Vol. 2. *Excavations.* London.

Peacock, D. P. S., and Peacock, A. 2008. The Enigma of 'Aydhab: A Medieval Islamic Port on the Red Sea Coast. *IJNA* 37 (1), 32–48.

Peacock, D. P. S., and Phillips, J. 2001. The Quarries. In Maxfield and Peacock 2001b, 131–191.

Peacock, D. P. S., and Williams, D. (eds.). 2007. *Food for the Gods: New Light on the Ancient Incense Trade.* Oxford.

Peacock, D. P. S., et al. 1997. Characterisation Studies and the Use of Mons Claudianus Granodiorite. In Peacock and Maxfield 1997, 315–337.

Peacock, D. P. S., et al. (eds.). 1999. *Myos Hormos—Quseir al-Qadim: A Roman and Islamic Port Site on the Red Sea Coast of Egypt. Interim Report, 1999.* Southampton, UK. Unpublished.

Peacock, D. P. S., et al. (eds.). 2000. *Myos Hormos—Quseir al-Qadim: A Roman and Islamic Port Site on the Red Sea Coast of Egypt. Interim Report, 2000.* Southampton, UK. Unpublished.

Peacock, D. P. S., et al. 2001a. The Central Complex. In Maxfield and Peacock 2001b, 11–56.

Peacock, D. P. S., et al. (eds.). 2001b. *Myos Hormos—Quseir al-Qadim: A Roman and Islamic Port Site on the Red Sea Coast of Egypt. Interim Report, 2001.* Southampton, UK. Unpublished.

Peacock, D. P. S., et al. (eds.). 2002. *Myos Hormos—Quseir al-Qadim: A Roman and Islamic Port Site. Interim Report 2002.* Southampton, UK. Unpublished.

Peacock, D. P. S., et al. (eds.). 2003. *Myos Hormos—Quseir al-Qadim: A Roman and Islamic Port Site. Interim Report, 2003.* Southampton, UK. Unpublished.

Peacock, D. P. S., et al. (eds.). 2007a. *The Ancient Red Sea Port of Adulis, Eritrea: Results of the Eritro-British Expedition, 2004–5.* Oxford.

Peacock, D. P. S., et al. 2007b. Basalt as Ships' Ballast and the Roman Incense Trade. In Peacock and Williams 2007, 28–70.

Pearson, L. 1960. *The Lost Histories of Alexander the Great*. New York and London.

Peden, A. J. 2001. *The Graffiti of Pharaonic Egypt: Scope and Roles of Informal Writings (c. 3100–332 B.C.)*. Leiden, Boston, and Cologne.

Pedersen, R. K. 2000. Under the Erythraean Sea: An Ancient Shipwreck in Eritrea. *Quarterly of the Institute of Nautical Archaeology* 27 (2–3), 3–12.

Pekáry, T. 1968. *Untersuchungen zu den römischen Reichsstrassen*. Bonn.

Peña, J. T. 1989. P. Giss. 69: Evidence for the Supplying of Stone Transport Operations in Roman Egypt and the Production of Fifty-Foot Monolithic Column Shafts. *JRA* 2, 126–132.

———. 2007. *Roman Pottery in the Archaeological Record*. Cambridge and New York.

Peppard, M. 2009. A Letter concerning Boats in Berenike and Trade on the Red Sea. *ZPE* 171, 193–198.

Perevolotsky, A. 1981. Orchard Agriculture in the High Mountain Region of Southern Sinai. *Human Ecology* 9 (3), 331–357.

Pestman, P. W. (ed.). 1980a. *Greek and Demotic Texts from the Zenon Archive (P. L. Bat. 20). Text*. Leiden.

———. 1980b. *Greek and Demotic Texts from the Zenon Archive (P. L. Bat. 20). Plates*. Leiden.

———. 1981a. *A Guide to the Zenon Archive (P. L. Bat. 21). A. Lists and Surveys*. Leiden.

———. 1981b. *A Guide to the Zenon Archive (P. L. Bat. 21). B. Indexes and Maps*. Leiden.

Pflaum, H. G. 1940. *Essai sur le Cursus publicus sous le haut-empire romain*. Paris.

Pharr, C. 1952. *The Theodosian Code and Novels and the Sirmondian Constitutions: A Translation with Commentary, Glossary, and Bibliography*. Princeton, NJ.

Phillips, C., et al. 2004. A Latin Inscription from South Arabia. *PSAS* 34, 239–250.

Phillips, J. 1997a. The Leather. In Peacock, D., and Maxfield V. (eds.). *The Roman Imperial Porphyry Quarries: Gebel Dokhan, Egypt. Interim Report, 1997*. P. 20. Southampton, UK. Unpublished.

———. 1997b. Punt and Aksum: Egypt and the Horn of Africa. *Journal of African History* 38 (3), 423–457.

———. 2003. Egypt, Nubia and Ethiopia. In Hawass, Z., and Brock L. P. (eds.), *Egyptology at the Dawn of the Twenty-first Century: Proceedings of the Eighth International Congress of Egyptologists Cairo, 2000*. Vol. 2. *History, Religion*. Pp. 434–442. Cairo and New York.

———. 2007. The Leather. In Peacock and Maxfield 2007, 389–395.

Phillips, J., et al. 2006. The Islamic Town. In Peacock and Blue 2006c, 155–173.

Phillipson, D. W. 2009. Aksum, the Entrepot, and Highland Ethiopia, 3rd–12th Centuries. In Mango 2009, 353–368.

Pierce, R. H. 2007. Strabo and the Eastern Desert of Egypt and Sudan. In Seland 2007, 33–44.

Pietersma, A., and Comstock, S. T. 1987. Coptic Martyrdoms in the Chester Beatty Library. *BASP* 24 (3–4), 143–163.

Pigulewskaja, N. 1969. *Byzanz auf den Wegen nach Indien: Aus der Geschichte des byzantinischen Handels mit dem Orient vom 4. bis 6. Jahrhundert*. Berlin and Amsterdam.

Pinch, G. 1993. *Votive Offerings to Hathor*. Oxford.

Pinder, M., and Parthy, G. (eds.). 1860. *Ravennatis Anonymi Cosmographia et Guidonis Geographia*. Berlin.

Pintozzi, L. A. 2007. Excavations at the *Praesidium et Hydreuma* at Siket. In Sidebotham and Wendrich 2007a, 358–367.

Pirelli, R. 1999. Deir el-Bahri, Hatshepsut Temple. In Bard and Shubert 1999, 234–237.

Plaziat, J., et al. 1995. Quaternary Changes in the Egyptian Shoreline of the Northwestern Red Sea and Gulf of Suez. *Quaternary International* 29–30, 11–22.

Plisson, G. 2005. Some Thoughts on Exchange Systems in the Red Sea Region and Indian Ocean. In Starkey, J. C. M. (ed.), *People of the Red Sea: Proceedings of Red Sea Project II Held in the British Museum October 2004*. Pp. 67–74. Oxford.

Pomey, P., and Tchernia, A. 1980/1981. Il tonnellaggio massimo delle navi mercantili romane. *Puteoli* 4–5, 29–57.

Posener, G. 1936. *La Première Domination perse en Égypte*. Cairo.

———. 1938. Le canal du Nil à la mer Rouge avant les Ptolémées. *CdÉ* 13, 258–273.

Potter, D. S. 1996. Palmyra and Rome: Odenathus' Titulature and the Use of *Imperium Maius*. *ZPE* 113, 271–285.

Potts, D. T. 1988. Trans-Arabian Routes of the Pre-Islamic Period. In Salles 1988, 127–162.

———. 1990. *The Arabian Gulf in Antiquity*. Vol. 2. *From Alexander the Great to the Coming of Islam*. Oxford.

———. 1994. Augustus, Aelius Gallus and the Periplus: A Re-Interpretation of the Coinage of San'â' Class B. In Nebes, N. (ed.), *Arabia Felix. Beiträge zur Sprache und Kultur des vorislamischen Arabien. Festschrift Walter W. Müller zum 60. Geburtstag*. Pp. 212–222. Wiesbaden.

———. 1996. The Parthian Presence in the Arabian Gulf. In Reade, J. (ed.), *The Indian Ocean in Antiquity*. Pp. 269–285. London and New York.

———. 1997. The Roman Relationship with the *Persicus sinus* from the Rise of Spasinou Charax (127 B.C.) to the Reign of Shapur II (A.D. 309–79). In Alcock, S. (ed.), *The Early Roman Empire in the East*. Pp. 89–107. Oxford.

———. 2008. The Sasanian Relationship with South Arabia: Literary, Epigraphic and Oral Historical Perspectives. *Studia Iranica* 37, 197–213.

———. 2009. The Archaeology and Early History of the Persian Gulf. In Potter, L. G. (ed.), *The Persian Gulf in History*. Pp. 27–56. New York.

Power, T. 2007. The "Arabians" of Pre-Islamic Egypt. In Starkey, J., et al. (eds.), *Natural Resources and Cultural Connections of the Red Sea*. Pp. 195–210. Oxford.

Préaux, C. 1978. *Le Monde hellénistique: La Grèce et l'Orient (323–146 av. J.-C.)*. Paris.

———. 1979. *L'Économie royale des Lagides*. New York.

Priaulx, O. de B. 1860. On Indian Embassies to Augustus. *JRAS* 17, 309–321.

———. 1861. On the Second Indian Embassy to Rome (Pliny Nat. Hist. VI.24). *JRAS* 18, 345–361.

———. 1862. On the Indian Embassies to Rome from the Reign of Claudius to the Death of Justinian. *JRAS* 19, 274–298.

———. 1863. On the Indian Embassies to Rome from the Reign of Claudius to the Death of Justinian. *JRAS* 20, 269–312.

Price, S. R. F. 1984. *Rituals and Power: The Roman Imperial Cult in Asia Minor*. Cambridge.

Prickett, M. 1979. Quseir Regional Survey. In Whitcomb, D. S., and Johnson, J. H. (eds.), *Quseir al-Qadim, 1978 Preliminary Report*. Pp. 257–352. Cairo and Princeton, NJ.

Pritchard, J. B. 1969. *Ancient Near Eastern Texts Relating to the Old Testament*. 3rd ed. *With Supplement*. Princeton, NJ.

Pucci, G. 1983. Pottery and Trade in the Roman Period. In Garnsey, P., et al. (eds.), *Trade in the Ancient Economy*. Pp. 105–117. Berkeley and Los Angeles.

Pulleyblank, E. G. 1999. The Roman Empire in Chinese Sources. *JAOS* 119 (1), 71–79.

Purdy, C. 1886. Une Reconnaissance entre Bérénice et Berber: Expédition Purdy-Colston. *BSkGÉ*, 2nd ser., 8, 431–445 and map.

Purser, B. H., et al. 1987. Carbonate, Evaporate, Siliciclastic Transitions in Quaternary Rift Sediments of the Northwestern Red Sea. *Sedimentary Geology* 53 (3–4), 247–267.

Puskás, I. 1987. Trade Contacts between India and the Roman Empire. In Pollet, G. (ed.), *India and the Ancient World: History, Trade and Culture Before A.D. 650*. Pp. 141–156. Leuven.

Radke, G. 1971. *Viae Publicae Romanae*. Stuttgart.

Raimondi, J. 1923a. *Le désert oriental égyptien du Nil à la mer Rouge: Ses richesses dans le passé, son importance dans l'avenir*. Cairo.

———. 1923b. Étude des ports de Ras Benas et de Bérénice sur le Mer Rouge et project de ligne de chemin de fer devant relier ces ports à Kom Ombo, sur le Nil. In Raimondi 1923a, 53–76.

Rajan, K. 1988. Seafaring Activities of Tamil Nadu. In Rao 1988, 22–24.

———. 1996. Early Maritime Activities of the Tamils. In Ray and Salles 1996, 97–108.

———. 1997. *Archaeological Gazetteer of Tamil Nadu*. Thanjavur, Tamil Nadu, India.

Rao, S. R. (ed.). 1988. *Maritime Archaeology of Indian Ocean Countries: Proceedings of the First International Conference on Marine Archaeology of Indian Ocean Countries—October 1987*. Goa, India.

Raschke, M. G. 1974a. Papyrological Evidence for Ptolemaic and Roman Trade with India. *Proceedings of the XIV International Congress of Papyrologists, Oxford, 24–31 July, 1974*. Pp. 241–246. London.

———. 1974b. Roman Overland Trade with India and China. *Echos du Monde Classique* 18, 37–47.

———. 1978. New Studies in Roman Commerce with the East. *ANRW* 2.9.2, 604–1378.

———. 1979. The Role of Oriental Commerce in the Economies of the Cities of the Eastern Mediterranean in the Roman Period. *Archaeological News* 8, 68–77.

Rathbone, D. 1983. Italian Wines in Roman Egypt. *Opus* 2, 81–98.

———. 1997. Prices and Price Formation in Roman Egypt. In Andreau, J., et al. (eds.), *Économie antique: Prix et formation des prix dans les economies antiques*. Entretiens d'archéologie et d'histoire. Pp. 183–244. Saint-Bertrand-de-Comminges, France.

———. 2000. The "Muziris" Papyrus (SB XVIII.13167): Financing Roman Trade with India. *BSAA* 46, 39–50.

———. 2009. Earnings and Costs: Living Standards and the Roman Economy (First to Third Centuries A.D.). In Bowman and Wilson 2009, 299–326.

Raunig, W. 2004. Adulis to Aksum: Charting the Course of Antiquity's Most Important Trade Route in East Africa. In Lunde and Porter 2004, 87–91.

Raven, S. 1984. *Rome in Africa*. London and New York.

Ray, H. P. 1986. *Monastery and Guild Commerce under the Sātavāhanas*. Delhi.

———. 1988. The Yavana Presence in Ancient India. *JESHO* 31 (3), 311–325.

———. 1993. A Resurvey of Roman Contacts with the East. *Topoi* 3 (2), 479–491.

———. 1994. *Winds of Change: Buddhism and the Maritime Links of Early South Asia*. Delhi.

————. (ed.). 1999. *Archaeology of Seafaring: The Indian Ocean in the Ancient Period*. Delhi.

————. 2005a. Far-flung Fabrics: Indian Textiles in Ancient Maritime Trade. In Barnes, R. (ed.), *Textiles in Indian Ocean Societies*. Pp. 17–37. London and New York.

————. 2005b. The Yavana Presence in India Reprint of *JESHO*, 1988, with an Addendum. In Boussac, M.-F., and Salles, J.-F. (eds.), *Athens, Aden, Arikamedu: Essays on the Interrelations between India, Arabia and the Eastern Mediterranean*. Pp. 75–95. New Delhi.

Ray, H. P., and Salles, J.-F. (ed.). 1996. *Tradition and Archaeology. Early Maritime Contacts in the Indian Ocean. Proceedings of the International Seminar Techno-Archaeological Perspectives of Seafaring in the Indian Ocean 4th cent. B.C.–15th cent. A.D. New Delhi, February 28–March 4, 1994*. Lyon and New Delhi.

Ray, S. C. 1991. A Revised Study into the Numismatic Evidence of the Indo-Roman Trade. In Jha, A. K. (ed.), *Coinage, Trade and Economy January 8th–11th, 1991, 3rd International Colloquium*. Pp. 138–144. Maharashtra, India.

Reardon, B. P. (ed.). 1989. *Collected Ancient Greek Novels*. Berkeley, CA.

Reddé, M. 2002. La présence militaire romaine dans le désert Oriental. *Topoi supplément* 3, 385–394.

————. 2003a. Les Fortins du désert Oriental d'Égypte et l'architecture militaire romaine. In Cuvigny 2003d, 235–262.

————. 2003b. Le paysage de la route. In Cuvigny 2003d, 39–49.

Reddé, M., and Brun, J.-P. 2003. L'architecture des *praesidia* et la genèse des dépotoirs. In Cuvigny 2003d, 73–185.

Reddé M., and Golvin, J.-C. 1986–1987. Du Nil à la mer Rouge: Documents anciens et nouveaux sur les routes du désert Oriental d'Égypte. *Karthago* 21, 5–64.

Reddé, M., et al. 2005. Oedenburg: Une agglomération d'époque romaine sur le Rhin Supérieur. *Gallia* 62, 215–277.

Redford, S., and Redford, D. B. 1989. Graffiti and Petroglyphs Old and New from the Eastern Desert. *JARCE* 26, 3–49.

Redmount, C. A. 1986. Wadi Tumilat Survey. *NARCE* 133, 19–23.

————. 1995. The Wadi Tumilat and the "Canal of the Pharaohs." *JNES* 54 (2), 127–135.

Redon, B. 2009. L'armée et les bains en Égypte hellénistique et romaine. *BIFAO* 109, 407–450.

Red Sea and Gulf of Aden Pilot. 1980. Taunton, Somerset, UK.

Régen, I., and Soukiassian, G. 2008. *Gebel Zeit II. Le materiel inscrit*. Cairo.

Reinach, A. J. 1910. Voyageurs et Pèlerins dans l'Égypte gréco-romain. *BSRAA* 13, 111–144.

————. 1911a. Premier Rapport sur les fouilles de Koptos. *BSFFA*, 14–69.

————.1911b. Rapports sur les fouilles de Koptos. *BSFFA*, 47–82.

————. 1913. *Catalogue des Antiquités égyptiennes recueillies dans les fouilles de Koptos en 1910 et 1911 exposées au Musée Guimet de Lyon*. Chalon-sur-Saône, France.

Reinach, S. 1892. Elephus. In Daremberg, C., and Saglio, E. (eds.), *Dictionnaire des antiquités grecques et romaines*. Vol. 2. Pp. 536–544. Paris.

Renan, E. 1873. Une nouvelle inscription nabatéenne, trouvée à Pouzzoles. *JA* 7th ser., 2, 366–384.

Renfrew, C. 1975. Trade as Action at a Distance: Questions of Integration and Communication. In Sabloff, J. A., and Lamberg-Karlovsky, C. C. (eds.), *Ancient Civilization and Trade*. Pp. 3–59. Albuquerque.

Al-Resseeni, I. M., et al. 1998. An Exploratory Survey of the Water Supply Structures on the Syrian and Egyptian Pilgrim Routes to Mecca and Medinah. In Mills, C. M., and Coles, G. (eds.), *Life on the Edge: Human Settlement and Marginality*. Pp. 127–138. Oxford.

Retsö, J. 1991. The Domestication of the Camel and the Establishment of the Frankincense Road from South Arabia. *Orientalia Suecana* 40, 187–219.

———. 2000. Where and What Was *Arabia Felix*. *PSAS* 30, 189–192.

———. 2003. *The Arabs in Antiquity: Their History from the Assyrians to the Umayyads*. London and New York.

Rice, E. E. 1983. *The Grand Procession of Ptolemy Philadelphus*. Oxford.

Richardson, Jr., L. 1992. *A New Topographical Dictionary of Ancient Rome*. Baltimore and London.

Richardson, S. 2002. Basketry, Matting and Cordage. In Peacock, D., et al., *Myos Hormos Quseir al-Qadim: A Roman-Islamic Port Site Interim Report 2002*. Pp. 77- 80. Southampton, UK. Unpublished.

Ricke, H., et al. 1967. *Joint Expedition 1960/61 with the Schweizerisches Institut für Ägyptische Bauforschung und Altertumskunde in Kairo: Ausgrabungen von Khor-Dehmit bis Bet El-Wali*. Chicago.

Rickman, G. 1971. *Roman Granaries and Store Buildings*. Cambridge.

Ridley, R. T. 1982. *Zosimus New History*. Sydney.

Ripinsky, M. 1975. The Camel in Ancient Arabia. *Antiquity* 49, 295–298.

———. 1983. Camel Ancestry and Domestication in Egypt and the Sahara. *Archaeology* 36, 21–27.

Robin, C. 1991. L'Arabie du Sud et la date du *Périple de la mer Érythrée* (nouvelles données). *JA* 279, 1–30.

———. 1997. The Date of the *Periplus of the Erythraean Sea* in the Light of South Arabian Evidence. In De Romanis and Tchernia 1997, 41–65.

———. 2005. Saba and the Sabaeans. In Gunter, A. C. (ed.), *Caravan Kingdoms: Yemen and the Ancient Incense Trade*. Pp. 8–19. Washington, DC.

Robin, C. J., and Gorea, M. 2002. Les vestiges antiques de la grotte de Hôq (Suqutra, Yémen). *CRAI*, fasc. 2, 409–445.

Roche, M.-J. 1996. Remarques sur les Nabatéens en Méditerranée. *Semitica* 45, 73–99.

Rodewald, C. 1976. *Money in the Age of Tiberius*. Manchester, UK.

Roe, A. 2005–2006. The Old *Darb al Arbein* Caravan Route and Kharga Oasis in Antiquity. *JARCE* 42, 119–129.

Roeder, G. 1959. *Die ägyptische Götterwelt*. Zurich and Stuttgart.

Rohl, D. (ed.). 2000. *The Followers of Horus: Eastern Desert Survey Report*. Vol. 1. Thames View, Abingdon, Oxon., UK.

Roll, I. 1995. Roads and Transportation in the Holy Land in the Early Christian and Byzantine Times. In Dassmann, A., and Engemann, J. (eds.), *Akten des XII. Internationalen Kongresses für christliche Archäologie Bonn 22.-28. September 1991*. Teil 2. Pp. 1166–1170. Münster and Vatican City.

Roller, D. W. 1998. *The Building Program of Herod the Great*. Berkeley, CA.

Rosen, W. 2007. *Justinian's Flea: Plague, Empire, and the Birth of Europe*. New York.

Rosenberger, V. 1996. Taprobane: Trauminsel oder der Beginn einer neuen Welt? *Laverna* 7, 1–16.

Rossignani, M. P. 1997. Milan: Discovery of Frankincense Lumps in a Roman Burial. In Avanzini 1997, 147–148.

Rostovtzeff, M. I. 1908. Zur Geschichte des Ost- und Südhandels im ptolemäisch-römischen Ägypten. *Archiv für Papyrusforschung 4*, 298–315.

———. 1932a. *Caravan Cities*. Oxford.

———. 1932b. Foreign Commerce of Ptolemaic Egypt. *JEBH* 4, 728–769.

———. 1979. *The Social and Economic History of the Roman Empire*. Revised 2nd ed. Oxford.

———. 1986. *The Social and Economic History of the Hellenistic World*. Vol. 2. Reprinted/reissued. Oxford.

Roth, J. P. 1999. *The Logistics of the Roman Army at War (264 B.C.–A.D. 235)*. Leiden, Boston, and Cologne.

Rothe, R. D., and Rapp Jr., G. R. 1995. Trace-Element Analysis of Egyptian Eastern Desert Tin and Its Importance to Egyptian Archaeology. *Proceedings of the Egyptian-Italian Seminar on Geosciences and Archaeology in the Mediterranean Countries Cairo, November 28–30/1993*. Pp. 229–244. Cairo.

Rowley-Conwy, P. 1988. The Camel in the Nile Valley: New Radiocarbon Accelerator (AMS) Dates from Qasr Ibrim. *JEA* 74, 245–248.

Rowley-Conwy, P., et al. 1999. Ancient DNA from Sorghum: The Evidence from Qasr Ibrim, Egyptian Nubia. In Van der Veen, M. (ed.), *The Exploitation of Plant Resources in Ancient Africa*. Pp. 55–61. New York.

Rubin, Z. 1989. Byzantium and Southern Arabia: The Policy of Anastasius. In French, D. H., and Lightfoot, C. S. (eds.), *The Eastern Frontier of the Roman Empire: Proceedings of a Colloquium Held at Ankara in September 1988*. Pp. 383–420. Oxford.

Ruffing, K. 1993. Das Nikanor-Archiv und der römische Süd- und Osthandel. *MBAH* 12 (2), 1–26.

———. 1999. Zum Weinhandel zwischen Italien und Indien im 1. Jh. n. Chr. *Laverna* 10, 60–80.

———. 2001. Einige Überlegungen zum Weinhandel im römischen Ägypten (1.-3. Jh. n. Ch.). *MBAH* 20 (1), 55–80.

———. 2002. Wege in den Osten: Die Routen des römischen Süd- und Osthandels (1. bis 2. Jahrhundert n. Chr.). In Olshausen, E., and Sonnabend, H. (eds.), *Stuttgarter Kolloquium zur historischen Geographie des Altertums 7, 1999. Zu Wasser und zu Land. Verkehrswege in der antiken Welt*. Pp. 360–378. Stuttgart.

Russell, N. 1981. *The Lives of the Desert Fathers: The Historia Monachorum in Aegypto*. London and Oxford.

Rutten, K. 2007. The Roman Fine Wares of ed-Dur (Umm al-Qaiwain, U.A.E.) and Their Distribution in the Persian Gulf and the Indian Ocean. *AAE* 18, 8–24.

El-Saghir, M., et al. 1986. *Le Camp romain de Louqsor (avec une étude des graffites gréco-romains du temple d'Amon)*. Cairo.

Salles, J.–F. 1988. (ed.). *L'Arabie et ses bordières I. Itinéraires et Voisinages. Séminaire de recherche 1985–1986*. Lyon.

———. 1992. Découvertes du Golfe Arabo-Persique aux époques grecque et romaine. In *L'Océan et les mers lointaines dans l'Antiquité (Actes du colloque de la Société des Professeurs d'Histoire Ancienne de l'Université Nantes-Angers 24–26 mai 1991)*. Pp. 79–97. Paris.

———. 1993. Hellénisme et traditions orientales à Failaka. In Invernizzi, A., and Salles, J.–F. (eds.), *Arabia Antiqua Hellenistic Centres around Arabia*. Pp. 223–255. Rome.

———. 1995. *The Periplus of the Erythraean Sea* and the Arab-Persian Gulf. In Boussac, M. F., and Salles, J.-F. (eds.). *Athens, Aden, Arikamedu: Essays on the Interrelations between India, Arabia and the Eastern Mediterranean*. Pp. 115–146. New Delhi.

———. 2005. The *Periplus of the Erythraean Sea* and the Arab-Persian Gulf. In Boussac, M.-F., and Salles, J. F. (eds.). *Athens, Aden, Arikamedu: Essays on the Interrelations between India, Arabia and the Eastern Mediterranean*. Pp. 115–146. Reprint. New Delhi.

Salles, J.-F., and Sedov, A. V. 2010. *Qāni': Le port antique du Ḥaḍramawt entre la Méditerranée, l'Afrique at l'Inde. Fouilles russes 1972, 1985–1989, 1991, 1993–1994 (Indicopleustoi)*. Turnhout, Belgium.

Salomon, R. 1991. Epigraphic Remains of Indian Traders in Egypt. *JNES* 111 (4), 731–736.

———. 1993. Addenda to Epigraphic Remains of Indian Traders in Egypt. *JNES* 113 (4), 593.

Salway, B. 2001. Travel, *Itineraria* and *Tabellaria*. In Adams and Laurence 2001, 22–66.

———. 2004. Sea and River Travel in the Roman Itinerary Literature. In Talbert, R., and Brodersen, K. (eds.), *Space in the Roman World: Its Perception and Presentation*. Pp. 43–96. Münster.

Sampsell, B. M. 2003. *A Traveler's Guide to the Geology of Egypt*. Cairo and New York.

Samuel, A. E. 1989. *The Shifting Sands of History: Interpretations of Ptolemaic Egypt*. Lanham, MD, New York, and London.

Sartre, M. 1981. La frontière méridionale de l'Arabie romaine. In Fahd, T. (ed.), *La Géographie administrative et politique d'Alexandre à Mahomet. Actes du Colloque de Strasbourg 14–16 juin 1979*. Pp. 77–92. Leiden.

Sartre, M. 2005. *The Middle East under Rome*. Cambridge, MA, and London.

Saud, A. S., et al. 1996. The Domestication of the Camel and Inland Trading Routes in Arabia. *Atlal* 14, 129–136.

Sayed, A. M. A. H. 1977. Discovery of the Site of the 12th Dynasty Port at Wâdi Gawâsîs on the Red Sea Shore. *RÉ* 29, 138–178.

———. 1979. Discovery of the Site of the 12th Dynasty Port at Wâdi Gawâsîs on the Red Sea Shore. In Reineke, W. F. (ed.), *Acts of the First International Congress of Egyptology*. Pp. 569–577. Berlin.

———. 1980. Observations on Recent Discoveries at Wadi Gawasis. *JEA* 66, 154–157.

———. 1983. New Light on the Recently Discovered Port on the Red Sea Shore. *Cd'É* 58 (115–116), 23–37.

———. 1984. Reconsideration of the Minaean Inscription of Zayd'il bin Zayd. *PSAS* 14, 93–99.

———. 1993. On the Non-existence of the Nile-Red Sea Canal (So Called Canal of Sesostris). during the Pharaonic Times. In Sayed, A. M. A. H, *The Red Sea in Antiquity. A Collection of Papers Published in the Arabic and European Periodicals*. Pp. 127–147. Alexandria.

———. 1999. Wadi Gasus. In Bard and Shubert 1999, 866–868.

———. 2003. The Land of Punt: Problems of the Archaeology of the Red Sea and the Southeastern Delta. In Hawass, Z., and Brock, L. P. (eds.), *Egyptology at the Dawn of the Twenty-first Century: Proceedings of the Eighth International Congress of Egyptologists Cairo, 2000*. Vol. 1. *Archaeology*. Pp. 432–439. Cairo and New York.

Scaife, C. H. O. 1935. Two Inscriptions at Mons Porphyrites (Gebel Dokhan). Also a Description, with Plans, of the Stations: between Kainopolis and Myos Hormos together with Some Other Ruins in the Neighborhood of Gebel Dokhan. *BFAFU* 3 (2), 58–104.

Scala, L. 2002. Une puits de Coptos: Essai de reconstition. *Topoi supplément* 3, 349–353.

Scarborough, J. 1982. Roman Pharmacy and the Eastern Drug Trade: Some Problems as Illustrated by the Example of Aloe. *Pharmacy in History* 24 (4), 135–143.

Scheidel, W. 2001. *Death on the Nile: Disease and the Demography of Roman Egypt.* Leiden, Boston, and Cologne.

———. 2002. A Model of Demographic and Economic Change in Roman Egypt after the Antonine Plague. *JRA* 15, 97–114.

Scheil, V. 1930. Inscriptions de Darius à Suez. *RAAO* 27, 93–97.

Schenk, H. 2000. Rouletted Ware and Other Imports of Tissamaharama, Observations on the Pottery Sequence from Southern Sri Lanka. In Taddei, M., and de Marco, G. (eds.), *South Asian Archaeology 1997: Proceedings of the Fourteenth International Conference of the European Association of South Asian Archaeologists, Held in the Istituto Italiano per l'Africa e l'Oriente, Palazzo Brancaccio, Rome, 7–14 July 1997.* Vol. 2. Pp. 653–677. Rome.

Schenke, G. 2001. Mumienporträts im römischen Ägypten: Totenbildnisse oder Privatporträts? *Cd'É* 76 (151–152), 281–289.

Schmid, S. G. 2007. La distribution de la céramique nabatéenne et l'organisation du commerce nabatéen de longue distance. *Topoi supplément* 8, 61–91.

Schmidt, A. 1979. *Drogen und Drogenhandel im Altertum.* Reprint ed. New York.

Schmidt-Colinet, A. 1995. (ed.). *Palmyra Kulturbegegnung im Grenzbereich.* Mainz.

Schmidt-Nielsen, K. 1964. *Desert Animals: Physiological Problems of Heat and Water.* Oxford.

Schneider, P. 2004. *L'Éthiopie et L'Inde: Interférences et confusions aux extrémités du monde antique (VIIIe siècle avant J.-C.–VIe siècle après J.-C.).* Rome.

Schopen, S. 1994. Doing Business for the Lord: Lending on Interest and Written Loan Contracts in the *Mūlasarvāstivāda-Vinaya. JAOS* 114 (4), 527–554.

Schwartz, J. 1953. Les Palmyréniens et l'Égypte. *BSRAA* 40, 63–81.

Schweinfurth, G. 1922. *Auf unbetretenen Wegen in Aegypten.* Hamburg and Berlin.

Schwinden, L. 1983. Handel mit Pfeffer und anderen Gewürzen im römischen Trier. *Funde und Ausgrabungen im Bezirk Trier* 15, 20–26.

Scullard, H. H. 1974. *The Elephant in the Greek and Roman World.* Ithaca, NY.

Searight, S. 2007. Navigating a Hazardous Sea. In Starkey, J., et al. (eds.), *Natural Resources and Cultural Connections of the Red Sea.* Pp. 121–127. Oxford.

Sedov, A. V. 1992. New Archaeological and Epigraphical Material from Qana (South Arabia). *AAE* 3, 110–137.

———. 1996. Qana' (Yemen) and the Indian Ocean: The Archaeological Evidence. In Ray and Salles 1996, 11–35.

———. 1997. Sea-trade of the Hadramawt Kingdom from the 1st to the 6th Century A.D. In Avanzini 1997, 365–383.

———. 2005. *Temples of Ancient Hadramawt.* Pisa.

———. 2007. The Port of Qana' and the Incense Trade. In Peacock, D., and Williams, D. (eds.), *Food for the Gods: New Light on the Ancient Incense Trade.* Pp. 71–111. Oxford.

Seeger, J. A. 2001. A Preliminary Report on the 1999 Field Season at Marsa Nakari. *JARCE* 38, 77–88.

Seeger, J. A. and Sidebotham, S. E. 2005. Marsa Nakari: An Ancient Port on the Red Sea. *EA* 26, 18–20.

Seeger, J. A., et al. 2006. A Brief Archaeological Survey of the Aqiq Region (Red Sea Coast), Sudan. *Sahara* 17, 7–18.

Seipel, W. (ed.). 1998. *Jemen: Kunst und Archäologie im Land der Königen von Saba.* Vienna.

Seland, E. H. 2005. Ancient South Arabia: Trade and Strategies of State Control as Seen in the *Periplus Maris Erythraei. PSAS* 35, 271–280.

———. 2006. *Indian Ocean in Antiquity: Trade and the Emerging State.* PhD diss. University of Bergen.

———. (ed.). 2007. *The Indian Ocean in the Ancient Period: Definite Places, Translocal Exchange.* Oxford.

———. 2010. *Ports and Political Power in the Periplus: Complex Societies aand Maritime Trade on the Indian Oceran in the First Century* A. D. Oxford.

Selvakumar, V., et al. 2005. Trial Excavations at Pattanam, Paravur Tuluk, Ernakulam District—A Preliminary Report. *JCHS* 2, 57–66.

Şerban, I. and Băluță, C. L. 1979. On Mithraism in the Army of Dacia Superior. In Bianchi, U. (ed.), *Mysteria Mithrae.* Pp. 573–578. Leiden.

Sethe, K. (ed.). 1904. *Hieroglyphische Urkunden der griechisch-römischen Zeit. I. Historische-bi-ographische Urkunden aus den zeiten der makedonischen Könige und der beiden ersten Ptolemäer.* Leipzig.

Sewell, R. 1904. Roman Coins Found in India. *JRAS,* 591–637.

Seyhrig, H. 1936. Inscription relative au commerce maritime de Palmyre. *Annuaire de l'Institut de Philologie et d'Histoire et Slaves 4. Melanges Franz Cumont.* Pp. 397–402. Brussels.

Shahîd, I. 1971. *The Martyrs of Najrân New Documents.* Brussels.

———. 1984. *Byzantium and the Arabs in the Fourth Century.* Washington, DC.

———. Byzantium in South Arabia. In Shahîd, I. (ed.), *Byzantium and the Semitic Orient before the Rise of Islam.* Pp. 25–94. London.

———. 1989. *Byzantium and the Arabs in the Fifth Century.* Washington, DC.

Shajan, K. P., et al. 2004. Locating the Ancient Port of Muziris: Fresh Findings from Pattanam. *JRA* 17 (I), 312–320.

Shajan, K. P., et al. 2005. Was Pattanam Ancient Muziris? *Man and Environment* 30(2) 66–73.

Shaw, B. D. 1979. The Camel in Roman North Africa and the Sahara: History, Biology and Economy. *BIFAN* 41, ser. B. 4: 663–721.

———. 1995. The Camel in Roman North Africa and the Sahara: History, Biology, and Human Economy. In Shaw, B. D. (ed.), *Environment and Society in Roman North Africa. Studies in Roman North Africa.* Pp. 663–721. Aldershot, UK.

———. 1984. Bandits in the Roman Empire. *Past and Present* 105, 3–52.

———. 2004. Bandits in the Roman Empire. In Osborne, R. (ed.), *Studies in Ancient Greek and Roman Society.* Pp. 326–374. Cambridge and New York.

Shaw, I. M. E. 1986. Chapter 10: A Survey at Hatnub. In Kemp, B. J. (ed.), *Amarna Reports III.* Pp. 189–212. London.

———. 1987. Chapter 13: The 1986 Survey at Hatnub. In Kemp, B. J. (ed.), *Amarna Reports IV.* Pp. 160–167. London.

————. 1994. Pharaonic Quarrying and Mining: Settlement and Procurement in Egypt's Marginal Areas. *Antiquity* 68 (258), 108–119.

————. 1999a. Sikait-Zubara. In Bard and Shubert 1999, 731–733.

————. 1999b. Wadi el-Hudi. In Bard and Shubert 1999, 871–872.

————. 2000. Egypt and the Outside World. In Shaw, I. (ed.), *The Oxford History of Ancient Egypt.* Pp. 314–329. Oxford.

————. 2002. Life on the Edge: Gemstones, Politics and Stress in the Deserts of Egypt and Nubia. In Friedman, R. (ed.), *Egypt and Nubia Gifts of the Desert.* Pp. 244–251. London.

Shaw, I. and Jameson, R. 1993. Amethyst Mining in the Eastern Desert: A Preliminary Survey at Wadi el-Hudi. *JEA* 79, 81–97.

Shaw, I., et al. 1999. Emerald Mining in Roman and Byzantine Egypt. *JRA* 12, 203–215.

El-Shazly, E. M. and Hassan, M. A. 1972. Geology and Radioactive Mineralization at Wadi Sikait-Wadi El-Gemal Area, Eastern Desert. *Egyptian Journal of Geology* 16 (2), 201–234.

Shea, W. S. 1977. A Date for the Recently Discovered Eastern Canal of Egypt. *BASOR* 226, 31–38.

Sheehan, P. Forthcoming. *Babylon of Egypt The Making of Old Cairo: An Archaeological Investigation into the Ancient Nucleus of the Medieval and Modern City* (unpublished manuscript).

El-Sheikh, H. A. 1992. Roman Expeditions to the Upper Nile. In Mandruzzato, A. (ed.), *Roma e l'Egitto nell'antichità classica. Cairo, 6–9 Febbraio 1989. Atti del I Congresso internazionale italo-egiziano.* Pp. 157–160. Rome.

Shepherd, R. 1993. *Ancient Mining.* London and New York.

Sherk, R. K. 1974. Roman Geographical Exploration and Military Maps. *ANRW* 2.1, 534–562.

Shinnie, P. L. 1960. Socotra. *Antiquity* 34, 100–110.

Shitomi, Y. 1976. On the Date of Composition of the *Periplus Maris Erythraei.* A Study of the South Arabian Epigraphic Evidence. *Memoirs of the Research Department of the Toyo Bunko (The Oriental Library)* 34, 15–45.

Siddall, M., et al. 2003. Sealevel Fluctuations during the Last Glacial Cycle. *Nature* 423, 853–858.

Siddall, M., et al. 2004. Understanding the Red Sea Response to Sea Level. *Earth and Planetary Science Letters* 225, 421–434.

Sidebotham, S. E. 1986. *Roman Economic Policy in the Erythra Thalassa 30 B.C.-A.D. 217.* Leiden.

————. 1989. Lure of the Desert Road. *Archaeology* 42 (4), 58–60.

————. 1990. Ship Graffiti from Mons Porphyrites. *BIFAO* 90, 339–345.

————. 1991a. A *Limes* in the Eastern Desert of Egypt: Myth or Reality? In Maxfield, V. A. and Dobson, M. J. (eds.). *Roman Frontier Studies 1989. Proceedings of the XVth International Congress of Roman Frontier Studies.* Pp. 494–497. Exeter, UK.

————. 1991b. Ports of the Red Sea and the Arabia-India Trade. In Begley, V. and De Puma, R. D. (eds.). *Rome and India: The Ancient Sea Trade.* Pp. 12–38. Madison, WI.

————. 1991c. Römische Straßen in der ägyptische Wüste. *AntW* 22 (3), 177–189.

————. 1991d. University of Delaware Archaeological Project at 'Abu Sha'ar, The 1990 Season. *NARCE* 153, 1–6.

————. 1992a. A Roman Fort on the Red Sea Coast. *Minerva* 3 (2), 5–8.

————. 1992b. The 1991 Season of Archaeological Fieldwork at 'Abu Sha'ar (Red Sea Coast), Egypt Conducted by the University of Delaware. *Archaeological News* 17 (1–4), 31–34, and pls. 15–18.

———. 1993. University of Delaware Archaeological Project at 'Abu Sha'ar: The 1992 Season. *NARCE* 161–162, 1–9.

———. 1994a. Preliminary Report on the 1990–1991 Seasons of Fieldwork at 'Abu Sha'ar (Red Sea Coast). *JARCE* 31, 133–158.

———. 1994b. University of Delaware Fieldwork in the Eastern Desert of Egypt, 1993. *DOP* 48, 263–275.

———. 1995a. The Excavations. In Sidebotham and Wendrich 1995, 21–27.

———. 1995b. Survey of the Hinterland. In Sidebotham and Wendrich 1995, 85–101.

———. 1996a. The Excavations. In Sidebotham and Wendrich 1996, 7–97.

———. 1996b. Newly Discovered Sites in the Eastern Desert. *JEA* 82, 181–192.

———. 1996c. Romans and Arabs in the Red Sea. *Topoi* 6 (2), 785–797.

———. 1996d. The Ship Graffito. In Sidebotham and Wendrich 1996, 315–317.

———. 1997a. Caravans Across the Eastern Desert of Egypt: Recent Discoveries on the Berenike-Apollinopolis Magna-Coptos Roads. In Avanzini 1997, 385–394.

———. 1997b. The Roman Frontier in the Eastern Desert of Egypt. In van-Waateringe, W. G., et al. (eds.). *Roman Frontier Studies 1995. Proceedings of the XVIth International Congress of Roman Frontier Studies.* Pp. 503–509. Oxford.

———. 1998a. The Coins. In Sidebotham and Wendrich 1998a, 181–192.

———. 1998b. The Excavations. In Sidebotham and Wendrich 1998a, 11–120.

———. 1998c. The Survey. In Sidebotham and Wendrich 1998a, 415–426.

———. 1999a. The Coins. In Sidebotham and Wendrich 1999, 183–199.

———. 1999b. The Excavations. In Sidebotham and Wendrich 1999, 3–94.

———. 1999c. Survey of the Hinterland. In Sidebotham and Wendrich 1999, 349–369.

———. 2000a. Coins. In Sidebotham and Wendrich 2000a, 169–178.

———. 2000b. The Excavations. In Sidebotham and Wendrich 2000a, 3–147.

———. 2000c. Map 78 Porphyrites et Claudianus Montes. In Talbert, R. J. A. (ed.), *Barrington Atlas of the Greek and Roman World.* Princeton, NJ.

———. 2000d. Map 78 Porphyrites et Claudianus Montes. In Talbert, R. J. A. (ed.), *Barrington Atlas of the Greek and Roman World. Map-by-Map Directory* II. Pp. 1158–1163. Princeton, NJ.

———. 2000e. Survey of the Hinterland. In Sidebotham and Wendrich 2000a, 355–377.

———. 2002a. From Berenike to Koptos: Recent Results of the Desert Route Survey. *Topoi supplément* 3, 415–438.

———. 2002b. Late Roman Berenike. *JARCE* 39, 217–240.

———. 2003. Ptolemaic and Roman Water Resources and Their Management in the Eastern Desert of Egypt. In Liverani 2003, 87–116.

———. 2007a. Coins. In Sidebotham and Wendrich 2007a, 200–210.

———. 2007b. Excavations. In Sidebotham and Wendrich 2007a, 30–165.

———. 2007c. Survey of the Hinterland. In Sidebotham and Wendrich 2007a, 295–303.

———. 2008a. Archaeological Evidence for Ships and Harbor Facilities at Berenike (Red Sea Coast), Egypt. In Hohlfelder 2008, 305–324.

———. 2008b. South Asian Archaeological Finds from Berenike, a Hellenistic-Roman Port on the Red Sea Coast of Egypt. The Background. In Raven, E. M. (ed.), *South Asian Ar-*

chaeology 1999. *Proceedings of the European Association of South Asian Archaeologists, Held at the Universiteit Leiden 5–9 July, 1999.* Pp. 223–228. Groningenn, Netherlands.

———. In preparation a. The Coins. In Sidebotham, S. E. and Wendrich, W. Z. (eds.). *Berenike 2001. Report on the Excavations at Berenike and the Survey of the Eastern Desert of Egypt.* Los Angeles.

———. In preparation b. The Excavations. In Sidebotham, S. E. and Wendrich, W. Z. (eds.). *Berenike 2001. Report on the Excavations at Berenike and the Survey of the Eastern Desert of Egypt.* Los Angeles.

Sidebotham, S. E. and Seeger, J. A. 1996. The Coins. In Sidebotham and Wendrich 1996, 179–196.

Sidebotham, S. E. and Wendrich, W. Z. (eds.). 1995. *Berenike 1994. Preliminary Report of the 1994 Excavations at Berenike (Egyptian Red Sea Coast) and the Survey of the Eastern Desert.* Leiden.

———. (eds.). 1996. *Berenike 1995. Preliminary Report of the 1995 Excavations at Berenike (Egyptian Red Sea Coast) and the Survey of the Eastern Desert.* Leiden.

———. (eds.). 1998a. *Berenike 1996. Report of the 1996 Excavations at Berenike (Egyptian Red Sea Coast). and the Survey of the Eastern Desert.* Leiden.

———. 1998b. Berenike: Archaeological Fieldwork at a Ptolemaic-Roman Port on the Red Sea Coast of Egypt: 1994–1998. *Sahara* 10, 85–96.

———. 1998c. Interpretative Summary and Conclusion. In Sidebotham and Wendrich 1998a, 445–454.

———. (eds.). 1999. *Berenike 1997. Report of the 1997 Excavations at Berenike and the Survey of the Egyptian Eastern Desert, including Excavations at Shenshef.* Leiden.

———. (eds.). 2000a. *Berenike 1998. Report of the 1998 Excavations at Berenike and the Survey of the Egyptian Eastern Desert, including Excavations in Wadi Kalalat.* Leiden.

———. 2000b. Interpretative Summary and Conclusion. In Sidebotham and Wendrich 2000a, 413–419.

———. 2001–2002. Berenike Archaeological Fieldwork at a Ptolemaic-Roman Port on the Red Sea Coast of Egypt 1999–2001. *Sahara* 13, 23–50.

———. 2002. Berenike: a Ptolemaic-Roman Port on the Ancient Maritime Spice and Incense Route. *Minerva* 13 (3), 28–31.

———. (eds.). 2007a. *Berenike 1999/2000. Report on the Excavations at Berenike, Including Excavations in Wadi Kalalat and Siket, and the Survey of the Mons Smaragdus Region.* Los Angeles.

———. 2007b. Interpretative Summary and Conclusion. In Sidebotham and Wendrich 2007a, 368–374.

Sidebotham, S. E. and Zitterkopf, R. E. 1995. Routes Through the Eastern Desert of Egypt. *Expedition* 37 (2), 39–52.

———. 1996. Survey of the Hinterland. In Sidebotham and Wendrich 1996, 357–409.

———. 1997. Survey of the Via Hadriana by the University of Delaware: The 1996 Season. *BIFAO* 97, 221–237.

———. 1998. Survey of the Via Hadriana: the 1997 season. *BIFAO* 98, 353–365.

———. 2005. Surveying the Via Hadriana: The Emperor Hadrian's Desert Highway in Egypt. *Minerva* 16 (6), 16–18.

Sidebotham, S. E., and Zych, I. 2010. Berenike: Archaeological Fieldwork at a Ptolemaic-Port on the Red Sea Coast of Egypt, 2008–2010. *Sahara* 21, 7–26 and pls. A1-A7.

Sidebotham, S. E., et al. 1989. Fieldwork on the Red Sea Coast: The 1987 Season. *JARCE* 26, 127–166.

Sidebotham, S. E., et al. 1991. Survey of the 'Abu Sha'ar-Nile Road. *AJA* 95 (4), 571–622.

Sidebotham, S. E., et al. 1996. Statuary and Cult Objects. In Sidebotham and Wendrich 1996, 229–243.

Sidebotham, S. E., et al. 2000a. Excavations in Wadi Kalalat. In Sidebotham and Wendrich 2000a, 379–402.

Sidebotham, S. E., et al. 2000b. Survey of the Via Hadriana: the 1998 Season. *JARCE* 37, 115–126.

Sidebotham, S. E., et al. 2001. The Roman Quarry and Installations in Wadi Umm Wikala and Wadi Semna. *JEA* 87, 135–170.

Sidebotham, S. E., et al. 2002. Five Enigmatic Late Roman Settlements in the Eastern Desert. *JEA* 88, 187–225.

Sidebotham, S. E., et al. 2004a. Preliminary Report on Archaeological Fieldwork at Sikait (Eastern Desert of Egypt), and Environs: 2002–2003. *Sahara* 15, 7–30.

Sidebotham, S. E., et al. 2004b. A Water Temple at Bir 'Abu Safa (Eastern Desert). *JARCE* 41, 149–159.

Sidebotham, S. E., et al. 2008. *The Red Land. The Illustrated Archaeology of Egypt's Eastern Desert.* Cairo and New York.

Sidebotham, S. E., et al. In preparation. Survey of the Via Nova Hadriana: Final Report.

Sijpesteijn, P. J. 1963. Der ΠΟΤΑΜΟΣ ΤΡΑΙΑΝΟΣ. *Aegyptus* 43, 70–83.

———. 1965. Trajan and Egypt. In *Papyrologica Lugduno-Batava Papyri Selectae* 13, 106–113.

———. 1987. *Customs Duties in Graeco-Roman Egypt.* Zutphen, Netherlands.

Siliotti, A. (ed.). 2001. *Belzoni's Travels, Narrative of the Operations and Recent Discoveries in Egypt and Nubia.* London.

Silva, R. 1985. Mantai—a Second Arikamedu? *Antiquity* 59 (225), 46–47.

Singer, S. 2007. The Incense Kingdoms of Yemen: An Outline History of the South Arabian Incense Trade. In Peacock, D. and Williams, D. (eds.). *Food for the Gods. New Light on the Ancient Incense Trade.* Pp. 4–27. Oxford.

Sinkankas, J. 1989. *Emerald and Other Beryls.* Prescott, AZ.

Sircar, D. C. 1957. *Inscriptions of Aśoka.* Delhi.

Skeat, T. C. 1977. A Letter from the King of the Blemmyes to the King of the Noubades. *JEA* 63, 159–170.

Slane, K. W. 1996. Other Ancient Ceramics Imported from the Mediterranean. In Begley, V., et al., *The Ancient Port of Arikamedu New Excavations and Researches 1989–1992.* Pp. 351–368. Paris.

Smallwood, E. M. (ed.). 1967. *Documents Illustrating the Principates of Gaius, Claudius and Nero.* Cambridge.

———. 1976. *The Jews Under Roman Rule from Pompey to Diocletian.* Leiden.

Smith, M. C., and Wright, H. T. 1988. The Ceramics from Ras Hafun in Somalia: Notes on a Classical Maritime Site. *Azania* 23, 115–141.

Soebadio, H. 1999. Indian-Indonesian Cultural Relations. In Behera, K. S. (ed.), *Maritime Heritage of India.* Pp. 72–79. New Delhi.

Solomon, J. 1995. The Apician Sauce—*Ius Apicianum*. In Wilkins, J., et al. (eds.), *Foods in Antiquity*. Pp. 115–131. Exeter, UK.

Speidel, M. A. 1992a. Roman Army Pay Scales. *JRS* 82, 87–106.

Speidel, M. P. 1982. Augustus' Deployment of the Legions in Egypt. *Cd'É* 57 (113), 120–124.

———. 1984. Palmyrene Irregulars at Koptos. *BASP* 21, 221–224.

———. 1988a. Nubia's Roman Garrison. *ANRW* 2.10.1, 767–798.

———. 1988b. Outpost Duty in the Desert: Building the Fort at Gholaia (Bu Njem, Libya). *Antiquités africaines* 24, 99–102.

———. 1992b. Nubia's Roman Garrison. In Speidel, M. P. (ed.), *Roman Army Studies*. Vol. 2. Pp. 240–274. Stuttgart.

Spekke, A. 1976. *The Ancient Amber Routes and the Geographical Discovery of the Eastern Baltic*. Chicago.

Sridhar, T. S. (ed.). 2005. *Alagankulam. An Ancient Roman Port City of Tamil Nadu (Excavation of Archaeological Sites in Tamil Nadu)*. Chennai.

Srinivas, R. 1988. Shipping in Ancient India. In Rao 1988, 5–7.

Starkey, J. and El Daly, O. (eds.). 2000. *Desert Travelers from Herodotus to T. E. Lawrence*. Durham.

Starr, C. G. 1982. *The Roman Empire 27 B.C.-A.D. 476. A Study in Survival*. New York and Oxford.

Stauffer, A. 1995. Kleider, Kissen, bunte Tücher Einheimische Textilproduktion und weltweiter Handel. In Schmidt-Colinet, A. (ed.), *Palmyra Kulturbegegnung im Grenzbereich*. Pp. 57–71. Mainz.

———. 1996. Textiles from Palmyra: Local Production and the Import and Imitation of Chinese Silk Weavings. In *Les Annales Archéologiques arabes syriennes: Revue d'Archéologie et d'Histoire* 42 (1996). Pp. 425–430. Damascus.

Steiner, R. C. 2004. A Jewish Aramaic (or Hebrew) *Laissez-Passer* from the Egyptian Port of Berenike. *JNES* 63 (4), 277–281.

Stern, E. M. 1991. Early Roman Glass in India. In Begley, V. and De Puma, R. D. (eds.). *Rome and India The Ancient Sea Trade*. Pp. 113–124. Madison, WI.

Sternberg el-Hotabi, H. 1994. Die verschollene Horusstele aus Aksum. In Behlmer, H. (ed.), . . . *Quaerentes Scientiam, Festgabe für Wolfhart Westendorf zu seinem 70. Geburtstag überreicht von seinem Schülern*. Pp. 189–194. Göttingen.

Stevenson, E. L. 1991. *Claudius Ptolemy The Geography*. New York.

Stoll, C.-P., Kefrig, U., and Miete, C. 1999. (eds.). *Wracktauchen. Die schönsten Wracks im Roten Meer*. Augsburg.

Stoneman, R. 1992. *Palmyra and its Empire; Zenobia's Revolt against Rome*. Ann Arbor, MI.

Strauch, I. and Bukharin, M. D. 2004. Indian Inscriptions from the Cave Ḥoq on Suquṭrā (Yemen). *Annali* 64, 121–138.

Sundelin, L. K. R. 1996. Plaster Jar Stoppers. In Sidebotham and Wendrich 1996, 297–308.

Suresh, S. 2004. *Symbols of Trade. Roman and Pseudo-Roman Objects Found in India*. New Delhi.

———. 2007. *Arikamedu: Its Place in the Ancient Rome-India Contacts*. New Delhi.

Swamy, L. N. 1999. Traditional Boats of Karnataka and their Building Practices. In Behera, K. S. (ed.), *Maritime Heritage of India*. Pp. 116–142. New Delhi.

Syme, R. 1983. *Historia Augusta Papers*. Oxford.

Tabula Peutingeriana. 1976. *Tabula Peutingeriana Codex Vindobonensis 324 Vollständige Faksimile-Ausgabe in Originalformat*. Graz.

Tait, J. G. 1930. (ed.). *Greek Ostraca in the Bodleian Library at Oxford and Various Other Collections.* Vol. 1. London.

Talbert, R. J. A. (ed.). 2000. *Barrington Atlas of the Greek and Roman World.* Princeton, NJ.

———. 2004. Cartography and Taste in Peutinger's Roman Map. In Talbert, R., and Brodersen, K. (eds.). *Space in the Roman World: Its Perception and Preservation.* Pp. 113–141. Münster.

———. 2010. *Rome's World. The Peutinger Map Reconsidered.* Cambridge and New York.

Tarn, W. W. 1929. Ptolemy II and Arabia. *JEA* 15, 9–25.

Taylor, J. 2002. *Petra and the Lost Kingdom of the Nabataeans.* Cambridge.

Tchernia, A. 1986. *Le vin de l'Italie romaine: Essai d'Histoire économique d'après les amphores.* Rome.

———. 1995. Moussons et monnaies: les voies du commerce entre le monde gréco-romain et l'Inde. *AHSS* No. 5, 991–1009.

———. 1997a. The Dromedary of Peticii and Trade with the East. In De Romanis and Tchernia 1997, 238–249.

———. 1997b. Winds and Coins: From the Supposed Discovery of the Monsoon to the *Denarii* of Tiberius. In De Romanis and Tchernia 1997, 250–276.

———. 1998. Arikamedu et le graffito naval d' Alagankulam *Topoi* 8, 447–463.

Teggart, F. J. 1939. *Rome and China: A Study of Correlations in Historical Events.* Berkeley, CA.

Teixidor, J. 1973. The Nabataean Presence at Palmyra. *Journal of the Ancient Near Eastern Society of Columbia University* 5, 405–409.

———. 1984. *Un port romain du désert. Palmyre et son commerce d'Auguste à Caracalla.* Paris.

Temin, P. 2001. A Market Economy in the Early Roman Empire. *JRS* 91, 169–181.

Thapar, R. 1992. Black Gold: South Asia and the Roman Maritime Trade. *South Asia* 15 (2), 1–27.

———. 1997a. *Aśoka and the Decline of the Mauryas.* Delhi and New York.

———. 1997b. Early Mediterranean Contacts with India: An Overview. In De Romanis and Tchernia 1997, 11–40.

Al-Thenayian, M. A. R. 1999. *An Archaeological Study of the Yemeni Highland Pilgrim Route between Ṣan'a' and Mecca.* Riyadh.

———. 2008. The Red Sea Tihami Coastal Ports in Saudi Arabia. *PSAS* 38, 289–299.

Thiel, J. H. 1967. *Eudoxus of Cyzicus—A Chapter in the History of the Sea-Route to India and the Route Round the Cape in Ancient Times.* Groningen.

Thissen, H. J. 1979. Demotische Graffiti des Paneions im Wadi Hammamat. *Enchoria* 9, 63–92.

Thomas, J. D. 1975. *The Epistrategos in Ptolemaic and Roman Egypt.* Part 1. *The Ptolemaic Epistrategos.* Opladen.

———. 1976. The Date of the Revolt of L. Domitius Domitianus. *ZPE* 22, 253–279.

Thomas, R. I. 2001a. Early Imperial Roman Amphora Stoppers. In Peacock, D., et al., *Myos Hormos—Quseir al-Qadim: A Roman and Islamic Port Site Interim Report, 2001.* Pp. 51–55. Southampton, UK. Unpublished.

———. 2001b. *Early Imperial Amphora Stoppers of the Egyptian Eastern Desert. Maritime Archaeology Masters Dissertation.* Southampton. Unpublished MA thesis.

———. 2002. The Vessel Stoppers. In Peacock, D., et al., *Myos Hormos—Quseir al Qadim: A Roman and Islamic Port Site Interim Report 2002.* Pp. 63–66. Southampton, UK. Unpublished.

———. 2006a. Trench 6P and Q. In Peacock and Blue 2006c, 151–154.

———. 2006b. Trench 15. In Peacock and Blue 2006c, 87–94.

Thomas, R. I., and Masser, P. 2006. Trench 8. In Peacock and Blue 2006c, 127–140.

Thomas, R. I., and Tomber, R. 2006. Vessel Stoppers. In Tomber, R., et al. (eds.), *Survey and Excavations: Mons Claudianus 1987–1993*. Vol. 3. *Ceramic Vessels and Related Objects*. Pp. 239–258. Cairo.

Thomas, R. I., and Whitewright, J. 2001. Roman Period Maritime Artefacts. In Peacock, D., et al., *Myos Hormos—Quseir al-Qadim: A Roman and Islamic Port Site Interim Report, 2001*. Pp. 37–40. Southampton, UK. Unpublished.

Thomas, R. I., et al. 2002. Maritime artefacts. In Peacock, D., et al., *Myos Hormos—Quseir al Qadim: A Roman and Islamic Port Site Interim Report 2002*. Pp. 81–83. Southampton, UK. Unpublished.

Thomas, T. K. 2007. Coptic and Byzantine Textiles in Egypt: Corpora, Collections, and Scholarly Perspectives. In Bagnall, R. S. (ed.), *Egypt in the Byzantine World, 300–700*. Pp. 137–162. Cambridge.

Thompson, F. H. 2003. *The Archaeology of Greek and Roman Slavery*. London.

Thompson, W. E. 1988. Insurance and Banking. In Grant, M. and Kitzinger, R. (eds.). *Civilization of the Ancient Mediterranean: Greece and Rome*. Vol. 2. Pp. 829–836. New York.

Thorley, J. 1971. The Silk Trade between China and the Roman Empire at its Height, *circa* A.D. 90–130. *GR* 2nd ser. 18, 71–80.

Thosar, H. S. 1991. Dhenukākata—The Earliest Metropolis of the Deccan with a Yavana Settlement. In Arora, U. P. (ed.), *Graeco-Indica. India's Cultural Contacts with the Greek World (In Memory of Demetrius Galanos (1760–1833). A Greek Sanskritist of Benares)*. Pp. 172–178. New Delhi.

Thrower, N. J. W. 1996. *Maps and Civilization. Cartography in Culture and Society*. Chicago and London.

Thür, G. 1987. Hypotheken-Urkunde eines Seedarlehens für eine Reise nach Muziris und Apographe für die Tetarte in Alexandreia. *Tyche* 2, 229–245.

———. 1988. Zum Seedarlehe κατά Μουζειριν P. Vindob. 40822. *Tyche* 3, 229–233.

Tibbetts, G. R. 1961. Arab Navigation in the Red Sea. *GJ* 127 (3), 322–334.

Tibi, A. 1996. Arabia's Relations with East Africa. *Aram* 8 (1–2), 237–241.

Todd, M. 1999. *Roman Britain*. 3rd ed. Oxford.

Török, L. 2005. *Transfigurations of Hellenism. Aspects of Late Antique Art in Egypt* A.D. *250–700*. Leiden and Boston.

Tola, F. and Dragonetti, C. 1991. India and Greece from Alexander to Augustus. In Arora, U. P. (ed.), *Graeco-Indica. India's Cultural Contacts with the Greek World (In Memory of Demetrius Galanos (1760–1833). A Greek Sanskritist of Benares)*. Pp. 119–149. New Delhi.

Toll, C. 1994. Two Nabataean Ostraca from Egypt. *BIFAO* 94, 381–382.

Tomber, R. S. 1993. Quantitative Approaches to the Investigation of Long-distance Exchange. *JRA* 6, 142–166.

———. 1998. "Laodicean" Wine Containers in Roman Egypt. In Kaper 1998a, 213–219.

———. 1999. The Pottery. In Sidebotham and Wendrich 1999, 123–159.

———. 2000a. Indo-Roman Trade: The Ceramic Evidence from Egypt. *Antiquity* 74, 624–631.

———. 2000b. The Roman Pottery. In Peacock, D., et al., *Myos Hormos—Quseir-al-Qadim: A Roman and Islamic Port Site on the Red Sea Coast of Egypt: Interim Report, 2000*. Pp. 53–56. Southampton, UK. Unpublished.

————. 2001. Pottery from the Roman Deposits. In Peacock, D., et al., *Myos Hormos—Quseir al-Qadim: A Roman and Islamic Port Site on the Red Sea Coast of Egypt: Interim Report,* 2001. Pp. 43–44. Southampton, UK. Unpublished.

————. 2002. Indian Fine Wares from the Red Sea Coast of Egypt. *Man and Environment* 27 (1), 25–29.

————. 2004a. Amphorae from the Red Sea and Their Contribution to the Interpretation of Late Roman Trade beyond the Empire. In Eiring, J., and Lund, J. (eds.), *Transport Amphorae and Trade in the Eastern Mediterranean: Acts of the International Colloquium at the Danish Institute at Athens, September 26–29, 2002.* Pp. 393–402. Athens.

————. 2004b. Rome and South Arabia: New Artefactual Evidence from the Red Sea. *PSAS* 34, 351–360.

————. 2005a. Aksumite and other Imported Ceramics from Early Historic Kamrej. *JIOA* 2, 99–102.

————. 2005b. Amphorae from Pattanam. *JCHS* 2, 67–68.

————. 2005c. Trade Relations in the Eastern Mediterranean and Beyond: the Egyptian-Indian Connection. In Briese, M. B. and Vaag, L. E. (eds.). *Trade Relations in the Eastern Mediterranean from the Late Hellenistic Period to Late Antiquity: The Ceramic Evidence. Acts from a Ph.D.-seminar for young scholars, Sandbjerg Manorhouse, 12–15 February 1998.* Pp. 221–233. Odense.

————. 2005d. Troglodites and Trogodites: Exploring Interaction on the Red Sea during the Roman Period. In Starkey, J. C. M. (ed.), *People of the Red Sea. Proceedings of Red Sea Project II Held in the British Museum October 2004.* Pp. 41–49. Oxford.

————. 2007a. Aksumite Sherds from Berenike 1996–2000. In Sidebotham and Wendrich 2007a, 175–182.

————. 2007b. Rome and Mesopotamia—Importers into India in the First Millennium A.D. *Antiquity* 81, 972–988.

————. 2008. *Indo-Roman Trade. From Pots to Pepper.* London.

Tomber, R. S., and Begley, V. 2000. Indian Pottery Sherds. In Sidebotham and Wendrich 2000a, 149–167.

Tomber, R. S., Graf, D., and Healey, J. F. Forthcoming. Pots with Writing. In Peacock, D. P. S. and Blue, L. (eds.), *Quseir al-Qadim 1999–2003.* Vol. 2. *The Finds.* Southampton.

Toynbee, J. M. C. 1973. *Animals in Roman Life and Art.* Ithaca, NY.

Traunecker, C. 2002. Le Panthéon du Ouadi Hammâmât. *Topoi supplément* 3, 355–383.

Trautmann, T. R. 1982. Elephants and Mauryas. In Mukherjee, S. N. (ed.), *India: History and Thought: Essays in Honour of A. L. Basham.* Pp. 254–281. Calcutta.

Tregenza, L. A. 1949. Notes on a Recent Journey from Abu Zawal to the Greiya Station II. *BFAFU* 11 (I), 127–135.

————. 1955. *The Red Sea Mountains of Egypt.* London, New York, and Toronto.

Tregenza, L. A., and Walker, J. 1949. Nabataean Inscriptions from the E. Desert of Egypt. *BFAFU* 11 (II), 151–160.

Treidler, H. 1959. Πτολεμαΐς Θηρῶν. In Ziegler, K (ed.), *Paulys Realencyclopädie der Classischen Altertumswissenschaften* 23 (2). Cols. 1870–1883. Stuttgart.

Tresson, P. 1922. *La Stèle de Koubân.* Cairo.

Tripati, S., and Raut, L. N. 2006. Monsoon Wind and Maritime Trade: A Case Study of Historical Evidence from Orissa, India. *Current Science* 90 (6), 864–871.

Tripati, S., et al. 2005. Use of Timber in Shipbuilding Industry: Identification and Analysis of Timber from Shipwrecks off Goa Coast, India. *Current Science* 89 (6), 1022–1027.

Tuck, S. L. 1997. *Creating Roman Imperial Identity and Authority: The Role of Roman Imperial Harbor Monuments.* PhD diss., University of Michigan. Ann Arbor.

———. 2008. The Expansion of Triumphal Imagery Beyond Rome: Imperial Monuments at the Harbors of Ostia and Lepcis Magna. In Hohlfelder 2008, 325–341.

Tucker, A. O. 1986. Frankincense and Myrrh. *Economic Botany* 49 (4), 425–433.

Tuplin, C. 1991. Darius' Suez Canal and Persian Imperialism. In Sancisi-Weerdenburg, H. and Kuhrt, A. (eds). *Achaemenid History VI Asia Minor and Egypt: Old Cultures in a New Empire. Proceedings of the Groningen 1988 Achaemenid History Workshop.* Pp. 237–283. Leiden.

Turner, P. J. 1989. *Roman Coins from India.* London.

Turner, P. J., and Cribb, J. 1996. Numismatic Evidence for the Roman Trade with Ancient India. In Reade, J. (ed.), *The Indian Ocean in Antiquity.* Pp. 309–319. London and New York.

Umehara, S. 1926. Deux grands découvertes archéologiques en Corée. *RAA* 2, 24–33.

Updegraff, R. T. 1988. The Blemmyes I, the Rise of the Blemmyes and the Roman Withdrawal from Nubia under Diocletian (with Additional Remarks by L. Török). *ANRW* 2.10.1, 44–106.

Valbelle, D., and Carrez-Maratray, J.-Y. 2000. *Le camp romain du Bas-Empire à Tell el Herr. Mission franco-égyptienne de Tell el-Herr (Nord Sinaï).* Paris.

Van Beek, G. W. 1958. Frankincense and Myrrh in Ancient South Arabia. *JAOS* 78, 141–152.

———. 1989. The Buzz: A Simple Toy from Antiquity. *BASOR* 275, 53–58.

Van den Bosch, L. P. 2001. India and the Apostolate of St. Thomas. In Bremmer, J. N. (ed.), *The Apocryphal Acts of Thomas.* Pp. 125–148. Leuven.

Vandersleyen, C. 1996. Les monuments de l'Ouadi Gaouasis et la possibilité d'aller au pays de Pount par la mer rouge. *RÉ* 47, 107–115.

Van der Veen, M. 1998. Gardens in the Desert. In Kaper 1998a, 221–242.

———. 2001. The Botanical Evidence. In Maxfield and Peacock 2001b, 173–247.

———. 2003. Trade and Diet at Roman and Medieval Quseir al-Qadim, Egypt: A Preliminary Report. In Neumann, K., et al. (eds.), *Food, Fuel and Fields: Progress in African Archaeobotany.* Pp. 207–212. Cologne.

———. 2004. The Merchants' Diet: Food Remains from Roman and Medieval Quseir al-Qadim. In Lunde and Porter 2004, 123–130.

Van der Venn, M., and Hamilton-Dyer, S. 1998. A Life of Luxury in the Desert? The Food and Fodder Supply to Mons Claudianus. *JRA* 11, 101–116.

Van der Vliet, J. 2002. Pisenthios de Coptos (569–632): Moine, évêque et saint. Autour d'ine-nouvelle édition de ses archives. *Topoi supplément* 3, 61–72.

Van Neer, W., and Ervynck, A. M. H. 1998. The Faunal Remains. In Sidebotham and Wendrich 1998a, 349–388.

———. 1999a. The Faunal Remains. In Sidebotham and Wendrich 1999, 325–348.

———. 1999b. Faunal Remains from Shenshef and Kalalat. In Sidebotham and Wendrich 1999, 431–444.

Van Neer, W., and Lentacker, A. 1996. The Faunal Remains. In Sidebotham.and Wendrich 1996, 337–355.

Van Neer, W., and Sidebotham, S. E. 2002. Animal Remains from the Fourth-Sixth Century A.D. Military Installations at Abu Sha'ar on the Red Sea coast of Egypt. In *Jennerstrasse 8 Tides of the Desert—Gezeiten der Wüste—Contributions to the Archaeology and Environmental History of Africa in Honor of Rudolph Kuper*. Pp. 171–195. Bonn.

Van Rengen, W. 1995. A new Paneion at Mons Porphyrites. *Cd'É* 70, 240–245.

———. 1997. La correspondance militaire (357–387). In Bingen, J., et al. 1997, 193–227.

———. 1999. Rock Art and Inscriptions on the Road to Bir Nakheil. In Peacock, D., et al. (eds.), *Myos Hormos—Quseir al-Qadim: A Roman and Islamic Port Site on the Red Sea Coast of Egypt: Interim Report, 1999*. Pp. 56–57. Southampton, UK. Unpublished.

———. 2001. The Inscription. In Maxfield and Peacock 2001b, 60–62.

———. 2007. The Written Evidence: Inscriptions and Ostraca. In Peacock and Maxfield 2007, 397–411.

Van Rengen, W., and Thomas, R. 2006. The Sebakh Excavations. In Peacock and Blue 2006c, 146–154.

Van Rengen, W., et al. 2006. Rock Art and Inscriptions. In Peacock and Blue 2006c, 17–26.

Van't Dack, E. 1962. Postes et télécomminications ptolémaïques. *Cd'É* 37, 338–341.

Van't Dack, E., and Hauben, V. H. 1978. L'apport égyptien á l'armée navale Lagide. In Maehler, H., and Strocka, V. M. (eds.), *Das ptolemäische Ägypten: Akten des internationalen Symposions 27.-29. September 1976 in Berlin*. Pp. 59–94. Mainz.

Varadarajan, L. 2005. Indian Boat Building Traditions: The Ethnological Evidence. In Boussac, M.-F., and Salles, J.-F. (eds.), *Athens, Aden and Arikamedu: Essays on the Interrelationships between India, Arabia and the Eastern Mediterranean*. Pp. 167–192. New Delhi.

Vasiliev, A. A. 1950. *Justin the First: An Introduction to the Epoch of Justinian the Great*. Cambridge, MA.

Vehling, J. D. 1936. *Apicius Cookery and Dining in Imperial Rome*. Chicago.

Veldmeijer, A. J. 1998. The Cordage. In Sidebotham and Wendrich 1998a, 237–252.

Veldmeijer, A. J., and Van Roode, S. M. 2004. Carrier Netting from the Ptolemaic-Roman Harbour Town of Berenike (Egyptian Red Sea Coast). *Antiguo Oriente* 2, 9–25.

Velissaropoulos, D. C. 1991. The Ancient Greek Knowledge of Indian Philosophy. In Arora, U. P. (ed.), *Graeco-Indica, India's Cultural Contacts with the Greek World (In Memory of Demetrius Galanos (1760–1833). A Greek Sanskritist of Benares)*. Pp. 257–279. New Delhi.

Venit, M. S. 2002. *Monumental Tombs of Ancient Alexandria: The Theater of he Dead*. Cambridge.

Venkatesan, P. 1988. Naval Battles and Shipwrecks Referred To in Tamil Epigraphs. In Rao 1988, 26–27.

Vercoutter, J. 1959. The Gold of Kush. *Kush* 7, 120–153.

Vergara, B. S., and De Datta, S. K. 1989. Oryza sativa L. In Westphal, E., and Jansen, P. C. M. (eds.), *Plant Resources of South-East Asia: A Selection*. Pp. 206–213. Wageningen, Netherlands.

Verhoogt, A. M. F. W. 1998. Greek and Latin Textual Material. In Sidebotham and Wendrich 1998a, 193–198.

Vermeeren, C. E. 1998. Wood and Charcoal. In Sidebotham and Wendrich 1998a, 331–348.

———. 1999a. The Use of Imported and Local Wood Species at the Roman Port of Berenike,

Red Sea Coast, Egypt. In van der Veen, M. (ed.), *The Exploitation of Plant Resources in An-cient Africa*. Pp. 199–204. New York.

———. 1999b. Wood and Charcoal. In Sidebotham and Wendrich 1999, 307–324.

———. 1999c. Wood and Charcoal from Shenshef. In Sidebotham and Wendrich 1999, 427–429.

———. 2000. Wood and Charcoal. In Sidebotham and Wendrich 2000a, 311–342.

Verri, E. 1994. Mar rosso, naufragio romano. *Archeologia Viva* 45, 52–57.

Vieillefond, J.-R. 1970. *Les "Cestes" de Julius Africanus: Étude sur l'ensemble des fragments avec édition, traduction et commentaries*. Florence and Paris.

Villeneuve, E. 2002. Océan Indien, île de Socotra. Bénis soient Abgar et les spéléologues! *Le Monde de la Bible* 145, 58.

———. 2003. Indischer Ozean Insel Sokotra. Gesegnet seien Abgar und die Höhlenforscher. *Welt und Umwelt der Bibel* 1, 72.

Villeneuve, F. 2005–2006. Response aux propositions de Mikhaïl Bukharin—Farasân Latin Inscriptions and Bukharin's Ideas: No *pontifex Herculis!* And Other Comments. *Arabia 3*, 289–296.

Villeneuve, F., et al. 2004a. Une inscription latine sur l'archipel Farasân, Arabie Séoudite, sud de la mer Rouge. *CRAI*, 419–429.

Villeneuve, F., et al. 2004b. Une inscription latine de l'archipel Farasān (sud de la mer Rouge) et son contexte archéologique et historique. *Arabia 2*, 143–190.

Vinson, S. 1994. *Egyptian Boats and Ships*. Princes Risborough, Buckinghamshire, UK.

Vogelsang-Eastwood, G. M. 1989. *Resist Dyed Textiles from Quseir al-Qadim*. Paris.

Volken, M. 2008. The Water Bag of Roman Soldiers. *JRA* 21, 264–274.

von Wissmann, H. 1978. Die Geschichte des Sabäerreichs und der Feldzug des Aelius Gallus. *ANRW* 2.9.1, 308–544.

Waard, P. W. F. 1989. Piper nigrum L. In Westphal, E., and Jansen, P. C. M. (eds.), *Plant Resources of South-East Asia: A Selection*. Pp. 225–230. Wageningen, Netherlands.

Wagner, G. 1987. *Les Oases d'Égypte à l'époque grecque, romaine et byzantine d'après les documents grecs (Recherches de papyrologie et d'épigraphie grecque)*. Cairo.

Wainwright, G. A. 1946. Zeberged: The Shipwrecked Sailor's Island. *JEA* 32, 31–38.

Wainwright, J. 2003. Maritime Artefacts. In Peacock, D., et al., *Myos Hormos—Quseir al-Qadim: A Roman and Islamic Port Site. Interim Report, 2003*. Pp. 71–73. Southampton, UK. Unpublished.

Walburg, R. 1991. Late Roman Copper Coins from Southern India. In Jha, K. (ed.), *Coinage, Trade and the Economy, January 8th-11th, 1991. 3rd International Colloquium*. Pp. 164–167. Maharashtra, India.

———. 2008. *Coins and Tokens from Ancient Ceylon (Forschungen zur Archäologie Außereuropäischer Kulturen 5)*. Wiesbaden.

Walker, S., and Bierbrier, M. 1997. *Ancient Faces: Mummy Portraits from Roman Egypt*. London.

Wallace, S. L. 1938/1969. *Taxation in Egypt from Augustus to Diocletian*. Princeton and New York.

Walser, A. V. 2001. Zur Rolle des Geldes im Handel zwischen dem Imperium Romanum, Südarabien und Indien in der frühen Kaiserzeit. *MBAH* 20 (2), 81–107.

Walters, C. C. 1974. *Monastic Archaeology in Egypt*. Warminster, UK.

Wang, H. 2004. *Money on the Silk Road: The Evidence from Eastern Central Asia to c. A.D. 800.* London.

Ward, C., and Zazzaro, C. 2007. Finds: Ship Evidence. In Bard and Fattovich 2007a, 135–163.

Ward, W. 2007. Aila and Clysma: The Rise of Northern Ports in the Red Sea in Late Antiquity. In Starkey, J., et al. (eds.), *Natural Resources and Cultural Connections of the Red Sea.* Pp. 161–171. Oxford.

Ward-Perkins, B. 2001. Specialisation, Trade, and Prosperity: An Overview of the Economy of the Late Antique Eastern Mediterranean. In Kingsley and Decker 2001a, 167–178.

Warmington, E. H. 1974. *The Commerce between the Roman Empire and India.* London.

Washer, J. 1998. *Roman Britain.* Thrupp, Stroud, Gloucestershire.

Watts, B. G., et al. 2004. Geochemistry and Petrography of Basalt Grindstones from the Kerak Plateau, Central Jordan. *Geoarchaeology* 19, 47–69.

Weeks, L., et al. 2002. A Recent Archaeological Survey on Soqotra: Report on the Preliminary Expedition Season, January 5th–February 2nd 2001. *AAE* 13, 95–125.

Weigall, A. E. P. 1913. *Travels in the Upper Egyptian Deserts.* Edinburgh and London.

Weisshaar, H.-J., and Wijeyapala, W. 2000. Tissamaharama Project (Sri Lanka): Excavations in the Citadel Area. In Taddei, M., and de Marco, G. (eds.), *South Asian Archaeology 1997. Proceedings of the Fourteenth International Conference of the European Association of South Asian Archaeologists Held in the Istituto italiano per l'Africa e l'Oriente. Palazzo Brancaccio, Rome, 7–14 July 1997.* Vol. 2. Pp. 633–645. Rome.

Wellmann, M. 1905. Elefant. In Wissowa, G. (ed.), *Paulys Realencyclopädie der Classischen Altertumswissenschaften* 5. Columns 2248–2257. Stuttgart.

Wellsted, J. R. 1836. Notice on the Ruins of Berenice. *JRGS* 36, 96–100.

———. 1838. *Travels in Arabia.* Vol. 2. London.

Welsby, D. 2003. The Kingdom of Kush: Rome's Neighbour on the Nile. In Liverani 2003, 65–78.

Wendrich, W. Z. 1995. Basketry and Cordage. In Sidebotham and Wendrich 1995, 69–84.

———. 1996. The Finds: Introduction. In Sidebotham and Wendrich 1996, 127–145.

———. 1998. Basketry and Matting. In Sidebotham and Wendrich 1998a, 253–264.

———. 1999. Basketry and Matting. In Sidebotham and Wendrich 1999, 277–284.

———. 2000. Basketry and Matting. In Sidebotham and Wendrich 2000a, 227–250.

———. 2007. Basketry and Matting. In Sidebotham and Wendrich 2007a, 228–250.

Wendrich, W. Z., and Van Neer, W. 1994. Preliminary Notes on Fishing Gear and Fish at the Late Roman Fort at 'Abu Sha'ar (Egyptian Red Sea Coast). In Van Neer, W. (ed.), *Fish Exploitation in the Past: Proceedings of the 7th Meeting of the ICAZ Fish Remains Working Group.* Pp. 183–189. Tervuren, Belgium.

Wendrich, W. Z., and Veldmeijer, A. J. 1996. Cordage and Basketry. In Sidebotham and Wendrich 1996, 269–296.

Wendrich, W. Z., et al. 2003. Berenike Crossroads: The Integration of Information. *JESHO* 46 (1), 46–87.

Wendrich, W. Z., et al. 2006. Berenike Crossroads: The Integration of Information. In Yoffee, N., and Crowell, B. L. (eds.), *Excavating Asian History: Interdisciplinary Studies in Archaeology and History.* Pp. 15–66. Tucson.

Wengrow, D. 2006. *The Archaeology of Early Egypt: Social Transformations in North-East Africa, 10,000 to 2650 B.C.* Cambridge and New York.

Westermann, W. L. 1924. Account of Lamp Oil from the Estate of Apollonius. *CP* 19 (3), 229–260.

———. 1925. The Greek Exploitation of Egypt. *Political Science Quarterly* 40 (4), 517–539.

Western Arabia and the Red Sea (Geographical Handbook Series), June 1946. Oxford.

Wheatley, P. 1961. *The Golden Khersonese: Studies in the Historical Geography of the Malay Peninsula Before A.D. 1500.* Kuala Lumpur.

Wheeler, R. E. M. 1955. *Rome Beyond the Imperial Frontiers.* New York.

Wheeler, R. E. M., et al. 1946. Arikamedu, an Indo-Roman Trading-Station on the East Coast of India. *Ancient India* 2, 17–125.

Whitcomb, D. S. 1979a. Islamic Pottery. In Whitcomb, D., and Johnson, J. (eds.), *Quseir al-Qadim, 1978 Preliminary Report.* Pp. 104–143. Cairo and Princeton, NJ.

———. 1979b. Trench Summaries. In Whitcomb, D. S. and Johnson, J. H. (eds.). *Quseir al-Qadim 1978 Preliminary Report.* Pp. 11–65. Cairo and Princeton, NJ.

———. 1982. Bir Kareim. In Whitcomb, D. S. and Johnson, J. H. (eds.). *Quseir al-Qadim 1980 Preliminary Report.* Pp. 391–396. Malibu, CA.

———. 1989a. Coptic Glazed Ceramics from the Excavations at Aqaba, Jordan. *JARCE* 26, 167–182.

———. 1989b. Evidence of the Umayyad Period from the Aqaba Excavations. In Bakhit, M. A., and Schick, R. (eds.), *The Fourth International Conference on the History of Bilād al Shām during the Umayyad Period. Proceedings of the Third Symposium 2–7 Rabī' 1408 A.H./24–29 October 1987.* English Section Vol. 2. Pp. 164–184. Amman, Jordan.

———. 1990. "Diocletian's" *miṣr* at 'Aqaba. *ZDPV* 106, 156–161.

———. 1994. *Ayla Art and Industry in the Islamic Port of Aqaba.* Chicago.

———. 1995. A Street and the Beach at Ayla: The Fall Season of Excavations at 'Aqaba, 1992. *ADAJ* 39, 499–507.

———. 1996. Quseir al-Qadim and the Location of Myos Hormos. *Topoi* 6 (2), 747–772.

———. 1999. Quseir al-Qadim. In Bard and Shubert 1999, 659–660.

Whitcomb, D. S., and Johnson, J. H. (eds.). 1979. *Quseir al-Qadim 1978 Preliminary Report.* Cairo and Princeton, NJ.

———. 1981. Quseir and the Red Sea Trade. *Archaeology* 34, 16–23.

———. 1981–1982. Season of Excavations at Quseir al-Qadim. *Oriental Institute Annual Report, 1981–1982,* 30–40.

———. (eds.). 1982a. *Quseir al-Qadim 1980 Preliminary Report.* Malibu, CA.

———. 1982b. 1982 Season of Excavations at Quseir al-Qadim. *NARCE* 120, 24–30.

White, K. D. 1984. *Greek and Roman Technology.* Ithaca, NY.

Whitehouse, D. 1989a. Begram Reconsidered. *Kölner Jahrbuch für Vor- und Frühgeschichte* 22, 151–157.

———. 1989b. Begram, the *Periplus* and Gandharan Art. *JRA* 2, 93–100.

———. 1990. The *Periplus Maris Erythraei. JRA* 3, 489–493.

———. 1996. Sasanian Maritime Activity. In Reade, J. (ed.), *The Indian Ocean in Antiquity.* Pp. 339–349. London and New York.

Whitehouse, D., and Williamson, A. 1973. Sasanian Maritime Trade. *Iran* 11, 29–49.

Whitewright, J. 2003. Maritime Artefacts. In Peacock, D., et al. (eds.), *Myos Hormos—Quseir al-Qadim: A Roman and Islamic Port Site: Interim Report, 2003.* Pp. 71–73. Southampton, UK. Unpublished.

———. 2007a. How Fast Is Fast? Technology, Trade and Speed under Sail in the Roman Red Sea. In Starkey, J., et al. (eds.), *Natural Resources and Cultural Connections of the Red Sea.* Pp. 77–87. Oxford.

———. 2007b. Roman Rigging Material from the Red Sea Port of Myos Hormos. *IJNA* 36 (2), 282–292.

Whitfield, S. 1999. *Life along the Silk Road.* Berkeley and Los Angeles.

Whittaker, C. R. 2002. Mental Maps: Seeing like a Roman. In McKechnie, P. (ed.), *Thinking like a Lawyer: Essays on Legal History and General History for John Cook on His Eightieth Birthday.* Pp. 81–112. Leiden, Boston, and Cologne.

———. 2004. *Rome and Its Frontiers: The Dynamics of Empire.* London and New York.

Whittaker, P. 2006. Trench 14. In Peacock and Blue 2006c, 84–87.

Whittaker, P., et al. 2006. Trench 10A, 10B and 10C. In Peacock and Blue 2006c, 74–81.

Wicker, F. D. P. 1998. The Road to Punt. *GJ* 164, 155–167.

Wicks, R. S. 1991. Money Use and the Control of Trade in Early Southeast Asia. In Jha, A. K. (ed.), *Coinage, Trade and the Economy, January 8th-11th, 1991. 3rd International Colloquium.* Pp. 84–98. Maharashtra, India.

Wiesehöfer, J. 1998. *Mare Erythraeum, Sinus Persicus* und *Fines Indiae:* Der Indische Ozean in hellenistischer und römischer Zeit. In Conermann, S. (ed.), *Der Indische Ozean in historischer Perspektive.* Pp. 9–36. Hamburg.

Wikander, Ö. 2000a. Canals. In Wikander, Ö. (ed.), *Handbook of Ancient Water Technology.* Pp. 321–330. Leiden, Boston, and Cologne.

———. 2000b. The Roman Empire. In Wikander, Ö. (ed.), *Handbook of Ancient Water Technology.* Pp. 657–658. Leiden, Boston, and Cologne.

Wilcken, U. 1920. Referate: Papyrus Urkunden. *Archiv für Papyrusforschung und Verwandte Gebiete* 6, 361–454.

———. 1963. *Grundzüge und Chrestomathie der Papyruskunde. Erster Band: Historischer Teil Zeite Hälfte: Chrestomathie.* Reprint. Hildesheim, Germany.

Wild, F. C. 2002. The Webbing from Berenike: A Classification. *ATN* 34, 9–16.

———. 2004. Sails, Sacking and Packing: Textiles from the First Century Rubbish Dump at Berenike, Egypt. In Alfaro, C., et al. (eds.), *Purpureae Vestes Actas del I Symposium Internacional sobre Textiles y Tintes del Mediterráneo en época romana (Ibiza, 8 al 10 de noviembre, 2002).* Pp. 61–67. Valencia, Spain.

———. Forthcoming. The Relief-Decorated Italian Sigillata. In Sidebotham, S. E., and Wendrich, W. Z. (eds.), *Berenike 2001: Report on the Excavations at Berenike and the Survey of the Eastern Desert of Egypt.* Los Angeles.

Wild, F. C., and Wild, J. P. 2001. Sails from the Roman Port at Berenike, Egypt. *IJNA* 30 (2), 211–220.

Wild, J. P. 1997. Cotton in Roman Egypt: Some Problems of Origin. *Al-Rāfidān* 18 *(Special Volume in Commemoration of the 70th Birthday of Professor Hideo Fujii),* 287–298.

———. 2006. Berenike: Archaeological Textiles in Context. In *Textiles In Situ: Their Find*

Spots in Egypt and Neighbouring Countries in the First Millennium C.E.. Pp. 175–255. Bern, Switzerland.

Wild, J. P., and Wild, F. C. 1996. The Textiles. In Sidebotham and Wendrich 1996, 245–256.

———. 1998. The Textiles. In Sidebotham, and Wendrich 1998a, 221–236.

———. 2000. Textiles. In Sidebotham and Wendrich 2000a, 251–274.

———. 2005. Rome and India: Early Roman Cotton Textiles from Berenike, Red Sea Coast of Egypt. In Barnes, R. (ed.), *Textiles in Indian Ocean Societies*. Pp. 11–16. London and New York.

———. 2008. Early Cotton Textiles from Berenike. In Raven, E. M. (ed.), *South Asian Archaeology 1999. Proceedings of the Fifteenth International Conference of the European Association of South Asian Archaeologists, Held at the Universiteit Leiden, 5–9 July, 1999*. Pp. 229–233. Groningen.

Wild, J. P., et al. 2007. Irrigation and the Spread of Cotton Growing in Roman Times. *ATN* 44, 16–18.

Wild, J. P., et al. 2008. Roman Cotton Revisited. In Alfaro, C. and Karali, L. (eds.), *Vestidos, Textiles y Tintes: Estudios sobre la producción de bienes de consumo en la Antigüedad. Purpureae Vestes II*. Pp. 143–147. Valencia.

Wilfong, T. 2000. Textual Remains. In Meyer, C., et al., *Bir Umm Fawakhir Survey Project, 1993: A Byzantine Gold-Mining Town in Egypt*. Pp. 25–26. Chicago.

Wilford, J. N. 2002. *The Mapmakers*. Rev. ed. London.

Wilhelm, A. 1937. Papyrus Tebtunis 33. *JRS* 27 (1), 145–151.

Wilkins, J. 1995a. General Introduction. In Wilkins, J., et al. (eds.), *Food in Antiquity*. Pp. 2–5. Exeter, UK.

———. 1995b. Introduction (to Part Four: Beyond the Greco-Roman World). In Wilkins, J., et al. (eds.), *Food in Antiquity*. Pp. 242–247. Exeter, UK.

Wilkinson, A. 1998. *The Garden in Ancient Egypt*. London.

Wilkinson, J. 1971. *Egeria's Travels: Newly Translated with Supporting Document and Notes*. London.

———. 1977. *Jerusalem Pilgrims before the Crusades*. Warminster, UK.

Wilkinson, J. G. 1832. Notes on a Part of the Eastern Desert of Upper Egypt. *JRGS* 2, 28–60.

———. 1835. *Topography of Thebes, and General View of Egypt*. London.

Will, E. 1996. Palmyre et les routes de la soie. In *Les Annales Archéologiques arabes syriennes: Revue d'Archéologie et d'Histoire* 42 (1996), 125–128.

Will, E. L. 1996. Mediterranean Shipping Amphoras from the 1941–50 Excavations. In Begley, V., et al., *The Ancient Port of Arikamedu: New Excavations and Researches, 1989–1992*. Vol. 1. Pp. 317–349. Pondicherry.

———. 2004a. Mediterranean Amphoras in India. In Eiring, J., and Lund, J. (eds.), *Transport Amphorae and Trade in the Eastern Mediterranean: Acts of the International Colloquium at the Danish Institute at Athens, September 26–29, 2002*. Pp. 433–440. Athens.

———. 2004b. The Mediterranean Shipping Amphoras from the 1989–92 Excavations. In Begley, V. (ed.), *The Ancient Port of Arikamedu: New Excavations and Researches, 1989–1992*. Vol. 2. Pp. 325–403. Paris.

Williams, D. F. 2004. The Eruption of Vesuvius and Its Implications for the Early Amphora Trade with India. In Eiring, J., and Lund, J. (eds.), *Transport Amphorae and Trade in the East-*

ern Mediterranean: Acts of the International Colloquium at the Danish Institute at Athens, September 26–29, 2002. Pp. 441–450. Athens.

Williams-Thorpe, O. 1988. Provenancing and Archaeology of Roman Millstones from the Mediterranean Area. *JAS* 15, 253–305.

Williams-Thorpe, O., and Thorpe, R. S. 1993. Geochemistry and Trade of Eastern Mediterranean Millstones from the Neolithic to Roman Periods. *JAS* 20, 263–320.

Wilson, A. 2000. Industrial Uses of Water. In Wikander, Ö. (ed.), *Handbook of Ancient Water Technology*. Pp. 127–149. Leiden, Boston, and Cologne.

———. 2002. Machines, Power and the Ancient Economy. *JRS* 92, 1–32.

———. 2009. Approaches to Quantifying Roman Trade. In Bowman and Wilson 2009, 213–249.

Wilson, N. G. 1994. *Photius. The Bibliotheca. A Selection Translated with Notes*. London.

Wilson, R. J. A. 1983. *Piazza Armerina*. Austin, TX.

Wilson, R. T. 1984. *The Camel*. New York and London.

Winkler, H. A. 1938. *Archaeological Survey of Egypt. Rock-Drawings of Southern Upper Egypt*. I. *Sir Robert Mond Desert Expedition. Season 1936–1937 Preliminary Report*. London.

Winter, E. 1987. Handel und Wirtschaft in sāsānidisch-(ost)römischen Verträgen und Abkommen. *MBAH* 6 (2), 46–74.

Winterbottom, S. 2001. Leather. In Maxfield and Peacock 2001b, 311–353.

Wipszycka, E. 1972. *Les ressources et les activités économiques des églises en Égypte du IVe au VIIIe siècle*. Brussels.

———. 2007. The institutional church. In Bagnall, R. S. (ed.), *Egypt in the Byzantine World, 300–700*. Pp. 331–349. Cambridge and New York.

Witt, R. E. 1971. *Isis in the Graeco-Roman World*. Ithaca, NY.

Wolff, C. 1999. Comment deviant-on brigand? *RÉA* 101 (3–4), 393–403.

Wolska-Conus, W. (ed.). 1968. *Cosmas Indicopleustès Topographie Chrétienne*. Tome I (Livres I–IV). Paris.

———. (ed.). 1970. *Cosmas Indicopleustès Topographie Chrétienne*. Tome II (Livre V). Paris.

———. (ed.). 1973. *Cosmas Indicopleustès Topographie Chrétienne*. Tome III (Livres VI–XII. Index). Paris.

Woolliscroft, D. J. 2001. *Roman Military Signalling*. Stroud, Gloucestershire.

Worrall, S. 2009. Made in China: A 1,200-Year-Old Shipwreck Opens a Window on Ancient Global Trade. *National Geographic*, June, 112–123.

Wriggins, S. H. 1996. *Xuanzang: A Buddhist Pilgrim on the Silk Road*. Boulder, CO.

Yeo, C. A. 1946. Land and Sea Transport in Imperial Italy. *TAPA* 77, 221–244.

Young, G. K. 1997. The Customs-Collector at the Nabataean Port of Leuke Kome (*Periplus Maris Erythraei* 19). *ZPE* 119, 266–268.

———. 2001. *Rome's Eastern Trade: International Commerce and Imperial Policy, 31 B.C.-A.D. 305*. London and New York.

Yoyotte, J. 1975. Les *sementiou* et l'exploitation des régions minières à l'Ancien Empire. *BSFE* 73, 44–55.

Yoyotte, J., and Charvet, P. 1997. *Strabon. Le Voyage en Égypte. Un regard romain*. Paris.

Zaccagnino, C. 1997. L'incenso e gli incensieri nel mondo greco. In Avanzini 1997, 101–120.

Zalat, S., and Gilbert, F. 2008. *Gardens of a Sacred Landscape: Bedouin Heritage and Natural History in the High Mountains of Sinai*. Cairo.

Zarins, J. 1996. Obsidian in the Larger Context of Predynastic/Archaic Egyptian Red Sea Trade. In Reade, J. (ed.), *The Indian Ocean in Antiquity*. Pp. 89–106. London and New York.

Zayadine, F. 1990. The Pantheon of the Nabataean Inscriptions in Egypt and the Sinai. *Aram* 2 (1–2), 151–174.

——. 1996. Palmyre, Pétra, la mer erythrée et les routes de la soie. In *Les Annales Archéologiques arabes syriennes: Revue d'Archéologie et d'Histoire* 42 (1996), 167–178.

Zeuner, F. E. 1963. *A History of Domesticated Animals*. London.

Ziethen, G., and Klingenberg, E. 2002. Merchants, Pilgrims and Soldiers on the Red Sea Route. In Freeman, P., et al. (eds.), *Limes XVIII. Proceedings of the XVIII International Congress of Roman Frontier Studies Held in Amman, Jordan (September 2000)*. Vol. 1. Pp. 379–385. Oxford.

Zitterkopf, R. E. 1998. Roman Construction Techniques in the Eastern Desert. In Kaper 1998a, 271–286.

Zitterkopf, R. E., and Sidebotham, S. E. 1989. Stations and Towers on the Quseir-Nile Road. *JEA* 75, 155–189.

Zohary, D., and Hopf, M. 2000. *Domestication of Plants in the Old World: The Origin and Spread of Cultivated Plants in West Africa, Europe and the Nile Valley*. 3rd ed. Oxford.

Zuckerman, C. 1990. The Military Compendium of Syrianus Magister. *JöB* 40: 209–224.

Zuhdi, B. 1996. La route de la soie et Palmyre, la ville des caravanes. In *Les Annales Archéologiques arabes syriennes: Revue d'Archéologie et d'Histoire* 42 (1996), 165–166.

Zvelebil, K. 1973. *The Smile of Murugan: On Tamil Literature of South India*. Leiden.

INDEX

amethysts, 24, 172

amla (Indian gooseberry), 229

Ammianus Marcellinus, 54

Ampelome/Ampelone, 175

amphoras: Aila-made, 199, 272, 273; at
Berenike, 231–34, 261; in Christian hermit
communities, 276; Cilician, 103, 108; gra-
fitto on, 75, 252; in India, 190, 191, 251;
ladikena, 232, 234; recycling toes of, 265;
stoppers for, 72–73, 241; used as fill in
construction, 62, 184, 262; in warehouse,
272, 273; for wine, 232–33

Anni Plocami, 72

Antinoopolis (Sheikh 'Ibada), 129

Antonine Itinerary, 158, 159

Aphilas, 248, 261

Aphrodite, 58, 83, 241, 242

Aphrodito/Aphrodites, 108, 110

Apollonopolis Magna (Edfu), 3, 28, 84, 133, 135,
160

Apollonos, 164

Apollonos Hydreuma, 154, 159, 165–66

Aqaba. *See* Aila/Aela/Aelana

Aqabat Najd Marqad, 252

Arabia, South: caravan routes of, 32, 33, 38;
coins to, 244, 246; graffiti at Berenike, 74–
75, 224; inscription, 211; merchants in
Berenike from, 224; as middlemen in
Ptolemaic trade, 37–38; Nabataeans and,
299; pottery from, 231; Ptolemaic trade
contacts with, 34, 35; turmoil in late
Roman period in, 260, 280. *See also*
Qana'/Kane'

Arabia Eudaimon, 200

al-'Aras, 119, 130, 131

Arikamedu, 235, 238

Aristonis, 159

aromatics: cost of, 250; cost of shipping, 216;
evidence for at Berenike, 230, 269, 270;
Ptolemaic office overseeing, 35; used in
medicine, 257–58. *See also* frankincense;
myrrh

Arsinoë/Cleopatris/Clysma, 51, 280, 281; as
important port, 178–79, 180; as likely place
for shipbuilding, 201; procuring water for,
101, 103

Arsinoite Nome, 181

Aśoka, 37

Atrash Northeast, 119, 130

Augustus, 167, 244, 245

Axum: coins from, 178, 187, 248–49, 261, 275,
277; as commercial emporium, 187, 261,
278; emeralds to, 236; inscriptions of, 72,
75; pottery from, 178, 185, 187, 231, 277–78;
war against Himyar by, 187, 188, 260, 280

Bab al-Mukhenig, 119, 130

Babylon (Egypt), 181

Badia', 105, 119, 130

balsam, 230

bamboo, 240

barley, 79

Barramiya, 102, 133

Barud, 105

Barygaza, 224, 231, 238, 247, 252

basalt, vesicular, 61, 200, 205, 236

Basilica Ulpia, 169

bathing/baths, 81, 99, 111, 117–18, 169

Bawab, 134

beads, 186, 191; 238–39; at Berenike, 76, 196,
223, 238–39; coral, 239; glass, 238; from
India and Sri Lanka, 192, 238, 276; plant
seed, 230

Bedouin, 63, 101–2, 115

Begram, 235

Bellefonds, L. M. A. Linant de, 93–94

Belzoni, Giovanni, 16

Berenike, 130, 133; connections with Nile Valley
of, 3–4; difficulties of excavating at, 18–
20; difficulties of maintaining, 12–13; early
modern visitors to, 16–17; environmental
setting of, 8–11; health and hygiene at, 80–
81; hinterland in, 66–67; as hub of Maritime Spice Route, 1–5; map location of, 2,
4, 67; natural harbors at, 9–11; Roman
authors on, 13–16; site plan, 10; women
and families at, 76–78

Berenike, early Roman period: control of trade
in, 252; decline at end of, 63; diet at, 76,
78–80; elephant enclosure at, 117; epidemic at, 221; ethnic composition of, 69–
76; evidence for bathing facility at, 81, 118;
evidence of corruption at, 253; graffito of
ship at, 202; harbor of, 60–61, 195, 197–
98, 205; Indian graffito at, 252; Indian
pottery at, 231; irrigation at, 114; Mediter-

ranean pottery at, 231–32; military presence at, 76, 77; ostraka at, 62, 69–71, 76, 102, 109, 199–200; Palmyrenes in, 154; papyri at, 71; personal names at, 70–74; political significance of, 85–86; population of, 68; religious buildings in, 81–85; robust activity at, 59, 62–63; sailcloth, rigging, etc. at, 199, 200; shipbuilding materials at, 198, 203–5; soldier figurine at, 77; stones exported from, 238; stones imported to, 236–37; trade area of, 196; trash deposits at, 199–200; water source for, 80, 108, 109

Berenike, late Roman period: antiques market at, 270; building techniques at, 56, 57; burials at, 279; Christian ecclesiastical complex at, 272, 274–75; coin from Axum at, 187, 248, 261, 275, 277; commercial/residential quarter at, 268–71; contact with India and Sri Lanka of, 261, 276; demise of, 279–81; diet at, 278; greater emphasis on local resources at, 278; harbors at, 272; hinterland of, 275–77; ply split braiding at, 261–62; possible light house at, 271; urban renewal at, 262–63; warehouse at, 272, 273; water source unknown at, 80, 278–79. *See also* Northern Shrine; Shrine of the Palmyrenes

Berenike, Ptolemaic era: building techniques at, 55–56, 57; diet at, 76; harbor at, 60–61; Indian pottery at, 75; industrial area at, 205; orthogonal plan of, 58. *See also* Serapis temple

Berenike-Apollonopolis Magna road: abandonment of, 149, 160; built-up section of, 144; cisterns on, 105–6; lack of special elephant accommodations along, 122; length of, 128; Ptolemaic use of, 28; stops/stations on, 135

Berenike-Koptos road: graffiti on, 72; length of, 128; origin of, 149; renewal/expansion of facilities on, 110, 154; replacement of stations on, 160–61; stops/stations on, 133–35, 159

beryl/emerald mines, 121, 172, 236. *See also* Sikait

Bezah, 134

Bezah West, 97, 107, 120, 132

Bint Abu Greiya, 133, 138

Bir Abu Hashim, 128

Bir Abu Safa, 93–95, 128

Bir Abu Sha'ar al-Qibli, 111

Bir al-Hammamat, 100, 144

Bir Fawakhir, 172

Bir Gidami, 173

Bir Handosi, 173

Bir Hawashiya, 129

Bir 'Iayyan, 107, 132, 186

Bir Jahaliya, 128

Bir Kareim, 102

Bir Menih, 42

Bir Nakheil, 102, 112

Bir Ria'da, 130

Bir Salah, 119, 130, 170

Bir Sayyala, 29

Bir Semna (Simiou), 116

Bir Umm Fawakhir, 100, 114, 116, 172, 173

bitumen, 23

Blemmyes, 266, 267, 280

Book of the Eparch, The, 270

Boswellia, 240–41

bowls, wooden, 60, 64, 230, 268

Bubastis, 181

Buddhism, 257

burials: along roads, 149–50; at Berenike, 263–64, 279

Cabalsi. *See* Abu Ghusun (Cabalsi)

camels, 25, 28, 38, 171; at Berenike, 79; for desert patrols, 151, 166; use in Eastern Desert of, 91, 155–56, 173

cameos, 238

Caracalla, 65, 226, 260, 267

caravans, 38, 151–53, 209–10

cedar, 205, 242

Celsus, Cornelius, 14

Cheops, 22

China, 223, 234–35, 254

Christians: at Berenike, 272, 274–75; in India, 256–57; settlements of, 115, 173, 182–83

cisterns: capacity of Ptolemaic-Early Roman, 103–5; capacity of Roman, 105; construction of Ptolemaic-early Roman, 105–6; construction of Roman, 106; covering of, 105

Clysma. *See* Arsinoë/Cleopatris/Clysma

coconuts, 228–29

carried by, 200; construction of, 201; costs of maintaining, 213–14; dimensions of, 195–96; mixed cargoes on, 217; pictorial representations of, 99, 189, 201–3; reuse of beams from, 239, 240, 242; sailcloth, rigging, etc. from, 199, 200; sewn-plank tradition of building, 198; speeds of, 213; two Roman construction methods for, 197; value of cargoes in, 217–18; wrecks in Red Sea, 198–99. See also *elephantegoi*

Shrine of the Palmyrenes: dedicated to Yarhibol/ Hierobol, 64, 65, 66, 84, 86, 226, 259, 260, 265, 267; end of, 267–68; later phases of, 264–65; pepper in, 226, 227; recycled teak beam in, 84, 85; stone sphinx in wall of, 59; temple pool offerings in, 268; wooden bowls in, 64, 230

Sibrit, 135

signal-watch towers, 101, 140–44, 152

silk, 244

Sikait, 90, 108, 115, 134, 145, 146

Sikait, Middle, 134, 144–45

Sikait, North, 134

Sikait/Nugrus road, 121

Siket, 62, 107–8, 110, 133, 163, 277

Simiou, 29, 51

Simmias, 29, 51, 143

Sinai, 24

skopeloi. See signal-watch towers

snail, land (escargot), 76, 229–30

Socotra (Dioscurida/Dioscurides), 189–90

sorghum, 228

Southeast Asia/Malay peninsula, 223, 238

Spasinou Charax (Mesene), 212

springs, 93

Sri Lanka: beads from, 192, 237, 238; coins to, 193, 244; products of, 193; red coral to, 238; sapphires from, 237; written sources on, 192–93

Strabo, 13, 62, 160, 177

Sukkari, 132

Syene (Aswan), 3, 128

Syrian fir, 242

Tal'at al-Arta, 129

Tamil-Brahmi, 75, 185, 252

Tamil Sangam poetry, 191, 224, 225, 251

Taw al-Kefare, 277

taxes, 34, 217, 219, 253

tax farmers, 34

teak, 84, 85, 203, 204–5, 239–40, 265

Tell al-Maskhuta, 179, 180, 181

Theodosius, 266

Tiberiane, 105, 145, 167

Tiberius, 62, 83, 167, 244, 245, 246

tin, 25

Tissamaharama (Sri Lanka), 193, 249

tombs, ring-cairn, 263–64

trade/trading: barter, 249; balance of, 245–47; costs of land vs. water, 212–16; government involvement in, 251–53; luxuries vs. necessities in, 249–51; profits from, 219; in Roman Berenike, 221–44; sources of capital for, 216–17, 219; taxes on, 217, 219; transport costs in, 212–16, 219; underground economy and, 220. *See also* India; ships

Trajan, 83, 108, 124, 180

travertine, 237

Trogodytes, 33–34, 43

Turin map, 23, 26

Umm Arba'een, 132

Umm Balad, 100, 105, 108, 117, 130

Umm Disi, 92–93

Umm Garahish, 135

Umm Gariya/Umm Ushra, 105, 134

Umm Heiran, 134, 173

Umm Howeitat/Umm Hayatat, 129

Umm Howeitat al-Bahri, 173

Umm Howeitat al-Qibli, 129

Umm Huyut, 131, 167

Umm Kebash, 134, 156

Umm Mureer, 132

Umm Sidri, 99, 119, 130

Umm Suwagi, 129

Veii, 50

Vetus Hydreuma (Wadi Abu Greiya), 130, 131, 133; forts at, 138, 139; garrison size of, 166; Indian pottery at, 231; in late Roman times, 275, 277; possible aqueduct at, 112–13; road near, 138; Roman reuse of Ptolemaic fort at, 149, 163

THE CALIFORNIA WORLD HISTORY LIBRARY

Edited by Edmund Burke III, Kenneth Pomeranz, and Patricia Seed

TEXT:	9.5/14 Scala
DISPLAY:	Scala Sans
COMPOSITOR:	Integrated Composition Systems
INDEXER:	Andrew Christenson
PRINTER AND BINDER:	Sheridan Books, Inc.